Reading STREET

Grade 4, Unit 1

This Land Is Your Land

PEARSON
Scott Foresman

scottforesman.com

Editorial Offices: Glenview, Illinois • Parsippany, New Jersey • New York, New York
Sales Offices: Boston, Massachusetts • Duluth, Georgia • Glenview, Illinois
Coppell, Texas • Sacramento, California • Mesa, Arizona

We dedicate Reading Street to
Peter Jovanovich.

His wisdom, courage,
and passion for education
are an inspiration to us all.

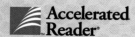
Accelerated Reader®

Cover Tim Jessell

About the Cover Artist

Tim Jessell draws and paints in Stillwater, Oklahoma. He and his wife are raising three great children, whom he coaches in many sports. When not playing catch or illustrating, Tim trains falcons for the sport of falconry. Occasionally, he can still be found making a racket behind his drum set, with kids dancing around.

ISBN-13: 978-0-328-24379-2

ISBN-10: 0-328-24379-5

Copyright © 2008 Pearson Education, Inc.

2 3 4 5 6 7 8 9 10 11 V063 16 15 14 13 12 11 10 09 08 07

CC:N1

Reading STREET

Where the Love of Reading Begins

Reading Street Program Authors

Peter Afflerbach, Ph.D.
Professor, Department of
Curriculum and Instruction
University of Maryland at
College Park

Camille L.Z. Blachowicz, Ph.D.
Professor of Education
National-Louis University

Candy Dawson Boyd, Ph.D.
Professor, School of Education
Saint Mary's College of California

Wendy Cheyney, Ed.D.
Professor of Special Education
and Literacy, Florida
International University

Connie Juel, Ph.D.
Professor of Education, School of
Education, Stanford University

Edward J. Kame'enui, Ph.D.
Professor and Director, Institute for
the Development of Educational
Achievement, University of Oregon

Donald J. Leu, Ph.D.
John and Maria Neag Endowed
Chair in Literacy and Technology
University of Connecticut

Jeanne R. Paratore, Ed.D.
Associate Professor of Education
Department of Literacy
and Language Development
Boston University

P. David Pearson, Ph.D.
Professor and Dean,
Graduate School of Education
University of California, Berkeley

Sam L. Sebesta, Ed.D.
Professor Emeritus,
College of Education,
University of Washington, Seattle

Deborah Simmons, Ph.D.
Professor, College of Education
and Human Development
Texas A&M University
(Not pictured)

Sharon Vaughn, Ph.D.
H.E. Hartfelder/Southland
Corporation Regents Professor
University of Texas

Susan Watts-Taffe, Ph.D.
Independent Literacy Researcher
Cincinnati, Ohio

Karen Kring Wixson, Ph.D.
Professor of Education
University of Michigan

Components

Student Editions (1–6)

Teacher's Editions (PreK–6)

Assessment
Assessment Handbook (K–6)

Baseline Group Tests (K–6)

DIBELS™ Assessments (K–6)

ExamView® Test Generator CD-ROM (2–6)

Fresh Reads for Differentiated Test Practice (1–6)

Online Success Tracker™ (K–6)*

Selection Tests Teacher's Manual (1–6)

Unit and End-of-Year Benchmark Tests (K–6)

Leveled Readers
Concept Literacy Leveled Readers (K–1)

Independent Leveled Readers (K)

Kindergarten Student Readers (K)

Leveled Reader Teaching Guides (K–6)

Leveled Readers (1–6)

Listen to Me Readers (K)

Online Leveled Reader Database (K–6)*

Take-Home Leveled Readers (K–6)

Trade Books and Big Books
Big Books (PreK–2)

Read Aloud Trade Books (PreK–K)

Sing with Me Big Book (1–2)

Trade Book Library (1–6)

Decodable Readers
Decodable Readers (K–3)

Strategic Intervention Decodable Readers (1–2)

Take-Home Decodable Readers (K–3)

Phonics and Word Study
Alphabet Cards in English and Spanish (PreK–K)

Alphabet Chart in English and Spanish (PreK–K)

Animal ABCs Activity Guide (K)

Finger Tracing Cards (PreK–K)

Patterns Book (PreK–K)

Phonics Activities CD-ROM (PreK–2)*

Phonics Activities Mats (K)

Phonics and Spelling Practice Book (1–3)

Phonics and Word-Building Board and Letters (PreK–3)

Phonics Songs and Rhymes Audio CD (K–2)

Phonics Songs and Rhymes Flip Chart (K–2)

Picture Word Cards (PreK–K)

Plastic Letter Tiles (K)

Sound-Spelling Cards and Wall Charts (1–2)

Strategies for Word Analysis (4–6)

Word Study and Spelling Practice Book (4–6)

Language Arts
Daily Fix-It Transparencies (K–6)

Grammar & Writing Book and Teacher's Annotated Edition, The (1–6)

Grammar and Writing Practice Book and Teacher's Manual (1–6)

Grammar Transparencies (1–6)

Six-Trait Writing Posters (1–6)

Writing Kit (1–6)

Writing Rubrics and Anchor Papers (1–6)

Writing Transparencies (1–6)

Practice and Additional Resources
AlphaBuddy Bear Puppet (K)

Alphasaurus Annie Puppet (PreK)

Amazing Words Posters (K–2)

Centers Survival Kit (PreK–6)

Graphic Organizer Book (2–6)

Graphic Organizer Flip Chart (K–1)

High-Frequency Word Cards (K)

Kindergarten Review (1)

Practice Book and Teacher's Manual (K–6)

Read Aloud Anthology (PreK–2)

Readers' Theater Anthology (K–6)

Research into Practice (K–6)

Retelling Cards (K–6)

Scott Foresman Research Base (K–6)

Skill Transparencies (2–6)

Songs and Rhymes Flip Chart (PreK)

Talk with Me, Sing with Me Chart (PreK–K)

Tested Vocabulary Cards (1–6)

Vocabulary Transparencies (1–2)

Welcome to Reading Street (PreK–1)

ELL
ELL and Transition Handbook (PreK–6)

ELL Comprehensive Kit (1–6)

ELL Posters (K–6)

ELL Readers (1–6)

ELL Teaching Guides (1–6)

Ten Important Sentences (1–6)

Digital Components
AudioText CDs (PreK–6)

Background Building Audio CDs (3–6)

ExamView® Test Generator CD-ROM (2–6)

Online Lesson Planner (K–6)

Online New Literacies Activities (1–6)*

Online Professional Development (1–6)

Online Story Sort (K–6)*

Online Student Editions (1–6)*

Online Success Tracker™ (K–6)*

Online Teacher's Editions (PreK–6)

Phonics Activities CD-ROM (PreK–2)*

Phonics Songs and Rhymes Audio CD (K–2)

Sing with Me/Background Building Audio CDs (PreK–2)

Songs and Rhymes Audio CD (PreK)

My Sidewalks Early Reading Intervention (K)

My Sidewalks Intensive Reading Intervention (Levels A–E)

Reading Street for the Guided Reading Teacher (1–6)

In ancient Greece, there was a golden fleece.

How do I help every child love to read?

It all starts with a "golden" collection of literature. *Reading Street* has funny stories, scary stories, real-life adventures! One story perfectly leads to the next—one concept is explored from many sides. Children have enough time to think about a big idea, learn, and enjoy.

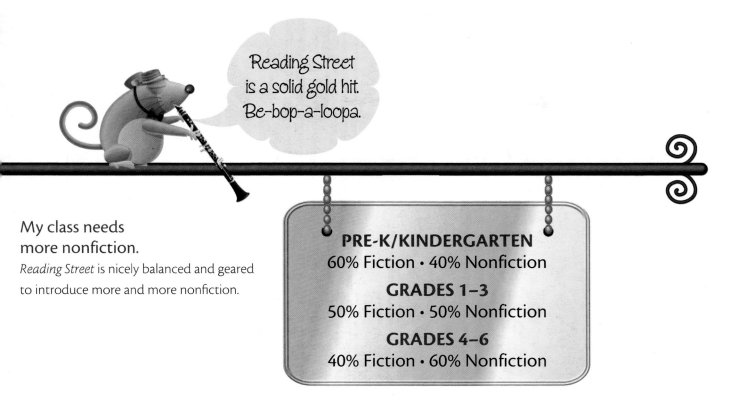

My class needs
more nonfiction.

Reading Street is nicely balanced and geared
to introduce more and more nonfiction.

PRE-K/KINDERGARTEN
60% Fiction • 40% Nonfiction

GRADES 1–3
50% Fiction • 50% Nonfiction

GRADES 4–6
40% Fiction • 60% Nonfiction

How do I get children to
think about what they read?

The literature in *Reading Street* is organized
around unit themes. Each selection
connects and expands the concept
to build deeper understanding.

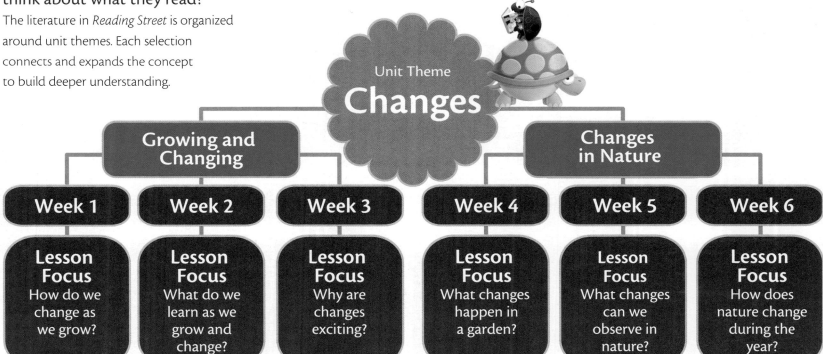

Unit Theme
Changes

Growing and Changing

Changes in Nature

Week 1	Week 2	Week 3	Week 4	Week 5	Week 6
Lesson Focus How do we change as we grow?	**Lesson Focus** What do we learn as we grow and change?	**Lesson Focus** Why are changes exciting?	**Lesson Focus** What changes happen in a garden?	**Lesson Focus** What changes can we observe in nature?	**Lesson Focus** How does nature change during the year?

Grade 1, Unit 3 Organization

There's never enough time
to cover content areas.

Every selection in *Reading Street* emphasizes
a science or social studies concept.
Your reading lessons become the tools
to meet content-area standards.

Don't lose sleep! You're on Reading Street.

Am I teaching the right skills at the right time?

You'll never have to worry about this question again. *Reading Street* prioritizes skills instruction so you place the correct emphasis on the most important skills at your grade. Built-in progress monitoring helps you zoom ahead or slow down, depending on your students' needs.

Help me prioritize my day!

Reading Street prioritizes the five core areas of reading instruction across the grades, so you know where to place your instructional emphasis. By assessing key predictors, you can ensure student success. (See below.)

PRIORITY SKILL	SUCCESS PREDICTOR
PHONEMIC AWARENESS	Blending and Segmenting
PHONICS	Word Reading
FLUENCY	Words Correct per Minute
VOCABULARY	Word Knowledge
COMPREHENSION	Retelling

Can I predict reading success?

The research says "YES!" Only *Reading Street* helps you monitor students' progress by assessing the research-based predictors of reading success.

Monitor Progress

Check Retelling Rubric 4 3 2 1

If... students have difficulty retelling the story,

then... use the Scoring Rubric for Retelling below to help move them toward fluent retelling.

SUCCESS PREDICTOR

I need a data management system.

Success Tracker is an online assessment and data management system that prescribes remediation, helps with grouping, and disaggregates and aggregates data.

Learn more at www.scottforesman.com/tours.

ix

One size never fits all.

How can I make sure every child reads?

One of the most important lessons our teachers taught us was that everyone is unique *and* the same. *Reading Street* provides a daily plan for whole-group teaching and for meeting with small groups to attend to specific needs. Don't you just love it?

We got style, we got class, we got fancy yellow pants.

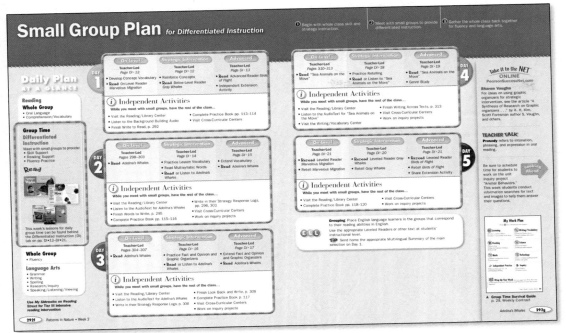

Teacher's Edition Grade 4 Unit 3

Give me a plan for group time.

Reading Street provides a daily plan for whole-group and small-group instruction. Assign the Independent Activities to the rest of the class when you meet with your small groups.

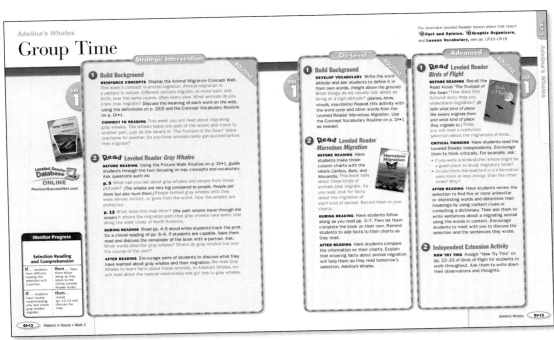

Teacher's Edition Grade 4 Unit 3

Help me teach my struggling and advanced readers.

Reading Street has daily instructional routines for both your Strategic Intervention and Advanced groups. See the Differentiated Instruction section at the back of the Teacher's Edition.

How can I support my English language learners?

Look for ELL instructional strategies, alternate comprehension lessons, and grade-level readers to build vocabulary and key concepts each week.

Q: Why did the chicken cross the road?
A: To get to the sidewalk!

What do I do when *Reading Street* isn't enough?

Every teacher knows that some students need more support. For those children, Scott Foresman provides *My Sidewalks*—an intensive reading intervention program that aligns perfectly with *Reading Street. My Sidewalks* accelerates reading development for children at risk.

B-A-W-K! It's so good it works with any core program.

What is Tier III Instruction?

Tier III instruction is for students with low reading skills and a lack of adequate progress. *My Sidewalks* provides sustained instruction, intensive language and concept development, and more focus on critical comprehension skills and strategies for Tier III students.

TIER I PRIMARY
Comprehensive Core Program

TIER II SECONDARY
Core Program Plus Strategic Intervention

TIER III TERTIARY
Intensive Reading Intervention

How does *My Sidewalks* support *Reading Street*?

My Sidewalks provides daily lessons for 30 weeks—for a minimum of 30 minutes a day. The oral language, vocabulary, and concepts developed in *My Sidewalks* parallel those in *Reading Street*.

Reading Street Student Edition

My Sidewalks Student Reader

When do I teach *My Sidewalks*?

Use *My Sidewalks* during group time, as a pull-out intervention program, or as a before- or after-school program. The *My Sidewalks* acceleration plan prioritizes skills so you teach less, more thoroughly.

Are you an adventurous reading teacher?

Do you love teaching with leveled text?

Reading Street for the Guided Reading Teacher will support you in organizing research-based reading instruction. It features the *Guide on the Side* to implement instruction around leveled text. All the resources are derived from *Reading Street* and its proven teaching methods.

I want to match my students to leveled text.

Reading Street for the Guided Reading Teacher organizes instruction around leveled text and helps you differentiate instruction. It's a complete guided reading program with leveled readers, lessons plans, practice, and assessment.

Does the program support *Reading Street*?

The scope and sequence, instructional routines, and teacher resources all align with *Reading Street*. Use the *Guide on the Side* as your main Teacher's Edition or to supplement your *Reading Street* Teacher's Edition.

Will I teach the skills my students need?

Reading Street for the Guided Reading Teacher provides a comprehensive scope and sequence that helps you pace instruction and prepare students for your state test.

READING

Pace Yourself

How do I know I am covering all the skills before the test?
This chart shows the instructional sequence from Scott Foresman Reading Street. You can use this pacing guide as is to ensure you're following a comprehensive scope and sequence, or you can adjust it to match your school/district focus calendar, curriculum map, or testing schedule.

BACK TO SCHOOL! →

	UNIT 1					UNIT 2					UNIT 3				
	WEEK 1	WEEK 2	WEEK 3	WEEK 4	WEEK 5	WEEK 6	WEEK 7	WEEK 8	WEEK 9	WEEK 10	WEEK 11	WEEK 12	WEEK 13	WEEK 14	WEEK 15
Comprehension Skill	Realism and Fantasy	Sequence of Events	Sequence of Events	Realism and Fantasy	Character and Setting	Main Idea and Details	Character	Main Idea and Details	Author's Purpose	Draw Conclusions	Cause and Effect	Author's Purpose	Draw Conclusions	Generalize	Compare/Contrast
Comprehension Strategy	Activate/Use Prior Knowledge	Summarize	Visualize	Monitor and Fix Up	Story Structure	Graphic Organizers	Visualize	Monitor and Fix Up	Predict	Ask Questions	Story Structure	Summarize	Ask Questions	Answer Questions	Monitor and Fix Up
Vocabulary Strategy/Skill	Context Clues/Homonyms	Word Structure/Compound Words	Reference Sources/Unfamiliar Words	Context Clues/Multiple-Meaning Words	Word Structure/Prefixes and Suffixes	Context Clues/Synonyms	Context Clues/Unfamiliar Words	Dictionary/Unfamiliar Words	Context Clues/Antonyms	Context Clues/Unfamiliar Words	Word Structure/Endings	Glossary/Unfamiliar Words	Word Structure/Compound Words	Context Clues/Unfamiliar Words	Dictionary/Unfamiliar Words
Fluency	Accuracy	Appropriate Pace/Rate	Express Characterization	Expression/Intonation	Appropriate Phrasing	Accuracy and Appropriate Pace/Rate	Express Characterization	Expression/Intonation	Appropriate Phrasing	Read Silently with Fluency	Expression/Intonation	Express Characterization	Appropriate Phrasing	Accuracy and Appropriate Pace/Rate	Read Silently with Fluency and Accuracy
Spelling/Word Work	Short Vowels VCCV	Plurals -s, -es	Adding -ed, -ing, -er, -est	Long Vowel Digraphs	Vowel Sounds in *out* and *toy*	Syllable Patterns V/CV, VC/V	Words Ending in -le	Compound Words	Words with *spl, thr, squ, str*	Digraphs *sh, th, ph, ch, tch*	Contractions	Prefixes *un-, re-, mis-, dis-*	Consonant Sounds /j/ and /k/	Suffixes -ly, -ful, -ness, -less	Words with *wr, kn, mb, gn*

	UNIT 4					UNIT 5					UNIT 6				
	WEEK 16	WEEK 17	WEEK 18	WEEK 19	WEEK 20	WEEK 21	WEEK 22	WEEK 23	WEEK 24	WEEK 25	WEEK 26	WEEK 27	WEEK 28	WEEK 29	WEEK 30
Comprehension Skill	Cause and Effect	Compare and Contrast	Generalize	Fact and Opinion	Plot and Theme	Compare and Contrast	Fact and Opinion	Sequence	Draw Conclusions	Author's Purpose	Main Idea	Cause and Effect	Fact and Opinion	Plot and Theme	Generalize
Comprehension Strategy	Answer Questions	Ask Questions	Activate and Use Prior Knowledge	Monitor and Fix Up	Graphic Organizers	Predict	Text Structure	Monitor and Fix Up	Summarize	Prior Knowledge	Text Structure	Graphic Organizers	Answer Questions	Visualize	Predict
Vocabulary Strategy/Skill	Word Structure/Endings	Word Structure/Compound Words	Context Clues/Multiple-Meaning Words	Context Clues/Multiple-Meaning Words	Word Structure/Endings	Context Clues/Synonyms	Context Clues/Antonyms	Word Structure/Compound Words	Context Clues/Unfamiliar Words	Context Clues/Homonyms	Word Structure/Prefixes	Context Clues/Antonyms	Glossary/Unfamiliar Words	Word Structure/Prefixes and Suffixes	Context Clues/Synonyms
Fluency	Accuracy and Appropriate Pace/Rate	Read Silently with Fluency and Accuracy	Characterization	Appropriate Phrasing	Expression/Intonation	Accuracy and Appropriate Pace/Rate	Read Silently with Fluency and Accuracy	Expression/Intonation	Express Characterization	Appropriate Phrasing	Accuracy and Appropriate Pace/Rate	Appropriate Phrasing	Read Silently with Fluency and Accuracy	Accuracy and Accuracy	Express Characterization
Spelling/Word Work	Plurals	Vowels with r	Prefixes pre-, mid-, over-, out-	Suffixes -er, -or, -ess, -ist	Syllable Pattern VCCCV	Syllable Patterns CVVC, CVV	Homophones	Vowel Sound in *ball*	More Vowel Sound in *ball*	Suffixes -y, -ish, -hood, -ment	Vowels in *tooth, cook*	Schwa	Words with -sion, -sion, -ture	Multisyllabic Words	Related Words

IT'S TEST TIME! — WHEN IS YOUR STATE TEST?

4   5

Guide on the Side Grade 3

Welcome to Reading Street!

GRADE 1

Student Edition (Unit 1)

Student Edition (Unit 2)

Student Edition (Unit 3)

Student Edition (Unit 4)

Student Edition (Unit 5)

5 Teacher's Editions
(1 per unit)

GRADE 2

Student Edition
(Units 1–3)

Student Edition
(Units 4–6)

6 Teacher's Editions
(1 per unit)

GRADE 3

Student Edition
(Units 1–3)

Student Edition
(Units 4–6)

6 Teacher's Editions
(1 per unit)

GRADE 4

Student Edition

6 Teacher's Editions
(1 per unit)

GRADE 5

Student Edition

6 Teacher's Editions
(1 per unit)

GRADE 6

Student Edition

6 Teacher's Editions
(1 per unit)

MORE READING SUPPORT

My Sidewalks Intensive
Reading Intervention (Levels A–E)

Reading Street for the Guided
Reading Teacher (Grades 1–6)

Ready, Teddy?
(On Reading Street, you're ready for everything and anything!)

Honey is yummy in my tummy.

Student Editions (1–6)

Teacher's Editions (PreK–6)

Assessment
Assessment Handbook (K–6)
Baseline Group Tests (K–6)
DIBELS™ Assessments (K–6)
Examview® Test Generator CD-ROM (2–6)
Fresh Reads for Differentiated Test Practice (1–6)
Online Success Tracker™ (K–6)*
Selection Tests Teacher's Manual (1–6)
Unit and End-of-Year Benchmark Tests (K–6)

Leveled Readers
Concept Literacy Leveled Readers (K–1)
Independent Leveled Readers (K)
Kindergarten Student Readers (K)
Leveled Reader Teaching Guides (K–6)
Leveled Readers (1–6)
Listen to Me Readers (K)
Online Leveled Readers Database (K–6)*
Take-Home Leveled Readers (K–6)

Trade Books and Big Books
Big Books (PreK–2)
Read Aloud Trade Books (PreK–K)
Sing with Me Big Book (1–2)
Trade Book Library (1–6)

Decodable Readers

Decodable Readers (K–3)

Strategic Intervention
Decodable Readers (1–2)

Take-Home Decodable Readers (K–3)

Phonics and Word Study

Alphabet Cards in English and Spanish
(PreK–K)

Alphabet Chart in English and Spanish
(PreK–K)

Animal ABCs Activity Guide (K)

Finger Tracing Cards (PreK–K)

Patterns Books (PreK–K)

Phonics Activities CD-ROM (PreK–2)*

Phonics Activities Mats (K)

Phonics and Spelling Practice Book (1–3)

Phonics and Word-Building Board and Letters
(PreK–3)

Phonics Songs and Rhymes Audio CD (K–2)

Phonics Songs and Rhymes Flip Chart (K–2)

Picture Word Cards (PreK–K)

Plastic Letter Tiles (K)

Sound-Spelling Cards and Wall Charts (1–2)

Strategies for Word Analysis (4–6)

Word Study and Spelling Practice Book (4–6)

Language Arts

Daily Fix-It Transparencies (K–6)

Grammar & Writing Book and
Teacher's Annotated Edition, The (1–6)

Grammar and Writing Practice Book
and Teacher's Manual (1–6)

Grammar Transparencies (1–6)

Six-Trait Writing Posters (1–6)

Writing Kit (1–6)

Writing Rubrics and Anchor Papers (1–6)

Writing Transparencies (1–6)

Practice and Additional Resources

AlphaBuddy Bear Puppet (K)

Alphasaurus Annie Puppet (PreK)

Amazing Words Posters (K–2)

Centers Survival Kit (PreK–6)

Graphic Organizer Book (2–6)

Graphic Organizer Flip Chart (K–1)

High-Frequency Word Cards (K)

Kindergarten Review (1)

Practice Book and Teacher's Manual (K–6)

Read Aloud Anthology (PreK–2)

Readers' Theater Anthology (K–6)

Research into Practice (K–6)

Retelling Cards (K–6)

Scott Foresman Research Base (K–6)

Skill Transparencies (2–6)

Songs and Rhymes Flip Chart (PreK)

Talk with Me, Sing with Me Chart (PreK–K)

Tested Vocabulary Cards (1–6)

Vocabulary Transparencies (1–2)

Welcome to Reading Street (PreK–1)

ELL

ELL and Transition Handbook (PreK–6)

ELL Comprehensive Kit (1–6)

ELL Posters (K–6)

ELL Readers (1–6)

ELL Teaching Guides (1–6)

Ten Important Sentences (1–6)

Digital Components

AudioText CDs (PreK–6)

Background Building Audio CDs (3–6)

ExamView® Test Generator
CD-ROM (2–6)

Online Lesson Planner (K–6)

Online New Literacies Activities (1–6)*

Online Professional Development (1–6)

Online Story Sort (K–6)*

Online Student Editions (1–6)*

Online Success Tracker™ (K–6)*

Online Teacher's Editions (PreK–6)

Phonics Activities CD-ROM (PreK–2)*

Phonics Songs and Rhymes
Audio CD (K–2)

Sing with Me/Background Building
Audio CDs (PreK–2)

Songs and Rhymes Audio CD (PreK)

My Sidewalks Early Reading Intervention (K)

My Sidewalks Intensive Reading Intervention (Levels A–E)

Reading Street for the Guided Reading Teacher (1–6)

* INTERACTIVE WHITEBOARD READY

We told you a moose was on the loose.

Reading Street Program Authors

Peter Afflerbach, Ph.D.
Professor, Department of
Curriculum and Instruction
University of Maryland at
College Park

Camille L.Z. Blachowicz, Ph.D.
Professor of Education
National-Louis University

Candy Dawson Boyd, Ph.D.
Professor, School of Education
Saint Mary's College of California

Wendy Cheyney, Ed.D.
Professor of Special Education
and Literacy, Florida
International University

Connie Juel, Ph.D.
Professor of Education, School of
Education, Stanford University

Edward J. Kame'enui, Ph.D.
Professor and Director, Institute for
the Development of Educational
Achievement, University of Oregon

Donald J. Leu, Ph.D.
John and Maria Neag Endowed
Chair in Literacy and Technology
University of Connecticut

Marvin D. Moose, Ph.D.
Reading Street University
(Hee-hee)

Jeanne R. Paratore, Ed.D.
Associate Professor of Education
Department of Literacy
and Language Development
Boston University

P. David Pearson, Ph.D.
Professor and Dean,
Graduate School of Education
University of California, Berkeley

Sam L. Sebesta, Ed.D.
Professor Emeritus,
College of Education,
University of Washington, Seattle

Deborah Simmons, Ph.D.
Professor, College of Education
and Human Development
Texas A&M University
(Not pictured)

Sharon Vaughn, Ph.D.
H.E. Hartfelder/Southland Corporation
Regents Professor
University of Texas

Susan Watts-Taffe, Ph.D.
Independent Literacy Researcher
Cincinnati, Ohio

Karen Kring Wixson, Ph.D.
Professor of Education
University of Michigan

Consulting Authors

Jim Cummins, Ph.D.
Professor
Department of Curriculum, Teaching and Learning, University of Toronto
Toronto, Ontario, Canada
English Language Learners

Lily Wong Fillmore, Ph.D.
Professor Emerita
Graduate School of Education
University of California, Berkeley
English Language Learners

Barbara Kay Foots, M.Ed.
Science Education Consultant
Houston, Texas
Science Integration

Georgia Earnest García, Ph.D.
Professor
Language and Literacy Division,
University of Illinois at Urbana-Champaign
English Language Learners

George González, Ph.D.
Professor (Retired)
School of Education, University of Texas
Pan-American, Edinburg
*English Language Learners,
Bilingual Education*

Valerie Ooka Pang, Ph.D.
Professor
School of Teacher Education
San Diego State University
Social Studies Integration

Sally M. Reis, Ph.D.
Professor and Department Head
Educational Psychology
University of Connecticut
Gifted and Talented

Consultants

V. Karen Hatfield, Ed.D.
Harrodsburg, Kentucky
Assessment

Lynn F. Howard, M.Ed.
Huntersville, North Carolina
Assessment

Student Edition Reviewers

Lahna Anhalt
Reading Coordinator
DeForest Area School District
DeForest, Wisconsin

Teresa M. Beard
Cary Elementary School
Cary, North Carolina

Ebony Cross
Glassmanor Elementary School
Oxon Hill, Maryland

Melisa G. Figurelli
Fourth and Fifth Grade Teacher
Hans Herr Elementary School
Lampeter, Pennsylvania

Jennifer Flynn
Second Grade Teacher
Weatherstone Elementary School
Cary, North Carolina

Linda Halbert
Centennial Elementary School
Springfield, Oregon

Angela Hartman
Hutto Elementary School
Hutto, Texas

Judy Holiday
Program Coordinator for
Special Education
Woodmen Center, Academy SD #20
Colorado Springs, Colorado

Victoria Holman
Third Grade Teacher
Mount Pleasant Elementary School
San Jose, California

Harriett Horton
Barnwell Elementary School
Alpharetta, Georgia

Mary Beth Huber
Elementary Curriculum Specialist
Calcasieu Parish School System
Lake Charles, Louisiana

Jeff James
Fay Wright Elementary School
Salem, Oregon

Debbie Jessen
Learning Strategist
Clifford J. Lawrence Jr. High School
Las Vegas, Nevada

Sherry Johnston
Literacy Coach
Bruce Elementary School
Milwaukee, Wisconsin

Carol Kelly
Hudson School
Union City, New Jersey

Linda Lindley
Fort Hall Elementary School
Pocatello, Idaho

Karen McCarthy
Goddard School
Brockton, Massachusetts

Patsy Mogush
Educational Coordinator
Central Kindergarten Center
Eden Prairie, Minnesota

Stacie Moncrief
Ventura Park Elementary School
Portland, Oregon

Nancy Novickis
Support Services
Douglass Valley Elementary School
United States Air Force Academy,
Colorado

Betty Parsons
Past President
Santa Clara Reading Council
San Jose, California

Greta Peay
Clark County School District
North Las Vegas, Nevada

Leslie Potter
Blackwood Elementary School
Blackwood, New Jersey

Cyndy Reynolds
Williams Elementary School
Georgetown, Texas

Sharyle Shaffer
Fourth Grade Teacher
Summit Elementary School
Smithfield, Utah

Barbara Smith
Goddard School
Brockton, Massachusetts

Jane Stewart
Lakeshore Elementary School
Monroe, Louisiana

Nancey Volenstine
Chinle Elementary School
Chinle, Arizona

Teacher's Edition Reviewers

Alyssa E. Agoston
First Grade Teacher
Elms Elementary School
Jackson, New Jersey

Laura Beltchenko
Wauconda CUSD #118
Wauconda, Illinois

Lisa Bostick
NSU Elementary Lab School
Natchitoches, Louisiana

Debra O. Brown
First Grade Teacher
McFadden School
Murfreesboro, Tennessee

Cheri S. DeLaune
Paulina Elementary School
Paulina, Louisiana

Dr. Susan B. Dold
Elementary English/Language Arts Staff
Development Coordinator
Memphis City Schools
Memphis, Tennessee

Amy Francis
Montview Elementary School
Aurora, Colorado

Dawn Julian
First Grade Teacher
Elms Elementary School
Jackson, New Jersey

Suzette Kelly
Woodmen-Roberts
Elementary School
Colorado Springs, Colorado

Suzanne Lank
Primary Teacher
Maury Elementary School
Alexandria, Virginia

Sharon Loos
Foothills Elementary School
Colorado Springs, Colorado

R. Franklin Mace
Title I Teacher
Bridgeview Elementary Center
South Charleston, West Virginia

Carol Masur
Second Grade Teacher
Elms Elementary School
Jackson, New Jersey

Jennifer D. Montgomery
Houston, Texas

Diana B. Nicholson
Cynthia Mann Elementary School
Boise, Idaho

Richard Potts
Memphis, Tennessee

Antonia Rogers
Richardson Independent
School District
Richardson, Texas

Audrey Sander
Brooklyn, New York

Dr. Johnny Warrick
Gaston County Schools
Gastonia, North Carolina

Diane Weatherstone
Second Grade Teacher
Elms Elementary School
Jackson, New Jersey

Becky Worlds
Charlotte, North Carolina

Later, Gator!

Table of Contents

Unit 1
This Land Is Your Land

Unit Opener.. 16a
Unit 1 Skills Overview 16c
Unit 1 Monitor Progress 16e
Grouping for AYP 16g
Theme Launch 16
Unit 1 Inquiry Project 17
Unit 1 Concept Development 17a

Because of Winn-Dixie 18a–39l
by Kate DiCamillo
Science in Reading
Fast Facts: Black Bears 36

Lewis and Clark and Me......40a–65l
by Laurie Myers
Social Studies in Reading
**They Traveled with
Lewis and Clark** 62

Grandfather's Journey 66a–87l
by Allen Say
Reading Online
A Look at Two Lands 84

The Horned Toad Prince 88a–111l
by Jackie Mims Hopkins
Science in Reading
**Horned Lizards and
Harvesting Ants** 108

Letters Home from Yosemite . .112a–133l
by Lisa Halvorsen
Poetry
This Land Is Your Land 130

Unit 1 Concept Wrap-Up 134a
Unit 1 Reading Poetry 134
Unit 1 Wrap-Up 138
Genre/Author Studies 139a
Author/Illustrator Biographies 139c
Glossary...................................... 139q
ELL Glossary 139w

Writing and Assessment WA1–WA18

Leveled Resources LR1–LR48

Differentiated Instruction ..... DI•1–DI•60

Teacher Resources TR1–TR25

Unit 2
Work & Play

Unit Opener..140a
Unit 2 Skills Overview 140c
Unit 2 Monitor Progress 140e
Grouping for AYP 140g
Theme Launch 140
Unit 2 Inquiry Project 141
Unit 2 Concept Development 141a

What Jo Did 142a–161l
by Charles R. Smith Jr.
Poetry
**Fast Break/Allow Me
to Introduce Myself** 158

Coyote School News 162a–187l
by Joan Sandin
Social Studies in Reading
**How to Start
a School Newspaper** 186

**Grace and
the Time Machine** 188a–211l
From *Starring Grace* by Mary Hoffman
adapted for Story Theater by Donald Abramson
Social Studies in Reading
What's There to Do? 210

**Marven of the
Great North Woods** 212a–239l
by Kathryn Lasky
Reading Online
Logging Camps 236

**So You Want
to Be President?** 240a–259l
by Judith St. George
Social Studies in Reading
Our National Parks 258

Unit 2 Concept Wrap-Up 260a
Unit 2 Reading Poetry 260
Unit 2 Wrap-Up 264
Glossary...................................... 265a
ELL Glossary 265g

Writing and Assessment WA1–WA18

Leveled Resources LR1–LR48

Differentiated Instruction ..... DI•1–DI•60

Teacher Resources TR1–TR25

Unit 3
Patterns in Nature

Unit Opener 266a
Unit 3 Skills Overview 266c
Unit 3 Monitor Progress 266e
Grouping for AYP 266g
Theme Launch 266
Unit 3 Inquiry Project 267
Unit 3 Concept Development 267a

The Stranger 268a–291l
by Chris Van Allsburg

Science in Reading
Time for a Change 288

Adelina's Whales 292a–313l
by Richard Sobol

Science in Reading
Sea Animals on the Move 310

How Night Came from the Sea 314a–337l
retold by Mary-Joan Gerson

Folk Literature
The Ant and the Bear 334

Eye of the Storm 338a–359l
by Stephen Kramer

Reading Online
Severe Weather Safety 356

The Great Kapok Tree 360a–383l
by Lynne Cherry

Science in Reading
Living in a World of Green 380

Unit 3 Concept Wrap-Up 384a
Unit 3 Reading Poetry 384
Unit 3 Wrap-Up 388
Glossary 389a
ELL Glossary 389g

Writing and Assessment WA1–WA18

Leveled Resources LR1–LR48

Differentiated Instruction . . . . . . DI•1–DI•60

Teacher Resources TR1–TR25

Unit 4
Puzzles and Mysteries

Unit Opener 390a
Unit 4 Skills Overview 390c
Unit 4 Monitor Progress 390e
Grouping for AYP 390g
Theme Launch 390
Unit 4 Inquiry Project 391
Unit 4 Concept Development 391a

The Houdini Box 392a–415l
by Brian Selznick

Science in Reading
So You Want to Be an Illusionist . . 412

Encantado: Pink Dolphin of the Amazon 416a–439l
by Sy Montgomery

Science in Reading
Mysterious Animals 436

The King in the Kitchen 440a–465l
by Margaret E. Slattery

Poetry
**A Man for All Seasonings/
A Confectioner/Expert** 464

Seeker of Knowledge 466a–487l
by James Rumford

Reading Online
Word Puzzles 484

Encyclopedia Brown and the Case of the Slippery Salamander 488a–507l
by Donald J. Sobol

Science in Reading
Young Detectives of Potterville Middle School 504

Unit 4 Concept Wrap-Up 508a
Unit 4 Reading Poetry 508
Unit 4 Wrap-Up 512
Glossary 513a
ELL Glossary 513g

Writing and Assessment WA1–WA18

Leveled Resources LR1–LR48

Differentiated Instruction . . . . . . DI•1–DI•60

Teacher Resources TR1–TR25

Unit 5
Adventures by Land, Air, and Water

Unit Opener 514a
Unit 5 Skills Overview 514c
Unit 5 Monitor Progress 514e
Grouping for AYP 514g
Theme Launch 514
Unit 5 Inquiry Project 515
Unit 5 Concept Development 515a

**Sailing Home: A Story
of a Childhood at Sea** 516a–537l
by Gloria Rand
Social Studies in Reading
Sharing a Dream 536

**Lost City: The Discovery
of Machu Picchu** 538a–559l
by Ted Lewin
Social Studies in Reading
Riding the Rails to Machu Picchu . . 556

**Amelia and Eleanor
Go for a Ride** 560a–581l
by Pam Muñoz Ryan
Reading Online
Women Explorers 578

Antarctic Journal 582a–607l
by Jennifer Owings Dewey
Social Studies in Reading
Swimming Towards Ice 604

Moonwalk 608a–629l
by Ben Bova
Science in Reading
A Walk on the Moon 626

Unit 5 Concept Wrap-Up 630a
Unit 5 Reading Poetry 630
Unit 5 Wrap-Up 634
Glossary 635a
ELL Glossary 635g

Writing and Assessment WA1–WA18

Leveled Resources LR1–LR48

Differentiated Instruction . . . DI•1–DI•60

Teacher Resources TR1–TR25

Unit 6
Reaching for Goals

Unit Opener 636a
Unit 6 Skills Overview 636c
Unit 6 Monitor Progress 636e
Grouping for AYP 636g
Theme Launch 636
Unit 6 Inquiry Project 637
Unit 6 Concept Development 637a

My Brother Martin 638a–659l
by Christine King Farris
Poetry
**Hopes and Dreams
of Young People** 658

Jim Thorpe's Bright Path . . . 660a–685l
by Joseph Bruchac
Social Studies in Reading
**Special Olympics,
Spectacular Athletes** 682

**How Tía Lola
Came to Visit Stay** 686a–711l
by Julia Alvarez
Social Studies in Reading
The Difficult Art of Hitting 708

**To Fly: The Story of
the Wright Brothers** 712a–737l
by Wendie C. Old
Reading Online
Early Flying Machines 734

**The Man Who Went to
the Far Side of the Moon** 738a–761l
by Bea Uusma Schyffert
Science in Reading
The Earth and the Moon 758

Unit 6 Concept Wrap-Up 762a
Unit 6 Reading Poetry 762
Unit 6 Wrap-Up 766
Glossary 767a
ELL Glossary 767g

Writing and Assessment WA1–WA18

Leveled Resources LR1–LR48

Differentiated Instruction . . . DI•1–DI•60

Teacher Resources TR1–TR25

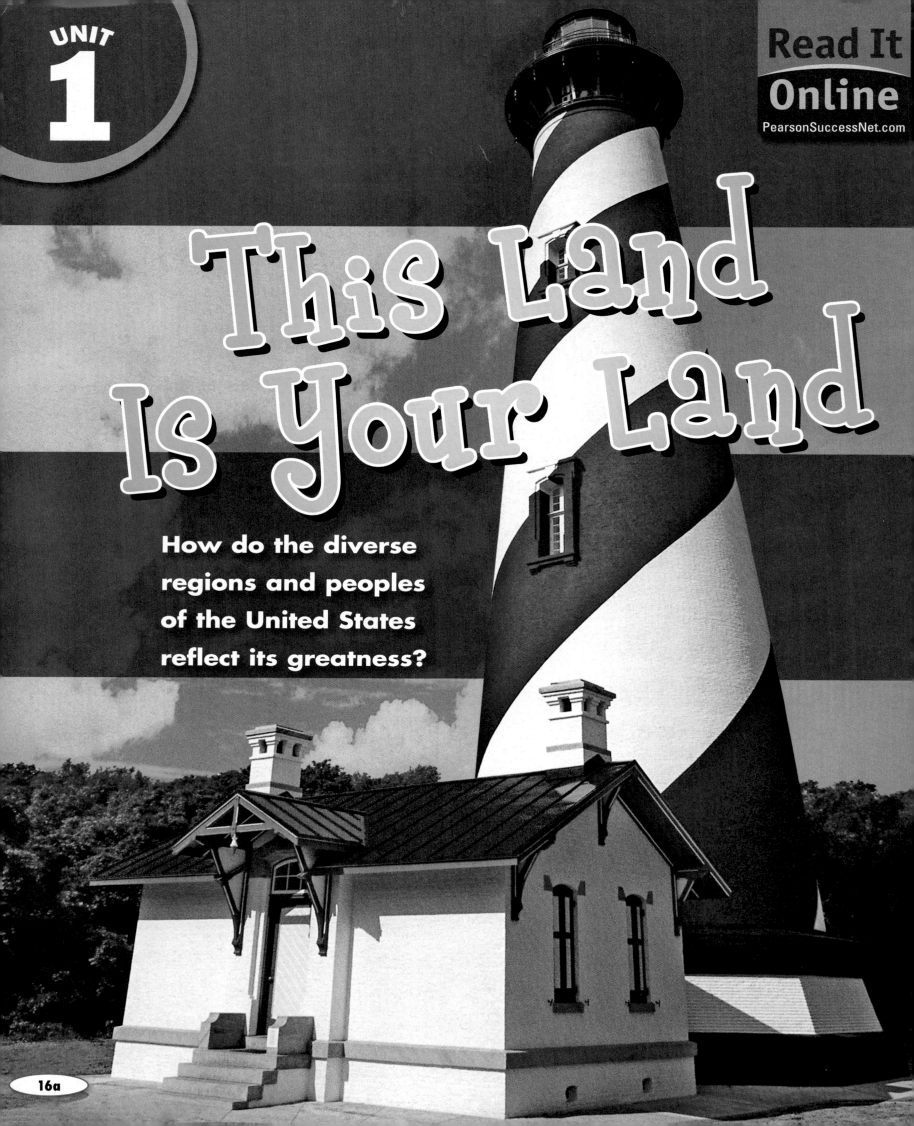

This Land Is Your Land

How do the diverse regions and peoples of the United States reflect its greatness?

Because of Winn-Dixie

A dog brings two people together in a Florida library.

REALISTIC FICTION

connect to **SOCIAL STUDIES**

Paired Selection

Fast Facts: Black Bears

EXPOSITORY NONFICTION

Lewis and Clark and Me

A group of men and their dog explore the Midwest.

HISTORICAL FANTASY

connect to **SOCIAL STUDIES**

Paired Selection

They Traveled with Lewis and Clark

NARRATIVE NONFICTION

Grandfather's Journey

A Japanese man makes his home in California.

HISTORICAL FICTION

connect to **SOCIAL STUDIES**

Paired Selection

A Look at Two Lands

ONLINE REFERENCE SOURCES

The Horned Toad Prince

A girl strikes a bargain on the Texas prairie.

MODERN FAIRY TALE

connect to **SOCIAL STUDIES**

Paired Selection

Horned Lizards and Harvesting Ants

EXPOSITORY NONFICTION

Letters Home from Yosemite

A traveler to Yosemite National Park recalls her trip.

NARRATIVE NONFICTION

connect to **SCIENCE**

Paired Selection

This Land Is Your Land

SONG

Unit 1
Skills Overview

Reading	Comprehension	**T** ◎ **Skill** Sequence ◎ **Strategy** Summarize **T** REVIEW **Skill** Author's Purpose	**T** ◎ **Skill** Author's Purpose ◎ **Strategy** Answer Questions **T** REVIEW **Skill** Cause and Effect
	Vocabulary	**T** ◎ **Strategy** Word Structure	**T** ◎ **Strategy** Word Structure
	Fluency	Tone of Voice	Pauses
Word Work	Spelling and Phonics	Short Vowels VCCV	Long *a* and *i*
Oral Language	Speaking/Listening/ Viewing	Dramatic Retelling Listen to a Story	Introduction Analyze an Illustration
Language Arts	Grammar, Usage, and Mechanics	**T** Declarative and Interrogative Sentences	**T** Imperative and Exclamatory Sentences
	Weekly Writing	Memoir Writing Trait: Word Choice	Journal Entry Writing Trait: Sentences
	Unit Process Writing	Personal Narrative	Personal Narrative
	Research and Study Skills	Map/Globe/Atlas	Skim and Scan
Integrate Science and Social Studies Standards		Time for SOCIAL STUDIES U.S. History, U.S. Geography	Time for SOCIAL STUDIES U.S. History, U.S. Geography, Economics

Big Idea How do the diverse regions and peoples of the United States reflect its greatness?

WEEK 3 	WEEK 4 	WEEK 5
70–87 **Grandfather's Journey/ A Look at Two Lands** HISTORICAL FICTION	92–111 **The Horned Toad Prince/ Horned Lizards & Harvesting Ants** MODERN FAIRY TALE	116–133 **Letters Home from Yosemite/ This Land Is Your Land** NARRATIVE NONFICTION 
What can we learn about the United States as we travel?	*What is unique about the landscape of the Southwest?*	*How does Yosemite reflect the unique qualities of the West?*
T Skill Sequence **Strategy** Graphic Organizers **T REVIEW Skill** Main Idea	**T Skill** Author's Purpose **Strategy** Story Structure **T REVIEW Skill** Sequence	**T Skill** Main Idea **Strategy** Graphic Organizers **T REVIEW Skill** Fact and Opinion
T Strategy Dictionary/Glossary	**T Strategy** Context Clues	**T Strategy** Word Structure
Tempo and Rate	Volume	Phrasing
Long *e* and *o*	Long *e*	Long *u* Sounds
Advertisement Listen to an Advertisement	Oral Report Analyze Photos	Debate Analyze a Photo
T Subjects and Predicates	**T** Compound Sentences	**T** Clauses and Complex Sentences
Postcard Writing Trait: Voice	E-mail Invitation Writing Trait: Focus/Ideas	Narrative Writing Writing Trait: Conventions
Personal Narrative	Personal Narrative	Personal Narrative
Electronic Media	Illustration/Caption/Label	Print Sources

 U.S. Geography, U.S. History   U.S. Geography, Sociology   Geology, Glaciology, Botany

Unit 1
Monitor Progress

Predictors of Reading Success		WEEK 1	WEEK 2	WEEK 3	WEEK 4
WCPM	**Fluency**	Tone of Voice 95–105 WCPM	Pauses 95–105 WCPM	Tempo and Rate 95–105 WCPM	Volume 95–105 WCPM
Vocabulary	**Vocabulary/ Concept Development** (assessed informally)	attention kindness understanding	pioneer settlers territories traveled	coast lush route	corral frontier rodeo
	Lesson Vocabulary	✿ ◉ **Strategy** Word Structure grand memorial peculiar positive prideful recalls selecting	✿ ◉ **Strategy** Word Structure docks migrating scan scent wharf yearned	✿ ◉ **Strategy** Dictionary/ Glossary amazed bewildered homeland longed sculptures still towering	✿ ◉ **Strategy** Context Clues bargain favor lassoed offended prairie riverbed shrieked
Retelling	**Text Comprehension**	✿ ◉ **Skill** Sequence ◉ **Strategy** Summarize	✿ ◉ **Skill** Author's Purpose ✿ ◉ **Strategy** Answer Questions	✿ ◉ **Skill** Sequence ◉ **Strategy** Graphic Organizers	✿ ◉ **Skill** Author's Purpose ◉ **Strategy** Story Structure

◉ Target Skill   ✿ SuccessTracker/Unit 1 Benchmark Tested Skills

Make Data–Driven Decisions

Data Management
- Assess
- Diagnose
- Prescribe
- Disaggregate

Classroom Management
- Monitor Progress
- Group
- Differentiate Instruction
- Inform Parents

Reading STREET

Success Tracker™

ONLINE CLASSROOM

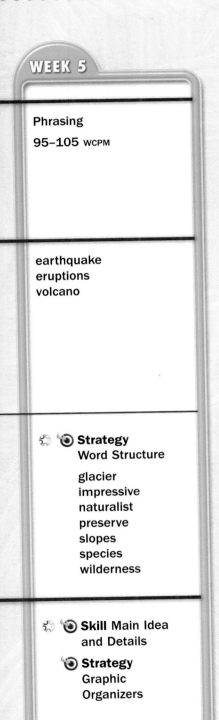

WEEK 5

Phrasing
95–105 WCPM

earthquake
eruptions
volcano

Strategy
Word Structure

glacier
impressive
naturalist
preserve
slopes
species
wilderness

Skill Main Idea
and Details

Strategy
Graphic
Organizers

Manage Data

- Assign the Unit 1 Benchmark Test for students to take online.

- SuccessTracker records results and generates reports by school, grade, classroom, or student.

- Use reports to disaggregate and aggregate Unit 1 skills and standards data to monitor progress.

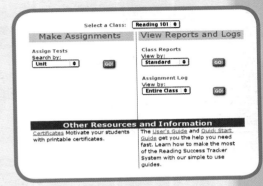

- Based on class lists created to support the categories important for AYP (gender, ethnicity, migrant education, English proficiency, disabilities, economic status), reports let you track adequate yearly progress every six weeks.

Group

- Use results from Unit 1 Benchmark Tests taken online through SuccessTracker to regroup students.

- Reports in SuccessTracker suggest appropriate groups for students based on test results.

On-Level

Strategic Intervention

Advanced

Individualize Instruction

- Tests are correlated to Unit 1 tested skills and standards so that prescriptions for individual teaching and learning plans can be created.

- Individualized prescriptions target instruction and accelerate student progress toward learning outcome goals.

- Prescriptions include resources to reteach Unit 1 skills and standards.

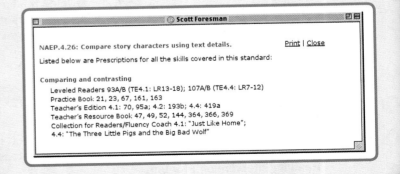

© Scott Foresman

NAEP.4.26: Compare story characters using text details.   Print | Close

Listed below are Prescriptions for all the skills covered in this standard:

Comparing and contrasting
Leveled Readers 93A/B (TE4.1: LR13-18); 107A/B (TE4.4: LR7-12)
Practice Book: 21, 23, 67, 161, 163
Teacher's Edition 4.1: 70, 95a; 4.2: 193b; 4.4: 419a
Teacher's Resource Book 47, 49, 52, 144, 364, 366, 369
Collection for Readers/Fluency Coach 4.1: "Just Like Home";
4.4: "The Three Little Pigs and the Big Bad Wolf"

Grouping for AYP

Diagnose and Differentiate

Diagnose

To make initial grouping decisions, use the Baseline Group Test or another initial placement test. Depending on children's ability levels, you may have more than one of each group.

Differentiate

If... student performance is **Below-Level** **then...** use the regular instruction and the daily Strategic Intervention lessons on pp. DI·2–DI·50.

If... student performance is **On-Level** **then...** use the regular instruction for On-Level learners throughout each selection.

If... student performance is **Advanced** **then...** use the regular instruction and the daily instruction notes and activities for Advanced learners, pp. DI·3–DI·51.

Group Time

On-Level	Strategic Intervention	Advanced
• Explicit instructional routines teach core skills and strategies.	• Daily Strategic Intervention lessons provide more intensive instruction, more scaffolding, more practice with critical skills, and more opportunities to respond.	• Daily Advanced lessons provide compacted instruction for accelerated learning, options for investigative work, and challenging reading content.
• Independent activities provide practice for core skills and extension and enrichment options.		
• Leveled readers (LR1–LR45) provide additional reading and practice with core skills and vocabulary.	• Reteach lessons (DI·52–DI·56) provide additional instructional opportunities with target skills.	• Leveled readers (LR1–LR45) provide additional reading tied to lesson concepts.
	• Leveled readers (LR1–LR45) build background for the selections and practice target skills and vocabulary.	

Additional opportunities to differentiate instruction:
- Reteach Lessons, pp. DI·52–DI·56
- Leveled Reader Instruction and Leveled Practice, LR1–LR45
- My Sidewalks on Scott Foresman Reading Street Intensive Reading Intervention Program

4–Step Plan for Assessment

1 **Diagnose and Differentiate**
2 **Monitor Progress**
3 **Assess and Regroup**
4 **Summative Assessment**

STEP 2 — Monitor Progress

- **Guiding comprehension questions** and skill and strategy instruction during reading
- **Monitor Progress boxes** to check comprehension and vocabulary
- **Weekly Assessments** on Day 3 for comprehension, Day 4 for fluency, and Day 5 for vocabulary
- **Practice Book** pages at point of use
- **Weekly Selection Tests** or **Fresh Reads for Differentiated Test Practice**

STEP 3 — Assess and Regroup

- **Days 3, 4, and 5 Assessments** Record results of weekly Days 3, 4, and 5 assessments in retelling, fluency, and vocabulary (pp. WA16–WA17) to track student progress.
- **Unit 1 Benchmark Test** Administer this test to check mastery of unit skills.
- The first opportunity for regrouping occurs at the end of Unit 2. Use weekly assessment information, Unit Benchmark Test performance, and the Unit 1 Assess and Regroup (p. WA18) to inform regrouping decisions at the end of Unit 2. See the time line below.

YOU ARE HERE
Begin Unit 1

SCOTT FORESMAN ASSESSMENT

Group Baseline Group Test → Regroup Units 1 and 2 (p. WA18) → Regroup Unit 3 → Regroup Unit 4 → Regroup Unit 5

1   5   10   15   20   25   30   END OF YEAR

OUTSIDE ASSESSMENT
Initial placement → Outside assessment for regrouping → Outside assessment for regrouping

Outside assessments (e.g., DIBELS) may recommend regrouping at other times during the year.

STEP 4 — Summative Assessment

- **Benchmark Assessment** Use to measure a student's mastery of each unit's skills.
- **End-of-Year Benchmark Assessment** Use to measure a student's mastery of program skills covered in all six units.

Unit 1
Theme Launch

Discuss the Big Idea

As a class, discuss the Big Idea question, *How do the diverse regions and peoples of the United States reflect its greatness?*

Point out that the United States is a large country, divided into regions, each with its unique geographic features, weather, and culture.

Ask students how physical environments may influence people's lifestyles, attitudes, or choice of work.

A good example of a region is America's Heartland, the center of the United States. Today, this rich flatland is the center of American farming. Here, people raise cattle and grow crops. In contrast, people living in a coastal area of the United States might enjoy boating or work in the fishing industry.

Theme and Concept Connections

Weekly lesson concepts help students connect the reading selections and the unit theme. Theme-related activities throughout the week provide opportunities to explore the relationships among the selections, the lesson concepts, and the unit theme.

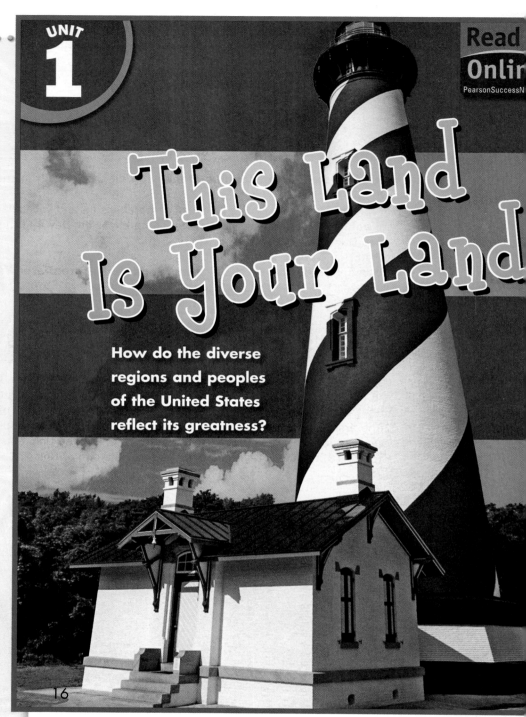

This Land Is Your Land

How do the diverse regions and peoples of the United States reflect its greatness?

16

CONNECTING CULTURES

Use the following selections to help students learn about the breadth and diversity of different regions of the United States.

Grandfather's Journey Have students discuss the different places Grandfather explored. Have them compare one of these places to their own communities.

Lewis and Clark and Me Have students discuss Lewis and Clark's journey. Students can share their thoughts about traveling on mighty rivers and trading with Native American tribes.

Because of Winn-Dixie

A dog brings two people together in a Florida library.

REALISTIC FICTION

Paired Selection

Fast Facts: Black Bears

EXPOSITORY NONFICTION

Lewis and Clark and Me

A group of men and their dog explore the Midwest.

HISTORICAL FANTASY

Paired Selection

They Traveled with Lewis and Clark

NARRATIVE NONFICTION

Grandfather's Journey

A Japanese man makes his home in California.

HISTORICAL FICTION

Paired Selection

A Look at Two Lands

ONLINE REFERENCE SOURCES

The Horned Toad Prince

A girl strikes a bargain on the Texas prairie.

MODERN FAIRY TALE

Paired Selection

Horned Lizards and Harvesting Ants

EXPOSITORY NONFICTION

Letters Home from Yosemite

A traveler to Yosemite National Park recalls her trip.

NARRATIVE NONFICTION

Paired Selection

This Land Is Your Land

SONG

17

Unit Inquiry Project

Natural Wonders

In the unit inquiry project, students choose a geographical attraction in the United States and research what makes it unique and appealing. Students may use print or online resources as available.

The project assessment rubric can be found on p. 134a. Discuss the rubric's expectations before students begin the project. **Rubric 4 3 2 1**

PROJECT TIMETABLE

WEEK	ACTIVITY/SKILL CONNECTION
1	**IDENTIFY QUESTIONS** Each student chooses a geographical attraction in the United States and browses a few Web sites or print reference materials to develop an inquiry question about what makes it unique and appealing.
2	**NAVIGATE/SEARCH** Students conduct effective information searches and look for text and images that can help them answer their questions about the region.
3	**ANALYZE** Students explore Web sites or print materials. They analyze the information they have found to determine whether or not it will be useful to them. Students print or take notes on valid information.
4	**SYNTHESIZE** Students combine relevant information they've collected from different sources to develop answers to their inquiry questions from Week 1.
5	**ASSESSMENT OPTIONS** **COMMUNICATE** Students prepare posters highlighting their geographical attractions and showing what makes them unique and appealing. Students can also design Web sites that travelers could use to find out more about the geographical attractions they researched.

Unit 1

This Land Is Your Land

CONCEPT QUESTION

How do the diverse regions and peoples of the United States reflect its greatness?

Expand the Concept
How does Yosemite reflect the unique qualities of the West?

Connect the Concept

Literature

Develop Language
earthquake, eruptions, volcano

Teach Content
Sierra Nevada
Types of Rocks
Glaciers
Redwood Forest

Writing
Narrative Writing

Internet Inquiry
Unique Qualities of the West

Time for Science

Expand the Concept
What is unique about the landscape of the Southwest?

Connect the Concept

Literature

Develop Language
corral, frontier, rodeo

Teach Content
Geography of the Southwest
Ranches of the Southwest

Writing
E-mail Invitation

Internet Inquiry
Southwestern Landscape

Time for Social Studies

Expand the Concept
What can we learn about the United States as we travel?

Connect the Concept

Literature

Develop Language
coast, lush, route

Teach Content
California's Geography
San Francisco
Wartime Conditions

Writing
Postcard

Internet Inquiry
Travel in the United States

Time for Social Studies

Expand the Concept
What experiences bring diverse peoples together?

Connect the Concept

Literature

Develop Language
attention, kindness, understanding

Teach Content
European Influence
Geography of the Southeast

Writing
Memoir

Internet Inquiry
Diversity

Time for Social Studies

Expand the Concept
What did Lewis and Clark learn on their journey?

Connect the Concept

Literature

Develop Language
pioneer, settlers, territories, traveled

Teach Content
Lewis and Clark
Midwestern Climate
Barter System
Western Expansion

Writing
Journal Entry

Internet Inquiry
Lewis and Clark's Discoveries

Oregon

Planning Guide for Common Curriculum Goals

Because of Winn-Dixie

Reading Street Teacher's Edition pages	Grade 4 Oregon Grade-Level Standards for English/Language Arts

Oral Language

Speaking/Listening Build Concept Vocabulary: 18l, 27, 33, 39c

EL.04.RE.10 Develop vocabulary by listening to and discussing both familiar and conceptually challenging selections read aloud across the subject areas.

EL.04.SL.04 Use a variety of descriptive words that help to convey a clear message.

Word Work

Short Vowels VCCV: 39i–39j

EL.04.WR.15 Spell correctly: syllables (word parts each containing a vowel sound, such as *sur-prise* or *e-col-o-gy*).

Reading

Comprehension Sequence: 18–19, 22–33, 36–39, 39b
Summarize: 18–19, 22–33

Vocabulary Lesson Vocabulary: 20b, 27, 33, 36
Word Structure: 20–21, 29, 39c

Fluency Tone of Voice: 18l–18m, 39a

Self-Selected Reading: LR1–9, TR16–17

Literature Genre—Realistic Fiction: 22
Reader Response: 34

EL.04.RE.01 Read aloud grade-level narrative text and informational text fluently and accurately with effective pacing, intonation, and expression; by the end of fourth grade, read aloud unpracticed grade-level text at a rate of 115–140 wcpm (words correct per minute).

EL.04.RE.09 Understand, learn, and use new vocabulary that is introduced and taught directly through informational text, literary text, and instruction across the subject areas.

EL.04.LI.03 Identify and/or summarize sequence of events, main ideas, and supporting details in literary selections.

Language Arts

Writing Memoir: 39g–39h

Six-Trait Writing Word Choice: 35, 39g–39h

Grammar, Usage, and Mechanics
Declarative and Interrogative Sentences: 39e–39f

Research/Study Map, Globe, Atlas: 39l

Technology New Literacies: 39k

EL.04.RE.18 Find information in specialized materials (e.g., atlas, magazine, catalog).

EL.04.WR.23 Write personal narratives: include ideas, observations, or memories of an event or experience; provide a context to allow the reader to imagine the world of the event or experience; use concrete sensory details; provide insight into why the selected event or experience is memorable.

Unit Skills

Writing Personal Narrative: WA2–9

Poetry: 134–137

Project/Wrap-Up: 138–139

EL.04.WR.04 Choose the form of writing that best suits the intended purpose—personal letter, letter to the editor, review, poem, report, or narrative.

EL.04.WR.23 Write personal narratives: include ideas, observations, or memories of an event or experience; provide a context to allow the reader to imagine the world of the event or experience; use concrete sensory details; provide insight into why the selected event or experience is memorable.

This Week's Leveled Readers

Intensive Intervention
SCOTT FORESMAN
SiDEWALKS
Intensive Intervention for Tier 3 Students

Below-Level

Nonfiction

EL.04.RE.06 Match reading to purpose—location of information, full comprehension, and personal enjoyment.

EL.04.LI.03 Identify and/or summarize sequence of events, main ideas, and supporting details in literary selections.

On-Level

Fiction

EL.04.RE.22 Make and confirm predictions about text by using prior knowledge and ideas presented in the text itself, including illustrations, titles, topic sentences, and important words.

EL.04.LI.03 Identify and/or summarize sequence of events, main ideas, and supporting details in literary selections.

Advanced

Nonfiction

EL.04.RE.05 Demonstrate listening comprehension of more complex text through class and/or small group interpretive discussions.

EL.04.LI.03 Identify and/or summarize sequence of events, main ideas, and supporting details in literary selections.

Content-Area Content Standards and Benchmarks in This Lesson

Science

SC.05.LS.01 Group or classify organisms based on a variety of characteristics. (Previews Grade 5 Benchmark)

SC.05.LS.03 Describe basic plant and animal structures and their functions. (Previews Grade 5 Benchmark)

SC.05.LS.03.01 Associate specific structures with their functions in the survival of the organism. (Previews Grade 5 Benchmark)

SC.05.LS.05 Describe the relationship between characteristics of specific habitats and the organisms that live there. (Previews Grade 5 Benchmark)

SC.05.LS.05.05 Describe the living and nonliving resources in a specific habitat and the adaptations of organisms to that habitat. (Previews Grade 5 Benchmark)

Social Studies

SS.05.GE.01 Define basic geography vocabulary such as concepts of location, direction, distance, scale, movement, and region using appropriate words and diagrams. (Previews Grade 5 Benchmark)

SS.05.GE.04.02 Identify the type of economic activity, population distribution, and cities found in regions of the United States. (Previews Grade 5 Benchmark)

SS.05.GE.07 Understand how physical environments are affected by human activities. (Previews Grade 5 Benchmark)

Oregon!

A FAMOUS OREGONIAN
Pietro Belluschi

Pietro Belluschi (1899–1994) was an Italian architect whose work is largely identified with the Pacific Northwest. He was involved in the design of more than one thousand buildings during his lifetime. Three of his works in Portland are the Equitable Building (1948), which is thought to be the first glass curtain-wall structure built in the United States; the Sutor House (1938); and Zion Lutheran Church (1950). Belluschi also designed the Portland Art Museum with other architects.

Students can . . .
Find photographs of buildings Pietro Belluschi designed. Ask students to create a collage of the buildings with the names and locations of each structure and a review of each building's design.

A SPECIAL OREGON PLACE
Corvallis

In the western part of the state, the Willamette and Mary's Rivers meet in the city of Corvallis. This city was originally called Marysville in 1851, but two years later it was renamed Corvallis, which is Latin for "heart of the valley." Oregon State University, which was founded as Corvallis College in 1858, is located here. The headquarters for the Siuslaw National Forest can be found in the city too. Thick forests of Douglas fir trees are common to the Corvallis area, and lumber sawmills are an important part of the local economy.

Students can . . .
Design a billboard of Corvallis attractions.

OREGON FUN FACTS
Did You Know?

- Kam Wah Chung & Co., in the town of John Day, was founded by "Doc" Ing Hay and Lung On as a general store and meeting place for local Chinese miners.

- For hundreds of years Native Americans in The Dalles area dried salmon, which preserved the fish in a lightweight yet nutritious form called salmon pemmican.

- At Paul Jensen Arctic Museum in Monmouth, visitors can see polar bears, musk oxen, and arctic wolves.

Students can . . .
Read an encyclopedia entry about arctic animals. Ask students to make a collector card about one species that includes its picture and facts about it.

Unit 1
This Land Is Your Land

CONCEPT QUESTION
How do the diverse regions and peoples of the United States reflect its greatness?

Week 1

What experiences bring diverse peoples together?

Week 2

What did Lewis and Clark learn on their journey?

Week 3

What can we learn about the United States as we travel?

Week 4

What is unique about the landscape of the Southwest?

Week 5

How does Yosemite reflect the unique qualities of the West?

EXPAND THE CONCEPT
What experiences bring diverse peoples together?

CONNECT THE CONCEPT

▶ **Build Background**
attention, kindness, understanding

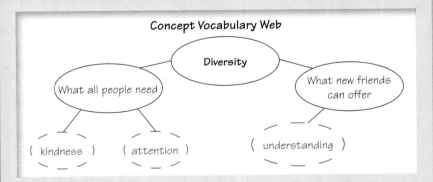

Concept Vocabulary Web

Diversity

What all people need

What new friends can offer

(kindness)　(attention)　(understanding)

▶ **Social Studies Content**
European Influence, Geography of the Southeast

▶ **Writing**
Memoir

▶ **Internet Inquiry**
Diversity

Preview Your Week

What experiences bring diverse people together?

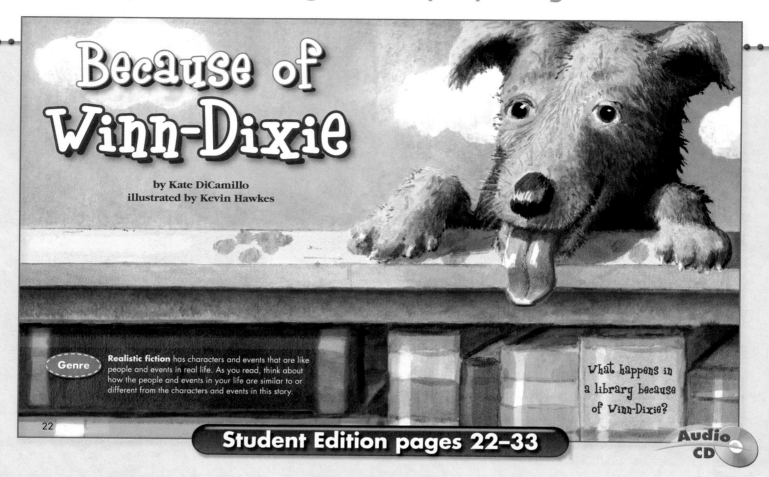

Because of Winn-Dixie

by Kate DiCamillo
illustrated by Kevin Hawkes

Genre Realistic fiction has characters and events that are like people and events in real life. As you read, think about how the people and events in your life are similar to or different from the characters and events in this story.

What happens in a library because of Winn-Dixie?

22

Student Edition pages 22–33

Audio CD

Genre	Realistic Fiction
🔊 **Vocabulary Strategy**	Word Structure
🔊 **Comprehension Skill**	Sequence
🔊 **Comprehension Strategy**	Summarize

Paired Selection

Reading Across Texts
Verify Facts About Black Bears

Genre
Expository Nonfiction

Text Features
Heads
Maps

Science in Reading

Expository Nonfiction

Genre
- Expository nonfiction provides information about people, places, animals, and other things in the real world.
- Expository nonfiction may give a few facts or it may describe a subject in depth with many facts.

Text Features
- A head above each paragraph tells you what the paragraph will be about.
- The map is important because it gives visual information to go along with the text.

Link to Science
Choose a favorite animal to research. Use the library or the Internet to find a complete description of that animal—where it lives, what it looks like, what it eats. Make a "Fast Facts" poster about your animal.

36

Fast Facts:
Black Bears

by Kathy Kranking

Where Are They?
There are more black bears in the world than any other kind of bear. Most of them live in forests and other wild places. That's why most people never see them. The people who first called these bears "black" lived in eastern North America, where the bears *are* black.

🐾 **Take a Stand**
Like other bears, black bears can stand upright as humans do. They may stand to see over tall grass or to sniff an odor in the breeze. Or they may stand to get to food that's hard to reach.

🐾 **Long, Sharp Claws**
Black bears have sharp claws that grow up to 2.5 inches (6.25 cm) long. The bears use their claws to climb, tear apart prey, dig for food, and make dens.

🐾 **Trees Are a Breeze**
Adult black bears are good at climbing trees. They usually go up to get food such as acorns or cherries.

Black Bear Habitat

Body Length: 4–6 feet (1.2–1.8 m)
Weight: 100–900 pounds (45–400 kg)
Life Span: About 30 years
Habitat: Woods, meadows, and swamps
Range: See orange areas on map.

🔊 **Sequence** Is sequence always important in what you read?

Student Edition pages 36–39

Audio CD

Read It
ONLINE
PearsonSuccessNet.com
- Student Edition
- Leveled Readers

Leveled Readers

◉ **Skill** Sequence

◉ **Strategy** Summarize

Lesson Vocabulary

Below-Level

On-Level

Advanced

ELL Reader
- Concept Vocabulary
- Text Support
- Language Enrichment

Integrate Social Studies Standards
- U.S. History
- U.S. Geography

✓ **Read**

Because of Winn-Dixie,
pp. 22–33

"Fast Facts: Black Bears,"
pp. 36–39

Leveled Readers

Below-Level
- Support Concepts

On-Level
- Develop Concepts

Advanced
- Extend Concepts
- Social Studies Extension Activity

ELL Reader

✓ **Build Concept Vocabulary**
  Diversity, pp. 18l–18m

✓ **Teach Social Studies Concepts**
  European Influence, p. 25
  Geography of the Southeast, p. 29

✓ **Explore Social Studies Center**
  Research Map Facts, p. 18k

Weekly Plan

READING

45–90 minutes

TARGET SKILLS OF THE WEEK

🎯 **Comprehension Skill**
Sequence

🎯 **Comprehension Strategy**
Summarize

🎯 **Vocabulary Strategy**
Word Structure

DAY 1
PAGES 18l–20b, 39a, 39e–39k

Oral Language

QUESTION OF THE WEEK *What experiences bring diverse people together?*

Read Aloud: "Child of the Silent Night," 18m
Build Concepts, 18l

Comprehension/Vocabulary

Comprehension Skill/Strategy Lesson, 18–19
🎯 Sequence **T**
🎯 Summarize
Build Background, 20a
Introduce Lesson Vocabulary, 20b
grand, memorial, peculiar, positive, prideful, recalls, selecting **T**

Read Leveled Readers

Grouping Options 18f–18g

Fluency

Model Tone of Voice, 18l–18m, 39a

DAY 2
PAGES 20–27, 39a, 39e–39k

Oral Language

QUESTION OF THE DAY *Can an elderly librarian and a little girl really be friends?*

Comprehension/Vocabulary

Vocabulary Strategy Lesson, 20–21
🎯 Word Structure **T**

Read *Because of Winn-Dixie,* 22–27

Grouping Options 18f–18g

🎯 Sequence **T**
🎯 Summarize
🎯 Word Structure
REVIEW Author's Purpose **T**
Develop Vocabulary

Fluency

Choral Reading, 39a

LANGUAGE ARTS

30–60 minutes

Trait of the Week

Word Choice

Grammar, 39e
Introduce Declarative and Interrogative Sentences **T**

Writing Workshop, 39g
Introduce Memoir
Model the Trait of the Week: Word Choice

Spelling, 39i
Pretest for Short Vowels VCCV

Internet Inquiry, 39k
Identify Questions

Grammar, 39e
Develop Declarative and Interrogative Sentences **T**

Writing Workshop, 39g
Improve Writing with Voice/Tone

Spelling, 39i
Teach the Generalization

Internet Inquiry, 39k
Navigate/Search

DAILY WRITING ACTIVITIES

Day 1 Write to Read, 18

Day 2 Words to Write, 21
Strategy Response Log, 22, 27

DAILY SOCIAL STUDIES CONNECTIONS

Day 1 Diversity Concept Web, 18l

Day 2 Time for Social Studies: European Influence, 25
Revisit the Diversity Concept Web, 27

DAILY SUCCESS PREDICTORS
for Adequate Yearly Progress

Monitor Progress and Corrective Feedback

Vocabulary Check Vocabulary, *18l*

RESOURCES FOR THE WEEK

- Practice Book, *pp. 1–10*
- Word Study and Spelling Practice Book, *pp. 1–4*
- Grammar and Writing Practice Book, *pp. 1–4*

- Selection Test, *pp. 1–4*
- Fresh Reads for Differentiated Test Practice, *pp. 1–6*
- The Grammar and Writing Book, *pp. 50–55*

Grouping Options for Differentiated Instruction
Turn the page for the small group lesson plan.

DAY 3 — PAGES 28–35, 39a, 39e–39k

Oral Language

QUESTION OF THE DAY *What do Miss Franny and Opal have in common?*

Comprehension/Vocabulary

Read *Because of Winn-Dixie,* 28–34

Grouping Options 18f–18g

- ◉ Summarize **T**
- ◉ Word Structure
- ◉ Author's Purpose **T**
- Develop Vocabulary

Reader Response

Selection Test

Fluency

Model Tone of Voice, 39a

Grammar, 39f
Apply Declarative and Interrogative Sentences in Writing **T**

Writing Workshop, 35, 39h
Write Now
Prewrite and Draft

Spelling, 39j
Connect Spelling to Writing

Internet Inquiry, 39k
Analyze Sources

Day 3 Strategy Response Log, 32
Look Back and Write, 34

Day 3 Time for Social Studies: Geography of the Southeast, 29
Revisit the Diversity Concept Web, 33

DAY 4 — PAGES 36–39a, 39e–39k

Oral Language

QUESTION OF THE DAY *Why might it cause problems when people move into bears' home territory?*

Comprehension/Vocabulary

Read "Fast Facts: Black Bears," 36–39

Grouping Options 18f–18g

Expository Nonfiction/
Text Features

Reading Across Texts

Content-Area Vocabulary

Fluency

Partner Reading, 39a

Grammar, 39f
Practice Declarative and Interrogative Sentences for Standardized Tests **T**

Writing Workshop, 39h
Draft and Revise

Spelling, 39j
Provide a Strategy

Internet Inquiry, 39k
Synthesize Information

Day 4 Writing Across Texts, 39

Day 4 Time for Social Studies: Research Map Facts, 18k

DAY 5 — PAGES 39a–39l

Oral Language

QUESTION OF THE WEEK *To wrap up the week, revisit the Day 1 question.*
Build Concept Vocabulary, 39c

Fluency

Read Leveled Readers

Grouping Options 18f–18g

Assess Reading Rate, 39a

Comprehension/Vocabulary

- ◉ Reteach Sequence, 39b **T**
- Idiom, 39b
- ◉ Review Word Structure, 39c **T**

Speaking and Listening, 39d
Dramatic Retelling
Listen to a Story

Grammar, 39f
Cumulative Review

Writing Workshop, 39h
Connect to Unit Writing

Spelling, 39j
Posttest for Short Vowels VCCV

Internet Inquiry, 39k
Communicate Results

Research/Study Skills, 39l
Map/Globe/Atlas

Day 5 Idiom, 39b

Day 5 Revisit the Diversity Concept Web, 39c

KEY ◉ = Target Skill   **T** = Tested Skill

Comprehension — Check Retelling, *34*	**Fluency** — Check Fluency wcpm, *39a*	**Vocabulary** — Check Vocabulary, *39c*

SUCCESS PREDICTOR

Small Group Plan for Differentiated Instruction

Daily Plan AT A GLANCE

Reading
Whole Group
- Oral Language
- Comprehension/Vocabulary

Group Time
Differentiated Instruction

Meet with small groups to provide:
- Skill Support
- Reading Support
- Fluency Practice

Read

This week's lessons for daily group time can be found behind the Differentiated Instruction (DI) tab on pp. DI·2–DI·11.

Whole Group
- Fluency

Language Arts
- Grammar
- Writing
- Spelling
- Research/Inquiry
- Speaking/Listening/Viewing

Use *My Sidewalks on Reading Street* for Tier III intensive reading intervention.

DAY 1

On-Level	Strategic Intervention	Advanced
Teacher-Led *Page DI·3*	**Teacher-Led** *Page DI·2*	**Teacher-Led** *Page DI·3*
• Develop Concept Vocabulary • **Read** On-Level Reader *Something to Do*	• Reinforce Concepts • **Read** Below-Level Reader *Florida Everglades: Its Plants & Animals*	• **Read** Advanced Reader *The Story of Libraries* • Independent Extension Activity

(i) Independent Activities

While you meet with small groups, have the rest of the class...

- Visit the Reading/Library Center
- Listen to the Background Building Audio
- Finish Write to Read, p. 18
- Complete Practice Book pp. 3–4
- Visit Cross-Curricular Centers

DAY 2

On-Level	Strategic Intervention	Advanced
Teacher-Led *Pages 24–27*	**Teacher-Led** *Page DI·4*	**Teacher-Led** *Page DI·5*
• **Read** *Because of Winn-Dixie*	• Practice Lesson Vocabulary • Read Multisyllabic Words • **Read** or Listen to *Because of Winn-Dixie*	• Extend Vocabulary • **Read** *Because of Winn-Dixie*

(i) Independent Activities

While you meet with small groups, have the rest of the class...

- Visit the Reading/Library Center
- Listen to the AudioText for *Because of Winn-Dixie*
- Finish Words to Write, p. 21
- Complete Practice Book pp. 5–6
- Write in their Strategy Response Logs, pp. 22, 27
- Visit Cross-Curricular Centers
- Work on inquiry projects

DAY 3

On-Level	Strategic Intervention	Advanced
Teacher-Led *Pages 28–33*	**Teacher-Led** *Page DI·6*	**Teacher-Led** *Page DI·7*
• **Read** *Because of Winn-Dixie*	• Practice Sequence and Summarize • **Read** or Listen to *Because of Winn-Dixie*	• Extend Vocabulary • **Read** *Because of Winn-Dixie*

(i) Independent Activities

While you meet with small groups, have the rest of the class...

- Visit the Reading/Library Center
- Listen to the AudioText for *Because of Winn-Dixie*
- Write in their Strategy Response Logs, p. 32
- Finish Look Back and Write, p. 34
- Complete Practice Book p. 7
- Visit Cross-Curricular Centers
- Work on inquiry projects

① Begin with whole class skill and strategy instruction.

② Meet with small groups to provide differentiated instruction.

③ Gather the whole class back together for fluency and language arts.

On-Level

Teacher-Led
Pages 36–39

- **Read** "Fast Facts: Black Bears"

Strategic Intervention

Teacher-Led
Page DI · 8

- Practice Retelling
- **Read** or Listen to "Fast Facts: Black Bears"

Advanced

Teacher-Led
Page DI · 9

- **Read** "Fast Facts: Black Bears"
- Genre Study

DAY 4

ⓘ Independent Activities

While you meet with small groups, have the rest of the class…

- Visit the Reading/Library Center
- Listen to the AudioText for "Fast Facts: Black Bears"
- Visit the Writing/Vocabulary Center
- Finish Writing Across Texts, p. 39
- Visit Cross-Curricular Centers
- Work on inquiry projects

On-Level

Teacher-Led
Page DI · 11

- **Reread** Leveled Reader *Something to Do*
- Retell *Something to Do*

Strategic Intervention

Teacher-Led
Page DI · 10

- **Reread** Leveled Reader *Florida Everglades: Its Plants & Animals*
- Retell *Florida Everglades: Its Plants & Animals*

Advanced

Teacher-Led
Page DI · 11

- **Reread** Leveled Reader The *Story of Libraries*
- Share Extension Activity

DAY 5

ⓘ Independent Activities

While you meet with small groups, have the rest of the class…

- Visit the Reading/Library Center
- Complete Practice Book pp. 8–10
- Visit Cross-Curricular Centers
- Work on inquiry projects

Grouping Place English language learners in the groups that correspond to their reading abilities in English.

Use the appropriate Leveled Reader or other text at students' instructional level.

TIP Send home the appropriate Multilingual Summary of the main selection on Day 1.

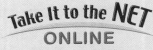
Take It to the NET
ONLINE
PearsonSuccessNet.com

P. David Pearson
For research on comprehension instruction, see the article "An Instructional Study" by J. Hansen and Scott Foresman author P. D. Pearson.

TEACHER TALK

Comprehension strategies are steps a reader takes to make sense of text. Strategies include monitoring comprehension, using graphic organizers, answering and asking questions, summarizing, and so on.

Be sure to schedule time for students to work on the unit inquiry project "Natural Wonders." This week students develop inquiry questions about geographical attractions in the United States.

Looking Ahead

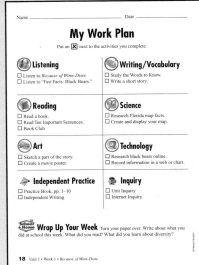

▲ **Group-Time Survival Guide**
p. 18, Weekly Contract

Because of Winn-Dixie **18g**

Customize Your Plan *by Strand*

ORAL LANGUAGE

Concept Development

What experiences bring diverse people together?

CONCEPT VOCABULARY

attention   kindness   understanding

BUILD

❑ **Question of the Week** Introduce and discuss the question of the week. This week students will read a variety of texts and work on projects related to the concept *diversity*. Post the question for students to refer to throughout the week. **DAY 1** *18d*

❑ **Read Aloud** Read aloud "Child of the Silent Night." Then begin a web to build concepts and concept vocabulary related to this week's lesson and the unit theme, This Land Is Your Land. Introduce the concept words *attention, kindness*, and *understanding* and have students place them on the web. Display the web for use throughout the week. **DAY 1** *18l–18m*

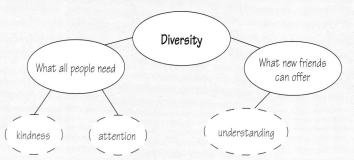

DEVELOP

❑ **Question of the Day** Use the prompts from the Weekly Planner to engage students in conversations related to this week's reading and the unit theme. **EVERY DAY** *18d–18e*

❑ **Concept Vocabulary Web** Revisit the Diversity Concept Web and encourage students to add concept words from their reading and life experiences. **DAY 2** *27*, **DAY 3** *33*

CONNECT

❑ **Looking Back/Moving Forward** Revisit the Diversity Concept Web and discuss how it relates to this week's lesson and the unit theme. Then make connections to next week's lesson. **DAY 5** *39c*

CHECK

❑ **Concept Vocabulary Web** Use the Diversity Concept Web to check students' understanding of the concept vocabulary words *attention, kindness*, and *understanding*. **DAY 1** *18l*, **DAY 5** *39c*

VOCABULARY

STRATEGY WORD STRUCTURE
When you are reading and see an unfamiliar word, you can look at the end of the word to help figure out the meaning. The base word, the word without the ending, will also help you understand the meaning.

LESSON VOCABULARY

grand   memorial
peculiar   positive
prideful   recalls
selecting

TEACH

❑ **Words to Know** Give students the opportunity to tell what they already know about this week's lesson vocabulary words. Then discuss word meaning. **DAY 1** *20b*

❑ **Vocabulary Strategy Lesson** Use the vocabulary strategy lesson in the Student Edition to introduce and model this week's strategy, *word structure*. **DAY 2** *20–21*

Vocabulary Strategy Lesson

PRACTICE/APPLY

❑ **Leveled Text** Read the lesson vocabulary in the context of leveled text. **DAY 1** *LR1–LR9*

Leveled Readers

❑ **Words in Context** Read the lesson vocabulary and apply word structure in the context of *Because of Winn-Dixie*. **DAY 2** *22–27*, **DAY 3** *28–34*

❑ **Writing/Vocabulary Center** Write a short story about the first time you met a friend. **ANY DAY** *18k*

Main Selection—Fiction

❑ **Homework** Practice Book pp. 4–5. **DAY 1** *20b*, **DAY 2** *21*

❑ **Word Play** Have students select two words from *Because of Winn-Dixie* and create a crossword puzzle. The words could be vocabulary words or other important words. **ANY DAY** *39c*

ASSESS

❑ **Selection Test** Use the Selection Test to determine students' understanding of the lesson vocabulary words. **DAY 3**

RETEACH/REVIEW

❑ **Reteach Lesson** If necessary, use this lesson to reteach and review *word structure*. **DAY 5** *39c*

COMPREHENSION

◉ SKILL SEQUENCE Events in a story occur in a certain order, or sequence. The sequence of events can be important to understanding the story.

◉ STRATEGY SUMMARIZE Summarizing is a short retelling of a portion of the text that includes the important information (main ideas).

TEACH

❏ **Skill/Strategy Lesson** Use the skill/strategy lesson in the Student Edition to introduce and model *sequence* and *summarize*. **DAY 1** 18-19

❏ **Extend Skills** Teach idiom. **ANY DAY** 39b

Skill/Strategy Lesson

PRACTICE/APPLY

❏ **Leveled Text** Apply *sequence* and *summarize* to read leveled text. **DAY 1** LR1-LR9

❏ **Skills and Strategies in Context** Read *Because of Winn-Dixie*, using the Guiding Comprehension questions to apply *sequence* and *summarize*. **DAY 2** 22-27, **DAY 3** 28-34

Leveled Readers

❏ **Skills and Strategies in Context** Read "Fast Facts: Black Bears," guiding students as they apply *sequence* and *summarize*. Then have students discuss and write across texts. **DAY 4** 36-39

Main Selection—Fiction

❏ **Homework** Practice Book pp. 3, 7, 8 **DAY 1** 19, **DAY 3** 33, **DAY 5** 39b

Paired Selection—Nonfiction

❏ **Fresh Reads for Differentiated Test Practice** Have students practice *sequence* with a new passage. **DAY 3**

ASSESS

❏ **Selection Test** Determine students' understanding of the selection and their use of *sequence*. **DAY 3**

❏ **Retell** Have students retell *Because of Winn-Dixie*. **DAY 3** 34-35

RETEACH/REVIEW

❏ **Reteach Lesson** If necessary, reteach and review *sequence*. **DAY 5** 39b

FLUENCY

SKILL TONE OF VOICE Tone of voice is the ability to add emotion to words. By varying your tone as you read aloud, you can bring the words to life, create the mood, and make the reading lively.

TEACH

❏ **Read Aloud** Model fluent reading by rereading "Child of the Silent Night." Focus on this week's fluency skill, tone of voice. **DAY 1** 18l-18m, 39a

PRACTICE/APPLY

❏ **Choral Reading** Read aloud selected paragraphs from *Because of Winn-Dixie*, emphasizing your tone of voice. Have students practice by doing three choral readings of the paragraphs. **DAY 2** 39a, **DAY 3** 39a

❏ **Partner Reading** Have partners practice reading aloud, calling attention to their tone of voice. As students reread, monitor their progress toward their individual fluency goals. **DAY 4** 39a

❏ **Listening Center** Have students follow along with the AudioText for this week's selections. **ANY DAY** 18j

❏ **Reading/Library Center** Have students reread a selection of their choice. **ANY DAY** 18j

❏ **Fluency Coach** Have students use Fluency Coach to listen to fluent readings or practice reading on their own. **ANY DAY**

ASSESS

❏ **Check Fluency** WCPM Do a one-minute timed reading, paying special attention to this week's skill—tone of voice. Provide feedback for each student. **DAY 5** 39a

Customize Your Plan *by Strand*

GRAMMAR

DECLARATIVE AND INTERROGATIVE SENTENCES A declarative sentence tells something and ends with a period. An interrogative sentence asks a question and ends with a question mark.

TEACH

❏ **Grammar Transparency 1** Use Grammar Transparency 1 to teach declarative and interrogative sentences. DAY 1 *39e*

Grammar Transparency 1

PRACTICE/APPLY

❏ **Develop the Concept** Review the concept of declarative and interrogative sentences and provide guided practice. DAY 2 *39e*

❏ **Apply to Writing** Have students review something they have written and improve it by adding interrogative sentences. DAY 3 *39f*

❏ **Test Preparation** Examine common errors in declarative and interrogative sentences to prepare for standardized tests. DAY 4 *39f*

❏ **Homework** Grammar and Writing Practice Book pp. 1–3. DAY 2 *39e,* DAY 3 *39f,* DAY 4 *39f*

ASSESS

❏ **Cumulative Review** Use Grammar and Writing Practice Book p. 4. DAY 5 *39f*

RETEACH/REVIEW

❏ **Daily Fix-It** Have students find and correct errors in grammar, spelling, and punctuation. **EVERY DAY** *39e–39f*

❏ **The Grammar and Writing Book** Use pp. 50–53 of The Grammar and Writing Book to extend instruction for declarative and interrogative sentences. **ANY DAY**

The Grammar and Writing Book

WRITING

Trait of the Week

WORD CHOICE Good writers choose their words carefully. Strong verbs, specific nouns, and vivid adjectives help writers elaborate on their ideas. Well-chosen words make writing clear and lively.

TEACH

❏ **Writing Transparency 1A** Use the model to introduce and discuss the Trait of the Week. DAY 1 *39g*

❏ **Writing Transparency 1B** Use the transparency to show students how word choice can improve their writing. DAY 2 *39g*

Writing Transparency 1A   **Writing Transparency 1B**

PRACTICE/APPLY

❏ **Write Now** Examine the model on Student Edition p. 35. Then have students write their own memoir. DAY 3 *35, 39h,* DAY 4 *39h*

> **Prompt** In *Because of Winn-Dixie,* Opal tells about her experiences moving to a new town. Think about a time that you were a newcomer to a place or situation. Use vivid words to write a memoir about that experience.

Write Now p. 35

❏ **Writing/Vocabulary Center** Write a short story about the first time you met a friend. **ANY DAY** *18k*

ASSESS

❏ **Writing Trait Rubric** Use the rubric to evaluate students' writing. DAY 4 *39h*

RETEACH/REVIEW

❏ **The Grammar and Writing Book** Use pp. 50–55 of The Grammar and Writing Book to extend instruction for declarative and interrogative sentences, voice/tone, and memoirs. **ANY DAY**

The Grammar and Writing Book

SPELLING

GENERALIZATION SHORT VOWELS VCCV Short *a, e, i, o,* and *u* are usually spelled *a: admire, e: method, i: finger, o: soccer,* and *u: custom*. A single vowel that comes before two consonants usually has a short sound.

TEACH

❏ **Pretest** Give the pretest for words with short vowels VCCV. Guide students in self-correcting their pretests and correcting any misspellings. **DAY 1** *39i*

❏ **Think and Practice** Connect spelling to the phonics generalization short vowels VCCV. **DAY 2** *39i*

PRACTICE/APPLY

❏ **Connect to Writing** Have students use spelling words to write a personal essay. Then review frequently misspelled words: *with, cousin.* **DAY 3** *39j*

❏ **Homework** Phonics and Spelling Practice Book pp. 1–4. **EVERY DAY**

RETEACH/REVIEW

❏ **Review** Review spelling words to prepare for the posttest. Then provide students with a spelling strategy—problem parts. **DAY 4** *39j*

ASSESS

❏ **Posttest** Use dictation sentences to give the posttest for words with short vowels VCCV. **DAY 5** *39j*

Spelling Words

1. admire	8. engine	15. flatten
2. magnet	9. sudden*	16. rascal
3. contest	10. finger*	17. gutter
4. method	11. accident	18. mammal
5. custom	12. mitten	19. happen*
6. rally	13. intend*	20. cannon
7. soccer	14. fabric	

Challenge Words

21. dungeon	23. festival	25. injury
22. magnify	24. thunderstorm	

*Word from the selection

RESEARCH AND INQUIRY

❏ **Internet Inquiry** Have students conduct an Internet inquiry on diversity. **EVERY DAY** *39k*

❏ **Map/Globe/Atlas** Review the features of a map, globe, and atlas. Discuss with students how these resources can be used to help develop their inquiry question. **DAY 5** *39l*

❏ **Unit Inquiry** Allow time for students to develop inquiry questions about geographical attractions in the United States. **ANY DAY** *17*

SPEAKING AND LISTENING

❏ **Dramatic Retelling** Have students select a scene from *Because of Winn-Dixie* and retell it from the point of view of one of the characters. **DAY 5** *39d*

❏ **Listen to a Story** Have students listen to a reading of a story that has a lot of dramatic tension. This could be a pre-recorded story or a story of your choice to read aloud. Follow this activity with a class discussion. **DAY 5** *39d*

Resources for
Differentiated Instruction

LEVELED READERS

▶ **Comprehension**
- 🎯 **Skill** Sequence
- 🎯 **Strategy** Summarize

▶ **Lesson Vocabulary**
- 🎯 **Word Structure**

memorial   grand   peculiar   prideful   recalls   selecting   positive

▶ **Social Studies Standards**
- U.S. History
- U.S. Geography

Leveled Reader Database

ONLINE

PearsonSuccessNet.com

Use the Online Database of over 600 books to

- Download and print additional copies of this week's leveled readers.

- Listen to the readers being read online.

- Search for more titles focused on this week's skills, topic, and content.

On-Level Reader

Something to Do by Carol Talley, illustrated by Don Dyen

Name _____   **Something to Do**

Sequence

- **Sequence** is the order of events.

Directions Use *Something to Do* to answer the following questions.

1. Skim through the book. Write down some of the clue words the author uses to indicate the sequence of events in the story.
   after, every morning, so, then, the next step, now

2. Reread page 5. What was the usual sequence of events every day after Grandpa moved in?
   Dad left to open the café; the boy left for school; Grandpa settled into his chair to watch TV and sleep; the boy and his dad returned home at the end of the day to find Grandpa still in his chair.

3. Reread pages 7 and 8. What was the order of Grandpa's reactions to the pyrography set?
   He asked what it was; he said he couldn't draw; he said he couldn't even read his own writing with a pen; he made one sign that said "Do not disturb! Sleeping!"

4. What was the sequence of events that led to Grandpa making his first fried pie?
   Dad gave Grandpa and the boy some pies to eat one night; Grandpa and Dad remembered the fried pies Grandma used to make; the boy suggested that they make some fried pies; the boy dragged Grandpa into the kitchen to try.

🎯 **On-Level Practice** TE p. LR5

Name _____   **Something to Do**

Vocabulary

Directions Rewrite each sentence using the form of the underlined word found in the box.

Check the Words You Know

☐ grand ☐ memorial ☐ peculiar ☐ positive
☐ prideful ☐ recalls ☐ selecting

Possible responses given.

1. Dad loves recalling the time when our family took a trip across the country.
   Dad often recalls the fried pies Grandma used to make.

2. Grandpa positively couldn't get along all by himself.
   Grandpa was positive he couldn't get along all by himself.

3. Grandma took pride in her fried pies.
   Grandma was prideful about her fried pies.

4. It's hard to select which flavor I want.
   Selecting a flavor is hard.

Directions For each word below, write the meaning of the word. Then write a sentence using the word. **Sentences will vary.**

5. peculiar   odd

6. grand   wonderful

7. memorial   something done in honor of someone

On-Level Practice TE p. LR6

Life Science

Florida Everglades: Its Plants & Animals by Patricia West

Below-Level Reader

Name _____   **Florida Everglades**

Sequence

- **Sequence** is the order of events.

Directions Use *Florida Everglades: Its Plants & Animals*. Answer the following questions.

1. What is the sequence of the information the author presents about black bears in the Florida Everglades?
   bear facts, bear trouble, bear food

2. Reread page 11. What sequence of events led to the protection of egrets?
   First, many egrets were killed for their feathers
   Next, the feathers were used to decorate hats
   Now, the egret is protected

3. Reread page 14. What sequence of events led to the protection of the Florida Everglades?
   First, many animals and plants lived in the Florida Everglades
   Next, many animals and plants almost went extinct
   Now, the Florida Everglades is a protected habitat

4. In what sequence does the selection tell about the plants and animals in the Florida Everglades?
   First, black bears
   Next, other animals
   Next, birds
   Next, plants
   Finally, plants and animals together

🎯 **Below-Level Practice** TE p. LR2

Name _____   **Florida Everglades**

Vocabulary

Directions Use the vocabulary words in the box to fill in the blanks in the sentences below.

Check the Words You Know

☐ grand ☐ memorial ☐ peculiar ☐ positive
☐ prideful ☐ recall ☐ select

1. I was **positive** the black bear had not seen me.

2. Many people support putting up a **memorial** sign for all the black bears killed crossing highways.

3. Black bears like to **select** the tastiest berries.

4. Besides the armadillo, another **peculiar** animal is the porcupine, with its unusual quills.

5. One of the most amazing habitats in North America is the **grand** Florida Everglades.

6. Nina could not **recall** where she had put her homework the night before.

7. People who live in Florida are **prideful** of many beautiful plants that grow in their state.

Directions Use a thesaurus to find antonyms for each of the words below. **Possible responses given.**

8. grand   ordinary, poor, small, minor

9. peculiar   normal, ordinary, usual, common

10. prideful   ashamed, humble

Below-Level Practice TE p. LR3

Advanced

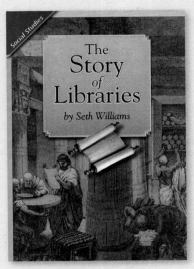

Advanced Reader

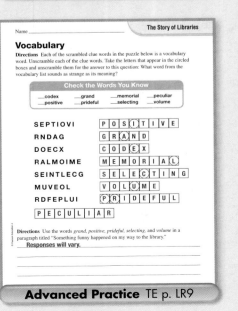

Advanced Practice TE p. LR8

Advanced Practice TE p. LR9

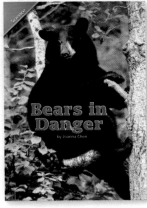

ELL Reader

ELL Poster 1

Teacher's Edition Notes

ELL notes throughout this lesson support instruction and reference additional resources at point of use.

Teaching Guide pp. 1–7, 212–213

- Multilingual summaries of the main selection
- Comprehension lesson
- Vocabulary strategies and word cards
- ELL Reader 4.1.1 lesson

ELL and Transition Handbook

Ten Important Sentences

- Key ideas from every selection in the Student Edition
- Activities to build sentence power

More Reading

Readers' Theater Anthology

- Fluency practice
- Five scripts to build fluency
- Poetry for oral interpretation

Leveled Trade Books

- Extended reading tied to the unit concept
- Lessons in the Trade Book Library Teaching Guide

School + Home

Homework

- Family Times Newsletter
- ELL Multilingual Selection Summaries

Take-Home Books

- Leveled Readers

Because of Winn-Dixie

18i

Cross-Curricular Centers

Listening

Listen to the Selections

MATERIALS
CD player, headphones,
AudioText CD, student book

`SINGLES`

LISTEN TO LITERATURE Listen to *Because of Winn-Dixie* and "Fast Facts: Black Bears" as you follow or read along in your book. Listen for the sequence of events that occur in *Because of Winn-Dixie*.

If there is anything you don't understand, you can listen again to any section.

Reading/Library

Read It *Again!*

MATERIALS
Collection of books for self-selected reading, reading logs, student book

`SINGLES`
`PAIRS`
`GROUPS`

Select a book you have already read. Record the title of the book in your reading log. You may want to read with a partner.

Choose from the following:

- **Leveled Readers**
- **ELL Readers**
- **Books or Stories Written by Classmates**
- **Books from the Library**
- ***Because of Winn-Dixie***

TEN IMPORTANT SENTENCES Read the Ten Important Sentences for *Because of Winn-Dixie*. Then locate the sentences in the student book.

BOOK CLUB Read other books that belong in the same genre of realistic fiction. Get together with a group to share your favorites and discuss what makes this genre so fun to read.

Art

Create a Poster

MATERIALS
Art materials

`SINGLES`

Imagine that *Because of Winn-Dixie* is being made into a movie. Draft a poster to convince people to see the movie.

1. **Draw a rough sketch of your favorite part of the story.**
2. **Under your sketch write three or four sentences to convince people to see the movie. Be sure to include something about the story.**

EARLY FINISHERS Use your draft to create a finished poster.

Because of Winn-Dixie

It's the best movie of the year!

What is a bear doing at the library? See <u>Because of Winn-Dixie</u> to find out!

Scott Foresman Reading Street Centers Survival Kit

Use the *Because of Winn-Dixie* materials from the Reading Street Centers Survival Kit to organize this week's centers.

Writing/Vocabulary

Write a Friend Story

MATERIALS **SINGLES**
Writing materials

Write a short story about the first time you met a friend.

1. **Use the following title or make up your own: "The First Time I Met _____." Fill in the blank with the name of a friend.**
2. **Use interesting details, such as the time of year, where and how you met, what time of day it was, what you were doing, and why you liked your friend.**

EARLY FINISHERS Write a paragraph about what you and your friend like to do together now.

Tom Peterson
Crashing into a New Friend
My friend Mark and I met when I crashed into him at the skateboard park. Luckily, we were both wearing a helmet and pads, so no one got hurt.

Social Studies

Research Map Facts

MATERIALS **SINGLES** **PAIRS** **GROUPS**
Map of Florida or the southeastern United States, tracing paper, self-sticking notes or index cards, writing materials

Use a map to find facts about Florida.

1. **Look at a map of Florida or southeastern United States and copy or trace it onto your own paper.**
2. **Find at least five facts about this region, such as the names of bodies of water or mountain ranges.**
3. **Write your facts on self-sticking notes or index cards and attach them to your map.**
4. **Display your map and facts in the classroom.**

EARLY FINISHERS Discuss reasons why you think people would want to visit Florida.

Technology

Search the Internet

MATERIALS **SINGLES** **PAIRS**
Internet access, writing materials

Search the Internet to learn more about black bears.

1. **Using a student-friendly search engine, type the keywords *black bears* into the search line.**
2. **Click on one or more Web site links listed to learn more about bears.**
3. **Use a word web, chart, or other graphic organizer to record interesting information about bears.**
4. **Follow classroom rules when searching the Internet.**

EARLY FINISHERS Tell a classmate about what you learned. If your friend did an Internet search too, ask what he or she learned.

ALL CENTERS

OBJECTIVES

- Build vocabulary by finding words related to the lesson concept.
- Listen for a sequence of events.

Concept Vocabulary

attention care and thoughtfulness
kindness treatment that does good rather than harm; gentleness
understanding comprehension

Monitor Progress

Check Vocabulary

If...	**then...** review the
students are unable to place words on the web,	lesson concept. Place the words on the web and provide additional words for practice, such as *love* and *care*.

SUCCESS PREDICTOR

DAY 1   **Grouping Options**

Reading
Whole Group
Introduce and discuss the Question of the Week. Then use pp. 18l–20b.

Group Time
Differentiated Instruction
Read this week's Leveled Readers. See pp. 18f–18g for the small group lesson plan.

Whole Group
Use p. 39a.

Language Arts
Use pp. 39e–39k.

Build Concepts

FLUENCY

MODEL TONE OF VOICE As you read "Child of the Silent Night" aloud, pay particular attention to intonation, using the rise and fall of your voice to provide rhythm for long sentences, signal questions and full stops, and emphasize important and emotionally-charged words.

LISTENING COMPREHENSION

After reading "Child of the Silent Night," use the following questions to assess listening comprehension.

1. **When did Laura's parents realize Laura had lost her sight and hearing?** *(They gradually realized it several months after Laura had gotten sick.)* **Sequence**

2. **What were the steps in Laura's recovery? Describe them in order.** *(At first she could only drink liquids and could not sit up. For a whole year, she couldn't walk. By the time she was five, she was nearly as strong as other children her age.)* **Sequence**

BUILD CONCEPT VOCABULARY

Start a web to build concepts and vocabulary related to this week's lesson and the unit theme.

- Draw the Diversity Concept Web.

- Read the sentence with the words *kindness* and *attention* again. Ask students to pronounce *kindness* and *attention* and discuss their meanings.

- Place *kindness* and *attention* in ovals attached to the oval *What all people need*. Explain that the words are connected to the concept. Then read the sentence in which *understanding* appears. Have students pronounce the word, place it on the Web, and provide reasons.

- Brainstorm additional words and categories for the Web. Keep the Web on display and add words throughout the week.

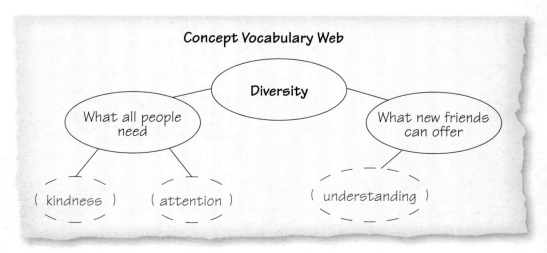

Concept Vocabulary Web

Child of the Silent Night

by Edith Fisher Hunter

For several months after the fever Laura had lain in a large old cradle in a darkened room. Gradually her father and mother discovered that the sickness had made her blind and deaf. For weeks she could only drink liquids and could not even sit up. It was a whole year before she could walk by herself again and it was not until she was about five years old that she was nearly as strong as most children her age.

Perhaps she would never have become very healthy if it had not been for her friend Mr. Asa Tenney. The Bridgman family called him Uncle Asa, but he was not a real uncle to them. Most people thought that Asa Tenney was a little odd. Although he seemed very old, he wasn't, really. But his clothes were. He didn't care about things like clothes. All he cared about were out-of-door things—like birds and flowers and brooks, and the little dumb animals that he found on his walks.

And now he had come to care about Laura Bridgman, too. In a way she seemed almost like one of the little helpless creatures of the woods. Like them, she could not tell people what she was thinking and what she wanted. But he knew that she wanted kindness and attention and love.

Mr. Tenney had no family of his own. When he discovered this little girl at neighbor Bridgman's house he felt that at last he had found someone who needed him.

Daniel and Harmony Bridgman, Laura's father and mother, were kindly people and wanted to do what they could for this poor child of theirs. But they had little time to give her. Mr. Bridgman was a busy farmer and a selectman of the town of Hanover. Mrs. Bridgman had two little boys younger than Laura to care for. In addition, she had to do all the things that any farm wife did in those days.

No, Mrs. Bridgman did not have much time to teach her little deaf, blind, mute daughter. Even if there had been time, how could she have taught Laura anything? Can a person who cannot see or hear or talk learn anything?

Asa Tenney was sure Laura could learn. He believed that she was learning every minute and that she wanted to learn a great deal more. He knew that he had plenty of time in which to teach her too.

He explained it to himself this way: "It is as though Laura is living in a room without windows or doors. I must make windows and doors into that room. Somehow, I must get behind the cloth band that she wears over her eyes and bring the light of understanding to her."

SKILLS ◆ STRATEGIES IN CONTEXT

Sequence
Summarize

OBJECTIVES

- Determine a sequence of events.
- Use sequence to summarize.

Skills Trace
Sequence

Introduce/Teach	TE: 4.1 18–19, 66–67; 4.5 560–561
Practice	TE: 25, 27, 73, 77, 567, 571 PB: 3, 7, 8, 23, 27, 28, 223, 227, 228
Reteach/Review	TE: 4.1 39b, 87b, 97, DI·52, DI·54; 4.5 531, 551, 581b, DI·54 PB: 36, 206, 216
Test	Selection Test: 1–4, 9–12, 89–92; Benchmark Test: Units 1, 5

INTRODUCE

Ask students to name things the class did yesterday or earlier in the day at school. Write three or four of these activities out of sequence. Then ask students to put the listed events in order from the first thing that happened to the last.

Have students read the information on p. 18. Explain the following:

- Identifying the sequence, or order, of events in a story can help you understand what you are reading.

- Summarizing main events and noting their order as you read can help you remember important information.

Use Skill Transparency 1 to teach sequence and summarize.

Comprehension

Skill
Sequence

Strategy
Summarize

 ## Sequence

- Events in a story occur in a certain order, or sequence. The sequence of events can be important to understanding a story.

- Sometimes events in a story are told out of sequence. Something that happened earlier might be told after something that happened later.

Main Event		**Main Event**	

Main Event   **Main Event**

 ### Strategy: Summarize

Good readers summarize. As they read, they pause to sum up the important ideas or events. This helps them remember the information. As you read a story, note the main events. After you read, ask yourself what the main events were and in what order they occurred.

Write to Read

1. Read "Going Batty." Make a graphic organizer like the one above to put the main events in order. Start with "Kindergarten class goes to Story Hour."

2. Use your graphic organizer to write a summary of the story. Include only the main events.

18

Strategic Intervention

Sequence Demonstrate the process for completing the graphic organizer on p. 18. Draw the time line on the board and number the tick marks on it from 1 to 4. Explain that students will write the main events that happened first, second, third, and fourth in the numbered spaces from left to right. Help students complete the numbered time line.

ELL

Access Content

Beginning/Intermediate For a Picture It! lesson on sequence, see the ELL Teaching Guide, pp. 1–2.

Advanced The title of the text on p. 19 is an idiom. Before students read "Going Batty," have volunteers tell what it means to "go batty." *(act crazy)* Discuss the title's humorous play on words, which emphasizes a crazy event involving real bats getting into the library.

Going Batty

Mrs. Koch's fourth-grade class walked down the hall to the library, just as they did every afternoon. At the door, their mouths dropped open. Hanging everywhere were bats—upside-down, little black bats. It took a few seconds before they realized the bats were paper. "What's with all the bats?" they asked Mr. Egan, the librarian. •

Mr. Egan laughed. "We had some excitement this morning." He went on to explain. •

"The day started quietly enough. I checked in some books and shelved new ones. Then a kindergarten class arrived for Story Hour. They sat in a circle while I began reading *Stellaluna*. You remember that story, don't you? It's about a little fruit bat. Well, suddenly the children yelled, 'Stellaluna! It's Stellaluna!' I love it when kids get excited about a story, but this was ridiculous! Then I saw they were pointing up. Somehow a little bat had gotten into the library! It was darting all over. Luckily, I was able to trap it in a box and take it outside. The kids all made paper bats to take its place." •

The fourth graders looked around the room hopefully. But there were no bats—no real ones, anyway. They all sighed. Sometimes little kids have all the luck. •

1 Skill Which grade is mentioned first in the story? Why do you suppose it is not the first event on your graphic organizer?

2 Skill What time word clues tell you that Mr. Egan is going to tell about events that happened earlier in the day?

3 Strategy See if you can summarize what Mr. Egan told the fourth graders. Be sure to give the events in order.

4 Strategy Now summarize the day's events in the library, not in the order in which you read about them but in the order in which they actually happened.

19

Available as **Skill Transparency** 1

Sequence

- Events in a story occur in a certain order, or **sequence**. The sequences of events can be important to understanding a story.

Directions Read the following passage. Then complete the time line below by putting the events in the order in which they happen.

When Charlie came home from visiting his grandparents in Florida, he told his friend Bill all about his trip. He told him how fun it was to take his first airplane flight to Florida and to look down on the houses and cars from so far up.

His grandparents then took him to the beach to pick up sharks' teeth along the coast. Later in the week, he went to an amusement park to ride the roller coasters. Bill wished he could have gone to Florida too.

Possible answers given.

1. Charlie took his first airplane flight to Florida.
2. Charlie went to the beach to find sharks' teeth.
3. Charlie went to an amusement park.
4. Charlie told Bill about his trip.
5. Bill wished he could have gone to Florida too.

School + Home **Home Activity** Your child completed a time line with the order of events from a short passage. Talk together about the main events of a typical day. Ask your child to put those events in sequential order using a simple time line.

▲ **Practice Book** p. 3

TEACH

1 SKILL Discuss why the first class mentioned is not the first event on the graphic organizer.

Think Aloud **MODEL** The graphic organizer shows the events in the order they occurred that day. The first class mentioned in the story is the fourth grade. Mr. Egan tells them what happened when the kindergarteners visited the library earlier that day. Because the fourth-grade class came to the library *after* the kindergarten class, it is not the first event in the graphic organizer.

3 STRATEGY Use the sequence of events to summarize what Mr. Egan said.

Think Aloud **MODEL** Mr. Egan read *Stellaluna*, a story about a bat, to kindergarteners. The kids started pointing and yelling "Stellaluna!" because they saw a real bat in the library. Mr. Egan caught the bat and brought it outside, and the kindergarteners made paper bats.

PRACTICE AND ASSESS

2 SKILL Clue words: *this morning*

4 STRATEGY Mr. Egan was reading a story about a bat to a kindergarten class when they saw a real bat in the library. He caught the bat, and the kids made paper bats. Mrs. Koch's fourth-grade class saw the paper bats hanging in the library, and Mr. Egan told them what happened that morning.

WRITE Have students complete steps 1 and 2 of the Write to Read activity. You might consider using this as a whole-class activity.

Monitor Progress	
🎯 Sequence	
If... students are unable to complete **Write to Read** on p. 18,	**then...** use Practice Book p. 3 to provide additional practice.

Students can learn more about their local library or other library resources available to them by using a student-friendly search engine and keywords such as their town or county name. Be sure to follow classroom rules for Internet use

Build Background Use ELL Poster 1 to build background and vocabulary for the lesson concept of diversity in inter-generational friendships.

▲ **ELL Poster** 1

Build Background

ACTIVATE PRIOR KNOWLEDGE

BEGIN A CONCEPT WEB about moving to a new place.

- Have students come up with as many things as they can about moving to a new place, such as new people to meet, new places to explore, and related feelings. Record student responses on the concept web. Add an idea of your own.

- Tell students that, as they read, they should look for other ideas or details from the story to add to the web.

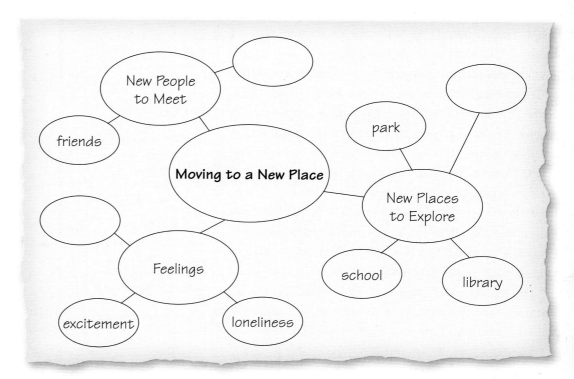

New People to Meet

friends

park

Moving to a New Place

New Places to Explore

Feelings

school

library

excitement

loneliness

▲ **Graphic Organizer** 16

BACKGROUND BUILDING AUDIO This week's audio explores the development of libraries. After students listen, discuss what they found out and what surprised them most about how libraries developed in the United States.

Background Building Audio

Introduce Vocabulary

WORDS-IN-CONTEXT CHART

Create a three-column chart in which students read lesson vocabulary words in context, think about meaning, and provide another example. Context may be phrases, as shown below, or sentences.

Word in Context	Meaning	Another Example
a <u>grand</u> time at the party	great	a grand birthday
<u>peculiar</u> noises not heard before	strange	an odd, peculiar smell coming from the garbage
to be <u>positive</u> the facts are correct	certain	positive the girl in the store was Tina
too <u>prideful</u> to admit a mistake	overly proud	Prideful students brag a lot.
<u>recalls</u> the past	remembers	recalls his childhood
<u>selecting</u> a library book	choosing	selecting the best snack

▲ **Graphic Organizer** 26

Read each item in the first column with students. Discuss what students know about each underlined word in context. Then have students provide a meaning and another example for each word until the chart is complete.

Activate Prior Knowledge

Use the word *grand* to point out that a word may have more than one meaning. Ask how having a *grand* time is different from having a *grand* house. (*A grand time is a very good or wonderful time, but a grand house is a large and fancy house.*) **Multiple Meanings**

At the end of the week, students can add other examples for lesson vocabulary words to their charts or add new selection words.

Use the Multisyllabic Word Routine on p. DI·1 to help students read multisyllabic words.

Lesson Vocabulary

WORDS TO KNOW

T grand excellent; very good

T memorial helping people to remember a person, thing, or event

T peculiar strange; unusual

T positive without doubt; sure

T prideful overly proud of oneself

T recalls calls back to mind; remembers

T selecting picking out; choosing

MORE WORDS TO KNOW

consisted was made up of
friendless without friends

T = Tested Word

Vocabulary

Directions Choose the word from the box that best matches each definition. Write the word on the line shown to the left.

recalls _____ 1. remembers

positive _____ 2. without doubt

grand _____ 3. excellent

peculiar _____ 4. strange

selecting _____ 5. picking out

Check the Words You Know
___grand
___memorial
___peculiar
___positive
___prideful
___recalls
___selecting

Directions Choose the word from the box that best matches the meaning of the underlined words. Write the word on the line shown to the left.

selecting _____ 6. She needed help <u>choosing</u> a book.

grand _____ 7. We had a <u>great</u> time in Florida.

memorial _____ 8. Greg saw a <u>statue that helps people remember</u> the town's early settlers.

positive _____ 9. I was <u>certain</u> that I had my keys with me.

prideful _____ 10. She is a person who <u>thinks a lot of herself</u>.

Write a Story

On a separate sheet of paper, write a story about becoming friends with someone new. Use as many vocabulary words as you can.
Stories should include words from the vocabulary list and details about making a new friend.

School + Home Home Activity Your child identified and used vocabulary words from *Because of Winn-Dixie*. With your child, create original sentences using the vocabulary words.

▲ **Practice Book** p. 4

Vocabulary Strategy

OBJECTIVE

⊙ Use word structure to determine word meaning.

INTRODUCE

Discuss the strategy for word structure by using the steps on p. 20.

TEACH

- Have students pay attention to words with the suffix *-ful* or *-al* as they read "The Storyteller."
- Model using word structure to determine the meaning of *prideful*.

Think Aloud **MODEL** If I cover the *-ful* suffix in this word, I see the base word *pride*. The suffix *-ful* can mean "full of," so a *prideful* person is "full of pride" or "very proud." That meaning makes sense in the context.

Words to Know

memorial

prideful

recalls

peculiar

grand

positive

selecting

Remember

Try the strategy. Then, if you need more help, use your glossary or a dictionary.

Vocabulary Strategy
for Suffixes

Word Structure Suppose you are reading and you come to a word you don't know. Does the word have *-ful* or *-al* at the end? You can use the suffix to help you figure out the word's meaning. The suffix *-ful* can make a word mean "full of _____," as in *careful*. The suffix *-al* can make a word mean "of or like _____," as in *fictional*.

1. Put your finger over the *-ful* or *-al* suffix.

2. Look at the base word. (That's the word without the suffix.) Put the base word in the phrase "full of _____" or "of or like _____."

3. Try that meaning in the sentence. Does it make sense?

As you read "The Storyteller," look for words that end with *-ful* or *-al*. Use the suffixes to help you figure out the meanings of the words.

DAY 2 Grouping Options

Reading
Whole Group Discuss the Question of the Day. Then use pp. 20–23.

Group Time Differentiated Instruction
Read *Because of Winn-Dixie*. See pp. 18f–18g for the small group lesson plan.

Whole Group Use p. 39a.

Language Arts
Use pp. 39e–39k.

Strategic Intervention

⊙ **Word Stucture** Show students how to separate a suffix from a base word: find the word *magical* in the first sentence on p. 21, cover the suffix *-al*, name the base word, and have students explain why Ms. Ada's storytelling mornings are called *magical*.

ELL

Access Content Use ELL Poster 1 to preteach vocabulary. Choose from the following to meet language proficiency levels.

Beginning Have students find clues on p. 21, paragraph 2 that describe a *prideful* person.

Intermediate Have pairs return to the words-in-context chart (p. 20b) and add more examples of the words in context.

Advanced Teach the lesson on pp. 20–21. Have students determine if any of these words have cognates in their home languages.

Resources for home-language words may include parents, bilingual staff members, bilingual dictionaries, or online translation sources.

The Storyteller

Thursday mornings at the James P. Guthrie Memorial Library are magical. That's because every Thursday morning Ms. Ada Landry tells stories to anyone who wants to listen. But she does not just tell the stories. She acts them out. She makes them come alive.

When Ms. Ada describes what she calls "a prideful person," she puffs out her chest and looks down her nose. She talks in a loud, boastful voice. When she tells about a sly person, she narrows her eyes and pulls up her shoulders. She talks in a shady kind of voice. When she recalls things that happened long ago, she gets a faraway look in her eyes, and she talks in a quiet, dreamy voice.

Ms. Ada's stories are entertaining, but they nearly always have a lesson in them too. A person who everyone thinks is a bit peculiar turns out to be kind or brave. A person who everyone thinks is grand proves to be cowardly or mean. A mistake or disaster ends up having a positive effect.

When it comes to selecting and telling stories, Ms. Ada is the best.

Words to Write

Write about what you like best about the library. Give reasons for your choice. Use some words from the Words to Know list.

21

PRACTICE AND ASSESS

- Have students determine the meanings of the remaining words and explain the strategy they used.
- Have students name other words with *-al* and *-ful* in "The Storyteller" and tell how the base word and suffix combine to give meaning.
- If you began a words-in-context chart (p. 20b), have students list more examples for the lesson vocabulary words and any other unfamiliar words in "The Storyteller."
- Have students complete Practice Book p. 5.

WRITE Writing should include several lesson vocabulary words as well as words related to libraries.

Monitor Progress

Word Structure

If... students need more practice with the lesson vocabulary,	**then...** use Tested Vocabulary Cards.

Vocabulary • Word Structure

- A **suffix** is a syllable added to the end of a base word to change its meaning or the way it is used in a sentence.
- The suffix *–ful* means "full of _____," as in *careful*. The suffix *–al* means "from, of, or like _____," as in *fictional*. You can use suffixes to help you figure out the meanings of words.

Directions Read the following story about a trip to the library. Then answer the questions below.

When I went to King Memorial School, there was a contest for telling a story about our town's original settlers. My friends and I formed a team and went to the local library. I was doubtful that our team would win until we talked to the town historian in the library. She told us the wonderful story of one brave pioneer family. To us, the story was a logical choice. I was really prideful when my team won the prize for telling our town's most colorful story.

1. What does the word *prideful* mean in the story?
   "full of pride"
2. What does the word *original* mean in the story?
   "from the origin"
3. What is the suffix in the word *wonderful*? What does *wonderful* mean?
   It means "full of"; *wonderful* means "full of wonder."
4. What does the suffix mean in the word *logical*? What does *logical* mean?
   It means "of"; *logical* means "of logic."
5. Think of another word that ends with either *–ful* or *–al*. Tell the meaning of the word. Then use it in an original sentence.
   Possible answer: *Beautiful* means "full of beauty"; The ocean looked beautiful at sunset.

Home Activity Your child identified suffixes in words to understand their meanings. With your child, read a short selection. Ask your child to point out words that use suffixes and what those words mean.

▲ **Practice Book** p. 5

Prereading Strategies

GENRE STUDY

Realistic Fiction

Because of Winn-Dixie is realistic fiction. Explain that in realistic fiction, although the story is fictional, the characters are believable and the events that happen are things that could happen in real life.

PREVIEW AND PREDICT

Have students preview the story title and illustrations and discuss who the characters might be and what might happen in the story. Encourage students to use lesson vocabulary words as they talk about what they expect to read.

Strategy Response Log

Ask Questions Have students write two questions they have about the story in their strategy response logs. Students will answer their questions in the Strategy Response Log activity on p. 27.

Because of Winn-Dixie

by Kate DiCamillo
illustrated by Kevin Hawkes

Genre **Realistic fiction** has characters and events that are like people and events in real life. As you read, think about how the people and events in your life are similar to or different from the characters and events in this story.

22

ELL

Access Content Help students understand the meaning of *library*, a false cognate in Spanish of *librería*, which means "bookstore."

Consider having students read the selection summary in English or in students' home languages. See the Multilingual Summaries in the ELL Teaching Guide, pp. 5–7.

What happens in a library because of Winn-Dixie?

23

SET PURPOSE

With students, discuss the picture on p. 23 of the story. Students can tell where they think the dog is and what he is doing. Have them tell what they hope to find out as they read the story.

Remind students to look for the sequence of events as they read.

STRATEGY RECALL

Students have now used these before-reading strategies:

- preview the selection to be aware of its genre, features, and possible content;
- activate prior knowledge about that content and what to expect of that genre;
- make predictions;
- set a purpose for reading.

Remind students to be aware of and flexibly use the during-reading strategies they have learned:

- link prior knowledge to new information;
- summarize text they have read so far;
- ask clarifying questions;
- answer questions they or others pose;
- check their predictions and either refine them or make new predictions;
- recognize the text structure the author is using, and use that knowledge to make predictions and increase comprehension;
- visualize what the author is describing;
- monitor their comprehension and use fix-up strategies.

After reading, students will use these strategies:

- summarize or retell the text;
- answer questions they or others pose;
- reflect to make new information become part of their prior knowledge.

Audio CD **AudioText**

Guiding Comprehension

1 🎯 **Sequence • Inferential**

Reread p. 25, paragraph 2. List in order the main events that happen in this paragraph.

First, Opal shows Winn-Dixie how to look in the window. Then Opal goes inside the library. Then Miss Franny Block sees the dog at the window and thinks he is a bear.

Monitor Progress
🎯 **Sequence**
If... students are unable to determine the sequence, : **then...** use the skill and strategy instruction on p. 25.

2 **Draw Conclusions • Inferential**

Why do you think Miss Franny Block is sitting on the floor behind her desk?

She is hiding or simply dropped to the floor in fear because she thinks she saw a bear at the window.

ndia Opal Buloni, known best as Opal, has recently moved to Naomi, Florida, with her preacher father. Shortly after her arrival, Opal rescues a scrappy dog that she names Winn-Dixie, after the store in which she finds him. She convinces her father, who often preaches about caring for the needy, that this dog is certainly in need. Thus a summer of adventures begins.

E L L

Extend Language Use the first paragraph on p. 24 to clarify that *Winn-Dixie* is the name of a grocery store chain in the southeastern United States and also the name of the dog in the story. Opal's full name is India Opal Buloni, but she is known by her middle name. The setting is Naomi, Florida. *Naomi* can also be the first name for a girl.

I spent a lot of time that summer at the Herman W. Block Memorial Library. The Herman W. Block Memorial Library sounds like it would be a big fancy place, but it's not. It's just a little old house full of books, and Miss Franny Block is in charge of them all. She is a very small, very old woman with short gray hair, and she was the first friend I made in Naomi.

It all started with Winn-Dixie not liking it when I went into the library, because he couldn't go inside, too. But I showed him how he could stand up on his hind legs and look in the window and see me in there, selecting my books; and he was okay, as long as he could see me. But the thing was, the first time Miss Franny Block saw Winn-Dixie standing up on his hind legs like that, looking in the window, she didn't think he was a dog. She thought he was a bear.

This is what happened: I was picking out my books and kind of humming to myself, and all of a sudden, there was this loud and scary scream. I went running up to the front of the library, and there was Miss Franny Block, sitting on the floor behind her desk. ❷

25

European Influence

Opal has just moved to a small town in Florida. Many groups of people have settled in Florida over the years. Native Americans were the first settlers, having lived in the area for at least 10,000 years. Florida is also the location of the first permanent European settlement in the United States. Spaniards founded the city of St. Augustine in 1565. Florida was under Spanish rule until 1821 when it became a United States territory. Florida became a state in 1845. Many ethnic groups now live in the state, but the influence of Spanish culture on Florida is significant. It is reflected in the names, food, and architecture of the state.

🎯 SKILLS ↔ STRATEGIES IN CONTEXT

Sequence

TEACH

- Remind students that it is important to keep track of the sequence, or order, of events in a story.
- Point out that when the sequence is hard to follow, it helps to visualize what is happening. Picturing the events mentally may help students figure out the order in which they happen.
- Model finding the sequence of events on p. 25, paragraph 2.

Think Aloud **MODEL** I read in the first sentence that Opal goes into the library. But Winn-Dixie can't go in, so she shows him how to look through a window. I try to picture what is happening. Opal probably showed her dog the window *before* she went in the library. Opal goes in and *then* Miss Franny sees the dog at the window.

PRACTICE AND ASSESS

Have students reread p. 25, paragraph 3. Ask them to list what happens first, next, and last. *(First Opal looks for books, then she hears a scream, and last she runs to the front of the library and sees Miss Franny sitting on the floor.)*

EXTEND SKILLS

Narration

Explain that narration is the recounting of events by a narrator, or storyteller. Have students read the first paragraph on p. 25 and discuss who is the narrator in the story. *(Opal)* Point out the pronoun *I* and explain that this story is narrated in the first-person. This means story events are told from the point of view of one of the characters.

Guiding Comprehension

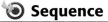

3 **Character • Inferential**

How does Miss Franny feel about bears? How do you know?

She is terrified of bears. She is trembling and shaking.

4 **Sequence • Literal**

When did a bear come into the Herman W. Block Memorial Library? What time words tell you when it happened?

It came into the library long ago. The words *a long time ago* tell you when it happened.

Monitor Progress
Sequence

If... students are unable to determine when the event happened,	**then...** use the skill and strategy instruction on p. 27.

Tech Files
ONLINE

Students can search the Internet to find out more about how bears behave. Have them use a student-friendly search engine and use the keywords *bear behavior*. Be sure to follow classroom rules for Internet use.

"Miss Franny?" I said. "Are you all right?"

"A bear," she said.

"A bear?" I asked.

"He has come back," she said.

"He has?" I asked. "Where is he?"

"Out there," she said and raised a finger and pointed at Winn-Dixie standing up on his hind legs, looking in the window for me.

"Miss Franny Block," I said, "that's not a bear. That's a dog. That's my dog. Winn-Dixie."

"Are you positive?" she asked.

"Yes ma'am," I told her. "I'm positive. He's my dog. I would know him anywhere."

Extend Language Point out familiar contractions in the phrases "That's a dog" or "I'm positive." Help students understand that *ma'am* is also a contraction and it means "madam," a polite term used to address, or speak to, a woman. Reinforce the idea that the apostrophe in a contraction indicates the omission of one or more letters.

Encourage students to record familiar and unusual contractions and their meanings in language journals, word lists, or computer files of English vocabulary.

Miss Franny sat there trembling and shaking. **3**

"Come on," I said. "Let me help you up. It's okay." I stuck out my hand and Miss Franny took hold of it, and I pulled her up off the floor. She didn't weigh hardly anything at all. Once she was standing on her feet, she started acting all embarrassed, saying how I must think she was a silly old lady, mistaking a dog for a bear, but that she had a bad experience with a bear coming into the Herman W. Block Memorial Library a long time ago, and she never had quite gotten over it. **4**

"When did that happen?" I asked her.

"Well," said Miss Franny, "it is a very long story."

27

Develop Vocabulary

PRACTICE LESSON VOCABULARY

Students orally respond to each question.

1. If you are *positive* that you know something, do you have any doubts or are you sure? (You are sure.)

2. If you are *selecting* a coat, are you picking it out or putting it away? (You are picking it out.)

3. If a person *recalls* a story, does this person have a good memory or a bad memory? (The person has a good memory.)

BUILD CONCEPT VOCABULARY

Review previous concept words with students. Ask if students have come across any words today in their reading that they would like to add to the Diversity Concept Web, such as *friend* and *ma'am*.

⊙ SKILLS ⟷ STRATEGIES IN CONTEXT

Sequence Summarize

TEACH

Read the second paragraph on p. 27. Have students find the time word clues *once* and *a long time ago*. Discuss how these clues help determine sequence. Then model how to summarize the sequence of events in this part of the story.

Think Aloud **MODEL** Now that I understand the sequence of events in this part of the story, I can summarize what is happening in my own words. Opal helps Miss Franny stand up and Miss Franny acts embarrassed. She says she will tell a story about something that happened a long time ago to explain her reaction to Opal's dog.

PRACTICE AND ASSESS

Have students work in pairs to find the sequence of events on p. 28 in order to write a short summary retelling what happens. To assess, make sure that summaries tell the main events in order and are written in students' own words.

Strategy Response Log

Answer Questions Have students review the questions they wrote at the beginning of the story. (See p. 22.) Provide the following prompt: *Have your questions about the story been answered yet? If so, write answers to your questions. Then write a new question about the rest of the story.*

If you want to teach this story in two sessions, stop here.

Guiding Comprehension

If you are teaching the story in two days, discuss the events that have happened so far and review the vocabulary.

5 🎯 **Vocabulary • Word Structure**

Have students use word structure to determine the meaning of *Memorial* on p. 28, paragraph 2.

Structure: The word has the base word *memory* and the suffix *-al*. Meaning: something that is a reminder of a person.

Monitor Progress

🎯 **Word Structure**

If... students have difficulty using word structure to determine the meaning of *memorial*,	**then...** use the vocabulary strategy instruction on p. 29.

6 **Dialogue • Critical**

Why do you think Miss Franny says "mosquitoes so big they could fly away with you" instead of just "big mosquitoes"?

Possible response: Her description is more exaggerated. The effect is to make the story more interesting by using vivid language.

DAY 3 Grouping Options

Reading
Whole Group Discuss the Question of the Day.

Group Time Differentiated Instruction
Read *Because of Winn-Dixie.* See pp. 18f–18g for the small group lesson plan.

Whole Group Discuss the Reader Response questions on page 34. Then use p. 39a.

Language Arts
Use pp. 39e–39k.

"That's okay," I told her. "I am like my mama in that I like to be told stories. But before you start telling it, can Winn-Dixie come in and listen, too? He gets lonely without me."

"Well, I don't know," said Miss Franny. "Dogs are not allowed **5** in the Herman W. Block Memorial Library."

"He'll be good," I told her. "He's a dog who goes to church." And before she could say yes or no, I went outside and got Winn-Dixie, and he came in and lay down with a *"huummmppff"* and a sigh, right at Miss Franny's feet.

She looked down at him and said, "He most certainly is a large dog."

"Yes ma'am," I told her. "He has a large heart, too."

"Well," Miss Franny said. She bent over and gave Winn-Dixie a pat on the head, and Winn-Dixie wagged his tail back and forth and snuffled his nose on her little old-lady feet. "Let me get a chair and sit down so I can tell this story properly."

28

ELL

Context Clues Help students use context to figure out the meaning of the expressions *little-miss-know-it-all* and *miss-smarty-pants* (p. 29). The meaning is given in the next sentence: *I thought I knew the answers to everything.*

"Back when Florida was wild, when it consisted of nothing but palmetto trees and mosquitoes so big they could fly away with you," Miss Franny Block started in, "and I was just a little girl no bigger than you, my father, Herman W. Block, told me that I could have anything I wanted for my birthday. Anything at all."

Miss Franny looked around the library. She leaned in close to me. "I don't want to appear prideful," she said, "but my daddy was a very rich man. A very rich man." She nodded and then leaned back and said, "And I was a little girl who loved to read. So I told him, I said, 'Daddy, I would most certainly love to have a library for my birthday, a small little library would be wonderful.'"

"You asked for a whole library?"

"A small one," Miss Franny nodded. "I wanted a little house full of nothing but books and I wanted to share them, too. And I got my wish. My father built me this house, the very one we are sitting in now. And at a very young age, I became a librarian. Yes ma'am."

"What about the bear?" I said.

"Did I mention that Florida was wild in those days?" Miss Franny Block said.

"Uh-huh, you did."

"It was wild. There were wild men and wild women and wild animals."

"Like bears!"

"Yes ma'am. That's right. Now, I have to tell you, I was a little-miss-know-it-all. I was a miss-smarty-pants with my library full of books. Oh, yes ma'am, I thought I knew the answers to everything. Well, one hot Thursday, I was sitting in my library with all the doors and windows open and my nose stuck in a book, when a shadow crossed the desk. And without looking up, yes ma'am, without even looking up, I said, 'Is there a book I can help you find?'"

29

Geography of the Southeast

Time for SOCIAL STUDIES

Florida, along with other southeastern states, forms part of the Atlantic Coastal Plain. The region's warm, sunny climate makes it a popular destination for tourists and retirees who enjoy swimming, fishing, and boating along miles of sandy coastlines. The climate also makes it a good place for agriculture. Cotton, vegetables, citrus fruits, peanuts, and tobacco all grow well in the Southeast, and farming has long been a way of life in the area.

VOCABULARY STRATEGY
Word Structure

TEACH

Read the second paragraph on p. 28. Model using word structure to determine the meaning of *Memorial*.

Think Aloud **MODEL** I recognize the suffix *-al* in the word *memorial*. I know *-al* can mean "of" or "like." When I cover the suffix with my finger, I can figure out that the base word is *memory*. So I think that this word has something to do with being "a memory of" someone or something. Since it is the Herman W. Block Memorial Library, perhaps the library was named in memory of Herman W. Block.

PRACTICE AND ASSESS

Have students use word structure to determine the meaning of *prideful* on p. 29, paragraph 2. *(full of pride)*

EXTEND SKILLS

Dialogue

Explain that dialogue is the conversation between two or more people. In print, dialogue is set off with quotation marks. Discuss how the author uses dialogue to develop the characters in this story. Ask students to find examples of words in the dialogue that reflect the region (e.g., "Yes ma'am"), the age of the characters (e.g., "In those days"), and the informal tone of the conversation (e.g., "Back when …," "Uh-huh").

Guiding Comprehension

7 **Author's Purpose • Critical**

Question the Author **Why do you think the author includes in the description how the bear smelled and how big he was?**

Possible response: The author wants to describe the bear with vivid details so we can picture it clearly and understand how frightened Miss Franny must have been.

Monitor Progress

REVIEW Author's Purpose

If... students have difficulty understanding the author's purpose in this section,	then... use the skill and strategy instruction on p. 31.

---

8 **Draw Conclusions • Critical**

Text to World **Using what you already know about bears, do you think Miss Franny should have thrown the book at the bear? Was she brave or foolish to do so? Explain.**

Possible response: Bears can be very dangerous and have been known to attack humans. Although Miss Franny acted bravely, it was probably foolish to hit the bear with the book.

---

7 "Well, there was no answer. And I thought it might have been a wild man or a wild woman, scared of all these books and afraid to speak up. But then I became aware of a very peculiar smell, a very strong smell. I raised my eyes slowly. And standing right in front of me was a bear. Yes ma'am. A very large bear."

"How big?" I asked.

"Oh, well," said Miss Franny, "perhaps three times the size of your dog."

"Then what happened?" I asked her.

"Well," said Miss Franny, "I looked at him and he looked at me. He put his big nose up in the air and sniffed and sniffed as if he was trying to decide if a little-miss-know-it-all librarian was what he was in the mood to eat. And I sat there. And then I thought, 'Well, if this bear intends to eat me, I am not going to let it happen without a fight. No ma'am.' So very slowly and very carefully, I raised up the book I was reading."

"What book was that?" I asked.

"Why, it was *War and Peace,* a very large book. I raised it up slowly and then I aimed it carefully and I threw it right at that **8** bear and screamed, 'Be gone!' And do you know what?"

30

Fluency Help students rephrase long, complex sentences into more manageable chunks. For example, the second sentence on p. 30, paragraph 5, could be rephrased this way:

"He put his big nose up in the air and sniffed and sniffed. He was trying to decide if he wanted to eat a little-miss-know-it-all librarian."

31

SKILLS ⟷ STRATEGIES IN CONTEXT

Author's Purpose REVIEW

TEACH

- To accomplish a purpose, an author uses vivid language to help readers visualize story events.

- Model determining the author's purpose using the first three paragraphs on p. 30.

MODEL As I read this part of the story, I notice lots of descriptive words. The bear had a strong, peculiar smell. He was three times the size of Opal's dog. I can imagine the bear's size and smell. I think the author's purpose is to help us picture the bear so we understand how Miss Franny felt.

PRACTICE AND ASSESS

- Have students read paragraph 6 on p. 32 to determine why they think the author includes the part about the bear keeping the book. *(The author probably wants to entertain us.)*

- To assess, use Practice Book p. 6.

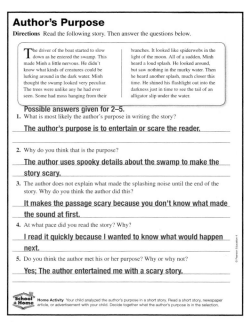

Author's Purpose

Directions Read the following story. Then answer the questions below.

The driver of the boat started to slow down as he entered the swamp. This made Minh a little nervous. He didn't know what kinds of creatures could be lurking around in the dark water. Minh thought the swamp looked very peculiar. The trees were unlike any he had ever seen. Some had moss hanging from their branches. It looked like spiderwebs in the light of the moon. All of a sudden, Minh heard a loud splash. He looked around, but saw nothing in the murky water. Then he heard another splash, much closer this time. He shined his flashlight out into the darkness just in time to see the tail of an alligator slip under the water.

Possible answers given for 2–5.
1. What is most likely the author's purpose in writing the story?

   The author's purpose is to entertain or scare the reader.

2. Why do you think that is the purpose?

   The author uses spooky details about the swamp to make the story scary.

3. The author does not explain what made the splashing noise until the end of the story. Why do you think the author did this?

   It makes the passage scary because you don't know what made the sound at first.

4. At what pace did you read the story? Why?

   I read it quickly because I wanted to know what would happen next.

5. Do you think the author met his or her purpose? Why or why not?

   Yes; The author entertained me with a scary story.

School + Home Home Activity Your child analyzed the author's purpose in a short story. Read a short story, newspaper article, or advertisement with your child. Decide together what the author's purpose is in the selection.

▲ **Practice Book** p. 6

Guiding Comprehension

9 ⊙ **Summarize • Inferential**

What happened in the story Miss Franny told about the bear? Summarize the story.

Possible response: Once, when Miss Franny was a young librarian, a bear walked into her library. She threw a book at it and the bear left with the book.

10 **Compare and Contrast • Inferential**

How are Opal and Miss Franny alike? Give details to support your answer.

Possible response: They are both lonely (Opal because she's new in town, and Miss Franny because all her old friends are dead). They both like books and libraries. They both sigh. Opal says she felt "the same way" as Miss Franny.

11 **Draw Conclusions • Critical**

Text to Self **Opal and Miss Franny are different from each other, but they become friends. Think about your own friends. Based on your experience, why do you think certain people become friends?**

Possible response: People become friends when they enjoy spending time together and have things in common.

Strategy Response Log

Summarize When students finish reading this selection, provide this prompt: Imagine you are writing a summary of *Because of Winn-Dixie* for a book cover. In four or five sentences, tell the most important events.

"No ma'am," I said.

"He went. But this is what I will never forget. He took the book with him."

"Nuh-uh," I said.

9 "Yes ma'am," said Miss Franny. "He snatched it up and ran."

"Did he come back?" I asked.

"No, I never saw him again. Well, the men in town used to tease me about it. They used to say, 'Miss Franny, we saw that bear of yours out in the woods today. He was reading that book and he said it sure was good and would it be all right if he kept it for just another week.' Yes ma'am. They did tease me about it." She sighed. "I imagine I'm the only one left from those days. I imagine I'm the only one that even recalls that bear. All my friends, everyone I knew when I was young, they are all dead and gone."

She sighed again. She looked sad and old and wrinkled. It was the same way I felt sometimes, being friendless in a new

10 town and not having a mama to comfort me. I sighed, too.

Winn-Dixie raised his head off his paws and looked back and forth between me and Miss Franny. He sat up then and showed Miss Franny his teeth.

"Well now, look at that," she said. "That dog is smiling at me."

"It's a talent of his," I told her.

"It is a fine talent," Miss Franny said. "A very fine talent." And she smiled back at Winn-Dixie.

"We could be friends," I said to Miss Franny. "I mean you and me and Winn-Dixie, we could all be friends."

Miss Franny smiled even bigger. "Why, that would be grand," she said, "just grand."

And right at that minute, right when the three of us had decided to be friends, who should come marching into the

32

E L L

Understanding Idioms Explain the expression "old pinch-faced Amanda Wilkinson" on p. 33 does not refer to the girl's age. The word *old* can refer to something we don't like. Have students find the meaning of *pinch-faced* by studying Amanda's picture. Encourage them to record English idioms and their meanings in journals, lists, or computer files.

Herman W. Block Memorial Library but old pinch-faced Amanda Wilkinson. She walked right up to Miss Franny's desk and said, "I finished *Johnny Tremain* and I enjoyed it very much. I would like something even more difficult to read now, because I am an advanced reader."

"Yes dear, I know," said Miss Franny. She got up out of her chair.

Amanda pretended like I wasn't there. She stared right past me. "Are dogs allowed in the library?" she asked Miss Franny as they walked away.

"Certain ones," said Miss Franny, "a select few." And then she turned around and winked at me. I smiled back. I had just made my first friend in Naomi, and nobody was going to mess that up for me, not even old pinch-faced Amanda Wilkinson. **11**

33

Develop Vocabulary

PRACTICE LESSON VOCABULARY

As a class, complete the following sentences orally. Possible responses are given.

1. A dog who is acting *peculiar* might (run around in circles).

2. When we observe *Memorial* Day, we are (remembering or honoring others).

3. A friend who is *prideful* is likely to (brag about herself).

4. A *grand* time with a friend is (great, wonderful).

BUILD CONCEPT VOCABULARY

Review previous concept words with students. Ask if students have come across any words today in their reading that they would like to add to the Diversity Concept Web, such as *select few* and *little-miss-know-it-all*.

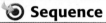 **STRATEGY SELF-CHECK**

Summarize

Have students identify the main events in the story and put them in order. Students can use these events they listed to write a summary of the story. Use Practice Book p. 7 for more practice.

SELF-CHECK

Students can ask themselves these questions to assess their understanding of the story.

- Did I list the main events of the story in the correct order?
- Does my summary include the most important events from the story?

Monitor Progress
⊙ **Sequence**

If... students are having difficulty listing events in order and writing a summary,	**then...** use the Reteach lesson on p. 39b.

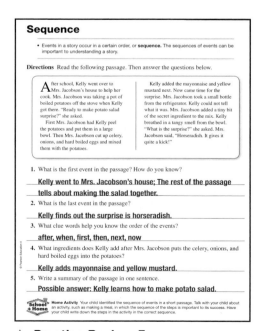

▲ **Practice Book** p. 7

MURDOCK LEARNING RESOURCE CENTER

Reader Response

Open for Discussion Personal Response

 Think Aloud **MODEL** I can visualize an older house full of library books. Miss Franny Block, the librarian, is sitting by her desk. She's telling Opal about the bear. Winn-Dixie is lying down by Miss Franny's feet.

Comprehension Check Critical Response

1. Responses will vary, but should describe a scene from the story and give reasons the scene is prize worthy. **Author's Purpose**

2. At first, Miss Franny is afraid of Winn-Dixie because she thinks he is a bear. At the end, she becomes his friend after the dog "smiles" at her. **Sequence**

3. Students should recognize that choices *a* and *c* are less important details that are not needed in a summary of the story. **Summarize**

4. Possible responses: *odd, strange, weird, unusual.* **Vocabulary**

 Look Back and Write For test practice, assign a 10–15 minute time limit. For assessment, see the Scoring Rubric at the right.

Retell

Have students retell *Because of Winn-Dixie.*

Monitor Progress

Check Retelling Rubric 4 3 2 1	
If... students have difficulty retelling the story,	then... use the Retelling Cards and the Scoring Rubric for Retelling on p. 35 to assist fluent retelling. **SUCCESS PREDICTOR**

 ELL

Check Retelling Have students use the story's illustrations to guide their retellings. Model how to retell the beginning of the story before students do their own retellings. For more ideas on assessing students' retellings, see the ELL and Transition Handbook.

Reader Response

Open for Discussion In your mind's eye, see the Herman W. Block Memorial Library. Tell about that place and what happened there.

1. This author has won prizes for her books. Why? Find a part of this story you think could win a prize. **Think Like an Author**

2. Think about the events in the story. How do Miss Franny's feelings about Winn-Dixie change from the beginning to the end? Why do they change? **Sequence**

3. When summarizing a story, you only include important details. Which two of the following statements would you leave out of a summary of the story? Why? **Summarize**

   a. The Herman W. Block Memorial Library is a little old house full of books.

   b. Miss Franny Block is afraid of Winn-Dixie because she thinks he is a bear.

   c. Amanda Wilkinson returns a book to the library.

4. Miss Franny Block describes the bear as having a *peculiar* smell. What other words might she have used in place of *peculiar*? Use a thesaurus. Remember that some synonyms will not be appropriate to describe the bear's smell. **Vocabulary**

 Look Back and Write Winn-Dixie is a dog with talent. What is that talent? Look back at page 32 and then write about Winn-Dixie's talent.

Meet author **Kate DiCamillo** on page 770.

34

Scoring Rubric | Look Back and Write

Top-Score Response A top-score response uses information from page 32 to describe Winn Dixie's special talent.

Example of a Top-Score Response Winn Dixie is a dog with a special talent: He can smile. When he smiles at Miss Franny, she smiles back. That is when Opal, Winn Dixie, and Miss Franny decide to be friends. Miss Franny says that smiling is a "very fine talent."

For additional rubrics, see p. WA10.

Write Now

Memoir

Prompt

In *Because of Winn-Dixie*, Opal tells about her experiences after moving to a new town. Think about a time that you were a newcomer to a place or situation. Now use vivid words to write a memoir about that experience.

Writing Trait

Vivid **word choice** helps readers imagine the story you are telling. Use vivid adjectives and strong verbs to describe your feelings and your experience.

Student Model

Introductory paragraph grabs reader's attention.

Vivid word choice helps the reader understand the narrator's feelings and experience.

Have you ever felt alone in a room full of people? That's how I felt the first day of chorus practice.

I always loved music—the thundering trumpet, the gentle flute. Most of all, I liked to sing. My mother suggested I join the school chorus. I was fearful, but I went to talk to the music teacher anyway. She was very caring. She said I could join.

The next day I shuffled into the music room. There were so many kids I didn't know. I was so nervous. Then the teacher started to play the piano. All the kids began to sing. The sound was enchanting! I felt part of the group.

Use the model to help you write your own memoir.

35

Write Now

Look at the Prompt Have students identify and discuss key words and phrases in the prompt. *(experiences, newcomer, vivid words, memoir)*

Strategies to Develop Word Choice

Have students

- draw an illustration or storyboard of their experience.
- search for precise adjectives in books or magazines.
- find the adjectives in their writing and try to replace them with more specific words.

NO: nice teacher

YES: generous, helpful teacher

For additional suggestions and rubric, see pp. 39g–39h.

Hints for Better Writing

- Carefully read the prompt.
- Use a graphic organizer to plan your writing.
- Support your ideas with information and details.
- Use words that help readers understand.
- Proofread and edit your work.

Scoring Rubric — Narrative Retelling

Rubric 4 3 2 1	4	3	2	1
Connections	Makes connections and generalizes beyond the text	Makes connections to other events, stories, or experiences	Makes a limited connection to another event, story, or experience	Makes no connection to another event, story, or experience
Author's Purpose	Elaborates on author's purpose	Tells author's purpose with some clarity	Makes some connection to author's purpose	Makes no connection to author's purpose
Characters	Describes the main character(s) and any character development	Identifies the main character(s) and gives some information about them	Inaccurately identifies some characters or gives little information about them	Inaccurately identifies the characters or gives no information about them
Setting	Describes the time and location	Identifies the time and location	Omits details of time or location	Is unable to identify time or location
Plot	Describes the problem, goal, events, and ending using rich detail	Tells the problem, goal, events, and ending with some errors that do not affect meaning	Tells parts of the problem, goal, events, and ending with gaps that affect meaning	Retelling has no sense of story

Retelling Plan

- ☑ **Week 1** Assess Strategic Intervention students.
- ☐ **Week 2** Assess Advanced students.
- ☐ **Week 3** Assess Strategic Intervention students.
- ☐ **Week 4** Assess On-Level students.
- ☐ **Week 5** Assess any students you have not yet checked during this unit.

Use the Retelling Chart on p. TR16 to record retelling.

Selection Test To assess with *Because of Winn-Dixie*, use Selection Tests, pp. 1–4.

Fresh Reads for Differentiated Test Practice For weekly leveled practice, use pp. 1–6.

Retelling

SUCCESS PREDICTOR

Science in Reading

PREVIEW/USE TEXT FEATURES

As students preview "Fast Facts: Black Bears," have them look at the head above each paragraph and examine the map. Then ask:

- **What information does the map show?** (*It shows where black bears live.*)

- **What are the main topics in the selection?** (*Where bears live, what their bodies are like, and what they eat*)

Link to Science

Discuss what a *fast fact* is, and have students organize the information about bears in a three-column chart.

DAY 4 Grouping Options

Reading

Whole Group Discuss the Question of the Day.

Group Time Differentiated Instruction
Read "Fast Facts: Black Bears." See pp. 18f–18g for the small group lesson plan.

Whole Group Use p. 39a.

Language Arts
Use pp. 39e–39k.

Science in Reading

Fast Facts: Black Bears

by Kathy Kranking

Expository Nonfiction

Genre

- Expository nonfiction provides information about people, places, animals, and other things in the real world.

- Expository nonfiction may give a few facts or it may describe a subject in depth with many facts.

Text Features

- Subheads tell you what each section will be about.

- The map gives visual information to go along with the text.

Link to Science

Choose a favorite animal to research. Use the library or the Internet to find a complete description of that animal—where it lives, what it looks like, what it eats. Make a "Fast Facts" poster.

Where Are They?

There are more black bears in the world than any other kind of bear. Most of them live in forests and other wild places. That's why most people never see them. The people who first called these bears "black" lived in eastern North America, where the bears *are* black.

36

Content-Area Vocabulary	Science

den	place where a wild animal lives; lair
keen	strong; vivid
prey	animals hunted and killed for food by another animal

Access Content Preview the selection with students by reading each head aloud and explaining the idioms. For example, *Trees Are a Breeze* means trees are easy to climb, *Working Out* refers to exercising, and *Chow Time* means it's time to eat.

Take a Stand

Like other bears, black bears can stand upright as humans do. They may stand to see over tall grass or to sniff an odor in the breeze. Or they may stand to get to food that's hard to reach.

Long, Sharp Claws

Black bears have sharp claws that grow up to 2.5 inches (6.25 cm) long. The bears use their claws to climb, tear apart prey, dig for food, and make dens.

Trees Are a Breeze

Adult black bears are good at climbing trees. They usually go up to get food such as acorns or cherries.

Black Bear Habitat

Body Length: **4-6 feet (1.2-1.8 m)**
Weight: **100-900 pounds (45-400 kg)**
Life Span: **About 30 years**
Habitat: **Woods, meadows, and swamps**
Range: **See orange areas on map.**

 **Sequence** Is sequence always important in what you read?

37

Bears in the Southeast

TIME FOR Science

Black bears can be found in the mountains and coastal plains of the Southeast. There, as elsewhere in the United States, people continue to move into areas once inhabited by wildlife, leaving less wild land on which the animals find food and shelter. Black bears generally are not a great threat to humans, but people and bears are encountering each other more and more. Reports of "nuisance" bears have greatly increased. In Florida: calls escalated from less than 100 in 1990 to 1,563 calls in 2004. Fortunately, only one fatal black bear attack has ever occurred in the southeastern United States.

EXPOSITORY NONFICTION

Use the sidebar on p. 36 to guide discussion.

- Explain that the purpose of expository nonfiction is to inform readers.
- Some pieces of expository nonfiction, such as this selection, contain heads describing the content of each section.
- Have students look at the heads and discuss how they can help readers understand nonfiction selections better. Point out how students can use heads before they read to predict the topics the selection will cover. They can use them after reading to recall or summarize what they've read.

Audio CD AudioText

Sequence

Possible response: No, sequence is not always important. In "Fast Facts: Black Bears," you don't have to read the paragraphs in sequence to understand the information.

Strategies for Nonfiction

USE MAPS Like other graphic sources, maps can help readers better understand a selection. Many maps include a title, labels, and a key. When expository nonfiction contains a map, readers may need to refer to it to answer test questions. Provide the following strategy.

Use the Strategy

1. Read the test question carefully to make sure you understand what is being asked.

2. Look at the map and its key to find out if it has the information you need to answer the question.

3. Use the key and labels to interpret the map and answer the question.

GUIDED PRACTICE Have students discuss how they would use the strategy to answer the following question.

What is the range for black bears shown on the map?

INDEPENDENT PRACTICE After students answer the following test question, discuss the process they used to find information.

Are black bears found where you live? Use details from the map to support your answer.

Bear Bodies

Bears of Many Colors

Black bears can be white, light brown, dark brown, cinnamon, blond, or blue-black. Most of the black bears that aren't black live in western North America. Sometimes western cubs from the same family are different colors.

Working Out

Even though they're big and bulky, black bears can really move. They can run 30 miles (48 km) per hour and swim as far as 2 miles (3.2 km) at a time. And they can leap short distances when they want to.

Heading Home

Even after wandering far off, black bears can find their way home. They use all of their senses to find the way back, especially their keen sense of smell. They may be the best "sniffers" of all the mammals in North America.

Tricky Tongues and Paws

Black bears have very long tongues. Their tongues come in handy for slurping food, such as insects, from hard-to-reach places.

They're also very good at using their paws. They can even unscrew jar lids to get at goodies that were left behind by careless campers!

38

Guided Practice Read the Guided Practice question. Have students match the key word *range* in the test question with the list under the map. Explain *range* refers to the regions where bears live. Encourage students to use the direction words *north, south, east,* and *west* in their descriptions of where bears live.

Chow Time

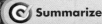
Hairy Neighbors

More and more people have been moving into areas that once were "bear country." Soon the bears start looking for food near people, and *that* causes problems.

Black Bear Menu

Black bears aren't picky eaters—they'll eat almost anything. Nuts, fruits, seeds, roots, grasses, and honey are all on a bear's menu. They'll also eat animals such as insects, fish, and rodents.

Bears Are Back

Black bears usually would rather run from people than hurt them. Even so, for many years some people shot or poisoned the bears until their numbers went way down. Today there are strict laws about when and where bears may be hunted, so they're making a big comeback. Hooray for black bears!

Reading Across Texts

Which facts about black bears could Miss Franny Block verify from her experience?

Writing Across Texts List the facts about black bears that Miss Block could verify.

Ⓒ Summarize What general statements summarize these facts?

39

CONNECT TEXT TO TEXT
Reading Across Texts

Have students review *Because of Winn-Dixie* to find details about Miss Franny's encounter with a bear. Point out they don't have to reread the entire story to answer the question, just the section where she describes her experiences.

Writing Across Texts Have students list details about Miss Franny's bear encounter in one column of a T-chart. In the second column, they can match these details with facts from "Fast Facts: Black Bears."

Ⓒ Summarize

Responses will vary, but should include general statements about black bears' habitat, behavior, and eating habits.

Fluency Assessment Plan

☑ **This week assess Advanced students.**
☐ **Week 2** Assess Strategic Intervention students.
☐ **Week 3** Assess On-Level students.
☐ **Week 4** Assess Strategic Intervention students.
☐ **Week 5** Assess any students you have not yet checked during this unit.

Set individual goals for students to enable them to reach the year-end goal.
• Current Goal: 95–105 WCPM
• Year-End Goal: 130 WCPM

For English language learners, emphasize repeated readings to build fluency with enjoyable passages in English, with as much teacher guidance as feasible.

 To develop fluent readers, use Fluency Coach.

DAY 5 Grouping Options

Reading
Whole Group
Revisit the Question of the Week.

Group Time
Differentiated Instruction
Reread this week's Leveled Readers. See pp. 18f–18g for the small group lesson plan.

Whole Group
Use p. 39b–39c.

Language Arts
Use pp. 39d–39l.

TONE OF VOICE
Fluency

DAY 1

Model Reread aloud "Child of the Silent Night" on p. 18m. Explain that you will use the rise and fall of your voice to show where the story includes questions and where it is full of emotion. Model for students as you read.

DAY 2

Choral Reading Read aloud paragraphs 3–6 on p. 28. Have students notice how your tone changes during dialogue to match the way people speak. Have students practice as a class, doing three choral readings of paragraphs 3–6.

DAY 3

Model Read aloud the last two paragraphs on p. 33. Have students notice how you raise your voice for questions and emphasize certain words, like *not even.* Practice as a class by doing three choral readings of these paragraphs.

DAY 4

Partner Reading Partners practice reading aloud the last two paragraphs on p. 33, three times. Have them use tone of voice to show Opal's feelings about Amanda, and then offer one another feedback.

Monitor Progress | Check Fluency WCPM

As students reread, monitor their progress toward their individual fluency goals. Current Goal: 95–105 words correct per minute. End-of-Year Goal: 130 words correct per minute.

If... students cannot read fluently at a rate of 95–105 words correct per minute,
then... make sure students practice with text at their independent level. Provide additional fluency practice, pairing nonfluent readers with fluent readers.

If... students already read at 130 words correct per minute,
then... they do not need to reread three to four times.

SUCCESS PREDICTOR

DAY 5

Assessment
Individual Reading Rate Use the Fluency Assessment Plan and do a one-minute timed reading of either selection from this week to assess students in Week 1. Pay special attention to this week's skill, tone of voice. Provide corrective feedback for each student.

RETEACH

Sequence

TEACH

Review the description of sequence on p. 18. Students can complete Practice Book p. 8 on their own or as a class. Discuss the graphic organizer on the Practice Book page. Point out that students should complete the phrases given for events 1, 2, and 5. They will write their own sentences to describe the third and fourth events in the passage.

ASSESS

Have students read p. 30, paragraph 5, in which Miss Franny tells Opal about the time she saw a bear in the library. Ask them to describe what happened first, next, and last. *(First, Miss Franny and the bear looked at each other. Then, the bear sniffed. Last, Miss Franny lifted up a book.)*

For additional instruction on sequence, see DI·52.

EXTEND SKILLS
Idiom

TEACH

An idiom is a phrase or expression whose meaning cannot be understood from the ordinary meaning of the words that form it. Students can determine the meaning of an idiom by figuring out what makes sense based on context.

• Identify idioms to help you better understand what you read.

• Understand that speakers from specific places use certain idioms.

Help students identify the idiom "has a large heart" on p. 28, paragraph 5, and use context to decide what it means.

ASSESS

Ask small groups to read the last paragraph on p. 29, find the idiom "nose stuck in a book," and write what it means. Then have them work together to write a list of other idioms they know and the meanings. Groups can share their lists with the class. To assess, make sure students understand that idioms have a nonliteral meaning.

OBJECTIVES

• Identify sequence of events.

• Identify and understand idioms.

Skills Trace	
Sequence	
Introduce/Teach	TE: 4.1 18-19, 66-67; 4.5 560-561
Practice	TE: 25, 27, 73, 77, 567, 571 PB: 3, 7, 8, 23, 27, 28, 223, 227, 228
▶ **Reteach/Review**	**TE: 4.1 39b, 87b, 97, DI·52, DI·54; 4.5 531, 551, 581b, DI·54 PB: 36, 206, 216**
Test	Selection Test: 1-4, 9-12, 89-92; Benchmark Test: Units 1, 5

ELL

Access Content Reteach the skill by reviewing the Picture It! lesson on sequence in the ELL Teaching Guide, pp. 1–2.

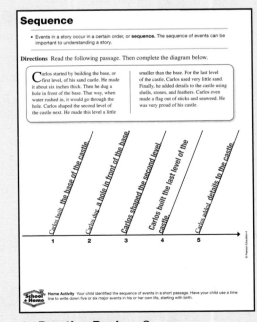

▲ **Practice Book** p. 8

SUCCESS PREDICTOR

Vocabulary and Word Study

VOCABULARY STRATEGY
Word Structure

SUFFIXES Remind students that the suffix *-ful* means "full of." For example, *prideful* means "full of pride." Another common suffix is *-ly*, meaning "in a way that is." Sometimes *-ful* and *-ly* are added to the end of a base word together, as in *pridefully*, which means "acting in a way that is full of pride." Have students use the suffixes to complete a chart like the one below. You may wish to add these base words: *skill, power, pity,* and *respect.*

Base Word	-ful	-ful + -ly	Word in Sentence
care	careful	carefully	She picked up the glass carefully.
hope			
fear			

Word Puzzles

Have students choose two vocabulary words or other important words from *Because of Winn-Dixie* and create crossword puzzles like the one below. Suggest students use a glossary, dictionary, or thesaurus to write meaning clues for each word. Students can exchange and solve each other's puzzles.

```
      p
      r
p e c u l i a r
      d
      e
      f
      u
      l
```

ACROSS:
odd, strange

DOWN:
boasting

BUILD CONCEPT VOCABULARY
Diversity

LOOKING BACK Remind students of the question of the week: *What experiences bring diverse people together?* Discuss how this week's Concept Web relates to the theme of diversity. Ask students if they have any words or categories to add. Discuss if words and categories are appropriately related to the concept.

MOVING FORWARD Preview the title of the next selection, *Lewis and Clark and Me.* Ask students which Concept Web words might apply to the new selection based on the title alone. Put a star next to these words on the Web.

Display the Concept Web and revisit the vocabulary words as you read the next selection to check predictions.

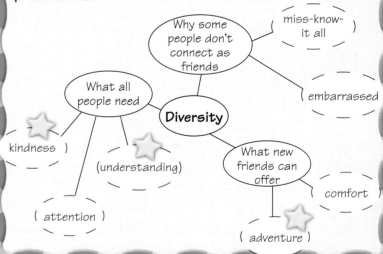

Monitor Progress
Check Vocabulary

If... students suggest words or categories that are not related to the concept,	**then...** review the words and categories on the Concept Web and discuss how they relate to the lesson concept.

SUCCESS PREDICTOR

Speaking and Listening

SPEAKING

Dramatic Retelling

SET-UP Have students choose a scene from *Because of Winn-Dixie* and retell it from the point of view of one of the characters. Set a time limit for the retelling.

PLANNING Have students decide from which character's point of view they will retell the scene. For example, students could portray the story from Winn-Dixie's point of view or the bear's point of view. Have students review the story to find important details for their retellings.

AUDIENCE Invite other students to provide constructive feedback. Discuss what makes a retelling interesting or easy to follow.

Delivery Tips
- Retell events in the order they happened.
- Focus on important events.
- Speak as if you are the character. Use the words, tone of voice, and movements you think the character would use.

LISTENING

Listen to a Story

Present a dramatic reading of a story to students. Read aloud a story of your choice or play a recording of a professional dramatic reading.

Then discuss what aspects of the story made it memorable, enjoyable, or full of dramatic tension. Guide students to consider the content, the organization, and the way it was presented.

You may want to practice this listening activity before students give their own dramatic retellings of *Because of Winn-Dixie*.

Have students answer these questions orally or in writing.

1. **How is the listening experience different from viewing a play or movie?** *(Responses will vary but should include a comparison between the two experiences.)*

2. **Why does listening to a dramatic reading spark your imagination?** *(Responses should include how the student imagines the actors, action, or setting.)*

E L L

Support Vocabulary Use the following to review and extend vocabulary and to explore lesson concepts further:
- ELL Poster 1, Days 3–5 instruction
- Vocabulary Activities and Word Cards in ELL Teaching Guide, pp. 3–4.

Assessment For information on assessing students' speaking and listening, see the ELL and Transition Handbook.

Grammar

Declarative and Interrogative Sentences

OBJECTIVES

- Define and identify declarative sentences.
- Define and identify interrogative sentences.
- Use declarative and interrogative sentences correctly in writing.
- Become familiar with declarative and interrogative sentence assessment on high-stakes tests.

Monitor Progress

Grammar

If... students have difficulty identifying declarative and interrogative sentences,	then... provide additional instruction and practice in The Grammar and Writing Book pp. 50–53.

DAILY FIX-IT

This week use Daily Fix-It Transparency 1.

Support Grammar See the Grammar Transition lessons in the ELL and Transition Handbook.

▲ **The Grammar and Writing Book**
For more instruction and practice, use pp. 50–53.

DAY 1 — Teach and Model

DAILY FIX-IT

1. My dog Bella is a real rascul? *(rascal.)*

2. Does stray dogs make good pets. *(Do; pets?)*

READING-GRAMMAR CONNECTION

Write these sentences from *Because of Winn-Dixie* on the board:

> *"Are you all right?"*
>
> *"That's my dog."*

Explain that the first sentence is an **interrogative sentence**. It asks a question and ends with a question mark. The second sentence is a **declarative sentence**. It tells something and ends with a period. Both sentences are simple sentences.

Display Grammar Transparency 1. Read aloud the definitions and sample sentences. Work through the items.

Declarative and Interrogative Sentences

A **sentence** is a group of words that expresses a complete thought. A sentence begins with a capital letter. A sentence that tells something is a **declarative sentence**. A declarative sentence ends with a period. A sentence that asks a question is an **interrogative sentence**. An interrogative sentence ends with a question mark.

Declarative Sentence   The library is full of interesting books.
Interrogative Sentence   How many of these books have you read?

Directions Write *D* if the sentence is declarative. Write *I* if the sentence is interrogative.

1. A person who works in a library is a librarian.   **D**
2. Are pets allowed in the library?   **I**
3. The librarian asked us to be quiet.   **D**
4. Hetty loves books about travel.   **D**
5. Can I do my homework at this table?   **I**

Directions Write each sentence with the correct end punctuation mark.
6. Who is your favorite author
   Who is your favorite author?
7. Do you prefer photographs or drawings in a book
   Do you prefer photographs or drawings in a book?
8. Our town library has a children's section
   Our town library has a children's section.
9. When a pigeon flew into the library, everyone laughed
   When a pigeon flew into the library, everyone laughed.
10. Where do I find the maps and dictionaries
    Where do I find the maps and dictionaries?

Unit 1 Because of Winn-Dixie   Grammar 1

▲ **Grammar Transparency** 1

DAY 2 — Develop the Concept

DAILY FIX-IT

3. I teaching my dog to rol over. *(I am teaching; roll)*

4. Dogs can learn to help blind people. Or works with the police. *(people or work)*

GUIDED PRACTICE

Review the concept of declarative and interrogative sentences.

- A **declarative sentence** is a statement that tells about something. It ends with a period.

- An **interrogative sentence** asks a question. It ends with a question mark.

- Declarative and interrogative sentences begin with capital letters and can be simple, compound, or complex.

HOMEWORK Grammar and Writing Practice Book p. 1. Work through the first two items with the class.

Declarative and Interrogative Sentences

A **sentence** is a group of words that expresses a complete thought. A sentence begins with a capital letter. A sentence that tells something is a **declarative sentence**. A declarative sentence ends with a period. A sentence that asks a question is an **interrogative sentence**. An interrogative sentence ends with a question mark.

Declarative Sentence   Florida was once a wild place.
Interrogative Sentence   Have you ever seen a bear?

Directions Read each sentence and add the correct end punctuation. Then write whether each sentence is declarative or interrogative.
1. In the old days, many people lived on farms .
   declarative
2. Wild animals roamed through the forests .
   declarative
3. Were the woods full of bears in those days ?
   interrogative

Directions Change each sentence to the kind named in ( ). Write the new sentence.
4. Grandpa likes telling stories. (interrogative)
   Does Grandpa like telling stories?
5. Are his stories always true? (declarative)
   His stories are always true.

Home Activity Your child learned about declarative and interrogative sentences. Have your child write two declarative and two interrogative sentences about something he or she did today.

▲ **Grammar and Writing Practice Book** p. 1

DAY 3 — Apply to Writing

DAILY FIX-IT

5. Our class study in the library every tuesday. *(studies; Tuesday)*

6. We read quietly for an our, we can read any book we like. *(hour. We)*

VARY YOUR SENTENCE STYLE

Point out that different kinds of sentences can make writing exciting. Explain that using interrogative sentences is one way to keep readers interested.

- Have students review something they have written to see if they can improve it by adding interrogative sentences.

HOMEWORK Grammar and Writing Practice Book p. 2.

Declarative and Interrogative Sentences

Directions Read the interrogative sentences. Then use your own ideas to write a declarative sentence that answers each question. **Possible answers:**

1. **Question** Why is it hard to move to a new place?
   Answer You don't have any friends in a new place.

2. **Question** Where would be a good place to make new friends?
   Answer You can make friends at school.

3. **Question** What kind of pet might make a good friend?
   Answer A dog might be a good friend.

4. **Question** What is a good way to make friends? You can ask people
   Answer if they want to play with you.

Directions Read the answers in the interview with Opal from *Because of Winn-Dixie*. Then write the questions you think she might be answering. **Possible answers:**

5. **Question** How did you feel when you first moved to Florida?
   Answer At first I felt really lonely.

6. **Question** Did you have any friends?
   Answer No, I didn't know anyone.

7. **Question** What did you do?
   Answer I spent a lot of time in the library.

Home Activity Your child learned how to use declarative and interrogative sentences in writing. Have your child ask a member of the family three questions and write down the questions and answers in interview form.

▲ **Grammar and Writing Practice Book** p. 2

DAY 4 — Test Preparation

DAILY FIX-IT

7. A bear is a large mamal? *(mammal.)*

8. Grizzly bears is bigger then black bears. *(are; than)*

STANDARDIZED TEST PREP

Test Tip

Keep an eye on helping verbs such as *is, are, has, have, does,* and *do.* They come before the subject of an interrogative sentence.

Declarative: The boys are playing with the dog.

Her dog looks like a bear.

Interrogative: Are the boys playing with the dog?

Does her dog look like a bear?

HOMEWORK Grammar and Writing Practice Book p. 3.

Declarative and Interrogative Sentences

Directions For each item, mark the letter of the word or the word and punctuation mark that completes each sentence.

1. You have to be quiet in a _____
   A library
   B library?
   C library.
   D Library

2. _____ many books did you get?
   A Who
   B how
   C How?
   D How

3. _____ get a library card?
   A Can I
   B I can
   C I can?
   D can I

4. Do you like adventure _____
   A stories.
   B stories
   C stories?
   D Stories

Directions For each item, mark the letter of the declarative or interrogative sentence that is correctly written.

5. A Are pets allowed in the library.
   B I'll leave my dog outside?
   C he is very well behaved.
   D Do I hear him barking?

6. A Our dog can shake hands
   B Does he come when you call.
   C can he catch a ball?
   D I'm teaching him to sit.

7. A The pound has many animals
   B Are they all puppies?
   C Would you like one as a pet?
   D some ran away from home?

8. A Why is his name Winn-Dixie.
   B Isn't that the name of a store.
   C It's a funny name for a dog.
   D Does he know his name.

9. A Was your dog a stray?
   B a stray has no home.
   C Can I adopt one.
   D Where did he come from.

10. A Dogs are fun
    B They make good friends.
    C Dogs are part of the family?
    D do you have a dog?

Home Activity Your child prepared for taking tests on declarative and interrogative sentences. Say declarative or interrogative and have your child say a sentence of the correct kind.

▲ **Grammar and Writing Practice Book** p. 3

DAY 5 — Cumulative Review

DAILY FIX-IT

9. I love to here Miss Block tell his stories. *(hear; her)*

10. Some off her stories are hard to believe *(of; believe.)*

ADDITIONAL PRACTICE

Assign pp. 50–53 in The Grammar and Writing Book.

EXTRA PRACTICE Grammar and Writing Practice Book p. 122.

ASSESSMENT

CUMULATIVE REVIEW Grammar and Writing Practice Book p. 4.

Declarative and Interrogative Sentences

Directions Write *D* if the sentence is declarative. Write *I* if the sentence is interrogative.

1. Opal loved to visit the library. **D**
2. What did her dog do? **I**
3. Did Opal have any friends? **I**
4. She made friends with the librarian. **D**

Directions Make each word group into a sentence by writing it with correct capitalization and punctuation. Write *D* if the sentence is declarative. Write *I* if the sentence is interrogative.

5. a bear once visited the library
   A bear once visited the library. **D**

6. it walked through the open door
   It walked through the open door. **D**

7. what did the librarian do
   What did the librarian do? **I**

8. would you have run away
   Would you have run away? **I**

Directions Change each sentence to the kind named in ( ). Write the new sentence.

9. The dog looks like a bear. (interrogative)
   Does the dog look like a bear?

10. Are bears dangerous? (declarative)
    Bears are dangerous.

11. An amazing story is called a tall tale. (interrogative)
    Is an amazing story called a tall tale?

12. Did the librarian tell a tall tale? (declarative)
    The librarian told a tall tale.

Home Activity Your child reviewed declarative and interrogative sentences. Read a newspaper article together. Have your child identify declarative and interrogative sentences in the article.

▲ **Grammar and Writing Practice Book** p. 4

Writing Workshop Memoir

OBJECTIVES

- Identify qualities of a memoir.
- Write a memoir with a distinctive voice or tone.
- Focus on word choice.
- Use a rubric.

Genre Memoir
Writer's Craft Voice/Tone
Writing Trait Word Choice

Word Choice Pair an English learner with a proficient English speaker to discuss pictures in books or magazines. Have them list colorful words from the discussion to use in writing, such as *friendly, picnic, caterpillar, broken, snowstorm,* and *furry.*

Writing Traits

FOCUS/IDEAS Descriptive details make the narrator's experience come alive.

ORGANIZATION/PARAGRAPHS The memoir tells a story with a beginning, middle, and end.

VOICE The writer's personality comes through clearly.

WORD CHOICE The writer uses vivid adjectives to describe the stray dog (*hungry, skinny*) and strong verbs (*wander, snoozing*) to describe actions.

SENTENCES Use of an interrogative sentence to open the memoir catches the reader's interest.

CONVENTIONS There is excellent control and accuracy, including effective use of an interrogative sentence.

DAY 1 Model the Trait

READING-WRITING CONNECTION

- *Because of Winn Dixie* uses exact words to describe Opal's experience in a new place.
- Choosing exact words helps to create a unique voice or tone.
- Students will write **memoirs,** choosing exact words to create a unique voice.

MODEL WORD CHOICE Display Writing Transparency 1A. Then discuss the model and the writing trait of word choice.

 Think Aloud I see many precise words in this memoir. For example, the writer describes Happy's tail by saying it "curled around like the letter *C.*" These specific words give me a clear picture of what Happy looks like. The writer also uses strong verbs such as *snoozing* and *wander.*

Memoir

A **memoir** tells about an interesting event or experience in your life. It may include information about how you felt, what you saw, or why you did something. Memoirs are also known as personal essays. A memoir that tells a person's life story is called an autobiography.

The Dog That Wouldn't Go Away

Introductory paragraph grabs reader's attention.
Have you ever heard of a pet that chose its owner? That's how Happy came to live with us.

Details bring scene to life for reader.
Happy turned up at our door late one evening, hungry and without a collar. He was a skinny brown dog with a white tail that curled around like the letter *C.* My mom gave him some food and said he'd probably wander home. He didn't. The next morning we found him snoozing in our garage. A week later he was still there.

Conclusion sums up importance of experience to narrator.
Happy became a member of our family. He taught me that if you want something in life really badly, the best thing to do is to hang in there.

Unit 1 Because of Winn-Dixie   Writing Model **1A**

▲ **Writing Transparency** 1A

DAY 2 Improve Writing

WRITER'S CRAFT
Voice/Tone

Display Writing Transparency 1B. Read the directions and work together to describe different voices.

 Think Aloud **VOICE/TONE** Tomorrow we will be writing a memoir about an interesting experience. My memoir should sound like "me." I'm going to write about when I first moved to this town. Even though it was hard, I'm a friendly and enthusiastic person. That voice should shine through in my memoir.

GUIDED WRITING Some students may need more help with voice. Work with them to identify the voice of Opal in *Because of Winn-Dixie.*

Voice

Voice shows a writer's personality. It reveals feelings and makes one person's writing sound different from everyone else's. A writer's voice gives a piece of writing its tone.

Directions Write the word: *funny, serious,* or *friendly* to describe the voice of each paragraph.

1. Lovell was the smartest dog I ever met. He was a collie that belonged to my uncle Ed. Lovell knew what to do in an emergency. Once he woke up at night and started barking because he smelled smoke. Uncle Ed got his family out of the house quickly. He said that someone might have got hurt if Lovell hadn't barked.
serious

2. Hey, Sal!
You won't believe what happened today! You know it's my birthday, don't you? Well, it looked like Mom and Dad had forgotten about it. There were no presents at breakfast, and I had to remind Mom what day it was. Then suddenly my dad came up from the basement carrying . . . Guess what? A puppy! It's brown and white. I'm going to teach it tricks. This is so awesome! You've got to come over now.
Jo
friendly

3. Our dog wasn't always called Uh-oh. When we bought him, his name was Rags. But as a puppy he was always getting into trouble around the house. He'd eat my sister's shoe or pull down a curtain or make a mess on the floor. And every time he did something wrong, we'd say "Uh-oh!" After a while, the name stuck!
funny

Directions Write two or three sentences about a pet you have known. Use a funny, serious, or friendly voice. **Possible answer:**

I love Cleo, my neighbor's cat. Cleo always purrs and wants to sit on my lap. Whenever I feel sad, Cleo knows just how to cheer me up.

Unit 1 Because of Winn-Dixie   Writer's Craft **1B**

▲ **Writing Transparency** 1B

DAY 3 Prewrite and Draft

READ THE WRITING PROMPT

on page 35 in the Student Edition.

In Because of Winn Dixie, Opal tells about her experiences after moving to a new town.

Think about a time that you were a newcomer to a place or situation.

Now use vivid words to write a memoir of that experience.

Writing Test Tips

- Include details that explain how you felt as well as what happened.
- Vary your sentences to make your writing more interesting to read.
- Use vivid adjectives and strong verbs to make the experience come alive.

GETTING STARTED Students can do any of the following:

- Make a graphic organizer to order their ideas.
- Close their eyes and replay the important experience in their minds, looking for specific details.
- Visualize a person who might read their memoir, and tell the story with this audience in mind.

DAY 4 Draft and Revise

EDITING/REVISING CHECKLIST

☑ Does my personality come through in my writing?

☑ Do specific details catch the reader's attention?

☑ Have I used any interrogative sentences?

☑ Are words with short vowels spelled correctly?

See *The Grammar and Writing Book,* pp. 50–55.

Revising Tips

Word Choice

- Support exact word choice by selecting words that bring details to life.
- Make sure nouns are specific and verbs are strong.
- Use specific words to describe your feelings.

PUBLISHING Students can find photographs or make drawings to illustrate their writing and bind their memoirs in a class anthology. Some students may wish to revise their work later.

ASSESSMENT Use the scoring rubric to evaluate students' work.

DAY 5 Connect to Unit Writing

Personal Narrative	
Week 1	Memoir 39g–39h
Week 2	Journal Entry 65g–65h
Week 3	Postcard 87g–87h
Week 4	E-mail Invitation 111g–111h
Week 5	Narrative Writing 133g–133h

PREVIEW THE UNIT PROMPT

Write a personal narrative about a time that you were a newcomer to a place or situation (a school, club, team, or neighborhood). Explain how you felt and what you found challenging or exciting.

APPLY

- A personal narrative is a story about an interesting experience or event in the storyteller's life.
- Vivid descriptions create an effective personal narrative.

Writing Trait Rubric

	4	3	2	1
Word Choice	Word choice strong and exact	Word choice adequate	Word choice weak, few examples of strong and exact choices	Dull and/or inaccurate word choices throughout
	Memoir clear and engaging with strong word choices	Memoir generally clear and engaging	Memoir weakened by lack of exact language	Memoir weak and/or confusing with ineffective language

Spelling & Phonics Short Vowels VCCV

Spelling Words

1. admire	11. accident
2. magnet	12. mitten
3. contest	13. intend*
4. method	14. fabric
5. custom	15. flatten
6. rally	16. rascal
7. soccer	17. gutter
8. engine	18. mammal
9. sudden*	19. happen*
10. finger*	20. cannon

Challenge Words

21. dungeon	24. thunderstorm
22. magnify	25. injury
23. festival	

*Word from the selection

Spelling/Phonics Support See the ELL and Transition Handbook for spelling support.

PRETEST

Use the Dictation Sentences from Day 5 to administer the pretest. Read the word, read the sentence, and then read the word again. Guide students in self-correcting their pretests and correcting any misspellings.

Monitor Progress

Spelling

If... students misspell more than 5 pretest words,	then... use words 1–10 for Strategic Intervention.
If... students misspell 1–5 pretest words,	then... use words 1–20 for On-Level practice.
If... students correctly spell all pretest words,	then... use words 1–25 for Advanced Learners.

HOMEWORK Spelling Practice Book, p. 1.

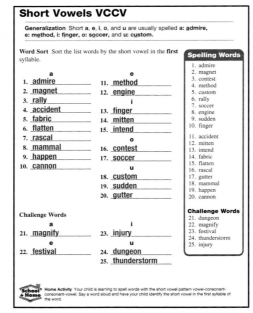

▲ **Spelling Practice Book** p. 1

TEACH

Vowels usually have the short sound when they are followed by two consonants. Write *sudden* on the board. Underline consonants *dd,* and circle the vowel *u.* Say *sudden* and identify *u* as a short vowel. Guide students in finding the VCCV pattern in *finger, intend,* and *happen.*

> VCCV
> *sudden*

FIND THE PATTERN Ask students to identify the VCCV pattern in each of the spelling words. For each word, have them tell whether the two consonants that follow the vowel are the same, as in *sudden,* or different, as in *finger.* Have students name the vowel and say the vowel sound in the first syllable of each word.

HOMEWORK Spelling Practice Book, p. 2.

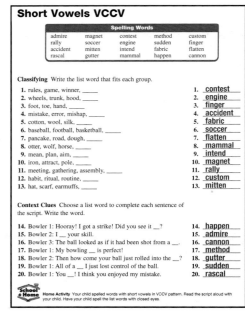

▲ **Spelling Practice Book** p. 2

DAY 3 Connect to Writing

WRITE A PERSONAL ESSAY

Ask students to use at least five spelling words to write a paragraph or two about an event from their life.

Frequently Misspelled Words

with   *cousin*

These words may seem easy to spell, but they are often misspelled by fourth-graders. Alert students to these frequently misspelled words. Make sure students pronounce the final *th* in *with*. Point out that the letters *ou* stand for the short *u* sound in *cousin*, and that the *z* sound is spelled with an *s*.

HOMEWORK Spelling Practice Book, p. 3.

Short Vowels VCCV

Proofread a Newspaper Column Circle five misspelled words in the newspaper column. Write the words correctly. Then write the sentence that has a punctuation mistake correctly.

Spelling Words
admire
magnet
contest
method
custom
rally
soccer
engine
sudden
finger
accident
mitten
intend
fabric
flatten
rascal
gutter
mammal
happen
cannon

Roof Rally
By Dan Green
Most days I (admire) that little (rascle) the squirrel. That furry little (mummal) is always busy. Its usual (costum) is to keep busy burying food all day long. On one recent day a squirrel decided to take a break. He brought twenty of his (cusins) and held a rally on my roof. The noise was terrible! How could this happen? Stop it, I shouted. They scampered over the gutter and ran away. It was good to have peace and quiet again.

1. admire   2. rascal
3. mammal   4. custom
5. cousins   6. "Stop it!" I shouted.

Proofread Words Circle the correctly spelled word. Write the word.

7. (cannon) cannen kannon   7. cannon
8. mignet (magnet) manget   8. magnet
9. (accident) ecident eccident   9. accident
10. ingune (engine) ingine   10. engine
11. soccor socor (soccer)   11. soccer
12. fabrik fibrak (fabric)   12. fabric

Frequently Misspelled Words
with
cousin

School Home **Home Activity** Your child identified misspelled words with short vowels in VCCV pattern. Say each spelling word. Ask your child to name the short vowel in the first syllable.

▲ **Spelling Practice Book** p. 3

DAY 4 Review

REVIEW SHORT VOWELS

Have pairs of students take turns giving each other clues about the spelling words. Tell them to give one clue about the word's meaning. For the other clue, students should say the vowel sound in the word's first syllable.

Spelling Strategy
Problem Parts

We all have words that are hard for us to spell.
Step 1: Ask yourself: Which part of the word gives me a problem?
Step 2: Underline your problem part.
Step 3: Picture the word. Focus on the problem part.

HOMEWORK Spelling Practice Book, p. 4.

Short Vowels VCCV

Spelling Words

admire	magnet	contest	method	custom
rally	soccer	engine	sudden	finger
accident	mitten	intend	fabric	flatten
rascal	gutter	mammal	happen	cannon

Riddle Read the riddle. To find the answer, write the list word that fits each clue. Then copy the numbered letters onto the numbered lines below.

Riddle: What weighs 5,000 pounds and wears glass slippers?

1. think highly of — a d m i r e
2. a meeting — r a l l y
3. the part that makes a car run — e n g i n e
4. attracts iron — m a g n e t
5. glove with no fingers — m i t t e n
6. a mischievous person — r a s c a l
7. your shirt is made of this — f a b r i c
8. a way of doing something — m e t h o d
9. what a steamroller can do — f l a t t e n
10. occur — h a p p e n
11. a game played with a round ball — s o c c e r
12. something that unexpectedly happens — a c c i d e n t
13. something to enter — c o n t e s t
14. a pinky — f i n g e r

Answer:
c i n d e r e l e p h a n t

School Home **Home Activity** Your child has learned to read, write, and spell words with the short vowel pattern VCCV. Ask your child to quiz your spelling of these words. Make a mistake with each word and have your child correct it.

▲ **Spelling Practice Book** p. 4

DAY 5 Posttest

DICTATION SENTENCES

1. I admire people who are kind.
2. A magnet picks up nails.
3. The girls won the contest.
4. Do you have a good method for doing homework?
5. It is our custom to stand during the parade.
6. We had a pep rally before the game.
7. Terry loves to play soccer.
8. The car's engine wouldn't start.
9. The car made a sudden turn.
10. I cut my finger.
11. No one was hurt in the accident.
12. I always seem to lose one mitten.
13. How do you intend to solve the puzzle?
14. The wool fabric made me itch.
15. I used my hand to flatten the clay.
16. That playful puppy is a rascal.
17. The leaves clogged the gutter.
18. A camel is a mammal.
19. I wonder what will happen next.
20. There is a cannon at the park.

CHALLENGE

21. A dungeon is dark and damp.
22. Glasses magnify small print.
23. We had fun at the holiday festival.
24. A tree fell during the thunderstorm.
25. The doctor treated Jed's injury.

- Formulate an inquiry question that is connected to this week's lesson focus.
- Effectively and efficiently find, evaluate, and communicate information related to an inquiry question using electronic sources.

New Literacies

Day 1	Identify Questions
Day 2	Navigate/Search
Day 3	Analyze
Day 4	Synthesize
Day 5	Communicate

NEW LITERACIES

Internet Inquiry Activity

EXPLORE DIVERSITY

Use the following 5-day plan to help students conduct this week's Internet inquiry activity on diversity. Remind students to follow classroom rules when using the Internet.

DAY 1

Identify Questions Discuss the meaning of *diversity* with students. Talk about how Opal and Miss Franny Block's friendship in *Because of Winn-Dixie* shows how common experiences can bring diverse people together. Brainstorm ideas for specific inquiry questions. For example, students might explore diversity in sports, multicultural music and arts, or organizations that promote tolerance. Have individuals, pairs, or small groups write an inquiry question they want to answer.

DAY 2

Navigate/Search Explain how to begin a simple Internet search using a student-friendly search engine. Tell students search engines find and list Web sites that match the keywords students enter. Help students determine appropriate keywords related to their inquiry questions. Discuss how to use search engine results to identify a few helpful Web sites.

DAY 3

Analyze Have students explore the Web sites they identified on Day 2. Tell them to scan each site for information that helps answer their inquiry question. After examining relevant and credible Web sites, students may want to revise their inquiry question based on the information available. Then they can choose a few sites to explore further.

DAY 4

Synthesize Have students synthesize information from Day 3. Remind them that when they synthesize, they combine relevant ideas and information from different sources to develop an answer to their inquiry question.

DAY 5

Communicate Have students share their inquiry results. They can use a word processing program to show their questions and answers.

RESEARCH/STUDY SKILLS
Map/Globe/Atlas

TEACH

Ask students how they could find the location of Naomi, Florida. Discuss using a map, globe, or atlas. Show examples of each type of source and use them to define the following terms:

- A **map** is an illustration of a place. It could be a drawing of your backyard or the solar system.

- A map's **legend** contains a **compass rose** showing direction, a **scale** showing distance, and a **key** showing symbols on the map and what they represent.

- A **globe** is a sphere with a map of the world on it.

- An **atlas** is a book that contains maps.

Have small groups take turns examining a globe and an atlas. Remind students to study the legend closely before using any map. Then ask:

1. **How would you find the country closest to Australia?** *(Possible response: Locate Australia on a globe and then find the country nearest to it.)*

2. **How would you figure out the number of miles between Washington, D.C. and New York City?** *(Possible response: Measure the distance on a map with a ruler and then use the scale to figure out the number of miles.)*

3. **How would you find a route to drive from Los Angeles to Miami?** *(Possible response: Look at a U.S. map that includes major highways.)*

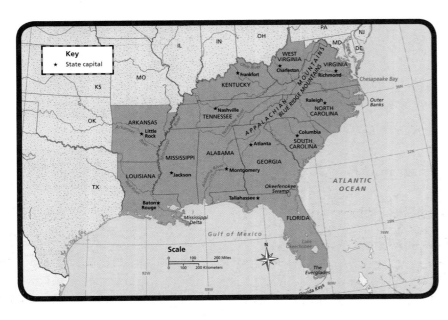

ASSESS

Check that students can name the parts of a map and explain the purpose of each part. Name specific locations and have students find them on the map.

For more practice or to assess students, use Practice Book pp. 9–10.

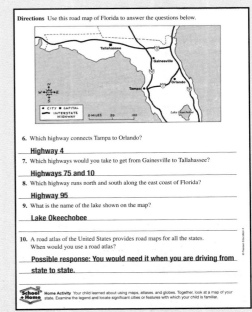

Map/Globe/Atlas

A **map** is a drawing of a place that shows where something is or where something happened. A map's **legend** has a **compass rose** to show direction, a **scale** to show distance, and a **key** to symbols. A **globe** is a sphere with a map of the world, and an **atlas** is a book of maps.

Directions Use this map of Florida to answer the questions below.

1. Which city is the farthest west?
   Apalachicola
2. Which city is on the Gulf of Mexico, Daytona Beach or Cedar Key?
   Cedar Key
3. Which city is north of Palm Bay, Melbourne or Fort Pierce?
   Melbourne
4. Name the city that is closest to Hollywood.
   Miami
5. Which city is approximately 75 miles east of Naples: Hollywood or Venice?
   Hollywood

▲ **Practice Book** p. 9

Directions Use this road map of Florida to answer the questions below.

6. Which highway connects Tampa to Orlando?
   Highway 4
7. Which highways would you take to get from Gainesville to Tallahassee?
   Highways 75 and 10
8. Which highway runs north and south along the east coast of Florida?
   Highway 95
9. What is the name of the lake shown on the map?
   Lake Okeechobee
10. A road atlas of the United States provides road maps for all the states. When would you use a road atlas?
    Possible response: You would need it when you are driving from state to state.

School + Home Home Activity Your child learned about using maps, atlases, and globes. Together, look at a map of your state. Examine the legend and locate significant cities or features with which your child is familiar.

▲ **Practice Book** p. 10

OBJECTIVES
- Review terms related to maps.
- Use maps, globes, and atlases to find information.

Assessment Checkpoints *for the Week*

Selection Assessment

Use pp. 1–4 of Selection Tests to check:

 Selection Understanding

 Comprehension Skill *Sequence*

 Selection Vocabulary

grand	prideful
memorial	recalls
peculiar	selecting
positive	

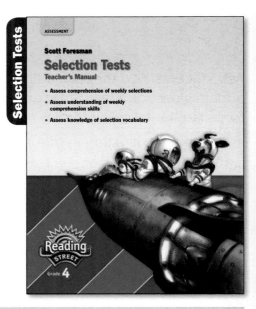

ASSESSMENT

Scott Foresman

Selection Tests
Teacher's Manual

- Assess comprehension of weekly selections
- Assess understanding of weekly comprehension skills
- Assess knowledge of selection vocabulary

Reading STREET
Grade 4

Leveled Assessment

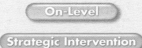
- On-Level
- Strategic Intervention
- Advanced

Use pp. 1–6 of Fresh Reads for Differentiated Test Practice to check:

 Comprehension Skill *Sequence*

 REVIEW Comprehension Skill
Authors' Purpose

 Fluency *Words Correct Per Minute*

ASSESSMENT   Teacher's Manual

Scott Foresman

Fresh Reads
for Differentiated Test Practice

Leveled passages—strategic intervention, on-level, and advanced—for

- Fluency checks
- Practice and application of weekly comprehension skills
- Answer key for all practice pages

Reading STREET
Grade 4

Managing Assessment

Use Assessment Handbook for:

 Observation Checklists

 Record-Keeping Forms

 Portfolio Assessment

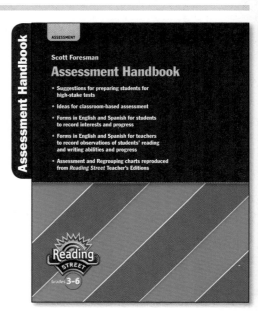

ASSESSMENT

Scott Foresman

Assessment Handbook

- Suggestions for preparing students for high-stake tests
- Ideas for classroom-based assessment
- Forms in English and Spanish for students to record interests and progress
- Forms in English and Spanish for teachers to record observations of students' reading and writing abilities and progress
- Assessment and Regrouping charts reproduced from *Reading Street* Teacher's Editions

Reading STREET
Grades 3–6

Oregon

Planning Guide for Common Curriculum Goals

Lewis and Clark and Me

Reading Street Teacher's Edition pages	Grade 4 Oregon Grade-Level Standards for English/Language Arts
Oral Language **Speaking/Listening** Build Concept Vocabulary: 40l, 53, 59, 65c Read Aloud: 40m **Viewing** Analyze an Illustration: 65d	**EL.04.RE.09** Understand, learn, and use new vocabulary that is introduced and taught directly through informational text, literary text, and instruction across the subject areas. **EL.04.RE.17** Locate information in titles, tables of contents, chapter headings, illustrations, captions, glossaries, indexes, graphs, charts, diagrams, and tables to aid understanding of grade-level text.
Word Work Long *a* and *i*: 65i–65j	**EL.04.WR.15** Spell correctly: syllables (word parts each containing a vowel sound, such as *sur-prise* or *e-col-o-gy*).
Reading **Comprehension** Author's Purpose: 40–41, 44–59, 62–65, 65b Answer Questions: 40–41, 44–59 **Vocabulary** Lesson Vocabulary: 42b, 53, 59, 62 Word Structure: 42–43, 51, 55, 65c **Fluency** Model Pauses: 40l–40m, 65a **Self-Selected Reading:** LR10–18, TR16–17 **Literature** Genre—Historical Fantasy: 44 Reader Response: 60	**EL.04.RE.07** Understand and draw upon a variety of comprehension strategies as needed— re-reading, self-correcting, summarizing, class and group discussions, generating and responding to essential questions, making predictions, and comparing information from several sources. **EL.04.RE.10** Develop vocabulary by listening to and discussing both familiar and conceptually challenging selections read aloud across the subject areas. **EL.04.RE.25** Determine the author's purpose, and relate it to details in the text.
Language Arts **Writing** Journal Entry: 65g–65h **Six-Trait Writing** Voice: 61, 65g–65h **Grammar, Usage, and Mechanics** Imperative and Exclamatory Sentences: 65e–65f **Research/Study** Skim and Scan: 65l **Technology** New Literacies: 65k	**EL.04.WR.10** Select a focus and a point of view based upon purpose, and audience. **EL.04.WR.12** Use words that describe, explain, or provide additional details and connections. **EL.04.WR.13** Use simple sentences and compound sentences in writing.
Unit Skills **Writing** Personal Narrative: WA2–9 **Poetry:** 134–137 **Project/Wrap-Up:** 138–139	**EL.04.WR.23** Write personal narratives: include ideas, observations, or memories of an event or experience; provide a context to allow the reader to imagine the world of the event or experience; use concrete sensory details; provide insight into why the selected event or experience is memorable.

This Week's Leveled Readers

Below-Level

The Long Trip West

Nonfiction

EL.04.RE.17 Locate information in titles, tables of contents, chapter headings, illustrations, captions, glossaries, indexes, graphs, charts, diagrams, and tables to aid understanding of grade-level text.

EL.04.RE.25 Determine the author's purpose, and relate it to details in the text.

On-Level

Lewis and Clark by Cindy Swan

Nonfiction

EL.04.RE.23 Draw inferences or conclusions about an author's meaning supported by facts and events from the text.

EL.04.RE.25 Determine the author's purpose, and relate it to details in the text.

Advanced

Two Great Rivers

Nonfiction

EL.04.RE.25 Determine the author's purpose, and relate it to details in the text.

EL.04.LI.03 Identify and/or summarize sequence of events, main ideas, and supporting details in literary selections.

Content-Area Content Standards and Benchmarks in This Lesson

Science

SC.05.LS.01.01 Classify a variety of living things into groups using various characteristics. (Previews Grade 5 Benchmark)

SC.05.LS.03 Describe basic plant and animal structures and their functions. (Previews Grade 5 Benchmark)

SC.05.LS.05 Describe the relationship between characteristics of specific habitats and the organisms that live there. (Previews Grade 5 Benchmark)

SC.05.LS.05.04 Explain the relationship between animal behavior and species survival. (Previews Grade 5 Benchmark)

SC.05.LS.06.01 Describe changes to the environment that have caused the population of some species to change. (Previews Grade 5 Benchmark)

Social Studies

SS.05.EC.01 Understand that all economic choices have costs and benefits, and compare options in terms of costs and benefits. (Previews Grade 5 Benchmark)

SS.05.EC.05.01 Distinguish between "barter" and "money" and how they facilitate the exchange of goods. (Previews Grade 5 Benchmark)

SS.05.GE.02 Examine and understand how to prepare maps, charts, and other visual representations to locate places and interpret geographic information. (Previews Grade 5 Benchmark)

Oregon!

AN EXPLORER OF OREGON
Meriwether Lewis

Meriwether Lewis (1774–1809) was an American explorer who, accompanied by fellow explorer Lt. William Clark, led the first expedition by land to the Pacific Northwest. Before beginning the expedition Lewis worked as a private secretary to President Thomas Jefferson. Congress set aside $2,500 for the exploration of the Louisiana Territory, and Lewis traveled to Philadelphia to study zoology, botany, and celestial navigation to prepare himself for the long journey.

Students can . . .
Read a children's book about another explorer. Ask students to write a brief summary of the explorer and his accomplishments.

A SPECIAL OREGON PLACE
Fort Vancouver

Fort Vancouver served as the headquarters and supply center for the fur-trading portion of the Hudson's Bay Company in the early 1800s. The fort became a popular meeting place for people in the Pacific Northwest and even provided American emigrants with the supplies they would need to settle in the Oregon Territory in the 1830s and 1840s. Today Fort Vancouver is a national historic site and is part of the 366-acre Vancouver National Historic Reserve.

Students can . . .
Research the design and structure of a fort. Ask students to draw a design for a Web site on the topic.

OREGON FUN FACTS
Did You Know?

- Malheur National Forest's name comes from the French word for "misfortune." In the 1820s fur trapper Peter Ogden named the area after his supplies were stolen there.

- Promoter Peter Burnett lured pioneers to Oregon in 1843 by telling tales of pigs that roamed the forests fully cooked and ready to be eaten.

- When Lewis and Clark's Corps of Discovery saw a beached whale near what is now Cannon Beach, they negotiated with Native Americans for three hundred pounds of whale blubber.

Students can . . .
Speculate about how Lewis and Clark negotiated for whale blubber with Native Americans and illustrate how they think the transaction might have looked.

Unit 1
This Land Is Your Land

CONCEPT QUESTION
How do the diverse regions and peoples of the United States reflect its greatness?

Week 1
What experiences bring diverse peoples together?

Week 2
What did Lewis and Clark learn on their journey?

Week 3
What can we learn about the United States as we travel?

Week 4
What is unique about the landscape of the Southwest?

Week 5
How does Yosemite reflect the unique qualities of the West?

EXPAND THE CONCEPT
What did Lewis and Clark learn on their journey?

CONNECT THE CONCEPT

▶ **Build Background**
pioneer, settlers, territories, traveled

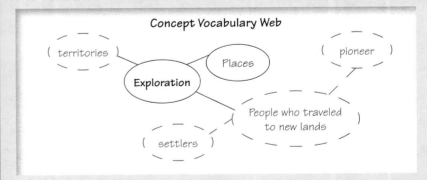

Concept Vocabulary Web

territories — Exploration — Places — pioneer

People who traveled to new lands

settlers

▶ **Social Studies Content**
Lewis and Clark, Midwestern Climate, Barter System, Western Expansion

▶ **Writing**
Journal Entry

▶ **Internet Inquiry**
Lewis and Clark's Discoveries

Preview Your Week

What did Lewis and Clark learn on their journey?

Lewis and Clark and Me

A DOG'S TALE

by Laurie Myers   illustrations by Michael Dooling

Genre *Historical fantasy* is based on real events in history, but it is a story that could never really happen—in this case, because a dog can't write. As you read, look for the facts on which this story is based.

44

Who will join Lewis and Clark on their journey of exploration?

Note to readers: The extracts from Meriwether Lewis's journal published in this excerpt retain their original spelling.

Student Edition pages 44–59

Audio CD

Genre	Historical Fantasy
Vocabulary Strategy	Word Structure
Comprehension Skill	Author's Purpose
Comprehension Strategy	Answer Questions

SOCIAL STUDIES

Paired Selection

Reading Across Texts
Compare Seaman, York, and Sacagawea

Genre
Narrative Nonfiction

Text Features
Introductory Paragraph
Large, Bold-faced Subheads
Realistic Pictures

Social Studies in Reading

Narrative Nonfiction

Genre
• Narrative nonfiction can give facts about a person and tell what he or she did in life.
• Biography and history are kinds of narrative nonfiction.

Text Features
• A short introductory paragraph gives the reader a reason to read on.
• Large, bold-faced subheads identify the historic person to be discussed.
• Realistic pictures give the reader an idea of what the historic person might have looked like.

Link to Social Studies
Do research to find out what places in the West have been named for Sacagawea (sometimes spelled Sacajawea). Write about one of them.

They Traveled with Lewis and Clark

by Elizabeth Massie

Meriwether Lewis and William Clark are known for exploring the vast land between St. Louis and the Pacific Ocean. But they could not have done it without the help of others.

York
African American Explorer

York was a member of Lewis and Clark's Corps of Discovery. He was about the same age as William Clark. The two had grown up together. Both were brave and strong. But there was one difference. Clark was a free man. York was a slave. York belonged to Clark.

Slaves had few rights. They could not vote or carry guns. They were supposed to eat and sleep apart from white people. Yet on the journey west, York proved in many ways that he was equal.

Some of the men could not swim. York could. Clark's journal describes how York swam into a river to gather greens for dinner. York hunted deer, buffalo, and elk. He served as a scout. He cut wood and cooked meals. He even cared for the other men when they were sick.

One day there was a heavy storm. The rain nearly washed Clark and others into the Missouri River. York thought they had been swept away. He ignored his own safety

Author's Purpose Based on your preview, how should this text be read?

62

Student Edition pages 62–65

Audio CD

Read It
ONLINE
PearsonSuccessNet.com

- Student Edition
- Leveled Readers

Time for
SOCIAL STUDIES

Leveled Readers

⊙ **Skill** Author's Purpose

⊙ **Strategy** Answer Questions

Lesson Vocabulary

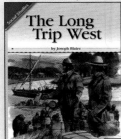

The Long Trip West
by Joseph Blaire

illustrated by Tom McNeely

Below-Level

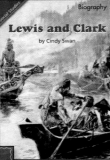

Biography
Lewis and Clark
by Cindy Swan

On-Level

Two Great Rivers
by Stephanie Sigue

Advanced

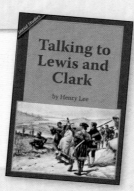

Talking to Lewis and Clark
by Henry Lee

ELL Reader

· Concept Vocabulary
· Text Support
· Language Enrichment

Integrate Social Studies Standards

- U.S. History
- Economics
- U.S. Geography

✓ **Read**

Lewis and Clark and Me, pp. 44–59

"They Traveled with Lewis and Clark," pp. 62–65

Leveled Readers

Below-Level   **On-Level**   **Advanced**

- Support Concepts
- Develop Concepts
- Extend Concepts
- Social Studies Extension Activity

ELL Reader

Talking to Lewis and Clark
by Henry Lee

✓ **Build Concept Vocabulary**

Exploration, pp. 40l–40m

✓ **Teach Social Studies Concepts**

Lewis and Clark, p. 47
Midwestern Climate, p. 51
Barter System, p. 57
Western Expansion, p. 63

✓ **Explore Social Studies Center**

Research Lewis and Clark, p. 40k

Weekly Plan

READING

45–90 minutes

TARGET SKILLS OF THE WEEK

- **Comprehension Skill**
Author's Purpose
- **Comprehension Strategy**
Answer Questions
- **Vocabulary Strategy**
Word Structure

DAY 1
PAGES 40l–42b, 65a, 65e–65k

Oral Language

QUESTION OF THE WEEK *What did Lewis and Clark learn on their journey?*

Read Aloud: "Johnny Appleseed," 40m
Build Concepts, 40l

Comprehension/Vocabulary

Comprehension Skill/Strategy Lesson, 40–41
- Author's Purpose **T**
- Answer Questions
Build Background, 42a
Introduce Lesson Vocabulary, 42b
docks, migrating, scan, scent, wharf, yearned **T**

Read Leveled Readers

Grouping Options 40f–40g

Fluency

Model Pauses, 40l–40m, 65a

DAY 2
PAGES 42–53, 65a, 65e–65k

Oral Language

QUESTION OF THE DAY *Why do you think the author chose to write this story from a dog's point of view?*

Comprehension/Vocabulary

Vocabulary Strategy Lesson, 42–43
- Word Structure **T**

Read *Lewis and Clark and Me,* 44–53

Grouping Options 40f–40g

- Author's Purpose **T**
- Answer Questions
- Word Structure **T**
- **REVIEW** Cause and Effect **T**
Develop Vocabulary

Fluency

Echo Reading, 65a

LANGUAGE ARTS

30–60 minutes

Trait of the Week

Sentences

Grammar, 65e
Introduce Imperative and Exclamatory Sentences **T**

Writing Workshop, 65g
Introduce Journal Entry
Model the Trait of the Week: Sentences

Spelling, 65i
Pretest for Long *a* and *i*

Internet Inquiry, 65k
Identify Questions

Grammar, 65e
Develop Imperative and Exclamatory Sentences **T**

Writing Workshop, 65g
Improve Writing with Transitions

Spelling, 65i
Teach the Generalization

Internet Inquiry, 65k
Navigate/Search

DAILY WRITING ACTIVITIES

Day 1 Write to Read, 40

Day 2 Words to Write, 43
Strategy Response Log, 44, 53

DAILY SOCIAL STUDIES CONNECTIONS

Day 1 Exploration Concept Web, 40l

Day 2 Time for Social Studies: Lewis and Clark, 47;
Climate of the Midwest, 51
Revisit the Exploration Concept Web, 53

DAILY SUCCESS PREDICTORS
for Adequate Yearly Progress

Monitor Progress and Corrective Feedback

Vocabulary — Check Vocabulary, 40l

RESOURCES FOR THE WEEK

- Practice Book, *pp. 11–20*
- Word Study and Spelling Practice Book, *pp. 5–8*
- Grammar and Writing Practice Book, *pp. 5–8*
- Selection Test, *pp. 5–8*
- Fresh Reads for Differentiated Test Practice, *pp. 7–12*
- The Grammar and Writing Book, *pp. 56–61*

Grouping Options for Differentiated Instruction

Turn the page for the small group lesson plan.

DAY 3 — PAGES 54–61, 65a, 65e–65k

Oral Language

QUESTION OF THE DAY *How would you describe the bond between Lewis and Seaman?*

Comprehension/Vocabulary

Read *Lewis and Clark and Me,* 54–60

Grouping Options 40f–40g

- 🎯 Author's Purpose **T**
- 🎯 Answer Questions
- 🎯 Word Structure **T**
- Develop Vocabulary

Reader Response

Selection Test

Fluency

Model Pauses, 65a

Grammar, 65f
Apply Imperative and Exclamatory Sentences in Writing **T**

Writing Workshop, 61, 65h
Write Now
Improve Writing with Prewrite and Draft

Spelling, 65j
Connect Spelling to Writing

Internet Inquiry, 65k
Analyze Sources

Day 3 Strategy Response Log, 58
Look Back and Write, 60

Day 3 Time for Social Studies: Barter System, 57
Revisit the Exploration Concept Web, 59

DAY 4 — PAGES 62–65a, 65e–65k

Oral Language

QUESTION OF THE DAY *In what ways can a person be an explorer, and what qualities make one an explorer?*

Comprehension/Vocabulary

Read *"They Traveled with Lewis and Clark,"* 62–65

Grouping Options 40f–40g

Narrative Nonfiction/ Text Features

Reading Across Texts

Content-Area Vocabulary

Fluency

Partner Reading, 65a

Grammar, 65f
Practice Imperative and Exclamatory Sentences for Standardized Tests **T**

Writing Workshop, 65h
Draft, Revise, and Publish

Spelling, 65j
Provide a Strategy

Internet Inquiry, 65k
Synthesize Information

Day 4 Writing Across Texts, 65

Day 4 Time for Social Studies: Western Expansion, 63

DAY 5 — PAGES 65a–65l

Oral Language

QUESTION OF THE WEEK *To wrap up the week, revisit the Day 1 question.*

Build Concept Vocabulary, 65c

Fluency

Read Leveled Readers

Grouping Options 40f–40g

Assess Reading Rate, 65a

Comprehension/Vocabulary

- 🎯 Reteach Author's Purpose, 65b **T**
- Imagery/Sensory Words, 65b
- 🎯 Review Word Structure, 65c **T**

Speaking and Viewing, 65d
Introduction
Analyze an Illustration

Grammar, 65f
Cumulative Review

Writing Workshop, 65h
Connect to Unit Writing

Spelling, 65j
Posttest for Long *a* and *i*

Internet Inquiry, 65k
Communicate Results

Research/Study Skills, 65l
Skim and Scan

Day 5 Imagery/Sensory Words, 65b

Day 5 Revisit the Exploration Concept Web, 65c

KEY 🎯 = Target Skill **T** = Tested Skill

Comprehension Check Retelling, *60*

Fluency Check Fluency WCPM, *65a*

Vocabulary Check Vocabulary, *65c*

SUCCESS PREDICTOR

Small Group Plan for Differentiated Instruction

Daily Plan AT A GLANCE

Reading
Whole Group
- Oral Language
- Comprehension/Vocabulary

Group Time

Differentiated Instruction

Meet with small groups to provide:
- Skill Support
- Reading Support
- Fluency Practice

Read

This week's lessons for daily group time can be found behind the Differentiated Instruction (DI) tab on pp. DI·12–DI·21.

Whole Group
- Fluency

Language Arts
- Grammar
- Writing
- Spelling
- Research/Inquiry
- Speaking/Listening/Viewing

Use *My Sidewalks on Reading Street* for Tier III intensive reading intervention.

DAY 1

On-Level	Strategic Intervention	Advanced
Teacher-Led *Page DI · 13*	**Teacher-Led** *Page DI · 12*	**Teacher-Led** *Page DI · 13*
• Develop Concept Vocabulary	• Reinforce Concepts	• **Read** Advanced Reader *Two Great Rivers*
• **Read** On-Level Reader *Lewis and Clark*	• **Read** Below-Level Reader *The Long Trip West*	• Independent Extension Activity

(i) Independent Activities

While you meet with small groups, have the rest of the class...

- Visit the Reading/Library Center
- Listen to the Background Building Audio
- Finish Write to Read, p. 40
- Complete Practice Book pp. 13–14
- Visit Cross-Curricular Centers

DAY 2

On-Level	Strategic Intervention	Advanced
Teacher-Led *Pages 46–53*	**Teacher-Led** *Page DI · 14*	**Teacher-Led** *Page DI · 15*
• **Read** *Lewis and Clark and Me*	• Practice Lesson Vocabulary	• Extend Vocabulary
	• Read Multisyllabic Words	• **Read** *Lewis and Clark and Me*
	• **Read** or Listen to *Lewis and Clark and Me*	

(i) Independent Activities

While you meet with small groups, have the rest of the class...

- Visit the Reading/Library Center
- Listen to the AudioText for *Lewis and Clark and Me*
- Finish Words to Write, p. 43
- Complete Practice Book pp. 15–16
- Write in their Strategy Response Logs, pp. 44, 53
- Visit Cross-Curricular Centers
- Work on inquiry projects

DAY 3

On-Level	Strategic Intervention	Advanced
Teacher-Led *Pages 54–59*	**Teacher-Led** *Page DI · 16*	**Teacher-Led** *Page DI · 17*
• **Read** *Lewis and Clark and Me*	• Practice Author's Purpose and Answer Questions	• Extend Author's Purpose and Answer Questions
	• **Read** or Listen to *Lewis and Clark and Me*	• **Read** *Lewis and Clark and Me*

(i) Independent Activities

While you meet with small groups, have the rest of the class...

- Visit the Reading/Library Center
- Listen to the AudioText for *Lewis and Clark and Me*
- Write in their Strategy Response Logs, p. 58
- Finish Look Back and Write, p. 60
- Complete Practice Book p. 17
- Visit Cross-Curricular Centers
- Work on inquiry projects

① Begin with whole class skill and strategy instruction.

② Meet with small groups to provide differentiated instruction.

③ Gather the whole class back together for fluency and language arts.

DAY 4

On-Level
Teacher-Led
Pages 62–65
- **Read** "They Traveled with Lewis and Clark"

Strategic Intervention
Teacher-Led
Page DI · 18
- Practice Retelling
- **Read** or Listen to "They Traveled with Lewis and Clark"

Advanced
Teacher-Led
Page DI · 19
- **Read** "They Traveled with Lewis and Clark"
- Genre Study

ⓘ Independent Activities

While you meet with small groups, have the rest of the class...

- Visit the Reading/Library Center
- Listen to the AudioText for "They Traveled with Lewis and Clark"
- Visit the Writing/Vocabulary Center
- Finish Writing Across Texts, p. 65
- Visit Cross-Curricular Centers
- Work on inquiry projects

DAY 5

On-Level
Teacher-Led
Page DI · 21
- **Reread** Leveled Reader *Lewis and Clark*
- Retell *Lewis and Clark*

Strategic Intervention
Teacher-Led
Page DI · 20
- **Reread** Leveled Reader *The Long Trip West*
- Retell *The Long Trip West*

Advanced
Teacher-Led
Page DI · 21
- **Reread** Leveled Reader *Two Great Rivers*
- Share Extension Activity

ⓘ Independent Activities

While you meet with small groups, have the rest of the class...

- Visit the Reading/Library Center
- Complete Practice Book pp. 18–20
- Visit Cross-Curricular Centers
- Work on inquiry projects

Grouping Place English language learners in the groups that correspond to their reading abilities in English.

Use the appropriate Leveled Reader or other text at students' instructional level.

TIP Send home the appropriate Multilingual Summary of the main selection on Day 1.

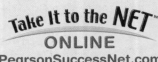

Take It to the NET™ ONLINE
PearsonSuccessNet.com

Peter Afflerbach
For ideas on implementing on-going assessment, see the article "STAIR" by Scott Foresman author Peter Afflerbach.

TEACHER TALK

Scaffolding is temporary support given as students learn a new skill. Scaffolded instruction includes direct explanations, crutches, and other support which is gradually removed as skills are mastered.

Looking Ahead ➤

Be sure to schedule time for students to work on the unit inquiry project "Natural Wonders." This week students conduct information searches for text and images to help them answer their questions.

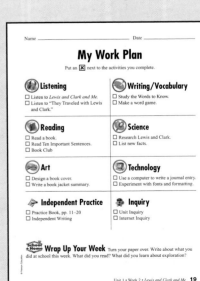

▲ **Group-Time Survival Guide**
p. 19, Weekly Contract

Lewis and Clark and Me **40g**

☑ Customize Your Plan *by Strand*

ORAL LANGUAGE

SOCIAL STUDIES

Concept Development

What did Lewis and Clark learn on their journey?

CONCEPT VOCABULARY

pioneer   settlers   territories   traveled

BUILD

☐ **Question of the Week** Introduce and discuss the question of the week. This week students will read a variety of texts and work on projects related to the concept *exploration*. Post the question for students to refer to throughout the week. **DAY 1** *40d*

☐ **Read Aloud** Read aloud "Johnny Appleseed." Then begin a web to build concepts and concept vocabulary related to this week's lesson and the unit theme, This Land Is Your Land. Introduce the concept words *pioneer, settlers, territories,* and *traveled* and have students place them on the web. Display the web for use throughout the week. **DAY 1** *40l-40m*

DEVELOP

☐ **Question of the Day** Use the prompts from the Weekly Plan to engage students in conversations related to this week's reading and the unit theme. **EVERY DAY** *40d-40e*

☐ **Concept Vocabulary Web** Revisit the Exploration Concept Web and encourage students to add concept words from their reading and life experiences. **DAY 2** *53,* **DAY 3** *59*

CONNECT

☐ **Looking Back/Moving Forward** Revisit the Exploration Concept Web and discuss how it relates to this week's lesson and the unit theme. Then make connections to next week's lesson. **DAY 5** *65c*

CHECK

☐ **Concept Vocabulary Web** Use the Exploration Concept Web to check students' understanding of the concept vocabulary words *pioneer, settlers, territories,* and *traveled.* **DAY 1** *40l,* **DAY 5** *65c*

VOCABULARY

⊙ **STRATEGY WORD STRUCTURE** When you are reading and see an unfamiliar word, you can look at the end of the word to help you figure out the meaning. The base word, the word without the ending, will also help you understand the meaning.

LESSON VOCABULARY

docks   wharf
migrating   yearned
scan
scent

TEACH

☐ **Words to Know** Give students the opportunity to tell what they already know about this week's lesson vocabulary words. Then discuss word meaning. **DAY 1** *42b*

☐ **Vocabulary Strategy Lesson** Use the vocabulary strategy lesson in the Student Edition to introduce and model this week's strategy, *word structure*. **DAY 2** *42-43*

Vocabulary Strategy Lesson

PRACTICE/APPLY

☐ **Leveled Text** Read the lesson vocabulary in the context of leveled text. **DAY 1** *LR10-LR18*

☐ **Words in Context** Read the lesson vocabulary and apply *word structure* in the context of *Lewis and Clark and Me.* **DAY 2** *44-53,* **DAY 3** *54-60*

Leveled Readers

☐ **Writing/Vocabulary Center** Make a word game. **ANY DAY** *40k*

☐ **Homework** Practice Book pp. 14–15. **DAY 1** *42b,* **DAY 2** *43*

Main Selection—Fiction

☐ **Word Play** Using a thesaurus, have students look up synonyms for words and then rate each word as to whether it has a positive or negative connotation. **ANY DAY** *65c*

ASSESS

☐ **Selection Test** Use the Selection Test to determine students' understanding of the lesson vocabulary words. **DAY 3**

RETEACH/REVIEW

☐ **Reteach Lesson** If necessary, use this lesson to reteach and review *word structure.* **DAY 5** *65c*

COMPREHENSION

◉ SKILL AUTHOR'S PURPOSE   The author's purpose is the reason or reasons the author has for writing. Authors may write to persuade, to inform, to entertain, or to express ideas and feelings. An author may have one or more reasons for writing.

◉ STRATEGY ANSWER QUESTIONS   Answering questions can help understand the author's purpose. Answers to questions may be in the text, but often students will need to combine details from the text with their prior knowledge.

TEACH

❏ **Skill/Strategy Lesson** Use the skill/strategy lesson in the Student Edition to introduce and model *author's purpose* and *answer questions*. **DAY 1** 40-41

❏ **Extend Skills** Teach imagery/sensory words. **ANY DAY** 65b

Skill/Strategy Lesson

PRACTICE/APPLY

❏ **Leveled Text** Apply *author's purpose* and *answer questions* to read leveled text. **DAY 1** LR10–LR18

Leveled Readers

❏ **Skills and Strategies in Context** Read *Lewis and Clark and Me*, using the Guiding Comprehension questions to apply *author's purpose* and *answer questions*. **DAY 2** 44-53, **DAY 3** 54-60

Main Selection—Fiction

❏ **Skills and Strategies in Context** Read "They Traveled with Lewis and Clark," guiding students as they apply *author's purpose* and *answer questions*. Then have students discuss and write across texts. **DAY 4** 62-65

❏ **Homework** Practice Book pp. 13, 17, 18 **DAY 1** 41, **DAY 3** 59, **DAY 5** 65b

Paired Selection—Nonfiction

❏ **Fresh Reads for Differentiated Test Practice** Have students practice *author's purpose* with a new passage. **DAY 3**

ASSESS

❏ **Selection Test** Determine students' understanding of the selection and their use of *author's purpose*. **DAY 3**

❏ **Retell** Have students retell *Lewis and Clark and Me*. **DAY 3** 60-61

RETEACH/REVIEW

❏ **Reteach Lesson** If necessary, reteach and review *author's purpose*. **DAY 5** 65b

FLUENCY

SKILL PAUSES   Pauses in reading are natural stopping points in a text. A fluent reader will pause at the end of phrases, after commas, and at the end of sentences to make it easier for listeners to understand the text.

TEACH

❏ **Read Aloud** Model fluent reading by rereading "Johnny Appleseed." Focus on this week's fluency skill, pauses. **DAY 1** 40l-40m, 65a

PRACTICE/APPLY

❏ **Echo Reading** Read aloud selected paragraphs from *Lewis and Clark and Me*, accentuating the pauses. Then practice as a class by doing three echo readings of the paragraphs. **DAY 2** 65a, **DAY 3** 65a

❏ **Partner Reading** Have partners practice reading aloud, inserting pauses, and offering each other feedback. As students reread, monitor their progress toward their individual fluency goals. **DAY 4** 65a

❏ **Listening Center** Have students follow along with the AudioText for this week's selections. **ANY DAY** 40j

❏ **Reading/Library Center** Have students reread a selection of their choice. **ANY DAY** 40j

❏ **Fluency Coach** Have students use Fluency Coach to listen to fluent readings or practice reading on their own. **ANY DAY**

ASSESS

❏ **Check Fluency** WCPM Do a one-minute timed reading, paying special attention to this week's skill—pauses. Provide feedback for each student. **DAY 5** 65a

Customize Your Plan *by Strand*

GRAMMAR

IMPERATIVE AND EXCLAMATORY SENTENCES An imperative sentence gives a command or makes a request. It usually begins with a verb and ends with a period. An exclamatory sentence shows strong feeling or surprise and ends with an exclamation mark.

TEACH

☐ **Grammar Transparency 2** Use Grammar Transparency 2 to teach imperative and exclamatory sentences. DAY 1 65e

Grammar Transparency 2

PRACTICE/APPLY

☐ **Develop the Concept** Review the concept of imperative and exclamatory sentences and provide guided practice. DAY 2 65e

☐ **Apply to Writing** Have students review something they have written and improve it by adding imperative and exclamatory sentences. DAY 3 65f

☐ **Test Preparation** Examine common errors in imperative and exclamatory sentences to prepare for standardized tests. DAY 4 65f

☐ **Homework** Grammar and Writing Practice Book pp. 5–7. DAY 2 65e, DAY 3 65f, DAY 4 65f

ASSESS

☐ **Cumulative Review** Use Grammar and Writing Practice Book p. 8. DAY 5 65f

RETEACH/REVIEW

☐ **Daily Fix-It** Have students find and correct errors in grammar, spelling, and punctuation. **EVERY DAY** 65e–65f

☐ **The Grammar and Writing Book** Use pp. 56–59 of The Grammar and Writing Book to extend instruction for imperative and exclamatory sentences. **ANY DAY**

The Grammar and Writing Book

WRITING

Trait of the Week

SENTENCES Good writers express their thoughts in lively, varied sentences. Sentences that have a natural flow as well as vary in structure and length create a rhythm and style.

TEACH

☐ **Writing Transparency 2A** Use the model to introduce and discuss the Trait of the Week. DAY 1 65g

☐ **Writing Transparency 2B** Use the transparency to show students how transitions can improve their writing. DAY 2 65g

Writing Transparency 2A   **Writing Transparency 2B**

PRACTICE/APPLY

☐ **Write Now** Examine the model on Student Edition p. 61. Then have students write their own journal entry. DAY 3 61, 65h, DAY 4 65h

> **Prompt** In *Lewis and Clark and Me*, Seaman tells about two memorable days of the expedition. Think about a memorable day in your own life. Now write a journal entry describing what happened on that special day.

Write Now p. 61

☐ **Writing/Vocabulary Center** Make a word game. **ANY DAY** 40k

ASSESS

☐ **Writing Trait Rubric** Use the rubric to evaluate students' writing. DAY 4 65h

RETEACH/REVIEW

☐ **The Grammar and Writing Book** Use pp. 56–61 of The Grammar and Writing Book to extend instruction for imperative and exclamatory sentences, transitions, and journal entry. **ANY DAY**

The Grammar and Writing Book

❶ Use assessment data to determine your instructional focus.

❷ Preview this week's instruction by strand.

❸ Choose instructional activities that meet the needs of your classroom.

SPELLING

GENERALIZATION LONG A AND I Long *a* is sometimes spelled *ai*, *eigh*, or *ay*: br**ai**d, w**eigh**, spr**ay**. Long *i* is sometimes spelled *igh*: s**igh**. The letter combinations *ai*, *eigh*, and *ay* usually stand for the long *a* sound. The letter combination *igh* usually stands for the long *i* sound.

TEACH

❑ **Pretest** Give the pretest for words with long *a* and *i*. Guide students in self-correcting their pretests and correcting any misspellings. DAY 1 65i

❑ **Think and Practice** Connect spelling to the phonics generalization for long *a* and *i*. DAY 2 65i

PRACTICE/APPLY

❑ **Connect to Writing** Have students use spelling words to write a journal entry. Then review frequently misspelled words: *vacation, always, might*. DAY 3 65j

❑ **Homework** Word Study and Spelling Practice Book pp. 5–8. EVERY DAY

RETEACH/REVIEW

❑ **Review** Review spelling words to prepare for the posttest. Then provide students with a spelling strategy—problem parts. DAY 4 65j

ASSESS

❑ **Posttest** Use dictation sentences to give the posttest for words with long *a* and *i*. DAY 5 65j

Spelling Words

1. sigh	8. braid	15. trait
2. right*	9. bait	16. highway
3. weigh*	10. grain*	17. frighten
4. eight	11. slight	18. dismay
5. detail	12. thigh	19. freight
6. height	13. tight*	20. sleigh
7. spray	14. raisin	

Challenge Words

21. eighteen	23. campaign	25. twilight
22. mayonnaise	24. daylight	

*Word from the selection

RESEARCH AND INQUIRY

❑ **Internet Inquiry** Have students conduct an Internet inquiry on Lewis and Clark's discoveries. EVERY DAY 65k

❑ **Skim and Scan** Review the strategies skimming and scanning and discuss how students can use these strategies to help in their search for text and images. DAY 5 65l

❑ **Unit Inquiry** Allow time for students to conduct information searches for text and images to help them answer their questions about the geographical attraction of their choice. ANY DAY 17

SPEAKING AND VIEWING

❑ **Introduction** Have students create an introduction for the dog Seaman to the imaginary American Dogs Hall of Fame show. DAY 5 65d

❑ **Analyze an Illustration** Have students analyze an art print from the old American West or a print depicting Lewis and Clark's journey and follow-up with a class discussion. DAY 5 65d

Resources for Differentiated Instruction

LEVELED READERS

▶ **Comprehension**

🎯 **Skill** Author's Purpose

🎯 **Strategy** Answer Questions

▶ **Lesson Vocabulary**

🎯 Word Structure

docks · migrating · scan · scent · wharf · yearned

▶ **Social Studies Standards**

• U.S. History
• Economics
• U.S. Geography

Leveled Reader Database

ONLINE

PearsonSuccessNet.com

Use the Online Database of over 600 books to

• Download and print additional copies of this week's leveled readers.

• Listen to the readers being read online.

• Search for more titles focused on this week's skills, topic, and content.

On-Level

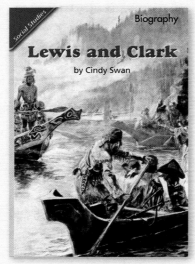

Social Studies · Biography
Lewis and Clark
by Cindy Swan

On-Level Reader

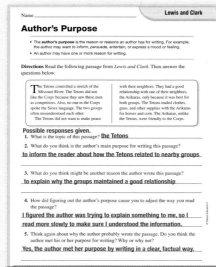

Name _____ Lewis and Clark

Author's Purpose

• The **author's purpose** is the reason or reasons an author has for writing. For example, the author may want to *inform, persuade, entertain,* or express a mood or feeling.
• An author may have one or more reason for writing.

Directions Read the following passage from *Lewis and Clark*. Then answer the questions below.

The Tetons controlled a stretch of the Missouri River. The Tetons did not like the Corps because they saw these men as competitors. Also, no one in the Corps spoke the Sioux language. The two groups often misunderstood each other. The Tetons did not want to make peace with their neighbors. They had a good relationship with one of their neighbors, the Arikaras, only because it was best for both groups. The Tetons traded clothes, guns, and other supplies with the Arikaras for horses and corn. The Arikaras, unlike the Tetons, were friendly to the Corps.

Possible responses given.
1. What is the topic of this passage? **the Tetons**

2. What do you think is the author's main purpose for writing this passage?
to inform the reader about how the Tetons related to nearby groups

3. What do you think might be another reason the author wrote this passage?
to explain why the groups maintained a good relationship

4. How did figuring out the author's purpose cause you to adjust the way you read the passage?
I figured the author was trying to explain something to me, so I read more slowly to make sure I understood the information.

5. Think again about why the author probably wrote the passage. Do you think the author met his or her purpose for writing? Why or why not?
Yes, the author met her purpose by writing in a clear, factual way.

🎯 **On-Level Practice** TE p. LR14

Name _____ Lewis and Clark

Vocabulary
Directions Read each sentence. Write the word from the box that best completes each sentence. Use each word only once.

Check the Words You Know
__docks __migrating __scan __scent
__translated __wharf __yearned

1. The captain of the ship told the sailor to **scan** the horizon for land.

2. The skies overhead are filled with the sounds of honking birds when the geese are **migrating** south for the winter.

3. The **wharf** was crowded with boxes of food.

4. Fishermen were lined up along the **docks** trying to catch the evening's meal from the waters below.

5. The young girl **yearned** to travel to faraway places.
Possible responses given.
Directions For each word below, write a sentence that uses the word correctly.

6. migrating **The migrating birds flew in V-formation.**

7. scan **If you scan the sky at night, you might see Venus.**

8. yearned **The student yearned to travel to faraway places.**

9. translated **My friend translated the Spanish signs for me.**

Responses will vary.
Directions Imagine that you have taken a trip by boat. On a separate sheet of paper, write a brief story in which you describe where you have been and what it feels like to be home. Use as many vocabulary words as possible in your story.

On-Level Practice TE p. LR15

Strategic Intervention

Social Studies
The Long Trip West
by Joseph Blaire

illustrated by Tom McNeely

Below-Level Reader

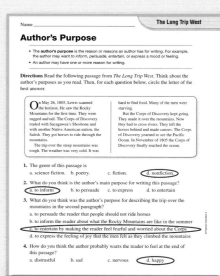

Name _____ The Long Trip West

Author's Purpose

• The **author's purpose** is the reason or reasons an author has for writing. For example, the author may want to *inform, persuade, entertain,* or express a mood or feeling.
• An author may have one or more reason for writing.

Directions Read the following passage from *The Long Trip West*. Think about the author's purposes as you read. Then, for each question below, circle the letter of the best answer.

On May 26, 1805, Lewis scanned the horizon. He saw the Rocky Mountains for the first time. They were rugged and tall. The Corps of Discovery traded with Sacagawea's Shoshone and with another Native American nation, the Salish. They got horses to ride through the mountains.
The trip over the steep mountains was tough. The weather was very cold. It was hard to find food. Many of the men were starving.
But the Corps of Discovery kept going. They made it over the mountains. Now they had to cross rivers. They left the horses behind and made canoes. The Corps of Discovery yearned to see the Pacific Ocean. In November of 1805 the Corps of Discovery finally reached the ocean.

1. The genre of this passage is
a. science fiction. b. poetry. c. fiction. **d. nonfiction.**

2. What do you think is the author's main purpose for writing this passage?
a. to inform b. to persuade c. to express d. to entertain

3. What do you think was the author's purpose for describing the trip over the mountains in the second paragraph?
a. to persuade the reader that people should not ride horses
b. to inform the reader about what the Rocky Mountains are like in the summer
c. to entertain by making the reader feel fearful and worried about the Corps
d. to express the feeling of joy that the men felt as they climbed the mountains

4. How do you think the author probably wants the reader to feel at the end of this passage?
a. distrustful b. sad c. nervous **d. happy**

🎯 **Below-Level Practice** TE p. LR11

Name _____ The Long Trip West

Vocabulary
Directions Choose the word from the box that best matches each definition. Write the word on the line. Use each word only once.

Check the Words You Know
__docks __migrating __scanned __scent
__translated __wharf __yearned

1. **docks** wharfs

2. **migrating** moving from one region to another

3. **scan** to glance at; look over hastily

4. **yearned** felt a longing or desire; desired earnestly

5. **wharf** a platform built on the shore or out from the shore beside which ships can load and unload

6. **scent** a smell

Directions Sort the words according to the description in each box.

Nouns
7. **docks**
8. **scent**
9. **wharf**

Words with Endings
10. **docks**
11. **migrating**
12. **scanned**
13. **translated**
14. **yearned**

Below-Level Practice TE p. LR12

Advanced

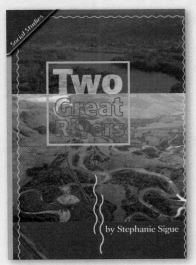

Advanced Reader

Name _____ Two Great Rivers

Author's Purpose

- The **author's purpose** is the reason or reasons an author has for writing. For example, the author may want to inform, persuade, entertain, or express a mood or feeling.
- An author may have one or more reason for writing.

Directions Read the following passage from *Two Great Rivers*. Then answer the questions below.

Floods and Flood Control

Flooding along the Mississippi can be a problem. When melting snow or heavy rains add lots of water to the river, the river overflows its banks. If the surrounding land is unable to absorb the water, flooding occurs. Since many acres of wetlands along the river have been drained and turned into farmland, more water has been forced into the river. Paved roads, parking lots, and even the roofs on buildings prevent rainwater from soaking into the ground. This increases run-off into the river and the chance of flooding. Severe flooding often results in damage to nearby homes and communities.

Several methods are used to control floods. One way is to plant trees, grass, and other plants to absorb the water. Another way to control flooding is to build levees. Levees raise the banks of the river so that they can hold more water. Floodways are areas of land that provide outlets for draining water when the river reaches flood level. They help to decrease flooding elsewhere.

Possible responses given.

1–2. Give two reasons for the author's purpose in writing this passage.
to inform the reader about Mississippi floods; to persuade that
flooding is a serious problem along the Mississippi

3. Support why you think this.
The author says flooding causes damage to homes and
communities.

4. Why does the author explain the human causes of flooding?
The author wants to convince the reader that humans are a big
part of the problem of flooding.

Advanced Practice TE p. LR17

Name _____ Two Great Rivers

Vocabulary

Directions Read each sentence. Write the word from the box that has the same meaning as the underlined word or phrase.

Check the Words You Know
__barges __conservationists __diminishing __expedition __reservoirs __route __silt __tributaries

1. We went on <u>large, flat-bottomed boats</u> to see how they operate. **barges**

2. A tree fell down in the storm and blocked the <u>road</u> to the store. **route**

3. Waterways get cloudy from <u>deposited dirt or sediment</u>. **silt**

4. My hopes of getting a bicycle are <u>becoming smaller</u>. **diminishing**

5. The scientists planned a <u>trip with a specific purpose</u> to study. **expedition**

Directions For each word, write a sentence that uses that word.

6. conservationists **Possible responses given.**
Conservationists believe that more needs to be done to protect
wildlife in Alaska.

7. reservoirs
There are many good reasons to build reservoirs.

8. tributaries
The fish that live in the river swim into tributaries to breed.

Advanced Practice TE p. LR18

ELL

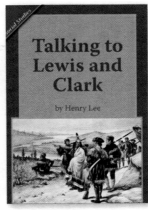

ELL Reader   **ELL Poster 2**

Teacher's Edition Notes

ELL notes throughout this lesson support instruction and reference additional resources at point of use.

Teaching Guide pp. 8–14, 214–215
- Multilingual summaries of the main selection
- Comprehension lesson
- Vocabulary strategies and word cards
- ELL Reader 4.1.2 lesson

ELL and Transition Handbook

Ten Important Sentences
- Key ideas from every selection in the Student Edition
- Activities to build sentence power

More Reading

Readers' Theater Anthology
- Fluency practice
- Five scripts to build fluency
- Poetry for oral interpretation

Leveled Trade Books

- Extended reading tied to the unit concept
- Lessons in the Trade Book Library Teaching Guide

Homework
- Family Times Newsletter
- ELL Multilingual Selection Summaries

Take-Home Books
- Leveled Readers

Cross-Curricular Centers

Listen to the Selections

MATERIALS
CD player, headphones, AudioText CD, student book

`SINGLES`

LISTEN TO LITERATURE Listen to *Lewis and Clark and Me* and "They Traveled with Lewis and Clark" as you follow or read along in your book. As you listen, think about reasons why the authors wrote these selections.

If there is anything you don't understand, you can listen again to any section.

Read It AGAIN!

MATERIALS
Collection of books for self-selected reading, reading logs, student book

`SINGLES`
`PAIRS`
`GROUPS`

Select a book you have already read. Record the title of the book in your reading log. You may want to read with a partner.

Choose from the following:

- **Leveled Readers**
- **ELL Readers**
- **Books or Stories Written by Classmates**
- **Books from the Library**
- *Lewis and Clark and Me*

TEN IMPORTANT SENTENCES Read the Ten Important Sentences for *Lewis and Clark and Me*. Then locate the sentences in the student book.

BOOK CLUB Write a letter to Laurie Myers, the author of *Lewis and Clark and Me*. Include any questions you have about the story. You might ask her how she decided to write from a dog's point of view or how much of the story is true.

Design a Book Cover

MATERIALS
Writing and art materials, student book

`SINGLES`

Create a book cover design for *Lewis and Clark and Me*.

1. Look at the art on pp. 44–59 of your book. For your book cover, use ideas from the story's art or ideas you thought of while reading.

2. Fold a large piece of paper in half. On the right half, draw your design for the front cover. Be sure to include the full title of the book and the names of the author and illustrator.

3. On the left half of the paper, draw your design for the back cover. You might show characters or events that you liked from the story.

EARLY FINISHERS On your back cover, write a short summary of what the story is about. Use vivid language that will make someone want to read the story.

Scott Foresman Reading Street Centers Survival Kit

Use the *Lewis and Clark* materials from the Reading Street Centers Survival Kit to organize this week's centers.

 **Writing/ Vocabulary**

Make a Word Game

MATERIALS **PAIRS**
Writing and art materials, slips of paper

Make a word game using the Words to Know on p. 42.

1. For each word, write a word clue or draw a picture clue on a slip of paper that will help someone guess that word. Write the actual word on the other side of the paper.
2. Exchange your clues with a partner. Use the clues to guess the words.

EARLY FINISHERS Choose one of the Words to Know and think of an action clue for it. Act out your clue for others to guess. *Drama*

 Social Studies

Research Lewis and Clark

MATERIALS **SINGLES**
Books on Lewis and Clark, writing materials **PAIRS**

Learn more about Lewis and Clark's expedition.

1. Using classroom resources, research to learn more about Lewis and Clark and their expedition.
2. Make a list of at least five new facts about their explorations.

EARLY FINISHERS Choose one of the facts from your list and find out more about it. Write a paragraph telling what you learned about that fact.

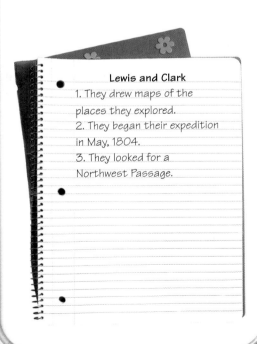

Lewis and Clark
1. They drew maps of the places they explored.
2. They began their expedition in May, 1804.
3. They looked for a Northwest Passage.

 Technology

Use a Computer

MATERIALS **SINGLES**
Computer, word processing program, student book **PAIRS**

Write a journal entry like the one by Captain Lewis on p. 53, written from Seaman's point of view.

1. Open a new document in your word processing program.
2. Write two to three sentences Seaman would write about Captain Lewis.
3. Add meaning by giving certain words a different font, type size, or both.
4. Follow classroom rules for saving or printing your journal entry.

EARLY FINISHERS Add pictures on your page using clip art from your word processing program. Select pictures that best fit your statements. Share your work with a partner.

Lewis is my **best** friend. I would do **anything** for him.

 **ALL CENTERS**

OBJECTIVES

- Build vocabulary by finding words related to the lesson concept.
- Listen for the author's purpose.

Concept Vocabulary

pioneer person who settles in a part of a country, preparing it for others

settlers people who takes up residence in a new country or place

territories land not admitted to a state but having its own lawmaking group

traveled journeyed

Monitor Progress

Check Vocabulary

If...	then... review the
students are unable to place words on the web,	lesson concept. Place the words on the web and provide additional words for practice, such as *Native Americans* and *Midwest.*

SUCCESS PREDICTOR

DAY 1 Grouping Options

Reading

Whole Group
Introduce and discuss the Question of the Week. Then use pp. 40l–42b.

Group Time
Differentiated Instruction
Read this week's Leveled Readers. See pp. 40f–40g for the small group lesson plan.

Whole Group
Use p. 65a.

Language Arts
Use pp. 65e–65k.

Build Concepts

FLUENCY

MODEL PAUSES Read "Johnny Appleseed" aloud, providing a model of a fluent, proficient oral reading for students. As you read, emphasize pauses to set off prepositional phrases and to indicate the ends of sentences or changes in topic.

LISTENING COMPREHENSION

After reading "Johnny Appleseed," use the following questions to assess listening comprehension.

1. **What do you think is the author's main purpose for writing this selection? Explain your reasoning.** *(Possible response: to inform; the author presents mostly statement of facts about a famous person in history, Johnny Appleseed.)* **Author's Purpose**

2. **Why do you think the author includes a description of how Johnny Appleseed looked?** *(Possible response: to help readers picture Johnny Appleseed and to support the opinion that Johnny wasn't interested in looks)* **Author's Purpose**

BUILD CONCEPT VOCABULARY

Start a web to build concepts and vocabulary related to this week's lesson and the unit theme.

- Draw the Exploration Concept Web.
- Read the sentence with the word *traveled* again. Ask students to pronounce *traveled* and discuss its meaning.
- Create an oval entitled *People who traveled to new lands.* Discuss how the word *traveled* is related to the concept *Exploration.* Read the sentences in which *pioneer, settlers,* and *territories* appear. Have students pronounce the words, place them on the Web, and provide reasons.
- Brainstorm additional words and categories for the Web. Keep the Web on display and add words throughout the week.

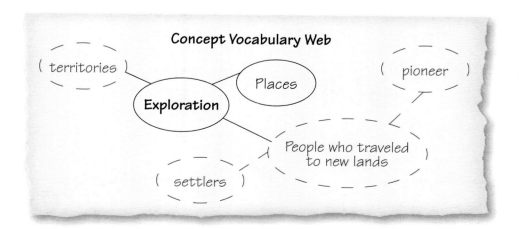

Concept Vocabulary Web

Johnny Appleseed

John Chapman was born in Massachusetts shortly before the beginning of the American Revolution. As the new nation began taking root, John Chapman became an American pioneer, and before long he would become a legend, earning the nickname Johnny Appleseed.

As a young man, Chapman set out alone traveling west from his birthplace. As he traveled, Appleseed claimed land, cleared it, and planted seeds. Johnny began by collecting apple seeds from cider presses. Until about the age of seventy, he traveled alone throughout the Midwest, planting apple trees on land he cleared. Johnny looked for good land that could support trees. Wherever he went, Johnny pulled weeds, took care of the soil, and planted apple seeds. He eventually owned over 1,000 acres of orchards throughout Ohio and Indiana. Johnny's dream was to enrich the land with blossoming apple trees for everyone to enjoy.

Johnny Appleseed worked hard caring for his orchards. He did not simply plant the seeds and abandon the orchards. He returned to care for the young trees as they grew. It is said that he traveled hundreds of miles simply to take care of one of his orchards. He was truly dedicated to his apple trees.

Johnny was a good-natured man, so he made friends with people wherever he went. He became friends with Native Americans and settlers in the territories he visited. Because he spent his time outdoors, he naturally respected the animals. He may even have shared his apples with them.

Johnny may have become well known because of his character. People noticed this friendly, kind-hearted man who planted and cared for apple orchards. To people he met along the way, he sold his apple seeds and saplings for a few pennies each. Sometimes he even gave away his apple trees. Some stories say that he accepted almost anything for payment, even old clothes. According to the stories, settlers didn't need money to buy Appleseed's trees.

Of course, those who told stories about Johnny Appleseed remembered to mention his unusual appearance. They said he traveled barefoot in ragged pants. According to the stories, he carried a pot that he sometimes wore as a hat! He cut holes in a coffee sack and wore it as a shirt. Johnny was also said to have very long hair that had seldom been cut. Can you imagine how he must have looked? But Johnny wasn't interested in looks. He was interested in apples. He was a happy man who shared his love of apples with others.

It's been many years since John Chapman roamed the Midwest planting trees. We may never be able to separate the fact from the fiction of his life. But, he will always be remembered as a spirited American pioneer who planted apple trees. He will always be an American legend. He will always be Johnny Appleseed.

Activate Prior Knowledge

Before students listen to the Read Aloud, have them share what they know about Johnny Appleseed and pioneer life in the United States.

Set Purpose

Read aloud the title and have students predict what the selection will be about.

Have students listen for clues that will help them determine the author's purpose for writing "Johnny Appleseed."

Creative Response

Have small groups use information from the selection to help them write and perform a skit about Johnny Appleseed. For example, students might act out a scene where Johnny accepts old clothes as payment for his apple seeds. **Drama**

Access Content Before reading, share this summary: This is the story of Johnny Appleseed, an American legend. He traveled across the United States planting apple trees and sharing his love of apples with other people.

Homework Send home this week's Family Times newsletter.

SKILLS ⟷ STRATEGIES IN CONTEXT

Author's Purpose
Answer Questions

OBJECTIVES

⊙ Determine the author's purpose.

⊙ Use strategies to answer questions about the author's purpose.

Skills Trace

⊙ **Author's Purpose**

Introduce/Teach	TE: 4.1 40–41, 88–89; 4.5 516–517
Practice	TE: 47, 57, 95, 103, 523, 529 PB: 13, 17, 18, 33, 37, 38, 203, 207, 208
Reteach/Review	TE: 4.1 31, 65b, 111b, DI-53, DI-55; 4.3 369; 4.5 537b, DI-52; 4.6 695 PB: 6, 146, 276
Test	Selection Test: 5–8, 13–16, 81–84; Benchmark Test: Unit 1

INTRODUCE

Read students a passage from a newspaper article. Ask students to identify the author's main purpose for writing: to persuade, to inform, to entertain, or to express ideas and feelings. *(Responses will vary based on the article.)*

Have students read the information on p. 40. Explain the following:

- When you try to determine the author's purpose for writing, it helps to remember the four main purposes authors have for writing.

- You may have to use what you already know and what you've read to answer questions about the author's purpose.

Use Skill Transparency 2 to teach author's purpose and answer questions.

Comprehension

Skill
Author's Purpose

Strategy
Answer Questions

⊙ Author's Purpose

Skill

- The author's purpose is the reason or reasons the author has for writing.

- An author may write to persuade, to inform, to entertain, or to express ideas and feelings.

	Author's Purpose	Why do you think so?
Before you read: What do you think it will be?		
As you read: What do you think it is?		

⊙ Strategy: Answer Questions

Strategy

Good readers know where to look for the answers to questions. They know that sometimes the answer to a question is in one place. Other times it is in several places. They know that sometimes they must use what they've read plus what they know to answer a question. That is what you usually have to do to answer a question about the author's purpose.

Write to Read

1. Read "Jefferson's Bargain." Make a graphic organizer like the one above to keep track of the author's purpose.

2. After you read the article, answer these questions: Do you think the author met his or her purpose? Why or why not?

40

Strategic Intervention

⊙ **Author's Purpose** Explain in greater detail the four common reasons for writing: to persuade, to inform, to entertain, and to express. Show students examples of familiar texts that illustrate each purpose and point out clues that help readers figure out the purpose.

ELL

Access Content

Beginning/Intermediate For a Picture It! lesson on author's purpose, see the ELL Teaching Guide, pp. 8–9.

Advanced Before reading "Jefferson's Bargain," have volunteers explain what a *bargain* is.

Jefferson's BARGAIN

About 200 years ago, when the United States was still new, our third President, Thomas Jefferson, had a big idea. He wanted to discover what lay west of the Mississippi River. This land was known as Louisiana.

Today one of our southern states is called Louisiana. But at that time, "Louisiana" was all of the land between the Mississippi River in the east and the Rocky Mountains in the west. This was an area of more than 800,000 square miles!

France said it owned this land. However, it was at war with England. It didn't want to fight another war with the United States over Louisiana. So France agreed to sell the land. President Jefferson got it for— are you ready?—less than 3 cents an acre!

The land became known as the Louisiana Purchase. In time it would become all or part of 13 states. But when Jefferson sent Lewis and Clark to explore this area in May of 1804, the two men and their group would enter a far-reaching wilderness.

1 **Skill** Preview the article. Do you think the author's purpose is to persuade, to inform, to entertain, or to express?

2 **Strategy** To answer the skill question, look at the title and skim the text. Do you see numbers and dates? What purpose do they suggest?

3 **Skill** Is the author's purpose what you thought it would be when you previewed the article? Why or why not?

4 **Strategy** Why did the author ask "are you ready?" in this paragraph?

41

Available as **Skill Transparency** 2

TEACH

1 **SKILL** Preview the article to predict the author's purpose.

 MODEL I'll preview the article by looking at the title and illustrations. The title is "Jefferson's Bargain." The map and document look old. I think the article is about something President Thomas Jefferson did when he was in office. The author's purpose is probably to inform.

2 **STRATEGY** Look at the title and skim the text to answer questions about the author's purpose.

MODEL I see the numbers *200 years ago; 800,000 square miles; 3 cents an acre;* and *13 states;* and the date *May of 1804* in the text. These numbers and dates are facts the author included in the article to describe something that happened a long time ago in American history. This suggests that the author's purpose is to inform.

PRACTICE AND ASSESS

3 **SKILL** Responses will vary but should include reasons why their prediction about the author's purpose matches or does not match the author's purpose they determined after reading the selection.

4 **STRATEGY** The phrase lets the reader know something surprising will come next.

WRITE Have students complete steps 1 and 2 of the Write to Read activity. You might consider using this as a whole-class activity.

Monitor Progress

🔄 Author's Purpose

If... students are unable to complete **Write to Read** on p. 40,	**then...** use Practice Book p. 13 to provide additional practice.

Author's Purpose

- The **author's purpose** is the reason or reasons the author has for writing.
- An author may write to persuade, to inform, to entertain, or to express ideas and feelings.

Directions Read the passage below. Use the graphic organizer to keep track of the author's purpose before and during reading, then answer the last question.

The Importance of Sacagawea

Even though it is hard to prove the facts about Sacagawea's life, many people believe that she was very helpful to Lewis and Clark on their expedition. Sacagawea was an Indian from the Shoshone tribe. She guided the explorers during their journey. She taught them about the wild plants and found them food in the wild. She even helped smooth the meetings between Lewis and Clark and the tribal leaders they met. Without Sacagawea's help, Lewis and Clark's journey would have been more difficult and dangerous.

Possible answers given.

	Author's Purpose	Why do you think so?
Before you read: What do you think it will be?	1. to inform us about Sacagawea and why she was important	2. The title previews what the author wants to inform us about.
As you read: What do you think it is?	3. to inform us of how Sacagawea helped Lewis and Clark	4. The author provides information believed to be true about Sacagawea.

5. Do you think the author met his or her purpose? Why or why not?

Yes; The author told us what Sacagawea did for Lewis and Clark.

School + Home Home Activity Your child identified the author's purpose in a passage. Work with your child to identify the author's purpose in an editorial in the newspaper.

Tech Files ONLINE

Students can learn more about Lewis and Clark's expedition by searching the Internet. Have them use a student-friendly search engine and the keywords *Lewis and Clark expedition*. Be sure to follow classroom rules for Internet use.

ELL

Build Background Use ELL Poster 2 to build background and vocabulary for the lesson concept of land and people in the Midwest.

▲ **ELL Poster** 2

Build Background

ACTIVATE PRIOR KNOWLEDGE

BEGIN A KWL CHART about Lewis and Clark and westward exploration.

• Give students a few minutes to write down whatever they know about the explorers Lewis and Clark and their expedition across the Midwest and West. Prompt them with categories from their Exploration and Discovery Concept Web from p. 40l. List their responses in the first column of a KWL chart.

• Give students two minutes to write three questions about what they would like to find out about Lewis and Clark's expedition. Record their questions in the second column of the chart. Add a question of your own.

• Tell students that, as they read, they should look for answers to their questions and note any new information to add to the chart.

Topic Lewis and Clark Expedition

K	W	L
President Jefferson wanted Lewis and Clark to explore the area bought by the Louisiana Purchase. Lewis and Clark traveled on the Missouri River and the Columbia River. Sacagawea, a Shoshone woman, helped guide Lewis and Clark.	What did the explorers see on their trip? What did they eat on their trip? What problems did they have on their trip?	

▲ **Graphic Organizer** 4

BACKGROUND BUILDING AUDIO This week's audio explores Lewis and Clark and their expedition. After students listen, discuss what they found out and how this information increased their understanding of the expedition.

 **Background Building Audio**

Introduce Vocabulary

CATEGORY CLUES

Give oral clues that help students think about the categories in which lesson vocabulary words belong.

Display the lesson vocabulary words. Have students identify words they know. Have them check their glossary for the meanings of any unfamiliar words. Then read aloud each set of three words listed below. Ask students for ideas about how the words in each group are related. ***Activate Prior Knowledge***

- search, peek, scan *(All are ways of looking.)*
- traveling, migrating, wandering *(All are ways of moving from one place to another.)*
- yearned, wished, hoped *(All are ways someone wanted something.)*
- odor, perfume, scent *(All are synonyms for a type of smell.)*
- pier, dock, wharf *(All have to do with where boats are kept.)*

Point out the word *scent.* Ask students how *scent, sent,* and *cent* are alike and different. Explain that homophones are words that sound alike but are spelled differently and have different meanings. Readers and writers use context clues to decide on the meaning and spelling of a homophone. ***Homophones***

Ask students if they know other words that sound the same but are spelled differently. *(Possible response: allowed, aloud)*

By the end of the week students should know the lesson vocabluary words. Have them demonstrate their knowledge by using the words in sentences. Have them identify any homophones.

Use the Multisyllabic Word Routine on p. DI·1 to help students read multisyllabic words.

BEFORE READING

Lesson Vocabulary

WORDS TO KNOW

T docks platforms built on the shore or out from the shore; wharves; piers

T migrating going from one region to another with the change in seasons

T scan to glance at; look over hastily

T scent a smell

T wharf platform built on the shore or out from the shore beside which ships can load or unload

T yearned felt a longing or desire

MORE WORDS TO KNOW

consult to seek information or advice from

leisurely without hurry; taking plenty of time

mutual done, said, or felt by each toward the other

T = Tested Word

Vocabulary

Directions Choose the word from the box that best matches each definition. Write the word on the line.

docks	1. platforms built on the shore or out from it; piers
scan	2. to look over hastily
scent	3. a smell
migrating	4. moving from one place to settle in another
wharf	5. another word for dock

Check the Words You Know

__docks
__migrating
__scan
__scent
__wharf
__yearned

Directions Choose the word from the box that best completes each statement. Write the word on the line shown to the left.

yearned	6. Josh _____ for home while he was on a long journey.
scent	7. Tanya could smell the _____ of the ocean in the air.
docks	8. Like the wharf in our hometown, these _____ are filled with sailors.
migrating	9. The people _____ to the West had to bring enough supplies to last the whole trip.
scan	10. I had to _____ the pages of the manual to find the diagram.

Write a Journal Entry

On a separate sheet of paper write a journal entry you might make after discovering a new part of the world. Use as many vocabulary words as you can.

Journal entries should include words from the vocabulary list and details about the new landscape.

Home Activity Your child identified and used vocabulary words from *Lewis and Clark and Me.* With your child, imagine you are walking along a busy waterfront. Write a short story together about your imaginary walk. Use as many vocabulary words as you can.

▲ **Practice Book** p. 14

Vocabulary Strategy

OBJECTIVE
Use word structure to determine word meaning.

INTRODUCE

Discuss the strategy for word structure using the steps on p. 42.

TEACH

- Have students take note of words with *-ed* or *-ing* as they read "Westward Ho!"
- Model identifying the base word to determine the meaning of *migrating*.

Think Aloud

MODEL When I cover the *-ing* ending, I see *migrat*. If I put back the final *e*, I recognize the word *migrate*. I know that birds migrate south in winter. I wonder if *migrating* has to do with moving from place to place. Yes, it makes sense that herds and flocks of animals could be on the move, or migrating.

DAY 2 **Grouping Options**

Reading

Whole Group Discuss the Question of the Day. Then use pp. 42–45.

Group Time Differentiated Instruction
Read *Lewis and Clark and Me.*
See pp. 40f–40g for the small group lesson plan.

Whole Group Use p. 65a.

Language Arts
Use pp. 65e–65k.

Words to Know

yearned
wharf
docks
scan
migrating
scent

Remember

Try the strategy. Then, if you need more help, use your glossary or a dictionary.

Vocabulary Strategy
for Endings

Word Structure Sometimes when you are reading, you may come across a word you don't know. Look at the end of the word. Does it have *-ed* or *-ing*? The ending *-ed* is added to a verb to make it past tense, or tell about past actions. The ending *-ing* is added to a verb to make it tell about present or ongoing actions. You may be able to use the ending to help you figure out the meaning of the word.

1. Put your finger over the *-ed* or *-ing* ending.

2. Look at the base word. Do you know what the base word means?

3. Try your meaning in the sentence. Does it make sense?

As you read "Westward Ho!" look for words that have the *-ed* or *-ing* ending. Use the ending to help you figure out the meanings of the words.

42

Strategic Intervention

Word Structure Have students find *waiting* on p. 43, paragraph 2. Have them cover the ending, name the base word, and use the words in this frame: *When I am __ for a bus, I do not like to __ a long time.*

Access Content Use ELL Poster 2 to preteach vocabulary. Choose from the following to meet language proficiency levels.

Beginning Show students how you scan the reading for the word *yearned*. Have them scan for the other words.

Intermediate Create a Word Rating Chart, rating words as *Know, Have Seen,* or *Don't Know.* Verify the meanings of *Have Seen.*

Advanced Teach the lesson on pp. 42–43. Students can report on terms such as *wharf* and *dock* in their home languages.

Resources for home-language words may include parents, bilingual staff members, bilingual dictionaries, or online translation sources.

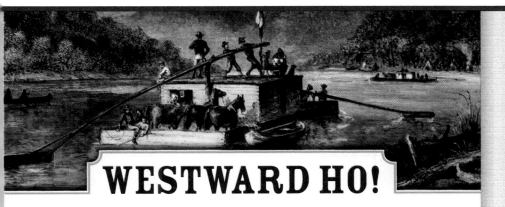

WESTWARD HO!

In the 1800s, America grew ever larger as land in the West was bought. As it grew, men and women of a certain kind yearned to travel west into the unknown. They had pioneer spirit.

There were no roads, of course. However, rivers made good highways for boats. In my mind I can see the pioneers with all their goods, waiting on the wharf in St. Louis. Sailors are busy loading and unloading ships. The pioneers load their belongings onto flatboats tied to the docks.

As they traveled, pioneers would scan the country for food and Indians. There were no grocery stores. And they never knew how the Indians would receive them. If the Indians were friendly, they might talk and trade. If a trapper were present, they were lucky. Trappers knew the country and the Indians well.

It must have been exciting to see this country for the first time. Pioneers saw endless herds and flocks of animals migrating. They breathed pure air full of the scent of tall grasses and wildflowers.

Words to Write

Imagine you are starting a trip to explore an unknown river. Describe your first day on the water. Use words from the Words to Know list.

43

Connect to Phonics

Word Study/Decoding Point out that the spelling of the base word often changes before adding an inflected ending. Model identifying the inflected ending and base word using *exciting* from p. 43, paragraph 4. Have students suggest other words they know with the inflected endings *–ed* and *–ing*. Have them identify the inflected ending and base in each word. Then have them identify the meaning of each word with and without the inflected ending.

PRACTICE AND ASSESS

- Have students determine the meanings of the remaining words and explain the strategy they used.

- Ask students for the base word and ending in the vocabulary word *yearned*. Discuss whether they know the meaning of *yearn*. Point out that if they do not know the meaning of a base word, they should think about the context—the surrounding words and sentences.

- If you offered category clues (p. 42b), have students create their own category clues using lesson vocabulary words.

- Have students complete Practice Book p. 15.

WRITE Writing should include several lesson vocabulary words as well as words related to river travel.

Monitor Progress	
Word Structure	
If... students need more practice with the lesson vocabulary,	**then...** use Tested Vocabulary Cards.

Vocabulary • Word Structure

- An **ending** is a letter or letters added to the end of a base word. Recognizing an ending will help you figure out the word's meaning.
- The ending *-ed* is added to a verb to make it past tense. The ending *-ing* is added to a verb to make it tell about present or ongoing actions.

Directions Read the following passage about a journey. Look for words ending in *-ed* and *-ing*. Then answer the questions below.

Enrique yearned for the unsettled land of the West. He was tired of living in such a busy town. So one day he packed up his things and headed for the docks. He started his journey migrating by boat. He planned to meet his uncle downriver. His uncle was also moving west and had offered him a ride on his wagon. When he arrived at the wharf, Enrique hopped off the boat and headed into town. The scent of freshly baked bread was in the air, which made him hungry. Enrique stopped to scan the row of shops for the bakery. Just then, Enrique heard his name being called from across the street. It was his uncle. "Are you ready for the journey of a lifetime?" asked his uncle. Enrique shouted, "More than you know!"

Possible answers given for 3, 5.

1. What does *yearned* mean? How does the ending change the base word?

   longed for; it makes it past tense.

2. What does *migrating* mean? What is the base word?

   traveling from one place to another; migrate

3. Rewrite the ninth sentence in the passage so that it uses the word *scanning*.

   Enrique began scanning the row of shops for the bakery.

4. If you added *-ed* to the noun *scent*, what kind of word does *scent* become?

   It changes from a noun into an adjective.

5. Write a sentence using an *-ed* and an *-ing* word.

   I looked at the door, waiting for it to open.

Home Activity Your child identified and used word endings to understand words in a passage. Have your child make a list of common verbs. Ask your child to change the meaning of the word by adding *-ed* and *-ing* to each word.

▲ **Practice Book** p. 15

Prereading Strategies

GENRE STUDY

Historical Fantasy

Lewis and Clark and Me: A Dog's Tale is historical fantasy. Use the individual words *historical* and *fantasy* to reinforce the idea that this genre combines both historic events that really happened and fantastic events that could not possibly happen, such as a dog as narrator.

PREVIEW AND PREDICT

Have students preview the story title and illustrations and discuss the historic events or people they think this story will cover. Encourage students to use lesson vocabulary words as they talk about what they expect to read.

Strategy Response Log

Predict Have students write their predictions in their strategy response logs. Students will confirm their predictions in the Strategy Response Log activity on p. 53.

Lewis and Clark and Me

— A DOG'S TALE —

by Laurie Myers   illustrations by Michael Dooling

Genre **Historical fantasy** is based on real events in history, but it is a story that could never really happen—in this case, because a dog can't write. As you read, look for the facts on which this story is based.

44

Build Background To help students understand the historical significance of Lewis and Clark's expedition, explain that the men were sent by President Thomas Jefferson to explore the Louisiana Purchase. This area included much of the land west of the Mississippi River to the Rocky Mountains.

Consider having students read the selection summary in English or in students' home languages. See the Multilingual Summaries in the ELL Teaching Guide, pp. 12–14.

Who will join Lewis and Clark on their journey of exploration?

Note to readers: The extracts from Meriwether Lewis's journal published in this excerpt retain their original spelling.

45

SET PURPOSE

Point out the subtitle *A Dog's Tale* and discuss what this subtitle tells about the story. Have students consider their discussion of historical fantasy and tell why they think this story is a fantasy.

Remind students to consider the author's purpose as they read.

STRATEGY RECALL

Students have now used these before-reading strategies:

- preview the selection to be aware of its genre, features, and possible content;
- activate prior knowledge about that content and what to expect of that genre;
- make predictions;
- set a purpose for reading.

Remind students that, as they read, they should monitor their own comprehension. If they realize something does not make sense, they can regain their comprehension by using fix-up strategies they have learned, such as:

- use phonics and word structure to decode new words;
- use context clues or a dictionary to figure out meanings of new words;
- adjust their reading rate—slow down for difficult text, speed up for easy or familiar text, or skim and scan just for specific information;
- reread parts of the text;
- read on (continue to read for clarification);
- use text features such as headings, subheadings, charts, illustrations, and so on as visual aids to comprehension;
- make a graphic organizer or a semantic organizer to aid comprehension;
- use reference sources, such as an encyclopedia, dictionary, thesaurus, or synonym finder;
- use another person, such as a teacher, a peer, a librarian, or an outside expert, as a resource.

After reading, students will use these strategies:

- summarize or retell the text;
- answer questions they or others pose;
- reflect to make new information become part of their prior knowledge.

Audio CD AudioText

Guiding Comprehension

The year is 1803. Lewis and Clark are planning their expedition to explore the territory west of the Mississippi River. Lewis is looking for a dog to accompany the expedition, and as the story opens, he meets a 150-pound Newfoundland dog named Seaman, who goes on to tell of their adventures.

① 🔍 **Author's Purpose • Inferential**
Question the Author **The author tells this story from Seaman's point of view. Why do you think she does this?**

Possible response: The author wants the story to be entertaining. Telling about the trip through the dog's eyes is an entertaining way to tell the story.

Monitor Progress	
🔍 **Author's Purpose**	
If... students have difficulty determining the author's purpose,	**then...** use the skill and strategy instruction on p. 47.

② **Character • Critical**
Text to Self **If you were Captain Lewis, would you choose Seaman to go with you on this trip?**

Possible response: Yes, I'd take Seaman because Lewis's trip is on a river. Seaman can swim and rescue drowning men. He can catch fish too.

"Seaman!"

I glance at the man beside me.

"Look alive. Here's buyers."

Something caught my attention beyond him, down the wharf—a group of men, but I saw only one. It was Lewis. He was a full head taller than the other men I had known on the docks. And he was dressed in a different way—white breeches and a short blue coat with buttons that shone in the sun. A tall pointed hat with a feather made him look even taller.

Lewis walked along the dock with a large stride. There was a purpose about him. My life on the wharves was good, but I was a young dog and yearned for more. At the time I didn't know exactly what. I sensed that this man was part of what I wanted. I sat straighter as he approached. The man who owned me stood straighter, too. Lewis slowed.

"Need a dog, sir?" my man asked.

"I'm lookin'," Lewis replied. He stooped down and looked me right in the eye. I wagged my tail and stepped forward. I wanted to sniff this strange man. He extended his hand for me. He didn't smell like any I had ever smelled, and it made me want to sniff him all over.

Lewis scratched the back of my neck, where I liked to be scratched.

46

"I'm headed out west, up the Missouri River," Lewis said. My man's face brightened.

"This dog be perfect, sir. These dogs can swim. Newfoundlands, they call them. Rescue a drowning man in rough water or in a storm. Look at these paws. You won't find another dog with paws like that. They's webbed." He spread my toes to show the webbing.

"So they are," Lewis replied. Lewis began feeling my chest and hindquarters. His hands were large and muscular.

"Water rolls off this coat," my man added. He pulled up a handful of my thick, dense double coat.

Lewis examined my coat and nodded. ❷

"I know the Mississippi, sir, but I don't know the Meesori," my man said.

"It's off the Mississippi, headin' northwest."

47

Lewis and Clark

Time for SOCIAL STUDIES

President Thomas Jefferson asked Meriwether Lewis and William Clark to explore the territory acquired by the Louisiana Purchase of 1803. Jefferson hoped they would discover a waterway leading to the Pacific Ocean. The two explorers led their Corps of Discovery westward along the Missouri and Columbia Rivers to the Pacific and back. Although a direct waterway to the Pacific doesn't exist, the explorers learned a great deal. For three years they kept journals about their expedition. They sketched and collected samples of the unusual plants and animals they saw. They also met and traded with Native American peoples such as the Mandan (in what is now North Dakota) and the Shoshone (in what is now Montana). The maps they drew of the areas they explored led a great number of explorers, traders, and settlers to make their way across the West.

🎯 **SKILLS** ↔ **STRATEGIES IN CONTEXT**

Author's Purpose

TEACH

- Remind students that authors often have more than one purpose, or reason, for writing, such as to entertain, to persuade, to inform, or to express ideas and feelings.

- Use p. 46 to model identifying the author's purpose for writing.

Think Aloud **MODEL** At the top of p. 46, I see facts about the explorers Lewis and Clark. At first, I thought the author's purpose was mostly to inform. As I read on, I find out that Seaman, a dog, is telling the story. Using a dog as a storyteller is a fun and unusual way to tell about this historic trip. I think one of the author's purposes is to entertain readers.

PRACTICE AND ASSESS

Have students work in pairs to reread p. 46. Have them list one or more of the author's purposes for writing this story with an explanation for each purpose. *(Possible responses: To entertain, the story is told by a dog; to inform, the reader learns that Lewis will travel westward, up the Missouri River.)*

Guiding Comprehension

3 **Text Structure • Critical**

At the bottom of p. 48, the author shows an excerpt from one of Captain Lewis's journals. What is a likely reason the author includes part of Captain Lewis's journal in the story?

Possible responses: The journal shows the story was based on an actual event. The contrast between Seaman's and Lewis's viewpoints makes the story more interesting to read.

4 **Cause and Effect • Literal**

Why does Seaman choose to ride in the back of the boat?

It is the highest place in the boat and it gives him the best view.

Monitor Progress	
REVIEW **Cause and Effect**	
If... students have difficulty identifying causes and effects,	**then...** use the skill and strategy instruction on p. 49.

Tech Files
ONLINE

Have students use a student-friendly search engine to to find out more about Lewis and Clark and their expedition. Use the keywords *Lewis and Clark*, *Corps of Discovery*, *Sacagawea*, *John Colter*, or *Pierre Cruzatte*. Be sure to follow classroom rules for Internet use.

"North, you say. Ah. It'll be cold up that river. Won't bother this one, though." He patted me firmly on the back.

Lewis stood and looked around. He found a piece of wood that had broken off a crate. He showed it to me, then threw it.

"Go," he said.

I wanted to go. I wanted to do whatever this man asked. But I belonged to another. I looked at my man.

"Go on," he said.

I ran for the stick and returned it to Lewis.

"How much?" Lewis asked.

"Twenty dollars. And a bargain at that."

Lewis looked down at me. I lifted my head proudly.

"Won't find a better dog than this. Perfect for your trip," my man said, trying to convince Lewis.

It wasn't necessary. Lewis wanted me. I could tell. He had liked me the minute he saw me. The feeling was mutual. Lewis paid my man twenty dollars.

"Does he have a name?" Lewis asked.

"I been callin' him Seaman, but you can name him anything you like."

"Come, Seaman," Lewis called.

As we walked away, my rope in his hand, he put his other hand on my head. After that, he didn't need a rope. I would follow this man to the ends of the Earth.

...the dog was of the newfoundland breed one that I prised
3 *much for his docility and qualifications generally for my journey....*
Meriwether Lewis   November 16, 1803

48

E L L

Activate Prior Knowledge Ask students to share what they know about journal writing. Have students identify the author of the journal entry on p. 48.

Squirrels

I caught fish off the docks. I chased animals in the woods. But hunting came alive for me on the river—the Ohio, Lewis called it.

I have always loved the water, so the day we boarded the boat and pushed out onto the Ohio River was just about the happiest day of my life. Lewis was excited, too. I could tell by the way he walked. And his voice was louder than usual.

The men were also excited. I could hear it in their voices. They didn't complain when they loaded the boat. Lewis was telling them what to load and how to load it. Anyway, that afternoon, Lewis and I and some men started down the river.

I rode in the back of the boat. It was the highest place and **4** gave me the best view. From there I could scan both banks and the water with just a glance. The first two weeks I couldn't get enough of it. There were animals I had not seen before. Smells I had not smelled. My skin tingled with excitement.

49

Cause and Effect REVIEW

TEACH

- Remind students a cause tells *why* something happened and an effect tells *what* happened.
- Explain that clue words such as *because* and *so* can signal causes and effects; sometimes the reader determines causes and effects without clue words.
- Model identifying cause-effect relationships using p. 49, paragraph 4.

Think Aloud

MODEL I want to know *why* Seaman rides in the back of the boat, but I don't see clue words in the sentence. I read on and find out the back of the boat is the highest place giving Seaman the best view. This tells me *why* Seamen rides in the back. To check, I can use my own words: Seaman rides in the back *because* it gives him a good view.

PRACTICE AND ASSESS

- Have students read the last paragraph on p. 49 and describe the effect new animals and smells have on Seaman. *(He gets excited.)*
- To assess, use Practice Book p. 16.

Cause and Effect

Directions Read the article. Then answer the questions below.

As more and more people wanted to move West, the ways they traveled changed to meet their needs. Many early settlers moved across the country by wagon. Wagons carried much more than saddlebags could carry on a horse. Wagons were also covered, which protected travelers from bad weather. Some people joined wagon trains. A wagon train was a group of wagons that traveled together. Traveling together in a wagon train kept people safer. Wagon trains were carefully planned out before they left for their journeys. People agreed to follow certain rules and elected officers to keep order along the way. Soon technology changed again, however, and people said good-bye to wagons and hello to railroads.

1. Why did people start using wagons instead of horses?
   People wanted to carry more things with them than would fit in saddlebags.

2. What was an effect of having a cover on a wagon?
   The things and people in the wagon were protected from the weather.

3. Why did people join wagon trains?
   People joined to be safe during long trips.

4. What was an effect of new technology?
   Possible answer: People started to ride on trains.

5. On a separate sheet of paper, explain why you think people stopped using wagons and started traveling on trains.
   Answers should express ideas about why people stopped using wagons and started using trains.

School Home **Home Activity** Your child read an article and answered questions about cause and effect. Read a short story with your child. Ask your child to identify causes and effects in the story.

▲ **Practice Book** p. 16

Lewis and Clark and Me **49**

Guiding Comprehension

5 🎯 **Vocabulary • Word Structure**

Have students name the base words and meanings for *hiring, hunting,* and *scanned* on p. 50.

Base words: *hire, hunt, scan.* Meanings: *hiring*—paying someone to do something for you; *hunting*—looking for animals to kill; *scanned*—looked out over an area.

Monitor Progress

🎯 **Word Structure**

If... students have difficulty using word structure to determine meanings,	**then**... use vocabulary strategy instruction on p. 51.

6 **Author's Craft • Inferential**

Question the Author **On p. 51, what is the author trying to tell you about Seaman when she writes, "It is impossible to describe the urge I felt. It was as strong as anything I had ever known. I had to get those squirrels."**

Possible response: By painting a vivid word picture, the author tells us Seaman is a hunting dog with very strong instincts to hunt.

7 **Character • Inferential**

The last paragraph on p. 51 describes Seaman's thoughts as the men guess why the squirrels are crossing the river. What do Seaman's thoughts tell you about him?

Possible response: He likes action. He doesn't like thinking about why it's happening. He wants to do something about it.

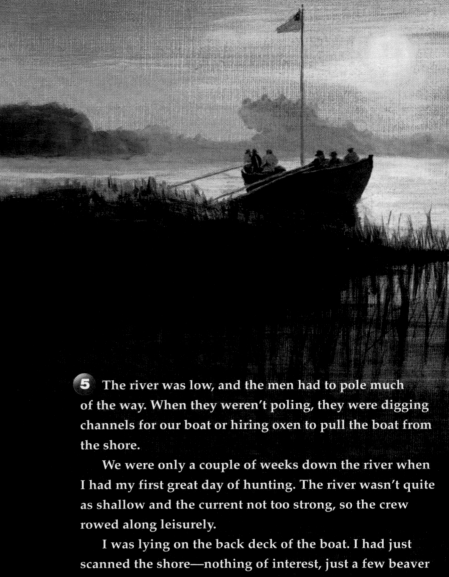

5 The river was low, and the men had to pole much of the way. When they weren't poling, they were digging channels for our boat or hiring oxen to pull the boat from the shore.

We were only a couple of weeks down the river when I had my first great day of hunting. The river wasn't quite as shallow and the current not too strong, so the crew rowed along leisurely.

I was lying on the back deck of the boat. I had just scanned the shore—nothing of interest, just a few beaver and a deer. I decided to close my eyes for a nap. I blinked a few times and was ready to lay my head on my paws when something on the water up ahead caught my eye.

50

Extend Language The word *project* (p. 51, paragraph 1) may be unfamiliar to students when used as a verb. Explain that it means "to give forth." Point out that its pronunciation and meaning differ from the more familiar noun *project.* Encourage students to find other words on these two pages that can be either nouns or verbs (Examples: *pole* on p. 50, paragraph 1, and *look* on p. 51, paragraph 2).

I stuck my nose in the air and sniffed. I recognized the scent immediately. Squirrel.

A squirrel on water? That was unusual. I had seen plenty of squirrels, but I had never seen one swim. There was something else strange. The smell of squirrel was especially strong. I had never known one squirrel to project so powerful a scent.

I stood to take a look. Right away I spotted a squirrel off the starboard side. He was swimming across the river. Another squirrel followed close behind. Without a second thought, I leaned over the side of the boat to get a better look.

I saw another squirrel. And another. I could not believe my eyes; hundreds of squirrels were crossing the river. The water up ahead was almost black with them. Every muscle in my body tightened to full alert.

Lewis was on the other side of the boat, talking to two of the men. I turned to him and barked.

"What is it?" he asked.

It is impossible to describe the urge I felt. It was as strong as anything I had ever known. I had to get those squirrels. **6**

I barked again. Lewis scanned the water ahead.

"Look at that," he said to the men. "Squirrels crossing the river. Now why would they do that?"

"Food?" one man suggested.

Lewis paused for a moment. "There are hickory nuts on both banks."

"Migrating?" suggested the other.

Lewis nodded. "Maybe. Or perhaps they're—"

I barked again. They were wasting time wondering why **7** the squirrels were crossing. It didn't matter. The squirrels were there. Hundreds of them, right in front of us. Sometimes men spend too much time thinking. They miss the fun of life.

51

⊙ VOCABULARY STRATEGY
Word Structure

TEACH

Read p. 50, paragraph 3. Model using word endings to identify the base word and understand the meaning of *scanned*. (Write *scanned* on the chalkboard.)

Think Aloud

MODEL When I come to the verb *scanned*, I see it has an *-ed* ending. So this action happened in the past. To help me understand this word, I'll cover the ending. I know the base word *scan* has to do with looking. *Scanned* probably means "looked at." To check, I'll try this meaning in the sentence, "I had just looked at the shore." That makes sense.

PRACTICE AND ASSESS

Have students identify two or three words with *-ed* or *-ing* endings on p. 51 and list these words in the first column of a three-column chart. Then have them write the base word in the second column. In the third column, they should give the meaning of the word or use it in another sentence to demonstrate their understanding.

Climate of the Midwest

Time for SOCIAL STUDIES

In the Midwest, summer and winter temperatures can differ greatly and weather changes may happen rapidly. Because land heats up and cools down more quickly than bodies of water, inland regions like the Midwest may have extreme temperature differences between their warmest months and coldest months of the year. For example, North Dakota may have a summer high of 111°F and a winter low of −44°F. When warm, moist air flowing north from the Gulf of Mexico collides with cool, dry air flowing south from Canada, the Midwest can experience sudden violent weather, such as tornadoes, blizzards, hailstorms, and rapid temperature changes. The climate of the Midwest may affect the lives of the people who live there.

Guiding Comprehension

8 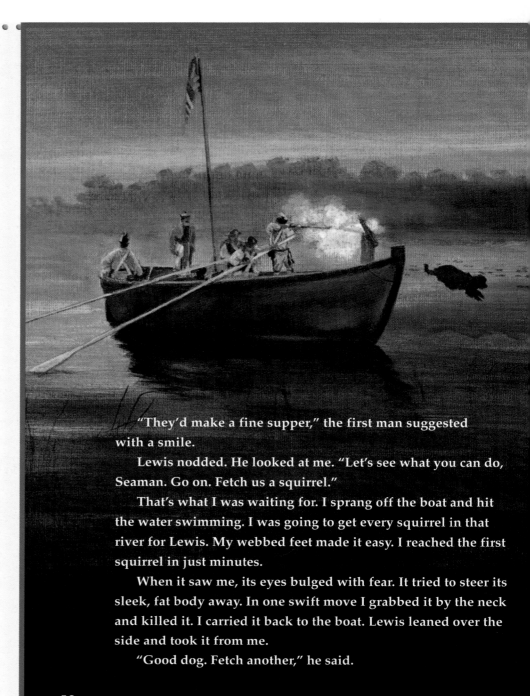 **Author's Purpose • Critical**

Question the Author **The author writes on p. 53, paragraph 7, that "... the look of pride on Lewis's face was better than all the men's praise added together." Why is the author telling you this?**

Possible response: She wants readers to connect to Seaman's feelings by thinking about how they feel when someone they respect or love is pleased with their work.

9 **Summarize • Inferential**

How has Seaman's life changed since Captain Lewis first stepped on the wharf in 1803?

Responses should include information about Seaman's life on the expedition, including his adventures riding on boats and catching squirrels for the men to eat.

"They'd make a fine supper," the first man suggested with a smile.

Lewis nodded. He looked at me. "Let's see what you can do, Seaman. Go on. Fetch us a squirrel."

That's what I was waiting for. I sprang off the boat and hit the water swimming. I was going to get every squirrel in that river for Lewis. My webbed feet made it easy. I reached the first squirrel in just minutes.

When it saw me, its eyes bulged with fear. It tried to steer its sleek, fat body away. In one swift move I grabbed it by the neck and killed it. I carried it back to the boat. Lewis leaned over the side and took it from me.

"Good dog. Fetch another," he said.

52

ELL

Understanding Idioms Explain the ideas of *cheering someone on* (p. 53, paragraph 3) and *cheering someone up.* The first means "to encourage someone to continue," the latter "to make someone happy." Encourage students to record similar or confusing idioms and their meanings in language journals, word lists, or computer files of English vocabulary.

The crew had stopped rowing, and the boat drifted slowly toward the mass of squirrels.

"Look at Captain Lewis's dog!" yelled one of the rowers.

I turned and started swimming again. I could hear the men cheering me on. In two strokes I was on another squirrel.

"Good dog!" Lewis yelled. "Go!"

"Go," the crew echoed. "Go, Seaman, go!"

I went. And went. Over and over, I went. I went until I was exhausted. I don't know how long it lasted. Maybe one hour. Maybe four.

All I know is that when I finished, there was a pile of squirrels in the boat. Lewis and the crew were laughing and cheering. All the rest of the day the men were patting me and saying, "Good dog" and "Good boy" and "We'll be eatin' good tonight." The admiration of the crew was great, but the look **8** of pride on Lewis's face was better than all the men's praise added together.

That night the men fried the squirrels, and we ate well.

In the three years that followed, I hunted almost every day. **9** But the squirrels on the Ohio were my favorite.

... observed a number of squirrels swiming the Ohio ... they appear to be making to the south; ... I made my dog take as many each day as I had occation for, they wer fat and I thought them when fryed a pleasent food ... he would take the squirel in the water kill them and swiming bring them in his mouth to the boat ....

Meriwether Lewis   September 11, 1803

53

Develop Vocabulary

Develop Vocabulary

PRACTICE LESSON VOCABULARY

Students orally respond *yes* or *no* to each question and provide a reason for each answer. Possible responses are given.

1. If you *yearned* to do something, were you trying to avoid it? *(No; if you yearned to do something, you wanted to do it.)*

2. Do *migrating* squirrels need new homes? *(Yes; migrating squirrels need new homes in the places they move to.)*

3. Is it possible to walk on a *wharf*? *(Yes; people can walk on a wharf because it is a platform above the water used to tie up boats.)*

BUILD CONCEPT VOCABULARY

Review previous concept words with students. Ask if students have come across any words today in their reading or elsewhere that they would like to add to the Exploration Concept Web, such as *adventures* or *Mississippi.*

STRATEGY SELF-CHECK

Answer Questions

Remind students that good readers ask and answer questions of the text when they have difficulty understanding what they are reading.

When discussing this strategy, have students answer these questions when they read: *What is the author trying to tell me? Why is this fact or event included in the story? Can the text be written more clearly? How would I say it instead?*

Remind students that sometimes answers are stated in the text and other times they are not.

Have students record their questions and responses in a T-chart.

SELF-CHECK

Students can ask themselves these questions to assess their understanding of the story.

- Did I identify the author's purpose for writing this page?
- How did answering questions help me understand the author's purpose?

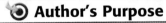

Monitor Progress	
Author's Purpose	
If... students have difficulty answering questions and identifying author's purpose,	**then...** revisit the skill lesson on pp. 40–41. Reteach as necessary.

Strategy Response Log

Confirm Predictions Have students review the predictions they made at the beginning of the story. (See p. 44.) Provide the following prompt: Was your prediction accurate? Revise your old prediction or make a new prediction about the rest of the story.

If you want to teach this story in two sessions, stop here.

Guiding Comprehension

If you are teaching this story in two days, discuss author's purpose as it relates to the story so far and review the vocabulary.

10 🔊 **Vocabulary • Word Structure**

Have students identify the base words and meanings for *listened, staring,* and *realized* on p. 54, paragraph 5.

Base words: *listen, stare, realize.* Meanings: *listened:* heard something; *staring:* looking at something; *realized:* understood.

Monitor Progress

🎯 **Word Structure**

If... students have difficulty using word structure to determine base words and meanings,	**then...** use vocabulary strategy instruction on p. 55.

---

11 **Draw Conclusions • Critical**

Is it reasonable for the Indians to think that Seaman is a bear? Why or why not?

Possible response: Yes, because Seaman is large and hairy like a bear, and he doesn't look like the dog the Indians have.

DAY 3 Grouping Options

Reading

Whole Group Discuss the Question of the Day.

Group Time Differentiated Instruction
Read *Lewis and Clark and Me.* See pp. 40f–40g for the small group lesson plan.

Whole Group Discuss the Reader Response questions on p. 60. Then use p. 65a.

Language Arts
Use pp. 65e–65k.

Bear-Dog

"Indians."

We had not been on the shore very long before I heard Lewis say the word.

Lewis and Clark and I had crossed the river to make some observations. That's when these Indians appeared. They were different from other people I had known—the boatmen and city folk.

I didn't sense that Lewis or Clark were concerned, so I wasn't. The Indians seemed friendly enough. Lewis talked to them. It wasn't until later that I realized Lewis gave the same talk to every group of Indians we met. He talked about the "great white father" in Washington.

10 The Indians listened patiently as one of the English-speaking Indians translated. Lewis used hand motions to help. As he talked on, it became obvious to me that the Indians were not interested in Lewis or what he was saying. They were staring at me. Finally, Lewis realized what was going on, and he invited the Indians to take a closer look.

They gathered around. They touched me. They whispered about me. They acted like they had never seen a dog before. Then I noticed an Indian dog standing to the side. I took one look at that animal and realized why they were so interested in me.

That dog could not have been more than twenty pounds. Newfoundlands can weigh up to 150 pounds, and I'm a large Newfoundland. If that scrawny dog was the only dog they had seen, then I was a strange sight indeed.

54

Context Clues Have students use context clues to figure out the meaning of *fetch* (p. 55, paragraph 9). Explain that this command, which means "to bring something back," is a common trick performed by dogs. If needed, remind students of a similar action that happened at the beginning of p. 48.

"Bear," one of the English-speaking Indians said.

I looked up. He was pointing at me.

"Dog," Lewis replied patiently.

The Indian looked at his own dog. He looked back at me.

"Bear," he said again.

Lewis looked at me and smiled. Clark was smiling, too.

I lifted my head.

"I guess he does look like a bear," Lewis said.

Lewis picked up a stick and threw it.

"Fetch," he said.

I fetched.

"Stay," he said.

I stayed.

55

⟳ VOCABULARY STRATEGY

Word Structure

TEACH

Read p. 54, paragraph 5. Model using word endings to identify the base word and understand the meaning of *realized*. (Write *realized* on the chalkboard.)

Think Aloud

MODEL When I come to the word *realized*, I notice that it has an *-ed* ending. I cover the ending, but I don't recognize the base word that is left—*realiz.* I know sometimes the spelling of the base word changes when endings are added. I think the base word is *realize*, and *realize* means "to understand something." Words that end in *-ed* tell about past actions, so *realized* probably means "understood." If I replace *realized* with *understood*, the sentence makes sense.

PRACTICE AND ASSESS

Have students read p. 55, paragraph 6. Have them identify and sort words ending in *-ed* or *-ing* using a T-chart. Beside each word, have students write its base word. *(-ed: looked, look; smiled, smile; lifted, lift; -ing: smiling, smile)* Then ask students to use each word in a sentence.

Guiding Comprehension

12 Vocabulary • Inferential

Why do the Indians call Seaman a "bear-dog"?

Possible response: The Indians don't have a word for a large dog like Seaman. For *horse*, they combined two words they had to describe something new. Since Seaman is a dog that is big like a bear, they use the word *bear-dog* to describe him.

13 Draw Conclusions • Critical

What is the significance of Lewis refusing to trade Seaman for the beaver pelts? Do you own something that is so valuable that you wouldn't trade it for anything?

Possible response: It shows that Seaman is more valuable to Lewis than the beaver pelts. Students should tell about things they own that are valuable to them.

14 Author's Purpose • Critical

What could the author's purpose be for using dialogue as well as Lewis's journal entry in this section of the story?

Possible response: The author uses dialogue to inform the reader about how the Indians created new words. The journal entry is used to show that this event really happened and to give us Lewis's thoughts about it.

Monitor Progress

Author's Purpose

| **If...** students have difficulty evaluating author's purpose, | **then...** use the skill and strategy instruction on p. 57. |

"Sit," he said.

I sat.

The Indians were impressed.

"Dog," Lewis said politely. Lewis was always nice.

The Indian who had called me "bear" turned to consult with his friends.

Finally, he turned.

"Bear-dog," he said with satisfaction.

Lewis smiled.

"Yes, I guess you could call him bear-dog."

Later, George Drouillard explained to us that the Indians don't have a separate word for *horse*. They call a horse "elk-

12 dog." I guess it made sense for them to call me a bear-dog.

The Indian suddenly turned and walked through the crowd to his horse. He pulled out three beaver skins. He held them out to Lewis.

"For bear-dog," he said.

It wasn't often that I saw Lewis surprised. He was then.

I took a step closer to Lewis.

Lewis looked the Indian square in the eye and said,

13 "No trade. Bear-dog special."

As we rode back to camp in the boat, Lewis said to me, "Three beaver skins! Can you believe that?"

No, I could not. The idea that Lewis and I would ever separate was unthinkable. Not many dogs and men fit together like Lewis and I. If you have ever experienced it, then you know what I'm talking about. And if you haven't, well, it's hard to explain. All I can tell you is that when a dog and a man fit like Lewis and I did, nothing can separate them. Lewis said it best.

"No trade."

56

Extend Language Have students compare English terms on p. 56 to equivalent terms in their home languages. *Indian, satisfaction,* or *special* are cognates in Spanish: *Indio, satisfacción, especial.* Resources for home language words may include parents, bilingual staff members, bilingual dictionaries, or online translation sources.

...one of the Shawnees a respectable looking Indian offered me
three beverskins for my dog with which he appeared much pleased...
of course there was no bargan, I had given 20$ for this dogg myself—

Meriwether Lewis   November 16, 1803

57

Author's Purpose
Answer Questions

TEACH

Model answering questions to identify the author's purpose for pp. 56–57.

Think Aloud **MODEL** To answer questions, I may need to look at more than one place in the story and think about what I already know. As I read the dialogue on p. 56, I see the author gives information about how the Indians created words for unfamiliar things and used beaver skins for trading. When I read Captain Lewis's journal on p. 57, I find out this event really happened and how Lewis felt about the trade. I know authors often write to inform, so that's probably why she included both the dialogue and the journal entry.

PRACTICE AND ASSESS

Have students use the question-the-author chart to evaluate the author's purpose.

Time for SOCIAL STUDIES

Barter System

As Lewis and Clark met with Native Americans during their expedition, they often traded with them for the goods they needed. This system of trading one set of goods for another instead of money is called a barter system. The fur trade between the Native Americans and the Europeans was an example of a barter system at work. In exchange for beaver, mink, and other pelts Native Americans had, French, Dutch, and American traders gave the Native Americans goods that they produced, such as iron axes and glass beads.

EXTEND SKILLS

Journal

Explain that a journal is a personal record of the writer's thoughts and daily events. Journal writing is usually kept private, but it is sometimes published if the writer or subject of the journal interests readers. Tell students that anyone can write a journal, and have them tell how their journals would be like or unlike Captain Lewis's journal.

Guiding Comprehension

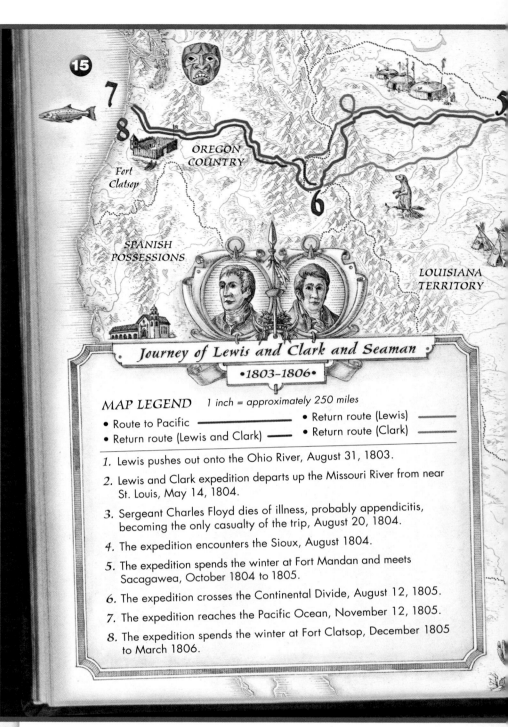

15 🔵 **Graphic Sources • Inferential**

What does the map on pp. 58–59 show?

It shows the routes of Lewis and Clark's 1803–1806 journey west to the Pacific and back east across what is now the United States.

16 🎯 **Answer Questions • Inferential**

Question the Author **Why do you think the author put numbers on certain spots on the map?**

The numbers show where important events occurred on the journey.

17 **Compare and Contrast • Critical**

Text to Text **How is this map of the United States similar to a U.S. map today? How is it different?**

Possible response: The states of New York, Pennsylvania, Virginia, Ohio, Kentucky, Tennessee, North Carolina, South Carolina, and Georgia all look the same as they do today. The rest of the land on the map is divided into different states today.

Strategy Response Log

Summarize When students finish reading the selection, provide this prompt: Think about the main events in *Lewis and Clark and Me*. Write four or five sentences summarizing the story in your own words.

Journey of Lewis and Clark and Seaman

•1803–1806•

MAP LEGEND   1 inch = approximately 250 miles

• Route to Pacific ——————   • Return route (Lewis) ——————
• Return route (Lewis and Clark) ——   • Return route (Clark) ——————

1. Lewis pushes out onto the Ohio River, August 31, 1803.
2. Lewis and Clark expedition departs up the Missouri River from near St. Louis, May 14, 1804.
3. Sergeant Charles Floyd dies of illness, probably appendicitis, becoming the only casualty of the trip, August 20, 1804.
4. The expedition encounters the Sioux, August 1804.
5. The expedition spends the winter at Fort Mandan and meets Sacagawea, October 1804 to 1805.
6. The expedition crosses the Continental Divide, August 12, 1805.
7. The expedition reaches the Pacific Ocean, November 12, 1805.
8. The expedition spends the winter at Fort Clatsop, December 1805 to March 1806.

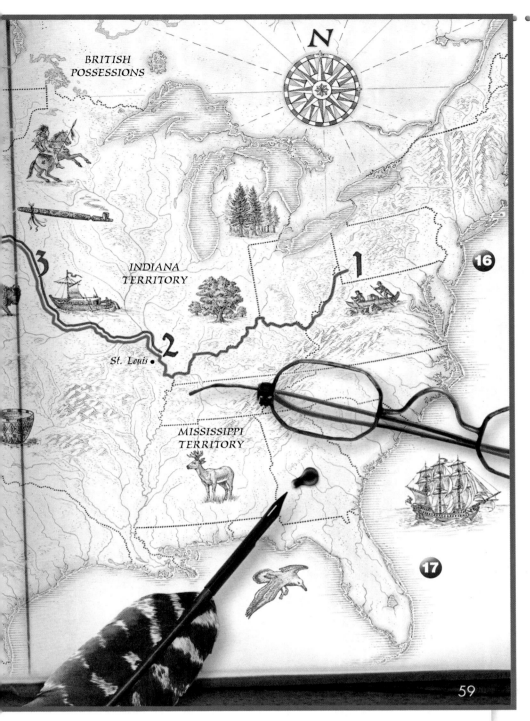

59

STRATEGY SELF-CHECK

Answer Questions

Ask students to explain the author's purpose for including the map at the end of the story. Encourage students to ask questions, such as: *What is the author trying to show me? (The author's purpose is to inform by showing the route of Lewis, Clark, and Seaman's journey.)* Remind them that answering questions about the author can help them identify the author's purpose. Use Practice Book p. 17.

SELF-CHECK

Students can ask themselves these questions to assess understanding of the selection.

- Was I able to identify the author's purpose for including the map?
- Did answering questions help me identify the author's purpose?

Monitor Progress

Author's Purpose

If... students have difficulty answering questions and identifying the author's purpose,	**then...** use the Reteach lesson on p. 65b.

Develop Vocabulary

PRACTICE LESSON VOCABULARY

Students orally respond to each question.

1. Are *docks* located near bodies of water or mountain ranges? *(bodies of water)*

2. Do you use your eyes or your ears when you *scan* something? *(your eyes)*

3. When you notice a *scent,* are you using your sense of taste or your sense of smell? *(sense of smell)*

BUILD CONCEPT VOCABULARY

Review previous concept words with students. Ask if students have met any words today in their reading or elsewhere that they would like to add to the Exploration Concept Web, such as *route, expedition,* and *departs.*

Author's Purpose

- The **author's purpose** is the reason or reasons the author has for writing.
- An author may write to persuade, to inform, to entertain, or to express ideas and feelings.

Directions Read the following passage. Then answer the questions below.

> Crossing the river was dangerous for the backpackers. If they lost their balance, the river's current could take them far downriver. But it was nearing sunset, and it would take too long for them to get back to the camp if they took another route. Elizabeth went first. She was a good swimmer and was not afraid of water.
>
> She made it safely to the other side. John followed her. The rushing water made him very nervous. He took one shaky step after another. All of a sudden, John was knocked off his feet. He was being carried downstream in the current. Elizabeth dove in after him, and luckily was able to tow John to shore.

Possible answers given.
1. What is most likely the author's purpose of the passage?
   The author is trying to entertain.

2. Why do you think that is the purpose?
   The author gives exciting details about John's rescue.

3. Where in the passage did the author write the most exciting detail? How do you know?
   the ending; The author builds the action there.

4. At what pace did you read this passage—fast, medium, or slow? Did you need to change your normal reading pace to understand it? Why or why not?
   I read the passage quickly because it didn't have a lot of facts to remember.

5. Do you think the author met his or her purpose? Why or why not?
   Yes, because I wanted to find out what would happen to the backpackers.

School Home Home Activity Your child identified the author's purpose in a passage. Have your child write a short story with a clear purpose in mind. See if you can determine your child's purpose after reading the story.

▲ **Practice Book** p. 17

Lewis and Clark and Me **59**

Reader Response

Open for Discussion Personal Response

 MODEL I think she probably knew a lot about dogs, and she must have researched Lewis and Clark's expedition.

Comprehension Check Critical Response

1. She wanted to show the words exactly as Lewis wrote them in his journal. **Author's Purpose**

2. Responses will vary but should include details from the text that support students' thinking. **Author's Purpose**

3. Possible response: Seaman loves Lewis. He expresses love by doing things for him, like hunting squirrels. **Answer Questions**

4. Responses will vary but should include at least one word from the Words to Know list and other words from the selection. **Vocabulary**

 Look Back and Write For test practice, assign a 10–15 minute time limit. For assessment, see the Scoring Rubric at the right.

Retell

Have students retell *Lewis and Clark and Me.*

Monitor Progress

Check Retelling Rubric 4 3 2 1

If... students have difficulty retelling the story,	then... use the Retelling Cards and the Scoring Rubric for Retelling on p. 61 to assist fluent retelling.

SUCCESS PREDICTOR

 **ELL**

Check Retelling Have students use the selection illustrations and section titles to guide their retellings. For more ideas on assessing students' retellings, see the ELL and Transition Handbook.

Reader Response

Open for Discussion A dog couldn't write a journal, could he? So how did the author, Laurie Myers, seem to get Seaman's words? Explain this mystery.

1. Reread the parts from Meriwether Lewis's journal. Some of the words are misspelled. Why didn't the author correct them? **Think Like an Author**

2. An author's purpose can be to help readers visualize a scene. Do you think this might have been one of Laurie Myers's purposes? Explain. **Author's Purpose**

3. How does Seaman feel about Lewis? How does he express these feelings? Use examples from the story to explain your answer. **Answer Questions**

4. What would you include in a newspaper ad for a Newfoundland like Seaman? Write an ad using words from the Words to Know list and the selection. **Vocabulary**

 Look Back and Write Seaman was a dog with special qualities. Reread page 47. List some of the qualities that made him special.

Meet author Laurie Myers on page 774 and illustrator Michael Dooling on page 780.

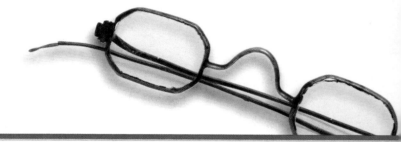

60

Scoring Rubric Look Back and Write

Top-Score Response will use details from page 47 to list some of Seaman's special qualities.

Example of a Top-Score Response Seaman is a dog with many special qualities. Because he is a Newfoundland, he is very good in the water. With webbed feet, he is a very good swimmer, and water rolls right off his coat. He could even rescue a drowning person.

For additional rubrics, see p. WA10.

Write Now

Journal Entry

Prompt

In *Lewis and Clark and Me,* Seaman tells about two memorable days of the expedition. Think about a memorable day in your own life. Now write a journal entry describing what happened on that special day.

Writing Trait

Vary the kinds of **sentences** in your journal entry. Include questions and interjections.

Student Model

Writer describes daily events.

This morning I woke up extra early. I got dressed and brushed my teeth as quickly as I could. I didn't want to be late for school. Why was I excited? It was our field trip!

Interrogative and exclamatory sentences catch the reader's interest.

My whole class had waited for weeks for this trip to the zoo. We arrived just as the zoo opened. What was the first stop on our list? It was the sea lions, of course! We were studying sea lions, so we had a million questions. What do they eat? How much do they weigh? Where do they live?

The sea lions were amazing to watch. Then their trainers shouted commands. Dive! Turn! Bark!

Writer engages reader in the final question.

Was I the only one who thought the animals were speaking right to me?

Use the model to help you write your own journal entry.

61

Write Now

Look at the Prompt Explain that each sentence in the prompt has a purpose.

- Sentence 1 presents a topic.
- Sentence 2 suggests students think about the topic.
- Sentence 3 tells what to write—a journal entry.

Strategies to Develop Sentences

Have students

- vary sentence lengths and types.
- avoid beginning sentences with the same words.

NO: We went to the zoo. We saw sea lions. We also saw tigers.

YES: At the zoo, we saw sea lions and tigers.

For additional suggestions and rubric, see pp. 65g–65h.

Writer's Checklist

☑ **Focus** Do sentences stick to the topic of a special day?

☑ **Organization** Do transitons show connections?

☑ **Support** Do details tell why this day was special?

☑ **Conventions** Are punctuation and spelling correct?

Scoring Rubric | Narrative Retelling

Rubric 4 3 2 1	4	3	2	1
Connections	Makes connections and generalizes beyond the text	Makes connections to other events, stories, or experiences	Makes a limited connection to another event, story, or experience	Makes no connection to another event, story, or experience
Author's Purpose	Elaborates on author's purpose	Tells author's purpose with some clarity	Makes some connection to author's purpose	Makes no connection to author's purpose
Characters	Describes the main character(s) and any character development	Identifies the main character(s) and gives some information about them	Inaccurately identifies some characters or gives little information about them	Inaccurately identifies the characters or gives no information about them
Setting	Describes the time and location	Identifies the time and location	Omits details of time or location	Is unable to identify time or location
Plot	Describes the problem, goal, events, and ending using rich detail	Tells the problem, goal, events, and ending with some errors that do not affect meaning	Tells parts of the problem, goal, events, and ending with gaps that affect meaning	Retelling has no sense of story

Retelling Plan

☑ **Week 1** Assess Strategic Intervention students.

☑ **This week assess Advanced students.**

☐ **Week 3** Assess Strategic Intervention students.

☐ **Week 4** Assess On-Level students.

☐ **Week 5** Assess any students you have not yet checked during this unit.

Use the Retelling Chart on p. TR16 to record retelling.

Retelling

Selection Test To assess with *Lewis and Clark and Me,* use Selection Tests, pp. 5–8.

Fresh Reads for Differentiated Test Practice For weekly leveled practice, use pp. 7–12.

SUCCESS PREDICTOR

Social Studies in Reading

PREVIEW/USE TEXT FEATURES

As students preview "They Traveled with Lewis and Clark," have them read the introductory paragraph and subheads and examine the realistic illustrations. After they preview, ask:

- **Why do you think the author included bold subheads?** (The subheads show the text is organized in two parts, and they identify the people described.)

- **How do the pictures add to your understanding of this text?** (Possible response: They help me imagine what the people looked like and how they dressed.)

Link to Social Studies

Help students determine appropriate reference sources to use, such as atlases or official state Web sites.

DAY 4 Grouping Options

Reading

Whole Group Discuss the Question of the Day.

Group Time Differentiated Instruction
Read "They Traveled with Lewis and Clark." See pp. 40f–40g for the small group lesson plan.

Whole Group Use p. 65a.

Language Arts
Use pp. 65e–65k.

Social Studies in Reading

Narrative Nonfiction

Genre

- **Narrative nonfiction can give facts about people and their lives.**

- **Biography and history are kinds of narrative nonfiction.**

Text Features

- **A short introductory paragraph gives a reason to read on.**

- **Large, bold-faced subheads identify the historic person to be discussed.**

- **Realistic pictures show what the historic person might have looked like.**

Link to Social Studies

Do research to find out what places in the West have been named for Sacagawea (sometimes spelled Sacajawea). Write about one of them.

62

They Traveled with Lewis and Clark

by Elizabeth Massie

Meriwether Lewis and William Clark are known for exploring the vast land between St. Louis and the Pacific Ocean. But they could not have done it without the help of others.

Content-Area Vocabulary | **Social Studies**

interpreted	translated from a foreign language
scout	person who is sent out to get information

York
African American Explorer

York was a member of Lewis and Clark's Corps of Discovery. He was about the same age as William Clark. The two had grown up together. Both were brave and strong. But there was one difference. Clark was a free man. York was a slave. York belonged to Clark.

Slaves had few rights. They could not vote or carry guns. They were supposed to eat and sleep apart from white people. Yet on the journey west, York proved in many ways that he was equal.

Some of the men could not swim. York could. Clark's journal describes how York swam into a river to gather greens for dinner. York hunted deer, buffalo, and elk. He served as a scout. He cut wood and cooked meals. He even cared for the other men when they were sick.

One day there was a heavy storm. The rain nearly washed Clark and others into the Missouri River. York thought they had been swept away. He ignored his own safety

Author's Purpose Based on your preview, how should this text be read?

63

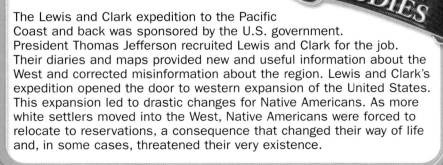

Western Expansion

The Lewis and Clark expedition to the Pacific Coast and back was sponsored by the U.S. government. President Thomas Jefferson recruited Lewis and Clark for the job. Their diaries and maps provided new and useful information about the West and corrected misinformation about the region. Lewis and Clark's expedition opened the door to western expansion of the United States. This expansion led to drastic changes for Native Americans. As more white settlers moved into the West, Native Americans were forced to relocate to reservations, a consequence that changed their way of life and, in some cases, threatened their very existence.

NARRATIVE NONFICTION

Use the sidebar on p. 62 to guide discussion.

- Explain narrative nonfiction recounts a true event or series of events. Biography and history are types of narrative nonfiction.

- Have students identify the clues that tell them this selection is narrative nonfiction. *(Possible response: Lewis and Clark were real explorers; subheads show we're learning about real people; introductory note explains the subject of the selection.)*

- Ask students if this selection is biography, history, or both, and why they think so. *(Possible response: It is both biography and history because it describes real people who were a part of the historic Lewis and Clark expedition.)*

 **AudioText**

Author's Purpose

Possible response: This text should be read slowly to make sure the reader understands historical facts about who the people are and why they are important.

Build Background Have students share what they know about African Americans and Native Americans in the United States during the early 1800s. Help students understand how York's and Sacagawea's lives were like and unlike the lives of white explorers.

Strategies for Nonfiction

USE ILLUSTRATIONS Explain to students that illustrations can support the text and sometimes even provide additional information. Readers can use them to locate information to answer test questions. Provide the following strategy.

Use the Strategy

1. Read the test question and locate a key word or phrase.

2. Scan the selection and illustrations. Notice how the illustrations help you understand and picture information in your mind. Look for matches between the illustrations and the key words from the test question.

3. When you find a match, use details from the illustration to help you answer the test question.

GUIDED PRACTICE Have students discuss how they would use the strategy to answer the following question.

How could Sacagawea carry a baby across hundreds of miles? Explain your thinking.

INDEPENDENT PRACTICE After students answer the following test question, discuss the process they used to find the information.

Do you think the tasks York did on the expedition were difficult? Explain your thinking.

and searched through the storm for the missing people. Clark wrote that when they found York he was "greatly agitated," worried that they were gone for good.

Native American tribes along the way were amazed at York. They had never seen a man with such dark skin. Some believed he had special powers. Historians think that meeting York made the Indians more willing to let the group move safely across their lands.

York worked hard on the long journey. Yet when it was over he received no pay. Clark did not give York his freedom for another ten years. Some believe York died in Tennessee. Others say he went back west to live with Indians he met on the expedition.

Sacagawea
Native American Guide

Sacagawea was sixteen years old when she joined the Corps of Discovery. She was a Shoshone Indian with a two-month-old baby. She was married to a French trader. Warriors from the Hidatsa tribe in North Dakota had kidnapped her when

64

Independent Practice Help students brainstorm words that describe the illustration of York on p. 63.

she was twelve. She had been taken hundreds of miles east. There, she learned the language of her new tribe.

Lewis and Clark needed someone who knew Indian languages. They hired Sacagawea's husband. Yet as it turned out, Sacagawea was more helpful than her husband.

Sacagawea interpreted for the explorers. She knew which plants were good to eat. She was familiar with some of the land over which they traveled. When Indians saw her, they knew that the corps was on a peaceful journey. A war party would not travel with a woman and her baby.

Once a storm nearly turned over one of the boats. Many important items fell into the water. While the men shouted and argued in the wind, Sacagawea saved the papers and other goods from the high waves. Lewis thought she was brave. He wrote: "The Indian woman to whom I ascribe equal fortitude and resolution with any person onboard . . . caught and preserved most of the light articles which were washed overboard."

At last the group reached western Montana, Shoshone land. This was the place of Sacagawea's birth. She discovered that her brother had become chief. She talked her brother into trading horses to the explorers. The men needed these horses to get over the Rocky Mountains.

Along with the men, Sacagawea made it to the Pacific Ocean and then back. Most people believe she died at age 25 at Fort Manuel, South Dakota. Some believe she died as a very old woman in 1884, among the Shoshone people in Wyoming.

Reading Across Texts

Seaman (the Newfoundland dog), York, and Sacagawea all helped Lewis and Clark. How did each help?

Writing Across Texts

Write a thank-you note from Lewis to one of those who helped him and Clark on their journey.

Summarize How do the subheads help you summarize?

65

CONNECT TEXT TO TEXT

Reading Across Texts

Have students use a three-column chart to record ways that Seaman, York, and Sacagawea each helped Lewis and Clark. Point out that, while they may remember some details from their reading, it will be helpful to skim the selections again to complete the chart.

Writing Across Texts Suggest students use their charts to help them write their thank-you notes. Have them take time to imagine how Lewis might feel about the recipient of his note before writing.

Summarize

Possible responses: The subheads name and briefly describe each person. They can be used to help identify the main idea of each part of the selection.

Fluency Assessment Plan

☑ **Week 1** Assess Advanced students.

☑ **This week assess Strategic Intervention students.**

☐ **Week 3** Assess On-Level students.

☐ **Week 4** Assess Strategic Intervention students.

☐ **Week 5** Assess any students you have not yet checked during this unit.

Set individual goals for students to enable them to reach the year-end goal.

• Current Goal: 95–105 WCPM

• Year-End Goal: 130 WCPM

Oral fluency depends not only on reading without halting but also on word recognition. After students read passages aloud for assessment, help them recognize unfamiliar English words and their meanings. Focus on each student's progress.

 To develop fluent readers, use Fluency Coach.

DAY 5 Grouping Options

Reading
Whole Group
Revisit the Question of the Week.

Group Time
Differentiated Instruction
Reread this week's Leveled Readers. See pp. 40f–40g for the small group lesson plan.

Whole Group
Use p. 65b–65c.

Language Arts
Use pp. 65d–65l.

PAUSES
Fluency

 DAY 1

Model Reread aloud "Johnny Appleseed" on p. 40m. Explain that you will pause in certain places as you read to make the reading easy for listeners to follow. You may also wish to model reading some text without pauses or using inappropriate pauses so students better understand effective use of pauses.

DAY 2

Echo Reading Read aloud paragraphs 1–4 after the introduction on p. 46. Have students notice how periods, dashes, and commas provide clues for pausing. Practice as a class by doing three echo readings of the paragraphs.

DAY 3

Model Read aloud p. 50. Have students notice how punctuation divides sentences into meaningful phrases and provides clues for pausing. Practice as a class by doing three echo readings.

DAY 4

Partner Reading Partners practice reading aloud p. 50, three times. Students should pause at commas, dashes, and at the ends of sentences. Have partners offer one another feedback.

Monitor Progress | Check Fluency WCPM

As students reread, monitor their progress toward their individual fluency goals. Current Goal: 95–105 words correct per minute. End-of-Year Goal: 130 words correct per minute.

If... students cannot read fluently at a rate of 95–105 words correct per minute,
then... make sure students practice with text at their independent level. Provide additional fluency practice, pairing nonfluent readers with fluent readers.

If... students already read at 130 words correct per minute,
then... they do not need to reread three to four times.

SUCCESS PREDICTOR

DAY 5

Assessment
Individual Reading Rate Use the Fluency Assessment Plan and do a one-minute timed reading of either selection for this week to assess students in Week 2. Pay special attention to this week's skill, pauses. Provide corrective feedback for each student.

RETEACH

Author's Purpose

TEACH

Review the definitions of *author's purpose* on p. 40. Students can complete Practice Book p. 18 on their own or as a class. Discuss the graphic organizer on the Practice Book page. Point out that students should answer questions 1–2 before they read the passage, questions 3–4 as they read, and question 5 after reading. For questions 2–3, students will complete phrases.

ASSESS

Have individuals read p. 54 and determine the author's purpose for including the last paragraph on that page. *(to inform, because the paragraph gives information about Newfoundlands and how they differ from the Indians' dog)*

For additional instruction on author's purpose, see DI·53.

EXTEND SKILLS

Imagery/Sensory Words

TEACH

Imagery, or sensory words, are words or phrases that help the reader experience the way things look, smell, taste, sound, or feel.

• Imagery can make characters and settings seem real by appealing to the reader's senses.

• Imagery may help establish the mood or dramatize the action.

Help students identify sensory words used to describe Lewis on p. 46, paragraphs 4 and 5, and describe how the words appeal to their senses.

ASSESS

Ask pairs to read p. 51, paragraph 3 ("I saw...."). Have them find two examples of imagery in the paragraph and write answers to these questions:

1. To which sense does each example appeal? *(sight and touch)*

2. How does the imagery help you better understand what you are reading?
(Possible response: It helps me picture the action of the scene.)

OBJECTIVES

• Determine the author's purpose for writing.

• Identify imagery and sensory words in a passage.

Skills Trace

Author's Purpose

Introduce/Teach	TE: 4.1 40–41, 88–89; 4.5 516–517
Practice	TE: 47, 57, 95, 103, 523, 529 PB: 13, 17, 18, 33, 37, 38, 203, 207, 208
▶ Reteach/Review	**TE: 4.1 31, 65b, 111b, DI•53, DI•55; 4.3 369; 4.5 537b, DI•52; 4.6 695 PB: 6, 146, 276**
Test	Selection Test: 5–8, 13–16, 81–84; Benchmark Test: Unit 1

Access Content Reteach the skill by reviewing the Picture It! lesson on author's purpose in the ELL Teaching Guide, pp. 8–9.

Author's Purpose

• The **author's purpose** is the reason or reasons the author has for writing.
• An author may write to persuade, to inform, to entertain, or to express ideas and feelings.

Directions Read the passage below. Use the graphic organizer to keep track of the author's purpose before and during reading, then answer the last question.

Don't Forget York
One special member of Lewis and Clark's expedition who was not in history books until recently was York. York was an African American slave of Clark's. In Clark's journals, it says that York hunted and found food for Clark and his men. It also says that York tried to make sure that Clark was safe during the trip. York was an important part of the expedition and will no longer be forgotten.

Possible answers given.

	Author's Purpose	Why Do You Think So?
Before you read: What do you think it will be?	1. inform us about York and not to forget him.	2. I looked at the title. It helps describe what the author will talk about.
As you read: What do you think it is?	3. to inform us about how York helped Lewis and Clark	4. The author provides facts about what York did during the expedition.

5. Do you think the author met his or her purpose? Why or why not?
Yes; The author gave us information we didn't already know about York.

School Home Home Activity Your child identified the author's purpose in a passage. Read an article or short story with your child. Ask your child the author's purpose before, during, and after reading.

▲ **Practice Book** p. 18

Vocabulary and Word Study

VOCABULARY STRATEGY
Word Structure

ENDINGS Remind students that the ending *-ed* is added to a verb to show action that happened in the past. The ending *-ing* is used for verbs telling about present or ongoing actions. Ask pairs to find five verbs in *Lewis and Clark and Me* that end in *-ed* or *-ing*. Have them write the verb, the base word, and then create a new verb by adding *-ed* or *-ing*. Then have partners take turns using the original and new forms of the verbs in example sentences.

Verb with Original Ending	Base word	Verb with New Ending
crossing	cross	crossed
blinked	blink	blinking

Word Connotations

Have small groups use a thesaurus to find synonyms for the word *scent*. Tell them to rate a few synonyms on a +/− scale to indicate whether each synonym has a positive or negative connotation. Use completed rating scales to discuss connotation—the feelings suggested by a word. Other words from the selection that students can rate include *complain*, *powerful*, and *admiration*.

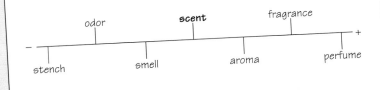

BUILD CONCEPT VOCABULARY
Exploration

LOOKING BACK Remind students of the question of the week: *What did Lewis and Clark learn on their journey?* Discuss how this week's Concept Web relates to the theme of exploration. Ask students if they have any words or categories to add. Discuss if words and categories are appropriately related to the concept.

MOVING FORWARD Preview the title of the next selection, *Grandfather's Journey*. Ask students which Concept Web words might apply to the new selection based on the title alone. Put a star next to these words on the Web.

Display the Concept Web and revisit the vocabulary words as you read the next selection to check predictions.

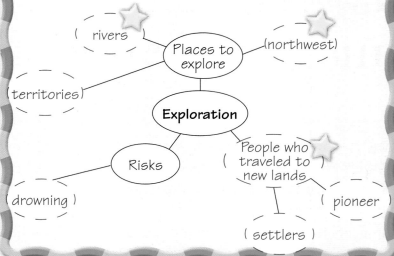

Monitor Progress

Check Vocabulary

If... students suggest words or categories that are not related to the concept,	**then**... review the words and categories on the Concept Web and discuss how they relate to the lesson concept.

SUCCESS PREDICTOR

Speaking and Viewing

SPEAKING

Introduction

SET-UP Have students imagine there is an American Dogs Hall of Fame that honors courageous and brave canines. Have them introduce the dog Seaman as a distinguished new member to this Hall of Fame.

TOPICS Ask students to review *Lewis and Clark and Me* to recall what Seaman was like—his physical characteristics, talents, and personality. Remind them their introductions should explain both who Seaman was and why he is a good choice for the Hall of Fame. Suggest they use strong adjectives to strengthen their descriptions.

AUDIENCE Remind speakers their audience wants to be entertained as well as informed. Instruct them to adjust the loudness of their voices with the back row of the audience in mind.

Delivery Tips
- Make a connection with your audience by looking directly at them.
- Vary your tone of voice.
- Speak with feeling to help convince the audience to share your opinions.
- Consider whether formal or informal language is appropriate for your speech.

VIEWING

Analyze an Illustration

Using library resources, display an illustration of an art print depicting Lewis and Clark's journey or another scene from the old American West. Have students examine the picture. Then ask students to answer the following questions:

1. **What is the setting or scene of the picture?**
2. **What details are most noticeable in the picture and why do you think the artist focused on them?**
3. **What is the artist trying to tell you about this moment in American history?**

(Responses will vary. Ask students to cite details to support their answers.)

ELL

Support Vocabulary Use the following to review and extend vocabulary and to explore lesson concepts further:
- ELL Poster 2, Days 3–5 instruction
- Vocabulary Activities and Word Cards in ELL Teaching Guide, pp. 10–11.

Assessment For information on assessing students' speaking and viewing, see the ELL and Transition Handbook.

Grammar   **Imperative and Exclamatory Sentences**

OBJECTIVES

- Define and identify imperative and exclamatory sentences.
- Distinguish between exclamatory sentences and interjections.
- Use imperative and exclamatory sentences correctly in writing.
- Become familiar with imperative and exclamatory sentence assessment on high-stakes tests.

Monitor Progress

Grammar

If... students have diffculty identifying imperative and exclamatory sentences,	**then...** provide additional instruction and practice in The Grammar and Writing Book pp. 56–59.

DAILY FIX-IT

This week use Daily Fix-It Transparency 2.

Spiral REVIEW

Grammar Support See the Grammar Transition lessons in the ELL and Transition Handbook.

▲ **The Grammar and Writing Book** For more instruction and practice, use pp. 56–59.

DAY 1   Teach and Model

DAILY FIX-IT

1. A big dog like seaman might frightin some people. *(Seaman; frighten)*

2. Do you think, he will bite me. *(think he; me?)*

READING-GRAMMAR CONNECTION

Write the following sentences:

Fetch us a squirrel.

This is an amazing dog!

Explain that the first example is an **imperative sentence**. It gives a command or makes a request and usually begins with a verb. The second example is an **exclamatory sentence**. It shows strong feeling or surprise and ends with an exclamation mark.

Display Grammar Transparency 2. Read aloud the definitions and sample sentences. Work through the items.

Imperative and Exclamatory Sentences

An **imperative sentence** gives a command or makes a request. It usually begins with a verb and ends with a period. The subject *(you)* is not shown. An **exclamatory sentence** shows strong feeling or surprise. It ends with an exclamation mark. An **interjection** also shows strong feeling and ends with an exclamation mark. An interjection is a word or group of words, not a complete sentence.

Imperative Sentence	Steer the boat upstream.
Exclamatory Sentences	This is an enormous river! How wide the river is!
Interjection	Amazing!

Directions Write *E* if the sentence is exclamatory. Write *I* if the sentence is imperative.

1. Keep your eyes open for rocks. — I
2. Give me the oar. — I
3. We're going to overturn! — E
4. Wow! That was a very close call! — E
5. Make sure that doesn't happen again. — I

Directions Write the correct end punctuation for each sentence. Then write *E* if the sentence is exclamatory and *I* if it is imperative.

6. Please catch some fish for supper — I
7. I can't believe how swift the current is — E
8. Use this pole for a fishing rod — I
9. I'm incredibly hungry — E
10. What a lot of fish you caught — E

Unit 1 Lewis and Clark and Me   Grammar **2**

▲ **Grammar Transparency** 2

DAY 2   Develop the Concept

DAILY FIX-IT

3. What a enormous country this is. *(an; is!)*

4. The Mississippi River. Is one of the biggest river in the world. *(River is; rivers)*

GUIDED PRACTICE

Review the concept of imperative and exclamatory sentences. Add the concept of interjections.

- An **imperative sentence** gives a command or makes a request.
- An **exclamatory sentence** shows strong feeling or surprise. It ends with an exclamation mark.
- An **interjection** also shows strong feeling or surprise, but it is not a complete sentence.

HOMEWORK Grammar and Writing Practice Book p. 5. Work through the first two items with the class.

Imperative and Exclamatory Sentences

An **imperative sentence** gives a command or makes a request. It usually begins with a verb and ends with a period. The subject (you) is not shown. An **exclamatory sentence** shows strong feeling or surprise. It ends with an exclamation mark. An **interjection** also shows strong feeling and ends with an exclamation mark. An interjection is a word or group of words, not a complete sentence.

Imperative Sentence	Lie down and stay.
Exclamatory Sentences	That is a gorgeous dog! What big paws he has!
Interjections	Wow! Ouch! Hurray! Oh, no!

Directions Read each sentence. Write *C* if the end punctuation is correct. Write *NC* if the end punctuation is not correct.

1. Show me your book about Lewis and Clark. — C
2. What an incredible journey they took. — NC
3. Please read me the paper you wrote about their expedition! — NC
4. That dog was amazing! — C
5. I can't believe the number of squirrels it caught. — NC

Directions Write a word or phrase that will make these sentences the kind named in ( ). **Possible answers:**

6. **Show** me the Missouri River on the map. (imperative)
7. **What** a long river it is! (exclamatory)
8. **Explain** why Lewis and Clark went on their expedition. (imperative)
9. **How** proud they must have been when they finished! (exclamatory)
10. **Don't** forget to finish reading your book on Lewis and Clark. (imperative)

School-Home CONNECTION   **Home Activity** Your child learned about imperative and exclamatory sentences. With your child, listen to a favorite television show and have your child identify examples of imperative and exclamatory sentences.

▲ **Grammar and Writing Practice Book** p. 5

DAY 3 Apply to Writing

5. The river was a heighway for Lewis and clark. *(highway; Clark)*

6. Tell me more about why they made her expedition? *(their; expedition.)*

MAKE YOUR WRITING EXCITING

Point out that commands and exclamations can give narrative writing a strong voice and an exciting style.

- Have students review something they have written to see if they can improve it by adding imperative and exclamatory sentences.

HOMEWORK Grammar and Writing Practice Book p. 6.

Imperative and Exclamatory Sentences

Directions Write an imperative sentence and an exclamatory sentence for each event.

1. going on a river trip **Possible answers:**
   imperative: **Get into the boat.**

   exclamatory: **The water is really cold!**

2. meeting a dog
   imperative: **Tell her not to jump up.**

   exclamatory: **What soft ears she has!**

3. looking at a map of the United States
   imperative: **Show me the route of Lewis and Clark.**

   exclamatory: **They went a long way!**

Directions Imagine that you are on a trip and you are writing a letter to a friend. Write one imperative sentence and one exclamatory sentence that you might include in the letter.

4. imperative: **Please write to me soon.**

5. exclamatory: **Bugs bit me all night!**

 Home Activity Your child learned how to use imperative and exclamatory sentences in writing. Have your child write something he or she was told to do that day as an imperative sentence. Ask your child what was exciting or interesting about the day. Have him or her write that as an exclamatory sentence.

▲ **Grammar and Writing Practice Book** p. 6

DAY 4 Test Preparation

7. Sacagawea is remembered because she help Lewis and Clark! *(helped; Clark.)*

8. She was only 16 years old, her husband was a French trader *(old. Her; trader.)*

STANDARDIZED TEST PREP

Test Tip

Remember that an imperative sentence generally begins with a verb.

Tell your dog to stay.

Sometimes, however, another word or phrase may come first.

Please *tell* your dog to stay.

A good rule to remember is "When the subject is an unspoken *you*, the sentence is imperative."

HOMEWORK Grammar and Writing Practice Book p. 7.

Imperative and Exclamatory Sentences

Directions For each item, mark the letter of the answer that best completes the type of sentence in ( ).

1. I love the way this story is told by ___ (exclamatory)
   A a dog.
   B a dog?
   C a dog.
   D a dog!

2. ___ the picture of Seaman swimming. (imperative)
   A Is that
   B I like
   C Show me
   D What is

3. What an incredible adventure ___ (exclamatory)
   A that was!
   B will we have.
   C would you like to go on?
   D is that?

4. ___ that page again. (imperative)
   A Are we reading
   B Please read
   C Will you read
   D How exciting to read

Directions For each item, mark the letter of the imperative or exclamatory sentence that is correctly written.

5. A Fetch, Seaman?
   B Please sell me your dog!
   C Tell me his name.
   D That's a great trick

6. A Go get those squirrels
   B Bring them back to the boat.
   C Wow! They taste wonderful.
   D Give the dog some?

7. A Tell me about Sacagawea!
   B She was incredibly young!
   C Show me her picture!
   D That's an amazing story?

8. **A** Explain who York was.
   B It's terrible that he was a slave?
   C What a brave man he was.
   D Find out more about him!

 Home Activity Your child prepared for taking tests on imperative and exclamatory sentences. Ask your child to write an example of each kind of sentence and to explain what makes it imperative or exclamatory.

▲ **Grammar and Writing Practice Book** p. 7

DAY 5 Cumulative Review

9. Its funny to read a story telled by a dog. *(It's; told)*

10. Ask the librarian for more books about the Lewis an Clark expedition? *(and; expedition.)*

ADDITIONAL PRACTICE

Assign pp. 56–59 in The Grammar and Writing Book.

EXTRA PRACTICE Grammar and Writing Practice Book p. 123.

ASSESSMENT

CUMULATIVE REVIEW Grammar and Writing Practice Book p. 8.

Imperative and Exclamatory Sentences

Directions Write *E* if the sentence is exclamatory. Write *I* if the sentence is imperative.

1. Don't let the dog jump into the river. **I**
2. Lend me a hand with this boat. **I**
3. We've got to save the missing people! **E**
4. Make sure you keep away from the shore. **I**
5. Seaman is a hero! **E**

Directions Make each word group into an imperative or exclamatory sentence by writing it with correct capitalization and punctuation. Identify imperative sentences with *I* and exclamatory sentences with *E*.

6. make room in the boat
   Make room in the boat. I

7. what a crowd there was on the wharf
   What a crowd there was on the wharf! E

8. ask sacagawea which of these plants we should eat
   Ask Sacagawea which of these plants we should eat. I

9. those plants will poison you
   Those plants will poison you! E

10. give me that dog for these beaver skins
    Give me that dog for these beaver skins. I

Directions Write the type of sentence named in ( ) for each event.

11. leading a camping trip (imperative) **Possible answers:**
    Stay together in the woods.

12. sailing on the Missouri River (exclamation)
    I've never seen such a wide river!

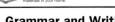 **Home Activity** Your child reviewed imperative and exclamatory sentences. Have your child find examples of imperative and exclamatory sentences in magazines, instructions, or other printed materials in your home.

▲ **Grammar and Writing Practice Book** p. 8

Writing Workshop   Journal Entry

OBJECTIVES

- Identify qualities of a journal entry.
- Write a journal entry with effective transitions.
- Focus on sentences.
- Use a rubric.

Genre Journal Entry
Writer's Craft Transitions
Writing Trait Sentences

Sentences Have language learners read their sentences aloud to check rhythm, completeness, and sense. Point out opportunities to change a declarative sentence to another type, or to vary sentence beginnings.

Writing Traits

FOCUS/IDEAS Strong supporting details help the reader experience the camping trip.

ORGANIZATION/PARAGRAPHS The entry describes the day in chronological order, using transitions to move through the events.

VOICE Writing is engaging and lively. The writer's feelings come through clearly.

WORD CHOICE The writer uses precise nouns to define the experience (*oatmeal, marshmallows*) and a strong interjection (*Yummy!*).

SENTENCES Use of interrogative and exclamatory sentences, including an interjection, catch the reader's interest.

CONVENTIONS There is excellent control and accuracy, including effective use of an exclamatory sentence.

DAY 1   Model the Trait

READING-WRITING CONNECTION

- *Lewis and Clark and Me* includes varied sentences, which keep the selection interesting.
- Transition words and phrases help link sentences and ideas together.
- Students will write a **journal entry** using a variety of sentences and smooth transitions.

MODEL SENTENCES Discuss Writing Transparency 2A. Then discuss the model and the writing trait of sentences.

 Think Aloud I see variety to the sentences in this journal entry. The writer ends the first paragraph by asking the reader a question: "Why does food taste so good when you're camping?" The writer also emphasizes the point with an exclamation, "Yummy!" These different kinds of sentences keep the writing interesting.

Journal Entry

A **journal entry** describes your thoughts and experiences during a day in your life. It is part of a journal, recording daily events over a period of weeks, months, or years.

Day 2 on the River

Writer describes daily events.
Dad got up early this morning and had the water boiling before I was awake. I was really stiff and a little cold from sleeping on the ground. The oatmeal was delicious. Why does food taste so good when you're camping?

Transition words link events.
Paddling was easy until we got to a beaver dam. Then we had to haul the canoe through the woods to get around it. Dad says that's called portaging.

Writer shows feelings.
I could barely move when we got to camp this evening. Now that we've had supper, I'm feeling better. I'm sitting on the beach in the last light. The sunset was incredible! Later, we're going to roast marshmallows over a campfire. Yummy!

Unit 1 Lewis and Clark and Me   Writing Model **2A**

▲ **Writing Transparency** 2A

DAY 2   Improve Writing

WRITER'S CRAFT
Transitions

Display Writing Transparency 2B. Read the directions and work together to practice using transitions.

 Think Aloud **TRANSITIONS** Tomorrow we will be writing a journal entry about a special day. To move from one idea to the next, we will use transitional words and phrases. If I just list my activities, the reader won't know what happened when. I'll use words like *first, next, then,* and *finally* to explain the sequence of my special day.

GUIDED WRITING Invite students to use some of the other transitional words or phrases listed at the top of the transparency in sentences of their own.

Transitions

Transitions are words or phrases that show a relationship between events or ideas. They help the reader by linking sentences or paragraphs. Examples of three common types of transitions are shown below.
  Time first, then, next, before, finally, at last, later, meanwhile, afterward
  Place above, below, beside, here, next to, near, there, opposite
  Comparison and Contrast however, but, too, and, on the other hand, like

Directions Choose a transition word or phrase from the box to complete the story. Write your answers on the lines below. Use each word or phrase only once. Capitalize words that begin sentences.

| afterward | first | finally | next to | however | at last | opposite | then |

Seaman, the Newfoundland dog, could hardly believe his eyes. **(1)** Hundreds of squirrels were swimming ___ the boat in the river. **(2)** They were heading for the ___ bank. Seaman wanted to catch the squirrels. **(3)** ___ his master was talking to some of the men. Seaman barked loudly. **(4)** ___ his master turned around and saw the squirrels.

"Go get them, Seaman," he said.

Seaman sprang off the boat into the river. **(5)** ___ he caught a squirrel. **(6)** ___ he brought it back to the boat in triumph. He kept on diving and bringing back squirrels. **(7)** ___ there was a pile of squirrels on the boat. **(8)** ___ the men fried the squirrels. They were delicious! **Possible answers:**

1. **next to**
2. **opposite**
3. **However,**
4. **At last** *or* **Finally**
5. **First**
6. **Then**
7. **Finally** *or* **At last**
8. **Afterward**

Unit 1 Lewis and Clark and Me   Writer's Craft **2B**

▲ **Writing Transparency** 2B

DAY 3 Prewrite and Draft

READ THE WRITING PROMPT

on page 61 in the Student Edition.

In Lewis and Clark and Me, *Seaman tells about two memorable days of the expedition.*

Think about a memorable day in your own life.

Now write a journal entry describing what happened on that special day.

Writing Test Tips

- Focus on two or three important or interesting events. Don't try to say everything about your day.
- Reflect on how events made you feel. Writing a journal is like talking to yourself!
- Vary your sentences to make your writing exciting and keep your readers interested.

GETTING STARTED Students can do any of the following:

- Make a list of the things that happened on the day they are describing.
- Tell the story of the day aloud to a partner.
- Ask themselves how events made them feel or what they learned from them.
- Use sentence variety to make their writing interesting.

DAY 4 Draft and Revise

EDITING/REVISING CHECKLIST

☑ Are events and ideas connected with transitional words or phrases?

☑ Do I explain how I feel about the day's events?

☑ Have I used any exclamatory sentences?

☑ Are words with the long *a* and *i* sounds spelled correctly?

See *The Grammar and Writing Book,* pp. 56–61.

Revising Tips

Sentences

- Support sentence variety by using declarative, interrogative, and exclamatory sentences.
- Vary sentence beginnings.
- Use transitions to make sentences flow smoothly.

PUBLISHING Have students contribute to a classroom anthology of journal entries. Students may wish to revise their work later.

ASSESSMENT Use the scoring rubric to evaluate students' work.

DAY 5 Connect to Unit Writing

Personal Narrative	
Week 1	Memoir 39g–39h
Week 2	Journal Entry 65g–65h
Week 3	Postcard 87g–87h
Week 4	E-mail Invitation 111g–111h
Week 5	Narrative Writing 133g–133h

PREVIEW THE UNIT PROMPT

Write a personal narrative about a time that you were a newcomer to a place or situation (a school, club, team, or neighborhood). Explain how you felt and what you found challenging or exciting.

APPLY

- A personal narrative is a story about an interesting experience or event in the storyteller's life.
- Journal entries describe the narrator's day-to-day life and thoughts.

Writing Trait Rubric

	4	3	2	1
Sentences	Good variety of sentence lengths and structures; uses transitions	Some variety of sentence lengths and structures; some transitions	Sentences generally lacking in fluency and variety; few transitions	Sentences choppy and dull; no transitions
	Journal entry flows smoothly	Journal entry generally flows smoothly	Inconsistent flow to journal entry	Journal entry boring or confusing with ineffective sentences

Spelling & Phonics Long *a* and *i*

Generalization

Connect to Phonics Long *a* is sometimes spelled *ai, eigh,* or *ay: braid, weigh, spray.* Long *i* is sometimes spelled *igh: sigh.* The letter combinations *ai, eigh,* and *ay* usually stand for the long *a* sound. The letter combination *igh* usually stands for the long *i* sound.

Spelling Words

1. sigh	11. slight
2. right*	12. thigh
3. weigh*	13. tight*
4. eight	14. raisin
5. detail	15. trait
6. height	16. highway
7. spray	17. frighten
8. braid	18. dismay
9. bait	19. freight
10. grain*	20. sleigh

Challenge Words

21. eighteen	24. daylight
22. mayonnaise	25. twilight
23. campaign	

*Word from the selection

Spelling/Phonics Support See the ELL and Transition Handbook for spelling support.

DAY 1 Pretest and Sort

PRETEST

Use the Dictation Sentences from Day 5 to administer the pretest. Read the word, read the sentence, and then read the word again. Guide students in self-correcting their pretests and correcting any misspellings.

Monitor Progress

Spelling

If... students misspell more than 5 pretest words,	**then...** use words 1–10 for Strategic Intervention.
If... students misspell 1–5 pretest words,	**then...** use words 1–20 for On-Level practice.
If... students correctly spell all pretest words,	**then...** use words 1–25 for Advanced Learners.

HOMEWORK Spelling Practice Book, p. 5.

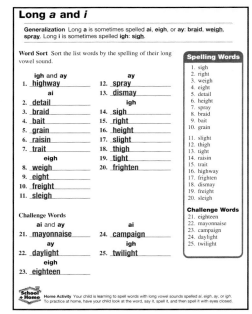

▲ **Spelling Practice Book** p. 5

DAY 2 Think and Practice

TEACH

The long *a* and long *i* sounds can be spelled in different ways. Write *highway* on the board. Underline the letters *igh* and *ay.* Say *highway* and point out that the letters *igh* spell the long *i* sound and the letters *ay* spell the long *a* sound. Guide students in finding the letters that stand for the long *a* sound in *grain* and *sleigh.*

hi<u>gh</u>w<u>ay</u>

MATCH SOUNDS AND SPELLINGS
Say and spell a list word. Have students name other list words that have the same long vowel spelling pattern.

HOMEWORK Spelling Practice Book, p. 6.

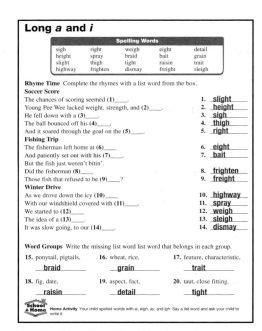

▲ **Spelling Practice Book** p. 6

DAY 3 — Connect to Writing

WRITE A JOURNAL ENTRY

Ask students to use at least five spelling words to write a journal entry.

Frequently Misspelled Words

vacation   always

might

These words may seem easy to spell, but they are often misspelled by fourth-graders. Alert students to these frequently misspelled words. Point out that *vacation* ends with *–tion*, *always* is one word, and *might* has the *igh* spelling pattern.

HOMEWORK Spelling Practice Book, p. 7.

Long a and i

Proofread Directions Read the following directions for making a wood puppet. Circle five misspelled words and write them correctly on the lines. Change the sentence fragments to a complete sentence and write the sentence.

Make sure you all ways work carefully with tools.
Measure wood for the hight you want.
Sand the wood in the direction of the grain.
Cut ate pieces for jointed arms and legs.
Spray on paint.
Braid some wool for hair.
Glue the hair on tite.
Add detale.
Make sure the puppet. Works with right and left hands.

		Spelling Words	
sigh	slight
right	thigh
weigh	tight
eight	raisin
detail	trait
height	highway
spray	frighten
braid	dismay
bait	freight
grain	sleigh

Frequently Misspelled Words
vacation
always
might

1. always   2. height
3. eight   4. tight
5. detail   6. Make sure the puppet works with right and left hands.

Finish the Sentences Circle the underlined list word that is spelled correctly. Write the word.

7. The freight/rate train has over 150 cars.   7. freight
8. This kind of raysin/raisin has no seeds.   8. raisin
9. The horses pulled the sleigh/slay.   9. sleigh
10. The thy/thigh bone is the strongest bone in the body. 10. thigh
11. Your answer is rite/right.   11. right
12. Generosity is a good freight/trait to have. 12. trait
13. "I forgot my homework," he said in dismay/dismeigh. 13. dismay
14. "Bring it in tomorrow," his teacher said with a sy/sigh. 14. sigh

School + Home **Home Activity** Your child identified misspelled words with ai, eigh, ay, and igh. Take turns quizzing each other on the spelling words.

▲ **Spelling Practice Book** p. 7

DAY 4 — Review

REVIEW LONG *a* AND LONG *i*

Have students write the spelling words on cards and cut the words apart, isolating the letters that spell the long vowel sound. Then have students mix up the cards and re-assemble the words.

Spelling Strategy Problem Parts

We all have words that are hard for us to spell.

Step 1: Ask yourself: Which part of the word gives me a problem?

Step 2: Underline your problem part.

Step 3: Picture the word. Focus on the problem part.

HOMEWORK Spelling Practice Book, p. 8.

Long a and i

		Spelling Words		
sigh	right	weigh	eight	detail
height	spray	braid	bait	grain
slight	thigh	tight	raisin	trait
highway	frighten	dismay	freight	sleigh

Analogies Write the list word that best completes the sentence.

1. *Ground* is to *floor* as *scare* is to ___.   1. frighten
2. *Cold* is to *cool* as *plait* is to ___.   2. braid
3. *Photo* is to *picture* as *moan* is to ___.   3. sigh
4. *Flat* is to *even* as *sled* is to ___.   4. sleigh
5. *Cup* is to *mug* as *small* is to ___.   5. slight
6. *Auto* is to *car* as *load* is to ___.   6. freight
7. *Phone* is to *call* as *disappointment* is to ___. 7. dismay

Word Search There are nine list words hidden in the puzzle. Circle and write each word you find.

D E T A I L W N R N Z I
G A R T R F K I I A I B
M A W H S Z A G N B V
T F Q Q T G C R H S E
M C I A O D I G T P J Q
Z O K V M B E R D B O
P F M A R U Q A H Y U T
J H O W T A V G H Q M X
U X O H H G I E W B E G
G C C G U E Z S E E S Z
H X P I H F A U I C R V
Q P A H O M K D A N C A

8. detail
9. eight
10. grain
11. right
12. highway
13. raisin
14. weigh
15. height
16. spray

School + Home **Home Activity** Your child has learned to read, write, and spell words with these spelling patterns: ai, eigh, ay, and igh. Take turns saying and spelling the list words.

8 Unit 1 Week 2 **Day 4**   **Spelling Practice Book**

▲ **Spelling Practice Book** p. 8

DAY 5 — Posttest

DICTATION SENTENCES

1. People sigh when they are sad.
2. Chad got all the answers right.
3. The scale shows how much you weigh.
4. One week is less than eight days.
5. Tell every detail of the story.
6. The wall's height is five feet.
7. Will you spray some water on the plants?
8. Ann wears her hair in a braid.
9. Bring your fishing pole and some bait.
10. The cow ate the grain.
11. There is a slight change of plans.
12. The thigh is part of the leg.
13. My clothes are too tight.
14. A dried grape is a raisin.
15. Kindness is a good trait.
16. Take the highway to the last exit.
17. Did the big dog frighten you?
18. To our dismay, we lost the game.
19. Trucks carry freight across the country.
20. The sleigh moved over the snow.

CHALLENGE

21. My brother is eighteen years old.
22. Put some mayonnaise on the sandwich.
23. The mayor ran a good campaign.
24. We left before daylight.
25. Fireflies come out at twilight.

OBJECTIVES

- Formulate an inquiry question that is connected to this week's lesson focus.
- Effectively and efficiently find, evaluate, and communicate information related to an inquiry question using electronic sources.

New Literacies	
Day 1	**Identify Questions**
Day 2	**Navigate/Search**
Day 3	**Analyze**
Day 4	**Synthesize**
Day 5	**Communicate**

NEW LITERACIES

Internet Inquiry Activity

EXPLORE LEWIS AND CLARK'S DISCOVERIES

Use the following 5-day plan to help students conduct this week's Internet inquiry activity on the discoveries Lewis and Clark made on their journey. Remind students to follow classroom rules when using the Internet.

DAY 1

Identify Questions Discuss the lesson focus question: *What did Lewis and Clark learn on their journey?* Ask students to think of questions they have about what Lewis and Clark learned. Have individuals, pairs, or small groups write an inquiry question they want to answer, such as: *What did they learn from Native American tribes they encountered?*

DAY 2

Navigate/Search Have students begin a simple Internet search using a student-friendly search engine. Discuss how to choose the best keywords related to students' inquiry questions. Explain keywords should be specific and relate directly to their topic. They can use trial and error with different keywords to narrow or expand their search to find relevant Web sites.

DAY 3

Analyze Have students explore the Web sites they identified on Day 2. Model ways students can analyze a site for credibility, reliability, and usefulness. For example, a museum or a government site is usually reliable, while a site created by an individual might not be accurate. Tell students to scan the best sites for information that helps answer their inquiry questions. They can print and highlight relevant information, if allowed, or take notes about it.

DAY 4

Synthesize Have students synthesize information from Day 3. Encourage students to think about the best way to organize the information they gathered.

DAY 5

Communicate Have students share their inquiry results. They may want to create a table in a word processing or spreadsheet program to list information that answers their inquiry question. For example, they could list information about different tribes Lewis and Clark encountered on their journey west.

RESEARCH/STUDY SKILLS
Skim and Scan

TEACH

Have students imagine they are writing a research report on Lewis and Clark's interactions with Native Americans. They have found several articles that might be helpful, but they don't have time to read them all. Explain that good researchers **skim** and **scan** a text to decide if it is useful.

- You may skim text to find the main ideas. When you skim, you read very quickly, paying most attention to these features:

  first and last paragraphs

  headings and subheadings

  summaries

  the first sentence of each paragraph.

- You may **scan** text to find answers to specific questions you have. When you scan, you move your eyes quickly down a page looking for specific words or phrases, such as **names, numbers,** or **dates.**

Have students skim a passage from a social studies or science textbook. After a few minutes, ask: **What main topics does this text cover?**

Then have students scan the passage to find five facts about specific people, places, dates, or ideas included in it. After a few minutes, ask: **What did you do to find the information quickly?**

ASSESS

Observe students as they work to check whether they can find information quickly and easily. Ask them to point out text features or words they used to find main ideas or to locate specific information to answer questions.

For more practice or to assess students, use Practice Book pp. 19–20.

Skim and Scan

To **scan** is to move one's eyes quickly down the page, seeking specific words and phrases. Scanning is used to find out if a resource will answer a reader's questions. Once a reader has scanned a document, he or she might go back and skim it.

To **skim** a document is to read the first and last paragraphs as well as using headings and other organizers as you move down the page. Skimming is used to quickly identify the main idea. You might also read the first sentence of each paragraph.

Directions Scan the passage to answer the questions below.

> **School's largest yard sale.** Northside School will hold its largest yard sale ever on Saturday, March 16. It will be located on the soccer field from 9 a.m. until 4 p.m. **Raising money for a class field trip.** The school is holding the sale to collect money for a class field trip to study the route taken by Lewis and Clarke. This is a cross-country trip, and the students need money for transportation, food, and lodging.
>
> **Toys, clothing, and furniture for sale.** Students' families will set up booths on the field. We've heard reports that many of the items for sale will be toys, games, clothes, furniture, and antiques. **Come early for the best selection.** It is best to arrive at the sale early to have the best pick of items. But, if you are not an early bird, you might find some half-price bargains at the end of the day.

1. When you scan this passage, what helps you find specific information?
   the titles of the paragraphs
2. In which paragraph would you find out if antiques will be for sale?
   the third paragraph
3. In which paragraph would you find out why the yard sale is being held?
   the second paragraph
4. In which paragraph would you find out the best time to go to the sale?
   the last paragraph
5. Can you find out about the prices of items by scanning this passage?
   no; None of the paragraph titles mentions prices.

▲ **Practice Book** p. 19

Directions Skim this letter to answer the questions below.

> Dear Mr. Lewis and Mr. Clark,
> I am a student at Gardner School in Portland, Oregon. My class is getting ready for a field trip that will cover part of the route you took to the Pacific Ocean.
> I can hardly imagine a two-year journey across half of the country without a car, train, or airplane. I think I would have gotten tired and lonely. I would have missed my home and family.
> But it must have been an amazing trip. Were you excited to see new landscapes? Were the people who you met along the way different from what you expected?
>
> Did you learn a lot from them? I think I would have liked traveling on horseback and in canoes.
> I wonder, were you ever scared? Did you worry about getting lost or getting sick? Were the wild animals frightening? You didn't have a map, although you had about 40 people traveling with you.
> I can't wait to see the route you took with my own eyes!
> Sincerely,
> Justin

6. What is a good way to skim this letter?
   Possible answer: Read the first sentence of each paragraph.
7. What is the topic of this letter?
   a student's upcoming field trip
8. Is the letter about the modern-day city of Portland? How can you tell?
   No; Only the first paragraph mentions Portland.
9. Does the letter indicate if Justin is impressed by Lewis and Clark's journey? How can you tell?
   Yes; The first sentence of the third paragraph uses "amazing."
10. Is Justin excited about the trip? What in the letter gave you that impression?
    Yes; The student says he "can't wait."

School Home **Home Activity** Your child learned about scanning and skimming to help find a main idea or information. Look at a newspaper or magazine with your child and have him or her skim it to find the main idea. Then ask your child to scan it for a particular piece of information.

▲ **Practice Book** p. 20

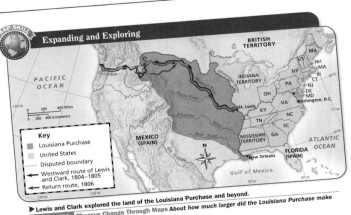

► Lewis and Clark explored the land of the Louisiana Purchase and beyond.
MAP SKILL **Observe Change Through Maps** *About how much larger did the Louisiana Purchase make the United States?*

Jefferson as President

After Washington left office, John Adams of Massachusetts served one term. But by 1801, a Virginian was once again President. Thomas Jefferson served two terms. During the Revolutionary War,

successes. In 1803, the United States bought a huge area of land from France. It stretched from the Mississippi River to the Rocky Mountains.

In 1804, Jefferson sent an expedition overland to the Pacific coast. It was led by two Virginians, **Meriwether Lewis** and **William Clark.**

Assessment Checkpoints *for the Week*

Selection Assessment

Use pp. 5–8 of Selection Tests to check:

 Selection Understanding

  **Comprehension Skill** *Authors' Purpose*

 Selection Vocabulary

docks	scent
migrating	wharf
scan	yearned

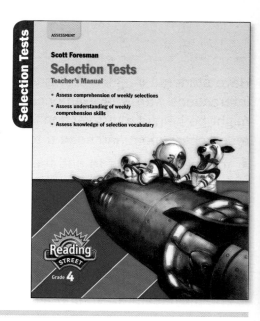

ASSESSMENT

Scott Foresman
Selection Tests
Teacher's Manual

- Assess comprehension of weekly selections
- Assess understanding of weekly comprehension skills
- Assess knowledge of selection vocabulary

Reading STREET Grade 4

Leveled Assessment

- On-Level
- Strategic Intervention
- Advanced

Use pp. 7–12 of **Fresh Reads for Differentiated Test Practice** to check:

  Comprehension Skill *Authors' Purpose*

 REVIEW Comprehension Skill
Cause and Effect

 Fluency *Words Correct Per Minute*

ASSESSMENT Teacher's Manual

Scott Foresman
Fresh Reads
for Differentiated Test Practice

Leveled passages—strategic intervention, on-level, and advanced—for

- Fluency checks
- Practice and application of weekly comprehension skills
- Answer key for all practice pages

Reading STREET Grade 4

Managing Assessment

Use Assessment Handbook for:

 Observation Checklists

Record-Keeping Forms

Portfolio Assessment

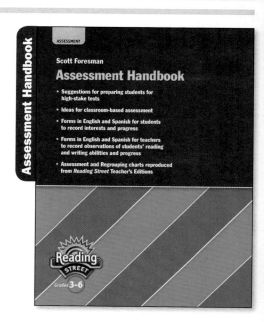

ASSESSMENT

Scott Foresman
Assessment Handbook

- Suggestions for preparing students for high-stake tests
- Ideas for classroom-based assessment
- Forms in English and Spanish for students to record interests and progress
- Forms in English and Spanish for teachers to record observations of students' reading and writing abilities and progress
- Assessment and Regrouping charts reproduced from *Reading Street* Teacher's Editions

Reading STREET Grades 3–6

Oregon

Planning Guide for Common Curriculum Goals

Grandfather's Journey

Reading Street Teacher's Edition pages	Grade 4 Oregon Grade-Level Standards for English/Language Arts
Oral Language **Speaking/Listening** Build Concept Vocabulary: 66l, 77, 81, 87c Read Aloud: 66m	**EL.04.RE.10** Develop vocabulary by listening to and discussing both familiar and conceptually challenging selections read aloud across the subject areas. **EL.04.SL.04** Use a variety of descriptive words that help to convey a clear message.
Word Work Long e and o: 87i–87j	**EL.04.WR.15** Spell correctly: syllables (word parts each containing a vowel sound, such as *sur-prise* or *e-col-o-gy*).
Reading **Comprehension** Sequence: 66–67, 70–81, 84–87, 87b Graphic Organizers: 66–67, 70–81 **Vocabulary** Lesson Vocabulary: 68b, 77, 81 Dictionary/Glossary: 68–69, 79, 87c **Fluency** Model Tempo and Rate: 66l–66m, 87a **Self-Selected Reading:** LR19–27, TR16–17 **Literature** Genre—Historical Fiction: 70 Reader Response: 82	**EL.04.RE.01** Read aloud grade-level narrative text and informational text fluently and accurately with effective pacing, intonation, and expression. **EL.04.RE.05** Demonstrate listening comprehension of more complex text through class and/or small group interpretive discussions across the subject areas. **EL.04.RE.17** Locate information in titles, tables of contents, chapter headings, illustrations, captions, glossaries, indexes, graphs, charts, diagrams, and tables to aid understanding of grade-level text. **EL.04.LI.01** Listen to text and read text to make connections and respond to a wide variety of significant works of literature, including poetry, fiction, non-fiction, and drama, from a variety of cultures and time periods that enhance the study of other subjects. **EL.04.LI.03** Identify and/or summarize sequence of events, main ideas, and supporting details in literary selections.
Language Arts **Writing** Postcard: 87g–87h **Six-Trait Writing** Focus/Ideas: 83, 87g–87h **Grammar, Usage, and Mechanics** Subjects and Predicates: 87e–87f **Research/Study** Electronic Media: 87l **Technology** New Literacies: 87k	**EL.04.WR.23** Write personal narratives: include ideas, observations, or memories of an event or experience. **EL.04.WR.25** Write informational reports: use more than one source of information, including speakers, books, newspapers, other media sources, and online information.
Unit Skills **Writing** Personal Narrative: WA2–9 **Poetry:** 134–137 **Project/Wrap-Up:** 138–139	**EL.04.WR.23** Write personal narratives: include ideas, observations, or memories of an event or experience; provide a context to allow the reader to imagine the world of the event or experience; use concrete sensory details; provide insight into why the selected event or experience is memorable.

This Week's Leveled Readers

Intensive Intervention

SCOTT FORESMAN

SiDEWALKS

Intensive Intervention for Tier 3 Students

Historical Fiction

Below-Level

EL.04.RE.19 Use structural features found in informational text (e.g., headings and sub-headings) to strengthen comprehension.
EL.04.LI.03 Identify and/or summarize sequence of events, main ideas, and supporting details in literary selections.

Nonfiction

On-Level

EL.04.RE.25 Determine the author's purpose, and relate it to details in the text.
EL.04.LI.03 Identify and/or summarize sequence of events, main ideas, and supporting details in literary selections.

Fiction

Advanced

EL.04.LI.03 Identify and/or summarize sequence of events, main ideas, and supporting details in literary selections.
EL.04.LI.04 Identify the main problem or conflict of the plot, and explain how it is resolved.

Content-Area Content Standards and Benchmarks in This Lesson

Science

SC.05.LS.04.02 Recognize that organisms are produced by living organisms of similar kind, and do not appear spontaneously from inanimate materials. (Previews Grade 5 Benchmark)

SC.05.LS.05 Describe the relationship between characteristics of specific habitats and the organisms that live there. (Previews Grade 5 Benchmark)

SC.05.LS.05.05 Describe the living and nonliving resources in a specific habitat and the adaptations of organisms to that habitat. (Previews Grade 5 Benchmark)

SC.05.LS.06 Describe how adaptations help a species survive. (Previews Grade 5 Benchmark)

Social Studies

SS.05.GE.04 Identify physical and human characteristics of regions in the United States and the processes that have shaped them. (Previews Grade 5 Benchmark)

SS.05.GE.05 Identify patterns of migration and cultural interaction in the United States. (Previews Grade 5 Benchmark)

SS.05.GE.05.02 Explain how migrations affect the culture of emigrants and native populations. (Previews Grade 5 Benchmark)

Oregon!

A FAMOUS OREGONIAN
Jesse Applegate

Jesse Applegate (1811–1888) was an American pioneer who traveled to Oregon. Applegate was born in Kentucky and began the westward move by traveling with his family to Missouri. They stayed there for more than twenty years before joining the "great emigration" along the Oregon Trail. There were more than nine hundred people on the trek, which Applegate later described in his book, *Day with the Cow Column in 1843.* Applegate served as a leader on the journey and was elected to the legislative committee of Oregon's provisional government.

Students can . . .
Shade in the Oregon Trail between Missouri and Oregon on an outline map of the United States.

A SPECIAL OREGON PLACE
Klamath Mountains

The Klamath Mountains are part of the Pacific mountain system. Named for the Klamath Native Americans, the mountains begin south of the Willamette Valley foothills and continue south 250 miles to California. The Klamath River is one of many that cross the Klamath Mountains. Most of the mountain region is protected within conservation areas, but lumber is still one of the top industries of the region, along with hunting, dairy, and tourism. The Oregon Caves National Monument and many national forests are part of this mountain range.

Students can . . .
Create a salt map of the Klamath Mountains. Ask students to paint the map and label points of interest.

OREGON FUN FACTS
Did You Know?

- In 1745 the British parliament spurred the exploration of the Pacific Northwest by promising an award of £20,000 to the individual who discovered a water route across the continent.

- Among the objects depicted on the state seal are mountains and forests, an elk, a covered wagon, a sheaf of wheat, a plow, and a pickax.

- A mature Port Orford cedar, which is in great demand as a construction material in Japan, can be valued at up to $50,000 on the open market.

Students can . . .
Compare the locations of Oregon and Japan on a globe or outline map of the world. Ask students to guess why certain cedar trees would be extremely valuable to the Japanese and list their guesses.

Unit 1
This Land Is Your Land

EXPAND THE CONCEPT

What can we learn about the United States as we travel?

CONCEPT QUESTION

How do the diverse regions and peoples of the United States reflect its greatness?

Week 1

What experiences bring diverse peoples together?

Week 2

What did Lewis and Clark learn on their journey?

Week 3

What can we learn about the United States as we travel?

Week 4

What is unique about the landscape of the Southwest?

Week 5

How does Yosemite reflect the unique qualities of the West?

CONNECT THE CONCEPT

▶ **Build Background**

coast, lush, route

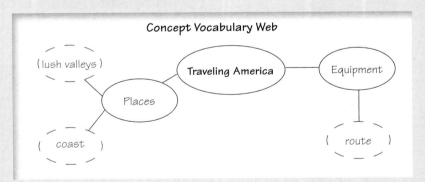

Concept Vocabulary Web

(lush valleys) — Places — Traveling America — Equipment

coast

route

▶ **Social Studies Content**

California's Geography, San Francisco, Wartime Conditions

▶ **Writing**

Postcard

▶ **Internet Inquiry**

Travel in the United States

Preview Your Week

What can we learn about the United States as we travel?

Grandfather's Journey

written and illustrated
by Allen Say

Genre Historical fiction is set in the past. It is a story in which some of the details are factual but in which others are made up or are loosely based on history. Look for the factual details as you read.

Where does a grandfather's journey take him and what does he learn along the way?

70

Student Edition pages 70–81

Audio CD

Genre	Historical Fiction
Vocabulary Strategy	Dictionary/Glossary
Comprehension Skill	Sequence
Comprehension Strategy	Graphic Organizers

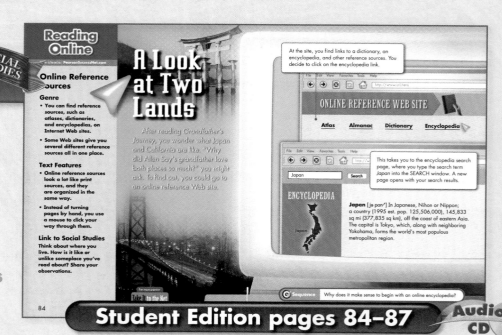

SOCIAL STUDIES

Paired Selection

Reading Across Texts

Compare Facts About Japan and California

Genre

Online Reference Sources

Text Features

Organized Like Print Sources
Mouse Used to Navigate Pages

Reading Online

www.PearsonSuccessNet.com

Online Reference Sources

Genre
- You can find reference sources, such as atlases, dictionaries, and encyclopedias, on Internet Web sites.
- Some Web sites give you several different reference sources all in one place.

Text Features
- Online reference sources look a lot like print sources, and they are organized in the same way.
- Instead of turning pages by hand, you use a mouse to click your way through them.

Link to Social Studies
Think about where you live. How is it like or unlike someplace you've read about? Share your observations.

A Look at Two Lands

After reading *Grandfather's Journey*, you wonder what Japan and California are like. "Why did Allen Say's grandfather love both places so much?" you might ask. To find out, you could go to an online reference Web site.

At the site, you find links to a dictionary, an encyclopedia, and other reference sources. You decide to click on the encyclopedia link.

ONLINE REFERENCE WEB SITE

Atlas **Almanac** **Dictionary** **Encyclopedia**

This takes you to the encyclopedia search page, where you type the search term *Japan* into the SEARCH window. A new page opens with your search results.

Japan | Search

ENCYCLOPEDIA

Japan

Japan [jə pan'] In Japanese, Nihon or Nippon; a country (1995 est. pop. 125,506,000), 145,833 sq mi (377,835 sq km), off the coast of eastern Asia. The capital is Tokyo, which, along with neighboring Yokohama, forms the world's most populous metropolitan region.

For more practice
Take It to the Net

84

Sequence Why does it make sense to begin with an online encyclopedia?

Student Edition pages 84–87

Audio CD

Read It
ONLINE
PearsonSuccessNet.com

- Student Edition
- Leveled Readers

Leveled Readers

◉ **Skill** Sequence
◉ **Strategy** Graphic Organizers
Lesson Vocabulary

Below-Level

On-Level

Advanced

ELL Reader
- Concept Vocabulary
- Text Support
- Language Enrichment

Time for
SOCIAL STUDIES

Integrate Social Studies Standards

- U.S. History
- U.S. Geography

✓ Read

Grandfather's Journey,
pp. 70–81

"A Look at Two Lands,"
pp. 84–87

Leveled Readers

 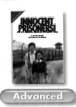

Below-Level   On-Level   Advanced

- Support Concepts
- Develop Concepts
- Extend Concepts

ELL Reader

✓ Build Concept Vocabulary

Traveling America, pp. 66l–66m

✓ Teach Social Studies Concepts

California's Geography, p. 73
San Francisco, p. 75
Wartime Conditions, p. 79

✓ Explore Social Studies Center

Follow the Adventure, p. 66k

Weekly Plan

READING

45-90 minutes

TARGET SKILLS OF THE WEEK

- **Comprehension Skill**
  Sequence
- **Comprehension Strategy**
  Graphic Organizers
- **Vocabulary Strategy**
  Dictionary/Glossary

LANGUAGE ARTS

30-60 minutes

Trait of the Week

Voice

DAY 1
PAGES 66l-68b, 87a, 87e-87k

Oral Language

QUESTION OF THE WEEK *What can we learn about the United States as we travel?*

Read Aloud: "Going Places," 66m
Build Concepts, 66l

Comprehension/Vocabulary

Comprehension Skill/Strategy Lesson, 66-67
- Sequence **T**
- Graphic Organizers

Build Background, 68a

Introduce Lesson Vocabulary, 68b
amazed, bewildered, homeland, longed, sculptures, still, towering **T**

Read Leveled Readers

Grouping Options 66f-66g

Fluency

Model Tempo and Rate, 66l-66m, 87a

Grammar, 87e
Introduce Subjects and Predicates **T**

Writing Workshop, 87g
Introduce Postcard
Model the Trait of the Week: Voice

Spelling, 87i
Pretest for Vowels Long *e* and *o*

Internet Inquiry, 87k
Identify Questions

DAY 2
PAGES 68-77, 87a, 87e-87k

Oral Language

QUESTION OF THE DAY *Why do you think traveling in the United States made the grandfather long to see even more?*

Comprehension/Vocabulary

Vocabulary Strategy Lesson, 68-69
- Dictionary/Glossary **T**

Read *Grandfather's Journey,* 70–77

Grouping Options 66f-66g

- Sequence **T**
- Graphic Organizers
- Dictionary/Glossary **T**
- **REVIEW** Main Idea **T**

Develop Vocabulary

Fluency

Choral Reading, 87a

Grammar, 87e
Develop Subjects and Predicates **T**

Writing Workshop, 87g
Improve Writing with Sequence

Spelling, 87i
Teach the Generalization

Internet Inquiry, 87k
Navigate/Search

DAILY WRITING ACTIVITIES	**Day 1** Write to Read, 66	**Day 2** Words to Write, 69 Strategy Response Log, 70, 77
DAILY SOCIAL STUDIES CONNECTIONS	**Day 1** Traveling America Concept Web, 66l	**Day 2** Time for Social Studies: California's Geography, 73; San Francisco, 75 Revisit Traveling America Concept Web, 66l

---

DAILY SUCCESS PREDICTORS
for Adequate Yearly Progress

Monitor Progress and Corrective Feedback

Vocabulary   Check Vocabulary, *66l*

RESOURCES FOR THE WEEK

- Practice Book, *pp. 21–30*
- Word Study and Spelling Practice Book, *pp. 9–12*
- Grammar and Writing Practice Book, *pp. 9–12*
- Selection Test, *pp. 9–12*
- Fresh Reads for Differentiated Test Practice, *pp. 13–18*
- The Grammar and Writing Book, *pp. 62–67*

Grouping Options for Differentiated Instruction

Turn the page for the small group lesson plan.

DAY 3
PAGES 78–83, 87a, 87e–87k

Oral Language

QUESTION OF THE DAY *What do you think the author of Grandfather's Journey would say are some positive and negative effects of moving to a new place?*

Comprehension/Vocabulary

Read *Grandfather's Journey*, 78–82

Grouping Options 66f–66g

- 🎯 Dictionary/Glossary **T**
- 🎯 Graphic Organizers
- Develop Vocabulary

Reader Response

Selection Test

Fluency

Model Tempo and Rate, 87a

Grammar, 87f
Apply Subjects and Predicates in Writing **T**

Writing Workshop, 83, 87h
Write Now
Prewrite and Draft

Spelling, 87j
Connect Spelling to Writing

Internet Inquiry, 87k
Analyze Sources

Day 3 Strategy Response Log, 80
Look Back and Write, 82

Day 3 Time for Social Studies: Wartime Conditions, 79
Revisit the Traveling America Concept Web, 81

DAY 4
PAGES 84–87a, 87e–87k

Oral Language

QUESTION OF THE DAY *Why do you think Allen Say's grandfather was fascinated by his journey through America?*

Comprehension/Vocabulary

Read "A Look at Two Lands," 84–87

Grouping Options 66f–66g

Online Reference Sources/Text Features

Reading Across Texts

Fluency

Partner Reading, 87a

Grammar, 87f
Practice Subjects and Predicates for Standardized Tests **T**

Writing Workshop, 87h
Draft, Revise, and Publish

Spelling, 87j
Provide a Strategy

Internet Inquiry, 87k
Synthesize Information

Day 4 Writing Across Texts, 87

Day 4 Time for Social Studies: Follow the Adventure, 66k

DAY 5
PAGES 87a–87l

Oral Language

QUESTION OF THE WEEK *To wrap up the week, revisit the Day 1 question.*

Build Concept Vocabulary, 87c

Fluency

Read Leveled Readers

Grouping Options 66f–66g

Assess Reading Rate, 87a

Comprehension/Vocabulary

- 🎯 Reteach Sequence, 87b **T**
- Paraphrase, 87b
- 🎯 Dictionary/Glossary, 87c **T**

Speaking and Listening, 87d
Advertisement
Listen to an Advertisement

Grammar, 87f
Cumulative Review

Writing Workshop, 87h
Connect to Unit Writing

Spelling, 87j
Posttest for Long *e* and *o*

Internet Inquiry, 87k
Communicate Results

Research/Study Skills, 87l
Electronic Media

Day 5 Paraphrase, 87b

Day 5 Revisit the Traveling America Concept Web, 87c

KEY 🎯 = Target Skill **T** = Tested Skill

Comprehension	Fluency	Vocabulary
Check Retelling, 82	Check Fluency WCPM, *87a*	Check Vocabulary, *87c*

SUCCESS PREDICTOR

Small Group Plan for Differentiated Instruction

Daily Plan AT A GLANCE

Reading
Whole Group
- Oral Language
- Comprehension/Vocabulary

Group Time
Differentiated Instruction

Meet with small groups to provide:
- Skill Support
- Reading Support
- Fluency Practice

Read

This week's lessons for daily group time can be found behind the Differentiated Instruction (DI) tab on pp. DI·22–DI·31.

Whole Group
- Fluency

Language Arts
- Grammar
- Writing
- Spelling
- Research/Inquiry
- Speaking/Listening/Viewing

Use *My Sidewalks on Reading Street* for Tier III intensive reading intervention.

DAY 1

On-Level
Teacher-Led
Page DI · 23
- Develop Concept Vocabulary
- **Read** On-Level Reader *Childhood in Pre-War Japan*

Strategic Intervention
Teacher-Led
Page DI · 22
- Reinforce Concepts
- **Read** Below-Level Reader *Grandpa's Scrapbook*

Advanced
Teacher-Led
Page DI · 23
- **Read** Advanced Reader *Innocent Prisoners!*
- Independent Extension Activity

ⓘ Independent Activities
While you meet with small groups, have the rest of the class...
- Visit the Reading/Library Center
- Listen to the Background Building Audio
- Finish Write to Read, p. 66
- Complete Practice Book pp. 23–24
- Visit Cross-Curricular Centers

DAY 2

On-Level
Teacher-Led
Pages 72–77
- Develop Concept Vocabulary
- **Read** *Grandfather's Journey*

Strategic Intervention
Teacher-Led
Page DI · 24
- Practice Lesson Vocabulary
- Read Multisyllabic Words
- **Read** or Listen to *Grandfather's Journey*

Advanced
Teacher-Led
Page DI · 25
- Extend Vocabulary
- **Read** *Grandfather's Journey*

ⓘ Independent Activities
While you meet with small groups, have the rest of the class...
- Visit the Reading/Library Center
- Listen to the AudioText for *Grandfather's Journey*
- Finish Words to Write, p. 69
- Complete Practice Book pp. 25–26
- Write in their Strategy Response Logs, pp. 70, 77
- Visit Cross-Curricular Centers
- Work on inquiry projects

DAY 3

On-Level
Teacher-Led
Pages 78–81
- **Read** *Grandfather's Journey*

Strategic Intervention
Teacher-Led
Page DI · 26
- Practice Sequence and Graphic Organizers
- **Read** or Listen to *Grandfather's Journey*

Advanced
Teacher-Led
Page DI · 27
- Extend Sequence and Graphic Organizers
- **Read** *Grandfather's Journey*

ⓘ Independent Activities
While you meet with small groups, have the rest of the class...
- Visit the Reading/Library Center
- Listen to the AudioText for *Grandfather's Journey*
- Write in their Strategy Response Logs, p. 80
- Finish Look Back and Write, p. 82
- Complete Practice Book p. 27
- Visit Cross-Curricular Centers
- Work on inquiry projects

① Begin with whole class skill and strategy instruction.

② Meet with small groups to provide differentiated instruction.

③ Gather the whole class back together for fluency and language arts.

DAY 4

On-Level
Teacher-Led
Pages 84–87

- **Read** "A Look at Two Lands"

Strategic Intervention
Teacher-Led
Page DI • 28

- Practice Retelling
- **Read** or Listen to "A Look at Two Lands"

Advanced
Teacher-Led
Page DI • 29

- **Read** "A Look at Two Lands"
- Genre Study

ⓘ Independent Activities

While you meet with small groups, have the rest of the class...

- Visit the Reading/Library Center
- Listen to the AudioText for "A Look at Two Lands"
- Visit the Writing/Vocabulary Center
- Finish Writing Across Texts, p. 87
- Visit Cross-Curricular Centers
- Work on inquiry projects

DAY 5

On-Level
Teacher-Led
Page DI • 31

- **Reread** Leveled Reader *Childhood in Pre-War Japan*
- Retell *Childhood in Pre-War Japan*

Strategic Intervention
Teacher-Led
Page DI • 30

- **Reread** Leveled Reader *Grandpa's Scrapbook*
- Retell *Grandpa's Scrapbook*

Advanced
Teacher-Led
Page DI • 31

- **Reread** Leveled Reader *Innocent Prisoners! Life in a Japanese American Interment Camp*
- Share Extension Activity

ⓘ Independent Activities

While you meet with small groups, have the rest of the class...

- Visit the Reading/Library Center
- Complete Practice Book pp. 28–30
- Visit Cross-Curricular Centers
- Work on inquiry projects

ⒺⓁⓁ

Grouping Place English language learners in the groups that correspond to their reading abilities in English.

Use the appropriate Leveled Readers or other text at students' instructional level.

TiP Send home the appropriate Multilingual Summary of the main selection on Day 1.

Take It to the NET™ ONLINE
PearsonSuccessNet.com

Camille Blachowicz
For activities to develop vocabulary, see a summary of the book *Teaching Vocabulary in all Classrooms* by Scott Foresman author Camille Blachowicz and Peter Fisher.

TEACHER TALK

Explicit instruction is teaching in which the teacher explains a skill (what it is and when and why to use it), models how to perform it, guides practice, and offers independent practice.

Be sure to schedule time for students to work on the unit inquiry project "Natural Wonders." This week students analyze the information they have found from Web sites or print materials.

Looking Ahead

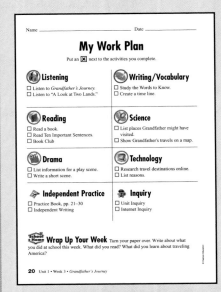

▲ **Group-Time Survival Guide** p. 20, Weekly Contract

☑ Customize Your Plan *by Strand*

ORAL LANGUAGE

Concept Development

What can we learn about the United States as we travel?

CONCEPT VOCABULARY
coast   *lush*   *route*

BUILD

❑ **Question of the Week** Introduce and discuss the question of the week. This week students will read a variety of texts and work on projects related to the concept *traveling America*. Post the question for students to refer to throughout the week. **DAY 1** *66d*

❑ **Read Aloud** Read aloud "Going Places." Then begin a web to build concepts and concept vocabulary related to this week's lesson and the unit theme, This Land Is Your Land. Introduce the concept words *coast, lush,* and *route* and have students place them on the web. Display the web for use throughout the week. **DAY 1** *66l–66m*

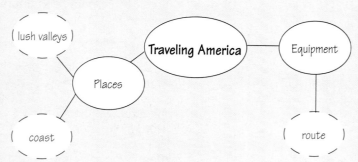

DEVELOP

❑ **Question of the Day** Use the prompts from the Weekly Plan to engage students in conversations related to this week's reading and the unit theme. **EVERY DAY** *66d–66e*

❑ **Concept Vocabulary Web** Revisit the Traveling America Concept Web and encourage students to add concept words from their reading and life experiences. **DAY 2** *77,* **DAY 3** *81*

CONNECT

❑ **Looking Back/Moving Forward** Revisit the Traveling America Concept Web and discuss how it relates to this week's lesson and the unit theme. Then make connections to next week's lesson. **DAY 5** *87c*

CHECK

❑ **Concept Vocabulary Web** Use the Traveling America Concept Web to check students' understanding of the concept vocabulary words *coast, lush,* and *route.* **DAY 1** *66l,* **DAY 5** *87c*

VOCABULARY

 **STRATEGY DICTIONARY/ GLOSSARY** When you are reading, you may come across a word whose meaning you know, but that meaning doesn't make sense in the sentence. This word may have more than one meaning. A dictionary or glossary will help you figure out the correct meaning.

LESSON VOCABULARY
amazed   sculptures
bewildered   still
homeland   towering
longed

TEACH

❑ **Words to Know** Give students the opportunity to tell what they already know about this week's lesson vocabulary words. Then discuss word meaning. **DAY 1** *68b*

❑ **Vocabulary Strategy Lesson** Use the vocabulary strategy lesson in the Student Edition to introduce and model this week's strategy, *dictionary/ glossary.* **DAY 2** *68–69*

Vocabulary Strategy Lesson

PRACTICE/APPLY

❑ **Leveled Text** Read the lesson vocabulary in the context of leveled text. **DAY 1** *LR19–LR27*

❑ **Words in Context** Read the lesson vocabulary and apply *dictionary/glossary skills* in the context of *Grandfather's Journey.* **DAY 2** *70–77,* **DAY 3** *78–82*

Leveled Readers

❑ **Writing/Vocabulary Center** Make a time line of Grandfather's travels. **ANY DAY** *66k*

Main Selection—Fiction

❑ **Homework** Practice Book pp. 24–25. **DAY 1** *68b,* **DAY 2** *69*

❑ **Word Play** Have small groups check the word meanings for *journey, journal, journalist,* and *sojourn* and then select one of the words and add it to a round-robin story. **ANY DAY** *87c*

ASSESS

❑ **Selection Test** Use the Selection Test to determine students' understanding of the lesson vocabulary words. **DAY 3**

RETEACH/REVIEW

❑ **Reteach Lesson** If necessary, use this lesson to reteach and review *dictionary/glossary.* **DAY 5** *87c*

❶ Use assessment data to determine your instructional focus.

❷ Preview this week's instruction by strand.

❸ Choose instructional activities that meet the needs of your classroom.

COMPREHENSION

◎ **SKILL SEQUENCE** Events in a story occur in a certain order, or sequence. The sequence of events can be important to understanding the story.

◎ **STRATEGY GRAPHIC ORGANIZERS** Creating charts, webs, diagrams or making lists can help organize your thoughts while reading. Using graphic organizers can help sequence the text while reading.

TEACH

☐ **Skill/Strategy Lesson** Use the skill/strategy lesson in the Student Edition to introduce and model *sequence* and *graphic organizers*. **DAY 1** *66-67*

Skill/Strategy Lesson

☐ **Extend Skills** Teach paraphrase. **ANY DAY** *87b*

PRACTICE/APPLY

☐ **Leveled Text** Apply *sequence* and *graphic organizers* to read leveled text. **DAY 1** *LR19-LR27*

Leveled Readers

☐ **Skills and Strategies in Context** Read *Grandfather's Journey*, using the Guiding Comprehension questions to apply *sequence* and *graphic organizers*. **DAY 2** *70-77*, **DAY 3** *78-82*

Main Selection—Nonfiction

☐ **Skills and Strategies in Context** Read "A Look at Two Lands," guiding students as they apply *sequence* and *graphic organizers*. Then have students discuss and write across texts. **DAY 4** *84-87*

Paired Selection—Nonfiction

☐ **Homework** Practice Book pp. 23, 27, 28 **DAY 1** *67*, **DAY 3** *81*, **DAY 5** *87b*

☐ **Fresh Reads for Differentiated Test Practice** Have students practice *sequence* with a new passage. **DAY 3**

ASSESS

☐ **Selection Test** Determine students' understanding of the selection and their use of *sequence*. **DAY 3**

☐ **Retell** Have students retell *Grandfather's Journey*. **DAY 3** *82-83*

RETEACH/REVIEW

☐ **Reteach Lesson** If necessary, reteach and review *sequence*. **DAY 5** *87b*

FLUENCY

SKILL TEMPO AND RATE The rate at which you read affects understanding. Using an appropriate tempo and reading rate can make the selection easier for a listener to understand. Good readers slow down at more difficult passages, group sentences that go together, and elongate pauses before new ideas. Using a quicker tempo and rate may cause the listener difficulty in understanding the selection.

TEACH

☐ **Read Aloud** Model fluent reading by rereading "Going Places." Focus on this week's fluency skill, tempo and rate. **DAY 1** *66l-66m, 87a*

PRACTICE/APPLY

☐ **Choral Reading** Read aloud selected paragraphs from *Grandfather's Journey*, modeling different reading rates and tempos. Have students practice as a class, doing three choral readings. **DAY 2** *87a*, **DAY 3** *87a*

☐ **Partner Reading** Have partners practice reading aloud, using appropriate tempo and rate, and offering each other feedback. As students reread, monitor their progress toward their individual fluency goals. **DAY 4** *87a*

☐ **Listening Center** Have students follow along with the AudioText for this week's selections. **ANY DAY** *66j*

☐ **Reading/Library Center** Have students reread a selection of their choice. **ANY DAY** *66j*

☐ **Fluency Coach** Have students use Fluency Coach to listen to fluent readings or practice reading on their own. **ANY DAY**

ASSESS

☐ **Check Fluency** WCPM Do a one-minute timed reading, paying special attention to this week's skill—tempo and rate. Provide feedback for each student. **DAY 5** *87a*

☑ Customize Your Plan *by Strand*

GRAMMAR

SKILL SUBJECTS AND PREDICATES Every sentence has a subject and a predicate. The subject is the part of the sentence that tells whom or what the sentence is about. All the words in the subject are called the complete subject. The simple subject is the most important word in the complete subject.

The predicate is the part of the sentence that tells what the subject is or does. All the words in the predicate are called the complete predicate. The simple predicate, or verb, is the most important word in the complete predicate.

TEACH

☐ **Grammar Transparency 3** Use Grammar Transparency 3 to teach subjects and predicates. **DAY 1** *87e*

Grammar Transparency 3

PRACTICE/APPLY

☐ **Develop the Concept** Review the concept of subjects and predicates and provide guided practice. **DAY 2** *87e*

☐ **Apply to Writing** Have students review something they have written and improve it by adding detalis to subjects and predicates. **DAY 3** *87f*

☐ **Test Preparation** Examine common errors in subjects and predicates to prepare for standardized tests. **DAY 4** *87f*

☐ **Homework** Grammar and Writing Practice Book pp. 9–11. **DAY 2** *87e*, **DAY 3** *87f*, **DAY 4** *87f*

ASSESS

☐ **Cumulative Review** Use Grammar and Writing Practice Book p. 12. **DAY 5** *87f*

RETEACH/REVIEW

☐ **Daily Fix-It** Have students find and correct errors in grammar, spelling, and punctuation. **EVERY DAY** *87e–87f*

☐ **The Grammar and Writing Book** Use pp. 62–65 of The Grammar and Writing Book to extend instruction for subjects and predicates. **ANY DAY**

The Grammar and Writing Book

WRITING

Trait of the Week

VOICE Good writers have a strong voice—a personality that comes through in the tone and style of their writing. Voice shows that a writer knows and cares about a topic. A strong voice speaks directly to readers and keeps their attention.

TEACH

☐ **Writing Transparency 3A** Use the model to introduce and discuss the Trait of the Week. **DAY 1** *87g*

☐ **Writing Transparency 3B** Use the transparency to show students how sequence can improve their writing. **DAY 2** *87g*

Writing Transparency 3A   **Writing Transparency 3B**

PRACTICE/APPLY

☐ **Write Now** Examine the model on Student Edition p. 83. Then have students write their own postcard. **DAY 3** *83, 87h*, **DAY 4** *87h*

> **Prompt** *Grandfather's Journey* describes how different places became important to the author's grandfather. Think about a place that you have visited and write a postcard describing that special place.

Write Now p. 83

☐ **Writing/Vocabulary Center** Make a time line of Grandfather's travels. **ANY DAY** *66k*

ASSESS

☐ **Writing Trait Rubric** Use the rubric to evaluate students' writing. **DAY 4** *87h*

RETEACH/REVIEW

☐ **The Grammar and Writing Book** Use pp. 62–67 of The Grammar and Writing Book to extend instruction for subjects and predicates, sequence, and postcards. **ANY DAY**

The Grammar and Writing Book

SPELLING

GENERALIZATION LONG _E_ AND _O_   Long _e_ is sometimes spelled _ee_ or _ea_: sw<u>ee</u>t, <u>ea</u>ch. Long _o_ is sometimes spelled _oa_ or _ow_: thr<u>oa</u>t, rainb<u>ow</u>. The letter combinations _ee_ and _ea_ usually stand for the long _e_ sound. The letter combinations _oa_ and _ow_ often stand for the long _o_ sound.

TEACH

❏ **Pretest** Give the pretest for words with long _e_ and _o_. Guide students in self-correcting their pretests and correcting any misspellings. DAY 1 _87i_

❏ **Think and Practice** Connect spelling to the phonics generalization for long _e_ and _o_. DAY 2 _87i_

PRACTICE/APPLY

❏ **Connect to Writing** Have students use spelling words to write a description. Then review frequently misspelled words: _whole, know._ DAY 3 _87j_

❏ **Homework** Word Study and Spelling Practice Book pp. 9–12. **EVERY DAY**

RETEACH/REVIEW

❏ **Review** Review spelling words to prepare for the posttest. Then provide students with a spelling strategy—problem parts. DAY 4 _87j_

ASSESS

❏ **Posttest** Use dictation sentences to give the posttest for words with long _e_ and _o_. DAY 5 _87j_

Spelling Words

1. sweet	8. float	15. eagle
2. each	9. foam	16. indeed*
3. three*	10. flown	17. rainbow
4. least	11. greet	18. grown
5. freedom*	12. season	19. seaweed
6. below	13. croak	20. hollow
7. throat	14. shallow	

Challenge Words

21. Halloween	23. underneath	25. cocoa
22. speedometer	24. seacoast	

*Word from the selection

RESEARCH AND INQUIRY

❏ **Internet Inquiry** Have students conduct an Internet inquiry on what travel might teach people about the United States. **EVERY DAY** _87k_

❏ **Electronic Media** Review the benefits of using electronic media and discuss how students can use this resource to find information. **DAY 5** _87l_

❏ **Unit Inquiry** Allow time for students to analyze the information they have found from the Web sites or print materials. **ANY DAY** _17_

SPEAKING AND LISTENING

❏ **Advertisement** Have students develop and present a radio advertisement that will persuade people to visit a city. Remind students that the city they select to advertise should be one that has tourist attractions, or unusual or interesting natural features that people want to see. **DAY 5** _87d_

❏ **Listen to an Advertisement** Have students listen to a classmate's radio advertisement offering feedback as to the effectiveness of the advertisement. **DAY 5** _87d_

Resources for
Differentiated Instruction

▶ **Comprehension**
  ◎ **Skill** Sequence
  ◎ **Strategy** Graphic Organizers
▶ **Lesson Vocabulary**
  ◎ Dictionary/Glossary

amazed bewildered homeland longed sculptures still towering

▶ **Social Studies Standards**
  • **U.S. Geography**
  • **U.S. History**

Leveled Reader Database
ONLINE
PearsonSuccessNet.com

Use the Online Database of over 600 books to

• Download and print additional copies of this week's leveled readers.

• Listen to the readers being read online.

• Search for more titles focused on this week's skills, topic, and content.

On-Level

Social Studies
Childhood
in Pre-War Japan

by Jana Martin

On-Level Reader

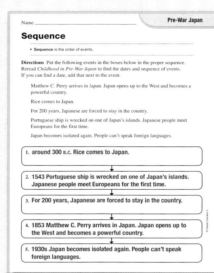

Name _____ Pre-War Japan

Sequence
• **Sequence** is the order of events.

Directions Put the following events in the boxes below in the proper sequence. Reread *Childhood in Pre-War Japan* to find the dates and sequence of events. If you can find a date, add that next to the event.

Matthew C. Perry arrives in Japan. Japan opens up to the West and becomes a powerful country.

Rice comes to Japan.

For 200 years, Japanese are forced to stay in the country.

Portuguese ship is wrecked on one of Japan's islands. Japanese people meet Europeans for the first time.

Japan becomes isolated again. People can't speak foreign languages.

1. around 300 B.C. Rice comes to Japan.

2. 1543 Portuguese ship is wrecked on one of Japan's islands. Japanese people meet Europeans for the first time.

3. For 200 years, Japanese are forced to stay in the country.

4. 1853 Matthew C. Perry arrives in Japan. Japan opens up to the West and becomes a powerful country.

5. 1930s Japan becomes isolated again. People can't speak foreign languages.

◎ **On-Level Practice** TE p. LR23

Name _____ Pre-War Japan

Vocabulary
Directions Fill in the blank with the word from the box that fits the definition.

Check the Words You Know
__amazed   __bewildered   __homeland   __longed
__sculptures __still   __towering

1. **longed** _____ wanted very much
2. **still** _____ to make quiet
3. **amazed** _____ greatly surprised
4. **homeland** _____ country that is one's home
5. **towering** _____ very high
6. **bewildered** _____ completely confused
7. **sculptures** _____ models made of stone or metal

Directions Write a brief paragraph discussing life in pre-war Japan, using as many vocabulary words as possible.

Responses will vary.
_____
_____
_____
_____
_____

◎ **On-Level Practice** TE p. LR24

Strategic Intervention

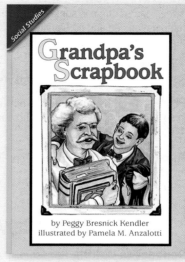

Social Studies
Grandpa's Scrapbook

by Peggy Bresnick Kendler
illustrated by Pamela M. Anzalotti

Below-Level Reader

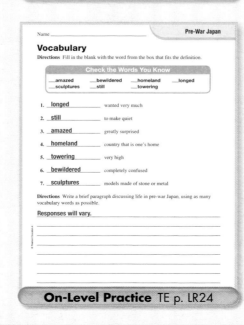

Name _____ Grandpa's Scrapbook

Sequence
• The **sequence** of events means the order in which the events happen.

Directions Fill in the table below. The events of *Grandpa's Scrapbook* are divided into two stages: Grandpa's childhood years and his early adult years. Fill in as many examples as you can for each category.

Childhood Years	Early Adult Years
adventures with Tim	cub pilot at age 22
swam in river	pilot's license in 1859
skating in winter	saw New Orleans and St. Louis
explored caves	worked on a steamboat
Laura Hawkins went along.	traveled on Mississippi River

◎ **Below-Level Practice** TE p. LR20

Name _____ Grandpa's Scrapbook

Vocabulary
Directions Fill in the blank with the word from the box that fits best.

Check the Words You Know
__amazed   __bewildered   __homeland   __longed
__sculptures __still   __towering

1. In Hannibal, Missouri, look for the **sculptures** of Tom Sawyer and Becky Thatcher.
2. The pine trees were **towering** over the raft as it moved downstream.
3. Sam Clemens's **homeland** was the area around Hannibal, Missouri.
4. Grandpa seemed **amazed** that we wanted to hear his stories again.
5. The water in this part of the river was deep and **still** _____.
6. Grandpa **longed** for the days of his youth.
7. Laura Hawkins looked **bewildered** when I asked her to enter the cave.

Directions Write a brief paragraph discussing Mark Twain's childhood on the Mississippi, using as many vocabulary words as possible.

Responses will vary.
_____
_____
_____
_____
_____

◎ **Below-Level Practice** TE p. LR21

Advanced

Advanced Reader

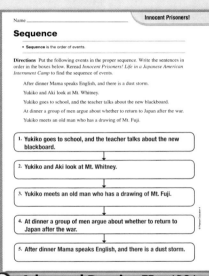

Name _____ **Innocent Prisoners!**

Sequence

• **Sequence** is the order of events.

Directions Put the following events in the proper sequence. Write the sentences in order in the boxes below. Reread *Innocent Prisoners! Life in a Japanese American Internment Camp* to find the sequence of events.

After dinner Mama speaks English, and there is a dust storm.

Yukiko and Aki look at Mt. Whitney.

Yukiko goes to school, and the teacher talks about the new blackboard.

At dinner a group of men argue about whether to return to Japan after the war.

Yukiko meets an old man who has a drawing of Mt. Fuji.

1. Yukiko goes to school, and the teacher talks about the new blackboard.

2. Yukiko and Aki look at Mt. Whitney.

3. Yukiko meets an old man who has a drawing of Mt. Fuji.

4. At dinner a group of men argue about whether to return to Japan after the war.

5. After dinner Mama speaks English, and there is a dust storm.

Advanced Practice TE p. LR26

Name _____ **Innocent Prisoners!**

Vocabulary

Directions Fill in the blank with the word from the box that fits the definition.

Check the Words You Know

___barracks   ___elections   ___horizon
___internment   ___naval

1. __elections__   an act of choosing by vote

2. __naval__   having to do with ships

3. __barracks__   housing for soldiers or prisoners

4. __internment__   placing people in camps

5. __horizon__   the line where earth meets sky

Directions Write a paragraph discussing life in an internment camp, using all the vocabulary words.

Responses will vary.

Advanced Practice TE p. LR27

ELL

Our Trip Out East
by Luz Nuncio Schick

ELL Reader

ELL Poster 3

Teacher's Edition Notes

ELL notes throughout this lesson support instruction and reference additional resources at point of use.

Teaching Guide pp. 15–21, 216–217

• Multilingual summaries of the main selection

• Comprehension lesson

• Vocabulary strategies and word cards

• ELL Reader 4.1.3 lesson

ELL and Transition Handbook

Ten Important Sentences

• Key ideas from every selection in the Student Edition

• Activities to build sentence power

More Reading

Readers' Theater Anthology

• Fluency practice

• Five scripts to build fluency

• Poetry for oral interpretation

Leveled Trade Books

• Extended reading tied to the unit concept

• Lessons in the Trade Book Library Teaching Guide

School + Home

Homework

• Family Times Newsletter

• ELL Multilingual Selection Summaries

Take-Home Books

• Leveled Readers

Cross-Curricular Centers

Listening

Listen to the Selections

MATERIALS
CD player, headphones, AudioText CD, student book

`SINGLES`

LISTEN TO LITERATURE Listen to *Grandfather's Journey* and "A Look at Two Lands" as you follow or read along in your book. Listen for the sequence of events that occurs in *Grandfather's Journey.*

If there is anything you don't understand, you can listen again to any section.

Reading/Library

Read It Again!

MATERIALS
Collection of books for self-selected reading, reading logs, student book

`SINGLES`
`PAIRS`
`GROUPS`

Select a book you have already read. Record the title of the book in your reading log. You may want to read with a partner.

Choose from the following:

- **Leveled Readers**
- **ELL Readers**
- **Books or Stories Written by Classmates**
- **Books from the Library**
- *Grandfather's Journey*

TEN IMPORTANT SENTENCES Read the Ten Important Sentences for *Grandfather's Journey.* Then locate the sentences in the student book.

BOOK CLUB Write a letter to Allen Say, the author and illustrator of *Grandfather's Journey.* Include questions and opinions about the story or his work as an author and illustrator.

Drama

Write a Scene

MATERIALS
Writing and art materials

`GROUPS`

Imagine a person from a different land is visiting your town. Write a scene about what your daily life is like.

1. List cast, settings, props, and costumes needed for the scene.
2. Write a short scene that shows a few things you do every day. Include dialogue and stage directions. Identify the speakers for the dialogue.

EARLY FINISHERS Draw pictures for your scene. Show what the set and costumes look like.

Cast: Nikki, Maria, Nikki's classmates

Settings: Inside Nikki's kitchen; school bus stop

Props: kitchen table and chairs, bowls of cereal, backpack

Costumes: jeans, t-shirt, sneakers; traditional Mexican blouse and skirt

MARIA (at kitchen table, smiles): Nikki! Hurry up, we'll be late for school.

NIKKI (enters breathing hard, grabs backpack): Sorry. I couldn't find my shoes. Are you ready to go? It's great that you're visiting my school, Maria.

Scott Foresman Reading Street Centers Survival Kit

Use the *Grandfather's Journey* materials from the Reading Street
Centers Survival Kit to organize this week's centers.

Writing/Vocabulary

Create a Time Line

MATERIALS
Student book, writing materials

`PAIRS`
`GROUPS`

Make a time line of Grandfather's travels.

1. Review the story and look for details about the places Grandfather visits and what he sees during his travels.
2. Make a time line summarizing Grandfather's travels. Be sure to list information in the order that it happens.
3. Look at the Words to Know on p. 68. Include some of these words in your time line.

EARLY FINISHERS Write a short postcard message from Grandfather to his family. Use your time line to tell about one of the places he visits.

Grandfather's Travels

Leaves his <u>homeland</u> in Japan. Takes a steamship across the Pacific Ocean to North America.

— Sees <u>towering</u> mountains and clear rivers.

Returns to village in Japan and gets married.

— Brings his bride to San Francisco Bay.

After his daughter is grown, he moves back to Japan with his family.

— Hiroshima

Moves back to his village after the war. He <u>longed</u> to visit California again, but he never does.

Social Studies

Follow the Adventure

MATERIALS
World map, writing materials, student book

`GROUPS`

Show Grandfather's travels on a world map.

1. Review the story to find details about Grandfather's travels.
2. In some cases, the author doesn't name specific places. Use a map and story clues to figure out likely places Grandfather might have visited. For example, which state(s) in the United States have "deserts with rocks"?
3. Make a list of places you think Grandfather visited.
4. Show Grandfather's travels on a world map and identify the places you think he visited.

EARLY FINISHERS Discuss with a partner the parts of Grandfather's travels you think were the hardest. Use your map and story clues to support your opinions.

Grandfather's Journey
starts in Japan
crosses Pacific Ocean
"deserts with rocks"
"endless farm fields"
"cities of factories"
New York City
"mountains and rivers"
San Francisco Bay
returns to Japanese village

ALL CENTERS

Technology

Research a Destination

MATERIALS
Internet access, printer, student book

`SINGLES`

Use the Internet to find a place you would like to visit.

1. Think of a place in the United States or another country you might like to visit, such as a city or town.
2. Using a student-friendly search engine, type in keywords for your search such as *travel Japan*.
3. Read the descriptions for the Web sites and decide which will give helpful and accurate information.
4. Make a list of reasons why this place is a good travel destination.
5. Follow classroom rules for searching the Internet and printing.

EARLY FINISHERS Print a picture of the place you wish to visit. Display your picture with your list of reasons.

Search Engine

travel Japan

Reasons I want to go to Japan

1. I would like to see Mt. Fuji.
2. The busy streets of Tokyo look exciting.
3. I liked the pictures of temples and other buildings I saw online.

OBJECTIVES

- Build vocabulary by finding words related to the lesson concept.
- Listen for sequence.

Concept Vocabulary

coast the land along the sea

lush having thick growth; covered with growing things

route way to go; road

Monitor Progress

Check Vocabulary

If...	then... review the
students are unable to place words on the web,	lesson concept. Place the words on the web and provide additional words for practice, such as *inland* and *directions.*

SUCCESS PREDICTOR

DAY 1 **Grouping Options**

Reading

Whole Group

Introduce and discuss the Question of the Week. Then use pp. 66l–68b.

Group Time

Differentiated Instruction

Read this week's Leveled Readers. See pp. 66f–66g for the small group lesson plan.

Whole Group

Use p. 87a.

Language Arts

Use pp. 87e–87k.

Build Concepts

FLUENCY

MODEL TEMPO AND RATE As you read "Going Places," model how to use an appropriate tempo and reading rate to make the selection easier for listeners to understand. Be sure to slow down at more difficult passages, group sentences that go together, and elongate pauses before new ideas. You may also wish to demonstrate the effect on meaning by reading a small part of the selection using a quicker tempo and rate.

LISTENING COMPREHENSION

After reading "Going Places," use the following questions to assess listening comprehension.

1. **If you were traveling east to west across the United States, what would you see just before the lush valleys of California?** *(the Rocky Mountains)* **Sequence**

2. **How is information in the selection organized?** *(She describes the sequence of what you would see traveling from east to west across the United States.)* **Text Structure**

BUILD CONCEPT VOCABULARY

Start a web to build concepts and vocabulary related to this week's lesson and the unit theme.

- Draw the Traveling America Concept Web.

- Read the sentence with the word *coast* again. Ask students to pronounce *coast* and discuss its meaning.

- Place *coast* in an oval attached to *Places*. Explain that a *coast* is one kind of place we'd see when traveling America. Read the sentences in which *lush* and *route* appear. Have students pronounce the words, place them on the Web, and provide reasons.

- Brainstorm additional words and categories for the Web. Keep the Web on display and add words throughout the week.

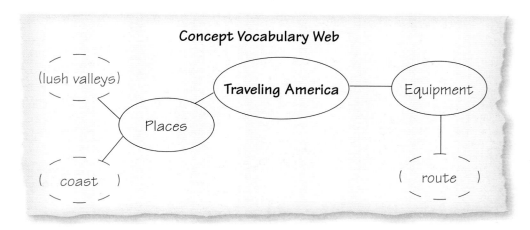

Concept Vocabulary Web

Going Places

By Harriet Webster

Our country stretches 1,600 miles from north to south and 2,800 miles from east to west. Coast to coast, that's nearly the same distance as from New York to London, passing over the Atlantic Ocean. Or think of it this way: If you traveled by car at a steady speed of sixty miles an hour, never once stopping for a break, it would take nearly forty-seven hours to cross the country. If you were to choose jet travel instead, the nonstop trip would take about five hours. From the edge of the Atlantic Ocean, you'd head inland and soar above the gentle rises of the Appalachian Mountains and the fertile farmlands of the Midwest. Depending upon your route, you might catch a glimpse of the Great Lakes to the north. Farther west, you'd look down on the endless prairies and cattle-grazing land. On the southern route, you might see desert below. Then you'd climb above the snow-capped Rockies before passing over the lush green valleys of California and the shores of the great Pacific Ocean.

That's a lot of territory! Think how challenging a cross-country expedition must have been for our forebears, who made their treks without the benefit of modern transportation. Parts of the Great Plains were so featureless and so flat that settlers drove stakes into the ground to show others where to go. Even today, that area is called Staked Plains. Another way they left directions for those who would follow was to sprinkle mustard seeds through the western valleys in the hope that a trail of bright yellow plants would signal the way.

There is so much to explore in the U.S.A. that you need never run out of discoveries to make or places to explore. A good way to keep track of what you have seen and to build on your knowledge is to keep a naturalist's scrapbook.

Activate Prior Knowledge

Before students listen to the Read Aloud, ask them to talk about any travels of their own in the United States.

Set Purpose

Read aloud the title and have students predict what the selection will be about.

Have students listen for the sequence in which the author describes traveling across the United States.

Creative Response

Have students imagine they are crossing the United States in an airplane, traveling from east to west. Partners can improvise a dialogue discussing what they see below the plane. *Drama*

Access Content Before reading, share this summary: This author imagines a journey across the United States and describes the main areas in the country.

Homework Send home this week's Family Times newsletter.

SKILLS ⟷ STRATEGIES IN CONTEXT

Sequence Graphic Organizers

OBJECTIVES

◎ Identify sequence of events.

◎ Use a graphic organizer to show sequence.

Skills Trace	
◎ Sequence	
Introduce/Teach	TE: 4.1 18–19, 66–67; 4.5 560–561
Practice	TE: 25, 27, 73, 77, 567, 571 PB: 3, 7, 8, 23, 27, 28, 223, 227, 228
Reteach/Review	TE: 4.1 39b, 87b, 97, DI·52, DI·54; 4.5 531, 551, 581b, DI·54 PB: 36, 206, 216
Test	Selection Test: 1–4, 9–12, 89–92; Benchmark Test: Units 1, 5

INTRODUCE

Have students think about the sequence the class follows to get ready for lunch each day. Perhaps students get their lunches, line up at the door, and walk to the cafeteria. Ask why the order of these events is important. *(Possible response: Students don't want to get to the cafeteria without their lunches.)* Explain that the sequence in stories and articles can also be important.

Have students read the information on p. 66. Explain the following:

• Sequence is the order in which events take place.

• A graphic organizer can help you remember the sequence of events in a story or article.

Use Skill Transparency 3 to teach sequence and graphic organizers.

Comprehension

Skill
Sequence

Strategy
Graphic Organizers

Sequence

• Sequence means the order in which things happen.

• Dates, times, and clue words such as *first, then, next,* and *last* can help you understand the order of events.

• Sometimes two or more events happen at the same time. Words such as *meanwhile* and *during* can show this.

First Event	→	Second Event	→	Third Event	→	Fourth Event

Strategy: Graphic Organizers

Using a graphic organizer can help you understand what you read. Some of these are webs, charts, and diagrams. For example, making a sequence chart like the one above can help you see the sequence. With some articles, you can fill in the organizer as you read. With others, you need to read the entire article before making the organizer.

Write to Read

1. Read "Moving to California." Make a graphic organizer like the one above to identify the sequence of important events in the article.

2. Reread the article, creating a web for "People Who Moved to California." Use your web to write a journal entry that a California resident might have written about the immigrants.

66

Strategic Intervention

◎ **Sequence** Talk about dates and clue words students can look for to help them determine the sequence. Give examples, such as *before, after, then, next, while, during that time,* and *later.* Let students offer other examples and use them in sentences. To help students develop the sequence chart on p. 66, have them find examples of clue words in "Moving to California." Help them determine the sequence from these clues.

E L L

Access Content

Beginning/Intermediate For a Picture It! lesson on sequence, see the ELL Teaching Guide, pp. 15–16.

Advanced Before reading "Moving to California," have volunteers use a map or globe to identify your state in relationship to California.

Moving to CALIFORNIA

Over time, many different groups of people have moved to California and made it their home. Because of this, California has a very diverse population today.

In 1542, a man from Spain named Juan Cabrillo entered California. Many people from Spain moved to California after that. Then, starting in 1841, many farmers from the United States moved to California.

After gold was found in California in 1848, thousands of people from Europe, Asia, and other parts of the world moved there. They hoped to become rich. Many of these people came from China.

By 1852, one out of every 10 people who lived in California was from China. But a new law in 1882 said that, for ten years, no one from China was allowed to move to the United States. During that same time, many people from Japan were moving to California.

Today, more people live in California than in any other state in the United States.

 1 Strategy Dates and clue words are important guides to sequence. Put three events from this paragraph on the sequence chart.

 2 Skill Which of the following events took place *first*? How do you know?
(a) People moved to California to become rich.
(b) Juan Cabrillo traveled to California.
(c) Farmers from the United States moved to California.

3 Skill Sometimes two events happen at the same time. Which event took place while people from Japan were moving to California?

4 Strategy Why can this information bring an end to the sequence chart?

67

Available as **Skill Transparency** 3

Sequence

- **Sequence** is the order in which things happen.
- Dates, times, and clue words such as *first, then, next,* and *last* can help you understand the order of events.

Directions Read the following passage. Then complete the diagram.

One rainy afternoon, Grandmother told me about the many places she had lived in her lifetime. The first place she lived was Austria, where she was born in 1920. But by 1925, her family had moved to Paris, France, and later to a small village in Belgium. After her eighteenth birthday, Grandmother came to New York City by herself. She hated the cold winters and knew the big city was not for her. Finally, Grandmother packed her bags and moved for the last time to a farm in North Carolina, where she has lived ever since.

First Event
1. Grandmother was born in Austria in 1920.

↓

Second Event
2. Grandmother had moved to France and Belgium by 1925.

↓

Third Event
3. Grandmother came to New York City.

↓

Fourth Event
4. Grandmother moved to a farm in North Carolina.

5. What clue words in the passage helped you to figure out the sequence of events?
first, in 1920, by 1925, then later, after, finally

Home Activity Your child used a graphic organizer to identify the sequence of events in a passage. With your child, draw a picture or write a summary of each of the main scenes in a favorite story on note cards. Arrange the note cards in the order in which the events occurred in the story.

TEACH

1 STRATEGY Use paragraph 2 to model how to create a graphic organizer.

Think Aloud **MODEL** I see that in 1542, Juan Cabrillo came to California. That's what I'll put first. People from Spain moved to California *after that*. The clue words tell me that is what happened next. Then I see that in 1841, farmers started coming to California. That must be the third event on the chart.

2 SKILL Determine a sequence of events.

Think Aloud **MODEL** I can use dates and clue words to help me. The third paragraph says people started coming to California to get rich *after* 1848. Juan Cabrillo traveled to California in 1542. Farmers moved to California in 1841. The year 1542 comes first, so that is the event that happened first.

PRACTICE AND ASSESS

3 SKILL People from China were not allowed to move to the United States.

4 STRATEGY The word *Today* brings us to the present time. The chart can't continue because we don't know what will happen in the future.

WRITE Have students complete steps 1 and 2 of the Write to Read activity. You might consider using this as a whole-class activity.

Monitor Progress

🔊 Sequence

If... students are unable to complete **Write to Read** on p. 66,	**then...** use Practice Book p. 23 to provide additional practice.

ONLINE

Students may want to learn more about what it was like for people who immigrated to this country. Have them use a student-friendly Internet search engine and the keyword *immigrants* to find Web sites about immigration to the United States.

ELL

Build Background Use ELL Poster 3 to build background and vocabulary for the lesson concept of traveling to America.

▲ **ELL Poster** 3

Build Background

ACTIVATE PRIOR KNOWLEDGE

CREATE A T-CHART about moving to a new country.

- Remind students that people have come to the United States from all over the world. Talk about the home countries of U.S. immigrants. Have students think about how life in these countries is like and unlike life in the United States and what it is like to move to a new country.

- Create a T-chart with the heads *Possible Difficulties* and *Good Experiences.* Have students describe experiences of new immigrants and identify in which column their ideas belong. Add a few ideas of your own.

- Tell students that, as they read *Grandfather's Journey,* they should look for new ideas about moving to a new country to add to the T-chart.

Possible Difficulties	Good Experiences
1. Miss family and friends left in home country	1. See new sights (mountains, oceans, cities, animals)
2. Learning a new language can be hard.	2. Meet new people, make new friends
3. Might have trouble communicating with others	3. Find a new job
4. Might not know customs or behaviors of new country	4. Find a safer place to live
5. People might not understand your customs or behaviors.	
6. Weather could be very different.	

▲ **Graphic Organizer** 25

BACKGROUND BUILDING AUDIO This week's audio explores the Japanese American National Museum. After students listen, talk together about what they learned and what surprised them most about this part of U.S. history.

Background Building Audio

Introduce Vocabulary

QUESTION AND ANSWER

Display the lesson vocabulary words. Give students the opportunity to tell whatever they already know about these words. Then ask oral questions such as those below. Students should respond *yes* or *no* and give reasons for their choices. **Activate Prior Knowledge**

- Would someone from the country be *amazed* to see *towering* skyscrapers? *(Yes)*
- Does a *bewildered* person understand something clearly? *(No)*
- Is your *homeland* a new place to visit? *(No)*
- Have you ever *longed* to see a friend who lives far away? *(Yes)*
- Are you likely to find *sculptures* in a museum? *(Yes)*
- Are you calm after you *still* your nerves? *(Yes)*

Have students identify the lesson vocabulary word that is made of two smaller words. *(homeland)* Ask how the meanings of the two words are combined in the compound word *homeland*. Ask students to analyze the two compound words in the More Words to Know list, *seacoast* and *steamship*. **Compound Words**

Have students use these steps for reading multisyllabic words. (See the Multisyllabic Word Routine on p. DI·1.)

1. **Look for Meaningful Word Parts** (base words, endings, prefixes, suffixes, roots) Think about the meaning of each part. Use the parts to read the word. Model: I see *-ing* at the end of *towering*. I know that a tower is something high, so *towering* must mean something that stands high over another thing.

2. **Chunk Words with No Recognizable Parts** Say each chunk slowly. Then say the chunks fast to make a word. Model: *sculp, tures—sculptures.*

At the end of the week, students can work in pairs to ask and answer their own *yes/no* questions about lesson vocabulary and other words from the story.

Lesson Vocabulary

WORDS TO KNOW

T amazed surprised greatly; struck with sudden wonder; astounded

T bewildered completely confused; puzzled

T homeland country that is your home; your native land

T longed wished very much; desired greatly

T sculptures works of art created by carving, modeling, casting, etc.

T still to make or become calm or quiet

T towering very high

MORE WORDS TO KNOW

seacoast land along the sea; seaboard

steamship ship moved by engines that work by the action of steam under pressure

T = Tested Word

Vocabulary

Directions Choose the word from the box that best completes each sentence. Write the word on the line shown to the left.

bewildered 1. The strange language of the country completely ___ her.

towering 2. She felt scared when she saw the ___ mountains.

homeland 3. The trip took her many miles from her ___.

amazed 4. She was ___ by the size of the city.

sculptures 5. The ___ at the museum were made out of marble.

longed 6. She ___ to see a familiar face.

Check the Words You Know
___amazed
___bewildered
___homeland
___longed
___sculptures
___still
___towering

Directions Circle the word that has the same or nearly the same meaning as the first word in each group.

7. longed — called — (yearned) — stretched
8. bewildered — (confused) — happy — angry
9. still — stir — (calm) — annoy
10. amazed — depressed — sleepy — (surprised)

Write an E-mail Message
Pretend you have just moved to a new country. On a separate sheet of paper write an email message to a friend back home explaining how you have adapted to life in this new place. Use as many vocabulary words as you can.
E-mail messages should include words from the vocabulary list and details about the new country.

Home Activity Your child identified and used vocabulary words from *Grandfather's Journey*. With your child, go on an imaginary trip halfway around the world. Use the vocabulary words to describe how you are feeling on the trip.

▲ **Practice Book** p. 24

Grandfather's Journey **68b**

Vocabulary Strategy

INTRODUCE

Discuss the strategy for using a dictionary or glossary by using the steps on p. 68.

TEACH

- Have students think about words with multiple meanings as they read "Becoming American."
- Model looking up meanings of *still*.

Think Aloud **MODEL** In the last sentence I see the word *still*. I know *still* can mean "yet," but that meaning doesn't fit here. I look up *still* in a dictionary and find several meanings. The one that fits best in the sentence is "to make calm or quiet." It makes sense to say, "Having a better life did not calm their feelings for their homeland."

Words to Know

homeland
bewildered
amazed
towering
sculptures
longed
still

Vocabulary Strategy
for Multiple-Meaning Words

Dictionary/Glossary Sometimes when you are reading, you may see a word whose meaning you know, but that meaning doesn't make sense in the sentence. It may be a word that has more than one meaning. You can use a dictionary or glossary to help you.

1. Try the meaning that you know. Does it make sense in the sentence?

2. If it doesn't make sense, look up the word in a dictionary or glossary to see what other meanings the word can have.

3. Find the entry for the word. The entries are in alphabetical order.

4. Read all the meanings given for the word. Try each in the sentence.

5. Choose the one that makes the best sense in the sentence.

As you read "Becoming American," look for words that can have more than one meaning. Use a dictionary or glossary to find meanings to try in the sentence. Which meaning makes sense?

68

DAY 2 Grouping Options

Reading

Whole Group Discuss the Question of the Day. Then use pp. 68–71.

Group Time Differentiated Instruction
Read *Grandfather's Journey.* See pp. 66f–66g for the small group lesson plan.

Whole Group Use p. 87a.

Language Arts
Use pp. 87e–87k.

Strategic Intervention

◉ **Dictionary/Glossary** Provide two sentences with the word *long*: *We long for summer. We must wait a long time.* Look up *long* in the student glossary and match each meaning to its context.

Access Content Use ELL Poster 3 to preteach vocabulary. Choose from the following to meet language proficiency levels.

Beginning Have students point out any words they are familiar with and say or gesture the meaning of each.

Intermediate Complete a vocabulary frame for an unfamiliar word. Predict the meaning and then verify it in a dictionary or glossary.

Advanced Teach the lesson on pp. 68–69. Have students ask and answer questions about the vocabulary words similar to the questions on p. 68b.

Resources for home-language words may include parents, bilingual staff members, bilingual dictionaries, or online translation sources.

Becoming American

People from around the world have been moving to the United States since it began. Full of hope, they left their homeland. They spent weeks crossing the treacherous ocean. Many arrived in strange cities that did not welcome them. The English language and the new mix of customs in America bewildered them. Often they could only get poorly paid jobs that others did not want.

However, they found much that amazed them. There was real freedom for American citizens. There was a feeling that anyone could work hard and have a better life. Towering buildings called skyscrapers soared into the sky. They seemed like sculptures that symbolized the power and promise of the new land.

All around the immigrants were energy and growth. They learned a new language and new customs. They worked tirelessly. They contributed to their new country. Sooner or later, the newcomers were accepted.

The new life did not take away the pain of loss, though. The new Americans longed for the sights and people they had left behind. Having a better life did not still their feelings for their homeland.

Words to Write

Pretend the year is 1900 and you have just come to the United States from another country. Write a letter home describing your new country. Use words from the Words to Know list.

69

PRACTICE AND ASSESS

- Have students determine the meanings of the remaining words and explain how they used the glossary to determine each meaning.
- Ask students which words have more than one definition in the glossary. Ask how they decided which meaning makes the most sense in this context.
- Have students work in pairs, asking each other *yes/no* questions like the ones on p. 68b about the vocabulary words.
- Have students complete Practice Book p. 25.

WRITE Letters should include several vocabulary words as well as words that describe a newcomer's view of the United States.

Monitor Progress

Dictionary/Glossary

If... students need more practice with the lesson vocabulary,	**then**... use Tested Vocabulary Cards.

Vocabulary • Dictionary/Glossary

- **Dictionaries** and **glossaries** provide alphabetical lists of words and their meanings.
- Sometimes looking at the words around an unfamiliar word can't help you figure out the word's meaning. If this happens, use a dictionary or glossary to find the meaning.

Directions Read the following story about traveling in the United States. Then answer the questions below. Use your glossary or a dictionary for help.

One year for summer vacation, my family took a long road trip around the United States. We visited national parks, where we drove along roads that went through towering mountains. I had to still my nerves just to look over the bluff. We went to art museums and studied sculptures carved ages ago. I was amazed to learn that people had created art before they could even read or write.

At the end of the trip, I longed for my home and my friends. But I will never forget the wonders I saw.

1. What is the meaning of the word *towering* as it is used in the story?
   very high
2. What is the other meaning of *bluff* not used in the story? What part of speech is it?
   The other meaning is "to fool or mislead"; verb
3. What is the meaning of *still* in the story?
   to make or become calm or quiet
4. Write an original sentence using the other meaning of *still* not used in the story.
   Possible answer: The lake looked very still.
5. To find the meaning of *longed*, you need to look at the entry for *long*. Which definition is used in story?
   wished very much; desired greatly

Home Activity Your child used a glossary to identify the intended definitions of multiple meaning words. Create and draw a comic together in which the confusion over the different meanings of a word has caused a funny outcome.

▲ **Practice Book** p. 25

Prereading Strategies

GENRE STUDY

Historical Fiction

Grandfather's Journey is historical fiction. Historical fiction is realistic fiction that takes place in the past and may include real people. Much of this story is based on the real experiences of the author's grandfather.

PREVIEW AND PREDICT

Have students preview the title and illustrations and discuss what they think *Grandfather's Journey* will be about. Encourage them to use lesson vocabulary words as they talk about their predictions.

Strategy Response Log

Graphic Organizer Have students draw a T-chart with the heads *Grandfather's Homeland* and *Grandfather's New Country*. Have them list facts about locations mentioned in the story as they read. Students will review and revise their T-charts in the Strategy Response Log activity on p. 77.

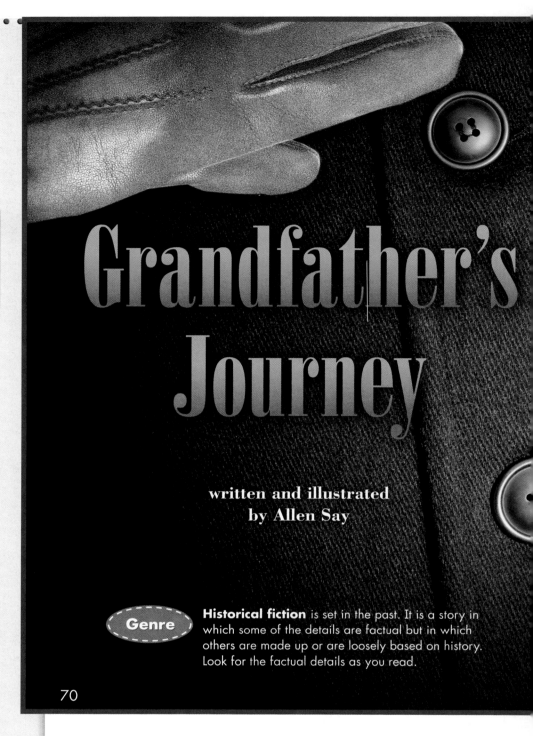

Grandfather's Journey

written and illustrated by Allen Say

Genre

Historical fiction is set in the past. It is a story in which some of the details are factual but in which others are made up or are loosely based on history. Look for the factual details as you read.

70

ELL

Access Content Lead a picture walk. The pictures span the grandfather's life, beginning and ending in Japan. Point out that the title refers to a lifelong journey.

Consider having students read the selection summary in English or in students' home languages. See the Multilingual Summaries in the ELL Teaching Guide, pp. 19–21.

Where does a grandfather's journey take him
and what does he learn along the way?

71

SET PURPOSE

Have students look at the illustration on p. 71. Tell them this is the grandfather in *Grandfather's Journey* as a young boy. Ask students what they hope to learn about this grandfather and the journey he takes.

Remind students that focusing on the sequence of events in this story will help them to understand what they read.

STRATEGY RECALL

Students have now used these before-reading strategies:

- preview the selection to be aware of its genre, features, and possible content;
- activate prior knowledge about that content and what to expect of that genre;
- make predictions;
- set a purpose for reading.

Remind students to be aware of and flexibly use the during-reading strategies they have learned:

- link prior knowledge to new information;
- summarize text they have read so far;
- ask clarifying questions;
- answer questions they or others pose;
- check their predictions and either refine them or make new predictions;
- recognize the text structure the author is using, and use that knowledge to make predictions and increase comprehension;
- visualize what the author is describing;
- monitor their comprehension and use fix-up strategies.

After reading, students will use these strategies:

- summarize or retell the text;
- answer questions they or others pose;
- reflect to make new information become part of their prior knowledge.

 **AudioText**

Guiding Comprehension

1 ⊙ **Sequence • Literal**

What did the grandfather do after the steamship landed in the New World?

He explored North America by train and riverboat.

Monitor Progress

⊙ **Sequence**

If... students are unable to identify the sequence of events,	**then...** use the skill and strategy instruction on p. 73.

2 **Compare and Contrast • Inferential**

In what ways was North America different from the grandfather's village in Japan? How do you know?

Possible response: North America had deserts and huge cities of factories. I know these things were unfamiliar to the grandfather because the author says they amazed, bewildered, and excited him.

My grandfather was a young man when he left his home in Japan and went to see the world.

He wore European clothes for the first time and began his journey on a steamship. The Pacific Ocean astonished him.

For three weeks he did not see land. When land finally appeared it was the New World.

72

Build Background Explain that a long time ago, European explorers referred to the Americas as the "New World" (p. 72, paragraph 3), full of opportunity and adventure. Subsequently, some immigrants referred to the United States this way too.

He explored North America by train and riverboat, and often walked for days on end. **1**

Deserts with rocks like enormous sculptures amazed him.

The endless farm fields reminded him of the ocean he had crossed.

Huge cities of factories and tall buildings bewildered and yet excited him. **2**

73

Sequence

TEACH

- Remind students that sequence is the order in which things happen.
- Explain that understanding the order of events in a story will help them to better understand the story.
- Model identifying the sequence of events on pp. 72–73.

Think Aloud

MODEL In the first sentence on p. 72, I learn that the grandfather has left his home in Japan. The next few paragraphs talk about his journey on a steamship. Then on the top of p. 73, I read that the grandfather explored North America by train and riverboat. The sentences that follow tell about all the things he saw.

PRACTICE AND ASSESS

- For practice, ask students this question: Did the grandfather buy European clothes before or after he got on the steamship? (*He had to buy the clothes before he got on the steamship because he wore them on the ship.*)
- To assess, have pairs write four important events from the story in the order in which they happened. (*Possible response: Grandfather left home, he got on a ship, he traveled for three weeks, and he explored North America.*)

California's Geography

Time for **SOCIAL STUDIES**

California is a state of great geographic diversity. Bordering the Pacific Ocean, it has almost 1,000 miles of coastline, including two enormous bays. California lays claim to Mount Whitney, the highest point in the continental United States, and the lowest, Death Valley. In the center of the state is the very productive farming region known as the Central Valley. This flat, fertile land extends for 400 miles and produces about 25% of America's foods.

Guiding Comprehension

3 **Characters • Critical**
Text to Self **Think about the grandfather's personality and spirit. In what ways does he remind you of yourself or someone you know?**

Responses will vary. The grandfather's courage, determination, confidence, adventurousness, or independence may remind students of themselves or friends.

4 **Main Idea • Inferential**
What is the main idea of p. 75, paragraph 1? What details support that idea?

Main idea: The grandfather loved California best. Supporting details: He liked the sunlight, the mountains, and the seacoast.

Monitor Progress
REVIEW Main Idea

If... students have difficulty identifying the main idea and supporting details,	**then...** use the skill and strategy instruction on p. 75.

5 **Draw Conclusions • Inferential**
How does the grandfather feel about North America? How can you tell?

Possible response: He is fascinated by it. After he marries his wife in Japan, he brings her back to California with him.

He marveled at the towering mountains and rivers as clear as the sky.

He met many people along the way. He shook hands with black men and white men, with yellow men and red men.

3 The more he traveled, the more he longed to see new places, and never thought of returning home.

74

Access Content Students may be familiar with the terms *black men* and *white men* (p. 74, paragraph 2), but not *yellow men* and *red men*. Explain these were terms sometimes used to refer to Asians and Native Americans. Discuss the cultural connotations of these historic terms and the terms ethnic groups use to name themselves today.

Of all the places he visited, he liked California **4** best. He loved the strong sunlight there, the Sierra Mountains, the lonely seacoast.

After a time, he returned to his village in Japan to marry his childhood sweetheart. Then he brought his bride to the new country.

They made their home by the San Francisco Bay and had a baby girl. **5**

San Francisco

Time for
SOCIAL STUDIES

San Francisco is one of the largest cities on the west coast of the United States. Built on and around more than forty hills, this unique city is a popular tourist attraction. Two well-known bridges, the Golden Gate Bridge and the Bay Bridge, connect the city to other parts of the Bay Area. San Francisco has one of the largest Asian populations in the continental United States. Of the more than 750,000 people that called San Francisco home in 2000, about 240,000 of them are people of Asian ancestry.

Main Idea (REVIEW)

TEACH

- Remind students that a main idea is an important point about the story's topic.
- Supporting details give more information about a main idea.

Think Aloud **MODEL** The first sentence says that the grandfather liked California best. The next sentence says that he liked the sunlight, the Sierra Mountains, and the lonely seacoast. These details tell what the grandfather liked about California. So the main idea must be the idea in the first sentence: *Grandfather liked California best.*

PRACTICE AND ASSESS

- Ask students to identify the main idea on p. 74. Have them name some details that support this idea. (*Main idea: Grandfather enjoyed traveling around North America. Supporting detail: He marveled at the towering mountains.*)
- To assess, use Practice Book p. 26.

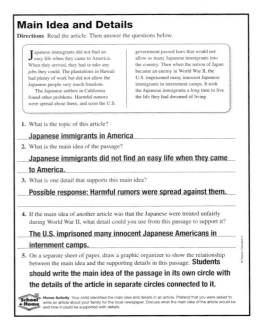

Main Idea and Details
Directions Read the article. Then answer the questions below.

Japanese immigrants did not find an easy life when they came to America. When they arrived, they had to take any jobs they could. The plantations in Hawaii had plenty of work but did not allow the Japanese people very much freedom.

The Japanese settlers in California found other problems. Harmful rumors were spread about them, and soon the U.S. government passed laws that would not allow as many Japanese immigrants into the country. Then when the nation of Japan became an enemy in World War II, the U.S. imprisoned many innocent Japanese immigrants in internment camps. It took the Japanese immigrants a long time to live the life they had dreamed of living.

1. What is the topic of this article?
   Japanese immigrants in America

2. What is the main idea of the passage?
   Japanese immigrants did not find an easy life when they came to America.

3. What is one detail that supports this main idea?
   Possible response: Harmful rumors were spread against them.

4. If the main idea of another article was that the Japanese were treated unfairly during World War II, what detail could you use from this passage to support it?
   The U.S. imprisoned many innocent Japanese Americans in internment camps.

5. On a separate sheet of paper, draw a graphic organizer to show the relationship between the main idea and the supporting details in this passage. **Students should write the main idea of the passage in its own circle with the details of the article in separate circles connected to it.**

School + Home **Home Activity** Your child identified the main idea and details in an article. Pretend that you were asked to write an article about your family for the local newspaper. Discuss what the main idea of the article would be and how it could be supported with details.

▲ **Practice Book** p. 26

Guiding Comprehension

6 **Draw Conclusions • Inferential**

Why would the grandfather leave a place he loved so much?

He missed his homeland too much to stay in the United States.

7 **Cause and Effect • Inferential**

Why did the grandfather buy a large house in the city?

Possible response: His daughter was accustomed to life in a big city because she had been raised in San Francisco. He wanted her to be comfortable.

8 🎯 **Sequence • Inferential**

Tell in order the important events in this story so far.

Possible response: The narrator's grandfather left Japan as a young man. He traveled in North America. He returned to Japan to marry. He came back and settled in California. He had a daughter. His daughter grew up. He took his family back to Japan with him.

As his daughter grew, my grandfather began to think about his own childhood. He thought about his old friends.

He remembered the mountains and rivers of his home. He surrounded himself with songbirds, but he could not forget.

Finally, when his daughter was nearly grown, he could wait no more. He took his family and returned to **6** his homeland.

76

Monitor Progress	
🎯 **Graphic Sources**	
If... students have difficulty recalling important story events in order,	**then...** use the skill and strategy instruction on p. 77.

🄴🄻🄻

Extend Language Students can infer meaning by breaking a word into its smaller parts. *Childhood* (p. 76, paragraph 1) can be broken into *child + hood*. The suffix *-hood* means "the state of," so *childhood* means "state of being a child." Have students analyze *songbirds* (p. 76, paragraph 2) and *homeland* (p. 76, paragraph 3) the same way.

Once again he saw the mountains and rivers of his childhood. They were just as he had remembered them.

Once again he exchanged stories and laughed with his old friends.

But the village was not a place for a daughter from San Francisco. So my grandfather bought a house in a large city nearby. **7**

8

77

 SKILLS ↔ STRATEGIES IN CONTEXT

Sequence Graphic Organizers

TEACH

- Remind students to use clue words to help them keep track of story events.
- Point out that a time line will help them organize story events in time order. Model creating a time line.
- Work with students to add other story events to the time line.

Think Aloud **MODEL** I look back through the story for clues to when things happened. I read that the grandfather left Japan as "a young man," so I'm going to write that on the first line. It says that "after a time" he went back to Japan and got married. Then he returned to San Francisco, where he and his wife had a baby girl. I write these events in that order on the time line.

PRACTICE AND ASSESS

Have students look at the time line and answer questions such as these: *Did the grandfather buy a house in Japan before or after his daughter was born? (After; he returned to Japan when his daughter was "nearly grown.")*

Strategy Response Log

Update Graphic Organizer Have students review the T-chart they began before reading the story. (See p. 70.) Have them add ideas based on what they've read so far.

If you want to teach this selection in two sessions, stop here.

Guiding Comprehension

If you are teaching the story in two days, discuss the sequence of events so far and review the vocabulary.

9 🔊 **Vocabulary • Dictionary/Glossary**

Have students use a dictionary to identify the meaning of *raised* as it is used on p. 78, paragraph 3.

Possible response: *Raised* means "looked after someone or something as it grew up."

Monitor Progress

🔊 Dictionary/Glossary

If... students are unable to use a dictionary to identify the meaning of *raised*,	**then...** use the vocabulary strategy instruction on p. 79.

---

10 **Simile • Inferential**

Explain the meaning of this sentence from p. 79: "Bombs fell from the sky and scattered our lives like leaves in a storm."

Possible response: Leaves in a storm blow and scatter in every direction. You can't predict where they will end up. The family's lives have been drastically changed, and the future is unpredictable.

DAY 3 Grouping Options

Reading
Whole Group Discuss the Question of the Day.

Group Time Differentiated Instruction
Read *Grandfather's Journey*. See pp. 66f–66g for the small group lesson plan.

Whole Group Discuss the Reader Response questions on p. 80. Then use p. 87a.

Language Arts
Use pp. 87e–87k.

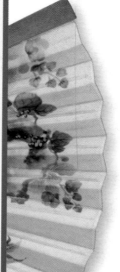

There, the young woman fell in love, married, and sometime later I was born.

When I was a small boy, my favorite weekend was a visit to my grandfather's house. He told me many stories about California.

9 He raised warblers and silvereyes, but he could not forget the mountains and rivers of California. So he planned a trip.

78

ⒺⓁⓁ

Context Clues Remind students that when they come to words they don't understand, they can read on to see if the context makes the meaning clear. Students may be unfamiliar with the *warblers* and *silvereyes* the grandfather raised (p. 78, paragraph 3), but if they read on, they will discover that the grandfather "never kept another songbird" (p. 79, paragraph 3).

But a war began. Bombs fell from the sky and scattered our lives like leaves in a storm. **10**

When the war ended, there was nothing left of the city and of the house where my grandparents had lived.

So they returned to the village where they had been children. But my grandfather never kept another songbird.

79

 VOCABULARY STRATEGY

Dictionary/ Glossary

TEACH

- Remind students that some words have more than one meaning. Readers sometimes need to check a dictionary or glossary to find the meaning that makes sense for the sentence.
- Model using a dictionary to identify the correct meaning of a multiple-meaning word.

Think Aloud **MODEL** On p. 78, paragraph 3, the author says, "He raised warblers and silvereyes." Warblers and silvereyes are birds, but I'm not sure what it means when it says he *raised* them. When I look up the word in the dictionary I see two definitions. The word *raised* can mean "to lift something up" or it can mean "to look after somebody until he or she is grown." Now I know the grandfather must have been looking after the birds until they were grown.

PRACTICE AND ASSESS

Have students use a dictionary to identify the meaning of *trip* as it is used in the last sentence on p. 78. *(journey; voyage)*

To assess, have them use this meaning in another sentence.

Wartime Conditions

Time for SOCIAL STUDIES

Japanese Americans suffered hardship and injustice in the United States during World War II. After Japan bombed Pearl Harbor on December 7, 1941, the United States declared war on Japan. Many Americans suspected *all* Japanese—even those who had grown up in the United States—of being traitors. In 1942, the U.S. government forced about 120,000 people of Japanese ancestry to leave their homes. They were imprisoned in camps with barbed wire fences and armed guards. At the same time, more than 20,000 Japanese American soldiers were serving in U.S. military units fighting bravely for their country: the United States.

Guiding Comprehension

11 🔵 **Graphic Organizers • Critical**

What events could be listed on a time line for the narrator's life?

Possible response: He grew up in Japan. He went to the United States as a young man. He had a daughter there. He stayed in the United States.

12 Theme • Inferential

What does the narrator mean when he says, "I think I know my grandfather now"?

Possible response: He understands how his grandfather thought and felt. He loves both countries, just as his grandfather did.

13 Plot • Critical

Text to World **Ask students to recall what they know of World War II. Why do they think this war prevented the grandfather from returning to the United States?**

Possible response: Japan and the United States were at war, and Japanese Americans in the U.S. were mistrusted.

Strategy Response Log

Summarize When students finish reading the selection, provide this prompt: Suppose you were asked to write a summary of *Grandfather's Journey* for a library catalog item. Summarize the story in a few sentences.

Tech Files ONLINE

Some students may want to know more about the grandfather's homeland of Japan. They can use a student-friendly search engine to learn more about this country. Suggest that they use the keyword *Japan.*

The last time I saw him, my grandfather said that he longed to see California one more time. He never did.

And when I was nearly grown, I left home and went to see California for myself.

After a time, I came to love the land my grandfather had **11** loved, and I stayed on and on until I had a daughter of my own.

80

ELL

Access Content Students may be unfamiliar with the phrase "I cannot still the longing in my heart" (p. 81, paragraph 1). Restate using the parallel structure "I cannot stop the desire in my heart". See if students can infer the meaning of the phrase "he longed to see California" (p. 80, paragraph 1).

But I also miss the mountains and rivers of my childhood. I miss my old friends. So I return now and then, when I cannot [still] the longing in my heart.

The funny thing is, the moment I am in one country, I am homesick for the other.

I think I know my grandfather now. I miss him **12** very much.

13

81

Develop Vocabulary

PRACTICE LESSON VOCABULARY

Write these vocabulary words on the board: *homeland, still, longed.* Then have students select the correct word for each blank.

1. My neighbor missed her _____ and hoped to return soon. *(homeland)*

2. She _____ to see her childhood friends again. *(longed)*

3. She could not _____ the aching in her heart. *(still)*

BUILD CONCEPT VOCABULARY

Review previous concept words with students. Ask if students have come across any words today in their reading or elsewhere that they would like to add to the Traveling America Concept Web, such as *mountains* and *rivers*.

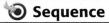 **STRATEGY SELF-CHECK**

Graphic Organizers

Remind students that good readers use graphic organizers to help them remember what they have read. Have each student complete a time line that shows the order of the most important events in this story. For more practice, use Practice Book p. 27.

SELF-CHECK

Have students ask themselves these questions to assess their understanding of the story.

- Did I list the most important story events on my time line?
- Did I list the events in the order in which they happened?

Monitor Progress

Sequence

If... students have difficulty using a graphic organizer to sequentially organize the events in this story,	**then...** use the Reteach lesson on p. 87b.

Sequence

- **Sequence** is the order in which things happen.
- Dates, times, and clue words such as *first, then, next,* and *last* can help you understand the order of events.

Directions Read the passage. Then answer the questions below.

The 442nd Regimental Combat Team, a brave team of Japanese American soldiers during World War II, had an interesting history. The team was made up of Japanese Americans from Hawaii and from the continental United States. These two groups grew up very differently. When they met for the first time in April of 1943 for training, they did not get along very well. They fought with each other constantly. But after they took a trip to an internment camp and saw how Japanese Americans were treated, they learned to respect each other. They trained hard from May until February of 1944.

In the spring, they left for combat in Europe. There they were joined by other battalions, including the 100th Infantry Battalion. The 442nd Regimental Combat Team served their country well and were honored with more than 9,000 Purple Hearts.

1. What major event is described first?
   The first event is when the soldiers met each other.

2. When did the team learn to appreciate each other?
   It happened after they took a trip to an internment camp.

3. What words tell you when the team left for combat in Europe?
   "in the spring"

4. Did the 100th Infantry Battalion join the 442nd Regimental Combat Team before or after they arrived in Europe? How do you know?
   after; You know because the passage says "there," meaning in Europe.

5. On a separate piece of paper, write the information from the passage in order using a graphic organizer. Graphic organizer should show the main events of the passage in the order in which they occurred.

School + Home Home Activity Your child has identified the order of events in a nonfiction article. Discuss the activities your child has to do in the upcoming week. Help your child put these activities in sequential order.

▲ **Practice Book** p. 27

Reader Response

Open for Discussion Personal Response

MODEL I think Grandfather would start by saying, "Coming to America was an incredible adventure."

Comprehension Check Critical Response

1. Possible responses: He wanted the characters to seem real. **Author's Purpose**

2. Grandfather travels to the U.S. He marries in Japan and settles in San Francisco. As his daughter grows, Grandfather thinks about his own childhood. ◉ *Sequence*

3. Beginning: Grandfather moves to the U.S. Middle: Grandfather marries and has a child. End: Grandfather returns to Japan. ◉ *Graphic Organizers*

4. List words: *amazed, bewildered.* Other words: *astonished, excited, marveled.* ◉ *Vocabulary*

Look Back and Write For test practice, assign a 10–15 minute time limit. For assessment, see the Scoring Rubric at the right.

Retell
Have students retell *Grandfather's Journey.*

Monitor Progress
Check Retelling 4 3 2 1 Rubric

If... students have difficulty retelling the story,	then... use the Retelling Cards and the Scoring Rubric for Retelling on p. 83 to assist fluent retelling.

SUCCESS PREDICTOR

Check Retelling Have students use the story's illustrations to guide their retellings. They can also use any graphic organizers they created showing the story's sequence. For more ideas on assessing students' retellings, see the ELL and Transition Handbook.

82

Reader Response

Open for Discussion Suppose Grandfather could describe his journey. What might he say? Examine each picture and tell what Grandfather might be saying about his experience.

1. Allen Say's paintings are like photographs, as if people had posed for them. Why do you think Mr. Say made his paintings so lifelike? *Think Like an Author*

2. Summarize what happens in Grandfather's life from the time he arrives in America until he returns to Japan. *Sequence*

3. Create a sequence organizer for the story with boxes for the story's beginning, middle, and end. Briefly describe what happens in each part of the story. *Graphic Organizers*

4. Which verbs on the Words to Know list tell how Grandfather felt as he journeyed to and then across North America? Find other verbs in the story to add to the list. *Vocabulary*

Look Back and Write Write a list of ten things that astonished Grandfather when he came to North America as a young man. Underline the one he liked best.

Meet author **and illustrator Allen Say on page 775.**

82

Scoring Rubric Look Back and Write

Top-Score Response A top-score response will use information from the selection to list ten things that surprised Grandfather when he came to North America. Students will underline the thing Grandfather liked best.

Example of a Top-Score Response 1) deserts 2) farm fields 3) huge cities 4) tall buildings 5) towering mountains 6) clear rivers 7) many different people 8) California 9) the Sierra Mountains 10) seacoast.

For additional rubrics, see p. WA10.

Write Now

Postcard

Prompt

Grandfather's Journey describes how different places became important to the author's grandfather.

Think about a place that you have visited. Now write a postcard describing that special place.

Student Model

Introductory paragraph connects the writer to the reader.

Writer uses figurative language to help describe the place.

Exclamatory sentences and an interjection make the voice lively.

Dear Melissa,

New York City is amazing! Do you remember when we saw Times Square on TV? Well, I'm here!

This morning we walked across the Brooklyn Bridge. I could see the Statue of Liberty out in the harbor. What a sight that was! Then we took a subway. It was like riding a roller coaster underground. We came up out of the subway at Times Square. Wow! I've never seen so many people. Tonight we are seeing a Broadway show.

See you soon,
Becca

Use the model to help you write your own postcard.

83

Write Now

Look at the Prompt Have students identify and discuss key words and phrases in the prompt. *(place that you have visited, postcard, describing)*

Strategies to Develop Voice

Have students:

- read their postcards aloud. Does the voice sound friendly and lively?
- add precise details about the place they are describing.
- revise words and phrases that do not sound friendly.

NO: This place is nice.

YES: Would you love it here? You bet!

For additional suggestions and rubric, see pp. 87g–87h.

Hints for Better Writing

- Carefully read the prompt.
- Use a graphic organizer to plan your writing.
- Support your ideas with information and details.
- Use words that help readers understand.
- Proofread and edit your work.

Scoring Rubric | Narrative Retelling

Rubric 4 3 2 1	4	3	2	1
Connections	Makes connections and generalizes beyond the text	Makes connections to other events, stories, or experiences	Makes a limited connection to another event, story, or experience	Makes no connection to another event, story, or experience
Author's Purpose	Elaborates on author's purpose	Tells author's purpose with some clarity	Makes some connection to author's purpose	Makes no connection to author's purpose
Characters	Describes the main character(s) and any character development	Identifies the main character(s) and gives some information about them	Inaccurately identifies some characters or gives little information about them	Inaccurately identifies the characters or gives no information about them
Setting	Describes the time and location	Identifies the time and location	Omits details of time or location	Is unable to identify time or location
Plot	Describes the problem, goal, events, and ending using rich detail	Tells the problem, goal, events, and ending with some errors that do not affect meaning	Tells parts of the problem, goal, events, and ending with gaps that affect meaning	Retelling has no sense of story

Retelling Plan

- ☑ **Week 1** Assess Strategic Intervention students.
- ☑ **Week 2** Assess Advanced students.
- ☑ **This week assess Strategic Intervention students.**
- ☐ **Week 4** Assess On-Level students.
- ☐ **Week 5** Assess any students you have not checked during this unit.

Use the Retelling Chart on p. TR16 to record retelling.

Selection Test To assess with *Grandfather's Journey*, use Selection Tests, pp. 9–12.

Fresh Reads for Differentiated Test Practice For weekly leveled practice, use pp. 13–18.

Retelling

SUCCESS PREDICTOR

Reading Online

- Examine the features of online reference sources.
- Compare and contrast across texts.

PREVIEW/USE TEXT FEATURES

As students preview "A Look at Two Lands," direct their attention to the map, URL entries, pictures, and captions. Discuss how these text features may remind them of features they have seen in print sources. Ask:

- **How do the graphic sources in this selection help readers?** *(They help readers visualize the information being presented.)*

- **How would you go from one page to another in an online reference source?** *(You would click a link with your mouse or type a new address into the window.)* If students need help understanding how to navigate in an online reference source, use the Technology Tools Box below.

Link to Social Studies

Brainstorm a list of places students have read about and ask them to describe each setting.

DAY 4 Grouping Options

Reading
Whole Group Discuss the Question of the Day.

Group Time **Differentiated Instruction**
Read "A Look at Two Lands." See pp. 66f–66g for the small group lesson plan.

Whole Group Use p. 87a.

Language Arts
Use pp. 87e–87k.

Reading Online

New Literacies: **PearsonSuccessNet.com**

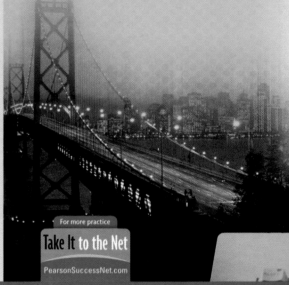

A Look at Two Lands

Online Reference Sources

Genre
- **You can find reference sources, such as atlases, dictionaries, and encyclopedias, on Internet Web sites.**
- **Some Web sites give you several different reference sources all in one place.**

Text Features
- **Online reference sources look a lot like print sources, and they are organized in the same way.**
- **Instead of turning pages by hand, you use a mouse to click your way through them.**

Link to Social Studies
Think about where you live. How is it like or unlike someplace you've read about? Share your observations.

After reading *Grandfather's Journey,* you wonder what Japan and California are like. "Why did Allen Say's grandfather love both places so much?" you might ask. To find out, you could go to an online reference Web site.

For more practice
Take It to the Net
PearsonSuccessNet.com

84

TECHNOLOGY TOOLS

Online Reference Sources

Search Window Type the keyword or phrase you want to research here. Most search windows are identified by a word like *SEARCH* or *GO*. Remember to click on the empty search window before typing.

 Back/Forward Instead of turning pages, online researchers click on these buttons. Click on the *Back* button to go to the previous Web site page. Click on the *Forward* button to return to the page you were on before you clicked on the *Back* button.

 Home When you click on the *Home* button, it takes you to the computer's home page, the first Web page you see when you go online. This page is like a table of contents in a book.

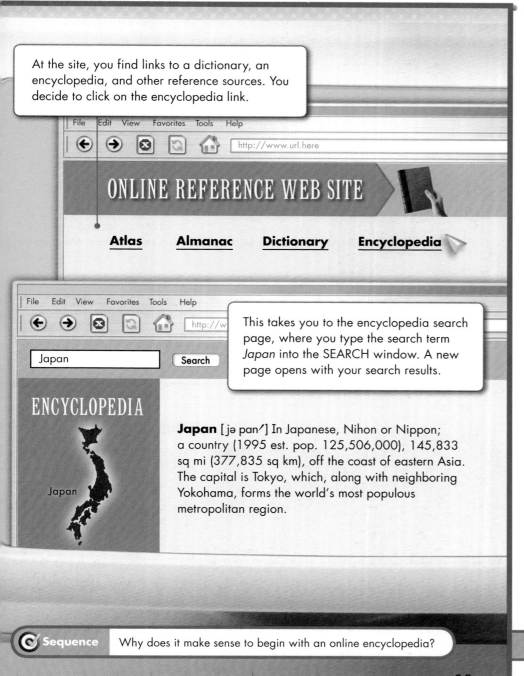

At the site, you find links to a dictionary, an encyclopedia, and other reference sources. You decide to click on the encyclopedia link.

File   Edit   View   Favorites   Tools   Help

http://www.url.here

ONLINE REFERENCE WEB SITE

Atlas   **Almanac**   **Dictionary**   **Encyclopedia**

File   Edit   View   Favorites   Tools   Help

http://w

Japan   Search

This takes you to the encyclopedia search page, where you type the search term *Japan* into the SEARCH window. A new page opens with your search results.

ENCYCLOPEDIA

Japan

Japan [jə pan′] In Japanese, Nihon or Nippon; a country (1995 est. pop. 125,506,000), 145,833 sq mi (377,835 sq km), off the coast of eastern Asia. The capital is Tokyo, which, along with neighboring Yokohama, forms the world's most populous metropolitan region.

 **Sequence**   Why does it make sense to begin with an online encyclopedia?

85

WEB-IQUETTE

Online Reference Sources

Tell students that while online reference sources are a quick and efficient way to find information, there are certain rules of etiquette they should follow:

- Check that you spell keywords correctly. Otherwise, you may not find the information you need.
- Be sure to follow the classroom rules for saving files, printing pages, and bookmarking Web sites.
- Use your research time wisely. Stay focused on finding answers to specific inquiry questions.
- Remember to record the URL address of any reference source you use. If allowed, print a page that shows the URL address or copy the URL from the address window and paste it into a new document. If you record the address by hand, make sure you copy every letter and symbol exactly as it is shown on the screen.

NEW LITERACIES: Online Reference Sources

Use the sidebar on p. 84 to guide discussion.

- Tell students that online reference sources are informational sources that can be found on the Internet. They contain similar information as encyclopedias, dictionaries, and atlases found on bookshelves.
- Point out the search window shown on p. 85. Explain that online resources have their own search engines. Students find information by typing keywords in the search window and clicking on the *Search* or *Go* button or link or pressing the *Enter* key on their keyboard.
- Discuss similarities and differences between online and print reference sources. Ask if students prefer using online or print reference sources and have them give reasons for their preferences.

Audio CD   AudioText

 **Sequence**

Possible response: An online encyclopedia would give general information about both countries. A researcher could search for more specific information after looking at the online encyclopedia.

ELL

Access Content Preview the selection with students, naming specific text features and discussing important terms, such as *online, Web site, link, search results, mouse,* and *click.*

Strategies for Navigation

USE GRAPHIC SOURCES Remind students that they can use graphic sources, such as maps, illustrations, photographs, time lines, and graphs, to help them find and understand information in an online reference source. Online references may also include short video or audio clips.

Use the Strategy

1. The next time you use an online encyclopedia, scan the screen for graphics. Look for pictures, charts, or other visuals that can help you understand the text better.

2. Compare the graphic sources to nearby text. Use the graphics to help you visualize information in the text.

3. Look for links to other graphic sources that may give you additional visual information. You may also be able to enlarge some graphics by clicking on them.

PRACTICE Think about the ways you use graphic sources when researching online at home and at school.

- Choose a place you would like to know more about. Make a list of graphic sources you could use to learn about this place. For example, to learn about the Arctic, a graph of temperatures might be helpful.

- The next time you access the Internet, try searching an online reference source to find graphics that tell you more about the place.

Now you decide to find out something about California. You find these results in an encyclopedia search.

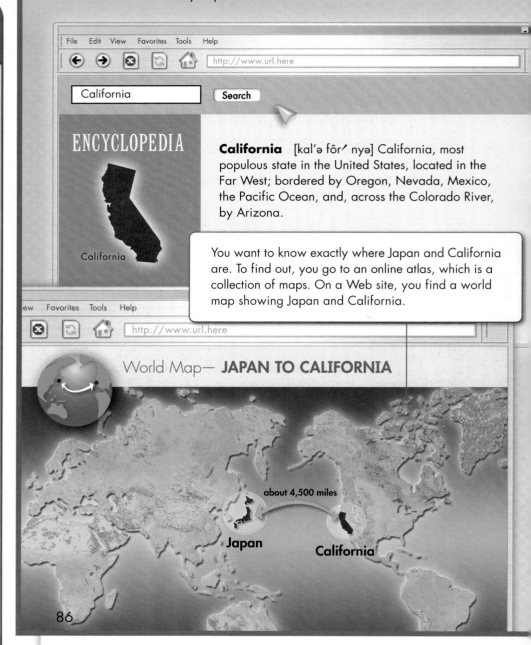

File   Edit   View   Favorites   Tools   Help

http://www.url.here

California   Search

ENCYCLOPEDIA

California

California [kal′ə fôr′ nyə] California, most populous state in the United States, located in the Far West; bordered by Oregon, Nevada, Mexico, the Pacific Ocean, and, across the Colorado River, by Arizona.

You want to know exactly where Japan and California are. To find out, you go to an online atlas, which is a collection of maps. On a Web site, you find a world map showing Japan and California.

Favorites   Tools   Help

http://www.url.here

World Map— **JAPAN TO CALIFORNIA**

about 4,500 miles

Japan   **California**

86

Guided Practice If time allows, have students log onto the Internet. Show them how to search for information in an online encyclopedia and access its graphic sources. Help students make connections between the steps they are doing and related vocabulary terms.

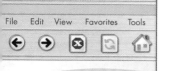

File　Edit　View　Favorites　Tools

On another Web site, you find these photographs of Japan and California. Now you are beginning to understand why Allen Say's grandfather loved both places so much.

Scenes from
JAPAN

Scenes from
CALIFORNIA

As you have learned from your research, Japan and California are far apart. Yet both contain a beauty that can appeal to many people.

Reading Across Texts

Both *Grandfather's Journey* and this article give information about Japan and California. In which place would you rather live? Choose one and list your reasons.

Writing Across Texts Write about why you would rather live in the place you chose.

Graphic Organizers | Which online source might have many lists and charts?

87

CONNECT TEXT-TO-TEXT

Reading Across Texts

Suggest students begin by reviewing the two texts. Have them identify specific details about the location and geography of each place. They can compare these details to help them decide which place they prefer.

Writing Across Texts Encourage students to use vivid and interesting details from their lists to help them explain why they would rather live in one place than the other.

Graphic Organizers

Possible response: An almanac includes facts about a lot of different topics. It would likely have many lists.

Fluency Assessment Plan

- ☑ **Week 1** Assess Advanced students.
- ☑ **Week 2** Assess Strategic Intervention students.
- ☑ **This week assess On-Level students.**
- ☐ **Week 4** Assess Strategic Intervention students.
- ☐ **Week 5** Assess any students you have not yet checked during this unit.

Set individual goals for students to enable them to reach the year-end goal.

- Current Goal: 95–105 WCPM
- Year-End Goal: 130 WCPM

English language learners may be able to decode some English words but still not know the meanings. Help students recognize that they will understand sentences better and read more fluently as they learn more English words.

To develop fluent readers, use Fluency Coach.

DAY 5 Grouping Options

Reading
Whole Group
Revisit the Question of the Week.

Group Time
Differentiated Instruction
Reread this week's Leveled Readers. See pp. 66f–66g for the small group lesson plan.

Whole Group
Use p. 87b–87c.

Language Arts
Use pp. 87d–87l.

TEMPO AND RATE

Fluency

 DAY 1

Model Reread aloud "Going Places" on p. 66m. Explain that, because the text has many statements of fact and details, you will use a slower tempo and rate to help listeners understand it better. Model for students as you read.

DAY 2

Choral Reading Read aloud p. 76 at a moderate tempo, pausing after phrases and between sentences. Have students notice how your tempo matches the slow, thoughtful pace of the writing. Have students practice as a class, doing three choral readings of p. 76.

DAY 3

Model Read aloud p. 81. Have students notice how your tempo matches the mood of the writing. Practice as a class by doing three choral readings.

DAY 4

Partner Reading Have partners practice reading aloud p. 81, three times, using appropriate tempo and rate. You might have them read quickly once so they hear how an inappropriate tempo affects meaning.

Monitor Progress — Check Fluency WCPM

As students reread, monitor their progress toward their individual fluency goals. Current Goal: 95–105 words correct per minute. End-of-Year Goal: 130 words correct per minute.

If… students cannot read fluently at a rate of 95–105 words correct per minute,
then… make sure students practice with text at their independent level. Provide additional fluency practice, pairing nonfluent readers with fluent readers.

If… students already read at 130 words correct per minute,
then… they do not need to reread three to four times.

SUCCESS PREDICTOR

DAY 5

Assessment
Individual Reading Rate Use the Fluency Assessment Plan and do a one-minute timed reading of the first selection from this week to assess students in Week 3. Pay special attention to this week's skill, tempo and rate. Provide corrective feedback for each student.

RETEACH

Sequence

TEACH

Review the definition of *sequence* on p. 66. Students can complete Practice Book p. 28 on their own or as a class. As they read the passage, have them look for clue words such as *then, later,* and *after* to help them understand the order of events. They can also ask themselves questions, such as: *What happened first? Then what happened? What happened last?*

ASSESS

Have students reread pp. 78–79 and tell what happened to the grandfather from the time the narrator was born until the grandfather died. *(He planned a trip to California but didn't go because the war began. During the war, his house was destroyed. After the war, he and his wife moved back to their childhood village.)*

For additional instruction on sequence, see DI·54.

EXTEND SKILLS

Paraphrase

TEACH

When you paraphrase, you put something in your own words.

- Paraphrasing should keep the ideas and meaning of the original text, but be simpler to read.
- A paraphrase should not include the reader's opinions.

Ask students to paraphrase pp. 73–74 in small groups. Students can discuss the text before agreeing on what they write down.

ASSESS

Have students write a paraphrase for pp. 76–77. They can ask themselves:

1. **Does my paraphrase show a good understanding of the pages?**
2. **Have I used my own words?**

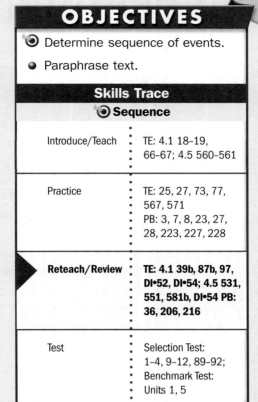

OBJECTIVES
- Determine sequence of events.
- Paraphrase text.

Skills Trace	
Sequence	
Introduce/Teach	TE: 4.1 18–19, 66–67; 4.5 560–561
Practice	TE: 25, 27, 73, 77, 567, 571 PB: 3, 7, 8, 23, 27, 28, 223, 227, 228
Reteach/Review	**TE: 4.1 39b, 87b, 97, DI•52, DI•54; 4.5 531, 551, 581b, DI•54 PB: 36, 206, 216**
Test	Selection Test: 1–4, 9–12, 89–92; Benchmark Test: Units 1, 5

ELL
Access Content Reteach the skill by reviewing the Picture It! lesson on sequence in the ELL Teaching Guide, pp. 15–16.

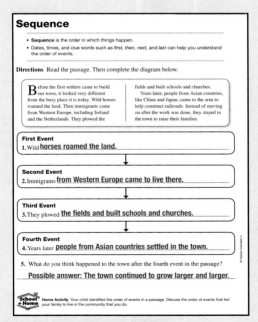

▲ **Practice Book** p. 28

SUCCESS PREDICTOR

Vocabulary and Word Study

VOCABULARY STRATEGY

Dictionary/ Glossary

MULTIPLE-MEANING WORDS Point out that many words have more than one meaning. Readers can look up the meanings of a word in a glossary or dictionary, but they must think about how the word is used in context to choose the appropriate definition. Have students use a dictionary to complete a chart listing different meanings for the words *lonely* and *country,* from *Grandfather's Journey* and identify the appropriate meaning for the context. Then have them choose another multiple-meaning word from the selection to add to the chart.

Story Word in Context	Dictionary Definitions	Number of Meanings That Fit
the *lonely* seacoast of California	1. feeling yourself alone and longing for company or friends 2. without many people 3. alone; isolated	2

Related Words

Tell students the root *jour* comes from a French word meaning "day." Have groups of four copy the following words on slips of paper, one word per slip: *journey, journal, journalist, sojourn.* Have each student choose a slip, check word meaning, and then use the word to add to a round-robin story that begins: "Last week, I set out on my travels."

journalist

journey

sojourn

journal

BUILD CONCEPT VOCABULARY

Traveling America

LOOKING BACK Remind students of the question of the week: *What can we learn about the United States as we travel?* Discuss how this week's Concept Web of vocabulary words relates to the theme of traveling in the United States. Ask students if they have any words or categories to add. Discuss whether words and categories are appropriately related to the concept.

MOVING FORWARD Preview the title of the next selection, *The Horned Toad Prince.* Ask students which Concept Web words might apply to the new selection based on the title alone. Put a star next to these words on the Web.

Display the Concept Web and revisit the vocabulary words as you read the next selection to check predictions.

	Monitor Progress
	Check Vocabulary

If... students suggest words or categories that are not related to the concept,	**then...** review the words and categories on the Concept Web and discuss how they relate to the lesson concept.

SUCCESS PREDICTOR

Speaking and Listening

SPEAKING

Advertisement

SET-UP Have students select one city in the United States—their own or another city—and develop a radio advertisement that will convince people to visit there.

RESEARCH Students can use classroom resources or the Internet to find noteworthy information about the city they have chosen. Suggest they look for unusual or interesting natural features, tourist attractions, people, events, and so on. Remind students to keep a record of their sources in order to validate their research.

DELIVERY Remind students that effective advertisements are focused and brief. Advertisers want audiences to get the point quickly and remember it. Some speakers use animated voice tones and humor in their delivery. Repetition of keywords and phrases is also common.

Rehearsal Tips

• Use a variety of tones of voice to emphasize different words and phrases while rehearsing. Select the most effective approaches.

• Tape yourself rehearsing the advertisement. Listen carefully and think about how you can make it better. Make appropriate changes.

• Practice your advertisement in front of a classmate. Ask for suggestions for improvement.

LISTENING

Listen to an Advertisement

Have each student listen critically to a classmate's radio advertisement. This step should be done during the rehearsal stage so speakers can use their partners' feedback to improve their advertisements. As students listen, they can analyze the effectiveness of the advertisement by answering questions such as these:

1. **How does the ad try to persuade you to visit the city? What is the most memorable language it uses?** *(Responses will vary but should cite specific examples.)*

2. **Are statements of opinion in the ad supported with facts and examples? How?** *(Responses will vary. Students should give examples of effective details and facts in the ads.)*

3. **How does the advertiser use voice tone, word emphasis, and repetition in the ad?** *(Responses should be supported by examples.)*

4. **What could the advertiser do to make this ad even more convincing?** *(Responses will vary but should include positive suggestions.)*

ELL

Support Vocabulary Use the following to review and extend vocabulary and to explore lesson concepts further:
• ELL Poster 3, Days 3–5 instruction
• Vocabulary Activities and Word Cards in ELL Teaching Guide, pp. 17–18

Assessment For information on assessing students' speaking and listening, see the ELL and Transition Handbook.

Vocabulary

SUCCESS PREDICTOR

Grammar **Subjects and Predicates**

OBJECTIVES

- Define and identify subjects and predicates.
- Distinguish between complete and simple subjects and predicates.
- Use subjects and predicates correctly in writing.
- Become familiar with subject and predicate assessment on high-stakes tests.

Monitor Progress

Grammar

| If... students have difficulty identifying subjects and predicates, | then... provide additional instruction and practice in The Grammar and Writing Book pp. 62–65. |

DAILY FIX-IT

This week use Daily Fix-It Transparency 3. *Spiral* REVIEW

Grammar Support See the Grammar Transition lessons in the ELL and Transition Handbook.

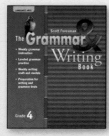

▲ **The Grammar and Writing Book**
For more instruction and practice, use pp. 62–65.

DAY 1 Teach and Model

DAILY FIX-IT

1. The hot springs at Yellowstone National Park is amazing? *(are amazing.)*

2. We saw an eagel. At our campsite. *(eagle at)*

READING-GRAMMAR CONNECTION

Write this sentence from *Grandfather's Journey* on the board:

> *The Pacific Ocean* astonished him.

Point out that the words underlined once are the **complete subject.** It tells whom or what the sentence is about. The words underlined twice are the **complete predicate.** It tells what the subject is or does.

Display Grammar Transparency 3. Read aloud the definitions and sample sentences. Work through the items.

Subjects and Predicates

Every sentence has a **subject** and a **predicate**. The **subject** is the part of the sentence that tells whom or what the sentence is about. All the words in the subject are called the **complete subject**. The **simple subject** is the most important word in the complete subject. A simple subject can be more than one word, as in *San Francisco*.

| Complete Subject | My grandfather from Japan traveled to California. |
| Simple Subject | My grandfather from Japan traveled to California. |

The **predicate** is the part of the sentence that tells what the subject is or does. All the words in the predicate are called the **complete predicate**. The **simple predicate**, or **verb**, is the most important word in the complete predicate. A simple predicate can be more than one word, as in *had lived*.

| Complete Predicate | My grandfather from Japan traveled to California. |
| Simple Predicate | My grandfather from Japan traveled to California. |

A **compound subject** is made up of two or more simple subjects. A **compound predicate** is made up of two or more simple predicates.

| Compound Subject | My sister and I were born in Japan. |
| Compound Predicate | We live and work in the United States. |

Directions Underline the complete subject of each sentence once. Underline the complete predicate twice.

1. My grandfather came from Japan.
2. He explored North America and settled in San Francisco.
3. His wife and daughter were born in Japan.
4. A terrible war destroyed his city.

Directions Circle the simple subject and the simple predicate of each sentence.

5. San Francisco was his favorite American city.
6. America's huge prairies reminded him of the ocean.
7. America has welcomed people from other lands.
8. This story will tell people about my grandfather's life.

Unit 1 Grandfather's Journey   Grammar **3**

▲ **Grammar Transparency** 3

DAY 2 Develop the Concept

DAILY FIX-IT

3. Mr and mrs. Kim entertained us in San Francisco. *(Mr. and Mrs.)*

4. They, were at the airport to great us. *(They were; greet)*

GUIDED PRACTICE

Review the concept of subjects and predicates.

- Every sentence has a **subject** and a **predicate.**

- The **subject** is the part of the sentence that tells whom or what the sentence is about.

- The **predicate** is the part of the sentence that tells what the subject is or does.

- A sentence that is missing a subject or a predicate is called a sentence fragment.

HOMEWORK Grammar and Writing Practice Book p. 9. Work through the first two items with the class.

Subjects and Predicates

Every sentence has a **subject** and a **predicate**. The **subject** is the part of the sentence that tells whom or what the sentence is about. All the words in the subject are called the **complete subject**. The **simple subject** is the most important word in the complete subject. A simple subject can be more than one word, as in *United States*.

| Complete Subject | The mountains in America reminded him of home. |
| Simple Subject | The mountains in America reminded him of home. |

The **predicate** is the part of the sentence that tells what the subject is or does. All the words in the predicate are called the **complete predicate**. The **simple predicate**, or **verb**, is the most important word in the complete predicate. A simple predicate can be more than one word, as in *was going*.

| Complete Predicate | The mountains in America reminded him of home. |
| Simple Predicate | The mountains in America reminded him of home. |

A **compound subject** is made up of two or more simple subjects. A **compound predicate** is made up of two or more simple predicates.

| Compound Subject | The forests and deserts amazed him. |
| Compound Predicate | He traveled and worked in the United States. |

Directions Look at the letters after each sentence. Circle the complete subject when you see *CS*, the simple subject when you see *SS*, the complete predicate when you see *CP*, and the simple predicate when you see *SP*.

1. The United States is home to millions of people from overseas. CP
2. This nation was founded by immigrants. SP
3. Many of the newcomers are from Asia. CS
4. Some become U.S. citizens. SS
5. More people are arriving every day. SP

Home Activity Your child learned about subjects and predicates. Ask your child to find sentences in a newspaper or magazine. Have him or her identify the simple subject and simple predicate in each sentence.

▲ **Grammar and Writing Practice Book** p. 9

DAY 3 Apply to Writing

DAILY FIX-IT

5. What an amazing sity San Francisco is. *(city; is!)*

6. My dad, my mom, my brother, and I. Went to chinatown. *(I went; Chinatown)*

ADD SPECIFIC DETAILS

Point out that specific details make writing more interesting to read.

• Have students review something they have written to see if they can improve it by adding specific details to subjects and predicates or by combining simple sentences into sentences with compound subjects or predicates.

HOMEWORK Grammar and Writing Practice Book p. 10.

Subjects and Predicates

Directions Each pair below has a simple subject and a verb. Add details to write an interesting sentence. Then underline the complete subject once and the complete predicate twice. **Possible answers:**

1. grandfather/traveled
The author's Grandfather traveled from Japan.

2. he/met
He met people from all over the country.

3. people/live
Many people live in cities.

4. mother/was born
Hanh's mother was born in Vietnam.

5. we/are learning
We are learning about American history.

6. I/will visit
I will visit New York City next summer.

7. United States of America/is
The United States of America is a great country.

8. visitors/come
Visitors from many other countries come to America.

9. schools/teach
Our schools teach people English.

10. Everyone/loves
Everyone in my class loves the Fourth of July.

Home Activity Your child learned how to use subjects and predicates in writing. Have your child write a sentence describing something he or she did today. Ask your child to identify the complete subject and the complete predicate of the sentence.

▲ **Grammar and Writing Practice Book** p. 10

DAY 4 Test Preparation

DAILY FIX-IT

7. Mr. Sakata, our neighbor, was borned in Japan? *(born; Japan.)*

8. He speaks English, he speaks and write Japanese. *(English. He; writes)*

STANDARDIZED TEST PREP

Test Tip

A simple subject can be more than one word, for example, a name:

San Francisco is a city in California.

A simple predicate can be more than one word, for example, a main verb and any helping verbs:

We are going to California.

HOMEWORK Grammar and Writing Practice Book p. 11.

Subjects and Predicates

Directions Mark the letter of the phrase that identifies the underlined word or words in each sentence.

1. Our family is going to California next summer.
   A simple subject
   B complete subject
   C simple predicate
   D complete predicate

2. San Francisco will be our first stop.
   A simple subject
   B complete subject
   C simple predicate
   D complete predicate

3. My mom promised us a visit to the Golden Gate Bridge.
   A simple subject
   B complete subject
   C simple predicate
   D complete predicate

4. We can ride in a cable car.
   A simple subject
   B complete subject
   C simple predicate
   D complete predicate

5. Our friends, the Kims, will entertain us.
   A simple subject
   B complete subject
   C simple predicate
   D complete predicate

6. Some other friends live in San Francisco too.
   A simple subject
   B complete subject
   C simple predicate
   D complete predicate

7. A travel agent booked our tickets.
   A simple subject
   B complete subject
   C simple predicate
   D complete predicate

8. Dad will take us to a ball game one night.
   A simple subject
   B complete subject
   C simple predicate
   D complete predicate

9. Fisherman's Wharf is a great place for dinner.
   A simple subject
   B complete subject
   C simple predicate
   D complete predicate

10. We are staying there for a week.
   A simple subject
   B complete subject
   C simple predicate
   D complete predicate

Home Activity Your child prepared for taking tests on subjects and predicates. Ask your child a question (What did you eat for lunch? When did you get home?). Have him or her write the answer in a complete sentence and identify the subject and predicate.

▲ **Grammar and Writing Practice Book** p. 11

DAY 5 Cumulative Review

DAILY FIX-IT

9. Your going to love the Rocky Mountains in colorado. *(You're; Colorado)*

10. They are higher then the mountains. Where we live. *(than; mountains where)*

ADDITIONAL PRACTICE

Assign pp. 62–65 in The Grammar and Writing Book.

EXTRA PRACTICE Grammar and Writing Practice Book p. 124.

ASSESSMENT

CUMULATIVE REVIEW Grammar and Writing Practice Book p. 12.

Subjects and Predicates

Directions Underline the complete subject of each sentence once. Underline the complete predicate twice.

1. The United States is a beautiful country.

2. Snow-capped mountains tower over the western plains.

3. Rich farmland provides food for millions of people.

4. Forests cover the ancient hills of the Northeast.

5. An amazing diversity of people live and work in the great cities.

Directions Look at the letters after each sentence. Write the simple subject when you see SS. Write the simple predicate when you see SP.

6. Many immigrants have made America their home. SP **have made**

7. They long for their old homes. SS **They**

8. Travel is fast these days. SS **Travel**

9. People can fly anywhere by airplane. SP **can fly**

10. The airplane has become a cure for homesickness! SP **has become**

Directions Write sentences using the pairs of words below. Use the noun as a simple subject and the verb as a simple predicate. Then underline the complete subject once and the complete predicate twice.

11. home/is **Possible answers:**
My home is in the United States.

12. country/has
This country has many beautiful places.

Home Activity Your child reviewed subjects and predicates. Ask your child to describe an object in the house in a sentence. Ask him or her to repeat the sentence and to identify the complete subject and complete predicate.

▲ **Grammar and Writing Practice Book** p. 12

Writing Workshop Postcard

- Identify qualities of a postcard.
- Write a postcard with events in sequence.
- Focus on voice.
- Use a rubric.

Genre Postcard
Writer's Craft Sequence
Writing Trait Voice

ELL

Voice Encourage English learners to use a bilingual dictionary if available, to find powerful verbs to express feelings. For example, *amazed* or *astounded* could express wonder. See more writing support in the ELL and Transition Handbook.

Writing Traits

FOCUS/IDEAS The writer selects ideas and details to interest his or her friend.

ORGANIZATION/PARAGRAPHS The postcard uses transition words to put experiences in order.

VOICE Writing is friendly and lively. The writer "talks" to the recipient.

WORD CHOICE The writer uses vivid details (*shark's fin, spider web*) to bring the scene to life.

SENTENCES Use of interrogative and exclamatory sentences catch the reader's interest.

CONVENTIONS There is excellent control and accuracy.

DAY 1 Model the Trait

READING-WRITING CONNECTION

- In *Grandfather's Journey,* the narrator uses his own unique voice to tell his grandfather's story.
- Like having a strong voice, telling a story in sequence keeps the reader engaged.
- Students will write a **postcard** in which they use their unique voice to describe events in sequence.

MODEL VOICE Discuss Writing Transparency 3A. Then discuss the model and the writing trait of voice.

 Think Aloud When I read this postcard aloud, it sounds friendly and enthusiastic. For example, the writer begins with an exclamation. "San Francisco is unbelievable!" There are other exclamations that show the writer's excitement. I can tell that the postcard is being written to a friend by the informal closing, "See you soon."

Postcard

A **postcard** is a brief message, with a picture on one side, sent by mail to friends or family. Often a postcard gives details about a place you are visiting on vacation and describes your feelings about being there.

Postcard from San Francisco

Writer talks directly to friend.
Sentences are varied and interesting.

Dear Maria,
    San Francisco is unbelievable! Do you remember those cable cars we saw on TV? I've been on one!

Events are described in order.

Writer uses figurative language.

Last night we had dinner in Chinatown. Dad ate shark's fin! This morning we saw the Golden Gate Bridge. It looked like a spider web in the fog. Tomorrow Mom and Dad want to go to the Japanese Cultural and Trade Center. My brother wants to go to a ball game. I can't make up my mind. There's so much to do!

See you soon,
Jasmine

Unit 1 Grandfather's Journey   Writing Model **3A**

▲ **Writing Transparency** 3A

DAY 2 Improve Writing

WRITER'S CRAFT
Sequence

Display Writing Transparency 3B. Read the directions and work together to put events in sequence.

 Think Aloud **SEQUENCE** Tomorrow we will be writing a postcard to a friend. I am going to pretend I'm writing my postcard from Los Angeles. It is important to describe the things I have been doing and seeing on my trip in sequence. It might get confusing for my reader if I present things out of order. I'll tell my friend what I did first, second, and third, all the way through to the end of my trip.

GUIDED WRITING Some students may need more help with sequence. Ask them to describe a day in their life, using words or phrases that help indicate sequence.

Sequence

Sequence is the order in which things happen in a story. Transition words such as *before, after, then, next,* and *finally* can tell you when something happens. Dates and times can also help you understand the order of events.
Transition word: He returned to Japan *after* exploring the United States.
Date: On *Monday* we were in San Francisco. On *Wednesday* we flew to Los Angeles.

Directions Read the summary of events from *Grandfather's Journey.* The events in the column below are out of order. Put the events in the correct sequence by numbering them in the order that they actually occurred. Write the numbers on the lines.

    Grandfather left Japan as a young man and went to the United States. Before returning home, he traveled throughout America. Later, he got married and settled in San Francisco, where he had a daughter. After many years, he took his family back to Japan.

    In 1941, the United States and Japan went to war. In 1945 the war was over, but Grandfather's home was destroyed. Finally, Grandfather returned to the village where he had been born.

1. **5** settles in San Francisco
2. **10** returns to village where he was born
3. **4** gets married
4. **3** returns to Japan as young man
5. **8** United States and Japan go to war
6. **1** leaves Japan as young man
7. **9** war ends
8. **2** travels throughout America
9. **6** has daughter
10. **7** takes family to Japan

Unit 1 Grandfather's Journey   Writer's Craft **3B**

▲ **Writing Transparency** 3B

DAY 3 — Prewrite and Draft

READ THE WRITING PROMPT

on page 83 in the Student Edition.

Grandfather's Journey *describes how different places became important to the author's grandfather.*

Think about a place that you have visited.

Now write a postcard describing that special place.

Writing Test Tips

- Choose carefully what you want to say. Space is limited on a postcard.
- Use vivid details. Make the recipient want to be where you are.
- Keep your voice friendly and lively. Remember that you are writing to someone you know well.
- Include a date to provide a sense of time.

GETTING STARTED Students can do any of the following:

- Make a word web about the place they are describing.
- Brainstorm places in the world they would like to visit and then find out more about those places.
- Think about the friend they might be writing to. What would that person want to hear about?
- Think of a catchy opening.

DAY 4 — Draft and Revise

EDITING/REVISING CHECKLIST

☑ Is the sequence of events easy to understand?

☑ Do all sentences have a subject and predicate?

☑ Have I varied my sentences?

☑ Are words with long *e* and *o* sounds spelled correctly?

See *The Grammar and Writing Book,* pp. 62–67.

Revising Tips

Voice

- Support a friendly and lively voice by using enthusiastic and informal language.
- Avoid overly formal greetings and closings.
- Read your postcard aloud to hear what the voice sounds like.

PUBLISHING Have students display their writing, with pictures of the places they described, on a bulletin board titled "Wish You Were Here!"

ASSESSMENT Use the scoring rubric to evaluate students' work.

DAY 5 — Connect to Unit Writing

Personal Narrative	
Week 1	Memoir 39g–39h
Week 2	Journal Entry 65g–65h
Week 3	Postcard 87g–87h
Week 4	E-mail Invitation 111g–111h
Week 5	Narrative Writing 133g–133h

PREVIEW THE UNIT PROMPT

Write a personal narrative about a time that you were a newcomer to a place or situation (a school, club, team, or neighborhood). Explain how you felt and what you found challenging or exciting.

APPLY

- A personal narrative is a story about an interesting experience or event in the storyteller's life.
- Tell about events in sequence to help readers follow what happens in your personal narrative.

Writing Trait Rubric

	4	3	2	1
Voice	Voice lively, enthusiastic, and friendly	Voice generally lively, enthusiastic, and friendly	Writer not very involved with topic	Writing flat; writer uninterested
	Postcard exciting and engaging	Postcard generally exciting and engaging	Postcard letter minimally engaging	Postcard unengaging

Spelling & Phonics Long *e* and *o*

● Spell words with long *e* and *o*.

Generalization

Connect to Phonics Long *e* is sometimes spelled *ee* or *ea*: sw<u>ee</u>t, <u>ea</u>ch. Long *o* is sometimes spelled *oa* or *ow*: thr<u>oa</u>t, rainb<u>ow</u>. The letter combinations *ee* and *ea* usually stand for the long *e* sound. The letter combinations *oa* and *ow* often stand for the long *o* sound.

Spelling Words

1. sweet	11. greet
2. each	12. season
3. three*	13. croak
4. least	14. shallow
5. freedom*	15. eagle
6. below	16. indeed*
7. throat	17. rainbow
8. float	18. grown
9. foam	19. seaweed
10. flown	20. hollow

Challenge Words

21. Halloween	24. seacoast
22. speedometer	25. cocoa
23. underneath	

*Word from the selection

Spelling/Phonics Support See the ELL and Transition Handbook for spelling support.

DAY 1 Pretest and Sort

PRETEST

Use the Dictation Sentences from Day 5 to administer the pretest. Read the word, read the sentence, and then read the word again. Guide students in self-correcting their pretests and correcting any misspellings.

Monitor Progress
Spelling

If... students misspell more than 5 pretest words,	then... use words 1–10 for Strategic Intervention.
If... students misspell 1–5 pretest words,	then... use words 1–20 for On-Level practice.
If... students correctly spell all pretest words,	then... use words 1–25 for Advanced Learners.

HOMEWORK Spelling Practice Book, p. 9.

Long *e* and *o*

Generalization Long e is sometimes spelled ee or ea: sweet, each. Long o is sometimes spelled oa or ow: throat, rainbow.

Word Sort Sort the list words by their long e and long o spellings.

ee and ea
1. seaweed

ee
2. sweet
3. three
4. freedom
5. greet
6. indeed

ea
7. each
8. least
9. season
10. eagle

oa
11. throat
12. float
13. foam
14. croak

ow
15. below
16. flown
17. shallow
18. rainbow
19. grown
20. hollow

Spelling Words
1. sweet
2. each
3. three
4. least
5. freedom
6. below
7. throat
8. float
9. foam
10. flown
11. greet
12. season
13. croak
14. shallow
15. eagle
16. indeed
17. rainbow
18. grown
19. seaweed
20. hollow

Challenge Words

ee and ow
21. Halloween

ea
24. underneath

ee and oa
22. seacoast

oa
25. cocoa

ee
23. speedometer

Challenge Words
21. Halloween
22. speedometer
23. underneath
24. seacoast
25. cocoa

Home Activity Your child is learning to spell words with long e and long o spelled ee, ea, oa, and ow. Have your child look at each word and point to the letters that make the long e and o sounds.

▲ **Spelling Practice Book** p. 9

DAY 2 Think and Practice

TEACH

The long *e* and long *o* sounds can be spelled in different ways. Write *seaweed* on the board. Underline the letters *ea* and *ee*. Say *seaweed* and point out that both *ee* and *ea* spell the long *e* sound. Guide students in finding the letters that stand for the long *o* sound in *float* and *rainbow*.

seaweed

MNEMONIC DEVICES Point out that since *ee* and *ea* sound the same and *oa* and *ow* sound the same, students must memorize the spellings. Challenge students to think of memory tricks that will help them remember the correct spellings of the list words.

HOMEWORK Spelling Practice Book, p. 10.

Long *e* and *o*

Spelling Words				
sweet	each	three	least	freedom
below	throat	float	foam	flown
greet	season	croak	shallow	eagle
indeed	rainbow	grown	seaweed	hollow

Opposites Write the list words that have the opposite or almost opposite meaning to the words below.

1. sour — 1. sweet
2. most — 2. least
3. sink — 3. float
4. dismiss — 4. greet
5. newborn — 5. grown
6. solid — 6. hollow
7. above — 7. below
8. all — 8. each
9. deep — 9. shallow
10. limits — 10. freedom

Words in Context Write a list word from the box to complete each sentence.

11. The ocean waves were white with ____. — 11. foam
12. Twins describe two people, and triplets describe ____ people. — 12. three
13. Spring is my favorite ____. — 13. season
14. When I was sick, I had a sore ____. — 14. throat
15. Some ocean plants are called ____. — 15. seaweed
16. When I lost my voice, I could only ____ like a frog. — 16. croak
17. The bald ____ is the national bird of the United States. — 17. eagle
18. Spelling is serious business, ____. — 18. indeed
19. I saw a ____ after the thunderstorm. — 19. rainbow
20. By the time I got the camera, the bird had ____ away. — 20. flown

Home Activity Your child wrote words with long e spelled ee or ea and long o spelled oa and ow. Say a word from the list and have your child write the word.

▲ **Spelling Practice Book** p. 10

DAY 3 Connect to Writing

WRITE A DESCRIPTION

Ask students to use at least five spelling words to write a description of an ocean, river, pond, or lake.

Frequently Misspelled Words

whole   know

These words may seem easy to spell, but they are often misspelled by fourth-graders. Alert students to these frequently misspelled words. Point out that /h/ is spelled *wh,* and /n/ is spelled *kn.*

HOMEWORK Spelling Practice Book, p. 11.

Long e and o

Proofread a Menu The restaurant owner is frantic! The new menus have errors that must be fixed before dinner tonight. Circle five misspelled words and write them correctly. Rewrite the sentence that has a capitalization error.

Spelling Words	
sweet	greet
each	season
three	croak
least	shallow
freedom	eagle
below	indeed
throat	rainbow
float	grown
foam	seaweed
flown	hollow

Seewead salad with vinegar and sesame seeds
Thre delight dish: shrimp, beef, and chicken
Hole crispy fried rainbow trout with lemon butter sauce
White hollo mushroom caps stuffed with crabmeat
Fresh vegetables in seeson
Chocolate cake with sweet whipped cream
Rootbeer float (vanilla or chocolate ice cream)
Coffee with hot milk foam
our Food is Organically grown.

Frequently Misspelled Words
whole
know

1. Seaweed   2. Three
3. Whole   4. hollow
5. season   6. Our food is organically grown.

Proofread Words Circle the correctly spelled word. Write the word

7. leest   (least)   lest   7. least
8. egle   (eagle)   eegle   8. eagle
9. (shallow) shalloe shallo   9. shallow
10. (greet) grete   graet   10. greet
11. throte throwt   (throat)   11. throat
12. floan   (flown)   flone   12. flown
13. beloa   (below)   belo   13. below
14. freedowm fredom   (freedom)   14. freedom
15. (indeed) indead   indede   15. indeed

School + Home **Home Activity** Your child identified misspelled words with ee, ea, oa, and ow. Ask your child to use each list word in a sentence.

▲ **Spelling Practice Book** p. 11

DAY 4 Review

REVIEW LONG *o* AND LONG *e*

Have students write the spelling words and circle each *ea.* Have them continue by circling *ee, oa,* and *ow.* If possible, they might use a different color for each letter combination.

Spelling Strategy Problem Parts

We all have words that are hard for us to spell.

Step 1: Ask yourself: Which part of the word gives me a problem?

Step 2: Underline your problem part.

Step 3: Picture the word. Focus on the problem part.

HOMEWORK Spelling Practice Book, p. 12.

Long e and o

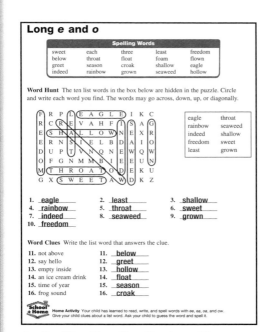

Spelling Words				
sweet	each	three	least	freedom
below	throat	float	foam	flown
greet	season	croak	shallow	eagle
indeed	rainbow	grown	seaweed	hollow

Word Hunt The ten list words in the box below are hidden in the puzzle. Circle and write each word you find. The words may go across, down, up, or diagonally.

eagle	throat
rainbow	seaweed
indeed	shallow
freedom	sweet
least	grown

1. eagle   2. least   3. shallow
4. rainbow   5. throat   6. sweet
7. indeed   8. seaweed   9. grown
10. freedom

Word Clues Write the list word that answers the clue.

11. not above   11. below
12. say hello   12. greet
13. empty inside   13. hollow
14. an ice cream drink 14. float
15. time of year   15. season
16. frog sound   16. croak

School + Home **Home Activity** Your child has learned to read, write, and spell words with ee, ea, oa, and ow. Give your child clues about a list word. Ask your child to guess the word and spell it.

▲ **Spelling Practice Book** p. 12

DAY 5 Posttest

DICTATION SENTENCES

1. Honey tastes <u>sweet</u>.

2. I think <u>each</u> of us has a sister.

3. Jake made <u>three</u> baskets.

4. At <u>least</u> it's not raining.

5. The army fought for <u>freedom</u>.

6. A basement is <u>below</u> the house.

7. Do you have a sore <u>throat</u>?

8. Can you <u>float</u> on your back?

9. My mom drinks coffee topped with milk <u>foam</u>.

10. The baby birds have <u>flown</u> away.

11. Did you <u>greet</u> your mom with a smile?

12. What <u>season</u> do you like best?

13. Some frogs <u>croak</u> at night.

14. The water is too <u>shallow</u> for swimming.

15. The <u>eagle</u> flew across the sky.

16. Your story is very good <u>indeed</u>.

17. We saw a <u>rainbow</u> after the storm.

18. The plant has <u>grown</u> very tall.

19. We saw <u>seaweed</u> under the water.

20. A mouse lives in the <u>hollow</u> log.

CHALLENGE

21. Do you dress up on <u>Halloween</u>?

22. Watch the <u>speedometer</u> to see how fast we are going.

23. The puppy hid <u>underneath</u> the bed.

24. The <u>seacoast</u> is rocky.

25. Do you like to drink hot <u>cocoa</u>?

OBJECTIVES

- Formulate an inquiry question that is connected to this week's lesson focus.

- Effectively and efficiently find, evaluate, and communicate information related to an inquiry question using electronic sources.

New Literacies	
Day 1	**Identify Questions**
Day 2	**Navigate/Search**
Day 3	**Analyze**
Day 4	**Synthesize**
Day 5	**Communicate**

NEW LITERACIES

Internet Inquiry Activity

EXPLORE TRAVEL IN THE UNITED STATES

Use the following 5-day plan to help students conduct this week's Internet inquiry activity on what travel might teach people about the United States. Remind students to follow classroom rules when using the Internet.

DAY 1

Identify Questions Discuss the lesson focus question: *What can we learn about the United States as we travel?* Brainstorm ideas with the class and write their contributions on the board. For example, students might want to find out more about a city, a landform, a national park, or even a particular form of transportation. Have students work individually, in pairs, or in small groups to write an inquiry question they want to answer. Remind them to keep their research focus narrow.

DAY 2

Navigate/Search Have students use student-friendly search engines for their Internet research. Discuss appropriate keywords to begin their searches. You may want to suggest they look for sites with virtual tours. Show students how to analyze search engine results. Students can ask themselves questions such as: *What is this site about? Who created it? What kind of information will I be likely to find here?* Check that students are able to identify sites relevant to their inquiry questions.

DAY 3

Analyze Have students explore the Web sites they identified on Day 2. Remind them to gather information from more than one site, take notes, and save their source information. If allowed, suggest they print photographs and other graphics that will help people visualize their research information.

DAY 4

Synthesize Have students synthesize information from Day 3. Remind them information can be organized in different ways. Sometimes it is appropriate to combine different ideas from their notes into paragraphs. Other times it is more effective to use a chart, diagram, web, or other graphic organizer.

DAY 5

Communicate Have students create posters that show something about what people can learn as they travel around America. Give students an opportunity to share their inquiry results.

RESEARCH/STUDY SKILLS
Electronic Media

TEACH

Ask students where they would find information for a report about immigrating to the United States from Japan. Students may mention library books, encyclopedias, or other reference materials. Remind them that a wealth of information can be found on electronic media. **Electronic media** includes any resources that require electricity to function.

Explain there are two types of electronic media, computer and non-computer sources. Invite students to brainstorm examples of both types.

- **Computer sources:** CD-ROMs, DVDs, and the Internet (including online sources such as Web sites, encyclopedias, newspapers, and so on).

- **Non-computer sources:** audiotapes, videotapes, DVDs, films, filmstrips, television shows, and radio.

Have pairs use electronic media from the classroom or library to find information about immigration to the United States from Japan. Each pair should research one computer source and one non-computer source. Ask:

1. What type of electronic media sources did you find? What kind of information did each source include?

2. Which source was more helpful? Why?

Responses will vary depending on electronic media sources students choose.

ASSESS

As students work, check whether they are able to use titles and source descriptions to select relevant electronic media and if they follow appropriate steps for accessing and evaluating information from each source.

For more practice or to assess students, use Practice Book pp. 29–30.

Assessment Checkpoints *for the Week*

Selection Assessment

Use pp. 9–12 of Selection Tests to check:

- [x] **Selection Understanding**
- [x] **Comprehension Skill** *Sequence*
- [x] **Selection Vocabulary**

amazed	sculptures
bewildered	still
homeland	towering
longed	

ASSESSMENT

Scott Foresman

Selection Tests
Teacher's Manual

- Assess comprehension of weekly selections
- Assess understanding of weekly comprehension skills
- Assess knowledge of selection vocabulary

Selection Tests

Reading STREET
Grade 4

Leveled Assessment

- On-Level
- Strategic Intervention
- Advanced

Use pp. 13–18 of Fresh Reads for Differentiated Test Practice to check:

- [x] **Comprehension Skill** *Sequence*
- [x] **REVIEW** **Comprehension Skill** *Main Idea*
- [x] **Fluency** *Words Correct Per Minute*

ASSESSMENT Teacher's Manual

Scott Foresman

Fresh Reads
for Differentiated Test Practice

Leveled passages—strategic intervention, on-level, and advanced—for
- Fluency checks
- Practice and application of weekly comprehension skills
- Answer key for all practice pages

Fresh Reads for Differentiated Test Practice

Reading STREET
Grade 4

Managing Assessment

Use Assessment Handbook for:

- [x] **Observation Checklists**
- [x] **Record-Keeping Forms**
- [x] **Portfolio Assessment**

ASSESSMENT

Scott Foresman

Assessment Handbook

- Suggestions for preparing students for high-stake tests
- Ideas for classroom-based assessment
- Forms in English and Spanish for students to record interests and progress
- Forms in English and Spanish for teachers to record observations of students' reading and writing abilities and progress
- Assessment and Regrouping charts reproduced from *Reading Street* Teacher's Editions

Assessment Handbook

Reading STREET
Grades 3–6

RESEARCH/STUDY SKILLS
Electronic Media

TEACH

Ask students where they would find information for a report about immigrating to the United States from Japan. Students may mention library books, encyclopedias, or other reference materials. Remind them that a wealth of information can be found on electronic media. **Electronic media** includes any resources that require electricity to function.

Explain there are two types of electronic media, computer and non-computer sources. Invite students to brainstorm examples of both types.

- **Computer sources:** CD-ROMs, DVDs, and the Internet (including online sources such as Web sites, encyclopedias, newspapers, and so on).

- **Non-computer sources:** audiotapes, videotapes, DVDs, films, filmstrips, television shows, and radio.

Have pairs use electronic media from the classroom or library to find information about immigration to the United States from Japan. Each pair should research one computer source and one non-computer source. Ask:

1. What type of electronic media sources did you find? What kind of information did each source include?

2. Which source was more helpful? Why?

Responses will vary depending on electronic media sources students choose.

ASSESS

As students work, check whether they are able to use titles and source descriptions to select relevant electronic media and if they follow appropriate steps for accessing and evaluating information from each source.

For more practice or to assess students, use Practice Book pp. 29–30.

Electronic Media

- There are two types of **electronic media**—computer and non-computer. Computer sources include computer software, CD-ROMs, and the Internet. Non-computer sources include audiotapes, videotapes, films, film strips, television, and radio.
- To find information on the Internet, use a search engine and type in your keywords. Be specific. It's a good idea to use two or more keywords.

Directions Use the list of electronic media below to answer the questions.

Electronic Media Source List
- "Interviews with Japanese Travelers" (Public Radio taped interview program)
- *Traveling in Japan* (CD-ROM with printable navigation maps)
- *The Japanese History Site* (Internet site that describes Japan's history)
- *Food in Japan* (DVD of Japan's most exotic foods)
- *The Japanese in America During World War II* (Filmstrip that shows life in the Japanese internment camps)

1. Which source would be helpful in writing a report on Japan for school?
   the Web site about Japan's history

2. Why would *Traveling in Japan* be a helpful source if you were planning a road trip around Japan?
   The CD-ROM has maps that you could print out.

3. Which source do you think was produced more recently: *Food in Japan* or *The Japanese in America During World War II*? Why?
   Food in Japan; it uses newer technology than a filmstrip.

4. What keywords might you type into a search engine to get the Web site *The Japanese History Site*?
   You could type in Japan and history.

5. If you needed to use a quote in your report about what travelers think about the United States, what source would you use?
   "Interviews with Japanese Travelers"

▲ **Practice Book** p. 29

Directions Use the Internet search results found on a search engine to answer the questions below.

WEB SEARCH

Results 1-3 of about 25,000
Search Results
History of **Immigration**
   Use the tool bar below to search through 1,000 primary source documents. First, type in the year of **immigration** and then the country from which the immigrants came.
My Story
   Hi! Welcome to my home page. My name is Ken, and I moved to this country 25 years ago with my wife and family. Learn about my story and my family by clicking on the icons to the right.
Japanese in the United States
   The *Japanese Immigrant Society*, together with the *Foundation to Support Diversity*, has supported the research found on this site. All information is for educational use only.

Possible answers given for 9–10.
6. If you click on the underlined link entitled History of Immigration, what kind of site will you be taken to?
   You will go to a site with documents about immigration history.

7. What does the information after each link tell you?
   It tells you the first few sentences on the Web sites.

8. What keyword was typed in to receive these search results?
   The keyword was "immigration."

9. Why might Ken's Web site not be useful for a school report?
   It is a personal home page, not a scholarly source.

10. Why might you be able to trust the information on the third link?
    The research was done by two organizations for educational reasons.

 Home Activity Your child learned about electronic media. With your child, review the rules of safe Internet searching and how to find helpful research articles on the Internet.

▲ **Practice Book** p. 30

Selection Assessment

Use pp. 9–12 of Selection Tests to check:

- ✅ **Selection Understanding**
- ✅ **Comprehension Skill** *Sequence*
- ✅ **Selection Vocabulary**

amazed   sculptures
bewildered   still
homeland   towering
longed

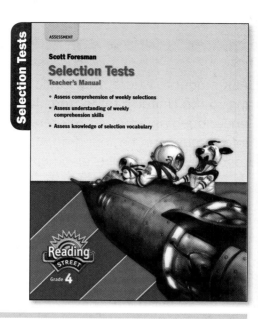

Leveled Assessment

Use pp. 13–18 of Fresh Reads for Differentiated Test Practice to check:

- ✅ **Comprehension Skill** *Sequence*
- ✅ **REVIEW** **Comprehension Skill** *Main Idea*
- ✅ **Fluency** *Words Correct Per Minute*

Managing Assessment

Use Assessment Handbook for:

- ✅ **Observation Checklists**
- ✅ **Record-Keeping Forms**
- ✅ **Portfolio Assessment**

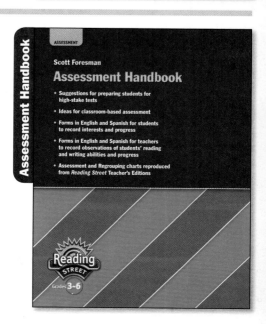

Unit 1
This Land Is Your Land

CONCEPT QUESTION
How do the diverse regions and peoples of the United States reflect its greatness?

Week 1
What experiences bring diverse peoples together?

Week 2
What did Lewis and Clark learn on their journey?

Week 3
What can we learn about the United States as we travel?

Week 4
What is unique about the landscape of the Southwest?

Week 5
How does Yosemite reflect the unique qualities of the West?

EXPAND THE CONCEPT
What is unique about the landscape of the Southwest?

CONNECT THE CONCEPT

▶ **Build Background**
corral, frontier, rodeo

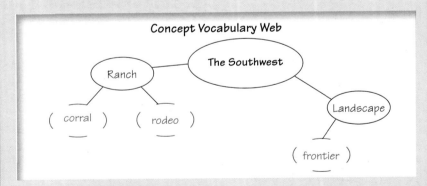

Concept Vocabulary Web

The Southwest — Ranch — (corral) (rodeo) — Landscape — (frontier)

▶ **Social Studies Content**
Geography of the Southwest, Ranches of the Southwest

▶ **Writing**
E-mail Invitation

▶ **Internet Inquiry**
Southwestern Landscape

Preview Your Week

What is unique about the landscape of the Southwest?

The Horned Toad Prince

by Jackie Mims Hopkins
illustrated by Michael Austin

Genre Modern fairy tales are fairy tales that are set in modern times. Like all fairy tales, they are stories with magical characters and events. As you read, think about how this story might be different if it were set in the long-ago time.

How could a horned toad possibly be a prince?

Student Edition pages 92–105

Audio CD

Genre	Modern Fairy Tale
⊙ **Vocabulary Strategy**	Context Clues
⊙ **Comprehension Skill**	Author's Purpose
⊙ **Comprehension Strategy**	Story Structure

Paired Selection

Reading Across Texts
Compare Fictional Horned Toad To Facts About Horned Lizards

Genre
Expository Nonfiction

Text Features
Captions
Descriptive Language

Science in Reading

Expository Nonfiction

Genre
- Expository nonfiction can tell about animals and where they live.
- The author sometimes organizes the text by explaining a series of events.

Text Features
- The author uses captions to explain photographs.
- The author uses descriptive language to tell about life in the Sonoran Desert.

Link to Science
Use reference materials to find out more about animals that camouflage themselves in the desert. Make a chart describing how these animals camouflage themselves and share it with your class.

Horned Lizards & Harvesting Ants

by John Brown

Imagine that you are on a journey to the Sonoran Desert, a vast area of flat land and canyons in the southwestern United States and northern Mexico. By day, you explore the many unique plants and animals. At night, you curl up in the safety of your desert home, a tent.

▲ A few clouds remain after last night's storm; the morning air feels cool and clean.

As we are having breakfast, we notice that last night's storm has knocked some of the fruit off the top of a nearby saguaro. This windfall has been discovered by a colony of harvester ants, who are busy pulling the seeds out of the sticky fruit and carrying them back to their hole. They are working very hard to get all the seeds inside their nest before it gets too hot for them to stay out in the sun.

▲ This harvester ant is wrestling to pull a saguaro seed out from the fruit. Imagine trying to pull a football out of a giant-sized sticky gumdrop—with your teeth!

ⓖ **Author's Purpose** If the purpose is to inform, how do you read this article?

108

Student Edition pages 108–111

Audio CD

Unit 1
This Land Is Your Land

CONCEPT QUESTION
How do the diverse regions and peoples of the United States reflect its greatness?

Week 1
What experiences bring diverse peoples together?

Week 2
What did Lewis and Clark learn on their journey?

Week 3
What can we learn about the United States as we travel?

Week 4
What is unique about the landscape of the Southwest?

Week 5
How does Yosemite reflect the unique qualities of the West?

Week 4

EXPAND THE CONCEPT
What is unique about the landscape of the Southwest?

CONNECT THE CONCEPT

▶ **Build Background**
corral, frontier, rodeo

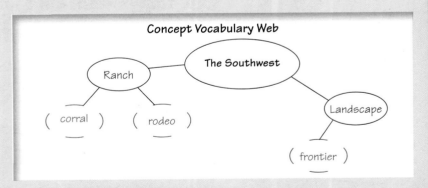

Concept Vocabulary Web

The Southwest — Ranch — (corral) — (rodeo) — Landscape — (frontier)

▶ **Social Studies Content**
Geography of the Southwest, Ranches of the Southwest

▶ **Writing**
E-mail Invitation

▶ **Internet Inquiry**
Southwestern Landscape

Preview Your Week

What is unique about the landscape of the Southwest?

The Horned Toad Prince

by Jackie Mims Hopkins
illustrated by Michael Austin

Genre Modern fairy tales are fairy tales that are set in modern times. Like all fairy tales, they are stories with magical characters and events. As you read, think about how this story might be different if it were set in the long-ago time.

How could a horned toad possibly be a prince?

Student Edition pages 92–105

Audio CD

Genre	Modern Fairy Tale
Vocabulary Strategy	Context Clues
Comprehension Skill	Author's Purpose
Comprehension Strategy	Story Structure

Paired Selection

Reading Across Texts
Compare Fictional Horned Toad To Facts About Horned Lizards

Genre
Expository Nonfiction

Text Features
Captions
Descriptive Language

Science in Reading

Horned Lizards & Harvesting Ants
by John Brown

Expository Nonfiction

Genre
- Expository nonfiction can tell about animals and where they live.
- The author sometimes organizes the text by explaining a series of events.

Text Features
- The author uses captions to explain photographs.
- The author uses descriptive language to tell about life in the Sonoran Desert.

Link to Science
Use reference materials to find out more about animals that camouflage themselves in the desert. Make a chart describing how these animals camouflage themselves and share it with your class.

Imagine that you are on a journey to the Sonoran Desert, a vast area of flat land and canyons in the southwestern United States and northern Mexico. By day, you explore the many unique plants and animals. At night, you curl up in the safety of your desert home, a tent.

▲ A few clouds remain after last night's storm; the morning air feels cool and clean.

As we are having breakfast, we notice that last night's storm has knocked some of the fruit off the top of a nearby saguaro. This windfall has been discovered by a colony of harvester ants, who are busy pulling the seeds out of the sticky fruit and carrying them back to their hole. They are working very hard to get all the seeds inside their nest before it gets too hot for them to stay out in the sun.

▲ This harvester ant is wrestling to pull a saguaro seed out from the fruit. Imagine trying to pull a football out of a giant-sized sticky gumdrop—with your teeth!

Author's Purpose If the purpose is to inform, how do you read this article?

108

Student Edition pages 108–111

Audio CD

Read It ONLINE
PearsonSuccessNet.com

- Student Edition
- Leveled Readers

Leveled Readers

🎯 **Skill** Author's Purpose

🎯 **Strategy** Story Structure

Lesson Vocabulary

Below-Level

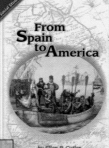

On-Level

Advanced

ELL Reader
- Concept Vocabulary
- Text Support
- Language Enrichment

Painting the Southwest

Time for SOCIAL STUDIES

Integrate Social Studies Standards
- U.S. Geography
- Sociology

✓ **Read**

The Horned Toad Prince, pp. 92–105

"Horned Lizards and Harvesting Ants," pp. 108–111

Leveled Readers

Below-Level **On-Level** **Advanced**

- Support Concepts
- Develop Concepts
- Extend Concepts
- Social Studies Extension Activity

ELL Reader

✓ **Build Concept Vocabulary**
The Southwest, pp. 88l–88m

✓ **Teach Social Studies Concepts**
Geography of the Southwest, p. 95
Ranches of the Southwest, p. 103

✓ **Explore Social Studies Center**
Write a Travel Description, p. 88k

Weekly Plan

READING

45–90 minutes

TARGET SKILLS OF THE WEEK

Comprehension Skill
Author's Purpose

Comprehension Strategy
Story Structure

Vocabulary Strategy
Context Clues

DAY 1
PAGES 88l–90b, 111a, 111e–111k

Oral Language

QUESTION OF THE WEEK *What is unique about the landscape of the Southwest?*

Read Aloud: "Growing Up in the Old West," 88m
Build Concepts, 88l

Comprehension/Vocabulary

Comprehension Skill/Strategy Lesson, 88–89
  Author's Purpose **T**
  Story Structure
Build Background, 90a
Introduce Lesson Vocabulary, 90b
bargain, favor, lassoed, offended, prairie, riverbed, shrieked **T**

Read Leveled Readers

Grouping Options 88f–88g

Fluency

Model Volume, 88l–88m, 111a

DAY 2
PAGES 90–99, 111a, 111e–111k

Oral Language

QUESTION OF THE DAY *In what ways is the Southwestern setting important to The Horned Toad Prince?*

Comprehension/Vocabulary

Vocabulary Strategy Lesson, 90–91
  Context Clues **T**

Read *The Horned Toad Prince*, 92–99

Grouping Options 88f–88g

  Author's Purpose **T**
  Story Structure
  Context Clues **T**
  REVIEW Sequence **T**
Develop Vocabulary

Fluency

Echo Reading, 111a

LANGUAGE ARTS

30–60 minutes

Trait of the Week

Focus/Ideas

Grammar, 111e
Introduce Compound Sentences **T**

Writing Workshop, 111g
Introduce E-mail Invitation
Model the Trait of the Week: Focus/Ideas

Spelling, 111i
Pretest for Vowel Long *e*

Internet Inquiry, 111k
Identify Questions

Grammar, 111e
Develop Compound Sentences **T**

Writing Workshop, 111g
Improve Writing with Know Your Purpose

Spelling, 111i
Teach the Generalization

Internet Inquiry, 111k
Navigate/Search

DAILY WRITING ACTIVITIES

Day 1 Write to Read, 88

Day 2 Words to Write, 91
Strategy Response Log, 92, 99

DAILY SOCIAL STUDIES CONNECTIONS

Day 1 The Southwest Concept Web, 88l

Day 2 Time for Social Studies: Geography of the Southwest, 95
Revisit The Southwest Concept Web, 99

DAILY SUCCESS PREDICTORS
for Adequate Yearly Progress

Monitor Progress and Corrective Feedback

Vocabulary — Check Vocabulary, 88l

RESOURCES FOR THE WEEK

- Practice Book, *pp. 31–40*
- Word Study and Spelling Practice Book, *pp. 13–16*
- Grammar and Writing Practice Book, *pp. 13–16*
- Selection Test, *pp. 13–16*
- Fresh Reads for Differentiated Test Practice, *pp. 19–24*
- The Grammar and Writing Book, *pp. 68–73*

Grouping Options for Differentiated Instruction

Turn the page for the small group lesson plan.

DAY 3 — PAGES 100-107, 111a, 111e-111k

Oral Language

QUESTION OF THE DAY *What important lesson did Prince Maximillian teach Reba Jo?*

Comprehension/Vocabulary

Read *The Horned Toad Prince,* 100–106

Grouping Options 88f–88g

- Author's Purpose **T**
- Story Structure
- Context Clues **T**
- Develop Vocabulary

Reader Response

Selection Test

Fluency

Model Volume, 111a

Grammar, 111f
Apply Compound Sentences in Writing **T**

Writing Workshop, 107, 111h
Write Now
Prewrite and Draft

Spelling, 111j
Connect Spelling to Writing

Internet Inquiry, 111k
Analyze Sources

Day 3 Strategy Response Log, 104
Look Back and Write, 106

Day 3 Time for Social Studies: Ranches of the Southwest, 103
Revisit The Southwest Concept Web, 88l

DAY 4 — PAGES 108-111a, 111e-111k

Oral Language

QUESTION OF THE DAY *How did the author tie in the features of the Southwest to the familiar fairy tale of a toad that turns into a prince?*

Comprehension/Vocabulary

Read *"Horned Lizards & Harvesting Ants,"* 108–111

Grouping Options 88f–88g

Expository Fiction

Reading Across Texts

Content-Area Vocabulary

Fluency

Partner Reading, 111a

Grammar, 111f
Practice Compound Sentences for Standardized Tests **T**

Writing Workshop, 111h
Draft, Revise, and Publish

Spelling, 111j
Provide a Strategy

Internet Inquiry, 111k
Synthesize Information

Day 4 Writing Across Texts, 111

Day 4 Time for Social Studies: Write a Travel Description, 88k

DAY 5 — PAGES 111a-111l

Oral Language

QUESTION OF THE WEEK *To wrap up the week, revisit the Day 1 question.*
Build Concept Vocabulary, 111c

Fluency

Read Leveled Readers

Grouping Options 88f–88g

Assess Reading Rate, 111a

Comprehension/Vocabulary

- Reteach Author's Purpose, 111b **T**
- Dialect, 111b
- Context Clues, 111c **T**

Speaking and Viewing, 111d
Oral Report
Analyze Photos

Grammar, 111f
Cumulative Review

Writing Workshop, 111h
Connect to Unit Writing

Spelling, 111j
Posttest for Long *e*

Internet Inquiry, 111k
Communicate Results

Research/Study Skills, 111l
Illustration/Caption/Label

Day 5 Dialect, 111b

Day 5 Revisit The Southwest Concept Web, 111c

KEY ◎ = Target Skill **T** = Tested Skill

Check Retelling, *107*

Check Fluency wcpm, *111a*

Check Vocabulary, *111c*

SUCCESS PREDICTOR

Small Group Plan for Differentiated Instruction

Daily Plan
AT A GLANCE

Reading
Whole Group
- Oral Language
- Comprehension/Vocabulary

Group Time
Differentiated Instruction

Meet with small groups to provide:
- Skill Support
- Reading Support
- Fluency Practice

Read

This week's lessons for daily group time can be found behind the Differentiated Instruction (DI) tab on pp. DI·32–DI·41.

Whole Group
- Fluency

Language Arts
- Grammar
- Writing
- Spelling
- Research/Inquiry
- Speaking/Listening/Viewing

Use My Sidewalks on Reading Street for Tier III intensive reading intervention.

DAY 1

On-Level
Teacher-Led
Page DI·33
- Develop Concept Vocabulary
- **Read** On-Level Reader *From Spain to America*

Strategic Intervention
Teacher-Led
Page DI·32
- Reinforce Concepts
- **Read** Below-Level Reader *Flash Flood*

Advanced
Teacher-Led
Page DI·33
- **Read** Advanced Reader *The Diné*
- Independent Extension Activity

(i) Independent Activities
While you meet with small groups, have the rest of the class...

- Visit the Reading/Library Center
- Listen to the Background Building Audio
- Finish Write to Read, p. 88
- Complete Practice Book pp. 33–34
- Visit Cross-Curricular Centers

DAY 2

On-Level
Teacher-Led
Pages 94–99
- **Read** *The Horned Toad Prince*

Strategic Intervention
Teacher-Led
Page DI·34
- Practice Lesson Vocabulary
- Read Multisyllabic Words
- **Read** or Listen to *The Horned Toad Prince*

Advanced
Teacher-Led
Page DI·35
- Extend Vocabulary
- **Read** *The Horned Toad Prince*

(i) Independent Activities
While you meet with small groups, have the rest of the class...

- Visit the Reading/Library Center
- Listen to the AudioText for *The Horned Toad Prince*
- Finish Words to Write, p. 91
- Complete Practice Book pp. 35–36
- Write in their Strategy Response Logs, pp. 92, 99
- Visit Cross-Curricular Centers
- Work on inquiry projects

DAY 3

On-Level
Teacher-Led
Pages 100–105
- **Read** *The Horned Toad Prince*

Strategic Intervention
Teacher-Led
Page DI·36
- Practice Author's Purpose and Story Structure
- **Read** or Listen to *The Horned Toad Prince*

Advanced
Teacher-Led
Page DI·37
- Extend Author's Purpose and Story Structure
- **Read** *The Horned Toad Prince*

(i) Independent Activities
While you meet with small groups, have the rest of the class...

- Visit the Reading/Library Center
- Listen to the AudioText for *The Horned Toad Prince*
- Write in their Strategy Response Logs, p. 104
- Finish Look Back and Write, p. 106
- Complete Practice Book p. 37
- Visit Cross-Curricular Centers
- Work on inquiry projects

① Begin with whole class skill and strategy instruction.

② Meet with small groups to provide differentiated instruction.

③ Gather the whole class back together for fluency and language arts.

DAY 4

On-Level	Strategic Intervention	Advanced
Teacher-Led *Pages 108–111*	**Teacher-Led** *Page DI · 38*	**Teacher-Led** *Page DI · 39*
• **Read** "Horned Lizards & Harvesting Ants"	• Practice Retelling • **Read** or Listen to "Horned Lizards & Harvesting Ants"	• **Read** "Horned Lizards & Harvesting Ants" • Genre Study

ⓘ Independent Activities

While you meet with small groups, have the rest of the class…

- Visit the Reading/Library Center
- Listen to the AudioText for "Horned Lizards & Harvesting Ants"
- Visit the Writing/Vocabulary Center
- Finish Writing Across Texts, p. 111
- Visit Cross-Curricular Centers
- Work on inquiry projects

DAY 5

On-Level	Strategic Intervention	Advanced
Teacher-Led *Page DI · 41*	**Teacher-Led** *Page DI · 40*	**Teacher-Led** *Page DI · 41*
• **Reread** Leveled Reader *From Spain to America* • Retell *From Spain to America*	• **Reread** Leveled Reader *Flash Flood* • Retell *Flash Flood*	• **Reread** Leveled Reader *The Diné* • Share Extension Activity

ⓘ Independent Activities

While you meet with small groups, have the rest of the class…

- Visit the Reading/Library Center
- Complete Practice Book pp. 38–40
- Visit Cross-Curricular Centers
- Work on inquiry projects

Grouping Place English language learners in the groups that correspond to their reading abilities in English.

Use the appropriate Leveled Reader or other text at students' instructional level.

TIP Send home the appropriate Multilingual Summary of the main selection on Day 1.

Take It to the NET™ ONLINE
PearsonSuccessNet.com

Edward Kame'enui
For an explanation of the techniques of direct instruction, see a summary of the book *Direct Instruction Reading* by D. Carnine, J. Silbert, and Scott Foresman author Edward Kame'enui.

TEACHER TALK

Phonics is instruction in the relationships between letters and sounds.

Looking Ahead

Be sure to schedule time for students to work on the unit inquiry project "Natural Wonders." This week students combine the information they have collected to answer their inquiry questions.

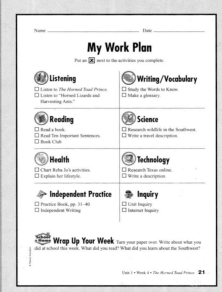

▲ **Group-Time Survival Guide** p. 21, Weekly Contract

The Horned Toad Prince **88g**

☑ Customize Your Plan *by Strand*

ORAL LANGUAGE

SOCIAL STUDIES

Concept Development

What is unique about the landscape of the Southwest?

CONCEPT VOCABULARY

corral   frontier   rodeo

BUILD

❑ **Question of the Week** Introduce and discuss the question of the week. This week students will read a variety of texts and work on projects related to the concept *The Southwest.* Post the question for students to refer to throughout the week. **DAY 1** *88d*

❑ **Read Aloud** Read aloud "Growing Up in the Old West." Then begin a web to build concepts and concept vocabulary related to this week's lesson and the unit theme, This Land Is Your Land. Introduce the concept words *corral, frontier,* and *rodeo* and have students place them on the web. Display the web for use throughout the week. **DAY 1** *88l–88m*

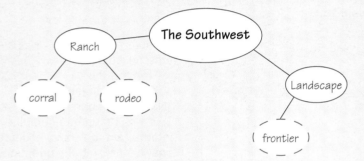

DEVELOP

❑ **Question of the Day** Use the prompts from the Weekly Plan to engage students in conversations related to this week's reading and the unit theme. **EVERY DAY** *88d–88e*

❑ **Concept Vocabulary Web** Revisit the The Southwest Concept Web and encourage students to add concept words from their reading and life experiences. **DAY 2** *99,* **DAY 3** *105*

CONNECT

❑ **Looking Back/Moving Forward** Revisit The Southwest Concept Web and discuss how it relates to this week's lesson and the unit theme. Then make connections to next week's lesson. **DAY 5** *111c*

CHECK

❑ **Concept Vocabulary Web** Use The Southwest Concept Web to check students' understanding of the concept vocabulary words *corral, frontier,* and *rodeo.* **DAY 1** *88l,* **DAY 5** *111c*

VOCABULARY

🔾 **STRATEGY CONTEXT CLUES**
Sometimes when you are reading you see an unfamiliar word. The author may use a synonym for the word to help you understand its meaning. A synonym has almost the same meaning as the unfamiliar word.

LESSON VOCABULARY

bargain	prairie
favor	riverbed
lassoed	shrieked
offended	

TEACH

❑ **Words to Know** Give students the opportunity to tell what they already know about this week's lesson vocabulary words. Then discuss word meaning. **DAY 1** *90b*

❑ **Vocabulary Strategy Lesson** Use the vocabulary strategy lesson in the Student Edition to introduce and model this week's strategy, *context clues.* **DAY 2** *90–91*

Vocabulary Strategy Lesson

PRACTICE/APPLY

❑ **Leveled Text** Read the lesson vocabulary in the context of leveled text. **DAY 1** *LR28–LR36*

Leveled Readers

❑ **Words in Context** Read the lesson vocabulary and apply *context clues* in the context of The Horned Toad Prince. **DAY 2** *92–99,* **DAY 3** *100–106*

❑ **Writing/Vocabulary Center** Make a glossary of words that name things found in the Southwest. **ANY DAY** *88k*

Main Selection—Fiction

❑ **Homework** Practice Book pp. 34–35. **DAY 1** *90b,* **DAY 2** *91*

❑ **Word Play** Have partners look through The Horned Toad Prince to find examples of idioms. Have students record the idioms on a T-Chart with the idiom and the meaning. Then have each pair choose one or two idioms to explain in words or with a captioned drawing. **ANY DAY** *111c*

ASSESS

❑ **Selection Test** Use the Selection Test to determine students' understanding of the lesson vocabulary words. **DAY 3**

RETEACH/REVIEW

❑ **Reteach Lesson** If necessary, use this lesson to reteach and review *context clues.* **DAY 5** *111c*

❶ Use assessment data to determine your instructional focus. ❷ Preview this week's instruction by strand. ❸ Choose instructional activities that meet the needs of your classroom.

COMPREHENSION

SKILL AUTHOR'S PURPOSE An author's purpose is the reason or reasons the author has for writing. An author may write to persuade, to inform, to entertain, and to express. An author may have one or more purposes for writing.

STRATEGY STORY STRUCTURE Story structure is how a fictional story is put together. The structure of a story includes how the story begins (the problem), how it builds through the middle (rising action and climax), and how it ends (resolution).

TEACH

❑ **Skill/Strategy Lesson** Use the skill/strategy lesson in the Student Edition to introduce and model *author's purpose* and *story structure*. **DAY 1** *88-89*

❑ **Extend Skills** Teach dialect. **ANY DAY** *111b*

Skill/Strategy Lesson

PRACTICE/APPLY

❑ **Leveled Text** Apply *author's purpose* and *story structure* to read leveled text. **DAY 1** *LR28-LR36*

❑ **Skills and Strategies in Context** Read *The Horned Toad Prince,* using the Guiding Comprehension questions to apply *author's purpose* and *story structure*. **DAY 2** *92-97,* **DAY 3** *100-106*

Leveled Readers

❑ **Skills and Strategies in Context** Read "Horned Lizards & Harvesting Ants," guiding students as they apply *author's purpose* and *story structure*. Then have students discuss and write across texts. **DAY 4** *108-111*

❑ **Homework** Practice Book pp. 33, 37, 38 **DAY 1** *89,* **DAY 3** *105,* **DAY 5** *111b*

Main Selection—Fiction

Paired Selection—Nonfiction

❑ **Fresh Reads for Differentiated Test Practice** Have students practice *author's purpose* with a new passage. **DAY 3**

ASSESS

❑ **Selection Test** Determine students' understanding of the selection and their use of *author's purpose*. **DAY 3**

❑ **Retell** Have students retell *The Horned Toad Prince*. **DAY 3** *106-107*

RETEACH/REVIEW

❑ **Reteach Lesson** If necessary, reteach and review *author's purpose*. **DAY 5** *111b*

FLUENCY

SKILL VOLUME Lowering and raising your voice during reading will make the story interesting and lively, as well as create a dramatic effect.

TEACH

❑ **Read Aloud** Model fluent reading by rereading "Growing Up in the Old West." Focus on this week's fluency skill, volume. **DAY 1** *88l-88m, 111a*

PRACTICE/APPLY

❑ **Echo Reading** Read aloud selected paragraphs from *The Horned Toad Prince,* adjusting the volume in your voice. Then practice as a class, doing three echo readings of the paragraphs. **DAY 2** *111a,* **DAY 3** *111a*

❑ **Partner Reading** Have partners practice reading aloud, lowering and raising the volume of their voices and offering each other feedback. As students reread, monitor their progress toward their individual fluency goals. **DAY 4** *111a*

❑ **Listening Center** Have students follow along with the AudioText for this week's selections. **ANY DAY** *88j*

❑ **Reading/Library Center** Have students reread a selection of their choice. **ANY DAY** *88j*

❑ **Fluency Coach** Have students use Fluency Coach to listen to fluent readings or practice reading on their own. **ANY DAY**

ASSESS

❑ **Check Fluency** WCPM Do a one-minute timed reading, paying special attention to this week's skill—volume. Provide feedback for each student. **DAY 5** *111a*

GRAMMAR

COMPUND SENTENCES A compound sentence is made up of two simple sentences joined by a comma and a connecting word such as *and, but,* or *or.* The two sentences in a compound sentence must have ideas that make sense together.

TEACH

❑ **Grammar Transparency 4** Use Grammar Transparency 4 to teach compound sentences.
DAY 1 *111e*

Grammar Transparency 4

PRACTICE/APPLY

❑ **Develop the Concept** Review the concept of compound sentences and provide guided practice. DAY 2 *111e*

❑ **Apply to Writing** Have students review something they have written and apply compound sentences. DAY 3 *111f*

❑ **Test Preparation** Examine common errors in compound sentences to prepare for standardized tests. DAY 4 *111f*

❑ **Homework** Grammar and Writing Practice Book pp. 13–15.
DAY 2 *111e*, DAY 3 *111f*, DAY 4 *111f*

ASSESS

❑ **Cumulative Review** Use Grammar and Writing Practice Book p. 16. DAY 5 *111f*

RETEACH/REVIEW

❑ **Daily Fix-It** Have students find and correct errors in grammar, spelling, and punctuation. **EVERY DAY** *111e-111f*

❑ **The Grammar and Writing Book** Use pp. 68–71 of The Grammar and Writing Book to extend instruction for compound sentences. **ANY DAY**

The Grammar and Writing Book

WRITING

Trait of the Week

FOCUS/IDEAS Good writers focus on a main idea and develop this idea with strong supporting details. Having a purpose, whether it is to inform, to persuade, or to entertain, helps keep focus on the main idea.

TEACH

❑ **Writing Transparency 4A** Use the model to introduce and discuss the Trait of the Week. DAY 1 *111g*

❑ **Writing Transparency 4B** Use the transparency to show students how having a clear purpose can improve their writing. DAY 2 *111g*

Writing Transparency 4A   **Writing Transparency 4B**

PRACTICE/APPLY

❑ **Write Now** Examine the model on Student Edition p. 107. Then have students write their own e-mail invitation. DAY 3 *107, 111h* DAY 4 *111h*

> **Prompt** In *The Horned Toad Prince*, the author has a clear purpose—to entertain. Think about an event that you would like to invite someone to. Now write an e-mail invitation with the purpose of informing family or friends of a special event.

Write Now p. 107

❑ **Writing/Vocabulary Center** Make a glossary of words that name things found in the Southwest. **ANY DAY** *88k*

ASSESS

❑ **Writing Trait Rubric** Use the rubric to evaluate students' writing. DAY 4 *111h*

RETEACH/REVIEW

❑ **The Grammar and Writing Book** Use pp. 68–73 of The Grammar and Writing Book to extend instruction for compound sentences, know your purpose, and e-mail invitations. **ANY DAY**

The Grammar and Writing Book

SPELLING

GENERALIZATION LONG E   Long e at the end of a word can be spelled *ie, ey,* and *y: calorie money happy*. When the letters *ie, ey,* and *y* come at the end of a word, they can stand for the long e sound.

TEACH

❑ **Pretest** Give the pretest for words with long e. Guide students in self-correcting their pretests and correcting any misspellings.   DAY 1 *111i*

❑ **Think and Practice** Connect spelling to the phonics generalization for long e.   DAY 2 *111i*

PRACTICE/APPLY

❑ **Connect to Writing** Have students use spelling words to write an e-mail to a friend. Then review frequently misspelled words: *finally, probably.*   DAY 3 *111j*

❑ **Homework** Word Study and Spelling Practice Book pp. 13–16.   **EVERY DAY**

RETEACH/REVIEW

❑ **Review** Review spelling words to prepare for the posttest. Then provide students with a spelling strategy—pronouncing for spelling.   DAY 4 *111j*

ASSESS

❑ **Posttest** Use dictation sentences to give the posttest for words with long e.   DAY 5 *111j*

Spelling Words

1. prairie*
2. calorie
3. honey
4. valley
5. money
6. finally
7. movie
8. country*
9. empty
10. city
11. rookie
12. hockey
13. collie
14. breezy
15. jury
16. balcony
17. steady
18. alley
19. trolley
20. misty

Challenge Words

21. frequency
22. parsley
23. journey
24. chimney
25. attorney

*Word from the selection

RESEARCH AND INQUIRY

❑ **Internet Inquiry** Have students conduct an Internet inquiry on the uniqueness of the southwestern landscape.   **EVERY DAY** *111k*

❑ **Illustration/Caption/Label** Review with students that illustrations can help readers understand information in fiction and nonfiction text. Review the fact that illustrations often have captions and labels that provide more information about the illustration. Illustrations also can enhance written and oral reports.   DAY 5 *111l*

❑ **Unit Inquiry** Allow time for students to combine the information they have collected to answer their inquiry questions.   **ANY DAY** *17*

SPEAKING AND VIEWING

❑ **Oral Report** Have students select a topic on the Southwest region and prepare an oral report. Possible topics include, but are not limited to, animals, plants, landforms, or other unique characteristics of the Southwest.   DAY 5 *111d*

❑ **Analyze Photos** Have students study the sequence of photographs on p. 111 and answer questions.   DAY 5 *111d*

Resources for
Differentiated Instruction

LEVELED READERS

▶ **Comprehension**
- ◎ **Skill** Author's Purpose
- ◎ **Strategy** Story Structure

▶ **Lesson Vocabulary**
- ◎ **Context Clues**

bargain   favor   lassoed   riverbed   prairie   shrieked   offended

▶ **Social Studies Standards**
- U.S. Geography
- Sociology

Leveled Reader Database ONLINE
PearsonSuccessNet.com

Use the Online Database of over 600 books to
- Download and print additional copies of this week's leveled readers.
- Listen to the readers being read online.
- Search for more titles focused on this week's skills, topic, and content.

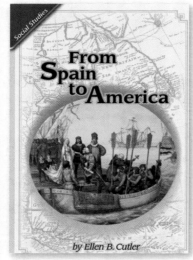

From Spain to America
by Ellen B. Cutler

On-Level Reader

Author's Purpose
- The **author's purpose** is the reason or reasons an author has for writing.
- An author may have one or more reason for writing. He or she may want to inform, persuade, entertain, or express a mood or feeling.

Directions Read the following passage. Then answer the questions below.

Columbus and his crew set sail in search of *oro*, the Spanish word for gold. They hoped to land in Asia, where they could fill their pockets with gold and other riches. Columbus believed he could reach the Asian countries of the Far East by sailing due west from Spain. His crew did not believe him. His men were angry and scared. They may have shrieked in fear, not knowing what lay ahead. His crew's distrust offended Columbus, but he still felt confident.

Possible responses given.

1. Why do you think the author describes the riches that Columbus hoped to find in Asia?
to help the reader understand why Columbus and his crew took the trip, even though they didn't know what lay ahead

2. What do you think is the author's main purpose for writing this passage?
to inform the reader of the reasons Columbus and his crew set sail for Asia

3. What might be another reason the author wrote this passage?
to express the feelings that Columbus and his crew felt on their trip

On-Level Practice TE p. LR32

Vocabulary
Directions Read each sentence. Write the word from the box that has the same meaning as the underlined word or phrase. Some words may be used more than once.

Check the Words You Know
__bargain   __favors   __lassoed   __offended
__prairie   __riverbed   __shrieked

1. __offended__   Yosh was hurt when Sarah left without saying good-bye to him.
2. __riverbed__   During the drought, you could see the floor of the channel in which the river used to flow.
3. __favors__   "Don't do me any acts of kindness by giving me a ride," huffed Mark.
4. __shrieked__   "You ruined my beautiful cake!" Milly said in a loud, sharp, shrill voice.
5. __prairie__   It's hard to play hide-and-seek in a large area of land with grass but few trees.
6. __offended__   The smell of the burning tire displeased Ms. Pauly.
7. __bargain__   Buying the used car for that amount of money was a great deal.
8. __lassoed__   The horse was caught with a long rope with a loop on one end.
9. __favors__   The crowd always prefers our team over any other.
10. __bargain__   At a flea market, we usually negotiate for the best price.

On-Level Practice TE p. LR33

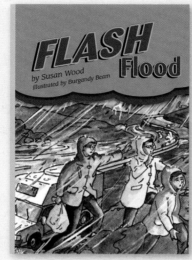

FLASH Flood
by Susan Wood
illustrated by Burgandy Beam

Below-Level Reader

Author's Purpose
- The **author's purpose** is the reason or reasons an author has for writing.
- An author may have one or more reasons for writing. He or she may want to inform, persuade, entertain, or express a mood or feeling.

Directions Read the following passage. Then answer the questions below.

Jimmy kept watching the river. The whipping wind shrieked outside the camper. Jimmy felt more and more nervous. "The dry ground of these riverbeds can become almost as hard as rocks. When it rains, the hardened riverbed cannot absorb all the water," the radio announcer said.

"Riverbeds can overflow during rain storms, flooding roads and houses. It happens really fast. That's why they are called flash floods. Drivers beware. In a flash it takes only two feet of water to wash away a car." Jimmy pictured rushing water overflowing a dry riverbed as he stared out the window.

1. This text is
  a. fiction.
  b. nonfiction.
  c. poetry.
  d. drama.
  c. entertain the reader by describing the fun and excitement Jimmy was having as he watched the river rise.
  d. inform the reader about what causes flash floods and how dangerous they are.

2. The author's main purpose for writing this passage was probably to
  a. show the importance of radio announcers.
  b. explain how campers can float.
  c. entertain the reader by making the reader feel scared and nervous.
  d. express a feeling of calm by describing the wind and rain.

4. The author writes the passage from the point of view of the boy, Jimmy, so that the reader knows what Jimmy is thinking and feeling. Why do you think the author does this?
  a. to inform the reader about what boys think of adults
  b. to express the mood of nervousness that Jimmy was feeling
  c. to persuade the reader that Jimmy knows a lot about campers
  d. to entertain the reader by making fun of Jimmy.

3. Another purpose the author may have had for writing this passage was to
  a. tell the reader that people should not worry about flash floods.
  b. express Jimmy's feeling of anger that he and his family were riding in a camper.

Below-Level Practice TE p. LR29

Vocabulary
Directions Match the words in column A with their synonyms in column B.

Check the Words You Know
__bargain   __favors   __lassoed   __offended
__prairie   __riverbed   __shrieked

Column A   **Column B**
1. lassoed — a. good deal
2. shrieked — b. good deeds
3. offended — c. roped
4. bargain — d. upset
5. favors — e. cried out
6. prairie — f. flat grassland

Directions Write a brief story or poem about a cowboy or cowgirl using the words *prairie*, *riverbed*, and *lassoed*.

Responses will vary. Students' stories or poems should use all three words correctly.

Below-Level Practice TE p. LR30

Advanced

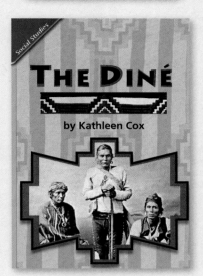

Advanced Reader

Name _____ The Diné

Author's Purpose

An author may have one or more **purpose**, or reason, for writing. He or she may want to inform, persuade, entertain, or express a mood or feeling.

Directions Read the following passage. Then answer the questions below.

The U.S. government finally let the Diné sign a second peace treaty in 1868. In return the Diné were given land in the Southwest. Their new reservation included their sacred Dinétah. The Diné were also given some livestock to replace what had been taken. They were given the right to make their own laws on this new reservation. Their days of raiding were over. The Diné had to promise to keep the peace, and they could no longer fight against the U.S. government.

The cavalry had destroyed Dinétah. Weeds grew throughout the once-plowed fields, dirt filled the ditches where water once flowed, and the lovely peach trees were reduced to tree stumps. But the Diné still had their four sacred mountains.

The Diné wanted to repair the damage. They performed ceremonies in honor of their Mother Earth. They prayed that Mother Earth would bless them again. Over time the Diné made a comeback. By 1890 their population rose to eighteen thousand people. The Diné also increased the size of their reservation until they owned more than fifteen million acres of land.

Possible responses given.

1. What do you think is the author's main purpose for writing this passage? Explain.

to inform the reader about what happened after the Diné signed the peace treaty in 1868 and returned to the Dinétah

2. What might be another reason the author wrote this passage? Explain.

to persuade the reader that the Diné were hard-working by telling how they made a comeback

3. Why do you think the author describes the way the cavalry had destroyed Dinétah?

to show how much work the Diné had to do to repair the damage

4. Why do you think the author describes how the Diné "performed ceremonies" and "prayed"?

The author wants to inform the reader of how important religion and sacred ceremonies were to the Diné.

Advanced Practice TE p. LR35

Name _____ The Diné

Vocabulary

Directions Choose the word from the box that best matches each definition. Write the word on the line.

Check the Words You Know

_ancestors	_cardinal points	_edible	_environmentalists
_hogans	_inhabited	_nomads	

1. _edible_ safe to eat

2. _cardinal points_ the four principal directions on the compass: north, south, east, and west

3. _environmentalists_ people who want to protect the land

4. _inhabited_ lived in a place

Directions Write the word from the box that belongs in each group.

5. buildings, houses, _hogans_

6. family, relatives, _ancestors_

7. wanderers, travelers, _nomads_

Directions Write a brief history of some of your ancestors. Use as many vocabulary words as you can. Use a separate sheet of paper if necessary.

Responses will vary.

Advanced Practice TE p. LR36

ELL

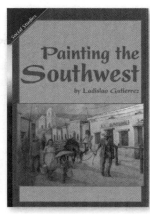

ELL Reader

ELL Poster 4

Teacher's Edition Notes

ELL notes throughout this lesson support instruction and reference additional resources at point of use.

Teaching Guide pp. 22–28, 218–219

- Multilingual summaries of the main selection
- Comprehension lesson
- Vocabulary strategies and word cards
- ELL Reader 4.1.4 lesson

ELL and Transition Handbook

Ten Important Sentences

- Key ideas from every selection in the Student Edition
- Activities to build sentence power

More Reading

Readers' Theater Anthology

- Fluency practice
- Five scripts to build fluency
- Poetry for oral interpretation

Leveled Trade Books

- Extended reading tied to the unit concept
- Lessons in the Trade Book Library Teaching Guide

Homework

- Family Times Newsletter
- ELL Multilingual Selection Summaries

Take-Home Books

- Leveled Readers

The Horned Toad Prince   **88i**

Cross-Curricular Centers

Listening

Reading/Library

Health

Listen to the Selections

MATERIALS | SINGLES
CD player, headphones, AudioText CD, student book

LISTEN TO LITERATURE Listen to *The Horned Toad Prince* and "Horned Lizards and Harvesting Ants" as you follow or read along in your book. As you listen, think about the authors' reasons for writing these selections.

If there is anything you don't understand, you can listen again to any section.

Audio CD

Read It Again!

MATERIALS | SINGLES PAIRS GROUPS
Collection of books for self-selected reading, reading logs, student book

Select a book you have already read. Record the title of the book in your reading log. You may want to read with a partner.

Choose from the following:

- Leveled Readers
- ELL Readers
- Books or Stories Written by Classmates
- Books from the Library
- *The Horned Toad Prince*

TEN IMPORTANT SENTENCES Read the Ten Important Sentences for *The Horned Toad Prince*. Then locate the sentences in the student book.

BOOK CLUB Look at p. 780 of the student book to help you begin an illustrator study of Michael Austin. Look at other books illustrated by Austin and get together with a group to share your favorite illustrations.

Classroom Library

Living on a Ranch

MATERIALS | SINGLES PAIRS GROUPS
Writing and art materials, student book, Graphic Organizer 26

Is living on a ranch a healthy lifestyle?

1. Find three or four activities Reba Jo does in *The Horned Toad Prince*.
2. List or draw the activities on a three-column chart.
   - Label the first column *What Reba Jo Does Outside*. List or draw outdoor activities in this column.
   - Label the second column *What Reba Jo Does Inside*. List or draw indoor activities in this column.
   - Label the third column *Time*. In this column, write an estimate of how much time you think she spends on each activity in a day.
3. Use your chart to write one or two sentences telling why Reba Jo probably has a healthy lifestyle.

EARLY FINISHERS Write a paragraph describing Reba Jo's daily life.

Reba Jo's Activities

Outside	Inside	Time
🐎		1 hour
	⭕	1/2 hour
	🎸	15 min.

Living on a ranch is a healthy lifestyle because you get to be outside a lot.

Scott Foresman Reading Street Centers Survival Kit

Use the *Horned Toad Prince* materials from the Reading Street
Centers Survival Kit to organize this week's centers.

Writing/Vocabulary

Social Studies

Technology

Create an *Illustrated Glossary*

MATERIALS
Student book, writing and art materials, Graphic Organizer 18

`SINGLES` `GROUPS`

Make a glossary of words that name things found in the Southwest, such as *cactus*.

1. Look through *The Horned Toad Prince* to find words describing the Southwest. Also include Words to Know from p. 90.
2. List three or four words in alphabetical order.
3. Draw a picture next to each word to show what it means.

EARLY FINISHERS Compare the Southwest to your own or another region. Use a Venn diagram to show the differences and similarities between the two regions.

Glossary of Southwest Words

1. cactus
2. horse
3. riverbed

Write a *Travel Description*

MATERIALS
Student book, social studies book, reference materials on the Southwest, writing materials

`SINGLES` `GROUPS`

Describe plants and animals of the Southwest.

1. Using classroom resources, find out about a plant or animal that lives in the Southwest.
2. Write a five-sentence description of the plant or animal that could appear in a travel brochure for the Southwest.

EARLY FINISHERS Make a class travel brochure of plants and animals of the Southwest. Add drawings, a cover, and a table of contents to complete your brochure.

The Coyote

The coyote lives in the Southwest. It sees and hears extremely well and is very fast. It runs up to 40 mph. The coyote even has its own way of communicating.

Plan a *Texas Trip*

MATERIALS
Computer, Internet access, writing and art materials

`SINGLES` `PAIRS` `GROUPS`

Search the Internet for a place to visit in Texas.

1. Log on to the Internet and find a search engine for students. Type the keyword *Texas* in the Search box. Click on one or more Web site links to find an interesting place to visit.
2. Choose a place to visit and write three or more sentences describing this place. Include the address of any Web site that gave you useful information.
3. Follow classroom rules when searching the Internet and printing.

EARLY FINISHERS With classmates, use your descriptions to choose the best place to visit in Texas. Compare your choice with other groups.

Search Engine

Texas

The capital of Texas is Austin. Almost 600,000 people live there. The Texas State Capitol is pink because it is made out of sunset red granite.

ALL CENTERS

Concept Vocabulary

corral pen for horses and cattle

frontier the farthest part of a settled country, where the wilds begin

rodeo a contest or exhibition of skill in roping cattle and riding horses and bulls

Monitor Progress

Check Vocabulary

If...	then...
students are unable to place words on the web,	review the lesson concept. Place the words on the web and provide additional words for practice, such as *settlement* and *prairie dog.*

SUCCESS PREDICTOR

DAY 1 — Grouping Options

Reading

Whole Group

Introduce and discuss the Question of the Week. Then use pp. 88l–90b.

Group Time

Differentiated Instruction

Read this week's Leveled Readers. See pp. 88f–88g for the small group lesson plan.

Whole Group

Use p. 111a.

Language Arts

Use pp. 111e–111k.

Build Concepts

FLUENCY

MODEL VOLUME As you read "Growing Up in the Old West," use a volume suited to the size of the room and the distance of the farthest listener. Model how to maintain an appropriate, steady volume while reading, making sure not to drop volume at the ends of sentences.

LISTENING COMPREHENSION

After reading "Growing Up in the Old West," use the following questions to assess listening comprehension.

1. **What was the author's purpose for writing "Growing Up in the Old West"?** *(Possible response: She wanted to inform people about what life was like for children growing up on the frontier.)* **Author's Purpose**

2. **What does the author think about the life of frontier children in the Old West?** *(Possible response: There were lots of fun things to do, so life in the Old West was never boring.)* **Author's Viewpoint**

BUILD CONCEPT VOCABULARY

Start a web to build concepts and vocabulary related to this week's lesson and the unit theme.

- Draw The Southwest Concept Web.
- Read the sentence with the word *frontier* again. Ask students to pronounce the word and discuss its meaning.
- Place *frontier* in an oval attached to *landscape*. Discuss how the landscape of the Southwest was once an isolated frontier. Read the sentence in which *corral* and *rodeo* appear. Have students pronounce the words, place them on the Web, and provide reasons.
- Brainstorm additional words and categories for the Web. Keep the Web on display and add words throughout the week.

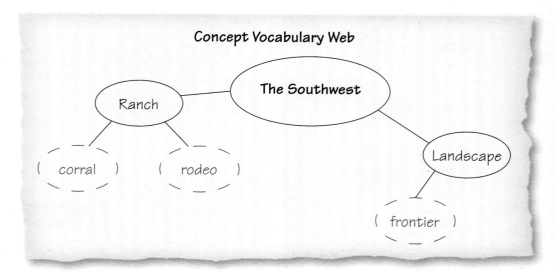

Concept Vocabulary Web

Growing Up in the Old West

⭐

By Judith Alter

Life on the frontier was hard work. There was little time for play, and many children lived in such isolation that they had few if any playmates. Nevertheless, youngsters on the frontier also had a whole world of wonder in which to play. If they had few ready-made amusements and little planned play, they quickly became skilled at inventing their own fun, and in a world of freedom, where there were few "don'ts," they became self-reliant.

Wild creatures formed part of a child's fun. Sometimes the lonely ranch child would have a live pet, though this usually did not work out for long. Sometimes a clever boy would capture a prairie dog, but that required patience. Youngsters used to catch toads and tie a string to them. And there were prairie chickens and rabbits to chase, even if one rarely caught them by hand.

Ranch children could have a free rodeo anytime they wandered to the corral. With calves to brand and young horses to rope, saddle, and ride for the first time, something was always going on.

There were swimming holes and creeks to fish in. One technique for fishing without a pole was to stir up the water with your hands until the fish were scared into jumping into the frog holes in the bank. Then one simply reached into the hole and pulled out the fish, hoping all the while that there were no water moccasin snakes in there with it.

Youngsters did play some of the same games their cousins were playing back east—statue, for example, in which one person swings another very fast by the hand and then lets go. The one who has been swung reels a few paces, then freezes into some strange position, the funnier the better. Even hide-and-seek and jump rope took on a difference when played in the great outdoors of the West.

For the days or months when weather forced children indoors there were homemade toys. Children also played cards, checkers, and dominoes. Small children played with cornhusk dolls or hand-carved toys. A popular toy was a jointed wooden bear that could, when properly handled, climb a rope.

Best of all, on long winter nights, was storytelling. This was the era of Indian battles, and during most of the years of settlement in the West, the Civil War was a very real and recent memory to people still living. Youngsters would sit on the knee of a parent or grandparent and hear tales of battles won and lost.

For those youngsters whose families lived close enough to a town, a Saturday trip there was the highlight of the week. Sometimes there were variety shows in town. For a few precious pennies, a youngster might see a sword swallower or a magician, a snake charmer or a juggler. Those same pennies might buy a peppermint or licorice stick.

From holidays to ordinary everyday delights, the Old West was a place of fun and amazement. There was never any complaint of: "But there's nothing to do!"

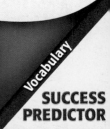

SKILLS ⟷ STRATEGIES IN CONTEXT

Author's Purpose
Story Structure

INTRODUCE

Display two familiar books. One should be an animated fairy tale or fantasy, such as *The Phantom Tollbooth*. The other should be an informational book, such as *The Nine Planets*. Identify the author of each book. Ask why these authors might have written their books. *(Possible response: The fantasy was written to entertain readers. The nonfiction was written to give information about a topic.)*

Have students read the information on p. 88. Explain the following:

- Authors write stories and articles for many different reasons.

- Identifying a story's structure can help you determine the author's purpose.

Use Skill Transparency 4 to teach author's purpose and story structure.

Comprehension

Skill
Author's Purpose

Strategy
Story Structure

Author's Purpose

- An author may write to persuade, inform, entertain, or express ideas or feelings. Often an author has more than one purpose.

- The kinds of ideas and the way the author organizes and states them can help you determine the author's purpose.

Ideas what they are how they are expressed	→	**Author's Purpose** persuade inform entertain express	←	**Text** title and any heads facts and information fictional characters and plot pattern of ideas

Strategy: Story Structure

Active readers note the structure of fictional stories, including the problem or goal, rising action (building up to the climax), climax (where the conflict is confronted), and outcome (where the conflict is resolved). Most stories are told in time order, or sequence, and are written to entertain, but some teach a lesson at the same time they entertain.

 Write to Read

1. As you read "The Fox and the Grapes," use a graphic organizer like the one above to figure out the author's purpose.

2. An author can have more than one purpose. Write the lesson about life that "The Fox and the Grapes" teaches.

88

Strategic Intervention

 Author's Purpose Review the four main purposes for writing: *to persuade, to inform, to entertain,* or *to express ideas or feelings*. Display additional books from your classroom library and model determining the author's purpose for each. Use titles, covers, illustrations, photographs, opening paragraphs, and so on to help explain the author's purpose. Then show an example of a book, such as one in the *Magic School Bus* series, that has more than one purpose.

ELL

Access Content

Beginning/Intermediate For a Picture It! lesson on author's purpose, see the ELL Teaching Guide, pp. 22–33.

Advanced Before reading "The Fox and the Grapes," have volunteers spell on the board the word that is represented phonetically in paragraph 2. *(delicious)*

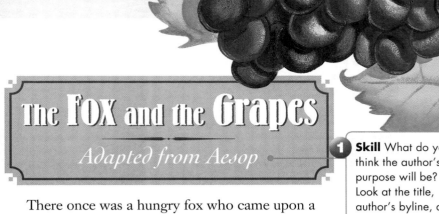

The Fox and the Grapes

Adapted from Aesop

There once was a hungry fox who came upon a grapevine wound around a high trellis. Hanging from the vine was a bunch of grapes.

"What DEE-LISH-US-looking grapes," the fox said to himself. "I think I'll just step up and grab a few." So he stood up on his hind legs under the trellis, but the grapes were out of reach.

"Hmmm," said the fox. "Those DEE-licious grapes are higher up than I thought." So the fox jumped up as high as he could, but the grapes were still out of reach.

"This is ridiculous," said the fox. "How hard can it be to grab some dee-licious grapes?" So the fox stepped back, took a running leap—and missed. The grapes were still out of reach.

"Humph!" said the fox, walking away with a little toss of his tail. "I thought at first those grapes looked delicious, but now I see they are sour."

1 Skill What do you think the author's purpose will be? Look at the title, author's byline, and illustrations for clues.

2 Strategy What is the problem in this story?
a) The grapes look delicious.
b) The fox is stealing the grapes.
c) The fox cannot reach the grapes.

3 Strategy Think about the way the story develops. Figure out the rising action, climax, and resolution of the story.

4 Skill In an Aesop's fable, the purpose is usually to teach a lesson about life. How is the fox's behavior an example of how not to act?

89

Available as **Skill Transparency** 4

TEACH

1 SKILL Preview the story and predict the author's purpose.

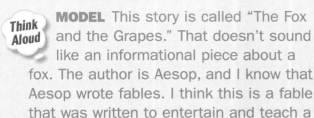 **MODEL** This story is called "The Fox and the Grapes." That doesn't sound like an informational piece about a fox. The author is Aesop, and I know that Aesop wrote fables. I think this is a fable that was written to entertain and teach a lesson.

2 STRATEGY Identify the story's problem.

Think Aloud **MODEL** The fox sees some grapes he wants to eat. He stands up on his hind legs to get them, but he can't reach them. So the problem in the story is c.

PRACTICE AND ASSESS

3 STRATEGY Rising action: The fox jumps high to try to get the grapes. Climax: The fox takes a running leap and still misses the grapes. Resolution: The fox gives up and says the grapes are sour.

4 SKILL The fox quits trying and says the grapes are no good anyway. The author is trying to say that people shouldn't make excuses for not trying when they can't get what they want right away.

WRITE Have students complete steps 1 and 2 of the Write to Read activity. You might consider using this as a whole-class activity.

Monitor Progress

Author's Purpose

If... students are unable to complete **Write to Read** on p. 88,	**then...** use Practice Book p. 33 to provide additional practice.

Author's Purpose

- The **author's purpose** is the reason or reasons for writing. An author may write to persuade, to inform, to entertain, or to express ideas and feelings.
- The kinds of ideas in the text, and the way the author organizes and states these ideas, can help you determine the purpose.

Directions Read the following passage. Then complete the diagram below.

When I smelled chili cooking in the kitchen, I knew I was in trouble. This wasn't just ordinary chili. This was "fibber's chili," which was invented by my great-aunt. She fed this chili to anyone she thought had told a fib or a lie. "One bite," she used to say, "and they can't help but tell you the whole truth."
I knew my mom was making it for me

now. Why? Yesterday I kicked a soccer ball into a window, and it broke. Of course, then I told my mother that the window smashed when a bird flew into it. I suppose now I could tell her that I'm too sick to eat. But then she'd serve me fibber's chili a second time! I've got to get up my courage and tell the truth.

Possible answers given for 1–4.

Examples of Ideas
1. A special chili **makes people tell the truth.**
2. The narrator has not told the truth about **a broken window.**

Author's Purpose
5. The author's purpose is to entertain.

Content of Text
3. comic details
4. narrator's worried feelings

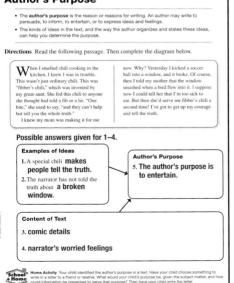 **Home Activity** Your child identified the author's purpose in a text. Have your child choose something to write in a letter to a friend or relative. What would your child's purpose be, given the subject matter, and how could information be presented to serve that purpose? Then have your child write the letter.

▲ **Practice Book** p. 33

Students can search the Internet to find out more about fairy tales or other fairy tales to read. Have them use a search engine for students and the keywords *fairy tales* or the name of a particular fairy tale. *The Horned Toad Prince* is based on the classic fairy tale *The Frog Prince.*

E L L

Build Background Use ELL Poster 4 to build background and vocabulary for the lesson concept of the uniqueness of the Southwest.

▲ **ELL Poster** 4

Build Background

ACTIVATE PRIOR KNOWLEDGE

BEGIN A FOUR-COLUMN CHART about fairy tales.

- Give each student a four-column chart (Graphic Organizer 27) with the headings *Settings, Characters, Story Events,* and *Lessons Learned.*
- Give students two or three minutes to write as many things as they can about typical settings, characters, story events, or lessons learned from familiar fairy tales. Compile some of their ideas in a chart on the chalkboard. Add an idea of your own.
- Tell students that, as they read, they should think about how *The Horned Toad Prince* is like and different from other fairy tales they know. You might have them return to their charts to answer the last Guided Comprehension question on p. 104 of this teacher's edition.

Fairy Tales			
Settings	Characters	Story Events	Lessons Learned
castles long ago	kings, queens, princesses, princes, frogs	animals turn into people people turn into animals	Don't judge people by their looks

▲ **Graphic Organizer** 27

BACKGROUND BUILDING AUDIO This week's audio explores animals of the Southwest. After students listen, invite them to tell what they learned about animals of the Southwest.

Background Building Audio

Introduce Vocabulary

VOCABULARY FRAMES

Create vocabulary frames that students can use to explore the meaning of lesson vocabulary words.

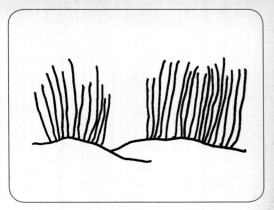

prairie

Word

Association or Symbol

Predicted definition: **Flat and grassy land**

One good sentence:

We saw herds of cattle on the prairie.

Verified definition:

A large area of level or rolling land with grass but few or no trees.

Another good sentence:

The prairie stretched out before us like a green blanket.

▲ **Graphic Organizer** 6

Go over the above vocabulary frame with students.

Then assign one lesson vocabulary word each to pairs of students. Have each pair discuss what they know about their assigned word and then work together to fill out a vocabulary frame for it. Have students share their work with other classmates. **Activate Prior Knowledge**

Suggest that students look for illustrations in the story that help explain word meanings. **Picture Clues**

By the end of the week, students should know the lesson vocabulary words. Have student pairs exchange their frame with another pair and demonstrate their knowledge by writing another good sentence for the framed word.

Lesson Vocabulary

WORDS TO KNOW

T bargain an agreement to trade or exchange; deal

T favor act of kindness

T lassoed roped; caught with a long rope with a loop on the end

T offended hurt the feelings of someone; made angry

T prairie large area of level or rolling land with grass but few or no trees

T riverbed channel in which a river flows or used to flow

T shrieked made a loud, sharp, shrill sound

MORE WORDS TO KNOW

sassy rude; lively, spirited

suspiciously without trust, doubtfully

twang to make a sharp, ringing sound

T = Tested Word

Vocabulary

Directions Draw a line to connect each word on the left with its definition on the right.

1. riverbed
2. favor
3. prairie
4. lassoed
5. bargain

a large area of level or rolling land with grass but few or no trees
a channel in which a river flows or used to flow
an agreement to trade; deal
act of kindness
roped; caught with a lasso

Directions In each statement below, the first pair of words has a certain relationship (such as the same meaning). To complete the statement, add a word that gives the second pair of words the same relationship as the first pair. For example, *neat* is to *messy* (opposite meanings) as *happy* is to *sad* (opposite meanings). Choose the word from the box and write it on the line shown to the left.

shrieked 6. *Laughed* is to *cried* as *whispered* is to _____.

offended 7. *Remembered* is to *recalled* as *angered* is to _____.

prairie 8. *Tree* is to *forest* as *grass* is to _____.

riverbed 9. *Train* is to *track* as *river* is to _____.

bargain 10. *Disagreement* is to *fight* as *deal* is to _____.

Check the Words You Know
☐ bargain
☐ favor
☐ lassoed
☐ offended
☐ prairie
☐ riverbed
☐ shrieked

Write a Fairy Tale
On a separate sheet of paper, write your own fairy tale about making a bargain. Use as many vocabulary words as you can.
Fairy tales should include words from the vocabulary list and details about making a bargain.

School + Home Home Activity Your child identified and used vocabulary words from *The Horned Toad Prince*. Together, create additional analogies, as shown in the second activity, to use with the vocabulary words.

▲ **Practice Book** p. 34

DAY 2

Vocabulary Strategy

OBJECTIVE

Use context clues to determine word meaning.

INTRODUCE

Discuss the strategy for synonyms as context clues using the steps on p. 90.

TEACH

- Have students think about lesson vocabulary words in context as they read "Tall Paul."
- Model using context clues to determine the meaning of *prairie*.

MODEL This sentence says Tall Paul could cross a mile of prairie in one step. The sentence before says he lived on the plains. I think the *plains* and *prairie* may be the same thing. I know the plains are a flat stretch of land. The synonym makes sense in the context: Tall Paul crossed a mile of the plains in one step.

Words to Know

prairie

lassoed

riverbed

bargain

favor

offended

shrieked

Remember

Try the strategy. Then, if you need more help, use your glossary or a dictionary.

Vocabulary Strategy
for Synonyms

Context Clues Sometimes when you are reading, you see a word you don't know. The author may give you a synonym for the word. A synonym is a word that has almost the same meaning as another word. Look for a synonym. It can help you understand the meaning of the word you don't know.

1. Look at the sentence in which the unknown word appears. The author may give a synonym in the same sentence.

2. If not, look at the sentences around the sentence with the unknown word. The author may use a synonym there.

3. Try the synonym in place of the word in the sentence. Does it make sense?

As you read "Tall Paul," look for synonyms to help you understand the meanings of the vocabulary words.

90

DAY 2 Grouping Options

Reading
Whole Group Discuss the Question of the Day. Then use pp. 90–93.

Group Time Differentiated Instruction
Read *The Horned Toad Prince.* See pp. 88f–88g for the small group lesson plan.

Whole Group Use p. 111a.

Language Arts
Use pp. 111e–111k.

Strategic Intervention

Context Clues Display the sentence: *The wind* shrieked *and whistled* through the trees. Have students tell which two words are synonyms.

Access Content Use ELL Poster 4 to preteach vocabulary. Choose from the following to meet language proficiency levels.

Beginning Use the Multilingual Lesson Vocabulary list that begins on p. 272 of the ELL Teaching Guide, as well as other home-language resources, to provide translations of the tested words.

Intermediate Ask Spanish-speaking students if they recognize the words *favor* and *offend.* These words have Spanish cognates: *favor* and *ofender.*

Advanced Teach the lesson on pp. 90–91. Have students report on the home-language words for some of the lesson vocabulary words.

Resources for home-language words may include parents, bilingual staff members, bilingual dictionaries, or online translation sources.

Tall Paul

Tall Paul was a cowboy who lived on the plains not so long ago. He was not just any cowboy, though. He was so long legged he could cross a mile of prairie in just one step. And he was so big and strong he lassoed and caught a whole herd of cattle with a single toss of his rope.

Tall Paul had a mighty big appetite too. He ate a mountain of flapjacks for breakfast. One time, out on the range, he got so thirsty he drank a river. The dry riverbed just lay there gasping for water.

Tall Paul felt bad about that so he struck a bargain with the sky.

The sky would bring a flood of rain. In return, the sky asked this favor: "I will help you if you do me this service. My servant, Wind, can't blow the clouds over that mountain there. I need you to flatten it a little for me."

Tall Paul said to the mountain, "Now don't be offended. I'll just take a little off the top." The mountain shrieked and screamed, but the deed was done. Tall Paul jumped on that mountain and turned it into a nice little mesa. In an instant, the rains began to fall.

Words to Write

Write your own tale about Tall Paul. Use some words from the Words to Know list.

91

PRACTICE AND ASSESS

- Have students determine the meanings of the remaining words and explain the context clues they used.

- Point out that context doesn't always offer enough clues to word meaning. Students may need to look up a word in the glossary or a dictionary for an exact definition.

- If students filled out a vocabulary frame (p. 90b), have them fill out another frame with a different vocabulary word.

- Have students complete Practice Book p. 35.

WRITE Tales should include several lesson vocabulary words as well as words that describe great size and strength.

Monitor Progress

Context Clues

If... students need more practice with the lesson vocabulary,	then... use Tested Vocabulary Cards.

Vocabulary • Context Clues

- Sometimes when you are reading, you see a word you don't know. The author may give you a **synonym** for the word. Synonyms are words with the same or similar meanings.
- Often you can recognize a synonym by noting a word set off by commas and preceded by the word *or* and *like*.

Directions Read the following passage. Then answer the questions below.

Once upon a time, there lived an old man. He lived on a prairie, or the plains, that seemed to stretch forever. One day, the old man took a walk and came upon two little boys fighting. One of the boys shrieked, or screeched, that the other boy had not carried out his half of a bargain.

"The deal," he screamed, "was that we would both dig for the treasure—not just me!" The little boy was obviously offended, or insulted, to be doing all the

work. "I'm not asking for favors. I just want you to do your share of digging," he said.

The boys stopped fighting when they saw the old man standing before them. The old man reached in his pocket and took out the largest ruby the boys had ever seen.

"If you agree never to fight again," said the man, "I will show you a treasure that is a million times greater than the one you are digging for."

1. What is the synonym for *prairie* used in the passage?
   The synonym is the _plains_.

2. What synonym for *shrieked* does the author use? How do you know?
   screeched; The word "or" suggests they mean the same thing.

3. Where in the passage is the synonym for *bargain*?
   "The deal" appears at the beginning of the next sentence.

4. In the passage, the synonym for *offended* is *insulted*. What is another synonym?
   Possible answer: angered

5. After reading the passage, you might describe the old man as mysterious. What is a synonym for *mysterious*?
   Possible answer: strange

Home Activity Your child identified synonyms that appeared as context clues in a passage. Play a naming game with your child by taking turns saying words that describe a feeling—such as *happy, sad,* or *angry*—and having the other person provide one or more synonyms.

▲ **Practice Book** p. 35

Prereading Strategies

GENRE STUDY

Modern Fairy Tale

The Horned Toad Prince is a modern fairy tale. Remind students that a fairy tale is a short story with magical characters and events. Explain that, unlike traditional fairy tales, a modern fairy tale is set in the present.

PREVIEW AND PREDICT

Have students preview the story title and illustrations and discuss what they think the story will be about and why they think it's called a modern fairy tale. Encourage students to use lesson vocabulary words as they talk about their predictions.

Strategy Response Log

Ask Questions Have students write a question about each of the characters pictured on pp. 92 and 93 in their strategy response logs. Students will answer their questions in the Strategy Response Log activity on p. 99.

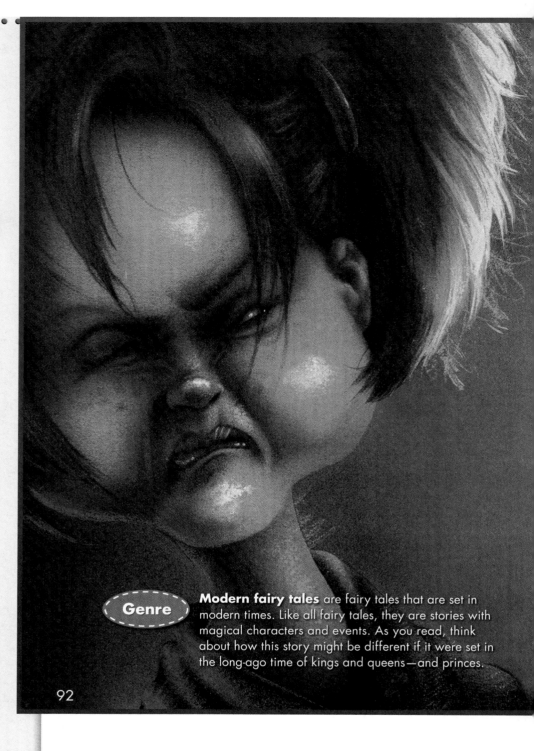

Genre

Modern fairy tales are fairy tales that are set in modern times. Like all fairy tales, they are stories with magical characters and events. As you read, think about how this story might be different if it were set in the long-ago time of kings and queens—and princes.

92

ELL

Access Content Lead a picture walk to get a sense of the setting of the Southwest: *prairie* (p. 94), *vulture* (p. 95), *cowgirl* (p. 96). This story contains many words associated with the Southwest, including Spanish.

Consider having students read the selection summary in English or in students' home languages. See the Multilingual Summaries in the ELL Teaching Guide, pp. 26–28.

The Horned Toad Prince

by Jackie Mims Hopkins

illustrated by Michael Austin

How could a horned toad possibly be a prince?

93

SET PURPOSE

Direct students' attention to the picture of the girl on p. 92 and the picture of the horned toad on p. 93. Explain that a horned toad is really a horned lizard and can be found in the western United States, Mexico, and Guatemala. Ask students what they want to find out about the girl and the horned toad as they read.

Remind students to think about the author's purpose as they read.

STRATEGY RECALL

Students have now used these before-reading strategies:

- preview the selection to be aware of its genre, features, and possible content;
- activate prior knowledge about that content and what to expect of that genre;
- make predictions;
- set a purpose for reading.

Remind students that, as they read, they should monitor their own comprehension. If they realize something does not make sense, they can regain their comprehension by using fix-up strategies they have learned, such as:

- use phonics and word structure to decode new words;
- use context clues or a dictionary to figure out meanings of new words;
- adjust their reading rate—slow down for difficult text, speed up for easy or familiar text, or skim and scan just for specific information;
- reread parts of the text;
- read on (continue to read for clarification);
- use text features such as headings, subheadings, charts, illustrations, and so on as visual aids to comprehension;
- make a graphic organizer or a semantic organizer to aid comprehension;
- use reference sources, such as an encyclopedia, dictionary, thesaurus, or synonym finder;
- use another person, such as a teacher, a peer, a librarian, or an outside expert, as a resource.

After reading, students will use these strategies:

- summarize or retell the text;
- answer questions they or others pose;
- reflect to make new information become part of their prior knowledge.

Audio CD AudioText

Guiding Comprehension

1 **Author's Craft • Inferential**

Question the Author **The author writes "a prairie storm could blow in quicker than a rattlesnake's strike." What is the author trying to tell you? Why do you think she uses these words?**

Possible response: Storms can begin suddenly on the prairie. Comparing a storm to a rattlesnake's strike helps the reader picture something happening fast, and rattlesnakes are common in this setting.

2 **Character • Inferential**

From what you have read so far, how would you describe Reba Jo?

Possible responses: She is happy, daring, fun-loving, curious, and independent.

3 ◎ **Author's Purpose • Inferential**

Question the Author **Why do you think Jackie Mims Hopkins wrote this story? How can you tell?**

Possible response: The author wrote this story to entertain readers. It is a fictional story, and the characters and illustrations are humorous.

Monitor Progress

◎ Author's Purpose

If... students are unable to determine the author's purpose,	**then...** use the skill and strategy instruction on p. 95.

Reba Jo loved to twang her guitar and sing while the prairie wind whistled through the thirsty sagebrush.

Singing with the wind was one of the ways Reba Jo entertained herself on the lonesome prairie. Sometimes she amused herself by racing her horse, Flash, against a tumbleweed cartwheeling across her daddy's land.

But her favorite pastime of all was roping. She lassoed cacti, water buckets, fence posts, and any unlucky critter that crossed her path.

94

ELL

Access Content Help students visualize the dry, lonesome prairie by describing or illustrating the plants mentioned on p. 94: sagebrush (paragraph 1), tumbleweed (paragraph 2), and cacti (paragraph 3).

One blustery morning, as she was riding the range looking for something to lasso, Reba Jo came upon a dry riverbed. Her daddy had warned her to stay away from these *arroyos*. He'd told her that a prairie storm could blow **1** in quicker than a rattlesnake's strike, causing a flash flood to rip through the riverbed. The swift water would wash away anything or anyone in its way.

Reba Jo knew she should turn back. But right at the edge of this gully she spied a vulture, all fat and sassy, sitting on top of a dried-up old well, just daring her to toss her spinning rope **2** around his long ugly neck. **3**

95

Geography of the Southwest

The southwestern United States includes Arizona, New Mexico, Oklahoma, and Texas. This region is known for its huge open spaces which include flat prairies and grasslands. The flat prairies are ideal for growing cotton, corn, and other crops. The grasslands help feed livestock. Other parts of the Southwest include desert regions, which are dry and very dusty, and higher plateaus or mountains, which have colder temperatures and heavier winter snows. Physical features that attract visitors include the Grand Canyon (Arizona), Painted Desert (Arizona), Carlsbad Caverns (New Mexico), Wichita Mountains (Oklahoma), and Rio Grande (Texas).

SKILLS ↔ STRATEGIES IN CONTEXT

Author's Purpose

TEACH

- Remind students that an author's purpose is the reason he or she has for writing.
- Review the four main purposes: to persuade, to inform, to entertain, or to express.
- Model finding the author's purpose using the text on p. 94 and the images on pp. 94–95.

Think Aloud **MODEL** I'll look first at the illustrations. The characters look more like cartoons than real people and animals, so I don't think the author is trying to provide factual information. Next I'll look for details in the text. I see parts where she makes me laugh—talking about Reba Jo racing a tumbleweed and lassoing cacti and "unlucky critters." Based on all of this, I think the author's purpose is to entertain.

PRACTICE AND ASSESS

Have students identify other elements on pp. 94–95 that show the author's purpose. *(Possible response: The vulture is described as "fat and sassy" with a "long ugly neck.")*

EXTEND SKILLS

Humorous Fiction

Tell students that humorous fiction is fiction that is designed to make readers laugh. Discuss how the author uses humor in *The Horned Toad Prince*. Have students identify examples on pp. 94–95 of humorous elements reflected in characters *(vulture)*, story events *(Reba Jo's lassoing)*, or word choices *("critter," "quicker than a rattlesnake's strike")*.

Guiding Comprehension

4 **Cause and Effect • Literal**

How did Reba Jo's hat end up in the well?

The wind blew it off her head.

5 **Sequence • Literal**

What did Reba Jo do after her hat fell off?

She looked into the well and started to cry.

Monitor Progress

REVIEW Sequence

If... students have difficulty identifying the sequence of events,	then... use the skill and strategy instruction on p. 97.

6 **Predict • Inferential**

What do you think will happen next?

Possible response: The horned toad might try to help Reba Jo get her hat.

Tech Files

ONLINE

Students can search an online encyclopedia or the Internet to find factual information about story elements. Suggest they use a student-friendly search engine and keywords based on story details such as *cowgirls*, *horned toads*, or *vultures* for their search. Be sure to follow classroom rules for Internet use.

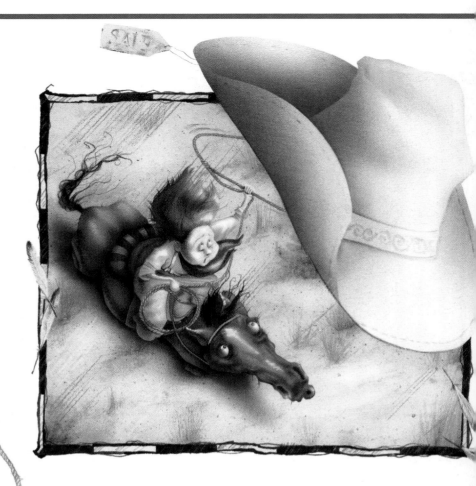

4 As Reba Jo's lasso whirled into the air, a great gust of wind came whipping through the *arroyo* and blew her new cowgirl hat right off her head and down to the bottom of the dusty old well.

5 Reba Jo scrambled to the edge of the well. She peered down into the darkness and commenced to crying. Suddenly she heard a small voice say, *"¿Qué pasa, señorita?"*

She looked around and wondered if the wind blowing through the *arroyo* was fooling her ears.

96

Context Clues Help students use context to figure out regionalisms. For example, *peck of trouble* (p. 97, paragraph 2) means "a lot of trouble."

Encourage students to record U.S. regionalisms and their meanings in language journals, word lists, or computer files of English vocabulary.

But then, there in the sand, she spotted a big fat horned toad looking up at her. "What's the matter, *señorita?*" he asked again.

"Oh," she cried, "the brand-new hat my daddy bought for me just blew down into this stinkin' old well. I'll never be able to get it out, and I'll be in a peck of trouble when he finds out I've been playin' down here near the *arroyo*."

97

SKILLS ⟷ STRATEGIES IN CONTEXT

Sequence REVIEW

TEACH

- To understand the story, readers need to understand the sequence, or order, in which things happen.

- Some stories use clue words, such as *first, next,* and *finally.*

- Use p. 96 to model identifying sequence.

Think Aloud **MODEL** I read that *as* Reba Jo whirls her lasso, a wind blows her hat off her head and into the well. The word *as* tells me these actions happen at the same time, and I can picture the wind blowing something away. The next paragraph tells me Reba Jo goes to the well, looks in it, and starts crying. That order makes sense. After she loses her hat, she looks for it in the well, gets upset, and starts crying.

PRACTICE AND ASSESS

- Have students read the first two paragraphs on p. 97 and tell what happens next in the story. (*A horned toad appears and asks Reba Jo what is wrong. She tells him she lost her hat.*)

- To assess, use Practice Book p. 36.

Sequence

Directions Read the following passage. Then answer the questions below.

Today I learned how to make green chili pie. First you must gather the ingredients—6 or 7 green chilies, 1 cup of grated Fontina cheese, 4 eggs, 2 cups light cream, salt, and pepper. Then preheat the oven to 425°. Butter the bottom of a pie pan and line it with chilies. Sprinkle the cheese over them. Mix the eggs, cream, salt, and pepper together in a bowl. Pour this mixture over the cheese. Bake the pie for 15 minutes. Then lower the heat to 325° and bake for 20–30 minutes longer. Test the pie for doneness by removing it from the oven and inserting a knife into the center. If the knife comes out clean, the pie is done. You may serve the pie hot or cold.

1. What is the first step in making green chili pie?
   The first step is gathering the ingredients.

2. What is the last step in making the pie?
   The final step is testing to see if the pie is cooked completely.

3. What step follows baking the pie for fifteen minutes? How do you know this is the next step?
   Lower the heat to 325° and bake the pie for 20–30 more minutes;
   The word *then* shows that this is the next step.

4. If these steps were written in a different order, would it matter? Why or why not?
   Possible answer: It could matter a lot; If you cooked the pie before all the ingredients were added, it would not taste right.

5. On a separate sheet of paper, explain the steps of a process you know well.
   Responses should include a number of correctly ordered steps in a process with which the student is familiar.

School Home **Home Activity** Your child identified the steps in a process. Perform a household chore with your child, like making a bed, and have your child name the steps that make up the process.

▲ **Practice Book** p. 36

The Horned Toad Prince 97

Guiding Comprehension

7 **Details • Literal**

What offer does the horned toad make to Reba Jo?

He will get Reba Jo's hat if she will do three things for him.

8 **Draw Conclusions • Critical**

Text to Self **Think about deals you have made with others. Does Reba Jo act the way you act when you make a deal? Explain why or why not.**

Responses will vary but should show the value of keeping a promise.

9 **Story Structure • Inferential**

What is the main problem at this point in this story?

Possible response: Reba Jo makes a deal with the horned toad to get her hat back, but she doesn't keep her end of the deal.

The horned toad looked at her slyly and said, "I'll fetch your *sombrero* for you if you will do

7 *tres pequeños* favors for me."

She sniffed and asked, "Three small favors? Like what?"

"All you have to do is feed me some chili, play your *guitarra* for me, and let me take a *siesta* in your *sombrero*."

"Some chili, a song, and a nap in my hat? I don't think so, *amigo*," replied Reba Jo.

"Okay, *señorita*, but do you mind if I follow you home and listen as you explain to your *padre* where your new *sombrero* is, and how it got there?"

"Good point, toad," Reba Jo said. "You've got yourself a deal."

Reba Jo placed the little critter in a splintered wooden bucket and carefully lowered him down the dry well, where he retrieved Reba Jo's hat.

98

Understanding Idioms Explain that "Wait up" (p. 99, paragraph 1) means "Wait for me." Encourage students to record other idioms that contain *wait*, such as *wait around* or *wait up for*. They can record these and other idioms in language journals, word lists, or computer files of English vocabulary.

Then, without so much as a *muchas gracias*, Reba Jo snatched her hat from the horned toad and galloped home. As she rode out of sight, she ignored the horned toad's cries of "*¡Espérate!* Wait up, *señorita*, wait up!" **8**

'Long about midday, when Reba Jo had sat down to eat, she heard a tap, tap, tapping at the ranch house door.

Reba Jo opened the door, but when she saw it was the fat horned toad, she slammed the door in his face.

His small voice called, "*Señorita, señorita, por favor.* Please let me come in." **9**

99

STRATEGY SELF-CHECK

Story Structure

Ask students to identify the author's purpose for writing this part of the story. *(Possible responses: to continue to entertain and to set up the conflict.)* Remind students to use story structure to help determine the author's purpose.

Have students identify key story elements such as the story's characters, setting, main problem, and rising action on a plot structure chart to determine the author's purpose.

SELF-CHECK

Students can ask themselves these questions to assess their abilities to use the skill and strategy.

- Did I identify the problem in this story?
- Was I able to describe the rising action?
- How does the story's organization help me identify the author's purpose?

Monitor Progress	
Story Structure	
If… students have difficulty describing story structure or determining author's purpose,	**then…** revisit the skill lesson on pp. 88–89. Reteach as necessary.

Develop Vocabulary

PRACTICE LESSON VOCABULARY

Have students respond *yes* or *no* to each question and provide reasons for their answers. Possible reasons are given.

1. Would you find a *riverbed* in a house? *(No; a riverbed is a place outside where a river flows or once flowed.)*

2. Can cacti and water buckets be *lassoed*? *(Yes; you can toss a looped rope around these items.)*

3. Do people like it when you do *favors* for them? *(Yes; people like it when you do acts of kindness for them.)*

BUILD CONCEPT VOCABULARY

Review previous concept words with students. Ask if students have come across any words today in their reading or elsewhere that they would like to add to The Southwest Concept Web, such as *horned toad* and *galloped*.

Strategy Response Log

Answer Questions Have students review the questions they wrote at the beginning of the story. (See p. 92.) Have students use what they have read to answer them. They can also record any additional questions they have.

If you want to teach this story in two sessions, stop here.

Guiding Comprehension

If you are teaching this story in two days, discuss the author's purpose and review vocabulary.

10 Character • Inferential

What kind of person is Reba Jo's father? How can you tell?

Possible response: He is honest and kind. He let the horned toad in his house and insisted that Reba Jo keep her bargain.

11 Vocabulary • Context Clues

Ask students to look for a synonym for *bargain* on p. 101 and use it to figure out the meaning of *bargain*.

Synonym: deal. Meaning: to make a deal.

Monitor Progress
** Context Clues**

If... students have difficulty using a synonym to determine meaning,	**then...** use the vocabulary strategy instruction on p. 101.

12 Draw Conclusions • Inferential

Why does Reba Jo give her chili to the horned toad?

Possible response: She knows her father expects her to keep her promises.

DAY 3 Grouping Options

Reading
Whole Group Discuss the Question of the Day.

Group Time Differentiated Instruction
Read *The Horned Toad Prince.* See pp. 88f–88g for the small group lesson plan.

Whole Group Discuss the Reader Response questions on p. 106. Then use p. 111a.

Language Arts
Use pp. 111e–111k.

The horned toad rapped on the door again. This time Reba Jo's father opened it and spotted the little fella on the porch.

"*Hola, señor,*" said the horned toad.

"Well howdy, mister toad. What brings you here?"

"A little deal that I made with your daughter, *señor.*"

"What's this all about, Reba Jo?" her father asked her.

Reba Jo admitted that the horned toad had done her a favor and in return she had promised to feed him some chili, play her guitar for him, and let him take a nap in her hat.

100

ELL

Access Content Explain that certain words in this story are spelled the way they are pronounced in the southwestern United States. *Fella* (p. 100, paragraph 1) is more commonly spelled *fellow,* just as *pardner* (p. 101, paragraph 1) is spelled *partner.* "Dadburn it!" (p. 101, paragraph 3) is a nonsense expression used to express anger.

"*Now, Reba Jo,*" said her daddy, "if you strike a **10** bargain in these parts, a deal's a deal. Come on in, pardner, you look mighty hungry." **11**

"I am indeed. *Yo tengo mucha hambre,*" said the horned toad. "I hope that is chili I smell." He peeked at Reba Jo's meal.

"Dadburn it!" Reba Jo muttered. She pushed her bowl of chili toward him. **12**

Soon the horned toad's belly was bulging. "Now, for a little *serenata,*" he said.

101

VOCABULARY STRATEGY

Context Clues

TEACH

- Remind students that sometimes context clues can help them figure out the meaning of unfamiliar words or phrases.

- A synonym is a type of context clue. Review the definition of synonym—a word that means almost the same thing as another word.

- Model using a synonym to help determine the meaning of *bargain* on p. 101.

Think Aloud **MODEL** In the first paragraph on p. 101, Reba Jo's dad says, "If you strike a bargain in these parts, a deal's a deal." I don't remember what a *bargain* is, but the word *deal* is used in the sentence in a way that tells me it means almost the same thing as *bargain. Deal* is a synonym for *bargain,* so I know a *bargain* must be a type of deal or agreement.

PRACTICE AND ASSESS

Have students return to p. 98 and read the first four paragraphs. Ask them to identify synonyms that help them understand the meaning of *siesta* and *sombrero* (*nap* and *hat*) and to model their thinking.

Guiding Comprehension

13 Character • Critical

What word would you use to describe the horned toad? Why?

Possible response: persuasive; he keeps getting Reba Jo to do what he wants.

14 Author's Craft • Critical

Question the Author **Why do you think the author writes, "You know dang well a kiss wasn't part of this deal, you low-life reptile" instead of "No, I won't give you a kiss"?**

Possible response: The author wants Reba Jo to sound thoroughly disgusted by the horned toad's request for a kiss. The words the author uses give a clearer picture of how Reba Jo feels.

15 👁 Author's Purpose • Inferential

What is the author's purpose for writing this part of the story? How can you tell?

Possible response: The author continues to entertain. The horned toad asks Reba Jo for a kiss; Reba Jo calls him a "low-life reptile" and "Lizard Lips."

Reba Jo stomped over, grabbed her guitar, and belted out a lullaby for her guest.

Then the drowsy little horned toad eyed Reba Jo's hat and yawned, saying, "That lovely music has made me *muy soñoliento*. I'm ready for my *siesta*."

"Forget it, Bucko," Reba Jo snapped. "You're not gettin' near my hat. No lizard cooties allowed!"

102

Monitor Progress	
👁 **Author's Purpose**	
If... students are unable to determine the author's purpose,	**then...** use the skill and strategy instruction on p. 103.

Understanding Idioms Use the picture on p. 102 to help students understand the phrase *belted out* means "sung loudly." Encourage students to record English idioms and their meanings in language journals, word lists, or computer files of English vocabulary.

"Now, señorita, remember what your wise *padre* said about striking a bargain in these parts," said the clever little horned toad.

"I know, I know," grumbled Reba Jo, "a deal's a deal." And with that, she flipped him into her hat.

"Before I take my *siesta*, I have just one more favor to ask," said the horned toad.

"Now what?" asked Reba Jo.

"Would you give me a kiss, *por favor?*" asked the horned toad.

"You've gotta be kiddin'!" shrieked Reba Jo. "You know dang well a kiss wasn't part of this deal, you low-life reptile." ⑭

"If you do this one last thing for me, we'll call it even, and I'll be on my way *pronto*," the horned toad said.

"You'll leave right away?" Reba Jo asked suspiciously. "You promise?"

"*Sí, te prometo,*" agreed the horned toad.

Reba Jo thought hard for a minute. She glared at the horned toad. "I can't believe I'm even considerin' this," she said, "but if it means you'll leave right now . . . pucker up, Lizard Lips." ⑮

103

Ranches of the Southwest

Time for SOCIAL STUDIES

In some parts of the Southwest, people raise herds of cattle and sheep on large areas of open grassland. Some ranches cover thousands of acres, and ranchers may use horses, trucks, and even small planes to check their land. Ranchers work long hours, and chores include building and fixing fences, checking ponds and tanks for water, moving animals from one grazing area to another, and rounding up animals that have strayed too far from their herds. Environmental influences, such as flooding, erosion, droughts, and fire, can all play a role in a rancher's ability to succeed.

SKILLS ↔ STRATEGIES IN CONTEXT

Author's Purpose Story Structure

TEACH

Review key story events thus far. Model how story structure can help students determine the author's purpose for this part of the story.

Think Aloud **MODEL** In this part of the story, Reba Jo finally gives the horned toad the three favors she promised. But now the horned toad wants a kiss too. Reba Jo doesn't want to kiss him, but when he promises to leave, she agrees. The author uses humorous story events and dialogue to build to the climax where the horned toad and Reba Jo finally work out their deal.

PRACTICE AND ASSESS

Have students add events to their plot structure charts and note any specific events or story elements that help them better understand the author's purpose.

EXTEND SKILLS

Slang

Define *slang* as informal, everyday language. Point out *cooties* on p. 102 and talk about how this word is used in the story and sometimes in real-life conversations. Explain that authors often use slang in dialogue to make characters sound like real people. Discuss other examples of slang, such as double negatives.

Guiding Comprehension

16 **Vocabulary • Context Clues**

What is a *caballero*? How can you tell?

A *caballero* is a gentleman. A handsome young caballero appears, and Reba Jo stares at the gentleman.

17 **Compare and Contrast • Inferential**

How has Reba Jo's attitude toward the horned toad changed?

She had been very anxious for him to go away. Now she is suggesting that they "get hitched and ride off into the sunset."

18 **Story Structure • Critical**

Text to Text **Use generalizations about fairy tales to compare and contrast this fairy tale to others you have read.**

While responses will vary, make sure students are able to identify general similarities and differences between modern and traditional fairy tales.

You might have them revisit their fairy tales charts used on p. 90a of the teacher's edition to help answer the question.

Strategy Response Log

Summarize When students finish reading the selection, provide this prompt: In four or five sentences, tell a friend the most important parts of the story.

Before Reba Jo could wipe the toad spit off her lips, a fierce dust devil spun into the yard, swept the horned toad off his feet, and whirled him around in a dizzying cloud of prairie dust.

When the dust cleared, there before Reba Jo stood a handsome young *caballero*.

"Who are you?" Reba Jo demanded, staring at

16 the gentleman.

"I am Prince Maximillian José Diego López de España."

"Whoa, how did this happen?" Reba Jo asked in amazement.

104

ELL

Activate Prior Knowledge Have students share any fairy tales or folk tales they know from family members or elsewhere that have similar story events, characters, or lessons as those found in *The Horned Toad Prince.*

"Many, many years ago when I came to this country, I offended the great spirit of the *arroyo*. The spirit put a spell on me and turned me into a horned toad. For many years I've been waiting for a cowgirl like you to break the spell. *Muchas gracias* for my freedom, *señorita*. Now I'll be leaving as I promised."

"Now hold on for just a dadburn minute," said Reba Jo, stepping in front of the nobleman. "I recollect my daddy readin' me a story where somethin' like this happened. Aren't we supposed to get hitched and ride off into the sunset?" **17**

With a twinkle in his eye, the *caballero* replied, *"Lo siento.* So sorry, Reba Jo, when you strike a bargain in these parts, a deal's a deal. *Adiós, señorita!"* **18**

105

Develop Vocabulary

PRACTICE LESSON VOCABULARY

As a class, answer the following questions orally.

1. When Reba Jo *shrieked,* did she speak softly or yell loudly? *(She yelled loudly.)*

2. When you have *offended* someone, have you insulted them or praised them? *(You have insulted them.)*

3. Is a *prairie* a flat grassy area or a peaked mountain? *(A prairie is a flat grassy area.)*

4. Is a *bargain* a type of agreement with someone or an argument? *(A bargain is a type of agreement with someone.)*

BUILD CONCEPT VOCABULARY

Review previous concept words with students. Ask if students have found any words today in their reading or elsewhere they would like to add to The Southwest Concept Web, such as *chili* and *dust*.

Story Structure

Have students complete their plot structure chart by describing the story's resolution. Review what they wrote about the story's problem, rising action, and climax. Discuss how story structure helps them identify the author's purpose for writing this story. Use Practice Book p. 37.

SELF-CHECK

Students can ask themselves these questions to assess their understanding of the story.

- Was I able to identify the key parts of the story structure?

- How did I use the structure to help me figure out the author's purpose for writing this story?

Monitor Progress
◉ **Author's Purpose**

If... students have difficulty determining the author's purpose after analyzing the story structure,	**then...** use the Reteach lesson on p. 111b.

Author's Purpose

- The **author's purpose** is the reason or reasons for writing. An author may write to persuade, to inform, to entertain, or to express ideas and feelings. The kinds of ideas in the text, and the way the author organizes and states these ideas, can help you determine the purpose.

Directions Read the following passage. Then answer the questions below.

> Riding in a hot-air balloon during the Albuquerque International Balloon Fiesta is inspiring. It is the chance of a lifetime. You would not believe the number of balloons that soar through the air at the same time. Each one's vibrant, colored patterns are unique. Peering over the edge of the balloon's basket, you can see tiny cars and buildings below. Even the mountains in the distance look small from this height. A rush of excitement fills your heart as the balloon soars higher into the clear, blue sky. All your worries and troubles are miles away.

Possible answers given for 1, 2, 4.
1. Give an example of an idea expressed in this passage.
   The author describes the unique balloons flying in the air.
2. How does the author organize ideas in the passage?
   The author praises the balloon fiesta, describes various balloons, and finally describes the experience of ballooning.
3. What do you think is the author's purpose?
   The author's purpose is to express ideas and feelings.
4. Do you think the author succeeds in meeting this purpose? Why or why not?
   The author meets his or her purpose, because as I read I felt the excitement of seeing and riding in a hot-air balloon.
5. Change the structure of this passage by creating a problem, rising action, a climax, and an outcome. What would be different about the passage with these additions?
   Students' answers should include that these changes would give the passage more suspense and tension.

Home Activity Your child answered questions to identify the author's purpose in a passage, and he or she created elements of a story structure. Read a favorite short story together. As you discuss the story, identify the problem, rising action, climax, and outcome.

▲ **Practice Book** p. 37

Reader Response

Open for Discussion Personal Response

Think Aloud

MODEL I knew the horned toad would show up at Reba Jo's door, but some parts of this story surprised me. I would ask Reba Jo why she didn't run away when the toad talked to her.

Comprehension Check Critical Response

1. Answers should show an understanding of what makes a good story (e.g., dialogue, dialect, drama). **Author's Purpose**

2. Possible response: If you trick someone, you may get tricked in return. **Author's Purpose**

3. Possible response: The most important event is Reba Jo's making a deal with the horned toad. **Story Structure**

4. Possible responses: *sagebrush, arroyo, dusty, rattlesnake.* **Vocabulary**

TEST PRACTICE

Look Back and Write For test practice, assign a 10–15 minute time limit. For assessment, see the Scoring Rubric at the right.

Retell

Have students retell *The Horned Toad Prince.*

Monitor Progress
Check Retelling Rubric 4 3 2 1

If... students have difficulty retelling the story,	then... use the Retelling Cards and the Scoring Rubric for Retelling on p. 107 to assist fluent retelling.

SUCCESS PREDICTOR

Check Retelling Go through the illustrations with students first, verifying they know character names and English words for items pictured. For more ideas on assessing students' retellings, see the ELL and Transition Handbook.

Reader Response

Open for Discussion Did you know what was going to happen in the story or were you surprised? What three questions would you ask Reba Jo if you could?

1. This story is fit for a storyteller. Find a part of the story that could be read the way a storyteller would. Why is that such a good part to read? Think Like an Author

2. An author's purpose can be to teach the reader an important lesson. What lesson do you think the author teaches in this story? Author's Purpose

3. What was the most important event in the story? Why do you think this? Story Structure

4. The words *prairie* and *riverbed* on the Words to Know list are clues to the story's setting. Identify other words in the story that hint at the Southwest setting. Vocabulary

TEST PRACTICE

Look Back and Write At the end of the story, the caballero says, "A deal's a deal." Explain what the deal is. Then tell whether or not you think it is a good deal and why.

Meet author Jackie Mims Hopkins on page 779 and illustrator Michael Austin on page 780.

Scoring Rubric **Look Back and Write**

Top-Score Response A top-score response uses information from the selection to describe the *caballero's* deal and to explain whether this is a good deal and why.

Example of a Top-Score Response While trapped as a frog, the caballero promised to leave if Reba Jo would kiss him. When she kissed him, he turned into a handsome prince. Reba Jo then asked if he was going to marry her, but he left as promised. I think this was a fair deal. Reba Jo didn't want the toad when he was ugly. She shouldn't be able to change her mind because he's a prince.

For additional rubrics, see p. WA10.

Write Now

E-mail Invitation

Prompt

In *The Horned Toad Prince,* the author has a clear purpose—to entertain.

Think about an event that you would like to invite someone to.

Now write an e-mail invitation with the purpose of informing family or friends about the special event.

Writing Trait

Focus your **ideas** on the main topic—your special event. Remind yourself of the purpose of your writing—to invite someone.

Student Model

Person invited is named.

The writer focuses clearly on the purpose of the writing.

Important information is clearly set out.

From: Isabella

Date: Thursday, May 1, 2008 6:22 pm

To: Grandma

Subject: Class play

Could you ever imagine your own granddaughter as a wicked stepsister? This Wednesday I will be. My class is putting on a play called Cinderella. I am writing this e-mail to invite you and Grandpa to come. My class made our own costumes and wrote a song. After the play, everyone is invited to stay for juice and cookies.

Here is the information:

Cinderella, a play by class 4-303

Wednesday, March 2, at 1:30 P.M.

Main Street School, 125 Main Street

Use the model to help you write your own e-mail invitation.

Write Now

Look at the Prompt Explain that each sentence in the prompt has a purpose.

- Sentence 1 presents a topic.
- Sentence 2 suggests students think about the topic.
- Sentence 3 tells what to write—an e-mail invitation.

Strategies to Develop Focus/Ideas

Have students

- eliminate wordiness.
- imagine they are receiving the invitation. What essential information would they need?

NO: Please come to the science fair!

YES: Please come to the science fair at noon on May 4! You'll see volcanoes and electricity displays.

For additional suggestions and rubric, see pp. 111g–111h.

Writer's Checklist

☑ **Focus** Do sentences stick to the invitation?

☑ **Organization** Are ideas in order?

☑ **Support** Do details give information about the event?

☑ **Conventions** Are grammar and spelling correct?

107

Scoring Rubric — Narrative Retelling

Rubric 4 3 2 1	4	3	2	1
Connections	Makes connections and generalizes beyond the text	Makes connections to other events, stories, or experiences	Makes a limited connection to another event, story, or experience	Makes no connection to another event, story, or experience
Author's Purpose	Elaborates on author's purpose	Tells author's purpose with some clarity	Makes some connection to author's purpose	Makes no connection to author's purpose
Characters	Describes the main character(s) and any character development	Identifies the main character(s) and gives some information about them	Inaccurately identifies some characters or gives little information about them	Inaccurately identifies the characters or gives no information about them
Setting	Describes the time and location	Identifies the time and location	Omits details of time or location	Is unable to identify time or location
Plot	Describes the problem, goal, events, and ending using rich detail	Tells the problem, goal, events, and ending with some errors that do not affect meaning	Tells parts of the problem, goal, events, and ending with gaps that affect meaning	Retelling has no sense of story

Retelling Plan

☑ **Week 1** Assess Strategic Intervention students.

☑ **Week 2** Assess Advanced students.

☑ **Week 3** Assess Strategic Intervention students.

☑ **This week assess On-Level students.**

☐ **Week 5** Assess any students you have not yet checked during this unit.

Use the Retelling Chart on p. TR16 to record retelling.

Selection Test To assess with *The Horned Toad Prince,* use Selection Tests, pp. 13–16.

Fresh Reads for Differentiated Test Practice For weekly leveled practice, use pp. 19–24.

SUCCESS PREDICTOR

Retelling

Science in Reading

OBJECTIVES

- Examine features of expository nonfiction.
- Practice a test-taking strategy.
- Compare and contrast across texts.

PREVIEW/USE TEXT FEATURES

Have students preview "Horned Lizards & Harvesting Ants," noting the photos and captions. Have them read the introductory paragraph. Then ask:

- **How do the captions in this selection help readers understand the topic?** *(The captions explain the photos and give more information about the topic.)*

- **Which descriptive words in the first paragraph help you visualize the Sonoran Desert?** *(vast area, flat land, canyons)*

Link to Science

Students can use both *desert animals* and *camouflage* as keywords when searching reference materials and then cross-reference to identify desert animals that use camouflage. Remind students of the value of using keywords when scanning the index or table of contents of print sources or while searching online.

DAY 4 Grouping Options

Reading

Whole Group Discuss the Question of the Day.

Group Time Differentiated Instruction
Read "Horned Lizards & Harvesting Ants." See pp. 88f–88g for the small group lesson plan.

Whole Group Use p. 111a.

Language Arts
Use pp. 111e–111k.

Science in Reading

Expository Nonfiction

Genre

- Expository nonfiction can tell about animals and where they live.

- The author sometimes organizes the text by explaining a series of events.

Text Features

- The author uses captions to explain photographs.

- The author uses descriptive language to tell about life in the Sonoran Desert.

Link to Science

Use reference materials to find out more about animals that camouflage themselves in the desert. Make a chart describing how these animals camouflage themselves and share it with your class.

108

Horned Lizards & Harvesting Ants

by John Brown

Imagine that you are on a journey to the Sonoran Desert, a vast area of flat land and canyons in the southwestern United States and northern Mexico. By day, you explore the many unique plants and animals. At night, you curl up in the safety of your desert home, a tent.

Content-Area Vocabulary | **Science**

armored	protected with a covering, such as a bony shell
camouflage	a disguised appearance that makes a person or animal look much like its surroundings
saguaro	a very tall, branching cactus of southern Arizona and neighboring regions

▲ A few clouds remain after last night's storm; the morning air feels cool and clean.

▲ This harvester ant is wrestling to pull a saguaro seed out from the fruit. Imagine trying to pull a football out of a giant-sized sticky gumdrop—with your teeth!

As we are having breakfast, we notice that last night's storm has knocked some of the fruit off the top of a nearby saguaro. This windfall has been discovered by a colony of harvester ants, who are busy pulling the seeds out of the sticky fruit and carrying them back to their hole. They are working very hard to get all the seeds inside their nest before it gets too hot for them to stay out in the sun.

Ⓒ Author's Purpose   If the purpose is to inform, how do you read this article?

109

EXPOSITORY NONFICTION

Use the sidebar on p. 108 to guide discussion.

- Explain that expository nonfiction informs readers about an object, topic, or theme.
- Expository nonfiction often uses maps, diagrams, photos, captions, or other features to present information visually, so readers can find and understand it more easily.
- As students read, have them look for ways the photos and captions add new information or help them understand points made in the selection.

 **AudioText**

Ⓒ Author's Purpose

Possible response: I would read the article slowly and carefully to make sure I understand and remember the information in it.

Ants of the Southwest

 TIME FOR **Science**

The southwestern United States is home for several ant species. In addition to harvester ants, honey ants also live in the region. Some of the worker ants in their highly organized society are known as *repletes*. A replete stores honey in its abdomen. When there is no food to be found, a replete can regurgitate, or throw up, the stored honey and feed the other ants with it. Fire ants are also found in the Southwest. These aggressive ants build large mounds up to two feet high. When a nest is disturbed, the fire ants rush out, biting and stinging whatever is near. Their bites are very painful.

ELL

Access Content Use the photographs to help students identify horned lizards and harvester ants and terms related to the desert setting.

TEST PRACTICE

Strategies for Nonfiction

USE CAPTIONS Remind students a caption is a title or sentence that accompanies a picture. When expository nonfiction like "Horned Lizards & Harvesting Ants" includes photographs with captions, students can sometimes use this information to answer test questions. Provide the following strategy.

Use the Strategy

1. Read the test question and locate a key word or phrase.
2. Scan the photographs looking for visual details related to the key word or phrase from the test question.
3. When you find a match, study the photograph and its caption for information that helps answer the test question.

GUIDED PRACTICE Have students discuss how they would use the strategy to answer the following question.

What does the horned lizard look like? Use a photograph and caption to support your answer.

INDEPENDENT PRACTICE After students answer the following test question, discuss the process they used to find information.

What is one source of food for harvester ants and how do they get it? Use details found in a photograph and caption in your answer.

I notice something out of the corner of my eye. It looked like a rock moved! We take a closer look and realize that it isn't a rock but a horned lizard. An amazing little lizard, it is so well camouflaged that you can hardly see it against the pebbles and sand. Up close it looks like a miniature dinosaur.

Some kinds of horned lizard eat almost nothing but ants, which they gobble up with their sticky tongue. They dart around, and with each quick flick of their tongue another ant disappears. The ants try to fight back, but their strong jaws make no impression on this armored ant-eating machine. We look around and find the lizard's little black droppings.

Resembling a miniature dinosaur, the horned lizard feasts on the ants. Look carefully and you can see an ant valiantly trying to fight back!

Independent Practice Review the Independent Practice question with students and ask them to identify its key words. *(harvester ant)* Remind them to look for a photograph related to the key words to answer the question. Point to different photographs in the selection and ask: *Would this photograph help me figure out what harvester ants eat? Why or why not?*

They crumble as you pick them up–they are made of nothing but the digested remains of dead ants!

These lizards have an amazing trick up their sleeve. Coyotes love to eat lizards, and if a coyote manages to see through a horned lizard's camouflage, the lizard is in big trouble. But if the coyote tries to bite the horned lizard, it squirts blood from its eyes into the coyote's mouth. The lizard's blood must taste disgusting to the coyote, which usually runs off in shock, giving the resourceful little lizard a chance to escape.

We watch the horned lizard having its ant breakfast as we finish ours.

Reading Across Texts

The "horned toad" in *The Horned Toad Prince* and the "horned lizard" in this article are the same animal. How are the two alike and different?

Writing Across Texts Make a chart showing the ways in which the fictional horned toad was like and unlike a real horned lizard.

ⓒ Text Structure   How has the author organized this text?

In slow motion we can see the horned lizard squirt blood from its eye.

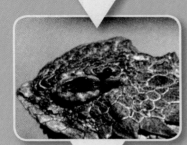

111

CONNECT TEXT TO TEXT

Reading Across Texts

Discuss the horned toad lizard in "The Horned Toad Prince" and the horned lizard in this article. Have students find descriptions of these animals in each selection and compare them.

Writing Across Texts Point out the advantages of using a Venn diagram for comparing and contrasting. Students can label the left part of the diagram *Fictional Horned Toad* and the right part *Real Horned Lizard* and record differences in the appropriate parts. They can label the overlapping part *How They Are Alike* and record similarities.

ⓒ Text Structure

Possible response: The author has organized the text as a series of events that happen while he is camping in the southwestern desert. However, he also includes information about and a description of horned lizards.

TIME FOR Science

Animal Survival

The horned lizard squirts blood from its eyes as a way to escape predators. Other animals of the Southwest have unusual survival mechanisms. The tiny kangaroo rat has such strong hind legs that it can cover almost 1,200 feet in a minute. It can also switch directions while in the air, confusing any animal that might be trying to catch it. When rattlesnakes sense danger, they can lift their tails and shake their rattles, creating a loud, buzzing sound that frightens potential predators.

Fluency Assessment Plan

- ☑ **Week 1** Assess Advanced students.
- ☑ **Week 2** Assess Strategic Intervention students.
- ☑ **Week 3** Assess On-Level students.
- ☑ **This week assess Strategic Intervention students.**
- ☐ **Week 5** Assess any students you have not yet checked during this unit.

Set individual goals for students to enable them to reach the year-end goal.

- Current Goal: 95–105 WCPM
- Year-End Goal: 130 WCPM

English learners benefit from assisted reading, with modeling by the teacher or by a skilled classmate. When the English learner reads the passage aloud, the more proficient reader assists by providing feedback and encouragement.

 To develop fluent readers, use Fluency Coach.

DAY 5   Grouping Options

Reading
Whole Group
Revisit the Question of the Week.

Group Time
Differentiated Instruction
Reread this week's Leveled Readers. See pp. 88f–88g for the small group lesson plan.

Whole Group
Use p. 111b–111c.

Language Arts
Use pp. 111d–111l.

VOLUME

Fluency

DAY 1

Model Reread aloud "Growing Up in the Old West" on p. 88m. Explain that you will match the volume of your voice to the size of the room so everyone can hear easily and maintain a steady volume. Model for students as you read.

DAY 2

Echo Reading Read aloud p. 96. Lower your volume to show how the toad speaks in a "small voice." Have students practice as a class using story cues to adjust their volume, doing three echo readings of p. 96.

DAY 3

Model Read aloud p. 99. Have students notice how your volume increases slightly when the toad cries out and drops slightly when he speaks in a small voice. Practice as a class by doing three echo readings.

DAY 4

Partner Reading Have partners practice reading aloud p. 99, three times. Suggest they use an appropriate volume for a small group and use story cues to adjust their volume for dramatic effect.

Monitor Progress   **Check Fluency WCPM**

As students reread, monitor their progress toward their individual fluency goals. Current Goal: 95–105 words correct per minute. End-of-Year Goal: 130 words correct per minute.

If… students cannot read fluently at a rate of 95–105 words correct per minute,
then… make sure students practice with text at their independent level. Provide additional fluency practice, pairing nonfluent readers with fluent readers.

If… students already read at 130 words correct per minute,
then… they do not need to reread three to four times.

SUCCESS PREDICTOR

DAY 5

Assessment
Individual Reading Rate Use the Fluency Assessment Plan and do a one-minute timed reading of either selection from this week to assess students in Week 4. Pay special attention to this week's skill, volume. Provide corrective feedback for each student.

RETEACH

◎ Author's Purpose

TEACH

Review the description of author's purpose on p. 88 and the four common purposes for writing. Students can complete Practice Book p. 38 on their own or as a class. Remind students to consider what happens and how the author tells about the events and characters. Ask, for example, if the ending of the passage is sad, funny, or scary and which purpose matches this ending.

ASSESS

Have students read about author Jackie Mims Hopkins on p. 779. Then have them determine the purpose of the passage. Remind them to consider the title of the page *(Meet Authors of Fairy Tales and Folk Tales)* and the contents before deciding on the purpose. *(to inform)*

For additional instruction on author's purpose, see DI·55.

EXTEND SKILLS

Dialect

TEACH

Dialect helps readers gain a sense of how characters from a particular group or region speak. Dialect differs from standard English in pronunciation, vocabulary, and grammar.

- Reading dialect may be difficult because words may be spelled in unconventional ways.
- Dialect gives a story a sense of realism and makes the characters more colorful.

Have students tell the meaning of *"howdy"* on p. 100, paragraph 3. *(It's a greeting like "hello.")* Ask them to identify the region of the father's dialect. *(the Southwest)* List greetings from other dialects.

ASSESS

Have pairs read p. 102, paragraph 3, and write answers to these questions:
1. **Which word in the last line is an example of dialect?** *(cooties)*
2. **What do you think *cooties* means?** *(annoying bugs or germs)*

OBJECTIVES

- ◎ Identify the author's purpose.
- ● Understand and recognize examples of regional dialect.

Skills Trace
◎ Author's Purpose

Introduce/Teach	TE: 4.1 40–41, 88–89; 4.5 516–517
Practice	TE: 47, 57, 95, 103, 523, 529 PB: 13, 17, 18, 33, 37, 38, 203, 207, 208
▶ Reteach/Review	**TE: 4.1 31, 65b, 111b, DI•53, DI•55; 4.3 369; 4.5 537b, DI•52; 4.6 695 PB: 6, 146, 276**
Test	Selection Test: 5–8, 13–16, 81–84; Benchmark Test: Unit 1

Access Content Reteach the skill by reviewing the Picture It! lesson on author's purpose in the ELL Teaching Guide, pp. 22–23.

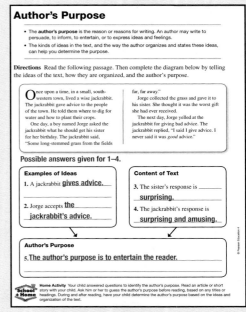

▲ **Practice Book** p. 38

SUCCESS PREDICTOR

Vocabulary and Word Study

VOCABULARY STRATEGY

 Context Clues

SYNONYMS Remind students that authors sometimes provide a synonym that can help readers understand an unfamiliar word. Have students locate the words listed on the left side of the T-chart in *The Horned Toad Prince*. Tell them to scan the nearby context to find related synonyms and list those synonyms on the right side the T-chart. Then challenge students to identify another word and synonym in the story.

Word in Story	Synonym Nearby
entertained (p. 94)	amused
arroyo (p. 95)	dry riverbed
flash flood (p. 95)	swift water
siesta (p. 98)	nap
caballero (p. 104)	gentlemen (or prince)

A Hunt for Idioms

Point out the idiom *strike a bargain* on p. 101. Discuss what an idiom is and the meaning of this expression. ("make a deal") Then have partners look through *The Horned Toad Prince* to find other examples of idioms. Examples include: *a peck of trouble* (p. 97), *wait up* (p. 99), *a deal's a deal* (p. 101), *hold on for a just a dadburn minute* (p. 105), *get hitched* (p. 105). Have each pair choose one or two idioms to explain in words or with a captioned drawing.

Idiom	Meaning
Strike a bargain	Make a deal

BUILD CONCEPT VOCABULARY

The Southwest

LOOKING BACK Remind students of the question of the week: *What is unique about the landscape of the Southwest?* Discuss how this week's Concept Web of vocabulary words relates to the theme of the Southwest. Ask students if they have any words or categories to add. Discuss whether words and categories are appropriately related to the concept.

MOVING FORWARD Preview the title of the next selection, *Letters Home from Yosemite*. Ask students which Concept Web words might apply to the new selection based on the title alone. Put a star next to these words on the Web.

Display the Concept Web and revisit the vocabulary words as you read the next selection to check predictions.

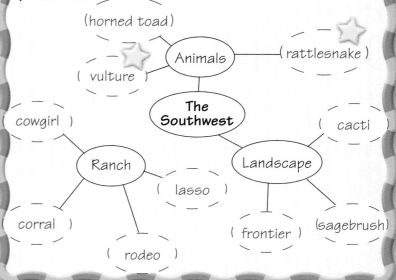

Monitor Progress

Check Vocabulary

If... students suggest words or categories that are not related to the concept,	**then...** review the words and categories on the Concept Web and discuss how they relate to the lesson concept.

SUCCESS PREDICTOR

Speaking and Viewing

SPEAKING

Oral Report

SET-UP Discuss animals, plants, landforms, and other aspects of the Southwest that make it a unique region. Have students select a topic on which they would like to report. Some students may choose to report on results of any Internet inquiries done this week.

PLANNING Suggest students brainstorm five questions they hope to answer about their topic. For example, students who are researching animals might ask questions such as: *Where can this animal be found? What does it look like? What does it eat? How does it get food? Who are its enemies?* Student reports can provide answers to these questions. Remind students to keep a record of their sources in order to validate their research.

VISUAL AIDS Encourage students to prepare visual aids to support and enhance their reports, such as photographs, illustrations, maps, diagrams, charts, and graphs.

Listening Tips

- Make eye contact with the speaker during a presentation.
- Take notes on the information being presented.
- Ask meaningful questions about the topic when the speaker is finished.

Support Vocabulary Use the following to review and extend vocabulary and to explore lesson concepts further:
- ELL Poster 4, Days 3–5 instruction
- Vocabulary Activities and Word Cards in ELL Teaching Guide, pp. 24–25

Assessment For information on assessing students' speaking, listening, and viewing, see the ELL and Transition Handbook.

VIEWING

Analyze Photos

Have students study the sequence of photographs on p. 111. They can work in small groups to answer the following questions orally or in writing.

1. **What is happening in these photos?** *(The horned lizard is squirting blood from its eye.)*

2. **What details are most noticeable? What details are least noticeable?** *(Possible response: The little squirt of blood is most noticeable. The horned toad's color is least noticeable.)*

3. **What is the initial impact of this photograph? Why do you think the author included it?** *(Possible response: I was a bit shocked to see blood squirting out of an animal's eye. The author probably included it so readers would understand how unusual this defense mechanism is.)*

They crumble as you pick them up—they are made of nothing but the digested remains of dead ants!

These lizards have an amazing trick up their sleeve. Coyotes love to eat lizards, and if a coyote manages to see through a horned lizard's camouflage, the lizard is in big trouble. But if the coyote tries to bite the horned lizard, it squirts blood from its eyes into the coyote's mouth. The lizard's blood must taste disgusting to the coyote, which usually runs off in shock, giving the resourceful little lizard a chance to escape.

We watch the horned lizard having its ant breakfast as we finish ours.

In slow motion we can see the horned lizard squirt blood from its eye.

Reading Across Texts
The "horned toad" in *The Horned Toad Prince* and the "horned lizard" in this article are the same animal. How are the two alike and different?

Writing Across Texts Make a chart showing the ways in which the fictional horned toad was like and unlike a real horned lizard.

Text Structure How has the author organized this text?

111

Grammar **Compound Sentences**

OBJECTIVES

- Define and identify compound sentences.
- Distinguish between simple sentences and compound sentences.
- Use compound sentences correctly in writing.
- Become familiar with compound sentence assessment on high-stakes tests.

Monitor Progress

Grammar

If... students have difficulty identifying compound sentences,	then... provide additional instruction and practice in The Grammar and Writing Book pp. 68–71.

DAILY FIX-IT

This week use Daily Fix-It Transparency 4.

Support Grammar See the Grammar Transition lessons in the ELL and Transition Handbook.

▲ **The Grammar and Writing Book**
For more instruction and practice, use pp. 68–71.

DAILY FIX-IT

1. She wanted to explore the vally but her father had warned her to be careful. *(valley, but)*

2. Yesterday she rodes at a steady pace for haf an hour. *(rode; half)*

READING-GRAMMAR CONNECTION

Write this sentence on the board:

> *Reba Jo made a promise, but she tried to break it.*

Explain that this is a **compound sentence.** When two simple sentences are joined by a comma and a connecting word such as *and, but,* or *or,* or when they are connected with a semicolon and no connecting words, they make a compound sentence.

Display Grammar Transparency 4. Read aloud the definitions and sample sentences. Work through the items.

Compound Sentences

A **compound sentence** is made up of two simple sentences joined by a comma and a connecting word such as *and, but,* or *or.*

Simple Sentences	The horned toad looks like a toad.
	It is really a lizard.
Compound Sentence	The horned toad looks like a toad, *but* it is really a lizard.

The two sentences in a compound sentence must have ideas that make sense together.

Directions Write *S* if the sentence is a simple sentence. Write *C* if the sentence is a compound sentence. Do not confuse a compound subject or predicate with a compound sentence.

1. Reba Jo loved to ride and play her guitar. **S**
2. The wind blew her hat away, and she rode after it. **C**
3. Reba Jo wanted her hat, but she was frightened. **C**
4. The horned toad spoke to her and found her hat. **S**
5. Give me some chili, or I will tell your father. **C**

Directions Join each pair of simple sentences to make a compound sentence. Use the word *and, but,* or *or.* Don't forget to add a comma.

6. The horned toad knocked on the door. Reba Jo's father let him in.
The horned toad knocked on the door, and Reba Jo's father let him in.

7. Reba Jo had made a promise. She did not want to keep it.
Reba Jo had made a promise, but she did not want to keep it.

8. She gave the horned toad some chili. He gobbled it up.
She gave the horned toad some chili, and he gobbled it up.

9. The toad asked Reba Jo to kiss him. At first she refused.
The toad asked Reba Jo to kiss him, but at first she refused.

10. A cowgirl had to kiss the horned toad. He would never become a prince.
A cowgirl had to kiss the horned toad, or he would never become a prince.

Unit 1 The Horned Toad Prince   Grammar **4**

▲ **Grammar Transparency** 4

DAILY FIX-IT

3. What a weird animul that is? *(animal; is!)*

4. Is a horned toad really a toad or is it a lizard. *(toad, or; lizard?)*

GUIDED PRACTICE

Review the concept of compound sentences.

- A **compound sentence** is made up of two simple sentences joined by a comma and a connecting word.
- The connecting words *and, but,* and *or* usually connect the simple sentences in a compound sentence.
- Run-on sentences can be fixed by making them compound sentences.

HOMEWORK Grammar and Writing Practice Book p. 13. Work through the first two items with the class.

Compound Sentences

A compound sentence is made up of two simple sentences joined by a comma and a connecting word such as *and, but,* or *or.*

Simple Sentences	Fairy tales are very old.
	Kids still enjoy them.
Compound Sentence	Fairy tales are very old, *but* kids still enjoy them.

The two sentences in a compound sentence must have ideas that make sense together.

Directions Write *S* after each simple sentence and *C* after each compound sentence. Do not confuse a compound subject or predicate with a compound sentence.

1. Fairy tales and other old stories are sometimes very scary. **S**
2. Witches, giants, or trolls can give little children nightmares. **S**
3. Fairy tale heroes are often in danger, but they usually win in the end. **C**
4. Often a poor girl marries a prince, or a poor boy marries a princess. **C**
5. The dragon is killed, and everybody lives happily ever after. **C**

Directions Join each pair of simple sentences to make a compound sentence. Use the word *and, but,* or *or.* Do not forget to add a comma.

6. The hero was small and young. He was very brave. **The hero was small and young, but [or and] he was very brave.**

7. She fell in love with the prince. He fell in love with her. **She fell in love with the prince, and he fell in love with her.**

8. You can fight the dragon. You can run away. **You can fight the dragon, or you can run away.**

9. He saw the woman in the tower. He wanted to save her. **He saw the woman in the tower, and he wanted to save her.**

10. The wolf knocked on the pigs' door. They wouldn't let him in. **The wolf knocked on the pigs' door, but they wouldn't let him in.**

Home Activity Your child learned about compound sentences. Encourage him or her to show you how the words *and, but,* and *or* can link simple sentences to form compound sentences.

▲ **Grammar and Writing Practice Book** p. 13

DAY 3 Apply to Writing

DAILY FIX-IT

5. Its a beautiful countrie. *(It's; country)*

6. My brother lives in Arizona. And my sister lives in new Mexico. *(Arizona, and; New)*

COMBINE SENTENCES

Point out that using only simple sentences can make your writing dull. Compound sentences help make writing smoother and more interesting.

- Have students review something they have written to see if they can improve it by combining simple sentences to form compound sentences.

HOMEWORK Grammar and Writing Practice Book p. 14.

Compound Sentences

Directions Complete each sentence by adding *and, but,* or *or* and one of the groups of words from the box.

> she sent them all away.   she would not marry anyone.
> her father gave her half his kingdom.   her father would lock her up in a tower.
> she fell in love with him.

1. The princess had many suitors, **but she would not marry anyone.**
2. She must marry, **or her father would lock her up in a tower.**
3. Many men came to see the princess, **but she sent them all away.**
4. Finally, a young farmer made her laugh, **and she fell in love with him.**
5. The princess got married, **and her father gave her half his kingdom.**

Directions Make a compound sentence by adding your own words to each item.
Possible answers:
6. I enjoy fairy tales, but **my brother likes mysteries.**
7. We can finish this story today, or **we can read it for homework.**
8. The hero killed the monster, and **everyone was happy.**
9. The old witch flew away, and **the sun came out again.**
10. The princess was locked up in a tower, but **the prince rescued her.**

 **Home Activity** Your child learned how to use compound sentences in writing. Have your child write a compound sentence about something he or she did today.

▲ **Grammar and Writing Practice Book** p. 14

DAY 4 Test Preparation

DAILY FIX-IT

7. Dont go near an arroyo. During thunderstorms. *(Don't; arroyo during)*

8. A flash flood might sweep through the riverbed, the water would carry you away? *(riverbed. The [or riverbed, and]; away.)*

STANDARDIZED TEST PREP

Test Tip

The comma connecting two simple sentences in a compound sentence goes before the connecting word, not after it.

No: *I have heard of a horned toad but, I have never seen one.*

Yes: *I have heard of a horned toad, but I have never seen one.*

HOMEWORK Grammar and Writing Practice Book p. 15.

Compound Sentences

Directions Mark the letter of the item that correctly completes each sentence.

1. Reba Jo lived on the prairie ___ she loved roping.
   A , or
   B , and
   C and
   D and,

2. Her hat blew off ___ it fell into a well.
   A but
   B or
   C , and
   D and

3. Reba Jo was scared ___ she wanted her hat.
   A and
   B or,
   C or
   D , but

4. The toad made an offer ___ Reba Jo accepted.
   A or
   B and
   C , but
   D , and

5. She could accept ___ she could go home.
   A , or
   B , but
   C but,
   D and,

6. She got the hat ___ she rode home.
   A , and
   B but
   C , or
   D and,

7. Reba Jo was rude ___ her father was polite.
   A but
   B , or
   C , but
   D and,

8. The horned toad came in ___ it ate some chili.
   A , or
   B , and
   C , but
   D but

9. She kissed the horned toad ___ she didn't want to.
   A , or
   B but
   C and,
   D , but

10. Was Reba Jo smart ___ was she foolish?
    A , or
    B , but
    C , and
    D and

 **Home Activity** Your child prepared for taking tests on compound sentences. Ask your child to write pairs of simple, related sentences about himself or herself and then connect them with *and, but,* or *or.*

▲ **Grammar and Writing Practice Book** p. 15

DAY 5 Cumulative Review

DAILY FIX-IT

9. The air in the desert is cleanest then in the city. *(cleaner than)*

10. At home the air isn't to clear but here you can see forever. *(too; clear, but)*

ADDITIONAL PRACTICE

Assign pp. 68–71 in The Grammar and Writing Book.

EXTRA PRACTICE Grammar and Writing Practice Book p. 125.

ASSESSMENT

CUMULATIVE REVIEW Grammar and Writing Practice Book p. 16.

Compound Sentences

Directions Circle *S* if the sentence is a simple sentence. Circle *C* if the sentence is a compound sentence. Do not confuse a compound subject or predicate with a compound sentence.

1. The Southwest is hot, dry, and mountainous.   **S**   C
2. The air is clear, and the colors are beautiful.   S   **C**
3. Sometimes it rains hard, but often it is very dry.   S   **C**
4. Visitors come from far away and camp.   **S**   C
5. Some visitors fall in love with the Southwest and settle there.   **S**   C

Directions Write the word you would use (*and, but,* or *or*) to join each pair of simple sentences into a compound sentence.

6. It is called a horned toad. It is really a lizard.   **but**
7. The country is beautiful. The people are friendly.   **and**
8. Was that an arroyo? Was it a canyon?   **or**
9. I'd love to stay. I have to go home.   **but**
10. We have had a great vacation. We plan to return.   **and**

Directions Read each sentence. Think of a simple related sentence. Make a compound sentence by adding *and, but,* or *or* and your sentence. **Possible answers:**

11. The desert is hot and dry, **but it gets cool at night.**

12. She could ride a horse, **and she loved to play her guitar.**

Home Activity Your child reviewed compound sentences. Ask your child to pretend that he or she has to explain compound sentences to someone who doesn't know what they are. Have your child "teach" the concept he or she has learned.

▲ **Grammar and Writing Practice Book** p. 16

Writing Workshop E-mail Invitation

- Identify qualities of an e-mail invitation.
- Write an e-mail invitation with a clear purpose.
- Focus on focus/ideas.
- Use a rubric.

Genre E-mail Invitation
Writer's Craft Know Your Purpose
Writing Trait Focus/Ideas

ELL

Focus/Ideas Talk with English learners about what they plan to write. Record ideas and help them generate language for support. Help them tighten their focus by eliminating unrelated details. See more writing support in the ELL and Transition Handbook.

Writing Traits

FOCUS/IDEAS The writer sticks to the topic (a party) and has a clear purpose (to invite a friend).

ORGANIZATION/PARAGRAPHS The invitation describes the event and clearly sets apart necessary information.

VOICE Writing is friendly and lively. The writer "talks" directly to the recipient.

WORD CHOICE The writer names specific characters (Cinderella, the horned toad) to help the reader and to add to the sense of fun.

SENTENCES Use of a variety of sentences catches the reader's interest.

CONVENTIONS There is excellent control and accuracy.

DAY 1 Model the Trait

READING-WRITING CONNECTION

- *The Horned Toad Prince* focuses on the idea of being true to your word.
- When writers know their purpose, they can better focus their ideas.
- Students will write an **e-mail invitation** with a specific purpose.

MODEL FOCUS/IDEAS Discuss Writing Transparency 4A. Then discuss the model and the writing trait of focus/ideas.

 Think Aloud All of the information in this invitation is focused on one event. The invitation begins with a sentence that gets the reader's attention. Then the writer presents all of the information you need to know about the event: who, what, where when, and why. All of the questions I might have as a reader are answered. There is also no information that is unnecessary or "off-topic."

E-mail Invitation

An **e-mail invitation** is a quick way to let friends know about an event. Like an invitation sent by regular mail, an e-mail invitation tells when and where the event is taking place, along with any other useful information. Unlike a regular invitation, it travels instantly, via the Internet.

Come to a Party!

Person invited is named. → Hey Jeanine,

Tone is lively and friendly. → Have you ever wanted to star in a fairy tale? Here's your chance! I'm having a party at my house next week, and you're invited. Everyone has to come as a favorite character from a fairy tale. You could be Cinderella, the Big Bad Wolf, Rapunzel, or Snow White's mean stepmother. You could even be that horned toad we read about in class last week!

Important information is clearly set out. → Here are the details:
When: Saturday, December 3 at 6:30 P.M.
Where: 47 Columbus Street
There'll be dessert and punch.
RSVP (That means let me know if you can make it.) Start working on your costume!

Amy

Unit 1 The Horned Toad Prince   Writing Model **4A**

▲ **Writing Transparency** 4A

DAY 2 Improve Writing

WRITER'S CRAFT
Know Your Purpose

Display Writing Transparency 4B. Read the directions and work together to identify the writer's purpose.

Think Aloud **KNOW YOUR PURPOSE** Tomorrow we will be writing an e-mail invitation to a friend or relative. I am going to invite my sister to a baseball game. I need to keep this purpose in mind as I write my invitation. I might have other things to ask my sister, such as whether I might borrow her guitar. But this invitation should stick to my purpose of inviting her to the game.

GUIDED WRITING On the board write *vacations.* Ask students what they might say about vacations if they wanted to entertain, inform, or persuade their readers.

Know Your Purpose

Authors write for different reasons, or **purposes.** They might want to inform, persuade, or entertain their readers. They might want to express their feelings or create a mood. Whatever reason an author has for writing, his or her purpose should be clear.

Directions Each numbered item describes the topic of a piece of writing. Match each topic with the letter of the purpose that best suits the topic.

A To entertain	B To inform	C To persuade

1. Why James Lopez should be president	C
2. The difference between tornadoes and hurricanes	B
3. A recipe for brownies	B
4. The day my hamster stole my lunch	A
5. What this school needs most	C
6. The funniest story I ever heard	A
7. Dogs should be kept on leashes	C
8. How to write a research paper	B
9. My most embarrassing moment	A
10. Lower the driving age	C

Directions Write two or three sentences about pets. Write with the purpose of informing, persuading, or entertaining your reader. **Possible answer:**

Mice are the best pets of all. They are friendly, cute, and clean. You can teach them tricks, and they don't sleep all day like hamsters.

Unit 1 The Horned Toad Prince   Writer's Craft **4B**

▲ **Writing Transparency** 4B

DAY 3 Prewrite and Draft

READ THE WRITING PROMPT

on page 107 in the Student Edition.

In The Horned Toad Prince, *the author has a clear purpose—to entertain.*

Think about an event that you would like to invite someone to.

Now write an e-mail invitation with the purpose of informing family or friends about the special event.

Writing Test Tips

- Make your event sound like fun. You want your reader to accept.
- Include all the necessary information: what, when, where.
- Remember that the main idea is to invite your reader to the event. Make sure the purpose comes across loud and clear.

GETTING STARTED Students can do any of the following:

- Make a chart with columns headed *What, When, Where,* and *Other Details.*
- Decide on the organization of their invitation.
- Think of ideas and details that will catch their reader's attention.

DAY 4 Draft and Revise

EDITING/REVISING CHECKLIST

☑ Is my purpose clear?

☑ Can any short sentences be combined into compound sentences?

☑ Is the important information easy to understand?

☑ Are words with a final long *e* sound spelled correctly?

See *The Grammar and Writing Book,* pp. 68–73.

Revising Tips

Focus/Ideas

- Check that your purpose—inviting a friend to an event—is absolutely clear.
- Make sure you have chosen details that make the event seem interesting and attractive.
- Remove information that does not focus on the main idea.

PUBLISHING Have students e-mail their invitations to each classmate, print out invitations they receive, and bind them in a "You're Invited" folder.

ASSESSMENT Use the scoring rubric to evaluate students' work.

DAY 5 Connect to Unit Writing

Personal Narrative

Week 1	Memoir 39g–39h
Week 2	Journal Entry 65g–65h
Week 3	Postcard 87g–87h
Week 4	E-mail Invitation 111g–111h
Week 5	Narrative Writing 133g–133h

PREVIEW THE UNIT PROMPT

Write a personal narrative about a time that you were a newcomer to a place or situation (a school, club, team, or neighborhood). Explain how you felt and what you found challenging or exciting.

APPLY

- A personal narrative is a story about an interesting experience or event in the storyteller's life.
- Think of your purpose when deciding what information to include in your personal narrative.

Writing Trait Rubric

	4	3	2	1
Focus/Ideas	Ideas well-focused; lively description of event	Ideas somewhat focused; description of event	Weak focus; event unclear	No focus; event unclear
	Purpose of invitation clear	Purpose of invitation generally clear	Purpose of invitation vague	Purpose of invitation unclear

Spelling & Phonics Long *e*

OBJECTIVE

● Spell words that end with the long *e*.

Generalization

Connect to Phonics Long *e* at the end of a word can be spelled *ie*, *ey*, and *y: calorie, money, happy.* When the letters *ie, ey,* and *y* come at the end of a word, they can stand for the long *e* sound.

Spelling Words

1. prairie*	11. rookie
2. calorie	12. hockey
3. honey	13. collie
4. valley	14. breezy
5. money	15. jury
6. finally	16. balcony
7. movie	17. steady
8. country*	18. alley
9. empty	19. trolley
10. city	20. misty

Challenge Words

21. frequency	24. chimney
22. parsley	25. attorney
23. journey	

*Word from the selection

Spelling/Phonics Support See the ELL and Transition Handbook for spelling support.

DAY 1 Pretest and Sort

PRETEST

Use the Dictation Sentences from Day 5 to administer the pretest. Read the word, read the sentence, and then read the word again. Guide students in self-correcting their pretests and correcting any misspellings.

Monitor Progress

Spelling

If... students misspell more than 5 pretest words,	then... use words 1–10 for Strategic Intervention.
If... students misspell 1–5 pretest words,	then... use words 1–20 for On-Level practice.
If... students correctly spell all pretest words,	then... use words 1–25 for Advanced Learners.

HOMEWORK Spelling Practice Book, p. 13.

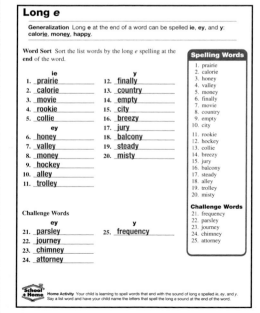

▲ **Spelling Practice Book** p. 13

DAY 2 Think and Practice

TEACH

Words that end with the long *e* sound often end with *ie, ey,* or *y.* Write *movie* on the board. Underline *ie.* Say *movie,* stressing the last syllable, and point out that the long *e* sound at the end of *movie* is spelled *ie.* Guide students in finding the letters that stand for the long *e* sound in *country* and *prairie.*

movi*e*

WORD CIRCLE Have small groups of students sit in a circle. Tell one student to say a list word, and have the next student say a list word that ends with the same letters. Continue around the circle until students cannot name any more similar list words. Then have them begin again with a new list word.

HOMEWORK Spelling Practice Book, p. 14.

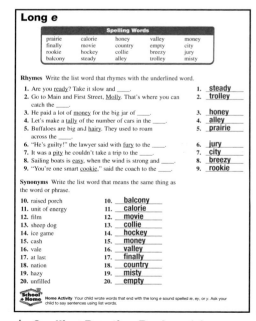

▲ **Spelling Practice Book** p. 14

DAY 3   Connect to Writing

WRITE AN E-MAIL

Ask students to use at least five spelling words to write an e-mail to a friend.

Frequently Misspelled Words

finally   *probably*

These words may seem easy to spell, but they are often misspelled by fourth-graders. Alert students to these frequently misspelled words. Make sure students correctly pronounce all the syllables in each word.

HOMEWORK Spelling Practice Book, p. 15.

Long e

Proofread an Ad Jan wrote this ad to sell her dog. Circle five misspelled words. Write the words correctly. Then write the sentence that has a capitalization mistake correctly.

Dog For Sale

This (colly) is a honey of a dog! Very nice and (steady) Likes to play ball and (hockie) too. We're not asking a lot of (monie) for this fine Dog. He needs a good home because we are (probablie) moving to the city.

Call: 555-888-1234

Spelling Words	
prairie	rookie
calorie	hockey
honey	collie
valley	breezy
money	jury
finally	balcony
movie	steady
country	alley
empty	trolley
city	misty

Frequently Misspelled Words

finally
probably

1. collie   2. steady
3. hockey   4. money
5. probably
6. We're not asking a lot of money for this fine dog.

Correct the Sentences Cross out the misspelled list word in each sentence. Write the word correctly.

7. Please put the trash cans in the ~~alley~~.   7. alley
8. It took the pioneers a long time to cross the ~~prairie~~.   8. prairie
9. Every spring, we put our potted plants on the ~~balcone~~.   9. balcony
10. The ~~miste~~ fog made it hard to see the road.   10. misty
11. The long trip is ~~finalee~~ over.   11. finally
12. The mailbox was ~~emptie~~.   12. empty
13. The ~~rokie~~ had a successful season.   13. rookie
14. I like ~~honee~~ on my toast.   14. honey
15. The ~~movee~~ was funny.   15. movie
16. I take the ~~trolee~~ to the shops.   16. trolley

School Home Activity Your child identified misspelled words that end with the long e sound spelled ie, ey, and y. Say a list word and spell, stopping before the letter or letters that spell the long e sound at the end of the word. Have your child complete the word.

▲ **Spelling Practice Book** p. 15

DAY 4   Review

REVIEW LONG e

Have pairs of students write the list words on individual note cards and turn the cards face down. Tell students to take turns turning two cards face up. If both words have the same long e ending, the student who turned up the cards keeps them.

Spelling Strategy Pronouncing for Spelling

We spell some words wrong because we say them wrong.

Step 1: Say the word correctly. Listen to the sound of each letter.

Step 2: Say the word again as you write it.

HOMEWORK Spelling Practice Book, p. 16.

Long e

Spelling Words				
prairie	calorie	honey	valley	money
finally	movie	country	empty	city
rookie	hockey	collie	breezy	jury
balcony	steady	alley	trolley	misty

Word Patterns Fill in the missing letters to write a list word.

1. C A L O R I E
2. M O V I E
3. C O L L I E
4. H O C K E Y
5. M O N E Y
6. V A L L E Y
7. F I N A L L Y
8. C O U N T R Y
9. M I S T Y
10. E M P T Y

Crossword Puzzle Use the clues below to solve the puzzle.

11. large town
14. high porch
17. flat land
18. sweet liquid

Down
12. cable car
13. firm
15. small street
16. panel

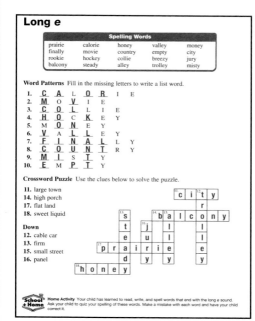

School Home Activity Your child has learned to read, write, and spell words that end with the long e sound. Ask your child to quiz your spelling of these words. Make a mistake with each word and have your child correct it.

▲ **Spelling Practice Book** p. 16

DAY 5   Posttest

DICTATION SENTENCES

1. Tall grass grew on the prairie.
2. Most foods have more than one calorie.
3. Bees make honey.
4. The river is down in the valley.
5. How do you earn money?
6. It is finally time for lunch.
7. What movie do you want to see?
8. The farm is out in the country.
9. I will refill your empty glass.
10. We rode the train into the city.
11. The rookie hit a home run.
12. Hockey is played on ice.
13. Is that big dog a collie?
14. Spring days are often breezy.
15. The jury listened to the judge.
16. Mom looked down at us from the balcony.
17. A steady rain fell all night long.
18. Park your car in the alley.
19. The trolley bell clanged.
20. We could hardly see through the misty fog.

CHALLENGE

21. What is the radio station's frequency?
22. We grew parsley in our garden.
23. The long journey took two days.
24. Smoke poured out of the chimney.
25. The attorney walked into the court.

OBJECTIVES

- Formulate an inquiry question that is connected to this week's lesson focus.
- Effectively and efficiently find, evaluate, and communicate information related to an inquiry question using electronic sources.

New Literacies

Day 1	Identify Questions
Day 2	Navigate/Search
Day 3	Analyze
Day 4	Synthesize
Day 5	Communicate

NEW LITERACIES

Internet Inquiry Activity

EXPLORE THE SOUTHWESTERN LANDSCAPE

Use the following 5-day plan to help students conduct this week's Internet inquiry activity on the uniqueness of the southwestern landscape. Remind students to follow classroom rules when using the Internet.

DAY 1

Identify Questions Discuss the lesson focus question: *What is unique about the landscape of the Southwest?* Brainstorm ideas for specific inquiry questions about the landscape of the Southwest. For example, students might want to learn more about unique landforms or plants and animals that thrive in this U.S. region. Have each student select an inquiry question to answer.

DAY 2

Navigate/Search Review how to conduct an Internet search using a student-friendly search engine or an online encyclopedia. Have students determine keywords related to their inquiry questions. As students study search engine results, point out specific URLs. Explain *URL* stands for *Uniform Resource Locator* and each Web site has a unique URL address. Discuss information students can infer from the URL, such as the letters *gov* used for government Web sites. Have students select a few sites to explore further.

DAY 3

Analyze Have students explore Web sites they identified on Day 2. Tell them to analyze each site carefully, searching for information related to their inquiry questions. Discuss how to distinguish relevant information and take notes. If allowed, students can print and highlight Web site information.

DAY 4

Synthesize Have students synthesize the information gathered on Day 3. Remind them they will need to combine ideas from different sources to try to come up with cohesive answers to their inquiry questions. Suggest they begin with an outline.

DAY 5

Communicate Encourage students to share their inquiry results in oral reports. They can create drawings or print photos with captions to help the class visualize what they learned about the uniqueness of the Southwest.

RESEARCH/STUDY SKILLS

Illustration/Caption/Label

TEACH

Discuss illustrations students have seen in books, encyclopedias, and magazines. Explain that illustrations often give readers information about the characters and events in a story or the subject of nonfiction texts. Display an illustration that includes a caption and label and review the following terms:

- An **illustration** can be a photograph, drawing, or diagram.

- A **caption** is the text that tells about the illustration. It is usually found below or next to the illustration.

- A **label** is a word or phrase that names part of an illustration.

Give pairs a textbook or other text with illustrations. Have them browse through the text, paying close attention to illustrations, captions, and labels. Then ask each pair to select an illustration and answer these questions:

1. What is the purpose of the illustration?

2. How does the illustration help you better understand the text?

3. How do the caption or labels help you understand the illustration?

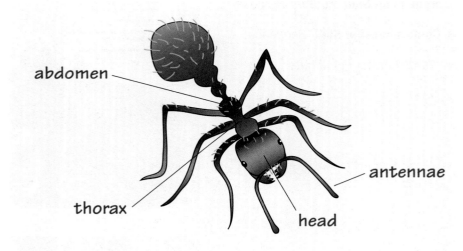

ASSESS

Ask students to describe the illustration and its caption or labels in their own words. They should be able to identify the purpose of the illustration and explain how the caption or labels provide further information about it.

For more practice or to assess students, use Practice Book pp. 39–40.

OBJECTIVES

- Review terms related to illustrations.
- Use illustrations to gather information.

Illustration/Caption/Label

- **Illustrations** and pictures can help readers understand information about characters and events in a story or a subject in a nonfiction article.
- A **caption** is the text that explains or gives more information about an illustration or picture. Captions usually appear below or to the side of the image.
- **Labels** also use text to provide information about illustrations and pictures. They can appear inside the image or above or below it.

Directions Study the illustrations and captions below.

prickly pear cactus

The prickly pear cactus, which grows in the American Southwest, has flat stems called pads. These stems are good at holding in water. For this reason, desert animals try to eat them. However, the prickly pear cactus protects itself with sharp, pointy spines that keep animals away.

saguaro cactus at maturity

The very large saguaro cactus grows from a very small seed. It takes many years for the saguaro to grow to its full size. These plants sometimes live 150 years. At that age, a saguaro may measure up to fifty feet high.

▲ **Practice Book** p. 39

Directions Use the illustrations and captions to answer the questions.
Possible answers given for 2, 5–10.
1. What is shown in these illustrations?

   The illustrations show two types of cactus plants.

2. What do the illustrations themselves show about the differences between the prickly pear cactus and the saguaro cactus?

   The prickly pear cactus is smaller than the saguaro cactus.

3. How large can a saguaro cactus grow?

   The saguaro cactus can grow fifty feet high.

4. How does the prickly pear cactus protect itself? How do you know?

   With sharp, pointy spines; the caption gives this information.

5. Why does the caption for the saguaro cactus include a detail about its seed, even though the illustration does not show this detail?

   The caption gives additional information, and the details about
   seeds are interesting because of the huge size of the cactus.

6. If the illustration of the prickly pear showed the kinds of animals that try to eat the plant's pads, what new information might the caption include?

   The caption would probably include the names of those animals.

7. What label might be added to the first illustration? Where would you place it?

   "Pads"; I might place it near the pads of the prickly pear.

8. What label might be added to the second illustration? Where would you place it?

   "Height: 50 feet"; I might place it to the side to show the height.

9. What kind of article might include these illustrations?

   An article about desert plants might include these illustrations.

10. Write a new caption that could be used for both images at once.

    Cacti come in different shapes and sizes.

 **Home Activity** Your child learned how to analyze illustrations and captions. Read a nonfiction article that contains no illustrations. Together, discuss what illustration you could add to help the reader understand the information in the article.

▲ **Practice Book** p. 40

The Horned Toad Prince **111I**

Assessment Checkpoints *for the Week*

Selection Assessment

Use pp. 13–16 of Selection Tests to check:

 Selection Understanding

  Comprehension Skill *Authors' Purpose*

 Selection Vocabulary

bargain	prairie
favor	riverbed
lassoed	shrieked
offended	

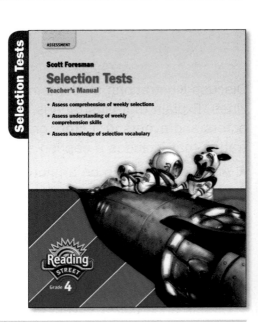

Selection Tests

Scott Foresman
Selection Tests
Teacher's Manual

- Assess comprehension of weekly selections
- Assess understanding of weekly comprehension skills
- Assess knowledge of selection vocabulary

Reading STREET Grade 4

Leveled Assessment

- On-Level
- Strategic Intervention
- Advanced

Use pp. 19–24 of **Fresh Reads for Differentiated Test Practice** to check:

 Comprehension Skill *Authors' Purpose*

 REVIEW Comprehension Skill *Sequence*

 Fluency *Words Correct Per Minute*

Fresh Reads for Differentiated Test Practice

Scott Foresman
Fresh Reads
for Differentiated Test Practice

Leveled passages—strategic intervention, on-level, and advanced—for
- Fluency checks
- Practice and application of weekly comprehension skills
- Answer key for all practice pages

Reading STREET Grade 4

Managing Assessment

Use Assessment Handbook for:

 Observation Checklists

 Record-Keeping Forms

 Portfolio Assessment

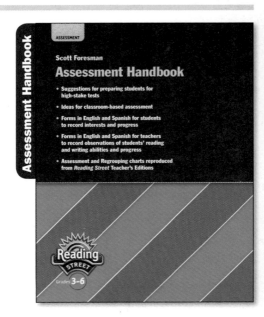

Assessment Handbook

Scott Foresman
Assessment Handbook

- Suggestions for preparing students for high-stake tests
- Ideas for classroom-based assessment
- Forms in English and Spanish for students to record interests and progress
- Forms in English and Spanish for teachers to record observations of students' reading and writing abilities and progress
- Assessment and Regrouping charts reproduced from *Reading Street* Teacher's Editions

Reading STREET Grades 3–6

Oregon

Planning Guide for Common Curriculum Goals

Letters Home from Yosemite

Reading Street Teacher's Edition pages	Grade 4 Oregon Grade-Level Standards for English/Language Arts
Oral Language **Speaking/Listening** Build Concept Vocabulary: 112l, 123, 127, 133c Read Aloud: 112m **Viewing** Analyze a Photo: 133d	**EL.04.RE.01** Read aloud grade-level narrative text and informational text fluently and accurately with effective pacing, intonation, and expression. **EL.04.RE.10** Develop vocabulary by listening to and discussing both familiar and conceptually challenging selections read aloud across the subject areas.
Word Work Long *u* Sounds: 133i–133j	**EL.04.WR.15** Spell correctly: syllables (word parts each containing a vowel sound, such as *sur-prise* or *e-col-o-gy*).
Reading **Comprehension** Main Idea: 112–113, 116–127, 133b Graphic Organizers: 112–113, 116–127 **Vocabulary** Lesson Vocabulary: 114b, 123, 127, 131 Word Structure: 114–115, 121, 133c **Fluency** Model Phrasing: 112l–112m, 133a **Self-Selected Reading:** LR37–45, TR16–17 **Literature** Genre—Narrative Nonfiction: 116 Reader Response: 128	**EL.04.RE.01** Read aloud grade-level narrative text and informational text fluently and accurately with effective pacing, intonation, and expression. **EL.04.RE.09** Understand, learn, and use new vocabulary that is introduced and taught directly through informational text, literary text, and instruction across the subject areas. **EL.04.RE.20** Identify and/or summarize sequence of events, main ideas, facts, supporting details, and opinions in informational and practical selections. **EL.04.LI.01** Listen to text and read text to make connections and respond to a wide variety of significant works of literature, including poetry, fiction, non-fiction, and drama, from a variety of cultures and time periods that enhance the study of other subjects.
Language Arts **Writing** Narrative Writing: 133g–133h **Six-Trait Writing** Conventions: 129, 133g–133h **Grammar, Usage, and Mechanics** Clauses and Complex Sentences: 133e–133f **Research/Study** Print Sources: 133l **Technology** New Literacies: 133k	**EL.04.WR.23** Write personal narratives: include ideas, observations, or memories of an event or experience. **EL.04.WR.31** Understand the organization of almanacs, newspapers, and periodicals and how to use those print materials.
Unit Skills **Writing** Personal Narrative: WA2–9 **Poetry:** 134–137 **Project/Wrap-Up:** 138–139	**EL.04.WR.23** Write personal narratives: include ideas, observations, or memories of an event or experience; provide a context to allow the reader to imagine the world of the event or experience; use concrete sensory details; provide insight into why the selected event or experience is memorable.

This Week's Leveled Readers

Intensive Intervention

SCOTT FORESMAN
SiDEWALKS

Intensive Intervention for Tier 3 Students

Below-Level

Nonfiction

EL.04.RE.01 Read aloud grade-level narrative text and informational text fluently and accurately with effective pacing, intonation, and expression.

EL.04.RE.20 Identify and/or summarize sequence of events, main ideas, facts, supporting details, and opinions in informational and practical selections.

On-Level

Nonfiction

EL.04.RE.20 Identify and/or summarize sequence of events, main ideas, facts, supporting details, and opinions in informational and practical selections.

EL.04.RE.28 Identify and analyze text that uses sequential or chronological order.

Advanced

Nonfiction

EL.04.RE.20 Identify and/or summarize sequence of events, main ideas, facts, supporting details, and opinions in informational and practical selections.

EL.04.LI.06 Use knowledge of the situation and setting and of a character's traits and motivations to determine the causes for that character's actions.

Content-Area Content Standards and Benchmarks in This Lesson

Math	Social Studies
MA.04.CE.01 Read, write, order, model, and compare whole numbers to one million, common fractions, and decimals to hundredths. **MA.04.ME.01** Select the most appropriate tool and U.S. customary unit to measure length, perimeter, weight, and volume. **MA.04.ME.06** Estimate the length of objects in inches, feet, and yards.	**SS.05.GE.01** Define basic geography vocabulary such as concepts of location, direction, distance, scale, movement, and region using appropriate words and diagrams. (Previews Grade 5 Benchmark)

Oregon!

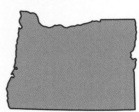

A FAMOUS OREGONIAN
Gordon Smith

Gordon Smith (1952–), an Oregon politician, was born in Pendleton. He graduated from Brigham Young University in 1976 and from Southwestern University in 1979, where he received his law degree. He entered politics in 1992, when he was elected into the Oregon Senate. In 1996 Smith was elected the first U.S. senator from eastern Oregon since 1938. Reelected in 2002, he continues to serve on major Senate committees, including the Energy and Natural Resources Committee and the Finance Committee.

Students can . . .
Learn about Gordon Smith's work in the U.S. Senate. Ask students to make a "mind map" with his name at the center and facts about him branching away from it.

A SPECIAL OREGON PLACE
Portland

Just south of Vancouver, Washington, on the Willamette River lies Portland, Oregon's largest city. Despite the fact that it is an urban and industrial center, Portland contains more than fourteen square miles of parkland, including Forest Park and the International Rose Test Garden, where hundreds of varieties of roses thrive in the city's climate. With more than five thousand wooded acres, Forest Park is the largest forested area within a city in the United States. A thirty-mile trail winds through the park, linking the cities of Portland and Gresham.

Students can . . .
Research different kinds of roses and other flowers that can be found in Portland's Forest Park and the International Rose Test Garden. Have students make a list of their findings.

OREGON FUN FACTS
Did You Know?

• Genetic tests indicate that Oregon's Kiger mustangs are related to those the Spanish conquistadors brought to North America more than five hundred years ago.

• The thunderegg has been the state rock since 1965. Thundereggs are as beautiful inside, with an array of colors, as they are plain on the outside.

• There is no hiking trail to the snowy peak of 11,239-foot Mount Hood. Climbing the mountain requires technical ability and highly specialized climbing equipment.

Students can . . .
Use an almanac to find the United States' tallest mountains. Ask students to create a graph illustrating Mt. Hood's height compared to those of other U.S. peaks.

Unit 1
This Land Is Your Land

CONCEPT QUESTION
How do the diverse regions and peoples of the United States reflect its greatness?

Week 1

What experiences bring diverse peoples together?

Week 2

What did Lewis and Clark learn on their journey?

Week 3

What can we learn about the United States as we travel?

Week 4

What is unique about the landscape of the Southwest?

Week 5

How does Yosemite reflect the unique qualities of the West?

Week 5

EXPAND THE CONCEPT
How does Yosemite reflect the unique qualities of the West?

CONNECT THE CONCEPT

▶ **Build Background**
earthquake, eruptions, volcano

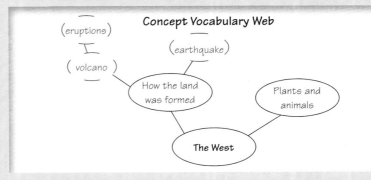

Concept Vocabulary Web

(eruptions) — (volcano) — (earthquake) — How the land was formed — Plants and animals — The West

▶ **Social Studies Content**
Sierra Nevada, Types of Rocks, Glaciers, Redwood Forest

▶ **Writing**
Narrative Writing

▶ **Internet Inquiry**
Unique Qualities of the West

Preview Your Week

How does Yosemite reflect the unique qualities of the West?

Letters Home from **Yosemite**

by Lisa Halvorsen

Yosemite National Park Visitor's Guide

Genre **Narrative nonfiction** tells the story of real people, places, or events. The narrator, or teller of the story, presents information in sequence. Notice this sequence as you read about Yosemite National Park.

Why do so many people travel to Yosemite National Park?

116

Student Edition pages 116–127

Audio CD

Genre Narrative Nonfiction
◉ **Vocabulary Strategy** Word Structure
◉ **Comprehension Skill** Main Idea
◉ **Comprehension Strategy** Graphic Organizers

Paired Selection

Reading Across Texts

Include a Natural Wonder from Yosemite in a Song

Genre

Song

Poetry

This Land Is Your Land

by Woody Guthrie

Song

Genre

- Songs are really poems. The lines rhyme and have rhythm so that they can be sung to a melody.
- Since patriotic songs are about a topic important to a whole nation, they are emotional and are widely sung.
- This song begins with the chorus, the part of the song that is repeated after each verse.
- The song's short phrases are easy to sing to the catchy melody.

Link to Social Studies
Make a four-column chart with the heads "Freedom," "Historical Events," "National Symbols," and "Landscape." Write the titles of other songs about the U.S. in the appropriate column(s).

"This Land Is Your Land." Words and Music by Woody Guthrie, TRO—Copyright 1956 (Renewed), 1958 (Renewed), 1970 (Renewed), 1972 (Renewed), Ludlow Music, Inc., New York, NY. Used by permission.

CHORUS:
This land is your land, this land is my land,
From California to the New York Island;
From the redwood forest to the Gulf Stream waters,
This land was made for you and me.

◉ **Prior Knowledge** Link the song's phrases to what you know about the U.S.

130

Student Edition pages 130–133

Audio CD

Read It
ONLINE
PearsonSuccessNet.com
• **Student Edition**
• **Leveled Readers**

Leveled Readers

⊙ **Skill** Main Idea
⊙ **Strategy** Graphic Organizers
Lesson Vocabulary

Below-Level

On-Level

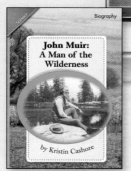

Advanced

E L L Reader
· Concept Vocabulary
· Text Support
· Language Enrichment

Integrate Science Standards
• Geology
• Glaciology
• Botany

✓ **Read**

Letters Home from Yosemite,
pp. 116–127

"This Land Is Your Land,"
pp. 130–133

Leveled Readers

Below-Level **On-Level** **Advanced**
• Support Concepts • Develop Concepts • Extend Concepts
• Science Extension
Activity

E L L Reader

✓ **Build**
Concept Vocabulary
The West, pp. 112l–112m

✓ **Teach**
Science Concepts
Sierra Nevada, p. 119
Types of Rocks, p. 121
Glaciers, p. 125
Redwood Forest, p. 131

✓ **Explore**
Science Center
Learn About Rocks!, p. 112k

Weekly Plan

READING

45–90 minutes

TARGET SKILLS OF THE WEEK

- **Comprehension Skill**
  Main Idea
- **Comprehension Strategy**
  Graphic Organizers
- **Vocabulary Strategy**
  Word Structure

LANGUAGE ARTS

30–60 minutes

Trait of the Week

Conventions

DAY 1
PAGES 112l–114b, 133a, 133e–133k

Oral Language

QUESTION OF THE WEEK *How does Yosemite reflect the unique qualities of the West?*

Read Aloud: "The Volcano Wakes," 112m
Build Concepts, 112l

Comprehension/Vocabulary

Comprehension Skill/Strategy Lesson, 112–113
- Main Idea **T**
- Graphic Organizers

Build Background, 114a

Introduce Lesson Vocabulary, 114b
glacier, impressive, naturalist, preserve, slopes, species, wilderness **T**

Read Leveled Readers

Grouping Options 112f–112g

Fluency

Model Phrasing, 112l–112m, 133a

Grammar, 133e
Introduce Clauses and Complex Sentences **T**

Writing Workshop, 133g
Introduce Narrative Writing
Model the Trait of the Week: Conventions

Spelling, 133i
Pretest for Long *u* Sounds

Internet Inquiry, 133k
Identify Questions

DAY 2
PAGES 114–123, 133a, 133e–133k

Oral Language

QUESTION OF THE DAY *Why did Congress establish Yosemite as a national park?*

Comprehension/Vocabulary

Vocabulary Strategy Lesson, 114–115
- Word Structure **T**

Read *Letters Home from Yosemite,* 116–123

Grouping Options 112f–112g

- Main Idea **T**
- Graphic Organizers
- Word Structure **T**
Develop Vocabulary

Fluency

Echo Reading, 133a

Grammar, 133e
Develop Clauses and Complex Sentences **T**

Writing Workshop, 133g
Improve Writing with Style

Spelling, 133i
Teach the Generalization

Internet Inquiry, 133k
Navigate/Search

DAILY WRITING ACTIVITIES

Day 1 Write to Read, 112

Day 2 Words to Write, 115
Strategy Response Log, 116, 123

DAILY SCIENCE CONNECTIONS

Day 1 The West Concept Web, 112l

Day 2 Time for Science: Sierra Nevada, 119;
Types of Rocks, 121
Revisit The West Concept Web, 123

DAILY SUCCESS PREDICTORS ➤
for Adequate Yearly Progress

Monitor Progress and Corrective Feedback

Vocabulary Check Vocabulary, *112l*

RESOURCES FOR THE WEEK

- Practice Book, *pp. 41–50*
- Word Study and Spelling Practice Book, *pp. 17–20*
- Grammar and Writing Practice Book, *pp. 17–20*
- Selection Test, *pp. 17–20*
- Fresh Reads for Differentiated Test Practice, *pp. 25–30*
- The Grammar and Writing Book, *pp. 74–79*

Grouping Options for Differentiated Instruction

Turn the page for the small group lesson plan.

DAY 3 PAGES 124–129, 133a, 133e–133k

Oral Language

QUESTION OF THE DAY *How does the author support her opinion that Yosemite is "one of the most awesome places on earth"?*

Comprehension/Vocabulary

Read *Letters Home from Yosemite,* 124–128

Grouping Options 112f–112g

Graphic Organizers

REVIEW Fact and Opinion **T**

Develop Vocabulary

Reader Response

Selection Test

Fluency

Model Phrasing, 133a

Grammar, 133f
Apply Clauses and Complex Sentences in Writing **T**

Writing Workshop, 129, 133h
Write Now
Prewrite and Draft

Spelling, 133j
Connect Spelling to Writing

Internet Inquiry, 133k
Analyze Sources

Day 3 Strategy Response Log, 126
Look Back and Write, 128

Day 3 Time for Science: Glaciers, 125
Revisit The West Concept Web, 127

DAY 4 PAGES 130–133a, 133e–133k

Oral Language

QUESTION OF THE DAY *What natural features of Yosemite are common in the western United States but not in other parts of the country?*

Comprehension/Vocabulary

Read *"This Land is Your Land,"* 130–133

Grouping Options 112f–112g

Song

Reading Across Texts

Content-Area Vocabulary

Fluency

Partner Reading, 133a

Grammar, 133f
Practice Clauses and Complex Sentences for Standardized Tests **T**

Writing Workshop, 133h
Draft, Revise, and Publish

Spelling, 133j
Provide a Strategy

Internet Inquiry, 133k
Synthesize Information

Day 4 Writing Across Texts, 133

Day 4 Time for Science: Redwood Forest, 131

DAY 5 PAGES 133a–133l

Oral Language

QUESTION OF THE WEEK *To wrap up the week, revisit the Day 1 question.*
Build Concept Vocabulary, 133c

Fluency

Read Leveled Readers

Grouping Options 112f–112g

Assess Reading Rate, 133a

Comprehension/Vocabulary

Reteach Main Idea, 133b **T**

Point of View, 133b

Word Structure, 133c **T**

Speaking and Viewing, 133d
Debate
Analyze a Photo

Grammar, 133f
Cumulative Review

Writing Workshop, 133h
Connect to Unit Writing

Spelling, 133j
Posttest for Long *u* Sounds

Internet Inquiry, 133k
Communicate Results

Research/Study Skills, 133l
Print Sources

Day 5 Point of View, 133b

Day 5 Revisit The West Concept Web, 133c

KEY = Target Skill **T** = Tested Skill

| Comprehension | Check Retelling, *128* | Fluency | Check Fluency WCPM, *133a* | Vocabulary | Check Vocabulary, *133c* |

SUCCESS PREDICTOR

Small Group Plan *for Differentiated Instruction*

Daily Plan
AT A GLANCE

Reading
Whole Group
- Oral Language
- Comprehension/Vocabulary

Group Time
Differentiated Instruction
Meet with small groups to provide:
- Skill Support
- Reading Support
- Fluency Practice

Read

This week's lessons for daily group time can be found behind the Differentiated Instruction (DI) tab on pp. DI·42–DI·51.

Whole Group
- Fluency

Language Arts
- Grammar
- Writing
- Spelling
- Research/Inquiry
- Speaking/Listening/Viewing

Use *My Sidewalks on Reading Street* for Tier III intensive reading intervention.

DAY 1

On-Level
Teacher-Led
Page DI · 43
- Develop Concept Vocabulary
- **Read** On-Level Reader *The Amazing Geography of the West*

Strategic Intervention
Teacher-Led
Page DI · 42
- Reinforce Concepts
- **Read** Below-Level Reader *This Land Is Our Land*

Advanced
Teacher-Led
Page DI · 43
- **Read** Advanced Reader *John Muir: A Man of the Wilderness*
- Independent Extension Activity

ⓘ Independent Activities
While you meet with small groups, have the rest of the class...
- Visit the Reading/Library Center
- Listen to the Background Building Audio
- Finish Write to Read, p. 112
- Complete Practice Book pp. 43–44
- Visit Cross-Curricular Centers

DAY 2

On-Level
Teacher-Led
Pages 118–123
- **Read** *Letters Home from Yosemite*

Strategic Intervention
Teacher-Led
Page DI · 44
- Practice Lesson Vocabulary
- Read Multisyllabic Words
- **Read** or Listen to *Letters Home from Yosemite*

Advanced
Teacher-Led
Page DI · 45
- Extend Vocabulary
- **Read** *Letters Home from Yosemite*

ⓘ Independent Activities
While you meet with small groups, have the rest of the class...
- Visit the Reading/Library Center
- Listen to the AudioText for *Letters Home from Yosemite*
- Finish Words to Write, p. 115
- Complete Practice Book pp. 45–46
- Write in their Strategy Response Logs, pp. 116, 123
- Visit Cross-Curricular Centers
- Work on inquiry projects

DAY 3

On-Level
Teacher-Led
Pages 124–127
- **Read** *Letters Home from Yosemite*

Strategic Intervention
Teacher-Led
Page DI · 46
- Practice Main Idea and Graphic Organizers
- **Read** or Listen to *Letters Home from Yosemite*

Advanced
Teacher-Led
Page DI · 47
- Extend Main Idea and Graphic Organizers
- **Read** *Letters Home from Yosemite*

ⓘ Independent Activities
While you meet with small groups, have the rest of the class...
- Visit the Reading/Library Center
- Listen to the AudioText for *Letters Home from Yosemite*
- Write in their Strategy Response Logs, p. 126
- Finish Look Back and Write, p. 128
- Complete Practice Book p. 47
- Visit Cross-Curricular Centers
- Work on inquiry projects

① Begin with whole class skill and strategy instruction.

② Meet with small groups to provide differentiated instruction.

③ Gather the whole class back together for fluency and language arts.

DAY 4

On-Level
Teacher-Led
Pages 130–133

- **Read** "This Land Is Your Land"

Strategic Intervention
Teacher-Led
Page DI · 48

- Practice Retelling
- **Read** or Listen to "This Land Is Your Land"

Advanced
Teacher-Led
Page DI · 49

- **Read** "This Land Is Your Land"
- Genre Study

(i) Independent Activities

While you meet with small groups, have the rest of the class...

- Visit the Reading/Library Center
- Listen to the AudioText for "This Land Is Your Land"
- Visit the Writing/Vocabulary Center
- Finish Writing Across Texts, p. 133
- Visit Cross-Curricular Centers
- Work on inquiry projects

DAY 5

On-Level
Teacher-Led
Page DI · 51

- **Reread** On-Level Reader *The Amazing Geography of the West*
- Retell *The Amazing Geography of the West*

Strategic Intervention
Teacher-Led
Page DI · 50

- **Reread** Leveled Reader *This Land Is Our Land*
- Retell *This Land Is Our Land*

Advanced
Teacher-Led
Page DI · 51

- **Reread** Leveled Reader *John Muir: A Man of the Wilderness*
- Share Extension Activity

(i) Independent Activities

While you meet with small groups, have the rest of the class...

- Visit the Reading/Library Center
- Complete Practice Book pp. 48–50
- Visit Cross-Curricular Centers
- Work on inquiry projects

Grouping Place English language learners in the groups that correspond to their reading abilities in English.

Use the appropriate Leveled Reader or other text at students' instructional level.

TiP Send home the appropriate Multilingual Summary of the main selection on Day 1.

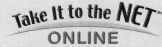

ONLINE
PearsonSuccessNet.com

Jeanne Paratore
For ideas for successful home-school programs, see the article "Home and School Together" by Scott Foresman author Jeanne Paratore.

TEACHER TALK

A **base word** is a word that can stand alone or take endings and affixes, such as *walk* or *happy*.

Looking Ahead

Be sure to schedule time for students to work on the unit inquiry project "Natural Wonders." This week students prepare posters highlighting their chosen geographical attractions.

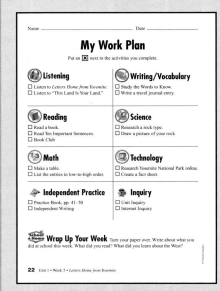

Name _____ Date _____

My Work Plan
Put an ☒ next to the activities you complete.

Listening
☐ Listen to *Letters Home from Yosemite.*
☐ Listen to "This Land Is Your Land."

Writing/Vocabulary
☐ Study the Words to Know.
☐ Write a travel journal entry.

Reading
☐ Read a book.
☐ Read Ten Important Sentences.
☐ Book Club

Science
☐ Research a rock type.
☐ Draw a picture of your rock.

Math
☐ Make a table.
☐ List the entries in low-to-high order.

Technology
☐ Research Yosemite National Park online.
☐ Create a fact sheet.

Independent Practice
☐ Practice Book, pp. 41–50
☐ Independent Writing

Inquiry
☐ Unit Inquiry
☐ Internet Inquiry

Wrap Up Your Week Turn your paper over. Write about what you did at school this week. What did you read? What did you learn about the West?

22 Unit 1 • Week 5 • *Letters Home from Yosemite*

▲ **Group-Time Survival Guide**
p. 22, Weekly Contract

Customize Your Plan *by Strand*

ORAL LANGUAGE

Concept Development

How does Yosemite reflect the unique qualities of the West?

CONCEPT VOCABULARY

earthquake   eruptions   volcano

BUILD

☐ **Question of the Week** Introduce and discuss the question of the week. This week students will read a variety of texts and work on projects related to the concept *The West*. Post the question for students to refer to throughout the week. **DAY 1** *112d*

☐ **Read Aloud** Read aloud "The Volcano Wakes." Then begin a web to build concepts and concept vocabulary related to this week's lesson and the unit theme, This Land Is Your Land. Introduce the concept words *earthquake, eruptions,* and *volcano* and have students place them on the web. Display the web for use throughout the week. **DAY 1** *112l–112m*

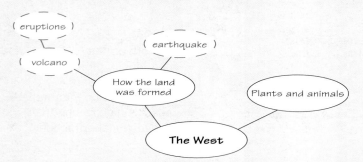

DEVELOP

☐ **Question of the Day** Use the prompts from the Weekly Plan to engage students in conversations related to this week's reading and the unit theme. **EVERY DAY** *112d–112e*

☐ **Concept Vocabulary Web** Revisit The West Concept Web and encourage students to add concept words from their reading and life experiences. **DAY 2** *123,* **DAY 3** *127*

CONNECT

☐ **Looking Back** Revisit The West Concept Web and discuss how it relates to this week's lesson and the unit theme. **DAY 5** *133c*

CHECK

☐ **Concept Vocabulary Web** Use The West Concept Web to check students' understanding of the concept vocabulary words *earthquake, eruptions,* and *volcano.* **DAY 1** *121l,* **DAY 5** *133c*

VOCABULARY

⟳ **STRATEGY WORD STRUCTURE** When you are reading and see an unfamiliar word, you can look at the end of the word to help figure out the meaning. The base word, the word without the ending, will also help you understand the meaning.

LESSON VOCABULARY

glacier   slopes
impressive   species
naturalist   wilderness
preserve

TEACH

☐ **Words to Know** Give students the opportunity to tell what they already know about this week's lesson vocabulary words. Then discuss word meaning. **DAY 1** *114b*

☐ **Vocabulary Strategy Lesson** Use the vocabulary strategy lesson in the Student Edition to introduce and model this week's strategy, *word structure.* **DAY 2** *114-115*

Vocabulary Strategy Lesson

PRACTICE/APPLY

☐ **Leveled Text** Read the lesson vocabulary in the context of leveled text. **DAY 1** *LR37-LR45*

☐ **Words in Context** Read the lesson vocabulary and apply *word structure* in the context of *Letters Home from Yosemite.* **DAY 2** *116-123,* **DAY 3** *124-128*

Leveled Readers

☐ **Writing/Vocabulary Center** Use the Words to Know to write a travel journal entry. **ANY DAY** *112K*

☐ **Homework** Practice Book pp. 44–45. **DAY 1** *114b,* **DAY 2** *115*

Main Selection—Nonfiction

☐ **Word Play** Discuss the fact that many of the words we use today come from Native American words. Using the sentences provided, have students identify objects whose names come from Native American languages. **ANY DAY** *133c*

ASSESS

☐ **Selection Test** Use the Selection Test to determine students' understanding of the lesson vocabulary words. **DAY 3**

RETEACH/REVIEW

☐ **Reteach Lesson** If necessary, use this lesson to reteach and review *word structure.* **DAY 5** *133c*

COMPREHENSION

👁 **SKILL MAIN IDEA** The main idea is the most important idea about the topic of a paragraph, passage, or article. The main idea is supported by small pieces of information, supporting details, that tell more about the main idea.

👁 **STRATEGY GRAPHIC ORGANIZERS** Creating charts, webs, diagrams or making lists can help organize thoughts while reading. Graphic organizers can be used before, during, or after reading to help you remember the main idea and supporting details.

TEACH

☐ **Skill/Strategy Lesson** Use the skill/strategy lesson in the Student Edition to introduce and model *main idea* and *graphic organizers*. **DAY 1** *112-113*

Skill/Strategy Lesson

☐ **Extend Skills** Teach point of view. **ANY DAY** *133b*

PRACTICE/APPLY

☐ **Leveled Text** Apply *main idea* and *graphic organizers* to read leveled text. **DAY 1** *LR37-LR45*

Leveled Readers

☐ **Skills and Strategies in Context** Read *Letters Home from Yosemite,* using the Guiding Comprehension questions to apply *main idea* and *graphic organizers*. **DAY 2** *116-123,* **DAY 3** *124-128*

Main Selection—Nonfiction

☐ **Skills and Strategies in Context** Read "This Land Is Your Land," guiding students as they identify *main ideas* and create *graphic organizers*. Then have students discuss and write across texts. **DAY 4** *130-133*

Paired Selection—Poetry

☐ **Homework** Practice Book pp. 43, 47, 48 **DAY 1** *113,* **DAY 3** *127,* **DAY 5** *133b*

☐ **Fresh Reads for Differentiated Test Practice** Have students practice *main idea* with a new passage. **DAY 3**

ASSESS

☐ **Selection Test** Determine students' understanding of the selection and their use of *main idea*. **DAY 3**

☐ **Retell** Have students retell *Letters Home from Yosemite*. **DAY 3** *128-129*

RETEACH/REVIEW

☐ **Reteach Lesson** If necessary, reteach and review *main idea*. **DAY 5** *133b*

FLUENCY

SKILL PHRASING Phrasing is grouping related words in a meaningful way. Phrasing allows the reader and listener to better understand the text.

TEACH

☐ **Read Aloud** Model fluent reading by rereading "The Volcano Wakes." Focus on this week's fluency skill, phrasing. **DAY 1** *112l-112m, 133a*

PRACTICE/APPLY

☐ **Echo Reading** Read aloud selected paragraphs from *Letters Home from Yosemite,* having students notice how the words are grouped in phrases, pausing briefly after clauses and punctuation marks. Then practice as a class, doing three echo readings. **DAY 2** *133a,* **DAY 3** *133a*

☐ **Partner Reading** Have partners practice reading aloud, reading with careful phrasing, and pausing briefly after clauses and punctuation marks. Have students offer each other feedback. As students reread, monitor their progress toward their individual fluency goals. **DAY 4** *133a*

☐ **Listening Center** Have students follow along with the AudioText for this week's selections. **ANY DAY** *112j*

☐ **Reading/Library Center** Have students reread a selection of their choice. **ANY DAY** *112j*

☐ **Fluency Coach** Have students use Fluency Coach to listen to fluent readings or practice reading on their own. **ANY DAY**

ASSESS

☐ **Check Fluency** WCPM Do a one-minute timed reading, paying special attention to this week's skill—phrasing. Provide feedback for each student. **DAY 5** *133a*

☑ Customize Your Plan *by Strand*

GRAMMAR

SKILL CLAUSES AND COMPLEX SENTENCES A clause is a group of words with a subject and a verb. A dependent clause cannot stand alone as a sentence. An independent clause can stand alone.

A sentence made up of a dependent clause and an independent clause is a complex sentence.

TEACH

❑ **Grammar Transparency 5** Use Grammar Transparency 5 to teach clauses and complex sentences. DAY 1 *133e*

Grammar Transparency 5

PRACTICE/APPLY

❑ **Develop the Concept** Review the concept of clauses and complex sentences and provide guided practice. DAY 2 *133e*

❑ **Apply to Writing** Have students review something they have written and add clauses and complex sentences to make their writing more interesting. DAY 3 *133f*

❑ **Test Preparation** Examine common errors in clauses and complex sentences to prepare for standardized tests. DAY 4 *133f*

❑ **Homework** Grammar and Writing Practice Book pp. 17–19. DAY 2 *133e*, DAY 3 *133f*, DAY 4 *133f*

ASSESS

❑ **Cumulative Review** Use Grammar and Writing Practice Book p. 20. DAY 5 *133f*

RETEACH/REVIEW

❑ **Daily Fix-It** Have students find and correct errors in grammar, spelling, and punctuation. **EVERY DAY** *133e-133f*

❑ **The Grammar and Writing Book** Use pp. 74–77 of The Grammar and Writing Book to extend instruction for clauses and complex sentences. **ANY DAY**

The Grammar and Writing Book

WRITING

Trait of the Week

CONVENTIONS Conventions are special rules for written language. Conventions are signals that writers use to make their meaning clear to readers.

TEACH

❑ **Writing Transparency 5A** Use the model to introduce and discuss the Trait of the Week. DAY 1 *133g*

❑ **Writing Transparency 5B** Use the transparency to show students how style can improve their writing. DAY 2 *133g*

Writing Transparency 5A **Writing Transparency 5B**

PRACTICE/APPLY

❑ **Write Now** Examine the model on Student Edition p. 129. Then have students write their own narrative. DAY 3 *129, 133h*, DAY 4 *133h*

> **Prompt** In *Letters Home from Yosemite*, the author tells about a special trip. Think about a trip you have taken—maybe for a vacation or family visit and write a narrative describing a special experience from that trip.

Write Now p. 129

❑ **Writing/Vocabulary Center** Write a travel journal entry. **ANY DAY** *112k*

ASSESS

❑ **Writing Trait Rubric** Use the rubric to evaluate students' writing. DAY 4 *133h*

RETEACH/REVIEW

❑ **The Grammar and Writing Book** Use pp. 74–79 of The Grammar and Writing Book to extend instruction for clauses and complex sentences, style, and narrative writing. **ANY DAY**

The Grammar and Writing Book

❶ Use assessment data to determine your instructional focus.

❷ Preview this week's instruction by strand.

❸ Choose instructional activities that meet the needs of your classroom.

SPELLING

GENERALIZATION LONG *U* SOUNDS   Long *u* has two sounds, /ü/ and /yü/, and several spellings, *u-consonant-e, ew, oo, ui,* and *u: excuse, threw, mood, cruise, pupil.* The letter patterns *u-consonant-e, ew, oo, ui,* and *u* can stand for /ü/ or /yü/.

TEACH

❏ **Pretest** Give the pretest for words with long *u* sounds. Guide students in self-correcting their pretests and correcting any misspellings. DAY 1 *133i*

❏ **Think and Practice** Connect spelling to the phonics generalization for long *u* sounds. DAY 2 *133i*

PRACTICE/APPLY

❏ **Connect to Writing** Have students use spelling words to write a postcard. Then review frequently misspelled words: *school, too.* DAY 3 *133j*

❏ **Homework** Phonics and Spelling Practice Book pp. 17–20. **EVERY DAY**

RETEACH/REVIEW

❏ **Review** Review spelling words to prepare for the posttest. Then provide students with a spelling strategy—steps for spelling new words. DAY 4 *133j*

ASSESS

❏ **Posttest** Use dictation sentences to give the posttest for words with long *u* sounds. **DAY 5** *133j*

Spelling Words

1. usual*	8. scooter	15. pupil
2. huge*	9. juice	16. groove
3. flute	10. cruise	17. confuse
4. mood	11. truth	18. humor
5. smooth	12. bruise	19. duty
6. threw	13. cruel	20. curfew
7. afternoon*	14. excuse	

Challenge Words

21. influence	23. nutrition	25. igloo
22. aluminum	24. accumulate	

*Word from the selection

RESEARCH AND INQUIRY

❏ **Internet Inquiry** Have students conduct an Internet inquiry on unique qualities of the American West. **EVERY DAY** *133k*

❏ **Print Sources** Discuss with students the variety of print sources available as well as their purpose. Have small groups analyze various print sources on national parks and answer questions about the sources. **DAY 5** *133l*

❏ **Unit Inquiry** Allow time for students to work on the posters highlighting their chosen geographical attractions. **ANY DAY** 17

SPEAKING AND VIEWING

❏ **Debate** Have students debate reasons for and against restricting vehicle access in the parks. Students need to choose a position and support their position with researched facts. **DAY 5** *133d*

❏ **Analyze a Photo** Have students analyze a photograph of Yosemite or another national park and answer questions about it. **DAY 5** *133d*

Resources for Differentiated Instruction

LEVELED READERS

▶ **Comprehension**
- ⦿ **Skill** Main Idea
- ⦿ **Strategy** Graphic Organizers

▶ **Lesson Vocabulary**
- ⦿ **Word Structure**

glacier · impressive · species · slopes · naturalist · preserve · wilderness

▶ **Science Standards**
- • Geology
- • Glaciology
- • Botany

Leveled Reader Database ONLINE

PearsonSuccessNet.com

Use the Online Database of over 600 books to

- Download and print additional copies of this week's leveled readers.
- Listen to the readers being read online.
- Search for more titles focused on this week's skills, topic, and content.

Life Science
Earth Science

The Amazing Geography of the West

by Vana Dougias

On-Level Reader

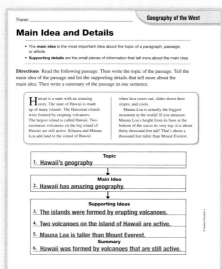

Name _____   Geography of the West

Main Idea and Details

- The **main idea** is the most important idea about the topic of a paragraph, passage, or article.
- **Supporting details** are the small pieces of information that tell more about the main idea.

Directions Read the following passage. Then write the topic of the passage. Tell the main idea of the passage and list the supporting details that tell more about the main idea. Then write a summary of the passage in one sentence.

Hawaii is a state with an amazing story. The state of Hawaii is made up of many islands. The Hawaiian islands were formed by erupting volcanoes. The largest island is called Hawaii. Two enormous volcanoes on the big island of Hawaii are still active. Kilauea and Mauna Loa add land to the island of Hawaii when lava oozes out, slides down their slopes, and cools.

Mauna Loa is actually the biggest mountain in the world! If you measure Mauna Loa's height from its base at the bottom of the sea to its very top, it is about thirty thousand feet tall! That's about a thousand feet taller than Mount Everest.

Topic
1. Hawaii's geography

Main Idea
2. Hawaii has amazing geography.

Supporting Ideas
3. The islands were formed by erupting volcanoes.
4. Two volcanoes on the island of Hawaii are active.
5. Mauna Loa is taller than Mount Everest.

Summary
6. Hawaii was formed by volcanoes that are still active.

⦿ **On-Level Practice** TE p. LR41

Name _____   Geography of the West

Vocabulary
Directions Choose the word from the box that best matches each clue. Write the word on the line.

Check the Words You Know
___ glacier   ___ impressive   ___ naturalist   ___ preserve
___ slopes   ___ species   ___ wilderness

1. __naturalist__ a person who studies plants or animals
2. __glacier__ a mass of ice that moves slowly
3. __wilderness__ an outdoor place with more animals than humans
4. __impressive__ able to have a strong effect on the mind or emotions
5. __species__ living things in a group that are very much alike

Possible responses given.
Directions Write a sentence using the new form of the vocabulary word.

6. preserving __Preserving special places in the United States is an important job.__
7. sloped __The hill sloped so much it was hard to climb.__
8. impressed __I impressed my teacher with my report.__
9. glaciers __Many mountains are covered with glaciers.__

On-Level Practice TE p. LR42

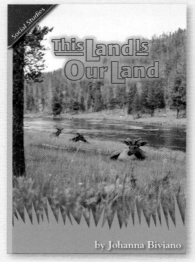

Social Studies

This Land Is Our Land

by Johanna Biviano

Below-Level Reader

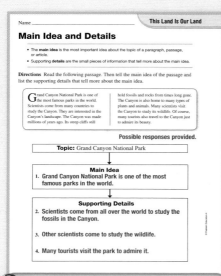

Name _____   This Land Is Our Land

Main Idea and Details

- The **main idea** is the most important idea about the topic of a paragraph, passage, or article.
- **Supporting details** are the small pieces of information that tell more about the main idea.

Directions Read the following passage. Then tell the main idea of the passage and list the supporting details that tell more about the main idea.

Grand Canyon National Park is one of the most famous parks in the world. Scientists come from many countries to study the Canyon. They are interested in the Canyon's landscape. The Canyon was made millions of years ago. Its steep cliffs still hold fossils and rocks from times long gone. The Canyon is also home to many types of plants and animals. Many scientists visit the Canyon to study its wildlife. Of course, many tourists also travel to the Canyon just to admire its beauty.

Possible responses provided.

Topic: Grand Canyon National Park

Main Idea
1. Grand Canyon National Park is one of the most famous parks in the world.

Supporting Details
2. Scientists come from all over the world to study the fossils in the Canyon.
3. Other scientists come to study the wildlife.
4. Many tourists visit the park to admire it.

⦿ **Below-Level Practice** TE p. LR38

Name _____   This Land Is Our Land

Vocabulary
Directions Match the word from Column A with its definition in Column B. Write the letter of the correct definition next to each word in Column A.

Check the Words You Know
___ glaciers   ___ impressive   ___ naturalists   ___ preserve
___ slopes   ___ species   ___ wilderness

Column A		Column B
_b_	1. naturalists	a. great masses of ice moving very slowly down mountains, along valleys, or over land areas
_e_	2. slopes	b. people who study living things
_c_	3. wilderness	c. a wild, uncultivated region with few or no people living in it
_a_	4. glaciers	d. to keep from harm or change; keep safe; protect
_d_	5. preserve	e. lines, surfaces, land, or other objects that go up or down at an angle

Directions Choose the word from the box that best completes each sentence. Write the word on the line.

6. Mt. McKinley in Alaska is the most __impressive__ mountain in America.
7. There are many different __species__ of plants and animals living in Yosemite National Park.
8. It is important to have national parks to __preserve__ our most beautiful places.
9. The skier did not expect to find such steep __slopes__.
10. People who hike in the __wilderness__ need to take along a map and plenty of water.

Below-Level Practice TE p. LR39

Advanced

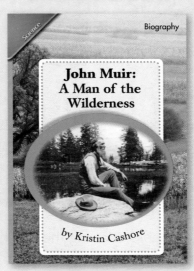

Biography

John Muir: A Man of the Wilderness

by Kristin Cashore

Advanced Reader

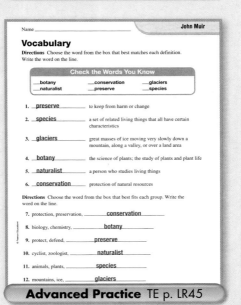

Name _____ John Muir

Main Idea and Details

- The **main idea** is the most important idea about the topic of a paragraph, passage, or article.
- **Supporting details** are the small pieces of information that tell more about the main idea.

Directions Read the following passage. Answer the following questions about the passage.

John Muir was one of our country's most important naturalists. Millions of people have read his books, and many have been influenced by his ideas. It is thanks to John Muir and others like him that many Americans today care about nature and the environment. People who work toward conservation today are acting in the spirit of this highly respected immigrant from Scotland.

John Muir is so admired that many parks, trails, and organizations are named after him. The John Muir Trust is a Scottish organization that works to protect the environment. The Muir Woods National Monument is a forest of protected redwood trees in California. The John Muir Trail runs for 211 miles through some of the most beautiful mountains in California. The John Muir Wilderness is a large area in California full of mountains, lakes, and streams. The Sierra Club that Muir established has also grown over the years, and today it does important conservation work all over the world.

Possible responses given.

1–2. What is the main idea of the first paragraph? Give one supporting detail.

John Muir was one of our country's most important naturalists. Many people have been influenced by his ideas.

3–4. What is the main idea of the second paragraph? Give one supporting detail.

John Muir is admired; many parks, trails, and organizations are named after him.

5–7. What is the main idea of the entire passage? Give two supporting details.

Muir was so important to conservation in America that he is still remembered today. Millions of people have read his books. Muir's Sierra Club has grown. It still does important conservation work.

Advanced Practice TE p. LR44

Name _____ John Muir

Vocabulary

Directions Choose the word from the box that best matches each definition. Write the word on the line.

Check the Words You Know
__botany __conservation __glaciers __naturalist __preserve __species

1. **preserve** to keep from harm or change

2. **species** a set of related living things that all have certain characteristics

3. **glaciers** great masses of ice moving very slowly down a mountain, along a valley, or over a land area

4. **botany** the science of plants; the study of plants and plant life

5. **naturalist** a person who studies living things

6. **conservation** protection of natural resources

Directions Choose the word from the box that best fits each group. Write the word on the line.

7. protection, preservation, **conservation**

8. biology, chemistry, **botany**

9. protect, defend, **preserve**

10. cyclist, zoologist, **naturalist**

11. animals, plants, **species**

12. mountains, ice, **glaciers**

Advanced Practice TE p. LR45

(ELL)

For Purple Mountain Majesties

by Al Cantu

ELL Reader

ELL Poster 5

Teacher's Edition Notes

ELL notes throughout this lesson support instruction and reference additional resources at point of use.

Teaching Guide pp. 29–35, 220–221
- Multilingual summaries of the main selection
- Comprehension lesson
- Vocabulary strategies and word cards
- ELL Reader 4.1.5 lesson

ELL and Transition Handbook

Ten Important Sentences
- Key ideas from every selection in the Student Edition
- Activities to build sentence power

More Reading

Readers' Theater Anthology
- Fluency practice
- Five scripts to build fluency
- Poetry for oral interpretation

Leveled Trade Books

- Extended reading tied to the unit concept
- Lessons in the Trade Book Library Teaching Guide

School + Home

Homework
- Family Times Newsletter
- ELL Multilingual Selection Summaries

Take-Home Books
- Leveled Readers

Letters Home from Yosemite

112i

Cross-Curricular Centers

Listen to the *Selections*

MATERIALS `SINGLES`
CD player, headphones, AudioText CD, student book

LISTEN TO LITERATURE Listen to *Letters Home from Yosemite* and "This Land Is Your Land" as you follow or read along in your book. Listen for the main ideas in *Letters Home from Yosemite*.

If there is anything you don't understand, you can listen again to any section.

Read It *Again!*

MATERIALS `SINGLES` `PAIRS` `GROUPS`
Collection of books for self-selected reading, reading logs, student book

Select a book you have already read. Record the title of the book in your reading log. You may want to read with a partner.

Choose from the following:

- **Leveled Readers**
- **ELL Readers**
- **Books or Stories Written by Classmates**
- **Books from the Library**
- *Letters Home from Yosemite*

TEN IMPORTANT SENTENCES Read the Ten Important Sentences for *Letters Home from Yosemite*. Then locate the sentences in the student book.

BOOK CLUB In a group discuss why you like or dislike the style of writing in *Letters Home from Yosemite*. Tell how the author might have written it differently and if you would enjoy reading it more that way.

Find the *Height*

MATERIALS `SINGLES` `PAIRS` `GROUPS`
Writing materials, student book

Make a table showing the heights of the different sights found in Yosemite National Park.

1. **On a piece of paper, draw a table like the one shown below.**
2. **Skim *Letters Home from Yosemite* in the student book to find the height of each sight listed.**
3. **Record the height for each sight in your table.**
4. **List the sights in order from lowest to highest.**

EARLY FINISHERS Use division to convert the height measures from feet to yards. Remember, there are 3 feet in a yard.

Yosemite Park Sights	Height (ft)
Bridalveil Fall	620
Sequoia Tree	300
El Capitan	3,600
Ribbon Fall	1,612
Mt. Lyell	13,114
Tioga Pass	9,945

Scott Foresman Reading Street Centers Survival Kit

Use the *Letters Home from Yosemite* materials from the Reading Street Centers Survival Kit to organize this week's centers.

 ## Writing/Vocabulary

 ## Science

Technology

Write a Travel Journal

MATERIALS SINGLES
Writing and art materials, student book

Write a travel journal entry about a real place you have visited, heard about, or seen in pictures.

1. Use *Letters Home from Yosemite* as a model for your writing.
2. Use facts and vivid details to explain what is special about the place and what you did or saw.

EARLY FINISHERS Draw a picture to go along with your travel journal entry. Draw the place itself or an interesting detail, such as a special tree or animal you saw.

Verona Dog Park
The Verona Dog Park has acres of prairie grass, tall apple trees, beautiful wild flowers, and dogs—lots of dogs! Every Saturday, my dogs Scout and Ruby and I hike the largest trail that loops around the park.

Learn About Rocks!

MATERIALS SINGLES GROUPS
Science articles or books on rock types, Internet access, writing and art materials

Learn about igneous, sedimentary, or metamorphic rocks.

1. Choose a rock type to research and list five important facts about it.
2. Draw a picture of your rock type or, if your teacher gives you permission, download and print a picture of it from the Internet.

EARLY FINISHERS Use your facts and picture to create a trading card about your rock type. Trade your card with a classmate.

Igneous Rock
Obsidian

Igneous Rocks
1. These rocks are made from lava.
2. Granite is a kind of igneous rock.
3. Basalt is a kind of igneous rock.

Search the Internet

MATERIALS SINGLES
Internet access, writing materials, tape recorder

Use the Internet to find out about Yosemite National Park.

1. Using a student-friendly search engine, type the keywords *Yosemite National Park* in the Search box. Follow classroom rules when searching the Internet.
2. Click on a Web site you believe will provide helpful, accurate information about Yosemite.
3. List at least four facts about Yosemite from the Web site, such as the number of visitors each year or types of wildlife species in the park.
4. Write a fact sheet, listing the facts you found.

EARLY FINISHERS Pretend you're a tour guide at the park. Make an audio tape describing the park to a visitor. *Drama*

Search Engine
Yosemite

Yosemite National Park Fact Sheet
• Yosemite Park is more than 750,000 acres.
• There are 800 miles of hiking trails.
• There are thousands of lakes and ponds.

 ALL CENTERS

- Build vocabulary by finding words related to the lesson concept.
- Listen for main ideas and details.

Concept Vocabulary

earthquake a shaking of Earth's surface caused by the sudden breaking of masses of rock along a fault.

eruptions processes of throwing forth

volcano opening in Earth's crust through which steam, ashes, and lava are forced out in periods of activity

Monitor Progress

Check Vocabulary

If...	then... review the
students are unable to place words on the web,	lesson concept. Place the words on the web and provide additional words for practice, such as *logging* and *meadows*.

SUCCESS PREDICTOR

DAY 1 Grouping Options

Reading

Whole Group

Introduce and discuss the Question of the Week. Then use pp. 112l–114b.

Group Time

Differentiated Instruction

Read this week's Leveled Readers. See pp. 112f–112g for the small group lesson plan.

Whole Group

Use p. 133a.

Language Arts

Use pp. 133e–133k.

Build Concepts

FLUENCY

MODEL PHRASING As you read "The Volcano Wakes," model how to group words in a meaningful way. While reading, be sure to use phrasing that keeps related words grouped together, such as prepositional phrases. Also use punctuation as cues for logical places to pause or take a breath.

LISTENING COMPREHENSION

After reading "The Volcano Wakes," use the following questions to assess listening comprehension.

1. **What is the main idea of the selection?** *(Possible response: After 123 years of inactivity, Mount St. Helens erupted in 1980.)* **Main Idea**

2. **How was Mount St. Helens formed?** *(Cooled lava, ash, and pumice from many different eruptions built up over thousands of years.)* **Details**

BUILD CONCEPT VOCABULARY

Start a web to build concepts and vocabulary related to this week's lesson and the unit theme.

- Draw The West Concept Web.
- Read the sentence with the word *earthquake* again. Ask students to pronounce *earthquake* and discuss its meaning.
- Place *earthquake* in an oval attached to *How the land was formed*. Discuss how *earthquake* is related to this concept. Read the sentences in which *eruptions* and *volcano* appear. Have students pronounce the words *volcano* and *eruptions*, place them on the Web, and give reasons.
- Brainstorm additional words and categories for the Web. Keep the Web on display and add words throughout the week.

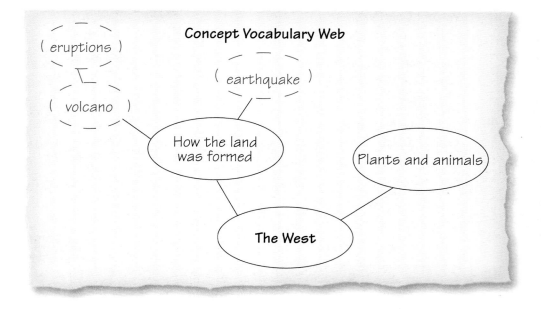

Concept Vocabulary Web
(eruptions)
(earthquake)
(volcano)
How the land was formed
Plants and animals
The West

THE VOLCANO WAKES

By Patricia Lauber

For many years the volcano slept. It was silent and still, big and beautiful. Then the volcano, which was named Mount St. Helens, began to stir. On March 20, 1980, it was shaken by a strong earthquake. The quake was a sign of movement inside St. Helens. It was a sign of a waking volcano that might soon erupt again.

Mount St. Helens was built by many eruptions over thousands of years. In each eruption hot rock from inside the earth forced its way to the surface. The rock was so hot that it was molten, or melted, and it had gases trapped in it. The name for such rock is magma. Once the molten rock reaches the surface it is called lava. In some eruptions the magma was fairly liquid. Its gases escaped gently. Lava flowed out of the volcano, cooled, and hardened. In other eruptions the magma was thick and sticky. Its gases burst out violently, carrying along sprays of molten rock. As it blasted into the sky, the rock cooled and hardened. Some of it rained down as ash—tiny bits of rock. Some rained down as pumice—frothy rock puffed up by gases.

Together the lava flows, ash, and pumice built a mountain with a bowl-shaped crater at its top. St. Helens grew to a height of 9,677 feet, so high that its peak was often hidden by clouds. Its big neighbors were built in the same way. Mount St. Helens is part of the Cascade Range, a chain of volcanoes that runs from northern California into British Columbia.

For well over a hundred years the volcano slept. Each spring, as winter snows melted, its slopes seemed to come alive. Wildflowers bloomed in meadows. Bees gathered pollen and nectar. Birds fed, found mates, and built nests. Bears lumbered out of their dens. Herds of elk and deer feasted on fresh green shoots. Thousands of people came to hike, picnic, camp, fish, paint, bird-watch, or just enjoy the scenery. Logging crews felled tall trees and planted seedlings.

These people knew that Mount St. Helens was a volcano, but they did not fear it. To them it was simply a green and pleasant mountain, where forests of firs stretched up the slopes and streams ran clear and cold.

The mountain did not seem so trustworthy to geologists, scientists who study the earth. They knew that Mount St. Helens was dangerous. It was a young volcano and one of the most active in the Cascade Range. In 1975 two geologists finished a study of the volcano's past eruptions. They predicted that Mount St. Helens would erupt again within 100 years, perhaps before the year 2000.

The geologists were right. With the earthquake of March 20, 1980, Mount St. Helens woke from a sleep of 123 years.

SKILLS ⟷ STRATEGIES IN CONTEXT

Main Idea
Graphic Organizers

OBJECTIVES

◎ Determine main idea and supporting details.

◎ Use a graphic organizer to identify main ideas and supporting details.

Skills Trace
◎ Main Idea and Details

Introduce/Teach	TE: 4.1 112–113; 4.2 240–241; 4.5 582–583
Practice	TE: 119, 123, 247, 251, 589, 595 PB: 43, 47, 48, 93, 97, 98, 233, 237, 238
Reteach/Review	TE: 4.1 75, 133b, DI-56; 4.2 225, 259b, DI-56; 4.4 475; 4.5 607b, DI-55 PB: 26, 86, 186
Test	Selection Test: 17–20, 37–40, 93–96; Benchmark Test: Unit 2

INTRODUCE

Write the topic "Hiking in National Parks" and add details: *Some parks have difficult trails that lead hikers to waterfalls and other natural wonders. Easy trails are also available.* Ask what might be the main idea in an article with this topic and details. (*National parks offer a wide range of trails for hikers.*)

Have students read the information on p. 112. Explain the following:

- Main ideas tell the central ideas of an article. Use a graphic organizer to record the most important points of an article.

- Supporting details expand on the main idea, providing more information about it.

Use Skill Transparency 5 to teach main idea and graphic organizers.

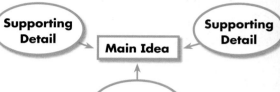

Comprehension

Skill
Main Idea and Details

Strategy
Graphic Organizers

 **Main Idea**
and Details

- The topic is what a paragraph, part of an article, or a whole article is about.

- The most important thing the author has to say about the topic is the main idea.

- The little pieces of information telling more about the main idea are the supporting details.

Supporting Detail → Main Idea ← Supporting Detail

Supporting Detail ↑

Strategy: Graphic Organizers

Active readers often use graphic organizers to help them understand what they read. Graphic organizers can be used before, during, or after reading. You can create a graphic organizer like the one above to help you remember the main idea and details.

Write to Read

1. Read "Send a Ranger!" Make a graphic organizer like the one above to help you understand the article.

2. Use your graphic organizer to help you write about a national park you have visited or would like to visit, and your reasons.

112

Strategic Intervention

◎ **Main Idea** Explain that a main idea is like the headline of a newspaper article. Display a few newspaper or magazine article headlines and ask pairs to discuss what kinds of details they would expect to read in the accompanying articles.

ELL

Access Content

Beginning/Intermediate For a Picture It! lesson on main idea and supporting details, see the ELL Teaching Guide, pp. 29–30.

Advanced Before reading "Send a Ranger!" point out the idiom *made up* in the first sentence of paragraph 1. Have volunteers rephrase this sentence.

SEND A RANGER!

The job of a ranger is made up of a lot of different jobs. • Park rangers are like police officers—they make sure people obey the rules of the park. Park rangers are like teachers—they take people on nature walks and tell them about important places in our history. Park rangers are like scientists—they keep track of information about plants and animals. Park rangers are like firefighters—they keep close watch to help put a stop to forest fires. Park rangers are like rescue workers—they hunt for people who are lost or hurt. •

Yes, the job of a park ranger is made up of a lot of different jobs. • In fact, Stephen Mather, the first director of the National Parks Service, has said: "If a trail is to be blazed, send a ranger; if an animal is floundering in the snow, send a ranger; if a bear is in a hotel, send a ranger; if a fire threatens a forest, send a ranger; and if someone is to be saved, send a ranger."

Does this sound like fun to you? Maybe you would like to be a park ranger.

> **1 Skill** The first sentence sounds like a big, overall main idea. Read on to see if this is so or if there is another bigger idea.

> **2 Skill** Is each example of a job a supporting detail or a new main idea?

> **3 Skill** Why do you think the author restated a sentence used earlier? Is this a clue about what the main idea is?

> **4 Strategy** On the graphic organizer, where would you put these additional jobs?

113

Available as **Skill Transparency** 5

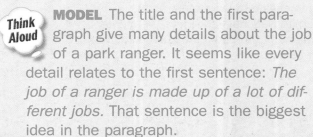

TEACH

1 SKILL Use paragraph 1 to model how to determine the main idea.

> **Think Aloud** **MODEL** The title and the first paragraph give many details about the job of a park ranger. It seems like every detail relates to the first sentence: *The job of a ranger is made up of a lot of different jobs.* That sentence is the biggest idea in the paragraph.

2 SKILL Discuss using a graphic organizer to record main ideas and details.

> **Think Aloud** **MODEL** If I wanted to complete a graphic organizer showing the main idea and details, I could use the first sentence of the article as the main idea. The examples of different jobs rangers do tell more about the main idea, so they could all be listed as supporting details.

PRACTICE AND ASSESS

3 SKILL The author restated the sentence to show that the second paragraph has the same main idea as the first paragraph.

4 STRATEGY The additional jobs the author mentions could be listed as supporting details on the graphic organizer.

WRITE Have students complete steps 1 and 2 of the Write to Read activity. If students have not visited a national park, have other students first describe their experiences or allow time for students to research a park.

Monitor Progress

 Main Idea

| **If...** students are unable to complete **Write to Read** on p. 112, | **then...** use Practice Book p. 43 to provide additional practice. |

Main Idea and Details

- The **main idea** is the most important idea from a paragraph, passage, or article.
- **Details** are small pieces of information that tell more about the main idea.

Directions Read the following passage. Then complete the diagram below.

Several people helped make Yellowstone National Park a protected place. In the 1600s and 1700s, fur trappers came through the area. They noticed its amazing features, such as geysers that shoot hot water high into the air. When they returned to towns and camps, they told stories about what they had seen.

Soon expeditions were organized to explore Yellowstone. The expedition led by Ferdinand Hayden in 1871 included a photographer and an artist who captured the beauty of Yellowstone in their pictures. They showed their pictures to Congress. In 1872, President Grant signed a law that made sure Yellowstone would be protected forever by making it the first national park.

Main Idea
1. Several people helped make Yellowstone a protected place.

Supporting Details
2. Fur trappers told stories about Yellowstone.
3. Expeditions came to explore Yellowstone.
4. Photographers and painters showed pictures of Yellowstone to Congress.
5. President Grant made Yellowstone into a national park.

School + Home **Home Activity** Your child read a short passage and identified the main idea and supporting details. Work with your child to create a graphic organizer that identifies the main idea and supporting details of an article about a natural area.

▲ **Practice Book** p. 43

Tech Files ONLINE Have students use a student-friendly search engine to learn more about Yosemite National Park. Have them enter the name of the park as the keywords for their search.

ELL

Build Background Use ELL Poster 5 to build background and vocabulary for the lesson concept of physical features of the West.

▲ ELL Poster 5

Build Background

ACTIVATE PRIOR KNOWLEDGE

BEGIN A KWL CHART about interesting natural sights in the West.

- Give students a few minutes to write what they know about natural sights found in the western United States. Have them think about what they know from books, travel brochures, postcards, TV programs, movies, or personal experiences. Record what students know in the first column of a KWL chart.

- Give students two minutes to write two questions they would like to answer as they read *Letters Home from Yosemite*. Write their questions in the second column of the KWL chart. Add a question of your own.

- Have students add any answers to their questions and any new information to the last column of the chart as they read.

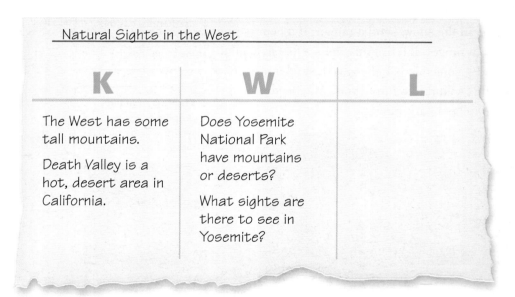

Natural Sights in the West

K	W	L
The West has some tall mountains. Death Valley is a hot, desert area in California.	Does Yosemite National Park have mountains or deserts? What sights are there to see in Yosemite?	

▲ **Graphic Organizer** 4

BACKGROUND BUILDING AUDIO This week's audio explores the work of a park ranger. After students listen, discuss the importance of preserving natural areas.

Background Building Audio

Introduce Vocabulary

ASK QUESTIONS

Display the lesson vocabulary words, and invite students to share what they already know about the meanings of these words. Have students look up the meanings of any unknown words in their glossary. Then ask the following questions to help students better understand the words' meanings. ***Activate Prior Knowledge***

• Is a ***glacier*** hot or cold? Is it large or small? Does it move quickly or slowly?

• How do you feel when you see an ***impressive*** sight in nature?

• In what kind of things does a ***naturalist*** study?

• If you want to ***preserve*** a forest, are you helping it or hurting it? Explain.

• What are the names of some animal ***species?***

• How are ***slopes*** different from mountain peaks?

• What sorts of things would you find in a ***wilderness?***

After discussing word meanings, students can write sentences that include lesson vocabulary words. You may wish to continue the activity using More Words to Know.

At the end of the week, students can work in pairs to ask and answer other questions involving lesson vocabulary.

Use the Multisyllabic Word Routine on p. DI·1 to help students read multisyllabic words.

Lesson Vocabulary

WORDS TO KNOW

T glacier a great mass of ice that moves very slowly down a mountain or along a valley, or spreading very slowly over a land area

T impressive able to impress the mind, feelings, conscience

T naturalist a person who studies living things

T preserve to keep from harm or change; protect

T slopes land that goes up or down at an angle

T species a set of related living things that share certain characteristics and that can interbreed

T wilderness a wild region with few or no people living in it

MORE WORDS TO KNOW

altitudes heights above Earth's surface

formations things that are formed

reservoir a place where water is collected and stored for use

T = Tested Word

Vocabulary

Directions Choose the word from the box that best matches each definition. Write the word on the line.

Check the Words You Know
—glacier
—impressive
—naturalist
—preserve
—slopes
—species
—wilderness

glacier _____ 1. a mass of ice moving very slowly down a mountain or along a valley

wilderness _____ 2. a wild place with few or no people living in it

preserve _____ 3. to keep from harm or change

naturalist _____ 4. a person who studies living things

species _____ 5. a set of related living things with similar characteristics

Directions Choose the word from the box that best matches the meaning of each underlined word. Write the word on the line.

slopes _____ 6. We went skiing down the snow-covered mountains.

impressive _____ 7. The scenery in the national park was magnificent.

preserve _____ 8. The park rangers want to keep changes from happening in the park.

glacier _____ 9. Long ago a large sheet of ice covered this whole area.

wilderness _____ 10. We camped out in a wild, isolated area.

Write a Poem
On a separate sheet of paper, write a poem about your favorite natural place. Use as many vocabulary words as you can.
Poems should include words from the vocabulary list and details about a natural place.

Home Activity Your child identified and used vocabulary words from *Letters Home from Yosemite*. Read a nonfiction article about a natural place with your child. Have your child create sentences in response to the article using the vocabulary words.

▲ **Practice Book** p. 44

Vocabulary Strategy

 Use word structure to determine word meaning.

INTRODUCE

Discuss the strategy for word structure by using the steps on p. 114.

TEACH

- Have students pay attention to words with the suffix *-ist* or *-ive* as they read "Letter from Denali."

- Model using a suffix to determine the meaning of *naturalist.*

Think Aloud **MODEL** If I cover the letters *-ist* in this word, I see the word *natural*. The suffix *-ist* can mean "one who is an expert in," so a *naturalist* could be a person who is an expert in natural things, or nature.

Words to Know

wilderness
preserve
species
naturalist
slopes
glacier
impressive

Remember

Try the strategy. Then, if you need more help, use your glossary or a dictionary.

Vocabulary Strategy
for Suffixes

Word Structure Suppose you are reading and you come to a word that has *-ist* or *-ive* at the end. You can use the suffix to help you figure out the word's meaning. The suffix *-ist* can make a word mean "one who is an expert in ____," as in *biologist,* an expert in biology. The suffix *-ive* can make a word mean "tending or inclined to ____," as in *active,* which means "tending to act."

1. Put your finger over the *-ist* or *-ive* suffix.

2. Look at the base word. Put the base word in the phrase "one who is an expert in ____" or "tending or inclined to ____."

3. Try that meaning in the sentence. Does it make sense?

As you read "Letter from Denali," look for words that end with *-ist* or *-ive.* Use the suffixes to help you figure out the meanings of the words.

114

DAY 2 **Grouping Options**

Reading
Whole Group Discuss the Question of the Day. Then use pp. 114–117.

Group Time Differentiated Instruction
Read *Letters Home from Yosemite.*
See pp. 112f–112g for the small group lesson plan.

Whole Group Use p. 133a.

Language Arts
Use pp. 133e–133k.

Strategic Intervention

Word Structure Write *naturalist* and *impressive* and draw a line before the suffix. Then show in words or pictures that a *naturalist* studies the *natural* world and *impressive* mountains *impress* visitors.

ELL

Access Content Use ELL Poster 5 to preteach vocabulary. Choose from the following to meet language proficiency levels.
Beginning Point out that *glacier* (p. 115, paragraph 3) is described as a "huge field of ice."
Intermediate After reading, have students fill out a word rating chart. Discuss words that students rate as *Have Seen* to consolidate meaning.
Advanced Teach the lesson on pp. 114–115. Have pairs take turns asking and answering questions about vocabulary words. (See p. 114b.)
Resources for home-language words may include parents, bilingual staff members, bilingual dictionaries, or online translation sources.

Letter from Denali

Dear Kevin,

Here we are in Denali National Park in Alaska. Denali is a gigantic park. It has more than 6 million acres of wilderness, so we certainly won't be seeing the whole park!

Denali was established to preserve the land and the animals and plants that live here. More than 650 species of flowering plants and 217 species of animals live in Denali! That's what the naturalist on the guided walk told us yesterday. She also said that to live in Denali year-round, a plant or animal species has to be able to survive long, cold winters.

Today we hiked up the lower slopes of Mt. McKinley. It is the highest mountain in North America, and it is part of Denali. We could see a giant glacier looking like a huge field of ice farther up on the mountain. It was a very impressive sight. Mt. McKinley has several glaciers, and some are more than 30 miles long!

I have taken a zillion pictures, but I really think this is a place you have to see in person.

Love,
Lisa

Words to Write

Write a letter to a friend. Describe a park or other natural setting that you have seen. Use some words from the Words to Know list.

115

PRACTICE AND ASSESS

- Have students determine the meanings of the remaining words and explain the strategy they used.
- Point out that the meaning of a suffix may not be enough information if the base word is not familiar. Students may need to look up a word in the glossary or a dictionary for an exact definition.
- Have students work in pairs, asking each other *either/or* questions like those on p. 114b about the vocabulary words, and any other words related to the natural world.
- Have students complete Practice Book p. 45.

WRITE Letters should include several lesson vocabulary words as well as words that describe the natural world.

Monitor Progress

Word Sturcture

If... students need more practice with the lesson vocabulary,	then... use Tested Vocabulary Cards.

Vocabulary • Word Structure

- A **suffix** is a syllable added to the end of a **base word** to change its meaning. You can use a suffix to figure out the meaning of an unfamiliar word.
- The suffix *-ist* can make a word mean "one who is an expert in." The suffix *-ive* means "tending or inclined to ____."

Directions Read the following passage. Then answer the questions below.

On our sunrise hike through the extensive wilderness, the naturalist told us that the park was filled with many species of animals. It was impressive to think that so many different animals could live in the same place. She also told us that to preserve the park, we needed to leave it like we had never been there. We couldn't take any flowers or plants with us, and we shouldn't leave our garbage there either. Unfortunately, visitors in the past had not been so careful. Restoring the park to its natural state is a massive job.

1. What is the suffix in the word *extensive*? What does it tell you about the meaning of the word?

   -ive; The word means "inclined to extend," or "goes on and on."

2. What does *naturalist* mean? How do you know?

   Naturalist means "a person who is an expert in nature"; The suffix *-ist* means "one who is an expert in."

3. What does *impressive* mean? How do you know?

   "tending to impress"; The suffix *-ive* means "tending to."

4. What does the word *massive* mean?

   It means "tending to mass," or "tending to be very large."

5. Write two other words that end in either *-ist* or *-ive.*

   Possible answers: biologist, captive

School + Home **Home Activity** Your child read a short passage and identified suffixes to understand words in a passage. Read an article with your child. Help your child to identify and circle the suffixes added to words in the article.

▲ **Practice Book** p. 45

Prereading Strategies

GENRE STUDY

Narrative Nonfiction

Letters Home from Yosemite is narrative nonfiction. Narrative nonfiction presents information about true events in a specific sequence, often in chronological order.

PREVIEW AND PREDICT

Have students preview the title and photographs and discuss the kinds of information the selection might provide. Encourage students to use lesson vocabulary words as they make predictions about the selection's content.

Strategy Response Log

Activate Prior Knowledge Have students write notes about what they already know about national parks in general and anything specific about Yosemite National Park. Students will monitor their comprehension by listing new information in the Strategy Response Log activity on p. 123.

Letters Home from Yosemite

by Lisa Halvorsen

Genre

Narrative nonfiction tells the story of real people, places, or events. The narrator, or teller of the story, presents information in sequence. Notice this sequence as you read about Yosemite National Park.

116

ELL

Access Content Lead a picture walk, pointing out the photographs and other items the author shows from her trip to Yosemite National Park.

Consider having students read the selection summary in English or in students' home languages. See the Multilingual Summaries in the ELL Teaching Guide, pp. 33–35.

Why do so many people travel to Yosemite National Park?

117

SET PURPOSE

Read the first page of the selection aloud as students follow along. Have them set a purpose about what they hope to learn as they read.

Remind students to look for main ideas and supporting details as they read.

STRATEGY RECALL

Students have now used these before-reading strategies:

- preview the selection to be aware of its genre, features, and possible content;
- activate prior knowledge about that content and what to expect of that genre;
- make predictions;
- set a purpose for reading.

Remind students to be aware of and flexibly use the during-reading strategies they have learned:

- link prior knowledge to new information;
- summarize text they have read so far;
- ask clarifying questions;
- answer questions they or others pose;
- check their predictions and either refine them or make new predictions;
- recognize the text structure the author is using, and use that knowledge to make predictions and increase comprehension;
- visualize what the author is describing;
- monitor their comprehension and use fix-up strategies.

After reading, students will use these strategies:

- summarize or retell the text;
- answer questions they or others pose;
- reflect to make new information become part of their prior knowledge.

Audio CD   AudioText

Guiding Comprehension

1 🎯 **Main Idea • Inferential**

Reread p. 119, paragraph 2. What is the main idea and one supporting detail?

Main idea: Yosemite is in the Sierra Nevada, a large mountain chain in California. Supporting detail: Yosemite is right in the middle of the Sierra Nevada range.

Monitor Progress

🎯 Main Idea/Details

If... students are unable to determine the main idea and a supporting detail,	**then**... use the skill and strategy instruction on p. 119.

---

2 **Draw Conclusions • Critical**

Based on what you have read, what can you conclude about the author? Give reasons to support your answer.

Possible responses: The author is excited about the trip because she is interested in nature and history. She uses exclamations and words such as *amazing* and *incredible*.

Tech Files
ONLINE

Have students choose a topic from pp. 118–119 and search the Internet or an electronic encyclopedia for more information. Remind students to use a student-friendly search engine and specific keywords for their search, such as *John Muir* or *Miwok Indians*. Be sure to follow classroom rules for Internet use.

Arrival in . . . *San Francisco*

As our plane touched down in San Francisco, I knew we were in for an exciting vacation. I'd been reading about Yosemite on the plane. I learned that it is America's third national park. Yosemite is known throughout the world for its amazing scenery. It has incredible waterfalls, rock formations, alpine lakes and meadows, and giant sequoia trees. It's located in the east central part of California and covers 1,170 square miles. That's an area about the size of Rhode Island!

Efforts to protect the wilderness around Yosemite began in 1864. That's when President Abraham Lincoln signed the Yosemite Grant deeding the land to California. Yosemite was finally established as a national park on Oct. 1, 1890, by an act of Congress.

Views of **Yosemite**

118

Access Content Point out measurements on pp. 118–119: 1,170 square miles, 430 miles, and 15.5 million acres. The metric equivalents are 3,042 square kilometers, 688 kilometers, and 6.2 hectares. Students can use a map to measure and compare the size of their state to understand these measurements.

Yosemite Valley

Topography

Our tour guide said that one of the first people to visit this area was John Muir, a Scottish naturalist. He fought hard to convince the U.S. government to preserve Yosemite as a national park. The name supposedly comes from the Indian name "yo'hem-iteh." That means grizzly bear.

Yosemite is right in the middle of the Sierra Nevada ❶ Mountains. These mountains stretch for 430 miles along California's eastern border. The area covers 15.5 million acres, which is about the size of Vermont, New Hampshire, and Connecticut combined! This is the highest and longest single continuous range of mountains in the lower 48 states (not including Alaska and Hawaii).

Native Americans were the first people to live in Yosemite, about 7,000 to 10,000 years ago. When explorers arrived at Yosemite Valley in the 1830s and 1840s, Southern Sierra Miwok Indians were living there. They called the Yosemite Valley "Ahwahnee" (Place of the Gaping Mouth). ❷

Sierra Nevadas from east of Tioga Pass

119

Sierra Nevada

TIME FOR Science

The Sierra Nevada is a mountain range that runs north and south along the eastern edge of California. This region once lay under the sea. Mountains formed as the sea bed was thrust upward. Melted rock from below Earth's surface cooled into granite formations. Glaciers from the Pleistocene (PLEYE stuh seen) Period helped shape the surface of the mountains, leaving high, unusual rock formations such as Half Dome and El Capitan in Yosemite Valley.

Much of the mining during the California Gold Rush took place in the Sierra Nevada. Later, logging became another important industry. Today, the area is known for its tourism and recreation.

SKILLS ↔ STRATEGIES IN CONTEXT

Main Idea

TEACH

- Remind students that the main idea makes an important point about the topic and has at least one supporting detail.
- Supporting details are smaller pieces of information that develop the main idea.
- Main ideas are not always stated directly.
- Model finding the main idea of p. 119, paragraph 2.

Think Aloud **MODEL** This paragraph does not have one most important statement, so I'll read each sentence and decide how they are related. The first sentence mentions Yosemite and the Sierra Nevada. The rest of the sentences tell where these mountains are located and how big they are. I think the main idea is that Yosemite is in the Sierra Nevada, a large mountain chain in California.

PRACTICE AND ASSESS

Have students read p. 119, paragraph 3. Ask which sentence is the main idea. *(Choice b)*

a) Yosemite Valley's name means "Place of the Gaping Mouth."

b) Native Americans lived in Yosemite long ago.

c) Explorers visited Yosemite in the 1830s and 1840s.

EXTEND SKILLS

Personal Essay

Explain that a personal essay is a brief discussion about a specific topic. It often includes informal language, and the author may share personal feelings and experiences as well as factual details. Have students find a sentence on p. 119 that shows the author is relating a personal experience.

Guiding Comprehension

3 **Compare and Contrast • Inferential**

How is a visit to Yosemite today different from when the first tourists arrived? How is it similar?

Possible responses: Millions more people visit each year than in the past. People use cars and buses to get to the park, instead of horses. The natural sights are probably the same. Some places still only can be reached on horseback. People still find the sights amazing.

4 🎯 **Vocabulary • Word Structure**

Have students use word structure to identify the base word for *impressive* on p. 121 and then give its meaning.

Base word: impress. Meaning: to have a strong effect on the mind.

Monitor Progress
🎯 **Word Structure**

If... students have difficulty using suffixes to determine word meaning,	**then...** use the vocabulary strategy instruction on p. 121.

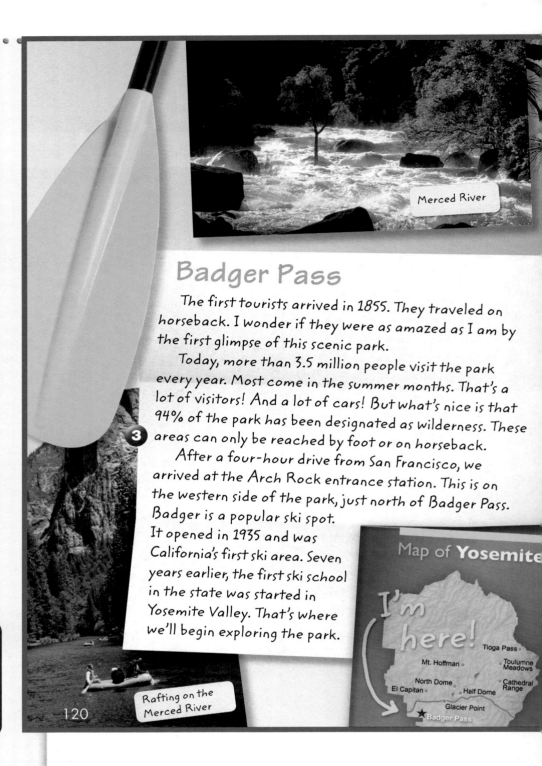

Merced River

Badger Pass

The first tourists arrived in 1855. They traveled on horseback. I wonder if they were as amazed as I am by the first glimpse of this scenic park.

Today, more than 3.5 million people visit the park every year. Most come in the summer months. That's a lot of visitors! And a lot of cars! But what's nice is that 94% of the park has been designated as wilderness. These areas can only be reached by foot or on horseback.

After a four-hour drive from San Francisco, we arrived at the Arch Rock entrance station. This is on the western side of the park, just north of Badger Pass. Badger is a popular ski spot. It opened in 1935 and was California's first ski area. Seven years earlier, the first ski school in the state was started in Yosemite Valley. That's where we'll begin exploring the park.

3

Map of **Yosemite**

I'm here!

Tioga Pass

Mt. Hoffman

Toulumne Meadows

North Dome

El Capitan

Half Dome

Cathedral Range

Glacier Point

★ Badger Pass

Rafting on the Merced River

120

ELL

Extend Language Point out the comparative adjectives *bigger*, *higher*, and *more impressive* (p. 121, paragraph 3). Explain these words compare two things. Comparatives are formed by adding *-er* to short adjectives or by placing the word *more* in front of longer adjectives. You can provide similar explanations of superlatives.

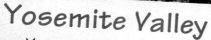

Yosemite Valley

Yosemite Valley

Yosemite Valley is only seven miles long and one mile wide, but it's where the most services are. Our campground is here, and so are many of the park's best natural attractions. It's the most heavily visited part of the park.

Today, we learned about the Miwok and Paiute people, and about the natural history of the park. Then we hopped on the shuttle bus to see famous sights like Yosemite Falls, El Capitan, and Happy Isles. One of my favorite places was Mirror Lake, where we saw Tenaya Canyon reflected in the water.

Bridalveil Creek/Fall

It seems that wherever we look, there's something bigger, higher, or more impressive than before. More than half of America's highest waterfalls are found in Yosemite. One of the prettiest is Bridalveil Fall. It is located near the entrance to Yosemite Valley.

The Ahwahneechee called Bridalveil Fall "Pohono." It means "spirit of the puffing wind." Sometimes hard winds actually blow the falls sideways! I'm glad I brought my raincoat because we got soaked by the spray on the way up! This waterfall is 620 feet high. That's as tall as a 62-story building!

Bridalveil Fall

121

TEACH

Read the first paragraph under the heading *Bridalveil Creek/Fall* on p. 121. Model using word structure to determine the meaning of *impressive*.

Think Aloud **MODEL** The word *impressive* has the suffix *-ive* at the end. I know the suffix *-ive* means "tending or inclined to." When I put my finger over the *-ive*, I see the base word *impress*. So *impressive* means "tending to or inclined to have a strong effect on the mind." Something that impresses me is special or amazing. I'll try that meaning in the sentence to see if it makes sense. The author keeps seeing impressive sights that amaze her.

PRACTICE AND ASSESS

Explain that the suffix *-ist* can make a word mean "a person who does or makes a ____" or "a person who is an expert in _____." Have students determine which meaning of *-ist* helps them define *tourists* on p. 120, paragraph 1. *(People who do a tour.)* To assess, have them use *tourists* in another sentence.

Types of Rocks

The three main types of rocks are igneous, sedimentary, and metamorphic. Igneous rocks are formed when melted rock from deep under Earth's surface rises up through cracks in Earth's crust and cools. Sedimentary rocks form when layers of decayed plants and animals and older rocks get compressed or harden. Metamorphic rocks are those that have changed from one form to another by either heat or pressure. The rock formations in and around Yosemite are made of granite, a type of igneous rock. Quartz and feldspar are two minerals commonly found in granite. Because of its hardness, granite is often used for building and paving.

Guiding Comprehension

5 ⊙ **Main Idea • Inferential**

Have students determine the main idea and supporting details on p. 122, paragraph 1.

Main idea: Giant sequoias are the world's largest trees and among the oldest trees on Earth. Supporting details: 300 feet tall and 40 feet around; can live more than 3,000 years

6 **Author's Craft • Critical**

Question the Author **Why do you think the author includes the names of several giant sequoias on p. 122?**

Possible response: Names of trees tell about their shape or size; the author includes the nicknames to help readers visualize the trees.

Monitor Progress
⊙ **Main Idea**

If... students have difficulty determining the main idea and supporting details,	**then...** use the skill and strategy instruction on p. 123.

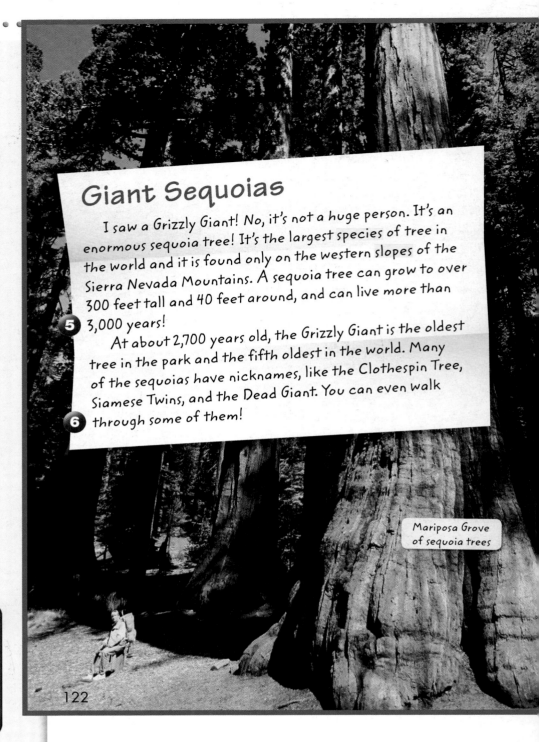

Giant Sequoias

I saw a Grizzly Giant! No, it's not a huge person. It's an enormous sequoia tree! It's the largest species of tree in the world and it is found only on the western slopes of the Sierra Nevada Mountains. A sequoia tree can grow to over 300 feet tall and 40 feet around, and can live more than 3,000 years!

At about 2,700 years old, the Grizzly Giant is the oldest tree in the park and the fifth oldest in the world. Many of the sequoias have nicknames, like the Clothespin Tree, Siamese Twins, and the Dead Giant. You can even walk through some of them!

Mariposa Grove of sequoia trees

122

E L L

Access Content Explain that a *cute teddy bear* (p. 123, paragraph 1) refers to a stuffed toy bear. Help students use context to understand the meaning of *dangerous* (rip open a tent; break into a car).

Bobcat

Yosemite Wildlife

I'm so excited! This morning on our way to Glacier Point we saw a black bear and her two cubs. The young ones were as cute as teddy bears. The ranger reminded us how dangerous these bears really are. They have a very strong sense of smell and will rip open a tent or even break into a car to get food! That's why we put all our food—and even our toothpaste—in the bear-proof metal box at the campground.

An adult black bear can weigh as much as 500 pounds. The average size is about 300 pounds. Not all of them are black. They may be brown, cinnamon, or sometimes tan. Between 300 to 500 bears live in the park.

We have seen a ton of mule deer since we arrived. They like to graze along the roadsides and in the meadows in the early morning and late afternoon. They can be just as aggressive as bears when approached. Mule deer have long ears like mules. They can run up to 35 miles an hour and can jump 24 feet in a single leap. You'd never know it from looking at them!

The park is also home to mountain lions, bobcats, coyotes, black-tailed jackrabbits, yellow-bellied marmots, rattlesnakes, and California bighorn sheep. Thousands of sheep once roamed the slopes of the Sierra Nevada Mountains. They were nearly wiped out by hunters, disease,

Mule deer

Black bear

Develop Vocabulary

PRACTICE LESSON VOCABULARY

Students orally respond *yes* or *no* to each question and provide a reason for each answer. Possible responses are given.

1. Does a *naturalist* study how people live in cities? *(No; a naturalist studies plants and animals in nature.)*

2. Would you likely find trees and streams in the *wilderness*? *(Yes; trees, streams, and wild animals can be found in the wilderness.)*

3. Is an *impressive* sight boring? *(No; an impressive sight is exciting or interesting.)*

BUILD CONCEPT VOCABULARY

Review previous concept words with students. Ask if students have come across any words today in their reading or elsewhere that they would like to add to The West Concept Web, such as *mountains* or *waterfalls*.

SKILLS ◄► STRATEGIES IN CONTEXT

Main Idea Graphic Organizer

TEACH

- Main ideas may or may not be stated directly. Have students identify some of the main ideas read thus far.
- A graphic organizer can help students record and remember main ideas and supporting details.
- Model using a main idea chart to determine the main idea of p. 122, paragraph 1.

Think Aloud

MODEL Sometimes taking a close look at supporting details helps me figure out the main idea. Details on this page tell about giant sequoia trees. I'll write these details in the boxes at the bottom of the chart. Next, I'll write a main idea that connects these details: Giant sequoias are the largest and one of the oldest species of trees in the world.

PRACTICE AND ASSESS

Have students reread the first three paragraphs on p. 123 and use a main idea chart to record main ideas and supporting details about Yosemite wildlife.

Strategy Response Log

Monitor Comprehension Have students review the notes on national parks and Yosemite they wrote before they began the selection. (See p. 116.) Then have students record three new facts they have learned about Yosemite, as well as questions they have about their reading.

If you want to teach this selection in two sessions, stop here.

Guiding Comprehension

If you are teaching the story in two days, discuss the main ideas presented so far and review the vocabulary.

7 **Fact and Opinion • Critical**

Which sentences in the first paragraph under the heading *Glacier Point* are statements of opinion? How can you tell?

The first and last sentences. They cannot be proved true or false.

8 **Graphic Sources • Critical**

The photograph on p. 125 shows El Capitan. Use it to draw a conclusion about the people who climb El Capitan?

Possible response: It shows how steep El Capitan is, so the climbers must be highly skilled and adventurous.

DAY 3 **Grouping Options**

Reading

Whole Group Discuss the Question of the Day.

Group Time Differentiated Instruction

Read *Letters Home from Yosemite.* See pp. 112f–112g for the small group lesson plan.

Whole Group Discuss the Reader Response questions on p. 128. Then use p. 133a.

Language Arts
Use pp. 133e–133k.

Steller's jay

and lack of food. A ranger said they were successfully reintroduced to the park in 1986.

More than 240 species of birds have been spotted in Yosemite. Some of them are endangered, like the willow flycatcher and the great gray owl. Some—like the bald eagle—just spend the winter in the park. My favorite is the Steller's jay, a noisy blue bird with a black crest. It will steal food off your plate if you don't watch out!

I also like to watch bats swooping through the air to catch insects. Did you know that one bat can eat up to 600 mosquito-sized insects in an hour? Yosemite has 15 species of bats. These include the rare spotted bat, which has big ears and three white spots on its back.

Glacier Point

7 The view from Glacier Point was totally awesome. It made me dizzy to look over the edge. It's 3,200 feet—a little more than a 1/2 mile—straight down to the floor of Yosemite Valley! In the distance I could see Yosemite Falls. I could also see El Capitan and Half Dome. I like the way light reflected off the bare rock surfaces at sunrise and sunset, "painting" them pink, purple, and gold.

The ranger told us that this is a good place to see peregrine falcons in flight. They can dive at speeds up to 200 miles per hour and catch their prey in mid-air. They nest in high places on very narrow rock ledges.

124

ELL

Context Clues Have students use context clues to understand unfamiliar terms such as *willow flycatcher*, *great gray owl,* and *Steller's jay* (p. 124, paragraph 1). The first sentence of the paragraph and the picture of a Steller's jay indicate that these are names for different species of birds.

El Capitan

El Capitan is Spanish for "the Captain." This is the biggest single block of granite on Earth. It is more than 3,600 feet from its base to its top. It's a favorite climbing spot for visitors from all over the world. It can take anywhere from several hours to several days to scale this rock. So it's not unusual to see people camped out on the rock ledges.

The highest single waterfall on the North American continent is Ribbon Fall. It plunges 1,612 feet off a cliff on the west side of El Capitan.

125

Glaciers

Glaciers form when the amount of snowfall is greater than the amount of snow that melts or evaporates. Over time, the weight of snow pressing downward forms an icy layer at the bottom. The melting and refreezing of this bottom layer causes a glacier to move. Glaciers may move from less than a foot to more than 100 feet in a day. The movement causes erosion because the glacier pushes rocks along its path and grinds the earth's surface as it moves. Glaciers may carve U-shaped valleys or create other identifiable shapes. They also leave behind large deposits of sand and rock.

SKILLS ⟷ STRATEGIES IN CONTEXT

Fact and Opinion REVIEW

TEACH

- Remind students that statements of fact can be proved true or false.
- Statements of opinion tell about a person's beliefs, feelings, or way of thinking that cannot be proved true or false.
- Model how to analyze the first sentence under the heading *Glacier Point*.

Think Aloud **MODEL** The sentence is a statement of opinion because the author writes that the view from Glacier Point is "totally awesome." She gives reasons that support her opinion, but it isn't a statement you can prove true or false.

PRACTICE AND ASSESS

- Have students read the text for *Glacier Point* and identify a statement of fact. Have them give reasons to support their answers. (Facts: *height of Glacier Point; speeds and nesting places of peregrine falcons.*)
- To assess, use Practice Book p. 46.

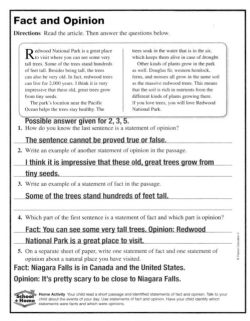

Fact and Opinion

Directions Read the article. Then answer the questions below.

Redwood National Park is a great place to visit where you can see some very tall trees. Some of the trees stand hundreds of feet tall. Besides being tall, the trees can also be very old. In fact, redwood trees can live for 2,000 years. I think it is very impressive that these old, great trees grow from tiny seeds.

The park's location near the Pacific Ocean helps the trees stay healthy. The trees soak in the water that is in the air, which keeps them alive in case of drought.

Other kinds of plants grow in the park as well. Douglas fir, western hemlock, ferns, and mosses all grow in the same soil as the massive redwood trees. This means that the soil is rich in nutrients from the different kinds of plants growing there. If you love trees, you will love Redwood National Park.

Possible answer given for 2, 3, 5.

1. How do you know the last sentence is a statement of opinion?
   The sentence cannot be proved true or false.

2. Write an example of another statement of opinion in the passage.
   I think it is impressive that these old, great trees grow from tiny seeds.

3. Write an example of a statement of fact in the passage.
   Some of the trees stand hundreds of feet tall.

4. Which part of the first sentence is a statement of fact and which part is opinion?
   Fact: You can see some very tall trees. Opinion: Redwood National Park is a great place to visit.

5. On a separate sheet of paper, write one statement of fact and one statement of opinion about a natural place you have visited.
   Fact: Niagara Falls is in Canada and the United States.
   Opinion: It's pretty scary to be close to Niagara Falls.

Home Activity Your child read a short passage and identified statements of fact and opinion. Talk to your child about the events of your day. Use statements of fact and opinion. Have your child identify which statements were facts and which were opinions.

▲ **Practice Book** p. 46

Guiding Comprehension

9 🎧 **Main Idea • Literal**

What does the author mean that "all together" Yosemite Falls are the highest in North America?

There are three sections of falls with a total height of 2,425 feet.

10 **Cause and Effect • Critical**

What causes more water to go over Yosemite Falls in the spring and early summer than near the end of summer?

In spring and early summer, snow high in the mountains melts. This causes large amounts of water to fall.

11 🎧 **Facts and Details • Literal**

Text to World **What important ideas and details have you learned about the physical features of Yosemite?**

Responses should include information about formations such as Glacier Point, El Capitan, and Yosemite Valley, as well as waterfalls and glaciers in the park.

Strategy Response Log

Summarize When students finish reading the selection, provide this prompt: Suppose that a friend was planning a visit to Yosemite. Summarize what you learned from the selection to help your friend decide what to see there.

Yosemite Falls

Yosemite Falls

9 All together, Yosemite Falls are the highest waterfalls in North America and rank number five in the world. There are actually three sections of falls, one on top of the other. The total drop is 2,425 feet, which is as high as 13 Niagara Falls!

In late spring and early summer, so much water goes over the falls that you can feel the ground shake! By the end of the summer, the falls may be no more than a **10** trickle. And some years they dry up all together.

126

ELL

Extend Language If students are unfamiliar with the word *differ* on p. 127, paragraph 4, name other words in the word family, such as *different* or *difference*. Have students tell how trees in Tioga Pass differ from the sequoias.

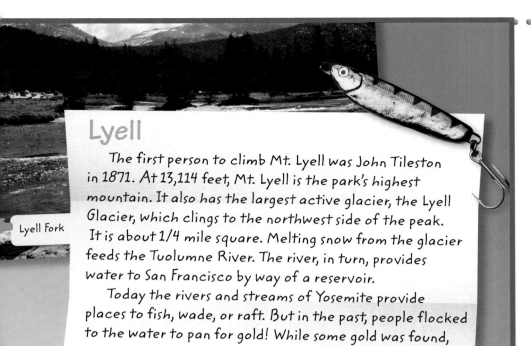

Lyell

The first person to climb Mt. Lyell was John Tileston in 1871. At 13,114 feet, Mt. Lyell is the park's highest mountain. It also has the largest active glacier, the Lyell Glacier, which clings to the northwest side of the peak. It is about 1/4 mile square. Melting snow from the glacier feeds the Tuolumne River. The river, in turn, provides water to San Francisco by way of a reservoir.

Today the rivers and streams of Yosemite provide places to fish, wade, or raft. But in the past, people flocked to the water to pan for gold! While some gold was found, the area did not yield as much of this precious metal as the foothills to the west of the park did.

Lyell Fork

Tioga Pass

On our last day we drove over Tioga Pass. It's 9,945 feet above sea level. It's the highest highway pass in the Sierra Nevada range and in all of California.

Because it's so high, many flowers and plants that grow here differ from those in lower elevations such as the Yosemite Valley. The trees are also small and stunted, because it's difficult for them to grow at such high altitudes.

Wherever you go—high in the mountains, or low in the valleys—Yosemite is truly one of the most awesome places on Earth! **11**

Tioga Pass

127

Develop Vocabulary

PRACTICE LESSON VOCABULARY

As a class, complete the following sentences orally. Possible responses given.

1. Two *species* of animals commonly found in Yosemite are (*black bears and mule deer*).

2. *Slopes* would likely be found (*on the sides of mountains and valleys.*)

3. A *glacier* would likely be found in (*a cold place with lots of snow.*)

4. When someone tries to *preserve* an area, he or she wants to (keep it from changing).

BUILD CONCEPT VOCABULARY

Review previous concept words with students. Ask if students have come across any words today in their reading or elsewhere that they would like to add to The West Concept Web, such as *valleys* or *gold*.

STRATEGY SELF-CHECK

Graphic Organizer

Ask students to determine the main idea for the selection. Use a main idea chart and list the main ideas from different parts of the selection as supporting details. Students can use this information to state the main idea of the entire selection. Use Practice Book p. 47.

SELF-CHECK

Students can ask themselves these questions to assess their understanding of the selection.

- Was I able to identify the main idea of the selection and the supporting details?
- How does a graphic organizer help me understand and remember the selection's main idea and supporting details?

Monitor Progress

Main Idea and Details

If... students have difficulty using a graphic organizer to identify the main idea and supporting details,	**then...** use the Reteach lesson on p. 133b.

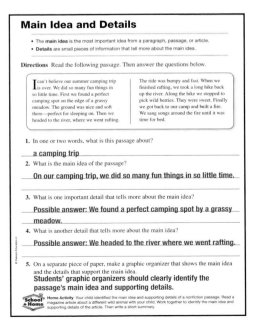

Main Idea and Details

- The **main idea** is the most important idea from a paragraph, passage, or article.
- **Details** are small pieces of information that tell more about the main idea.

Directions Read the following passage. Then answer the questions below.

I can't believe our summer camping trip is over. We did so many fun things in so little time. First we found a perfect camping spot on the edge of a grassy meadow. The ground was nice and soft there—perfect for sleeping on. Then we headed to the river, where we went rafting. The ride was bumpy and fast. When we finished rafting, we took a long hike back up the river. Along the hike we stopped to pick wild berries. They were sweet. Finally we got back to our camp and built a fire. We sang songs around the fire until it was time for bed.

1. In one or two words, what is this passage about?
   a camping trip

2. What is the main idea of the passage?
   On our camping trip, we did so many fun things in so little time.

3. What is one important detail that tells more about the main idea?
   Possible answer: We found a perfect camping spot by a grassy meadow.

4. What is another detail that tells more about the main idea?
   Possible answer: We headed to the river where we went rafting.

5. On a separate piece of paper, make a graphic organizer that shows the main idea and the details that support the main idea.
   Students' graphic organizers should clearly identify the passage's main idea and supporting details.

Home Activity Your child identified the main idea and supporting details of a nonfiction passage. Read a magazine article about a different wild animal with your child. Work together to identify the main idea and supporting details of the article. Then write a short summary.

▲ **Practice Book** p. 47

Reader Response

Open for Discussion Personal Response

Think Aloud

MODEL There are many amazing sights in Yosemite. I love waterfalls, so I would put visiting the falls near the top of my list.

Comprehension Check Critical Response

1. Possible response: Using letters and photographs makes the selection more interesting because it feels like you're really there. ***Author's Purpose***

2. The main idea is stated in the first sentence. Details include the rock formations and their colors at sunrise and sunset. ⊙ ***Main Idea***

3. Main idea: People visit Yosemite to see the scenery and wildlife. Details: Unusual rock formations. Plants and wildlife: giant sequoias, mule deer, brown bears. ⊙ ***Graphic Organizers***

4. Responses should include Words to Know to describe wonders such as mountains with glaciers or wildlife. ⊙ ***Vocabulary***

TEST PRACTICE ✓ **Look Back and Write** For test practice, assign a 10–15 minute time limit. For assessment, see the Scoring Rubric at the right.

Retell

Have students retell *Letters Home from Yosemite*.

Monitor Progress
Check Retelling Rubric ④③②①

If... students have difficulty retelling the selection,	**then...** use the Retelling Cards and the Scoring Rubric for Retelling on p. 129 to assist fluent retelling.

SUCCESS PREDICTOR

ELL

Check Retelling Have students use the subheads to guide their retellings. Let students listen to other retellings before attempting their own. For more ideas on assessing students' retellings, see the ELL and Transition Handbook.

Reader Response

Open for Discussion Make a list of the things you'll do on a future trip to Yosemite. Put the best thing at the top.

1. Why do you think the author chose to use letters and photographs to tell about Yosemite? **Think Like an Author**

2. Reread the letter from Glacier Point on page 124. What sentence states the main idea of the passage? What supporting details can you find? **Main Idea and Details**

3. Create a main idea chart for the selection. Draw a box on top of your paper and record the selection's main idea in it. Next, connect boxes to it and fill them in with details that support the main idea. **Graphic Organizers**

4. The author uses the word *impressive* to describe many wonders in Yosemite. Tell about some of these wonders, and explain how they would be impressive. Use words from the Words to Know list. **Vocabulary**

TEST PRACTICE ✓ **Look Back and Write** At Yosemite, someone says, "It all started with Abraham Lincoln." What does this person mean? Reread page 118 and then explain the statement.

Meet author Lisa Halvorsen on page 773.

128

Scoring Rubric Look Back and Write

Top-Score Response A top-score response uses information from page 118 to explain the statement, "It all started with Abraham Lincoln."

Example of a Top-Score Response In 1864, President Lincoln signed a document called the Yosemite Grant. It gave Yosemite and the land around it to California. In 1890, Yosemite became a national park through an act of Congress.

For additional rubrics, see p. WA10.

Write Now
Narrative Writing

Prompt

In *Letters Home from Yosemite*, the author tells about a special trip.

Think about a trip you have taken—maybe for a vacation or family visit.

Now write a narrative describing a special experience from that trip.

Writing Trait

Conventions are rules about grammar, spelling, punctuation, and capitalization. Correct conventions will make your narrative smooth.

Student Model

Writer uses <u>conventions</u>, including commas, to help readers read fluently.

Writer uses figurative language to help describe interesting incidents.

Compound sentences, different sentence lengths, and an exclamation add to style.

> Last summer, my family and I got lucky. We got an extra day of vacation. We were visiting my cousins in Minnesota, and I didn't want to say good-bye. Finally, we headed to the airport. I cried the whole way. When we got to the airport, they told us our plane was delayed. There was nothing to do but sit and wait. I didn't think it could get any worse, but it did. Suddenly the sky got very dark, as if a curtain had been drawn.
>
> Then there was an announcement. Our flight was canceled, and there were no more flights until the next day. Mom called my aunt and uncle. They came back to the airport to pick us up, and we were back at their house before the first raindrop fell. It was the best thunderstorm ever!

Use the model to help you write your own narrative.

129

Write Now

Look at the Prompt Have students identify and discuss key words and phrases in the prompt. *(trip, narrative, special experience)*

Strategies to Develop Conventions

Have students

- read their narratives aloud, pausing at each comma and stopping at each period.
- trade stories with a partner to peer-edit.
- use a dictionary to confirm spelling of unfamiliar words.

NO: It was a disasterous huricane!

YES: It was a disastrous hurricane!

For additional suggestions and rubric, see pp. 133g–133h.

Hints for Better Writing

- Carefully read the prompt.
- Use a graphic organizer to plan your writing.
- Support your ideas with information and details.
- Use words that help readers understand.
- Proofread and edit your work.

Scoring Rubric — Expository Retelling

Rubric 4 3 2 1	4	3	2	1
Connections	Makes connections and generalizes beyond the text	Makes connections to other events, texts, or experiences	Makes a limited connection to another event, text, or experience	Makes no connection to another event, text, or experience
Author's Purpose	Elaborates on author's purpose	Tells author's purpose with some clarity	Makes some connection to author's purpose	Makes no connection to author's purpose
Topic	Describes the main topic	Identifies the main topic with some details early in retelling	Identifies the main topic	Retelling has no sense of topic
Important Ideas	Gives accurate information about events, steps, and ideas using details and key vocabulary	Gives accurate information about events, steps, and ideas with some detail and key vocabulary	Gives limited or inaccurate information about events, steps, and ideas	Gives no information about events, steps, and ideas
Conclusions	Draws conclusions and makes inferences to generalize beyond the text	Draws conclusions about the text	Is able to draw few conclusions about the text	Is unable to draw conclusions or make inferences about the text

Retelling Plan

☑ **Week 1** Assess Strategic Intervention students.

☑ **Week 2** Assess Advanced students.

☑ **Week 3** Assess Strategic Intervention students.

☑ **Week 4** Assess On-Level students.

☑ **This week assess any students you have not yet checked during this unit.**

Use the Retelling Chart on p. TR17 to record retelling.

Selection Test To assess with *Letters Home from Yosemite*, use Selection Tests, pp. 17–20.

Fresh Reads for Differentiated Test Practice For weekly leveled practice, use pp. 25–30.

Retelling

SUCCESS PREDICTOR

Poetry

PREVIEW/USE TEXT FEATURES

Have students preview the illustrations and subheadings in "This Land Is Your Land" and scan some of the text in the song's chorus and verses. After students preview, ask:

How is a chorus different from verses in a song? *(The chorus is repeated; the other verses are sung only once.)*

Link to Social Studies

Have students brainstorm in groups. To help identify songs to list on the chart, hum or give clues about a few familiar songs from a songbook. Then students can name the song and consider the most suitable category for it.

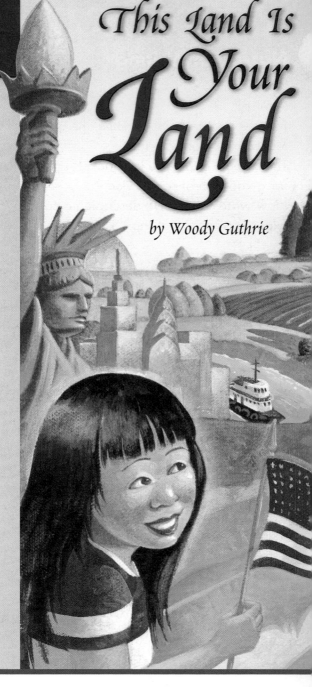

Poetry

Song

Genre

- **Songs are really poems. The lines rhyme and have rhythm so that they can be sung to a melody.**
- **Patriotic songs are about a topic important to a whole nation.**
- **This song begins with the chorus, the part of the song that is repeated after each verse.**
- **The song's short phrases are easy to sing to the catchy melody.**

Link to Social Studies

Make a four-column chart with the heads Freedom, Historical Events, National Symbols, and Landscape. Write the titles of other songs about the U.S. in the appropriate column(s).

"This Land Is Your Land." Words and Music by Woody Guthrie. TRO—Copyright 1956 (Renewed), 1958 (Renewed), 1970 (Renewed), 1972 (Renewed), Ludlow Music, Inc., New York, NY. Used by permission.

This Land Is Your Land

by Woody Guthrie

130

Content-Area Vocabulary	Science
Gulf Stream	a current of warm water in the Atlantic. It flows out of the Gulf of Mexico, north along the East coast of the United States, and then northeast across the Atlantic toward the British Isles.
redwood	a very large evergreen sequoia tree of California and Oregon coastal regions

Build Background In this context, *land* means "country." Woody Guthrie was a famous folk singer from Oklahoma who wrote more than 1,000 songs. His songs reflect the spirit of America. "This Land Is Your Land" is one of his most familiar songs.

DAY 4 Grouping Options

Reading
Whole Group Discuss the Question of the Day.

Group Time Differentiated Instruction
Read "This Land Is Your Land." See pp. 112f–112g for the small group lesson plan.

Whole Group Use p. 133a.

Language Arts
Use pp. 133e–133k.

CHORUS:

This land is your land, this land is my land,
From California to the New York Island;
From the redwood forest to the Gulf Stream waters,
This land was made for you and me.

Prior Knowledge | Link the song's phrases to what you know about the U.S.

131

SONG

Use the sidebar on p. 130 to guide discussion.

- Explain that a song is a poem set to music. Songs usually use rhyme. Point out that only the first two lines of this song's chorus end with rhyming words.

- A chorus is a set of lines repeated between verses. Some songs have many verses.

- Tell students a chorus may give the main idea of a song. The verses may give more details. Ask students to identify the main idea of the chorus. *(The U.S. belongs to everyone who lives there.)*

Audio CD AudioText

Prior Knowledge

Have students share their experiences and personal reactions to the areas and landforms of the United States mentioned in the song.

Redwood Forest

TIME FOR Science

Redwoods are the tallest trees that grow today. Two species of redwood trees grow in California, as mentioned in the song. *Sequioa sempervirens,* known as the giant sequoia, grows in the fog belt along the northern coast. *Sequoiadendron giganteum,* known as the coast redwood, grows in the Sierra Nevadas. Giant sequoias can live up to 3,500 years. Coast redwoods can grow to more than 300 feet tall. The scientific name *sequoia* was chosen to honor the Cherokee leader Sequoyah. Redwood is used to make furniture and house shingles. Burls, or knots, are often carved into decorative objects such as bowls.

Strategies for Poetry

IDENTIFY THEME Identifying the theme of a poem or song can help students answer test questions. Provide the following strategy.

Use the Strategy

1. Read the test question and think carefully about what it is asking.

2. Reread the poem or song and think about the message the author is trying to convey. State the theme in your own words. Make sure you can find evidence to support this message.

3. Remember themes can be stated in different ways. If a multiple-choice test question asks you to choose the statement that best represents the theme of a poem or song, find the answer choice closest to the theme you stated. For a short-answer test question, write your theme statement and support it with examples and evidence from the poem or song.

GUIDED PRACTICE Have students discuss how they would use the strategy to answer the following question.

What is the theme of "This Land Is Your Land"? Provide two details to support your answer.

INDEPENDENT PRACTICE After students answer the following test question, discuss the process they used to find information.

What is the theme of another popular folk song, such as "You Are My Sunshine" or "America the Beautiful"? Name the song and use details to support your answer.

VERSE 1

As I was walking that ribbon of highway,
I saw above me that endless skyway;
I saw below me that golden valley;
This land was made for you and me.

[CHORUS]

VERSE 2

I've roamed and rambled and I followed my footsteps
To the sparkling sands of her diamond deserts;
And all around me a voice was sounding:
This land was made for you and me.

[CHORUS]

 Draw Conclusions How does the songwriter feel about the U.S.?

132

ELL

Guided Practice Write the Guided Practice test question on the board. Help students understand what supporting evidence is. Provide a theme statement for the song and have students offer details from the song that support this theme.

VERSE 3

When the sun came shining, and I was strolling,
And the wheat fields waving and the dust clouds rolling,
As the fog was lifting a voice was chanting:
This land was made for you and me.

[CHORUS]

Reading Across Texts

The song does not mention any of the natural wonders described in *Letters Home from Yosemite*. Which wonder from Yosemite would you like to include in the song?

Writing Across Texts Write a verse for "This Land Is Your Land" that describes the wonder you chose.

CONNECT TEXT TO TEXT

Reading Across Texts

Have students work in small groups to review some of the natural wonders described in *Letters Home from Yosemite* before they each choose one to include in a song.

Writing Across Texts Have students write descriptive words and phrases in a web for the wonder they chose. Clap out the rhythm as you say or sing a verse from "This Land Is Your Land." Suggest they try to follow the same rhyme scheme, rhythm, and repeated lines from the original song as they write their verses.

○ Draw Conclusions

Possible response: The songwriter is awed by the natural and man-made features of the United States and feels the variety and beauty of the land belong to each and every one of us.

Fluency Assessment Plan

- ☑ **Week 1** Assess Advanced students.
- ☑ **Week 2** Assess Strategic Intervention students.
- ☑ **Week 3** Assess On-Level students.
- ☑ **Week 4** Assess Strategic Intervention students.
- ☑ **Week 5 This week assess any students you have not yet checked during this unit.**

Set individual goals for students to enable them to reach the year-end goal.
- Current Goal: 95–105 WCPM
- Year-End Goal: 130 WCPM

Provide opportunities for English language learners to read aloud to younger children. This allows them to practice their oral reading and improve their fluency.

To develop fluent readers, use Fluency Coach.

DAY 5 Grouping Options

Reading
Whole Group
Revisit the Question of the Week.

Group Time
Differentiated Instruction
ReRead this week's Leveled Readers. See pp. 112f–112g for the small group lesson plan.

Whole Group
Use p. 133b–133c.

Language Arts
Use pp. 133d–133l.

PHRASING
Fluency

DAY 1

Model Reread aloud "The Volcano Wakes" on p. 112m. Explain that you will use phrasing to keep related words grouped together. Point out how phrasing makes sentences easier to understand. Model for students as you read.

DAY 2

Echo Reading Read aloud the last paragraph of "Badger Pass," p. 120. Have students notice how you group words in phrases, pausing briefly after clauses and punctuation marks. Practice as a class by doing three echo readings.

DAY 3

Model Read aloud "Lyell" on p. 127. Have students notice how you use commas that set off clauses as clues to grouping related words within sentences. Practice as a class by doing three echo readings of "Lyell."

DAY 4

Partner Reading Have partners practice reading aloud "Lyell," p. 127, three times. Students should read with careful phrasing and offer each other feedback.

Monitor Progress | Check Fluency WCPM

As students reread, monitor their progress toward their individual fluency goals. Current Goal: 95–105 words correct per minute. End-of-Year Goal: 130 words correct per minute.

If... students cannot read fluently at a rate of 95–105 words correct per minute,
then... make sure students practice with text at their independent level. Provide additional fluency practice, pairing nonfluent readers with fluent readers.

If... students already read at 130 words correct per minute,
then... they do not need to reread three to four times.

SUCCESS PREDICTOR

DAY 5

Assessment
Individual Reading Rate Use the Fluency Assessment Plan and do a one-minute timed reading of either selection from this week to assess students in Week 5. Pay special attention to this week's skill, phrasing. Provide corrective feedback for each student.

RETEACH

Main Idea

TEACH

Review the definitions of *topic, main idea,* and *supporting details* on p. 112. Students can complete Practice Book p. 48 on their own or as a class. Point out that students should add phrases or sentences to complete each box on the Practice Book page. For example, *Yosemite* is a topic. To become a main idea, it needs to be stated as a complete sentence.

ASSESS

Have pairs determine the main idea and supporting details of p. 124, paragraph 1. *(Main idea: There are more than 240 species of birds in Yosemite. Supporting details: willow flycatcher, great gray owl, bald eagle, and Steller's jay)*

For additional instruction on main idea and supporting details, see DI·56.

EXTEND SKILLS
Point of View

TEACH

The point of view of a story is the perspective from which readers see the action.

- In first-person point of view, words such as *I* and *me* show that the narrator is a character in the story.
- In third-person point of view, the narrator is not a character in the story. The writer uses words such as *he, she, it,* and *they* to tell about characters.

Work with students to identify the point of view on p. 118, paragraph 1. *(first person)* Have students support their answers by identifying clue words.

ASSESS

Have students write several sentences about an event at school, using first-person point of view. Ask:

1. **Did you use words like *I* and *me*?**
2. **Did you tell what happened from the narrator's perspective?**

OBJECTIVES

- Determine main idea and supporting details.
- Identify point of view.

Skills Trace
Main Idea and Details

Introduce/Teach	TE: 4.1 112–113; 4.2 240–241; 4.5 582–583
Practice	TE: 119, 123, 247, 251, 589, 595 PB: 43, 47, 48, 93, 97, 98, 233, 237, 238
▶ Reteach/Review	**TE: 4.1 75, 133b, DI•56; 4.2 225, 259b, DI•56; 4.4 475; 4.5 607b, DI•55 PB: 26, 86, 186**
Test	Selection Test: 17–20, 37–40, 93–96; Benchmark Test: Unit 2

ELL

Access Content Reteach the skill by reviewing the Picture It! lesson on main idea and supporting details in the ELL Teaching Guide, pp. 29–30.

Main Idea and Details

- The **main idea** is the most important idea from a paragraph, passage, or article.
- **Details** are small pieces of information that tell more about the main idea.

Directions Read the passage. Then complete the diagram below.

Yosemite National Park has many rules for people to follow in order to preserve the park. One rule is that hunting of any animals is not allowed. Hunting would change the food supply for animals in the park. Hunting in a busy park could also be dangerous to humans. Riding a bike off an official trail is against the rules too. This could ruin the plant life growing in natural areas. Another rule prohibits people from feeding animals. It is not safe for the animals or the visitors. Wild animals might get used to being fed and be unable to feed themselves in the wild. Finally, people cannot remove plants or rocks as souvenirs. If visitors follow these and other rules of the park, Yosemite will continue to be a beautiful, natural place to visit.

Possible answers given.

Main Idea
1. Yosemite has **rules to preserve the park.**

Supporting Ideas
2. Hunting **is not allowed.**
3. **Riding a bike through meadows is not allowed.**
4. Feeding animals **is against the rules.**
5. **Collecting rocks and plants is against the rules.**

Home Activity Your child read a short passage and identified its main idea and supporting details. Have your child write a paragraph about his or her favorite place. Then help your child create a graphic organizer that identifies the main idea and supporting details of the paragraph.

▲ **Practice Book** p. 48

SUCCESS PREDICTOR

Vocabulary and Word Study

VOCABULARY STRATEGY

Word Structure

SUFFIXES Remind students that the suffixes *-ist, -er,* and *-or* mean "one who is an expert in" or "one who does." For example, *naturalist* means "a nature expert." Have students look through the selection for more words that end with suffixes *-ist, -er* or *-or*. Have them list the words and their meanings.

Words Ending in *-ist, -er, -or*	Meanings
narrator	one who narrates, or tells a story
explorers	
tourists	
visitors	

Native American Words

Point out that many place names such as *Yosemite* and other words used in English today come from Native American words. Ask students if they can identify the following objects whose names come from Native American languages:

1. Taino word for a bed tied between two trees (hammock)
2. Micmac word for a curved piece of wood used for sliding down snow-covered hills (toboggan)
3. Inuit word for small boat where one person is completely enclosed and uses a double-ended paddle (kayak)
4. Algonquin word for a small, chattering mammal (chipmunk)
5. Tupi word for a mountain lion (cougar)

BUILD CONCEPT VOCABULARY

This Land Is Your Land

LOOKING BACK Remind students of the Big Idea question: *How do the diverse regions and peoples of the United States reflect its greatness?* Discuss the Big Idea question. Then ask students how the concept vocabulary from each week of this unit relates to the unit theme *This Land Is Your Land* and the Big Idea question. Ask students if they have any words or categories to add. If time permits, create a Unit Concept Web.

Monitor Progress

Check Vocabulary

If... students suggest words or categories that are not related to the concept,	**then**... review the words and categories on the Concept Web and discuss how they relate to the lesson concept.

SUCCESS PREDICTOR

Speaking and Viewing

SPEAKING

Debate

SET-UP Tell students the federal government makes rules about the use of motorized vehicles, such as snowmobiles, in national parks such as Yosemite. Have students debate reasons for and against restricting vehicle access in the parks. You may wish to have them research details about this policy. Then have them choose a position and give a short speech to the class.

ORGANIZATION Tell students to open their speech with a clear statement of an opinion and then list reasons that support the opinion. They should end with a summary of their position.

AUDIENCE Remind speakers to speak loud enough so the entire audience can hear them. Remind students in the audience to be respectful of speakers. They should listen respectfully, even when someone with an opposing view is speaking.

Planning Tips
- Think ahead about the arguments that speakers with opposing views often make.
- Try to come up with arguments that show why opposing reasons are not sound.

VIEWING

Analyze a Photo

Using library or Internet sources, show students a striking photograph of Yosemite or another national park. Then ask students to answer the following questions in pairs or small groups:

1. **What statement is the photographer making with this photograph?** (*Students should be able to draw reasoned conclusions about the photographer's point of view.*)

2. **Compare and contrast the photograph with photographs found in *Letters Home from Yosemite*. What new details do you notice in each photograph?** (*Responses will vary.*)

3. **How did viewing the picture again give you better understanding of the selection?** (*Responses should compare opinions of the reading before and after viewing the photographs again.*)

4. **Create a question about the photographs to ask a partner.** Avoid questions that can be answered yes or no.

ELL

Support Vocabulary Use the following to review and extend vocabulary and to explore lesson concepts further:
- ELL Poster 5, Days 3–5 instruction
- Vocabulary Activities and Word Cards in ELL Teaching Guide, pp. 31–32.

Assessment For information on assessing students' speaking, listening, and viewing, see the ELL and Transition Handbook.

Grammar **Clauses and Complex Sentences**

OBJECTIVES

- Define and identify clauses and complex sentences.
- Distinguish between dependent clauses and independent clauses.
- Use clauses and complex sentences correctly in writing.
- Become familiar with clause and complex sentence assessment on high-stakes tests.

Monitor Progress

Grammar

| If... students have difficulty identifying clauses and complex sentences, | then... provide additional instruction and practice in The Grammar and Writing Book pp. 74–77. |

DAILY FIX-IT

This week use Daily Fix-It Transparency 5.

Spiral REVIEW

Grammar Support See the Grammar Transition lessons in the ELL and Transition Handbook.

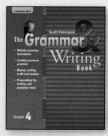

▲ **The Grammar and Writing Book**
For more instruction and practice, use pp. 74–77.

DAY 1 — Teach and Model

DAILY FIX-IT

1. As we approached the waterfall. We slipped on the smoothe rocks. *(waterfall, we; smooth)*

2. What a amazing waterfall this is? *(an; is!)*

READING-GRAMMAR CONNECTION

Write the following sentence:

> As our plane touched down,
> I grew very excited.

Explain that this is a **complex sentence.** It is made up of **two clauses,** an **independent clause** (underlined twice) and a **dependent clause** (underlined once). The independent clause can stand alone as a sentence; the dependent clause cannot: it is a sentence fragment.

Display Grammar Transparency 5. Read aloud the definitions and sample sentences. Work through the items.

Clauses and Complex Sentences

A clause is a group of words with a subject and a verb. A **dependent clause** begins with a word such as *because* or *when*. It cannot stand alone as a sentence. An **independent clause** can stand alone.

    Dependent Clause   when we first saw Yosemite
    Independent Clause   It was a beautiful fall day.

A sentence made up of a dependent clause and an independent clause is a **complex sentence.**

    Complex Sentences   When we first saw Yosemite, it was a beautiful fall day.
                         It was a beautiful fall day when we first saw Yosemite.

Other words that often introduce a dependent clause are *since, although, if, until, unless, as, after,* and *before.* When a dependent clause comes first in a complex sentence, it is followed by a comma.

Directions Write *I* if the underlined group of words is an independent clause. Write *D* if it is a dependent clause.

1. When we arrived at the campground, the rain had stopped. — **D**
2. After we ate our supper, we went for a hike. — **I**
3. We hiked until the sun set. — **D**
4. I would run if I saw a bear. — **I**
5. Before we went to bed, we lit a campfire. — **D**

Directions Write the clause in the sentence that is named in ( ).

6. Although we started late, we hiked fifteen miles. (dependent)
Although we started late
7. We were pitching our tent when we saw the bear. (dependent)
when we saw the bear
8. As we slowly moved away, the bear looked up. (independent)
the bear looked up

Unit 1 Letters Home from Yosemite   Grammar **5**

▲ **Grammar Transparency** 5

DAY 2 — Develop the Concept

DAILY FIX-IT

3. Winter's in the park can be crool. *(Winters; cruel)*

4. I want to go winter camping but Dad says its too cold. *(camping, but; it's)*

GUIDED PRACTICE

Review the concept of clauses and complex sentences.

- A **clause** is a group of words with a subject and a verb
- An **independent clause** can stand alone as a sentence; a **dependent clause** cannot.
- A dependent clause begins with a word such as *when, if,* or *as.*
- A **complex sentence** consists of a dependent clause and an independent clause.

HOMEWORK Grammar and Writing Practice Book p. 17. Work through the first two items with the class.

Clauses and Complex Sentences

A clause is a group of words with a subject and a verb. A **dependent clause** begins with a word such as *because* or *when*. It cannot stand alone as a sentence. An **independent clause** can stand alone.

    Dependent Clause   when I was eight
    Independent Clause   My family visited Yosemite.

A sentence made up of a dependent clause and an independent clause is a **complex sentence.**

    Complex Sentences   When I was eight, my family visited Yosemite.
                         My family visited Yosemite when I was eight.

Other words that often introduce a dependent clause are *since, although, if, until, unless, as, after,* and *before.* When a dependent clause comes first in a complex sentence, it is followed by a comma.

Directions Write *I* if the underlined group of words is an independent clause. Write *D* if it is a dependent clause.

1. People visit Yosemite because it is so beautiful. — **D**
2. When you see El Capitan, you'll be amazed. — **D**
3. If you go there, visit Yosemite Falls. — **I**
4. You will probably see a bear before you leave. — **I**
5. After I returned, I read a book about the park. — **D**

Directions Combine each pair of simple sentences. Use the word in ( ). Write the complex sentence.

6. I'll visit all the national parks. I'm grown up. (when)
I'll visit all the national parks when I'm grown up.
7. I'm only ten years old. I have to travel with my family. (since) **I have to travel with my family since I'm only ten years old.**

Home Activity Your child learned about clauses and complex sentences. Encourage him or her to show you how words such as because, when, although, and if can link simple sentences to form complex sentences.

▲ **Grammar and Writing Practice Book** p. 17

DAY 3 · Apply to Writing

DAILY FIX-IT

5. You will see lots of wildlife. If your patient. *(wildlife if you're)*

6. It's unusual to see a Bobcat, but you might be lucky? *(bobcat; lucky.)*

VARY SENTENCE STYLE

Explain that using only simple or compound sentences can make your narrative dull. Complex sentences add variety and interest to writing.

• Have students review something they have written to see if they can improve it by adding dependent clauses to form complex sentences.

HOMEWORK Grammar and Writing Practice Book p. 18.

Clauses and Complex Sentences

Directions Make complex sentences by choosing clauses from the box to combine with the clauses below. Write your sentences on the lines. Use correct capitalization and punctuation.

Indians were living there	if you get too close
you will want to return	because it is so beautiful
it is still mostly wilderness	

1. When explorers reached Yosemite, **When explorers reached Yosemite, Indians were living there.**

2. Many people visit Yosemite **Many people visit Yosemite because it is so beautiful.**

3. Although millions of tourists visit the park, **Although millions of tourists visit the park, it is still mostly wilderness.**

4. A mule deer can be dangerous **A mule deer can be dangerous if you get too close.**

5. After you have visited once, **After you have visited once, you will want to return.**

Directions Think of a place you would like to visit. Write three complex sentences about the place. Use the words in ( ). **Possible answers:**

6. (because) **I'd like to see the Grand Canyon because my dad says it's beautiful.**

7. (if) **If I get the chance, I'll go there.**

8. (when) **When I'm there, I'll ride a burro.**

School-Home Connection **Home Activity** Your child learned how to use clauses and complex sentences in writing. Ask your child a *why* question. Have him or her write a complex sentence to answer it. Ask your child to explain why the answer is a complex sentence.

▲ **Grammar and Writing Practice Book** p. 18

DAY 4 · Test Preparation

DAILY FIX-IT

7. If the weather's nice we'll spent the afternoon hiking. *(nice, we'll spend)*

8. Some of the thunderstorms here is very severe *(are very severe.)*

STANDARDIZED TEST PREP

Test Tip

When a dependent clause comes first in a complex sentence, put a comma after it. There is no comma when it comes last.

First: When you get there, you'll be amazed.

Last: You'll be amazed when you get there.

HOMEWORK Grammar and Writing Practice Book p. 19.

Clauses and Complex Sentences

Directions Mark the letter of the independent clause in each group.

1. A when the tourists arrived
   B if you are camping
   C it is bigger than Rhode Island
   D although there are many cars

2. A unless you want an angry bear
   B don't tease the animals
   C until they can smell you
   D as we were driving by

3. A before we went to sleep
   B since we had our backpacks
   C after we ate lunch
   D we pitched our tent

4. **A** we went too near the falls
   B because we were soaking wet
   C when the wind blows hard
   D if you want to stay dry

Directions Mark the letter of the word that completes each sentence.

5. ___ there are bobcats, we didn't see any.
   A Although
   B And
   C Until
   D As

6. I've been starving ___ we arrived here.
   A or
   B but
   C since
   D because

7. We stopped hiking ___ we got too cold.
   A or
   B unless
   C although
   D when

8. ___ you go out at night, you might see an owl.
   A If
   B Until
   C But
   D Although

9. ___ we go to bed, we safely store our food.
   A Unless
   B Before
   C Or
   D After

10. ___ I was hiking, I saw a large brown animal.
    A And
    B As
    C Until
    D If

School-Home Connection **Home Activity** Your child prepared for taking tests on clauses and complex sentences. Have your child find complex sentences in a newspaper article. Ask him or her to identify the independent and dependent clauses in each sentence.

▲ **Grammar and Writing Practice Book** p. 19

DAY 5 · Cumulative Review

DAILY FIX-IT

9. Did you took any good photographs! *(take; photographs?)*

10. Take a picture of Jim and I? *(me.)*

ADDITIONAL PRACTICE

Assign pp. 74–77 in The Grammar and Writing Book.

EXTRA PRACTICE Grammar and Writing Practice Book p. 126.

ASSESSMENT

CUMULATIVE REVIEW Grammar and Writing Practice Book p. 20.

Clauses and Complex Sentences

Directions Write the dependent clause in each sentence.

1. Although they are small, peregrine falcons are very fast.
   Although they are small

2. A jay will steal your food if you don't watch out.
   if you don't watch out

3. Sheep had almost vanished from the park before they were brought back.
   before they were brought back

4. Because bears are so greedy, store food in a metal box.
   Because bears are so greedy

5. If you enjoy wildlife, Yosemite is a good place to visit.
   If you enjoy wildlife

Directions Combine each pair of simple sentences. Use the word in ( ). Write the complex sentence. **Possible answers:**

6. The first tourists traveled by foot. There were no cars. (because) **The first tourists traveled by foot because there were no cars.**

7. Most visitors stay in one area. The park is huge. (although) **Most visitors stay in one area although the park is huge.**

8. The rocks seem to change color. The sun shines on them. (when) **The rocks seem to change color when the sun shines on them.**

9. You will see a bat. You watch closely. (if) **You will see a bat if you watch closely.**

10. Don't go near that waterfall. You want to get wet. (unless) **Don't go near that waterfall unless you want to get wet.**

School-Home Connection **Home Activity** Your child reviewed clauses and complex sentences. Ask your child to tell you something about his or her day using complex sentences with the words when, because, and if.

▲ **Grammar and Writing Practice Book** p. 20

Writing for Tests **Narrative Writing**

OBJECTIVES

- Write a narrative for a test.
- Identify key words in a prompt.
- Focus on conventions.
- Use a rubric.

Genre Narrative Writing
Writer's Craft Style
Writing Trait Conventions

Conventions Identify a particular grammar convention that presents difficulty for a child or a small group. Explicitly teach the English convention using an appropriate lesson in the ELL and Transition Handbook.

Writing Traits

FOCUS/IDEAS The writer has a main idea (Flying to NYC alone as a six-year-old) and a clear purpose (to entertain).

ORGANIZATION/PARAGRAPHS The writer describes events in sequence—the order that they occurred.

VOICE The writing has a friendly, informal tone.

WORD CHOICE Strong verbs (*was hopping, screamed, roared*) make the writing lively.

SENTENCES Sentences vary in length and type, creating a smooth style.

CONVENTIONS There is excellent control and accuracy, including use of both compound and complex sentences.

DAY 1 Model the Trait

READING-WRITING CONNECTION

- When you write a response for tests, remember that using conventions accurately will strengthen your answer by making your writing clear and easy to read.

- Think about how the writer uses conventions in *Letters Home from Yosemite* to make the selection a pleasure to read.

MODEL CONVENTIONS Discuss Writing Transparency 5A. Then discuss the model and the writing trait of conventions.

 I see that the writer of this narrative has paid close attention to punctuation, capitalization, and grammar. I am able to read the narrative without having to stop to ask myself questions like "What word is that supposed to be?" or "Why isn't this period followed by a capital letter?"

Writing for Tests

Prompt Think about a time when you took a <u>trip</u>—maybe for a vacation or a family visit. What <u>experience</u> stays in your mind? Write a <u>narrative</u>, describing this event to a <u>friend or family member</u>.

Flying Solo

Compound and complex sentences create a flowing style.
> When I was six years old, I flew to New York City alone! I had been on an airplane only once before, and I was hopping up and down with excitement. A hostess held my hand as I waved goodbye to my mom and dad. She took me onto the plane and helped me fix the seat belt.

Author uses vivid words and images to recall interesting incidents.
> The plane roared when it took off. I tried to squeeze my armrest, but I grabbed the lady sitting next to me instead. She screamed! Later I spilled orange juice over her dress. I loved making my seat go backwards and forwards. After I did this for a while, the lady next to me found another place to sit.

Sentences vary in style and length.
> My aunt met me at the airport. I stayed with her for two weeks, but I remember that flight best of all.

Unit 1 *Letters Home from Yosemite*   Writing Model **5A**

▲ **Writing Transparency** 5A

DAY 2 Improve Writing

WRITER'S CRAFT
Style

Display Writing Transparency 5B. Read the directions and work together to practice creating a smooth style.

 STYLE Tomorrow we will be writing a narrative about a trip we have taken. I am going to write about my hiking trip in the Adirondack Mountains. I can create a smooth style for my narrative by combining short, simple sentences into longer compound or complex sentences. Instead of saying, "We hiked for hours. I was very thirsty," I can combine these sentences. "After hiking for hours, I was very thirsty."

GUIDED WRITING If students have difficulty composing long sentences, suggest that they write about a place using short simple sentences. Have them combine their simple sentences using a variety of connecting words.

Style

Too many short simple sentences can make your writing dull and choppy. Create a smooth, flowing **style** by combining simple sentences to create compound or complex sentences.

Simple Sentences   We were tired. We wanted to reach the summit.
Compound Sentence   We were tired, but we wanted to reach the summit.
Complex Sentence   Although we were tired, we wanted to reach the summit.

Directions Combine the two short, choppy sentences. Use the word in ( ). Write the compound or complex sentence. **Possible answers:**

1. It was after noon. We reached the summit. (when)
   <u>It was after noon when we reached the summit.</u>

2. We were hungry. We hadn't eaten lunch. (because)
   <u>We were hungry because we hadn't eaten lunch.</u>

3. There was a cold wind. We felt warm inside. (but)
   <u>There was a cold wind, but we felt warm inside.</u>

4. Dad spotted an eagle. My brother saw our car far below. (and)
   <u>Dad spotted an eagle, and my brother saw our car far below.</u>

5. We started down. We took many photographs. (before)
   <u>Before we started down, we took many photographs.</u>

6. We reached the car. I wanted to go up again. (after)
   <u>After we reached the car, I wanted to go up again.</u>

Directions Write a short narrative about a place that you love to visit. Include at least one compound sentence and one complex sentence. **Possible answer:**

<u>I like many places, but I like the basketball courts at Grove Street best.</u>
<u>When I'm there, I'm always happy. The sound of the balls bouncing is like</u>
<u>music to me. If I ever get the money, I'll have my own basketball court.</u>

Unit 1 *Letters Home from Yosemite*   Writer's Craft **5B**

▲ **Writing Transparency** 5B

DAY 3 Prewrite and Draft

READ THE WRITING PROMPT

on page 129 in the Student Edition.

In Letters Home from Yosemite, the author tells about a special trip.

Think about a trip you have taken—maybe for a vacation or family visit.

Now write a narrative describing a special experience from that trip.

Writing Test Tips

1. **Read the prompt carefully.**
   - Find key words.
   - Consider your purpose and audience.
2. **Develop a plan.** Think about what you want to say before writing. Fill out a graphic organizer, such as a story sequence chart showing beginning, middle, and end or a T-chart for a comparison/contrast essay.
3. **Support your ideas.** Use facts, examples, and details to strengthen your response. Avoid making general statements that are unsupported.
4. **Use a variety of sentence structures.** Include complex and compound sentences, varied sentence beginnings, and sentences of different lengths and types.
5. **Choose clear, precise words.** Use words that create pictures and help readers understand what you mean.
6. **Check your writing.** If this is a timed test, neatly add, delete, or change words and make corrections in spelling, punctuation, or grammar instead of recopying. Use legible handwriting. Reread your work before handing it in.

DAY 4 Draft and Revise

EDITING/REVISING CHECKLIST

☑ **Focus** Do sentences stick to the topic of the trip and one memorable experience?

☑ **Organization** Is the narrative developed in a logical, sequential order with transition words?

☑ **Support** Do specific words make the narrative interesting and engaging? Is the voice lively?

☑ **Conventions** Have I indented correctly to make my organization clear? Have I used correct punctuation and capitalization to make the narrative easy to read?

See *The Grammar and Writing Book,* pp. 74–79.

Revising Tips

Conventions

- Make sure that sentences are complete, with correct capitalization and punctuation.
- Use verbs in the same tense—generally the past tense—when telling a story.
- Check that connecting words are used correctly in compound and complex sentences.

ASSESSMENT Use the scoring rubric to evaluate students' work.

DAY 5 Connect to Unit Writing

Personal Narrative	
Week 1	Memoir 39g–39h
Week 2	Journal Entry 65g–65h
Week 3	Postcard 87g–87h
Week 4	E-mail Invitation 111g–111h
Week 5	Narrative Writing 133g–133h

PREVIEW THE UNIT PROMPT

Write a personal narrative about a time that you were a newcomer to a place or situation (a school, club, team, or neighborhood). Explain how you felt and what you found challenging or exciting.

APPLY

- A personal narrative is a story about an interesting experience or event in the storyteller's life.
- Keep readers interested in your personal narrative with a varied sentence style.

Writing Trait Rubric

	4	3	2	1
Conventions	Excellent control and accuracy; very few or no errors	Solid control and accuracy; some errors	Weak control; several errors	Serious errors
	Narrative clear and easy to read	Narrative generally clear; errors that do not interfere with meaning	Narrative confusing at times; errors that distort meaning	Narrative unclear; errors that obscure meaning

Spelling & Phonics Long *u* Sounds

Generalization

Connect to Phonics Long *u* has two sounds, /ü/ and /yü/, and several spellings, *u-consonant-e, ew, oo, ui,* and *u*: ex*cuse*, th*rew*, m*ood*, cr*uise*, *pupil*. The letter patterns *u-consonant-e, ew, oo, ui,* and *u* can stand for /ü/ or /yü/.

Spelling Words

1. usual*	11. truth
2. huge*	12. bruise
3. flute	13. cruel
4. mood	14. excuse
5. smooth	15. pupil
6. threw	16. groove
7. afternoon*	17. confuse
8. scooter	18. humor
9. juice	19. duty
10. cruise	20. curfew

Challenge Words

21. influence	24. accumulate
22. aluminum	25. igloo
23. nutrition	

*Word from the selection

Spelling/Phonics Support See the ELL and Transition Handbook for spelling support.

DAY 1 Pretest and Sort

PRETEST

Use the Dictation Sentences from Day 5 to administer the pretest. Read the word, read the sentence, and then read the word again. Guide students in self-correcting their pretests and correcting any misspellings.

Monitor Progress

Spelling

If... students misspell more than 5 pretest words,	**then...** use words 1–10 for Strategic Intervention.
If... students misspell 1–5 pretest words,	**then...** use words 1–20 for On-Level practice.
If... students correctly spell all pretest words,	**then...** use words 1–25 for Advanced Learners.

HOMEWORK Spelling Practice Book, p. 17.

Long *u* Sounds

Generalization Long u has two sounds, /ü/ and /yü/, and several spellings, u-consonant-e, ew, oo, ui, and u: ex*cuse*, th*rew*, m*ood*, cr*uise*, pupil.

Word Sort Sort the list words by the long e spelling at the end of the word.

u-consonant-e
1. huge
2. flute
3. excuse
4. confuse

ew
5. threw
6. curfew

oo
7. mood
8. smooth
9. afternoon
10. scooter
11. groove

ui
12. juice
13. cruise
14. bruise

u
15. usual
16. truth
17. cruel
18. pupil
19. humor
20. duty

Challenge Words

oo
21. igloo

u
22. influence
23. aluminum
24. nutrition
25. accumulate

Spelling Words
1. usual
2. huge
3. flute
4. mood
5. smooth
6. threw
7. afternoon
8. scooter
9. juice
10. cruise
11. truth
12. bruise
13. cruel
14. excuse
15. pupil
16. groove
17. confuse
18. humor
19. duty
20. curfew

Challenge Words
21. influence
22. aluminum
23. nutrition
24. accumulate
25. igloo

Home Activity Your child is learning to spell words with long u sounds spelled u-consonant-e, ew, oo, ui, and u. Have your child say the words and listen for the two different long u sounds.

▲ **Spelling Practice Book** p. 17

DAY 2 Think and Practice

TEACH

The long *u* sounds, /ü/ and /yü/, can be spelled *u-consonant-e, ew, oo, ui,* and *u*. Write *confuse* on the board. Underline *use*. Say *confuse* and explain that the long *u* sound in *confuse* is /yü/ and the letters *use* spell /yüz/. Guide students in identifying and spelling the long *u* sound in *curfew, smooth, bruise,* and *humor*.

con<u>fuse</u>

SAY AND SORT Have pairs of students write the list words on note cards and sort the words into two groups: /ü/ words and /yü/ words. Then have them sort each group by spelling pattern.

HOMEWORK Spelling Practice Book, p. 18.

Long *u* Sounds

Spelling Words

usual	huge	flute	mood	smooth
threw	afternoon	scooter	juice	cruise
truth	bruise	cruel	excuse	pupil
groove	confuse	humor	duty	curfew

Antonyms Write the list word that has the opposite or nearly the opposite meaning as the word.

1. kind	1.	cruel
2. evening	2.	afternoon
3. rough	3.	smooth
4. dishonesty	4.	truth
5. caught	5.	threw

Synonyms Write the list word that has the same or nearly the same meaning as the word.

6. atmosphere	6.	mood
7. instrument	7.	flute
8. ridge	8.	groove
9. sail	9.	cruise
10. forgive	10.	excuse

Definitions Write the list word that fits the definition.

11.	curfew	the time when children must be indoors
12.	pupil	a student
13.	bruise	discolored skin caused by an injury
14.	scooter	a riding toy with a platform, wheels, and a handlebar
15.	humor	funny or amusing quality
16.	juice	liquid taken from fruit or vegetables
17.	huge	enormous
18.	duty	a task a person is required to do
19.	usual	ordinary
20.	confuse	perplex, mix up

Home Activity Your child wrote words with long u sounds spelled u-consonant-e, ew, oo, ui, and u. Say a list word and have your child write it.

▲ **Spelling Practice Book** p. 18

DAY 3 Connect to Writing

WRITE A POSTCARD

Ask students to use at least five spelling words to write a postcard from a real or imaginary trip.

Frequently Misspelled Words

school   too

These words may seem easy to spell, but they are often misspelled by fourth-graders. Alert students to these frequently misspelled words. Point out that the letters *ch* stand for /k/ in *school*. Discuss the differences in usage between *to, two,* and *too.*

HOMEWORK Spelling Practice Book, p. 19.

Long *u* Sounds

Proofread a Script Read the script that a DJ will read on the radio. Circle six spelling errors and write the words correctly. Add quotation marks where they are needed.

Spelling Words
usual
huge
flute
mood
smooth
threw
afternoon
scooter
juice
cruise
truth
bruise
cruel
excuse
pupil
groove
confuse
humor
duty
curfew

DJ: Good (afternune) listeners. Today, we're taking a (crewse) down memory lane. I'm going to play some (smoothe) sounds from the past. But first, here's a word from our sponsor.

Commercial Spot: Is it breakfast as usual? How about a huge energy boost? Drink some OranGee orange (juce) today. Don't confuse it with other breakfast drinks!

DJ: Now, it's time for the news! A high (schewl) pupil suffered a huge (bruze) when he fell off his scooter. "I have no clue what happened," said the student.

1. afternoon   2. cruise
3. smooth   4. juice
5. school   6. bruise

Frequently Misspelled Words
school
too

Proofread Words Circle the word that is spelled correctly. Write the word.

7. Abby likes to read stories that have some (humor) hewmor.   7. humor
8. The captain (threw) thru a life jacket to each passenger.   8. threw
9. "There is no excus (excuse) for this mess," said Mom.   9. excuse
10. It's always a good idea to tell the (truth) truth.   10. truth
11. "Don't stay out past curfoo (curfew) Dad warned.   11. curfew
12. The (huge) hug truck rattled the windows as it passed our house.   12. huge

Home Activity Your child identified misspelled words with *u*-consonant-*e*, *ew*, *oo*, *ui*, and *u*. Ask your child to use list words to make up a radio announcement or commercial.

▲ **Spelling Practice Book** p. 19

DAY 4 Review

REVIEW LONG *u* SOUNDS

Distribute graph paper and have each student make up a word search puzzle using at least ten spelling words. Then have students exchange puzzles with a partner and solve each other's puzzles.

Spelling Strategy Steps for Spelling New Words

Step 1: Look at the word. Say it and listen to the sounds.

Step 2: Spell the word aloud.

Step 3: Think about its spelling. Is there anything special to remember?

Step 4: Picture the word with your eyes shut.

Step 5: Look at the word and write it.

Step 6: Cover the word. Picture it and write it again. Check its spelling.

HOMEWORK Spelling Practice Book, p. 20.

Long *u* Sounds

Word Puzzle Figure out the code to complete the list words.

A	B	C	D	E	F	G	H	I	J	K	L	M	N	O	P	Q	R	S	T	U	V	W	X	Y	Z
17	7	14	21	10	16	4	13	23	12		6	1	25	20	19		3	18	26	9	24	22	2		8

1. S C O O T E R
2. H U G E
3. A F T E R N O O N
4. C R U I S E
5. B R U I S E
6. F L U T E
7. T R U T H
8. J U I C E
9. C R U E L
10. E X C U S E
11. P U P I L
12. H U M O R
13. G R O O V E
14. D U T Y
15. C U R F E W
16. C O N F U S E
17. U S U A L
18. M O O D

Spelling Words
usual
huge
flute
mood
smooth
threw
afternoon
scooter
juice
cruise
truth
bruise
cruel
excuse
pupil
groove
confuse
humor
duty
curfew

Home Activity Your child has learned to read, write, and spell words with the long *u* sound spelled *u*-consonant-*e*, *ew*, *oo*, *ui*, or *u*. Write each long *u* spelling and ask your child to add letters to write a list word with that spelling.

▲ **Spelling Practice Book** p. 20

DAY 5 Posttest

DICTATION SENTENCES

1. I gave the waiter my usual order.
2. The hot air balloon was huge.
3. Liz plays the flute in the band.
4. Drew is in a happy mood today.
5. That is a smooth stone.
6. I threw the ball.
7. The sun came out by afternoon.
8. I wear a helmet when I ride a scooter.
9. This juice is sweet.
10. The cruise ship sailed away from the port.
11. Jim always told the truth.
12. The ball hit me and caused a bruise.
13. Don't be cruel to your pets.
14. Please excuse me for bumping you.
15. Each pupil brought a book.
16. My bike's tire made a groove in the mud.
17. The map may confuse her.
18. Judy has a fine sense of humor.
19. It is your duty to walk the dog.
20. Come home before curfew.

CHALLENGE

21. What factors will influence your choice?
22. We recycle our aluminum cans.
23. Good nutrition keeps us healthy.
24. When we accumulate lots of toys, we give some away.
25. The girls built an igloo from snow.

NEW LITERACIES

OBJECTIVES

- Formulate an inquiry question that is connected to this week's lesson focus.
- Effectively and efficiently find, evaluate, and communicate information related to an inquiry question using electronic sources.

New Literacies

Day 1	Identify Questions
Day 2	Navigate/Search
Day 3	Analyze
Day 4	Synthesize
Day 5	Communicate

NEW LITERACIES

Internet Inquiry Activity

EXPLORE UNIQUE QUALITIES OF THE WEST

Use the following 5-day plan to help students conduct this week's Internet inquiry activity on the unique qualities of the American West. Remind students to follow classroom rules when using the Internet.

DAY 1

Identify Questions Discuss the lesson focus question: *How does Yosemite reflect the unique qualities of the West?* Brainstorm ideas for inquiry questions about landforms and other natural attractions found in Yosemite. Have students write an inquiry question they want to answer.

DAY 2

Navigate/Search Have students identify keywords to begin their search. If a search is unsuccessful, help students revise their keywords. Point out that government- or education-based organizations probably have more useful and credible information than travel company sites. Have them identify a few sites to explore in depth on Day 3.

DAY 3

Analyze Have students explore the Web sites identified on Day 2. They should scan each site to locate relevant information that helps answer their inquiry questions. Then, have them take notes or, if allowed, print out information and pictures and highlight useful facts and details. Remind students to record their sources carefully, including Web site addresses.

DAY 4

Synthesize Have students synthesize what they learned on Day 3 by combining information from different sources in a logical order. Remind them to restate the information in their own words and add their own ideas.

DAY 5

Communicate Have students share their inquiry results by creating a travel poster describing an attraction at Yosemite. They can use a word processing program to create the document and illustrate it with clip art, drawings, or printed Web site photographs.

RESEARCH/STUDY SKILLS
Print Sources

TEACH

Ask students where they might find information on another national park. Display examples of various print sources and discuss the purpose and features of each type.

- **Print sources** include textbooks, trade books, encyclopedias, dictionaries, almanacs, atlases, magazines, newspapers, newsletters, government and community pamphlets, and other printed reference materials.

- When selecting print sources for research, think about the **purpose** of each type of source. For example, history textbooks or trade books are good sources for information about people and events from the past; newspapers and magazines are good sources for information about people living today and current events.

- To find information in a print source, think about its **organization.** The **table of contents, index,** or **headings** show what information the source includes and how it is organized.

Distribute print sources with information on national parks to small groups. Have each group study its source. Then discuss these questions:

1. **What is the purpose of the source?**

2. **How is the information organized?**

3. **Suppose you needed information such as camping fees or details about an area affected by a recent forest fire. Which sources would probably have the most up-to-date information?**

Newsletter

Magazine

Pamphlet

ASSESS

As groups work, have them fill in a note card about the print source. Suggest they identify the type of source, the title, and a description of the information it contains. They may also record how it is organized, how current it is, how easy it is to use, and how they might use it for a research project.

For more practice or to assess students, use Practice Book pp. 49–50.

Print Sources

- Libraries contain many sources of information for students to use. You can use a library database or a card catalog to identify and locate these materials. In both cases, you can search for materials by author, title, or subject.
- **Print sources** include encyclopedias, newspapers, magazines, dictionaries, and other reference books.

Directions Study this school's list of available print resources.

Newspapers	Encyclopedias
Hillside School News (school newspaper)	*Encyclopedia of History Makers,* vol. I
Hillside Streets (community paper)	*Encyclopedia of the Nation,* vol. I–X
Daily Globe (metropolitan city paper)	*Encyclopedia of Nature,* vol. I–II
	Encyclopedia of Science, vol. I–IV
	Encyclopedia of Women, vol. I–II
Magazines	
History for Young People	**Dictionaries**
Mathematics Today	*Kenner's Dictionary of Common Words and Phrases*
The Natural World	*The Student's Dictionary*
Go Go Go Travel Monthly	*Theisen's Dictionary of Medicine*
Sports U.S.A.	

▲ **Practice Book** p. 49

Directions Imagine that you are writing a report on Yosemite National Park. Use the list of print sources to answer the questions below.
Possible answers given.

1. What print source would you use first for your report on Yosemite? Explain.
   I would use an encyclopedia to get an overview.

2. Why might a newspaper not be the first place you looked for information?
   Newspapers report mostly current events and might not have much general information.

3. What magazine(s) might have information you could use for your report?
   The Natural World, Go Go Go Travel Monthly

4. Which source(s) might have interesting photographs for your report?
   Magazines might include more pictures or graphics.

5. How might you use a dictionary while writing your report?
   I might use it to find the definition of an unfamiliar word.

6. Suggest a topic you might check in a library's card catalog for information.
   Yosemite National Park

7. Name three listed sources unlikely to have much information on Yosemite.
   Hillside School News, Hillside Streets, History for Young People

8. Which encyclopedia might help you find information on animals in Yosemite?
   Encyclopedia of Nature

9. How might you use an author's name to find information for this report?
   I might see if an author who has written once about Yosemite has written any other useful books.

10. What print sources would have up-to-date information on a fire at Yosemite?
    A newspaper or magazine would have it, because in general they are updated more frequently.

School + Home Home Activity Your child learned about print sources. Take a trip together to your local library. Find and browse through the sections of print sources.

▲ **Practice Book** p. 50

Assessment Checkpoints *for the Week*

Selection Assessment

Use pp. 17–20 of Selection Tests to check:

 Selection Understanding

  Comprehension Skill *Main Idea*

 Selection Vocabulary

glacier	slopes
impressive	species
naturalist	wilderness
preserve	

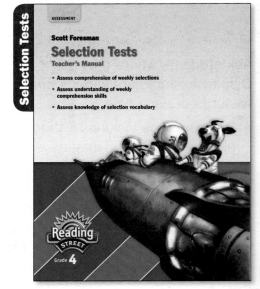

ASSESSMENT

Scott Foresman

Selection Tests
Teacher's Manual

- Assess comprehension of weekly selections
- Assess understanding of weekly comprehension skills
- Assess knowledge of selection vocabulary

Reading STREET
Grade 4

Leveled Assessment

On-Level
Strategic Intervention
Advanced

Use pp. 25–30 of Fresh Reads for Differentiated Test Practice to check:

 Comprehension Skill *Main Idea*

 REVIEW Comprehension Skill
Fact and Opinion

 Fluency *Words Correct Per Minute*

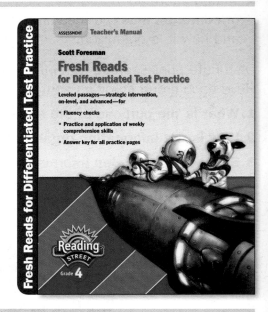

ASSESSMENT Teacher's Manual

Scott Foresman

Fresh Reads
for Differentiated Test Practice

Leveled passages—strategic intervention, on-level, and advanced—for

- Fluency checks
- Practice and application of weekly comprehension skills
- Answer key for all practice pages

Reading STREET
Grade 4

Managing Assessment

Use Assessment Handbook for:

 Observation Checklists

 Record-Keeping Forms

Portfolio Assessment

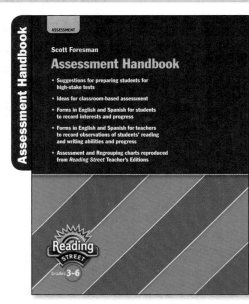

ASSESSMENT

Scott Foresman

Assessment Handbook

- Suggestions for preparing students for high-stake tests
- Ideas for classroom-based assessment
- Forms in English and Spanish for students to record interests and progress
- Forms in English and Spanish for teachers to record observations of students' reading and writing abilities and progress
- Assessment and Regrouping charts reproduced from *Reading Street* Teacher's Editions

Reading STREET
Grades 3–6

Unit 1
Concept Wrap-Up

How do the diverse regions and peoples of the United States reflect its greatness?

Students are ready to express their understanding of the unit concept question through discussion and wrap-up activities and to take the Unit 1 Benchmark Test.

Unit Poetry

Use the poetry on pp. 134-137 to help students appreciate poetry and further explore their understanding of the unit theme, This Land Is Your Land. It is suggested that you

- **read the poems aloud**
- **discuss and interpret the poems with students**
- **have students read the poems for fluency practice**
- **have students write interpretive responses**

Unit Wrap-Up

Use the Unit Wrap-Up on pp. 138-139 to discuss the unit theme, This Land Is Your Land, and to have students show their understanding of the theme through cross-curricular activities.

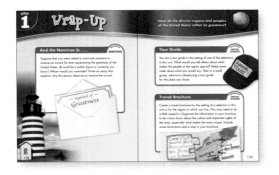

Unit Project

On p. 17, you assigned students a unit-long inquiry project, a poster highlighting a geographical attraction in the United States. Students have investigated, analyzed, and synthesized information during the course of the unit as they prepared their posters. Schedule time for students to present their projects. The project rubric can be found to the right.

Unit Inquiry Project Rubric

4	3	2	1
• Research is accurate and very detailed. Sources are reliable and relevant to inquiry question.	• Research is generally accurate and detailed. Most sources are reliable and relevant.	• Research includes inaccuracies, irrelevant information, or little detail. Some sources are unreliable.	• Research is not accurate, detailed, or relevant. Most sources are unreliable.
• Poster is informative, well organized, and visually appealing.	• Poster is informative, but has minor inconsistencies in organization or visually distracting elements.	• Poster is somewhat informative and visually appealing, but parts are unclear.	• Poster shows little or no information or organization. It is not visually appealing.

Unit 1
Reading Poetry

- Listen and respond to poems.
- Identify how meaning is conveyed through word choice.
- Read poetry fluently.
- Connect ideas and themes across texts.

Model Fluent Reading

Read "We're All in the Telephone Book" aloud. Tell students to listen for the rhythm of the poem. Is the language graceful and flowing, or clumsy and awkward? Point out that the rhythm of a poem helps readers make sense of it.

Discuss the Poem

1 Draw Conclusions • Inferential

Which names does the poet mention in the poem? Why might he include these names?

Possible responses: He includes the names Anderson, Zabowski, and Rockefeller. He might include them to show that people of many different backgrounds are included in the phone book.

2 Details and Facts • Critical

Why is a rich man like Rockefeller listed after Hughes, the poet, in the phone book? Why do you think the poet thinks this is important?

Possible response: Rockefeller is listed after Hughes because the phone book lists people in alphabetical order. The poet is pointing out that the phone book treats all people as equals. Wealth does not matter.

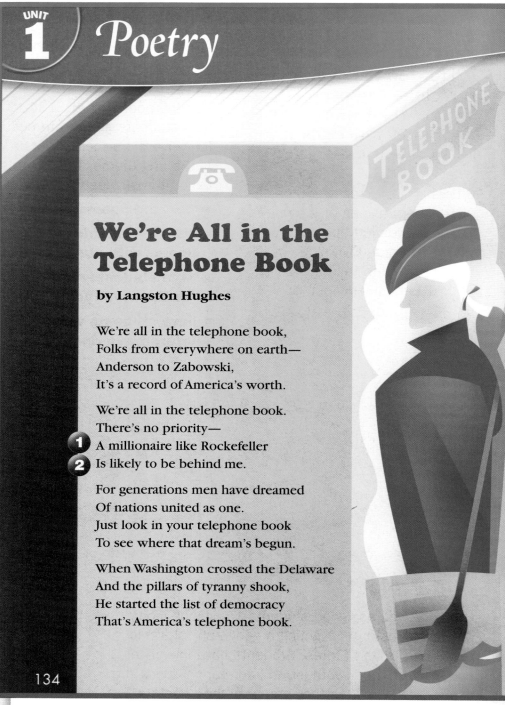

We're All in the Telephone Book

by Langston Hughes

We're all in the telephone book,
Folks from everywhere on earth—
Anderson to Zabowski,
It's a record of America's worth.

We're all in the telephone book.
There's no priority—
1 A millionaire like Rockefeller
2 Is likely to be behind me.

For generations men have dreamed
Of nations united as one.
Just look in your telephone book
To see where that dream's begun.

When Washington crossed the Delaware
And the pillars of tyranny shook,
He started the list of democracy
That's America's telephone book.

134

 **Practice Fluent Reading**

Have partners take turns reading "We're All in the Telephone Book" aloud. Tell students to listen for the rhythm of the poem. Is it easy to read aloud? Does the language flow? Then have students listen to the AudioText of the poem and compare and contrast their readings with the CD recording.

Audio CD Audio Text

Speak Up

by Janet S. Wong

You're Korean, aren't you?

Why don't you speak Korean?

Say something Korean.

C'mon. Say something.

Say some other stuff.
Sounds funny.
Sounds strange.

Listen to me?

But I'm American,
can't you see?

But I was born here.

Yes.

Just don't, I guess.

I don't speak it.
I can't.

Halmoni. Grandmother.
Haraboji. Grandfather.
Imo. Aunt.

Hey, let's listen to you
for a change.

Say some foreign words.

Your family came from
somewhere else. **1**
Sometime.

So was I. **2**

135

WRITING POETRY

Have students write their own poem that is a dialogue between two
people. Encourage students to have their speakers learn something
about each other through their dialogue.

Model Fluent Reading

Explain to students that "Speak Up" is a
conversation between two people. Read
the poem aloud, using your tone of voice to
express each speaker's emotions.

Discuss the Poem

1 Dialogue • Inferential
**What does the Korean American mean
when he or she says that the other
speaker's family came "from somewhere
else"?**

Possible response: The Korean American
is pointing out that America is a land of
immigrants. Most Americans can trace
their roots back to someplace outside of
the United States.

2 Compare and Contrast • Inferential
**How are the two speakers alike? How
are they different?**

Possible responses: The first speaker
thinks the second one "sounds funny"
when he or she speaks Korean. Both
speakers were born in America, and their
families came from other countries.

Unit 1
Reading Poetry

Model Fluent Reading

Read "City I Love" aloud. Have students pay attention to the repetition of sounds, words, and phrases in the poem. Ask them to name some of the repetitions they hear in the poem.

Discuss the Poem

1 **Alliteration • Literal**

What are some examples of alliteration, or words beginning with the same sounds?

Possible responses: Examples of alliteration include *swishes, swashes, sputters, of sweepers swooshing* and *pulse with people…pacing to must-get-there places.*

2 **Setting • Inferential**

What is the setting of this poem? How does the poet create a picture of it?

Possible responses: The poem is set in a city. The poet describes the city during the morning, afternoon, and night of a typical day.

CITY I LOVE

by Lee Bennett Hopkins

In the city
I live in—
city I love—
mornings wake
to
swishes, swashes,
sputters
of sweepers
swooshing litter
from gutters.

In the city
I live in—
city I love—
afternoons pulse
with
people hurrying,
scurrying—
races of faces
pacing to
must-get-there
places.

In the city
I live in—
city I love—
nights shimmer
with lights
competing
with stars
above
unknown heights.

In the city
I live in—
city I love—
as dreams
start to creep
my city
of senses
lulls
me
to
sleep. **2**

136

Practice Fluent Reading

Have partners practice and present "City I Love" in a choral reading. Tell students to stress or emphasize the sounds, words, and phrases that are repeated in the poem.

Audio CD Audio Text

Midwest Town

by Ruth De Long Peterson

Farther east it wouldn't be on the map—
Too small—but here it rates a dot and a name.
In Europe it would wear a castle cap
Or have a cathedral rising like a flame.

But here it stands where the section roadways meet.
Its houses dignified with trees and lawn;
The stores hold *tête-à-tête* across Main Street;
The red brick school, a church—the town is gone.

America is not all traffic lights,
And beehive homes and shops and factories;
No, there are wide green days and starry nights, ❶
And a great pulse beating strong in towns like these. ❷

137

WRITING POETRY

Have students write a poem about their neighborhood, city, or another special place. Suggest that students use imagery, or words that appeal to one or more of the five senses, to help readers imagine the place they are describing.

Model Fluent Reading

Tell students to use punctuation, not line breaks, to tell them when to pause when reading poetry. Read "Midwest Town" aloud. Pause briefly after commas and slightly longer after semicolons, periods, and dashes.

Discuss the Poem

❶ Imagery • Inferential
What images does the poet use to describe this town? To which senses do these images appeal?

Possible responses: The poet uses images like *houses…with trees and lawn, the red brick school, green days,* and *starry nights* to help you "see" the town.

❷ Compare and Contrast • Inferential
How is the town in this poem different from other towns in the United States? Which do you think the poet prefers?

Possible responses: The speaker says this town doesn't have *traffic lights, beehive homes, shops,* or *factories.* The poet seems to prefer the small town described in the poem. She says it has "a great pulse beating strong."

Connect Ideas and Themes

Remind students that this unit deals with how the diverse regions and people of the United States reflect its greatness. Ask students to discuss how the diversity of people and places in the United States is described in these four poems. What might the four poets say makes America great?

Unit 1
Wrap-Up

OBJECTIVES

- Critically analyze unit theme.
- Connect content across selections.
- Combine content and skills in meaningful activities that build literacy.
- Respond to unit selections through a variety of modalities.

THIS LAND IS YOUR LAND

Discuss the Big Idea

How do the diverse regions and peoples of the United States reflect its greatness?

Write the unit theme and Big Idea question on the board. Ask students to think about the selections they have read in the unit. Discuss how each selection and lesson concept can help them answer the Big Idea question from this unit.

Model this for students by choosing a selection and explaining how the selection and lesson concept address the Big Idea.

And the Nominee Is . . .

connect to **WRITING**

Suppose that you were asked to nominate someone to receive an award for best representing the greatness of the United States. (It could be a public figure or someone you know.) Whom would you nominate? Write an essay that explains why this person deserves to receive the award.

~ Symbol of ~
Greatness

138

How do the diverse regions and peoples of the United States reflect its greatness?

Tour Guide

connect to SOCIAL STUDIES

You are a tour guide in the setting of one of the selections in this unit. What would you tell others about what makes the people or the region special? Make some notes about what you would say. Then in a small group, take turns role-playing a tour guide for the place you chose.

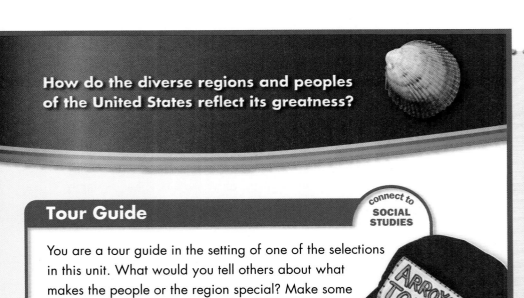

Travel Brochure

connect to SOCIAL STUDIES

Create a travel brochure for the setting of a selection in this unit or for the region in which you live. (You may need to do a little research.) Organize the information in your brochure to let visitors know about the culture and important sights of the area, especially what makes the area unique. Include some illustrations and a map in your brochure.

139

ACTIVITIES

And the Nominee Is ...

Write an Essay Tell students to begin by making a list of people who they might nominate for this award. Then have each student focus on one person. You may want to give students time to research well-known figures or interview people they know. Remind them to organize ideas carefully before they begin to write.

Tour Guide

Describe a Region Students should first review the selections in this unit and choose one of the settings. Then they can jot down ideas about what a tour guide might say about this place and the people who live there. Encourage them to use appealing sensory details in their presentations, emphasizing what is special about the region and its residents.

Travel Brochure

Create a Travel Brochure Have each student choose a setting and think of categories of information to include about it, such as "fast facts," weather, attractions to see, fun things to do, and so on. Students can draw pictures and maps or print online images to illustrate their brochures. Create a bulletin board of completed brochures.

Genre and Author Study

GENRE STUDY

Explain that understanding the conventions and elements of a genre can help students

- know what to expect and better understand a story
- recognize a genre when the genre is not identified
- gain insight into the author's purpose or author's thoughts
- read more critically
- create and organize their own writing

Think Aloud **MODEL** If I'm reading a story that I know is a fantasy, I know to look for fantastical elements. If I don't know the genre but am reading a story filled with events that could not happen or creatures that could not exist, I know I'm reading fantasy. Comparing fantasy stories and recognizing the best ones could help me create my own fantasy tale.

Historical Fiction

Point out the definition of historical fiction on p. 768. Add that selections in this genre combine facts and imagination to bring history to life. Imagined conversations, emotions, or people draw readers into historic settings and events. As students look at the chart, ask how *Grandfather's Journey* and *Amelia and Eleanor Go for a Ride* accomplish this.

Other Genres/Other Features

As opportunities arise, use the chart at the right to guide students in other genre studies. Help students recognize the characteristics of the genre and to make comparisons among genres.

Genre Study

What do you like to read? Poetry? Science fiction? Expository nonfiction? Select a favorite genre and do a study. For example, a genre study of historical fiction might compare *Grandfather's Journey* and *Amelia and Eleanor Go for a Ride*.

Try It
- Define the genre.
- Set up a chart with special features of the genre.
- Read two or more examples of the genre.
- Compare selections and complete the chart.

Historical fiction is a story with some factual details and others that are loosely based on history.

Title	Topic	Historical Facts	Fictional Elements
Grandfather's Journey by Allen Say	The journey of the author's grandfather from Japan to California and back	Stories told by Say's grandfather. Japanese immigration to California WWII	Exact feelings of Say's grandfather are interpreted by Say.
Amelia and Eleanor Go for a Ride by Pam Muñoz Ryan	Friendship between Amelia Earhart and Eleanor Roosevelt	Earhart and Roosevelt flew together.	No one knows what Eleanor and Amelia talked about.

Charts for other genres will have different headings. For example, a chart for realistic fiction might have the headings Title, Characters, Setting, Problem/Solution, or Realistic Details.

768

Other Genres and Their Features

Genre	Characteristics
Expository nonfiction	topic, organization, text features, style
Biography	main subject, facts, organization, illustrations
Mystery	detective, suspects, plot, clues, style
Science fiction	theme, science-related plot, characters, futuristic setting
Myth	country or culture of origin, characters, plot
Legend	hero, hero's traits, setting, conflict
Fantasy	characters, setting, plot, fantastical elements
Narrative poetry	subject, plot, rhyme, rhythm
Lyric poetry	subject, figurative language, sound devices, rhythm

Author Study

Do you have a favorite selection? Make a note of the author's name and look for books by that author. You will probably enjoy other works by him or her.

Try It

- Find three or four works by one author.
- Read the book jackets or use the Internet to learn about the author's life to see what may have influenced his or her writing.
- Read the author's works.
- Compare topics, genres, and so on.
- Tell which work is your favorite and why.

Read this author study of Charles R. Smith.

Charles R. Smith, Storyteller and Poet

Charles R. Smith has three loves—photography, writing, and basketball. It makes sense that he has written stories and poems about basketball and has illustrated them with his photographs. His story "What Jo Did" is about a girl who can dunk a basketball, much to the surprise of some neighborhood boys. His poems "Fast Break" and "Allow Me to Introduce Myself" use short lines and rhyme to help the reader feel the fast pace of a basketball game. Both his story and his poems are fun to read.

769

Additional Questions to Consider

- Where and when did/does the author live? How did this affect his or her work?
- Why was the author drawn to his or her favorite genre or topic?
- Are events in the author's life reflected in his or her work?
- Can you identify with any ideas or events from the author's life?
- How does knowing more about the author help you better understand his or her work?

AUTHOR STUDY

Explain to students that an author study is a great opportunity to learn more about favorite authors and their writing. Reading other works by the same author can help students

- identify an author's craft
- make connections to similar genres of writing
- experience good writing models

Author's Craft

Authors make choices about the elements, the language, and the style of their works. By studying an author's work, students will begin to see the writing traits of their favorite authors. Are their characters funny? Are their books easy to read? Do they have great illustrations? Identifying choices an author makes helps students understand their own interests.

Genre

An author study can also help students understand genres. Are all the books by their favorite author science fiction? Does the author write only biographies of famous sports legends? Connecting with a genre can encourage students to read similar works of the same genre by other authors.

Writing

What inspires your favorite author to write? How does he or she come up with ideas? These are the kinds of discoveries students will make by doing an author study. When students experience good writing models, they learn to understand the writing process. Imitating the style of their favorite authors is a great springboard for writing.

DISCUSS AUTHORS

The following information will add to students' understanding of the writing done by the authors whose biographical information appears on pages 770–771.

- Writers of any kind of fiction need good imaginations and storytelling skills, but writers of realistic fiction also need the research skills of a nonfiction writer.

- Writers of realistic fiction need to know about the settings of their stories and the details that would surround their characters. They may use places they know or research new places, but either way, they need to get the details right.

- Writers of realistic fiction must also be good observers of human nature and of people's lives. This is because more than settings have to be realistic; the events that occur, the problems people face, and the feelings and reactions characters have must be realistic as well, or readers will not connect with the story.

Meet Authors of Realistic Fiction

Julia Alvarez
The author of *How Tía Lola Came to ~~Visit~~ Stay*, p. 690

Julia Alvarez grew up in the Dominican Republic, a beautiful tropical island. When she was ten, her family moved to the United States. It was difficult starting over in a New York City school. Ms. Alvarez says, "Not understanding the language, I had to pay close attention to each word—great training for a writer." Ms. Alvarez wrote *How Tía Lola Came to ~~Visit~~ Stay* about an aunt like the ones she had in the Dominican Republic. **Other books about immigrant children: *In the Year of the Boar and Jackie Robinson* and *The Magic Shell***

Kate DiCamillo
The author of *Because of Winn-Dixie*, p. 22

Kate DiCamillo grew up in a small town in Florida. "I had a dog I loved. I spent a lot of time dressing Nanette up—in a green ballet tutu and then later as a disco dancer." After college, Ms. DiCamillo moved to Minneapolis and got a job at a bookstore. "I wrote *Because of Winn-Dixie* because I was homesick for Florida," she said. Since then, Ms. DiCamillo has written three award-winning books. She no longer works at the bookstore. **Other books: *The Tiger Rising* and *The Tale of Despereaux***

Mary Hoffman
The author of *Grace and the Time Machine*, p. 192

Mary Hoffman, who lives in England, is best known for her books about Grace. In 1991, Ms. Hoffman published *Amazing Grace*. This book told the story of Grace, a young black girl who insisted she could play the role of Peter Pan, a white boy, even though everyone told her she couldn't. Ms. Hoffman has said, "Grace is really me—a little girl who loved stories." **Other books: *Amazing Grace* and *Boundless Grace***

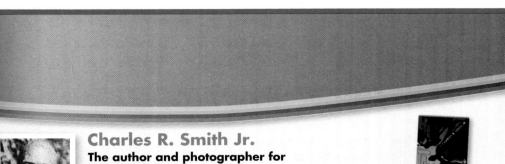

Charles R. Smith Jr.
The author and photographer for "What Jo Did," p. 146

Charles R. Smith Jr. loves photography, writing, and basketball. These three interests all came together for his book *Tall Tales: Six Amazing Basketball Dreams.* "What Jo Did" is just one of the stories in this book. Before he began writing books, Mr. Smith worked as a photographer. "The jobs paid the bills but were boring for me. So I decided to begin a series of photos called Street Basketball in New York." These photos were the beginning of *Rim Shots,* a book of photos, poems, and thoughts about basketball. For his next book, he decided to use infrared film. The film responds to heat and makes unusual colors. You can see the effect in "What Jo Did." **Other books: *Tall Tales: Six Amazing Basketball Dreams* and *Loki & Alex: The Adventures of a Dog & His Best Friend***

Donald J. Sobol
The author of *Encyclopedia Brown and the Case of the Slippery Salamander,* p. 492

Donald J. Sobol was born in New York City in 1924. *Encyclopedia Brown: Boy Detective,* his first story about this famous character, was published in 1963. Since then, he has written more than twenty books about Encyclopedia Brown. In most of these books, there are ten mysteries, with the solutions to the mysteries at the back of the book. Mr. Sobol once said, "Readers constantly ask me if Encyclopedia Brown is a real boy. The answer is no. He is, perhaps, the boy I wanted to be—doing the things I wanted to read about but could not find in any book when I was ten." **Other books: *Encyclopedia Brown Sets the Pace* and *Encyclopedia Brown and the Case of the Jumping Frogs***

771

More About Julia Alvarez

Ms. Alvarez was a teacher for a while. Then, her first novel, *How the Garcia Girls Lost Their Accents,* was successful, and she was able to start writing full time. She now lives on a farm in Vermont and writes novels, essays, and poetry. She wrote *How Tía Lola Came to ~~Visit~~ Stay* for her nephew when he was ten.

More About Mary Hoffman

Mary Hoffman has written more than eighty books on all sorts of topics. Since the success of *Amazing Grace,* Ms. Hoffman has written more books about Grace's dreams and adventures, including her trip to West Africa. Musical plays about Grace have been performed throughout the United States, and there are even Grace dolls.

More About Donald J. Sobol

Now in his eighties, Mr. Sobol lives in Florida and continues to write Encyclopedia Brown stories for a new generation of fans.

ONLINE

Students can use a student-friendly search engine to learn more about the authors on these pages and find additional works by the authors.

DISCUSS AUTHORS

The following information will add to students' understanding of the writing done by the authors whose biographical information appears on pages 772–773.

- Writers of expository nonfiction may write to explain, to give directions, to persuade, or to share information.

- Because expository nonfiction is not a story, there is no plot. As a result, writers must find other ways to organize information. A writer might use chronological order or a cause-and-effect or compare-and-contrast structure. A writer might also use sequential order, as in the numbered steps for directions.

- When an author wants to be persuasive, he or she selects the facts, ideas, and opinions that will guide the reader to reach a specific conclusion. Students can recognize persuasive writing if the writing asks them to think, believe, or do something. It is a good idea in these cases to get more facts on the topic, in order to discover whether you truly agree with the point being made.

- For some authors, writing expository nonfiction is their job. This applies to newspaper reporters, magazine writers, and encyclopedia writers, as well as authors of nonfiction books. They research a topic that interests them and write about it. However, some authors are scientists or historians, and they are simply writing about the topics they know best.

Meet Authors of Expository Nonfiction

Stephen Kramer
The author of *Eye of the Storm,* p. 342

Stephen Kramer says, "I write science books because I love science and want to share my excitement with young readers. I also hope that my books might inspire some of my readers to become scientists!" **Other books: *Caves* and *Hidden Worlds***

Sy Montgomery
The author of *Encantado,* p. 420

For *Encantado,* Sy Montgomery traveled to Peru and Brazil to study and even swim with dolphins. She says "It is my hope in writing for kids that my readers find we share the same dream: a world in which people, animals, land, plants, and water all are seen as precious and worthy of protection." **Other books: *The Snake Scientist* and *The Man-Eating Tigers of Sundarbans***

Richard Sobol
The author and photographer of *Adelina's Whales,* p. 296

Richard Sobol got the idea for *Adelina's Whales* while in Baja California, where Adelina's father was his whale guide. Mr. Sobol hopes his books inspire kids to value and protect the gray whale and other endangered animals. **Other books: *An Elephant in the Backyard* and *Seal Journey***

Judith St. George
The author of *So You Want to Be President?* p. 244

Judith St. George first discovered writing when she wrote a play in sixth grade. After publishing several books about American history, she decided to write about the presidency. She thought, "How about making my book on Presidents amusing and fun as well as informative?" **Another book: *So You Want to Be an Inventor?***

772

Meet Authors of Narrative Nonfiction and Journals

Jennifer Owings Dewey
The author and illustrator of _Antarctic Journal,_ p. 586

Jennifer Owings Dewey traveled to Antarctica for _Antarctic Journal._ During her four months there, she drew the animals and landscape, took photographs, and wrote in her journal. Friends and family saved the letters she wrote home. All these went into her book. **Other books about Antarctica: _An Extreme Dive Under the Antarctic Ice_ and _Antarctic Ice_**

Lisa Halvorsen
The author of _Letters Home from Yosemite,_ p. 116

Lisa Halvorsen has visited more than 40 countries on six continents. "Writing opens up a lot of doors," says Ms. Halvorsen. "It gives me a chance to travel, learn about places, and meet people I might not meet if I weren't a writer." **Other books: _Letters Home from the Grand Canyon_ and _Letters Home from Yellowstone_**

Ted Lewin
The author and illustrator of _Lost City,_ p. 542

Ted Lewin loves to travel. He writes and illustrates books about his trips. For _Lost City,_ he hiked the jungle trail to Machu Picchu in Peru. **Other books: _Gorilla Walk_ and _Elephant Quest_**

Bea Uusma Schyffert
The author of _The Man Who Went to the Far Side of the Moon,_ p. 742

Growing up in Sweden, Bea Uusma Schyffert didn't hear much about space travel. After spending time in the United States, however, she says she became "a space geek." To uncover quirky facts about Michael Collins's mission, Ms. Schyffert visited NASA and "asked their space historians all kinds of odd questions." **Other books about space: _Flying to the Moon_ and _Apollo 11_**

773

More About Stephen Kramer

Stephen Kramer says, "I've been picking up leaves, looking at flowers, and learning about animals for as long as I can remember." Mr. Kramer studied biology in college. Now he teaches fourth grade near Vancouver, Washington.

More About Jennifer Owings Dewey

Jennifer Owings Dewey loves to study and write about animals and nature. She says, "I enjoy traveling to remote or wild places to do research." She has written more than twenty nonfiction books for children. She says, "I like writing about extreme environments—cold and hot, dry and wet." She also writes about the amazing variety of animals on Earth. "Writing about the world we live in prevents running out of ideas," she says.

More About Ted Lewin

Ted Lewin has photographed gorillas in Uganda and rhinos in Nepal. He watched a tiger from an elephant's back in India, and he has been much too close to grizzly bears, rattlesnakes, and bison. Mr. Lewin grew up in Buffalo, New York, where he says he had "two brothers, one sister, two parents, a lion, an iguana, a chimpanzee, and an assortment of more conventional pets." The lion only stayed a short time. His mother donated it to the Buffalo Zoo.

ONLINE

Students can search electronic reference works to find out more about these authors and the topics covered in their expository writing. Keywords might include authors' names, interesting facts, or the topic of their work.

DISCUSS AUTHORS

The following information will add to students' understanding of the writing done by the authors whose biographical information appears on pages 774–775.

- A writer of historical fiction must have a sense of the importance of past events and an appreciation of how history can be a key to understanding what the world is like today.

- Writers of historical fiction need the story-telling skills of a fiction writer and the research skills of a nonfiction writer.

- These authors must study the time periods of their stories. They need to get to know as much as possible about the real people and events that surround the fictional elements of their stories. Events and places need to be correct, but so do smaller details. Using details about clothing, transportation, food, housing, tools, and other aspects of daily life are vital to creating successful historical fiction.

Meet Authors of Historical Fiction

Laurie Myers
The author of *Lewis and Clark and Me*, p. 44

Laurie Myers says she got the idea for *Lewis and Clark and Me* after reading about Meriwether Lewis and his dog. "I've had many dogs over the years, and I've been closer to some than others. I saw in Seaman and Lewis a unique closeness that I wanted to express." **Another book: *Surviving Brick Johnson***

Gloria Rand
The author of *Sailing Home*, p. 520

Sailing Home is the fifth book about sailing that Gloria Rand has written and her husband, Ted Rand, who died in 2005, illustrated. Gloria and Ted Rand lived on Mercer Island, off the coast of Washington state. So it is not surprising that they enjoyed making books together about the sea that surrounded them. They also loved hiking in the forest near their home. **Other books: *The Cabin Key* and *Fighting for the Forest***

Pam Muñoz Ryan
The author of *Amelia and Eleanor Go for a Ride*, p. 564

Pam Muñoz Ryan has always admired Amelia Earhart and Eleanor Roosevelt. "When I read something about their meeting, I couldn't wait to write a book about it. I sat in a library and finally found the old newspaper articles. Later, Brian Selznick found a photograph from the very evening. It actually happened!"
Another book: *How Do You Raise a Raisin?*

774

Joan Sandin

The author and illustrator of *Coyote School News*, p. 166

Joan Sandin grew up in Tucson, Arizona. *Coyote School News* is based on a real school newspaper called *Little Cowpuncher*. Schoolchildren in southern Arizona wrote articles for the paper from 1932 to 1943. Their teacher was Eulalia Bourne. Ms. Sandin explains, "Coyote School is a fictionalized school with fictionalized students, but it was inspired by the *Little Cowpuncher* papers." **Other books about school papers: *The Young Journalist's Book* and *Extra! Extra!***

Allen Say

The author and illustrator of *Grandfather's Journey*, p. 70

Allen Say was born in Japan. When he was 16, he moved to California. Remembering his grandfather's tales, he was excited about the move. But when he arrived, he was lonely and unhappy. Mr. Say often writes about people who are part of two cultures. **Other books: *Tea with Milk* and *The Lost Lake***

Brian Selznick

The author and illustrator of *The Houdini Box*, p. 396

Brian Selznick says, "Houdini really did die on Halloween, but in Detroit while on tour, not in New York, as in my story. I sent Houdini and his wife home so Victor could find them there that day. As for the Houdini box, I made it up— or at least I thought I did. Shortly after I wrote this story I found a newspaper article dated 1974, with the headline 'Magician's Box Still Being Sought.' Supposedly, on the 100th anniversary of Houdini's birth, 'a box containing his cherished secrets would be made public….' The article also said that the box had not yet been found." **Other books: *The Doll People* and *Riding Freedom*.**

775

More About Joan Sandin

Joan Sandin grew up in Tucson, Arizona. "I walked a mile to grade school through the desert, with roadrunners and quail for company," she says. As a child, she loved to draw. Art was her favorite subject in school. Today she has written several books and illustrated many more. Ms. Sandin's best friend in high school, María Amado, lived on a ranch near Tucson when she was young. María attended Sópori School, "a school very much like Coyote School," says Ms. Sandin. María's brother, sister, and cousins all wrote articles for the *Little Cowpuncher*.

More About Allen Say

When he was six years old, Allen Say dreamed of becoming a cartoonist. At age twelve, he apprenticed himself to his favorite cartoonist, Noro Shinpei, and young Allen studied with Shinpei for four years. In the United States, after high school, Say wandered unhappily from job to job, city to city, painting along the way. He knew he had to settle down and earn a living, and he decided on advertising photography. This proved to be a good career choice, but Mr. Say still wanted to write—and paint. He relates, "My first children's book was done in my photo studio, between shooting assignments." He now writes and illustrates full time.

Tech Files
ONLINE

Students can use a student-friendly search engine to learn more about the authors and their subjects. Keywords might include authors' names or the settings or events of the historical fiction.

DISCUSS AUTHORS

The following information will add to students' understanding of the writing done by the authors whose biographical information appears on pages 776–777.

- Writers of biographies are called **biographers.** Writers of autobiographies are called **autobiographers.**

- Biographers must do a lot of research to recreate the life and times of the people about whom they write.

- Because autobiographers write about themselves, they can use their memories. However, they might still do research about locations they visited. They might also talk to relatives and friends who went through events, problems, or changes with them.

- Biographies and autobiographies are works of nonfiction. However, some writers include fictional elements, such as dialogue and details that make the subject "come alive." These fictional elements are based on research and evidence. Dialogue should include words or ideas that the person would likely have said in a given situation, and details should be true to the time and place of the story.

- An autobiography is usually told from the first-person point of view because the writer is writing about himself or herself. A biography is usually written in the third person.

Meet Authors of Biography

Joseph Bruchac
The author of *Jim Thorpe's Bright Path*, p. 664

Joseph Bruchac, who is of Abenaki Indian descent, grew up admiring Jim Thorpe. "One of my dearest friends," said Mr. Bruchac, "was a Pueblo/Apache elder named Swift Eagle. For many years, Swift Eagle told me stories about Jim Thorpe, who had been a personal friend of his." Bruchac adds, "I think that all of us, whatever our backgrounds, can find inspiration from our unique heritages." **Other books: *Arrow over the Door* and *A Boy Called Slow***

Christine King Farris
The author of *My Brother Martin*, p. 642

Christine King Farris's main goal in writing *My Brother Martin* was to let children know that her brother, Martin Luther King Jr., was an ordinary child. She says, "I want children to understand as they are growing up that they, too, can become great individuals." Even as a child, her brother seems to have known that. "It all goes back to what Martin said to my mother. He said, 'You know, Mother dear, one day I'm going to turn this world upside down.' And that is exactly what he did." **Other books about Civil Rights: *Martin's Big Words* and *Let It Shine***

Kathryn Lasky
The author of *Marven of the Great North Woods*, p. 216

Kathryn Lasky has written more than one hundred books. Like *Marven of the Great North Woods*, many of her books are based on real events. She is not concerned that her readers learn a lot or get a message from her writing. She says, "What I do hope is that they come away with a sense of joy—indeed, celebration—about something they have sensed of the world in which they live." **Other books: *The Man Who Made Time Travel* and *Born in the Breezes***

776

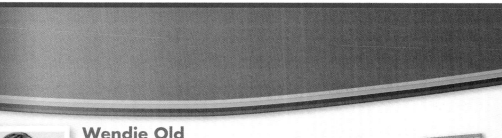

Wendie Old
The author of *To Fly,* p. 716

Wendie Old's life is filled with books. For over thirty years, she has been a children's librarian near Baltimore, Maryland. She has also written many biographies and picture books for children. To honor the one-hundredth anniversary of the flight at Kitty Hawk, Ms. Old decided to write about the Wright brothers. "This was fun," she says, "because I LOVE flying and have always been interested in the first flight." Ms. Old sees the Wright brothers' lives as proof that anyone can fulfill big dreams. As she points out, "The problems of flight were solved, not by people with huge amounts of money from the government, but by small-town bicycle repairmen." **Other books about flight: *The Wright Brothers and Other Pioneers of Flight* and *Sky Pioneer***

James Rumford
The author and illustrator of *Seeker of Knowledge,* p. 470

James Rumford began writing books in his forties. Before that, he worked for the Peace Corps and taught English all over the world, including Africa, the Middle East, and Asia. He currently lives in Hawaii, where he runs a small publishing company. Mr. Rumford can speak or translate many languages. For *Seeker of Knowledge,* he taught himself hieroglyphics. "I think all kids are like Jean-François Champollion," says Mr. Rumford. "When they're 10, 11, 12 years old, most of them have a clear picture of what they want to do." Mr. Rumford wants kids to know that dreams can come true with hard work. **Other books: *Traveling Man* and *The Island-below-the-Star***

777

More About Joseph Bruchac

Joseph Bruchac says, "Jim Thorpe struck me as a true American hero. The fact that part of my own heritage was American Indian made Jim even more special to me." Mr. Bruchac also says that he feels closer to Jim Thorpe and his story because of Swift Eagle's friendship with Thorpe.

More About Christine King Farris

Christine King Farris was close in age to her brother Martin Luther King Jr. The two of them played together a lot as they were growing up. Ms. Farris thinks her brother can be a role model for all children. Ms. Farris is a Professor of Education at a college in Atlanta, Georgia.

More About Kathryn Lasky

When Kathryn Lasky was growing up in the suburbs of Indianapolis, Indiana, her mother encouraged her to write. Ms. Lasky relates, "She said, 'Kathy, you love words. And you have such a great imagination. You should be a writer.' My mom always thought I was the best, even when teachers didn't."

ONLINE

Students can use a student-friendly search engine to learn more about the authors and their subjects. Keywords might include authors' names; the names of the subjects of the biographies; or an event, place, or time period mentioned in the author information or in the stories.

DISCUSS AUTHORS

The following information will add to students' understanding of the writing done by the authors whose biographical information appears on pages 778–779.

Science Fiction

- Writers of science fiction need to have an interest in science—because good science fiction needs to include some scientific facts, theories, or ideas.

- Even in science fiction, writers need to make sure the reactions and emotions of the characters are believable, or readers will not connect with the story.

Fantasy

- Most writers of fantasy have read a lot of fairy tales, myths, and legends. Their imaginations have been fed by the impossible situations or amazing creatures of these classic stories.

- Like all other successful fiction, fantasy needs to involve believable reactions, issues, and emotions for readers to connect with the stories.

Fairy Tales and Folk Tales

- Fairy tales and folk tales highlight human behavior and what a culture values. Behavior that a culture values will lead to a happy ending.

- Fairy tales and folk tales are often passed down for generations. The writers who record them usually appreciate the histories behind the stories. The tales may also reflect their own values or their own cultures.

Ben Bova
The author of *Moonwalk*, p. 612

Ben Bova calls upon the latest in scientific knowledge to write his books about the future. In the past, he predicted the first U.S. trip to the moon, virtual reality, video games, and possible life on Mars. Now, he predicts that we will one day enjoy tours in space and discovery of extraterrestrial life. We'll see—he's been right so far! **Other science fiction books: *The Wonderful Flight to the Mushroom Planet* and *The Forgotten Door***

Lynne Cherry
The author and illustrator of *The Great Kapok Tree*, p. 364

Lynne Cherry says, "I wrote *The Great Kapok Tree* so that children would know about the threat to the world's rain forests and, hopefully, try to save them. All my life I've been a nature lover. Natural settings have always provided me with places for my thoughts to wander and my imagination to fly." **Other books: *A River Ran Wild* and *The Armadillo from Amarillo***

Chris Van Allsburg
The author and illustrator of *The Stranger*, p. 272

Chris Van Allsburg started out as a sculptor, drawing only in the evenings for fun. One day an author and artist friend came for dinner and saw Mr. Van Allsburg's drawings. He thought they were amazing and showed them to his editor. Before long, Mr. Van Allsburg published his first picture book, *The Garden of Abdul Gasazi*. **Other books: *The Garden of Abdul Gasazi* and *Zathur***

Meet Authors of Fairy Tales and Folk Tales

Mary-Joan Gerson
The author of *How Night Came from the Sea*, p. 318

Mary-Joan Gerson became interested in writing books for children when she and her husband were in Nigeria serving with the Peace Corps. After she returned to the United States, she wanted to write books so that American children could learn about Africa. Ms. Gerson travels to learn about cultures. *How Night Came from the Sea* grew out of a trip she made to Brazil, where she went to experience the Yoruba culture. In addition to her work as a writer, Ms. Gerson is a psychologist and a faculty member at New York University. **Other books: *People of Corn* and *Why the Sky Is Far Away***

Jackie Mims Hopkins
Author of *The Horned Toad Prince*, p. 92

Jackie Mims Hopkins wasn't much of a reader as a young girl. "I didn't enjoy reading any book of length. I couldn't sit still long enough to read." Now she is an author and a librarian! Ms. Hopkins got the idea for *The Horned Toad Prince* when she was researching horned toads for another book. "I realized there weren't many stories about them. I decided it was time to write a story about the little critters," she says. "I started thinking about which fairy tale could be used with a horned toad as the main character. 'The Frog Prince' was a perfect match." **Another book: *The Three Armadillies Tuff***

779

More About Ben Bova

Ben Bova has been writing science fiction for over fifty years. A scientist in his own right, Bova has worked on major research projects, including one that helped prepare *Apollo 11* for flight. In his books, he combines his understanding of science with the ability to tell great stories that are full of adventure. Particularly popular is his "Grand Tour" series of books, which tell of humans who explore and colonize the solar system in the future.

More About Lynne Cherry

Lynne Cherry wrote the first, rough version of *The Great Kapok Tree* while riding on a train from Connecticut to Washington, D.C. However, she traveled to the Amazon rain forest in Brazil to research the illustrations.

More About Chris Van Allsburg

Chris Van Allsburg relates that his stories start with his seeing pictures in his mind. He says that if he can figure out what the pictures mean, he can discover the story that is waiting to be written.

ONLINE

Students can use a student-friendly search engine, using author's names as keywords. Students might also search out other folk tales or fairy tales, the science behind the science fiction, or the cultures or settings of the stories.

DISCUSS ILLUSTRATORS

The following information will add to students' understanding of the work done by the illustrators whose biographical information appears on pages 780–783.

- An illustrator must use the author's words and his or her own knowledge and imagination to create images to go with those words.

- Often an illustrator can rely on his or her own experiences to come up with images. However, in some cases, an illustrator must do research. He or she may need to determine the right clothes, transportation, or objects used by the characters in a story, or the plants, houses, and scenery of a location. This is especially important for a story with an historical or real-world setting. For science fiction, a knowledge of the scientific aspects of the story is necessary.

- Sometimes illustrators and authors work closely together. Other times, a story is completed and given to an illustrator, and the illustrator must fit the pictures to the words.

- Sometimes illustrations simply help readers visualize a story. Sometimes they are a necessary part of the information being shared, as the reader may have no knowledge of the location, people, objects, or events being described.

- Encourage students to look carefully at illustrations as they read. Ask them to think about what those illustrations contribute to the stories.

Meet Illustrators

Michael Austin
The illustrator of *The Horned Toad Prince*, p. 92

"*The Horned Toad Prince* stood out to me right away because of its personality and energy," Michael Austin said. As an artist, Mr. Austin has always had a "strange point of view." He enjoys drawing because it gives him a chance to "draw things my own way, strange or not." **Another book: *Late for School***

Michael Dooling
The illustrator of *Lewis and Clark and Me*, p. 44

Michael Dooling did research before illustrating *Lewis and Clark and Me*. He often asks family and friends to pose in historical costumes that he draws or paints. "Every day at my house is like Halloween!" he says. He also visits schools to teach children about history and art. He comes dressed in a colonial costume and takes children through the steps of making picture books. **Another book: *The Amazing Life of Benjamin Franklin***

Carla Golembe
The illustrator of *How Night Came from the Sea*, p. 318

Carla Golembe is an artist, writer, and teacher. Her paintings have been displayed in art galleries. Of her art she says, "My paintings are the product of my dreams and experiences." Ms. Golembe loves to travel to warm places. When she paints jungles or oceans, she thinks of her experiences in Mexico, Belize, and Hawaii.
Other books: *People of Corn* and *Why the Sky Is Far Away*

780

Kevin Hawkes

The illustrator of *Marven of the Great North Woods*, p. 216

Kevin Hawkes never planned to be an artist, but always loved art classes in school. His first job out of college was producing cartoons for Saturday morning television. In his words, "I was horrible!" When he went to work in the children's section of a bookstore, he read picture books morning, noon, and night. This helped him get a feel for his own style, which he has used in more than thirty books for children. Mr. Hawkes lives with his family and assorted pets (a beagle, a bunny, a large iguana, various fish, and a hamster named Crabby) on an island off the coast of Maine. **Other books: *Dreamland* and *The Librarian Who Measured the Earth***

Brett Helquist

The illustrator of *Encyclopedia Brown and the Case of the Slippery Salamander*, p. 492

Brett Helquist is best known as the illustrator of the Lemony Snicket books, *A Series of Unfortunate Events*. While illustrating those books might seem like enough danger for one man, Mr. Helquist has also illustrated many other children's books. He was born in Ganado, Arizona, and grew up in Orem, Utah. He studied art at Brigham Young University in Provo, Utah. Soon after graduating from college, he moved to New York City. He and his wife live in Brooklyn. **Other books: *It Came from Beneath the Bed* and *Bud Barkin, Private Eye***

781

More About Michael Dooling

Michael Dooling has always loved to read and draw. He loved adventure stories, mysteries, history, and any story where the characters had great costumes. Because of his fascination with the past, he particularly enjoys illustrating books about history. His research for these books has taken him to Ellis Island; Mount Vernon; Monticello; Williamsburg, Virginia; and many other places. Mr. Dooling often visits schools and shares his experiences with students.

More About Carla Golembe

Carla Golembe writes, "I have always loved to create things—paintings, stories, illustrations of imaginary worlds. When I was a child, my mother and I would go to the library every week. Being without a book to read was unimaginable, both then and now." Ms. Golembe has received numerous awards for her work. In addition to illustrating books, she teaches at the Art School of the Boca Raton Museum of Art and does presentations for school children and adults.

ONLINE

Students can use a student-friendly search engine to learn more about the illustrators on these pages or elsewhere in the book. Students may wish to find the personal Web pages for some of the illustrators.

More About S. D. Nelson

S. D. Nelson is a member of the Standing Rock Sioux tribe in the Dakotas. He writes, "My people are known as the Sioux or Lakota. My ancestors were the people of the Buffalo, for the Buffalo gave them most of their food, their warm robes, and the lodge skins of their tipis." Mr. Nelson's paintings are modern interpretations of traditional Lakota images. He also does traditional crafts, painting on animal skins and bone, creating rawhide drums, and doing beading on leather. Mr. Nelson's artwork has appeared on book covers and CD covers, and his paintings hang in galleries and private homes. He has written and illustrated numerous award-winning children's books.

More About Ted Rand

Ted Rand spent his early years traveling the world. He once said, "I saw Hitler speak in Munich. You had to feel something was coming (but) I was too dumb to be scared." He later joined the Naval Air Corps as a navigator in the Pacific during World War II. Mr. Rand became an important and successful graphic artist, and when he was 37, *Time* magazine named him a "Newsmaker of Tomorrow." However, he will be best remembered for the 78 children's books he illustrated through the years. Mr. Rand died at his home on Mercer Island, March 2005, aged 89.

Tech Files
ONLINE

Students can use a student-friendly search engine to find out about awards given for book illustration. Have students locate an award-winning illustrator whose images they like, and then pick a book they might like to read illustrated by that artist.

S. D. Nelson
The illustrator of *Jim Thorpe's Bright Path*, p. 664

S. D. Nelson often creates illustrations in the style of his Lakota ancestors. He was eager to illustrate a story about Thorpe, whom he admired as a boy. He says, "Jim Thorpe is a wonderful example of someone who struggled against many difficulties in order to make his dream come true. I hope young people today will be inspired by his true life story."

Ted Rand
The illustrator of *Sailing Home*, p. 520

Ted Rand was an award-winning illustrator of children's books until his death in 2005. He often collaborated with his wife, Gloria Rand, who writes books for children. The Rands made their home on Mercer Island, which is off the coast of Washington state. **Other books: *The Cabin Key* and *Fighting for the Forest***

David Small
The illustrator of *So You Want to Be President?* p. 244

David Small draws political cartoons for newspapers and illustrates children's books. *So You Want to Be President?* was a perfect opportunity for him to combine these two interests. "I hope readers will laugh first, and then begin to think a little more deeply," Mr. Small says. "Caricatures are not only funny pictures of people. The best ones make us see familiar faces in a new way. They exaggerate prominent aspects of a face to make us re-examine our heroes and other public figures in a different, more human light. The book concerns Presidents as the human beings they all are." **Another book: *Imogene's Antlers***

782

Chris Soentpiet
The illustrator of *My Brother Martin*, p. 642

Chris Soentpiet has illustrated almost twenty award-winning children's books. He felt honored to be asked to illustrate *My Brother Martin*. Mr. Soentpiet says, "It was exciting to work with the sister of Dr. King. When I was young, in school we celebrated his birthday every year. Dr. King was and still is one of my heroes. Mrs. Christine King Farris and her family played such an important part in Dr. King's childhood. I hope this book will tell boys and girls that Dr. King was just like them when he was their age." **Other books: *Peacebound Trains* and *Around Town***

Matthew Trueman
The illustrator of *The King in the Kitchen*, p. 440

Matthew Trueman's family moved from the United States to Italy when he was four. He remembers, "I didn't know Italian at first, so I spent a lot of time drawing by myself. I didn't have very many toys, but if I had paper and something to draw with, I could play with castles, robots, mountains, airplanes, soldiers, horses, swords, …anything I could think of." He now lives in the United States, where he creates illustrations for children's books, magazines, newspapers, and advertisements. Before he illustrates a story, Mr. Trueman tries to form a picture of the characters. He says, "The first and most important part for me is finding the characters—the way a director might experiment with different actors for a film. If I get the characters right, they become almost like real people to me, and they act out the story." Of the characters in *The King in the Kitchen*, he says, "I like the way the King and his daughter seem a little crazy." **Other books with plays: *12 Fabulously Funny Fairy Tale Plays* and *Theatre for Young Audiences***

783

More About Chris Soentpiet

Chris Soentpiet was born in South Korea. When he was only six, his mother died. A year later, his father was killed in a car accident. He and his older sister were adopted by the Soentpiets, an American family who lived in Hawaii. Since his new family spoke no Korean, Chris had to learn English quickly. Many years later, while researching the illustrations for a book titled *Peacebound Trains*, he was reunited with his Korean brothers and sisters. Chris writes, "The books I create reflect my interest in people, history, and culture." He says that for his books with a historical theme, he is very careful to make sure that what he paints is historically accurate.

Students can use a student-friendly search engine to find images of historic time periods, real places, or real people illustrated in the books and compare them with the illustrators' interpretations of those times and places.

Glossary

Glossary

How to Use This Glossary

This glossary can help you understand and pronounce some of the words in this book. The entries in this glossary are in alphabetical order. There are guide words at the top of each page to show you the first and last words on the page. A pronunciation key is at the bottom of every other page. Remember, if you can't find the word you are looking for, ask for help or check a dictionary.

The entry word is in dark type. It shows how the word is spelled and how it is divided into syllables.

The pronunciation is in parentheses. It also shows which syllables are stressed.

Part-of-speech labels show the function or functions of an entry word and any listed form of that word.

an·ces·tor (an′ses′tər), *NOUN.* person from whom you are descended, such as your great-grandparents: *Their ancestors had come to the United States in 1812.* ❏ *PLURAL* **an·ces·tors.**

Sometimes, irregular and other special forms will be shown to help you use the word correctly.

The definition and example sentence show you what the word means and how it is used.

784

Aa

a·board (ə bôrd′), *ADVERB.* on board; in or on a ship, train, bus, airplane, etc.: *"All aboard!" shouted the conductor, and everyone rushed for the train.*

a·bun·dance (ə bun′dəns), *NOUN.* quantity that is a lot more than enough: *There is an abundance of apples this year.*

af·ford (ə fôrd′), *VERB.* to give as an effect or a result; provide; yield: *Reading a good book affords real pleasure.* ❏ *VERB* **af·ford·ed, af·ford·ing.**

al·ti·tude (al′tə tüd), *NOUN.* a high place: *At some altitudes, snow never melts.*

a·maze (ə māz′), *VERB.* to surprise greatly; strike with sudden wonder; astound: *He was amazed at how different the strand of hair looked under a microscope.* ❏ *VERB* **a·mazed, a·maz·ing.**

am·phib·i·an (am fib′ē ən), *NOUN.* any of many cold-blooded animals with backbones and moist, scaleless skins. Their young usually have gills and live in water until they develop lungs for living on land. Frogs, toads, newts, and salamanders are amphibians. ❏ *PLURAL* **am·phib·i·ans.**

an·ces·tor (an′ses′tər), *NOUN.* person from whom you are descended, such as your great-grandparents: *Their ancestors had come to the United States in 1812.* ❏ *PLURAL* **an·ces·tors.**

an·cient (ān′shənt), *ADJECTIVE.* of times long past: *In Egypt, we saw the ruins of an ancient temple built 6000 years ago.* (Ancient comes from the Latin word *ante* meaning "before.")

an·tic·i·pa·tion (an tis′ə pā′shən), *NOUN.* act of anticipating; looking forward to; expectation: *In anticipation of a cold winter, they cut extra firewood.*

ap·pear (ə pir′), *VERB.* to be seen; come in sight: *One by one, the stars appear.* ❏ *VERB* **ap·peared, ap·pear·ing.**

a·quar·i·um (ə kwâr′ē əm), **1.** *NOUN.* tank or glass bowl in which fish or other water animals and water plants are kept in water. **2.** *NOUN.* building used for showing collections of live fish, water animals, and water plants.

as·tro·naut (as′trə nòt), *NOUN.* pilot or member of the crew of a spacecraft. ❏ *PLURAL* **as·tro·nauts.**

astronaut

at·las (at′ləs), *NOUN.* book of maps.

a·vi·a·tion (ā′vē ā′shən), *NOUN.* science or art of operating and navigating aircraft.

a·vi·a·tor (ā′vē ā′tər), *NOUN.* person who flies an aircraft; pilot.

a·void (ə void′), *VERB.* to keep away from; keep out of the way of: *We avoided driving through large cities on our trip.* ❏ *VERB* **a·void·ed, a·void·ing.**

awk·ward (òk′wərd), *ADJECTIVE.* not easily managed: *This is an awkward corner to turn.*

Bb

back·board (bak′bôrd), *NOUN.* in basketball, the flat, elevated surface of glass, plastic, or wood, on which the basket is mounted. Bank shots are bounced off the backboard.

bar·gain (bär′gən), *NOUN.* agreement to trade or exchange; deal: *You can't back out on our bargain.*

a in hat	ò in open	sh in she
ā in age	ô in all	th in thin
â in care	ô in order	ŦH in then
ä in far	oi in oil	zh in measure
e in let	ou in out	ə = a in about
ē in equal	u in cup	ə = e in taken
ėr in term	ú in put	ə = i in pencil
i in it	ü in rule	ə = o in lemon
ī in ice	ch in child	ə = u in circus
o in hot	ng in long	

785

bawl (bòl), *VERB.* to shout or cry out in a noisy way: *a lost calf bawling for its mother.* ❏ *VERB* **bawled, bawl·ing.**

be·wil·der (bi wil′dər), *VERB.* to confuse completely; puzzle: *bewildered by the confusing instructions.* ❏ *VERB* **be·wil·dered, be·wil·der·ing.**

bi·ol·o·gist (bī ol′ə jist), *NOUN.* a scientist who studies living things, including their origins, structures, activities, and distribution.

bluff¹ (bluf), *NOUN.* a high, steep slope or cliff.

bluff¹

bluff² (bluf), *VERB.* to fool or mislead, especially by pretending confidence: *She bluffed the robbers by convincing them that the police were on the way.*

board·ing school (bôr′ding skül), *NOUN.* school with buildings where the pupils live during the school term.

bow¹ (bou), *VERB.* to bend the head or body in greeting, respect, worship, or obedience: *The people bowed before the queen.* ❏ *VERB* **bowed, bow·ing.**

bow² (bō), **1.** *NOUN.* weapon for shooting arrows. A bow usually consists of a strip of flexible wood bent by a string. **2.** *NOUN.* a looped knot: *The gift had a bow on top.*

bow³ (bou), *NOUN.* the forward part of a ship, boat, or aircraft.

bril·liant (bril′yənt), *ADJECTIVE.* shining brightly; sparkling: *brilliant sunshine.*

brisk (brisk), *ADJECTIVE.* keen; sharp: *A brisk wind was blowing from the north.*

bus·tle (bus′əl), *VERB.* to be noisily busy and in a hurry: *The children were bustling to get ready for the party.* ❏ *VERB* **bus·tled, bus·tling.**

Cc

can·o·py (kan′ə pē), *NOUN.* the uppermost layer of branches in forest trees.

ca·pa·ble (kā′pə bəl), *ADJECTIVE.* having fitness, power, or ability; able; efficient; competent: *He was such a capable student that everyone had great hopes for his future.*

cap·sule (kap′səl), *NOUN.* the enclosed front section of a rocket made to carry instruments, astronauts, etc., into space. In flight, the capsule can separate from the rest of the rocket and go into orbit or be directed back to Earth.

car·go (kär′gō), *NOUN.* load of goods carried by a ship, plane, or truck: *The freighter had docked to unload a cargo of wheat.*

ce·les·tial (sə les′chəl), *ADJECTIVE.* of the sky or outer space: *The sun, moon, planets, and stars are celestial bodies.*

chant (chant), *VERB.* to call over and over again: *The football fans chanted, "Go, team, go!"* ❏ *VERB* **chant·ed, chant·ing.**

cho·rus (kôr′əs), *NOUN.* anything spoken or sung all at the same time: *The children greeted the teacher with a chorus of "Good morning."*

cock·pit (kok′pit′), *NOUN.* the place where the pilot sits in an airplane.

colo·nel (kėr′nl), *NOUN.* a military rank below general.

con·duct (kon′dukt for noun; kən dukt′ for verb), **1.** *NOUN.* way of acting; behavior thought of as good or bad: *Her conduct was admirable.* **2.** *VERB.* to direct; manage: *The teacher conducted our efforts.* ❏ *VERB* **con·duct·ed, con·duct·ing.**

con·fide (kən fīd′), *VERB.* to tell as a secret: *He confided his troubles to his brother.* ❏ *VERB* **con·fid·ed, con·fid·ing.**

con·front (kən frunt′), *VERB.* to face boldly; oppose: *Once she confronted her problems, she was able to solve them easily.* ❏ *VERB* **con·front·ed, con·front·ing.**

con·scious (kon′shəs), *ADJECTIVE.* aware of what you are doing; awake: *About five minutes after fainting, he became conscious again.*

con·sist (kən sist′), *VERB.* to be made up of; be formed: *A week consists of seven days.* ❏ *VERB* **con·sist·ed, con·sist·ing.**

Con·sti·tu·tion (kon′stə tü′shən), *NOUN.* the written set of fundamental principles by which the United States is governed.

con·sult (kən sult′), *VERB.* to seek information or advice from; refer to: *You can consult travelers, books, or maps for help in planning a trip abroad.* ❏ *VERB* **con·sult·ed, con·sult·ing.**

conduct (def. 2)

a in hat	ò in open	sh in she
ā in age	ô in all	th in thin
â in care	ô in order	ŦH in then
ä in far	oi in oil	zh in measure
e in let	ou in out	ə = a in about
ē in equal	u in cup	ə = e in taken
ėr in term	ú in put	ə = i in pencil
i in it	ü in rule	ə = o in lemon
ī in ice	ch in child	ə = u in circus
o in hot	ng in long	

787

continent•daring

con·ti·nent (kon′tə nənt), *NOUN.* one of the seven great masses of land on the Earth. The continents are North America, South America, Europe, Africa, Asia, Australia, and Antarctica. (*Continent* comes from two Latin words, *com* meaning "in" or "together" and *tenere* meaning "to hold.")

con·trap·tion (kən trap′shən), *NOUN.* device or gadget.

con·ver·gence (kən vėr′jəns), *NOUN.* act or process of meeting at a point. (*Convergence* comes from two Latin words, *com* meaning "in" or "together" and *vergere* meaning "incline.")

cord (kôrd), *NOUN.* measure of quantity for cut wood, equal to 128 cubic feet. A pile of wood 4 feet wide, 4 feet high, and 8 feet long is a cord.

cow·ard (kou′ərd), *NOUN.* person who lacks courage or is easily made afraid; person who runs from danger, trouble, etc.

coy·o·te (kī ō′tē or kī′ōt), *NOUN.* a small, wolflike mammal living in many parts of North America. It is noted for loud howling at night.

cra·dle (krā′dl), *NOUN.* a frame to support weight.

crime (krīm), *NOUN.* activity of criminals; violation of law: *Police forces combat crime.*

crum·ble (krum′bəl), *VERB.* to fall to pieces; decay: *The old wall was crumbling away at the edges.* ☐ *VERB* **crum·bled, crum·bling.**

cur·i·os·i·ty (kyur′ē os′ə tē), *NOUN.* an eager desire to know: *She satisfied her curiosity about animals by visiting the zoo every week.* (*Curiosity* comes from the Latin word *cure* meaning "care.")

Dd

dan·gle (dang′gəl), *VERB.* to hang and swing loosely. ☐ *VERB* **dan·gled, dan·gling.**

dangle

dap·pled (dap′əld), *ADJECTIVE.* marked with spots; spotted.

dar·ing (dâr′ing), *ADJECTIVE.* bold; fearless; courageous: *Performing on a trapeze high above a crowd is a daring act.*

788

decipher•drab

de·ci·pher (di sī′fər), **1.** *VERB.* to make out the meaning of something that is puzzling or not clear: *I can't decipher this poor handwriting.* **2.** *VERB.* to change something in cipher or code to ordinary language; decode. ☐ *VERB* **de·ci·phered, de·ci·pher·ing.**

de·part (di pärt′), *VERB.* to go away; leave: *Your flight departs at 6:15.* ☐ *VERB* **de·part·ed, de·part·ing.** (*Depart* comes from the Latin word *departire* meaning "to divide.")

de·pot (dē′ pō), *NOUN.* a railroad or bus station.

depot

des·ti·na·tion (des′tə nā′shən), *NOUN.* place to which someone or something is going or is being sent.

de·struc·tion (di struk′shən), *NOUN.* great damage; ruin: *The storm left destruction behind it.*

dig·ni·fied (dig′nə fīd), *ADJECTIVE.* having dignity; noble; stately: *The queen has a dignified manner.*

dis·may (dis mā′), *NOUN.* sudden, helpless fear of what is about to happen or what has happened: *I was filled with dismay when the basement began to flood.*

dock (dok), *NOUN.* platform built on the shore or out from the shore; wharf; pier. Ships load and unload beside a dock. ☐ *PLURAL* **docks.**

dol·phin (dol′fən), *NOUN.* any of the numerous sea mammals related to the whale, but smaller. Dolphins have beaklike snouts and remarkable intelligence. ☐ *PLURAL* **dol·phins.**

dor·mi·to·ry (dôr′mə tôr′ē), *NOUN.* a building with many rooms in which people sleep. Many colleges have dormitories for students whose homes are elsewhere.

drab (drab), *ADJECTIVE.* not attractive; dull; monotonous: *the drab houses of the smoky, dingy mining town.*

a in hat	ō in open	sh in she
ā in age	ô in all	th in thin
â in care	ô in order	ŦH in then
ä in far	oi in oil	zh in measure
e in let	ou in out	ə = a in about
ē in equal	u in cup	ə = e in taken
ėr in term	ü in put	ə = i in pencil
i in it	ü in rule	ə = o in lemon
ī in ice	ch in child	ə = u in circus
o in hot	ng in long	

789

draft•encounter

draft (draft), **1.** *NOUN.* current of air: *I caught cold by sitting in a draft.* **2.** *NOUN.* a rough copy: *She made two drafts of her book report before she handed in the final form.*

drag (drag), **1.** *NOUN.* the force acting on an object in motion, in a direction opposite to the object's motion. It is produced by friction. **2.** *VERB.* to pull or move along heavily or slowly; pull or draw along the ground: *We dragged the heavy crates out of the garage. I dragged along on my sprained ankle.* ☐ *VERB* **dragged, drag·ging.**

drib·ble (drib′əl), *VERB.* to move a ball along by bouncing it or giving it short kicks: *dribble a basketball or soccer ball.* ☐ *VERB* **drib·bled, drib·bling.**

dude (düd), **1.** *NOUN.* in the western parts of the United States and Canada, person raised in the city, especially an easterner who vacations on a ranch. **2.** *NOUN.* guy; fellow (slang). ☐ *PLURAL* **dudes.**

duke (dük), *NOUN.* nobleman of the highest title, ranking just below a prince.

dun·geon (dun′jən), *NOUN.* a dark underground room or cell to keep prisoners in.

dunk (dungk), *VERB.* to shoot a basketball by leaping, so that the hands are above the rim, and throwing the ball down through the netting. ☐ *VERB* **dunked, dunk·ing.**

dwell (dwel), *VERB.* to make your home; live: *He dwells in the city.* ☐ *VERB* **dwelled, dwell·ing.**

Ee

el·e·gant (el′ə gənt), *ADJECTIVE.* having or showing good taste; gracefully and richly refined; beautifully luxurious: *The palace had elegant furnishings.*

em·bar·rass·ment (em bar′əs mənt), *NOUN.* shame; an uneasy feeling: *He blushed in embarrassment at such a silly mistake.*

en·chant (en chant′), *VERB.* to delight greatly; charm: *The music enchanted us all.* ☐ *VERB* **en·chant·ed, en·chant·ing.** ☐ *ADJECTIVE* **en·chant·ing.**

en·coun·ter (en koun′tər), *NOUN.* an unexpected meeting: *The explorers had a surprising encounter with a polar bear.*

encounter

790

endurance•exposure

en·dur·ance (en dür′əns), *NOUN.* power to last and to withstand hard wear: *It takes great endurance to run a marathon.*

endurance

en·grave (en grāv′), *VERB.* to cut deeply in; carve in; carve in an artistic way: *The jeweler engraved my initials on the back of the watch.* ☐ *VERB* **en·graved, en·grav·ing.**

es·cape (e skāp′), *VERB.* to get out and away; get free: *The bird escaped from its cage.* ☐ *VERB* **es·caped, es·cap·ing.**

es·cort (e skôrt′), *VERB.* to go with another to give protection, show honor, provide companionship, etc. ☐ *VERB* **es·cort·ed, es·cort·ing.**

etch (ech), **1.** *VERB.* to engrave a drawing or design on a metal plate, glass, etc. **2.** *VERB.* to impress deeply: *Her face was etched in my memory.* ☐ *VERB* **etched, etch·ing.**

ex·e·cute (ek′sə kyüt), *VERB.* to carry out; do: *He executed her instructions.* ☐ *VERB* **ex·e·cut·ed, ex·e·cut·ing.**

ex·hale (eks hāl′), *VERB.* to breathe out: *We exhale air from our lungs.* ☐ *VERB* **ex·haled, ex·hal·ing.**

ex·hib·it (eg zib′it), *NOUN.* display or public showing: *The village art exhibit drew 10,000 visitors.*

ex·ile (eg′zil or ek′sil), *VERB.* to be forced to leave your country or home, often by law as a punishment; banish: *Napoleon was exiled to Elba.* ☐ *VERB* **ex·iled, ex·il·ing.**

ex·pect (ek spekt′), *VERB.* to think something will probably happen: *They expected the hurricane to change directions.* ☐ *VERB* **ex·pect·ed, ex·pect·ing.**

ex·po·sure (ek spō′zhər), *NOUN.* condition of being without protection; condition of being uncovered.

a in hat	ō in open	sh in she
ā in age	ô in all	th in thin
â in care	ô in order	ŦH in then
ä in far	oi in oil	zh in measure
e in let	ou in out	ə = a in about
ē in equal	u in cup	ə = e in taken
ėr in term	ü in put	ə = i in pencil
i in it	ü in rule	ə = o in lemon
ī in ice	ch in child	ə = u in circus
o in hot	ng in long	

791

Glossary

Ff

fas·ci·nate (fas′n āt), *VERB.* to interest greatly; attract very strongly; charm: *She was fascinated by the designs, colors in African art.* ❑ *VERB* **fas·ci·nat·ed, fas·ci·nat·ing.**

fa·vor (fā′vər), *NOUN.* act of kindness: *Will you do me a favor?*

fee·bly (fē′blē), *ADVERB.* weakly; without strength: *She walked feebly when she was first recovering from the flu.*

flex (fleks), *VERB.* to bend: *She flexed her stiff arm slowly.* ❑ *VERB* **flexed, flex·ing.**

flex·i·ble (flek′sə bəl), **1.** *ADJECTIVE.* easily bent; not stiff; bending without breaking: *Leather, rubber, and wire are flexible.* **2.** *ADJECTIVE.* able to change easily to fit different conditions: *My mother works from our home, and her hours are very flexible.*

flexible (def. 1)

for·bid·ding (fər bid′ing), *ADJECTIVE.* causing fear or dislike; looking dangerous or unpleasant: *The coast was rocky and forbidding.*

fore·cast (fôr′kast′), *NOUN.* statement of what is coming; prediction: *What is the weather forecast today?* ❑ *PLURAL* **fore·casts.**

for·ma·tion (fôr mā′shən), *NOUN.* series of layers or deposits of the same kind of rock or mineral. ❑ *PLURAL* **for·ma·tions.**

foul (foul), *VERB.* to make an unfair play against. ❑ *VERB* **fouled, foul·ing.**

fra·grant (frā′grənt), *ADJECTIVE.* having or giving off a pleasing odor; sweet-smelling: *fragrant roses.*

friend·less (frend′les), *ADJECTIVE.* to be without people who know and like you.

frost (fröst), **1.** *NOUN.* a freezing condition; temperature below the point at which water freezes: *Frost came early last winter.* **2.** *NOUN.* moisture frozen on or in a surface; feathery crystals of ice formed when water vapor in the air condenses at a temperature below freezing: *On cold fall mornings, there is frost on the grass.*

frus·tra·tion (fru strā′shən), *NOUN.* a feeling of anger and helplessness, caused by bad luck, failure, or defeat.

fu·ri·ous·ly (fyùr′ē əs lē), *ADVERB.* with unrestrained energy, speed, etc.

792

Gg

gash (gash), *NOUN.* a long, deep cut or wound.

gen·e·ra·tion (jen′ə rā′shən), **1.** *NOUN.* all people born about the same time. Your parents and their siblings and cousins belong to one generation; you and your siblings and cousins belong to the next generation. **2.** *NOUN.* about thirty years, or the time from the birth of one generation to the birth of the next generation. There are three generations in a century. ❑ *PLURAL* **gen·e·ra·tions.**

gen·ius (jē′nyəs), *NOUN.* person having very great natural power of mind: *Shakespeare was a genius.*

gla·cier (glā′shər), *NOUN.* a great mass of ice moving very slowly down a mountain, along a valley, or over a land area. Glaciers are formed from snow on high ground wherever winter snowfall exceeds summer melting for many years.

gleam (glēm), *VERB.* to flash or beam with light: *The car's headlights gleamed through the rain.* ❑ *VERB* **gleamed, gleam·ing.**

glid·er (gli′dər), *NOUN.* aircraft without an engine. Rising air currents keep it up in the air.

glider

glimpse (glimps), **1.** *NOUN.* a short, quick view or look: *I caught a glimpse of the falls as our train went by.* **2.** *NOUN.* a short, faint appearance: *There was a glimpse of truth in what they said.* ❑ *PLURAL* **glimp·ses.**

glint (glint), *NOUN.* a gleam; flash: *The glint in her eye showed that she was angry.*

glo·ri·ous (glôr′ē əs), *ADJECTIVE.* magnificent; splendid: *a glorious day.* (*Glorious* comes from the Latin word *gloria* meaning "praise.")

grand (grand), *ADJECTIVE.* excellent; very good: *We had a grand time at the party last night.*

gran·ite (gran′it), *NOUN.* made from a very hard gray or pink rock that is formed when lava cools slowly underground: *a granite countertop.*

griz·zly (griz′lē), **1.** *ADJECTIVE.* grayish; gray. **2.** *NOUN.* grizzly bear; a large, gray or brownish gray bear of western North America.

a	in hat	ò	in open	sh	in she
ā	in age	ō	in all	th	in thin
â	in care	ô	in order	ŦH	in then
ä	in far	oi	in oil	zh	in measure
e	in let	ou	in out	ə = a in about
ē	in equal	u	in cup	ə = e in taken
ėr	in term	ù	in put	ə = i in pencil
i	in it	ü	in rule	ə = o in lemon
ī	in ice	ch	in child	ə = u in circus
o	in hot	ng	in long	

793

Hh

hang·ar (hang′ər), *NOUN.* building for storing aircraft. ❑ *PLURAL* **hang·ars.**

hatch¹ (hach), **1.** *VERB.* to come out of an egg: *One of the chickens hatched today.* **2.** *VERB.* to keep an egg or eggs warm until the young come out: *The heat of the sun hatches turtles' eggs.*

hatch² (hach), *NOUN.* a trapdoor covering an opening in an aircraft's or ship's deck.

heave (hēv), **1.** *VERB.* to lift with force or effort: *The heavy cargo plane heaved off the runway.* **2.** *VERB.* to rise and fall alternately: *The waves heaved in the storm.* ❑ *VERB* **heaved, heav·ing.**

her·mit (hėr′mit), *NOUN.* person who goes away from others and lives alone.

hi·e·ro·glyph (hi′ər ə glif), *NOUN.* picture, character, or symbol standing for a word, idea, or sound. The ancient Egyptians used hieroglyphics instead of an alphabet like ours. ❑ *PLURAL* **hi·e·ro·glyphs.**

home·land (hōm′land′), *NOUN.* country that is your home; your native land.

hoop (hüp *or* hüp), *NOUN.* ring; round, flat band: *a hoop for embroidery, a basketball hoop.*

ho·ri·zon (hə ri′zn), *NOUN.* line where the Earth and sky seem to meet; skyline. You cannot see beyond the horizon.

howl·ing (hou′ling), *ADJECTIVE.* very great: *a howling success.*

hum·ble (hum′bəl), *ADJECTIVE.* not proud; modest: *to be humble in spite of success.*

hyp·no·tize (hip′nə tiz), *VERB.* to put someone into a state resembling deep sleep, but more active, in which the person acts according to the suggestions of the person who brought about the condition. ❑ *VERB* **hyp·no·tized, hyp·no·tiz·ing.**

Ii

ice·berg (is′bėrg′), *NOUN.* a large mass of ice, detached from a glacier and floating in the sea. About 90 percent of its mass is below the surface of the water. ❑ *PLURAL* **ice·bergs.**

iceberg

794

im·mense (i mens′), *ADJECTIVE.* very large; huge; vast: *An ocean is an immense body of water.*

im·pact (im′pakt), *NOUN.* action of striking one thing against another; collision: *The impact of the heavy stone against the windowpane shattered the glass.*

im·pres·sive (im pres′iv), *ADJECTIVE.* able to have a strong effect on the mind or feelings; able to influence deeply.

in·con·sol·a·ble (in′kən sō′lə bəl), *ADJECTIVE.* not able to be comforted; brokenhearted: *The girl was inconsolable because her kitten was lost.*

in·fe·ri·or (in fir′ē ər), *ADJECTIVE.* not very good; below most others; low in quality: *an inferior grade of coffee.*

in·jus·tice (in jus′tis), *NOUN.* lack of justice, fairness, lawfulness: *We were angry at the injustice of the new rule.*

in·land (in′lənd), *ADVERB.* in or toward the interior: *He traveled inland from New York to Chicago.*

Jj

jer·sey (jėr′zē), *NOUN.* shirt that is pulled over the head, made of soft, knitted cloth: *Members of the hockey team wear red jerseys.*

Ll

la·goon (lə gün′), *NOUN.* pond or small lake, especially one connected with a larger body of water.

land·lord (land′lôrd′), *NOUN.* person who owns buildings or land that is rented to others.

las·so (la′ sō), *VERB.* to catch with a long rope with a loop on one end. ❑ *VERB* **las·soed, las·so·ing.**

lei·sure·ly (lē′zhər lē), *ADVERB.* without hurry; taking plenty of time: *He walked leisurely across the bridge.*

link (lingk), *NOUN.* anything that joins or connects, as a loop of a chain does: *a link between his love of art and his career.*

liz·ard (liz′ərd), *NOUN.* any of many reptiles with long bodies and tails, movable eyelids, and usually four legs. Some lizards have no legs and look much like snakes. Iguanas, chameleons, and horned toads are lizards. ❑ *PLURAL* **liz·ards.**

a	in hat	ò	in open	sh	in she
ā	in age	ō	in all	th	in thin
â	in care	ô	in order	ŦH	in then
ä	in far	oi	in oil	zh	in measure
e	in let	ou	in out	ə = a in about
ē	in equal	u	in cup	ə = e in taken
ėr	in term	ù	in put	ə = i in pencil
i	in it	ü	in rule	ə = o in lemon
ī	in ice	ch	in child	ə = u in circus
o	in hot	ng	in long	

795

long•memorial

long (lòng), **1.** *ADJECTIVE.* measuring a great distance from end to end: *A year is a long time.* **2.** *VERB.* to wish very much; desire greatly: *long to see a good friend.* ❑ *VERB* **longed, long•ing.**

loom (lüm), *VERB.* to appear dimly or vaguely as a large, threatening shape: *A large iceberg loomed through the thick fog.* ❑ *VERB* **loomed, loom•ing.**

lull (lul), *VERB.* to soothe with sounds or caresses; cause to sleep: *The soft music lulled me to sleep.* ❑ *VERB* **lulled, lull•ing.**

lum•ber•jack (lum′bər jak′), *NOUN.* person whose work is cutting down trees and sending the logs to the sawmill; woodsman; logger.

lu•nar (lü′nər), *ADJECTIVE.* of, like, or about the moon: *a lunar landscape.*

lurk (lèrk), *VERB.* to move about in a secret and sly manner: *Several people were seen lurking near the house before it was robbed.* ❑ *VERB* **lurked, lurk•ing.**

Mm

ma•gi•cian (mə jish′ən), *NOUN.* person who entertains by art or skill of creating illusions, especially a sleight of hand: *The magician pulled not one, but three rabbits out of his hat!*

maj•es•ty (maj′ə stē), *NOUN.* title used in speaking to or of a king, queen, emperor, empress, etc.: *Your Majesty, His Majesty, Her Majesty.*

man•u•al (man′yü əl), **1.** *ADJECTIVE.* done with the hands: *Digging a trench with a shovel is manual labor.* **2.** *NOUN.* a small book that helps its readers understand and use something; handbook: *A manual came with my pocket calculator.*

mar•vel (mär′vəl), *VERB.* to be filled with wonder; be astonished: *She marveled at the beautiful sunset.* ❑ *VERB* **mar•veled, mar•vel•ing.**

mas•sive (mas′iv), *ADJECTIVE.* big and heavy; bulky: *a massive boulder.*

me•chan•i•cal (mə kan′ə kəl), *ADJECTIVE.* like a machine; automatic; without expression: *The performance was very mechanical.*

me•mo•ri•al (mə môr′ē əl), *ADJECTIVE.* helping people to remember some person, thing, or event: *memorial services.*

memorial

mesquite•mutual

me•squite (me skēt′), *ADJECTIVE.* any of several trees or bushes common in the southwestern United States and Mexico, which often grow in dense clumps or thickets. Mesquite pods furnish a valuable food for cattle. The wood is used in grilling food.

mi•grate (mi′grāt), *VERB.* to go from one region to another with the change in the seasons: *Most birds migrate to warmer countries in the winter.* ❑ *VERB* **mi•grat•ed, mi•grat•ing.**

migrate

min•i•a•ture (min′ē ə chùr or min′ə chər), *NOUN.* anything represented on a small scale: *In the museum, there is a miniature of the famous ship.* ❑ *PLURAL* **min•i•a•tures.**

min•is•ter (min′ə stər), *NOUN.* member of the clergy; spiritual guide; pastor.

mir•a•cle (mir′ə kəl), *NOUN.* a wonderful happening that is contrary to, or independent of, the known laws of nature: *His family considered his complete recovery from the accident to be a miracle.*

mod•ule (moj′ül), *NOUN.* a self-contained unit or system within a larger system, often designed for a particular function: *The lunar module circled the moon.*

mon•u•ment (mon′yə mənt), *NOUN.* something set up to honor a person or an event. A monument may be a building, pillar, arch, statue, tomb, or stone.

monument

mu•tu•al (myü′chü əl), *ADJECTIVE.* done, said, felt, etc., by each toward the other; both given and received: *They had mutual affection for each other.*

a in hat	ò in open	sh in she
ā in age	ò in all	th in thin
â in care	ô in order	ŦH in then
ä in far	oi in oil	zh in measure
e in let	ou in out	ə = a in about
ē in equal	u in cup	ə = e in taken
ėr in term	ú in put	ə = i in pencil
i in it	ü in rule	ə = o in lemon
ī in ice	ch in child	ə = u in circus
o in hot	ng in long	

naturalist•payroll

Nn

nat•ur•al•ist (nach′ər ə list), *NOUN.* person who makes a study of living things.

nau•ti•cal (nò′tə kəl), *ADJECTIVE.* of or about ships, sailors, or navigation.

nav•i•ga•tion (nav′ə gā′shən), *NOUN.* skill or process of finding a ship's or aircraft's position and course.

no•ble (nō′bəl), *ADJECTIVE.* high and great by birth, rank, or title; showing greatness of mind; good: *a noble person.*

nour•ish•ing (nèr′ish ing), **1.** *ADJECTIVE.* keeping well-fed and healthy; producing health and growth: *a nourishing diet.* **2.** *ADJECTIVE.* supporting, encouraging.

nu•mer•ous (nü′mər əs), *ADJECTIVE.* very many: *The child asked numerous questions.*

Oo

oath (ōth), *NOUN.* a solemn promise: *The oath bound him to secrecy.*

of•fend (ə fend′), *VERB.* to hurt the feelings of someone; make angry; displease; pain: *My friend was offended by my laughter.* ❑ *VERB* **of•fend•ed, of•fend•ing.**

out•spo•ken (out′spō′kən), *ADJECTIVE.* not reserved; frank: *an outspoken person.*

Pp

pal•ette (pal′it), **1.** *NOUN.* a thin board, usually oval or oblong, with a thumb hole at one end, used by painters to lay and mix colors on. **2.** *NOUN.* set of colors used by a painter. ❑ *PLURAL* **pal•ettes.**

pan•to•mime (pan′tə mim), *VERB.* to express by gestures: *They pantomimed being hungry by pointing to their mouths and their stomachs.* ❑ *VERB* **pan•to•mimed, pan•to•mim•ing.**

pantomime

par•lor (pär′lər), **1.** *NOUN.* formerly, a room for receiving or entertaining guests; sitting room. **2.** *NOUN.* room or set of rooms used for various business purposes; shop: *a beauty parlor, an ice cream parlor.*

pay•roll (pā′rōl′), *NOUN.* list of persons to be paid and the amount that each one is to receive.

peasant•prideful

peas•ant (pez′nt), *NOUN.* farmer of the working class in Europe, Asia, and Latin America.

pe•cul•iar (pi kyü′lyər), *ADJECTIVE.* strange; odd; unusual: *It was peculiar that the fish market had no fish last Friday.*

plush (plush), *ADJECTIVE.* luxurious; expensive; stylish: *a plush office.*

pol•i•tics (pol′ə tiks), *NOUN SINGULAR OR PLURAL.* the work of government; management of public business: *Our senator has been engaged in politics for many years.*

pol•len (pol′ən), *NOUN.* a fine, yellowish powder released from the anthers of flowers. Grains of pollen carried by insects, wind, etc., to the pistils of flowers fertilize the flowers.

pol•li•nate (pol′ə nāt), *VERB.* to carry pollen from anthers to pistils; bring pollen to. Flowers are pollinated by bees, bats, birds, wind, etc. ❑ *VERB* **pol•li•nat•ed, pol•li•nat•ing.**

por•ridge (pôr′ij), *NOUN.* food made of oatmeal or other grain boiled in water or milk until it thickens.

pos•i•tive (poz′ə tiv), *ADJECTIVE.* permitting no question; without doubt; sure: *We have positive evidence that the Earth moves around the sun.*

po•ten•tial (pə ten′shəl), *NOUN.* something possible: *a potential for danger.*

prair•ie (prâr′ē), **1.** *NOUN.* a large area of level or rolling land with grass but few or no trees, especially such an area making up much of central North America. **2.** *NOUN.* (regional) a wide, open space.

pre•serve (pri zėrv′), *VERB.* to keep from harm or change; keep safe; protect: *Good nutrition helps preserve your health.* ❑ *VERB* **pre•served, pre•serv•ing.**

preserve— fly preserved in amber

pride•ful (prid′fəl), *ADJECTIVE.* haughty; having too high an opinion of oneself.

a in hat	ò in open	sh in she
ā in age	ò in all	th in thin
â in care	ô in order	ŦH in then
ä in far	oi in oil	zh in measure
e in let	ou in out	ə = a in about
ē in equal	u in cup	ə = e in taken
ėr in term	ú in put	ə = i in pencil
i in it	ü in rule	ə = o in lemon
ī in ice	ch in child	ə = u in circus
o in hot	ng in long	

Glossary

pri·or·i·ty (pri ôr′ə tē), *NOUN.* something given attention before anything else: *The young couple's first priority was to find a pleasant house.*

pro·mote (prə mōt′), *VERB.* to raise in rank, condition, or importance: *Pupils who pass the test will be promoted to the next higher grade.* □ *VERB* **pro·mot·ed, pro·mot·ing.**

pul·pit (púl′pit), *NOUN.* platform or raised structure in a church from which the minister preaches.

pulse (puls), **1.** *NOUN.* the regular beating of the arteries caused by the rush of blood into them after each contraction of the heart. By feeling a person's pulse in the artery of the wrist, you can count the number of times the heart beats each minute. **2.** *NOUN.* any regular, measured beat: *the pulse in music.* □ *PLURAL* **pul·ses.**

Qq

quaint (kwānt), *ADJECTIVE.* strange or odd in an interesting, pleasing, or amusing way: *Many old photographs seem quaint to us today.*

quar·an·tine (kwôr′ən tēn′ or kwär′ən tēn′), *NOUN.* detention, isolation, and other measures taken to prevent the spread of an infectious disease.

quiv·er (kwiv′ər), *VERB.* to shake; shiver; tremble: *The dog quivered with excitement.* □ *VERB* **quiv·ered, quiv·er·ing.**

Rr

re·call (ri kôl′), *VERB.* to call back to mind; remember: *I can recall stories told to me when I was a small child.* □ *VERB* **re·called, re·call·ing.**

re·cruit·er (ri krüt′ər), *NOUN.* a person who gets new members, who gets people to join or come: *The college recruiter attended our football game to watch our quarterback.*

ref·er·ence (ref′ər əns), *ADJECTIVE.* used for information or help: *The reference librarian can find the article that you need.*

reign (rān), **1.** *VERB.* to rule: *A king reigns over his kingdom.* **2.** *VERB.* to exist everywhere; prevail: *On a still night, silence reigns.* □ *VERB* **reigned, reign·ing.**

re·mote (ri mōt′), *ADJECTIVE.* out of the way; secluded.

rep·tile (rep′til), *NOUN.* any of many cold-blooded animals with backbones and lungs, usually covered with horny plates or scales. Snakes, lizards, turtles, alligators, and crocodiles are reptiles. Dinosaurs were reptiles. □ *PLURAL* **rep·tiles.**

re·seat (rē sēt′), *VERB.* to sit again. □ *VERB* **re·seat·ed, re·seat·ing.**

re·sem·blance (ri zem′bləns), *NOUN.* similar appearance; likeness: *Twins often show great resemblance.*

res·er·va·tion (rez′ər vā′shən), **1.** *NOUN.* arrangement to have a room, a seat, etc., held in advance for your use later on: *make a reservation for a room in a hotel.* **2.** *NOUN.* land set aside by the government for a special purpose: *an Indian reservation.*

res·er·voir (rez′ər vwär), *NOUN.* place where water is collected and stored for use: *This reservoir supplies the entire city.*

re·sist·ance (ri zis′təns), *NOUN.* thing or act that resists; opposing force; opposition: *Air resistance makes a feather fall more slowly than a pin.*

re·spon·si·bil·i·ty (ri spon′sə bil′ə tē), *NOUN.* the act or fact of taking care of someone or something; obligation: *We agreed to share responsibility for planning the party.*

rift (rift), *NOUN.* a split; break; crack: *The sun shone through a rift in the clouds.*

rille (ril), *NOUN.* a long, narrow valley on the surface of the moon.

rim (rim), *NOUN.* an edge, border, or margin on or around anything: *the rim of a wheel, the rim of a glass.*

riv·er·bed (riv′ər bed′), *NOUN.* channel in which a river flows or used to flow.

round·up (round′up′), *NOUN.* act of driving or bringing cattle together from long distances.

rud·der (rud′ər), *NOUN.* a flat piece of wood or metal hinged vertically to the rear end of an aircraft and used to steer it.

rug·ged (rug′id), *ADJECTIVE.* covered with rough edges; rough and uneven: *rugged ground.*

rugged

ruin (rü′ən), *NOUN.* often ruins, *PL.* what is left after a building, wall, etc., has fallen to pieces: *the ruins of an ancient city.* (*Ruin* comes from the Latin word *ruina* meaning "a collapse.")

a in hat	ó in open	sh in she
ā in age	ò in all	th in thin
â in care	ô in order	ŦH in then
ä in far	oi in oil	zh in measure
e in let	ou in out	ə = a in about
ē in equal	u in cup	ə = e in taken
ėr in term	ú in put	ə = i in pencil
i in it	ü in rule	ə = o in lemon
ī in ice	ch in child	ə = u in circus
o in hot	ng in long	

rum·ble (rum′bəl), *VERB.* to make a deep, heavy, continuous sound: *Thunder was rumbling in the distance.* □ *VERB* **rum·bled, rum·bling.**

runt (runt), *NOUN.* animal, person, or plant that is smaller than the usual size. If used about a person, *runt* is sometimes considered offensive.

Ss

sal·a·man·der (sal′ə man′dər), *NOUN.* any of numerous animals shaped like lizards, but related to frogs and toads. Salamanders have moist, smooth skin and live in water or in damp places. □ *PLURAL* **sal·a·man·ders.**

sas·sy (sas′ē), *ADJECTIVE.* lively; spirited: *a sassy attitude.*

scan (skan), *VERB.* to glance at; look over hastily. □ *VERB* **scanned, scan·ning.**

scent (sent), *NOUN.* a smell: *The scent of roses filled the air.*

schol·ar (skol′ər), *NOUN.* a learned person; person having much knowledge: *The professor was a famous scholar.* □ *PLURAL* **schol·ars.** (*Scholar* comes from the Greek word *schol* meaning "discussion.")

sculp·ture (skulp′chər), **1.** *NOUN.* the art of making figures by carving, modeling, casting, etc. Sculpture includes the cutting of statues from blocks of marble, stone, or wood, casting in bronze, and modeling in clay or wax. **2.** *NOUN.* sculptured work; piece of such work. □ *PLURAL* **sculp·tures.**

sculpture (def. 2)

sea·coast (sē′kōst′), *NOUN.* land along the ocean or sea; seaboard: *the seacoast of Maine.*

seek·er (sēk′ər), *NOUN.* one who tries to find; one who searches: *That judge is a seeker of truth.*

se·lect (si lekt′), *VERB.* to pick out; choose: *Select the book you want.* □ *VERB* **se·lect·ed, se·lect·ing.**

shat·ter (shat′ər), *VERB.* to break into pieces suddenly: *A stone shattered the window.* □ *VERB* **shat·tered, shat·ter·ing.**

shield (shēld), *VERB.* to protect; defend: *They shielded me from unjust punishment.* □ *VERB* **shield·ed, shield·ing.**

shim·mer (shim′ər), *VERB.* to gleam or shine faintly: *Both the sea and the sand shimmered in the moonlight.* □ *VERB* **shim·mered, shim·mer·ing.** □ *ADJECTIVE* **shim·mer·ing.**

shriek (shrēk), *VERB.* to make a loud, sharp, shrill sound. People sometimes shriek because of terror, anger, pain, or amusement. □ *VERB* **shrieked, shriek·ing.**

sil·hou·ette (sil′ü et′), *NOUN.* a dark image outlined against a lighter background: *Silhouettes of skyscrapers could be seen against the moonlit sky.*

silhouette

slith·er (sliŦH′ər), *VERB.* to go with a sliding motion: *The snake slithered into the weeds.* □ *VERB* **slith·ered, slith·er·ing.**

slope (slōp), *NOUN.* any line, surface, land, etc., that goes up or down at an angle: *If you roll a ball up a slope, it will roll down again.* □ *PLURAL* **slopes.**

so·ci·e·ty (sə sī′ə tē), **1.** *NOUN.* the people of any particular time or place: *twentieth-century society, American society.* **2.** *NOUN.* company; companionship: *I enjoy their society.*

sol·emn·ly (sol′əm lē), *ADVERB.* seriously; earnestly; with dignity.

so·lo (sō′lō), **1.** *ADJECTIVE.* without a partner, teacher, etc.; alone: *The flying student made her first solo flight.* **2.** *ADVERB.* on one's own, alone: *to fly solo.*

spe·cies (spē′shēz), *NOUN.* a set of related living things that all have certain characteristics. Spearmint is a species of mint.

spec·i·men (spes′ə mən), *NOUN.* one of a group or class taken to show what the others are like; sample: *He collects specimens of all kinds of rocks and minerals.*

speech·less (spēch′lis), *ADJECTIVE.* not able to talk: *He was speechless with wonder.*

a in hat	ó in open	sh in she
ā in age	ò in all	th in thin
â in care	ô in order	ŦH in then
ä in far	oi in oil	zh in measure
e in let	ou in out	ə = a in about
ē in equal	u in cup	ə = e in taken
ėr in term	ú in put	ə = i in pencil
i in it	ü in rule	ə = o in lemon
ī in ice	ch in child	ə = u in circus
o in hot	ng in long	

spellbound•taunt

spell·bound (spel′bound′), *ADJECTIVE.* too interested to move; fascinated: *The children were spellbound by the circus performance.*

sphere (sfir), *NOUN.* ball or globe. The sun, moon, Earth, and stars are spheres.

splen·dor (splen′dər), *NOUN.* magnificent show; glory.

spur (spėr), *NOUN.* a metal point or pointed wheel, worn on a rider's boot heel for urging a horse on. ❑ *PLURAL* **spurs.**

stag·ger (stag′ər), *VERB.* to become unsteady; waver: *The troops staggered because of their exhaustion.* ❑ *VERB* **stag·gered, stag·ger·ing.**

stall (stȯl), *VERB.* to stop or bring to a standstill, usually against your wish: *The engine stalled.* ❑ *VERB* **stalled, stall·ing.**

steam·ship (stēm′ship′), *NOUN.* ship moved by engines that work by the action of steam under pressure.

stern¹ (stėrn), *ADJECTIVE.* harshly firm; hard; strict: *a stern parent.*

stern² (stėrn), *NOUN.* the rear part of a ship or boat.

still (stil), **1.** *ADJECTIVE.* staying in the same position or at rest; without motion; motionless: *to stand or lie still. The lake is still today.* **2.** *VERB.* to make or become calm or quiet: *The father stilled the crying baby.* ❑ *VERB* **stilled, stil·ling.**

stump (stump), *VERB.* to puzzle: *The riddle stumped me.* ❑ *VERB* **stumped, stump·ing.**

sub·merge (səb mėrj′), *VERB.* to put under water; cover with water: *A big wave momentarily submerged us.* ❑ *VERB* **sub·merged, sub·merg·ing.**

sum·mon (sum′ən), *VERB.* to stir to action; rouse: *We were summoning our courage before entering the deserted house.* ❑ *VERB* **sum·moned, sum·mon·ing.**

sur·face (sėr′fis), **1.** *NOUN.* the top of the ground or soil, or of a body of water or other liquid: *The stone sank beneath the surface of the water.* **2.** *NOUN.* the outward appearance: *He seems rough, but you will find him very kind below the surface.* **3.** *VERB.* to rise to the surface: *The submarine surfaced.*

surge (sėrj), *NOUN.* a swelling motion; sweep or rush, especially of waves: *Our boat was upset by a surge.*

sus·pi·cious·ly (sə spish′əs lē), *ADVERB.* without trust; doubtfully.

swat (swät), *VERB.* to hit sharply or violently: *swat a fly.* ❑ *VERB* **swat·ted, swat·ting.**

Tt

taunt (tȯnt), *VERB.* to jeer at; mock; reproach: *My classmates taunted me for being the teacher's pet.* ❑ *VERB* **taunt·ed, taunt·ing.**

804

teem (tēm), *VERB.* to be full of; abound; swarm: *The swamp teemed with mosquitoes.* ❑ *VERB* **teemed, teem·ing.**

tem·ple (tem′pəl), *NOUN.* building used for the service or worship of God or gods. ❑ *PLURAL* **tem·ples.** (*Temple* comes from the Latin word *templum* meaning "temple.")

ter·race (ter′is), *VERB.* to form into flat, level land with steep sides; terraces are often made in hilly areas to create more space for farming. ❑ *VERB* **ter·raced, ter·rac·ing.** (*Terrace* comes from the Latin word *terra* meaning "earth, land.")

terrace

ter·ror (ter′ər), *NOUN.* great fear: *The dog has a terror of thunder.*

thick·et (thik′it), *NOUN.* bushes or small trees growing close together: *We crawled into the thicket and hid.* ❑ *PLURAL* **thick·ets.**

tim·id (tim′id), *ADJECTIVE.* easily frightened; shy: *The timid child was afraid of the dark.*

tor·rent (tȯr′ənt), *NOUN.* a violent, rushing stream of water: *The mountain torrent dashed over the rock.* (*Torrent* comes from the Latin word *torrentum* meaning "boiling.")

torrent

tow·er·ing (tou′ər ing), **1.** *ADJECTIVE.* very high: *a towering mountain peak.* **2.** *ADJECTIVE.* very great: *Developing a polio vaccine was a towering achievement.*

a in hat	ȯ in open	sh in she
ā in age	ȯ in all	th in thin
â in care	ȯ in order	ŦH in then
ä in far	oi in oil	zh in measure
e in let	ou in out	ə = a in about
ē in equal	u in cup	ə = e in taken
ėr in term	ū in put	ə = i in pencil
i in it	ü in rule	ə = o in lemon
ī in ice	ch in child	ə = u in circus
o in hot	ng in long	

805

translate•vanish

trans·late (tran slāt′ or tranz lāt′), *VERB.* to change from one language into another: *translate a book from French into English.* ❑ *VERB* **trans·lat·ed, trans·lat·ing.** (*Translate* comes from the Latin word *trans,* which means "across, through, or behind.")

trans·mis·sion (tran smish′ən or tranz mish′ən), *NOUN.* passage of electromagnetic waves from a transmitter to a receiver: *When transmission is good, even foreign radio stations can be heard.*

treas·ur·y (trezh′ər ē), *NOUN.* money owned; funds: *We voted to pay for the party out of the club treasury.*

trench (trench), *NOUN.* any ditch; deep furrow: *to dig a trench for a pipe.*

tri·umph (trī′umf), *NOUN.* victory; success: *The exploration of outer space is a great triumph of modern science.*

trop·i·cal (trop′ə kəl), *ADJECTIVE.* of or like the regions 23.45 degrees north and south of the equator where the sun can shine directly overhead: *tropical heat.*

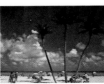

tropical

trudge (truj), *VERB.* to walk wearily or with effort. *We trudged up the hill.* ❑ *VERB* **trudged, trudg·ing.**

twang (twang), *VERB.* to make or cause to make a sharp, ringing sound: *The banjos twanged.* ❑ *VERB* **twanged, twang·ing.**

Uu

un·be·liev·a·ble (un′bi lē′və bəl), *ADJECTIVE.* incredible; hard to think of as true or real: *an unbelievable lie.*

un·cov·er (un kuv′ər), *VERB.* to make known; reveal; expose: *The reporter uncovered a scandal.* ❑ *VERB* **un·cov·ered, un·cov·er·ing.**

un·ex·plain·a·ble (un ek splān′ə bəl), *ADJECTIVE.* not able to be explained; mysterious.

Vv

vain (vān), *ADJECTIVE.* having too much pride in your looks, ability, etc.: *a good-looking but vain person.*

van·ish (van′ish), *VERB.* to disappear, especially suddenly: *The sun vanished behind a cloud.* ❑ *VERB* **van·ished, van·ish·ing.**

806

ve·hi·cle (vē′ə kəl), *NOUN.* device for carrying people or things, such as a car, bus, airplane, etc. Cars and trucks are motor vehicles. Rockets are space vehicles.

ven·ture (ven′chər), *VERB.* to dare to come or go: *We ventured out on the thin ice and almost fell through.* ❑ *VERB* **ven·tured, ven·tur·ing.**

Ww

wharf (wȯrf), *NOUN.* platform built on the shore or out from the shore, beside which ships can load and unload. ❑ *PLURAL* **wharves.**

wil·der·ness (wil′dər nis), *NOUN.* a wild, uncultivated region with few or no people living in it.

wilderness

with·stand (wiŦH stand′), *VERB.* to stand against; hold out against; resist; endure: *These heavy shoes will withstand much hard wear.* ❑ *VERB* **with·stood, with·stand·ing.**

won·drous (wun′drəs), *ADJECTIVE.* wonderful; marvelous, remarkable.

wreck·age (rek′ij), *NOUN.* what is left behind after the destruction of a motor vehicle, ship, building, train, or aircraft: *The hurricane left behind much wreckage.*

Yy

yearn (yėrn), *VERB.* to feel a longing or desire; desire earnestly: *I yearned for home.* ❑ *VERB* **yearned, yearn·ing.**

a in hat	ȯ in open	sh in she
ā in age	ȯ in all	th in thin
â in care	ȯ in order	ŦH in then
ä in far	oi in oil	zh in measure
e in let	ou in out	ə = a in about
ē in equal	u in cup	ə = e in taken
ėr in term	ū in put	ə = i in pencil
i in it	ü in rule	ə = o in lemon
ī in ice	ch in child	ə = u in circus
o in hot	ng in long	

807

English/Spanish Selection Vocabulary List

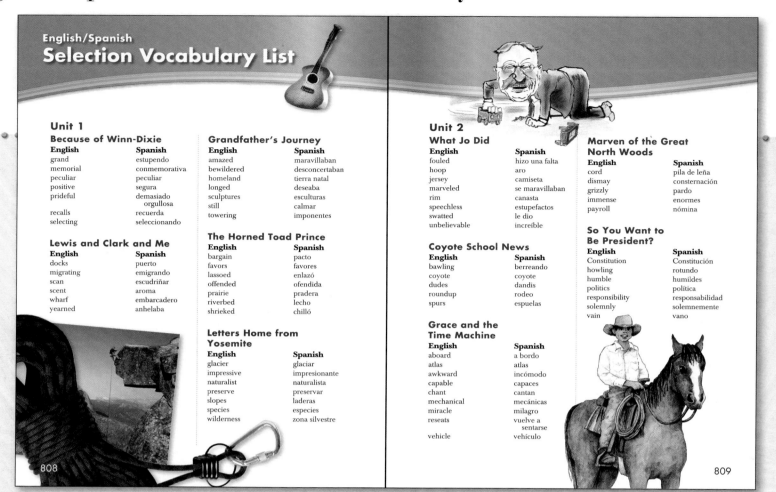

English/Spanish
Selection Vocabulary List

Unit 1

Because of Winn-Dixie

English	Spanish
grand	estupendo
memorial	conmemorativa
peculiar	peculiar
positive	segura
prideful	demasiado orgullosa
recalls	recuerda
selecting	seleccionando

Lewis and Clark and Me

English	Spanish
docks	puerto
migrating	emigrando
scan	escudriñar
scent	aroma
wharf	embarcadero
yearned	anhelaba

Grandfather's Journey

English	Spanish
amazed	maravillaban
bewildered	desconcertaban
homeland	tierra natal
longed	deseaba
sculptures	esculturas
still	calmar
towering	imponentes

The Horned Toad Prince

English	Spanish
bargain	pacto
favors	favores
lassoed	enlazó
offended	ofendida
prairie	pradera
riverbed	lecho
shrieked	chilló

Letters Home from Yosemite

English	Spanish
glacier	glaciar
impressive	impresionante
naturalist	naturalista
preserve	preservar
slopes	laderas
species	especies
wilderness	zona silvestre

Unit 2

What Jo Did

English	Spanish
fouled	hizo una falta
hoop	aro
jersey	camiseta
marveled	se maravillaban
rim	canasta
speechless	estupefactos
swatted	le dio
unbelievable	increíble

Coyote School News

English	Spanish
bawling	berreando
coyote	coyote
dudes	dandis
roundup	rodeo
spurs	espuelas

Grace and the Time Machine

English	Spanish
aboard	a bordo
atlas	atlas
awkward	incómodo
capable	capaces
chant	cantan
mechanical	mecánicas
miracle	milagro
reseats	vuelve a sentarse
vehicle	vehículo

Marven of the Great North Woods

English	Spanish
cord	pila de leña
dismay	consternación
grizzly	pardo
immense	enormes
payroll	nómina

So You Want to Be President?

English	Spanish
Constitution	Constitución
howling	rotundo
humble	humildes
politics	política
responsibility	responsabilidad
solemnly	solemnemente
vain	vano

808

809

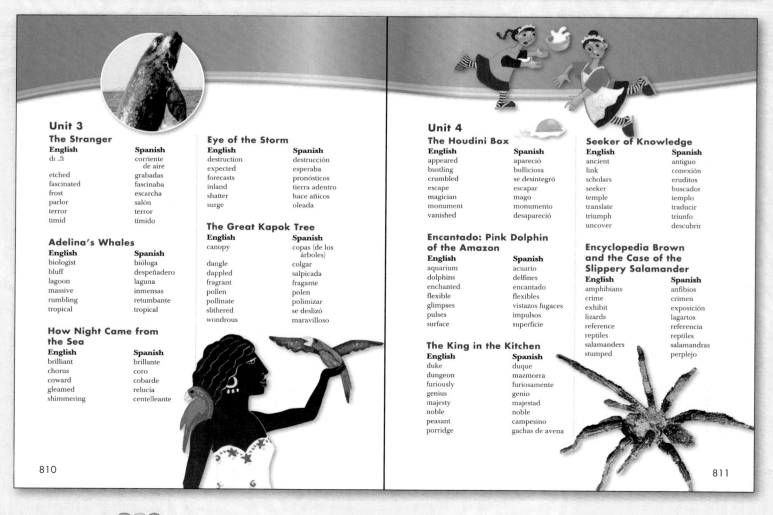

Unit 3

The Stranger

English	Spanish
drift	corriente de aire
etched	grabadas
fascinated	fascinaba
frost	escarcha
parlor	salón
terror	terror
timid	tímido

Adelina's Whales

English	Spanish
biologist	bióloga
bluff	despeñadero
lagoon	laguna
massive	inmensas
rumbling	retumbante
tropical	tropical

How Night Came from the Sea

English	Spanish
brilliant	brillante
chorus	coro
coward	cobarde
gleamed	relucía
shimmering	centelleante

Eye of the Storm

English	Spanish
destruction	destrucción
expected	esperaba
forecasts	pronósticos
inland	tierra adentro
shatter	hace añicos
surge	oleada

The Great Kapok Tree

English	Spanish
canopy	copas (de los árboles)
dangle	colgar
dappled	salpicada
fragrant	fragante
pollen	polen
pollinate	polimizar
slithered	se deslizó
wondrous	maravilloso

Unit 4

The Houdini Box

English	Spanish
appeared	apareció
bustling	bulliciosa
crumbled	se desintegró
escape	escapar
magician	mago
monument	monumento
vanished	desapareció

Encantado: Pink Dolphin of the Amazon

English	Spanish
aquarium	acuario
dolphins	delfines
enchanted	encantado
flexible	flexibles
glimpses	vistazos fugaces
pulses	impulsos
surface	superficie

The King in the Kitchen

English	Spanish
duke	duque
dungeon	mazmorra
furiously	furiosamente
genius	genio
majesty	majestad
noble	noble
peasant	campesino
porridge	gachas de avena

Seeker of Knowledge

English	Spanish
ancient	antiguo
link	conexión
scholars	eruditos
seeker	buscador
temple	templo
translate	traducir
triumph	triunfo
uncover	descubrir

Encyclopedia Brown and the Case of the Slippery Salamander

English	Spanish
amphibians	anfibios
crime	crimen
exhibit	exposición
lizards	lagartos
reference	referencia
reptiles	reptiles
salamanders	salamandras
stumped	perplejo

810

811

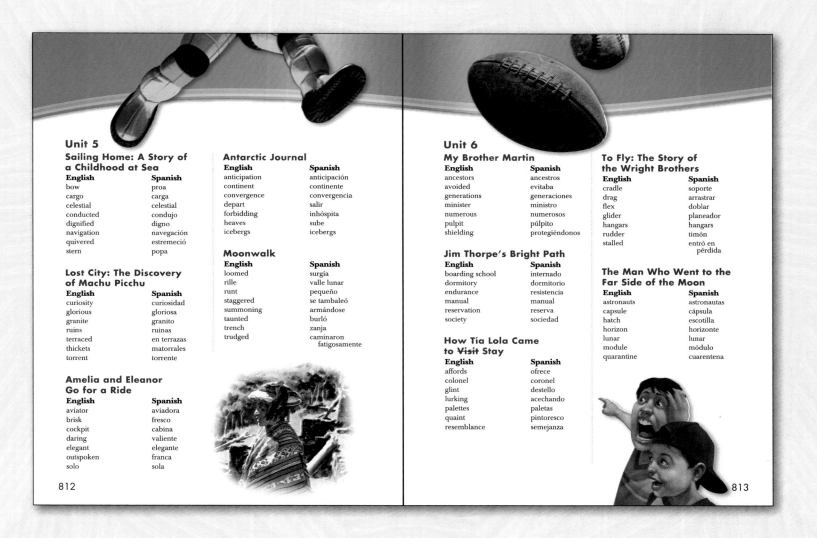

Unit 5

Sailing Home: A Story of a Childhood at Sea

English	Spanish
bow	proa
cargo	carga
celestial	celestial
conducted	condujo
dignified	digno
navigation	navegación
quivered	estremeció
stern	popa

Lost City: The Discovery of Machu Picchu

English	Spanish
curiosity	curiosidad
glorious	gloriosa
granite	granito
ruins	ruinas
terraced	en terrazas
thickets	matorrales
torrent	torrente

Amelia and Eleanor Go for a Ride

English	Spanish
aviator	aviadora
brisk	fresco
cockpit	cabina
daring	valiente
elegant	elegante
outspoken	franca
solo	sola

Antarctic Journal

English	Spanish
anticipation	anticipación
continent	continente
convergence	convergencia
depart	salir
forbidding	inhóspita
heaves	sube
icebergs	icebergs

Moonwalk

English	Spanish
loomed	surgía
rille	valle lunar
runt	pequeño
staggered	se tambaleó
summoning	armándose
taunted	burló
trench	zanja
trudged	caminaron fatigosamente

Unit 6

My Brother Martin

English	Spanish
ancestors	ancestros
avoided	evitaba
generations	generaciones
minister	ministro
numerous	numerosos
pulpit	púlpito
shielding	protegiéndonos

Jim Thorpe's Bright Path

English	Spanish
boarding school	internado
dormitory	dormitorio
endurance	resistencia
manual	manual
reservation	reserva
society	sociedad

How Tía Lola Came to Visit Stay

English	Spanish
affords	ofrece
colonel	coronel
glint	destello
lurking	acechando
palettes	paletas
quaint	pintoresco
resemblance	semejanza

To Fly: The Story of the Wright Brothers

English	Spanish
cradle	soporte
drag	arrastrar
flex	doblar
glider	planeador
hangars	hangars
rudder	timón
stalled	entró en pérdida

The Man Who Went to the Far Side of the Moon

English	Spanish
astronauts	astronautas
capsule	cápsula
hatch	escotilla
horizon	horizonte
lunar	lunar
module	módulo
quarantine	cuarentena

812

813

Acknowledgments

Acknowledgments

Text

22: *Because of Winn-Dixie.* Copyright © 2000 by Kate DiCamillo; Cover Illustration Copyright © 2000 by Chris Sheban. Reprinted by permission of Candlewick Press, Inc., Cambridge, MA; **36:** "Fast Facts: Black Bears" by Kathy Kranking as appeared in *Ranger Rick,* August 1995. © Kathy Kranking. Reprinted with permission of the author; **44:** Text excerpt and selected illustrations from *Lewis and Clark and Me, A Dog's Tale* by Laurie Myers, illustrated by Michael Dooling. Text © 2002 by Laurie Myers, illustrations © 2002 by Michael Dooling. Reprinted by permission of Henry Holt and Company, LLC; **70:** From *Grandfather's Journey* by Allen Say. Copyright © 1993 by Allen Say. Reprinted by permission of Houghton Mifflin Company. All rights reserved; **92:** From *The Horned Toad Prince* by Jackie Mims Hopkins. Illustrated by Michael Austin. Text © 2000 by Jackie Mims Hopkins. Illustrations © 2000 by Michael Austin. Reprinted by permission of Peachtree Publishers; **108:** "Horned Lizards and Harvesting Ants," from *Journey into the Desert* by John Brown, copyright © 2002 by John Brown. Reprinted by permission of Oxford University Press, Inc.; **116:** From *Letters Home from Yosemite* by Lisa Halvorsen, Blackbirch Press. © 2000, Blackbirch Press. Reprinted by permission of The Gale Group; **130:** "This Land Is Your Land." Words and Music by Woody Guthrie. TRO - Copyright 1956 (Renewed), 1958 (Renewed), 1970 (Renewed), 1972 (Renewed), Ludlow Music, Inc., New York, NY. Used by permission; **134:** "We're All in the Telephone Book" from *The Collected Poems of Langston Hughes* by Langston Hughes, copyright © 1994 by The Estate of Langston Hughes. Used by permission of Alfred A. Knopf, a division of Random House, Inc.; **135:** "Speak Up" from *Good Luck Gold And Other Poems* by Janet S. Wong. Copyright © 1994 by Janet S. Wong. Reprinted with permission of Margaret K. McElderry Books, an imprint of Simon & Schuster Children's Publishing Division. All rights reserved; **136:** "City I Love" by Lee Bennett Hopkins. Copyright © 2002 by Lee Bennett Hopkins. First appeared in *Home to Me: Poems Across America,* published by Orchard Books. Reprinted by permission of Curtis Brown, Ltd.; **137:** "Midwest Town" by Ruth De Long Peterson, *The Saturday Evening Post,* Nov. 13, 1954. © 1954 (renewed). Used by permission of The Saturday Evening Post Society; **146:** "What Jo Did," from *Tall Tales: Six Amazing Basketball Dreams* by Charles R. Smith Jr., copyright © 2000 by Charles R. Smith Jr. Used by permission of Dutton Children's Books, A Division of Penguin Young Readers Group, A Member of The Penguin Group (USA) Inc., 345 Hudson Street, New York, NY 10014. All rights reserved; **158:** "Fast Break," from *Rimshots: Basketball Pix, Rolls and Rhythms* by Charles R. Smith Jr., copyright © 1999 by Charles R. Smith Jr. Used by permission of Dutton Children's Books, A Division of Penguin Young Readers Group, A Member of Penguin Group (USA) Inc., 345 Hudson Street, New York, NY 10014. All rights reserved; **160:** "Allow Me to Introduce Myself," from *Short Takes: Fast Break Basketball Poetry* by Charles R. Smith Jr., copyright © 2001 by Charles R. Smith Jr. Used by permission of Dutton Children's Books, A Division of Penguin Young Readers Group, A Member of Penguin Group (USA) Inc., 345 Hudson Street, New York, NY 10014. All rights reserved; **166:** Text and illustrations from *Coyote School News* by Joan Sandin. Copyright © 2003 by Joan Sandin. Reprinted by permission of Henry Holt and Company, LLC; **192:** "Grace and the Time Machine" adapted from *Starring Grace* by Mary Hoffman, Frances Lincoln Books, London. Copyright text © 2000 Mary Hoffman c/o Rogers, Coleridge & White Ltd., 20 Powis Mews, London W11 1JN. Reprinted by permission; **210:** "What's There to Do?" formerly titled "Help an Elderly Neighbor with Yard Work" and "Put on an Outdoor Arts-and-Crafts Show" from *101 Outdoor Adventures* by Samantha Beres, copyright © 2002 by Dutton Children's Books. Used by permission of Dutton Children's Books, A Division of Penguin Young Readers Group, A Member of Penguin Group (USA) Inc., 345 Hudson Street, New York, NY 10014. All rights reserved; **216:** From *Marven of the Great North Woods* by Kathryn Lasky Knight, illustrated by Kevin Hawkes. Text copyright © 1997 by Kathryn Lasky Knight. Illustrations copyright © 1997 by Kevin Hawkes. Reprinted by permission of Harcourt, Inc.; **239:** Adaptation of "Cook Shanty & Bunkhouse" from the Paul Bunyan Logging Camp Web site, paulbunyancamp.org. Reprinted by permission of the Paul Bunyan Logging Camp Museum, Eau Claire, WI; **244:** From *So You Want to Be President?* by Judith St. George, illustrations by David Small, copyright © 2000 by Judith St. George, text, copyright © 2000 by David Small, illustrations. Used by permission of Philomel Books, A Division of Penguin Young Readers Group, A Member of Penguin Group (USA) Inc., 345 Hudson Street, New York, NY 10014. All rights reserved; **260:** "His Hands", from *My Man Blue* by Nikki Grimes, copyright © 1999 by Nikki Grimes. Used by permission of Dial Books for Young Readers, A Division of Penguin Young Readers Group, A Member of Penguin Group (USA) Inc., 345 Hudson Street, New York, NY 10014. All rights reserved; **261:** "Homework" by Russell Hoban from *Egg Thoughts and Other Frances Songs.* Copyright © 1964 by Russell Hoban. Reprinted by permission of David Higham Associates Ltd.; **262:** "Lem Lonnigan's Leaf Machine" from *Here's What You Do When You Can't Find Your Shoe* by Andrea Perry. Text copyright © 2003 by Andrea Perry. Reprinted with the permission of Atheneum Books for Young Readers, an imprint of Simon & Schuster Children's Publishing Division; **272:** From *The Stranger* by Chris Van Allsburg. Copyright © 1986 by Chris Van Allsburg. Reprinted by permission of Houghton Mifflin Company. All rights reserved; **296:** From *Adelina's Whales* by Richard Sobol, copyright © 2003 by Richard Sobol. Used by permission of Dutton Children's Books, A Division of Penguin Young Readers Group, A Member of Penguin Group (USA) Inc., 345 Hudson Street, New York, NY 10014. All rights reserved; **318:** *How Night Came from the Sea* retold by Mary-Joan Gerson, illustrations by Carla Golembe. Text copyright © 1994 by Mary-Joan Gerson. Illustrations copyright © 1994 by Carla Golembe. Reprinted by permission of Goodman Associates Literary Agents as authorized agent for Mary-Joan Gerson and Carla Golembe; **334:** "The Ant and the Bear" from *Spirit of the Cedar People: More Stories and Paintings of Chief Lelooska* edited by Christine Normandin. A DK Ink Book, 1998. Reprinted by permission of the Estate of Don Lelooska Smith, Lelooska Foundation, www.lelooska.org; **342:** From *Eye of the Storm* by Stephen Kramer, photographs by Warren Faidley, copyright © 1997 by Stephen Kramer, text. Used by permission of G. P. Putnam's Sons, A Division of Penguin Young Readers Group, A Member of Penguin Group (USA) Inc., 345 Hudson Street, New York, NY 10014. All rights reserved; **364:** From *The Great Kapok Tree: A Tale of the Amazon Rain Forest,* copyright © 1990 by Lynne Cherry, reprinted by permission of Harcourt, Inc.; **380:** From *Living in a World of Green* by Tanya Lee Stone. Copyright © 2001 Blackbirch Press, Inc. Used by permission of Thomson Learning; **384:** "Autumn" by Charlotte Zolotow from *River Winding* by Charlotte Zolotow. Copyright © 1970 by Carlotte Zolotow. Reprinted by permission of Scott Treimel NY. All rights reserved; **386:** "Early Spring" from *Navajo: Visions and Voices Across the Mesa* by Shonto Begay. Copyright © 1995 by Shonto Begay. Reprinted by permission of Scholastic Inc.; **396:** From *The Houdini Box* by Brian Selznick. Copyright © 1991 by Brian Selznick. Reprinted and edited with the permission of Atheneum Books for Young Readers, Simon & Schuster Children's Publishing Division. All rights reserved; **412:** "So You Want to Be an Illusionist," from *Who Was Harry Houdini?* by Tui T. Sutherland, illustrated by John O'Brien, copyright © 2002 by Tui T. Sutherland, text. Used by permission of Grosset & Dunlap, A Division of Penguin Young Readers Group, A Member of Penguin Group (USA) Inc., 345 Hudson Street, New York, NY 10014. All rights reserved; **420:** Abridged from *Encantado: Pink Dolphin of the Amazon* by Sy Montgomery with photographs by Dianne Taylor-Snow. Text copyright © 2002 by Sy Montgomery. Photographs copyright © 2002 by Dianne Taylor-Snow. Reprinted by permission of Houghton Mifflin Company. All rights reserved; **444:** From "The King in the Kitchen" by Margaret E. Slattery in *30 Plays from Favorite Stories,* edited by Sylvia E. Kamerman. Copyright © 1964, 1997 by Plays/Sterling Partners, Inc. Reprinted by permission; **464:** "A Man for All Seasonings" from *The Spouse in the House* by Richard Armour, 1975, McGraw-Hill Book Company. Reprinted by permission of Geoffrey Armour; **465:** "A Confectioner" from *A Lollygag of Limericks* by Myra Cohn Livingston. Copyright © 1978 by Myra Cohn Livingston. Used by permission of Marian Reiner; **470:** From *Seeker of Knowledge: The Man Who Deciphered Egyptian Hieroglyphs* by James Rumford. Copyright © 2000 by James Rumford. Reprinted by permission of Houghton Mifflin Company. All rights reserved; **486:** "What is Picture Stories?" and "In the Desert" from www.instituteofthefuture.org. Used by permission of Rahul Bhargava, Institute of the Future; **492:** From *Encyclopedia Brown and the Case of the Slippery Salamander* by Donald J. Sobol and illustrated by Warren Chang, copyright © 1999 by Donald J. Sobol. Used by permission of Random House Children's Books, a division of Random House, Inc.; **508:** "Who Knows?" by Fatou Ndiaye Sow, translated by Véronique Tadjo from *Talking Drums: A Selection of Poems from Africa South of the Sahara* edited and illustrated by Véronique Tadjo. © A & C Black Publishers, 2000. Reprinted by permission; **509:** "Poetry" from *Eleanor Farjeon's Poems for Children* by Eleanor Farjeon. Copyright 1938 by Eleanor Farjeon. Copyright renewed 1966 by Gervase Farjeon. Reprinted by permission of Harold Ober Associates Incorporated; **510:** "The Seed" from *Always Wondering* by Aileen Fisher. Copyright © 1991 by Aileen Fisher. Used by permission of Marian Reiner; **511:** "Carolyn's Cat" from *When Whales Exhale and Other Poems* by Constance Levy. Copyright © 1996 by Constance Levy (A Margaret K. McElderry Book). Reprinted by permission of Marian Reiner; **520:** *Sailing Home: A Story of a Childhood at Sea* by Gloria Rand, illustrated by Ted Rand. Text copyright © 2001 by Gloria Rand. Illustrations © 2001 by Ted Rand. Reprinted by arrangement with North-South Books Inc., New York. All rights reserved; **542:** From *Lost City: The Discovery of Machu Picchu* by Ted Lewin, copyright © 2003 by Ted Lewin. Used by permission of Philomel Books, A Division of Penguin Young Readers Group, A Member of Penguin Group (USA) Inc., 345 Hudson Street, New York, NY 10014. All rights reserved; **564:** From *Amelia and Eleanor Go for a Ride* by Pam Munoz Ryan, illustrated by Brian Selznick. Text copyright © 1999 by Pam Munoz Ryan, illustrations copyright © by Brian Selznick. Published by Scholastic Press/Scholastic Inc. Reprinted by permission; **586:** From *Antarctic Journal: Four Months at the Bottom of the World* by Jennifer Owings Dewey. Copyright © 2001 by Jennifer Owings Dewey. Used by permission of HarperCollins Publishers; **612:** "Moonwalk" by Ben Bova. Copyright © 2002 by Ben Bova. Reprinted with permission of Ben Bova and *Boys' Life,* November 2002, published by the Boy Scouts of America; **630:** "The Best Paths," from *Toasting Marshmallows: Camping Poems* by Kristine O'Connell George. Text copyright © 2001 by Kristine O'Connell George. Reprinted by permission of Clarion Books/Houghton Mifflin Company. All rights reserved; **631:** "Roller Coasters" by X. J. Kennedy. First appeared in *The Kite That Braved Old Orchard Beach,* published by Margaret K. McElderry Books. Copyright © 1991 by X. J. Kennedy. Reprinted by permission of Curtis Brown, Ltd.; **632:** "The Door" by Miroslav Holub from *Miroslav Holub: Selected Poems,* translated by Ian Milner and George Theiner. Copyright © 1967 by Miroslav Holub. Translation copyright © 1967 Penguin Books. Reproduced by permission of Penguin Books Ltd.; **642:** From *My Brother Martin* by Christine King Farris, illustrated by Chris Soentpiet. Text copyright © 2003 Christine King Farris. Illustrations copyright © 2003 Chris Soentpiet. Reprinted with the permission of Simon & Schuster Books for Young Readers, an imprint of Simon & Schuster Children's Publishing Division; **658:** "Haiku" by Cristina Beecham, *Skipping Stones,* Sept.-Oct. 2003. Reprinted with permission, Skipping Stones Magazine (www.SkippingStones.org); **659:** "When You Hope, Wish, and Trust" by Ek Ongkar K. Khalsa, *Skipping Stones,* Sept.-Oct. 2003. Reprinted with permission, Skipping Stones Magazine (www.SkippingStones.org); **659:** "My Life Is a Buried Treasure" by Dawn Withrow, *Ten-Second Rainshowers: Poems by Young People,* compiled by Sandford Lyne, Simon & Schuster Books for Young Readers, 1996; **664:** *Jim Thorpe's Bright Path* by Joseph Bruchac. Text copyright © 2004 by Joseph Bruchac, illustrations copyright © 2004 by S. D. Nelson. Permission arranged with Lee & Low Books Inc., New York, NY 10016; **690:** "Two Happy Months in Vermont" from *How Tia Lola Came to ~~Visit~~ Stay.* Copyright © 2001 by Julia Alvarez. Published by Dell Yearling and in hardcover by Alfred A. Knopf Children's Books, a division of Random House, New York. Reprinted by permission of Susan Bergholz Literary Services, New York. All Rights Reserved; **708:** From *Sadaharu Oh: A Zen Way of Baseball* by Sadaharu Oh and David Falkner, copyright © 1984 Sadaharu Oh and David Falkner. Used by permission of Times Books, a division of Random House, Inc.; **716:** Excerpts from *To Fly: The Story of the Wright Brothers* by Wendie C. Old. Text copyright © 2000 by Wendie C. Old. Abridged and reprinted by permission of Houghton Mifflin Company. All rights reserved; **737:** "Clement Ader's Eole" from First Flight Web site, http://firstflight.open.ac.uk. Used by permission of Dr. Peter Whalley; **742:** From *The Man Who Went to the Far Side of the Moon* by Bea Uusma Schyffert. Copyright © 1999 by Bea Uusma Schyffert. Reprinted with the permission of Chronicle Books LLC, San Francisco. www.chroniclebooks.com; **758:** "The Earth and the Moon" (originally titled "Earth", "The Moon" and "Exploring the Moon"), from *Scott Foresman Science,* Grade 4. Copyright © 2006 Pearson Education, Inc.; **762:** "Dream Dust" from *The Collected Poems of Langston Hughes* by Langston Hughes, copyright © 1994 by The Estate of Langston Hughes. Used by permission of Alfred A. Knopf, a division of Random House, Inc.; **762:** "Martin Luther King" from *No Way of Knowing: Dallas Poems* by Myra Cohn Livingston. Copyright © 1980 by Myra Cohn Livingston. Used by permission of Marian Reiner; **763:** "Martin Luther King Day" by X. J. Kennedy. First appeared in *The Kite That Braved Old Orchard Beach,* published by Margaret K. McElderry Books. Copyright © 1991 by X. J. Kennedy. Reprinted by permission of Curtis Brown, Ltd.; **764:** "Fall Football", from *Fearless Fernie: Hanging out with Fernie and Me* by Gary Soto, copyright © 2002 by Gary Soto, text. Used by permission of G. P. Putnam's Sons, A Division of Penguin Young Readers Group, A Member of Penguin Group (USA) Inc., 345 Hudson Street, New York, NY 10014. All rights reserved; **765:** "First Men on the Moon" by J. Patrick Lewis. © J. Patrick Lewis, 1998. Reprinted by permission of the author.

Illustrations

Cover: Tim Jessell; **17, 22-33:** ©Kevin Hawkes; **21, 489:** Barry Gott; **37, 96, 259, 312, 515, 558, 612-622, 812:** Peter Bollinger; **48, 130-132:** Robert Crawford; **70:** Dave Stevenson; **89-91:** Laura Ovresat; **134-136:** Patrick Corrigan; **141, 192-208:** Matt Faulkner; **186:** Sachiko Yoshikawa; **189:** Shelly Hehenberger; **210:** Stephen Kroninger; **215:** Erika Le Barre; **260-262:** Lee White; **361:** Richard Downs; **391, 444, 462, 811:** Matthew Trueman; **391, 492-502:** Brett Helquist; **412-415:** Vitali Konstantinov; **441-443:** Christine Benjamin; **464:** Amy Vangsgard; **508-510, 609:** Joel Nakamura; **517:** Dan Andreasen; **630-632:** Franklin Hammond; **637, 664-680:** S.D. Nelson; **637, 690-706, 813:** Macky Pamintuan; **658:** Stephen Daigle; **662-663:** Gwen Connelly; **709-711:** SuLing Wang; **713:** Mark Neely; **756:** Bea Uusma Schyffert; **762-764:** Rafael Lopez.

Photographs

Every effort has been made to secure permission and provide appropriate credit for photographic material. The publisher deeply regrets any omission and pledges to correct errors called to its attention in subsequent editions.

Unless otherwise acknowledged, all photographs are the property of Scott Foresman, a division of Pearson Education.

Photo locators denoted as follows: Top (T), Center (C), Bottom (B), Left (L), Right (R), Background (Bkgd).

4: ©Laurance B. Aiuppy/Getty Images; **6:** ©Paul King/Getty Images; **8:** ©Stewart Cohen/Getty Images; **10:** (TL, TR) ©ChiselVision/Corbis; **12:** ©Jerry Lofaro/Courtesy of Konica Minolta Business Solutions/American Artists Represents; **14:** ©Jerry Lofaro/Courtesy of Konica Minolta Business Solutions/American Artists Represents; **16:** ©Royalty-Free/Corbis; **17:** Corel; **20:** ©Stockbyte; **36:** ©Steve Kaufman/Corbis; **37:** (BL) ©Art Wolfe/Getty Images, (CR) ©Norbert Rosing/NGS Image Collection; **38:** (TR) ©George D. Lepp/Corbis, (BR) ©Art Wolfe/Photo Researchers, Inc., (Bkgd) ©Tim Davis/Photo Researchers, Inc.; **39:** (TCL) ©George F. Mobley/NGS Image Collection, (TR) ©Joe McDonald; **41:** (T) ©Royalty-Free/Corbis, (TR) Corbis; **42:** Getty Images; **43** ©Bettmann/Corbis; **46**: Getty Images; **48:** Getty Images; **53** Getty Images; **57:** Getty Images; **58:** Getty Images; **62:** ©brt Photo/Mira; **63:** ©Michael Haynes; **64:** (R) ©Michael Haynes, (TR) ©The Newark Museum/Art Resource, NY; **65:** Andreas Von Einsiedel/©DK Images; **67:** (BL) ©Arnold Genthe/Corbis, (TR) ©Bill Varie/Corbis; **69:** (TL) ©Joseph Sohm/Corbis, (TR) Corbis; **82:** ©Royalty-Free/Corbis; **84:** (TR) ©Dallas and John Heaton/Corbis, (BR) ©Roger Ressmeyer/Corbis; **87:** (TL) ©Dex Image, (TR) ©Orion Press/Getty Images, (CL) ©Roger Ressmeyer/Corbis, (CR) ©Ken Biggs/Getty Images; **113:** (B) ©Robert Y. Ono/Corbis, (BC) Getty Images; **114:** ©Royalty-Free/Corbis; **115:** (TL) ©Royalty-Free/Corbis, (TR) Corbis; **116:** (C) ©David Muench/Corbis, (TL, TR, CR) Getty Images; **117:** Getty Images; **118:** Getty Images; **119:** (CR) Getty Images, (BC) Corel, (T) ©Sam Clemens/Getty Images; **120:** (TC, BL) Corel; **121:**(TL) ©Sam Clemens/Getty Images, (TR) Royalty-Free/Corbis, (BR) Corel; **122:** ©Harvey Lloyd/Getty Images; **123:** (CR) ©Royalty-Free/Corbis, (BR, T) Corel; **124:** (TL) ©Boyle & Boyle/Animals Animals/Earth Scenes, (CR) ©Don Mason/Corbis; **125:** (C, BL) Getty Images; **126:** ©Royalty-Free/ Corbis; **127:** (BR, TR) Getty Images, (TC) Corel, (CR) ©Phil Schermeister/Corbis; **128** ©Royalty-Free/Corbis; **138:** ©Laurance B. Aiuppy/Getty Images; **139:** Getty Images; **140:** ©Paul King/Getty Images; **143:** (TR, BC) Getty Images; **145** ©Royalty-Free/Corbis; **156:** (BR, BC) Getty Images; **163:** ©Yann Arthus-Bertrand/Corbis; **164:** Getty Images; **165:** ©Macduff Everton/Corbis; **190:** ©Jim Sugar/Corbis; **191:** ©W. A. Sharman/Corbis; **213:** ©ThinkStock/SuperStock; **232:** (BL, TR) Courtesy the Lasky Family; **236:** ©W. J. Lubken/Corbis; **237:** Corbis; **238:** (BL) ©E. F. Keller/Corbis, (BR) ©Bluford W. Muir/Corbis; **239:** ©Minnesota Historical Society/Corbis; **241:** ©William Manning/Corbis; **258:** Getty Images; **259:** (TL, CL) ©Royalty-Free/Corbis, (CR) ©Jeffrey Greenberg/Photo Researchers, Inc., (BC, BL) Getty Images, (TR) ©David Muench/Corbis; **264:** (BL) ©Paul King/Getty Images, (CR, CC) Getty Images; **266:** ©Stewart Westmoreland/ Corbis; **267:** (BCR) ©Warren Faidley/Weatherstock, (TC) ©Stewart Cohen/ Getty Images; **269** (T, BR) Getty Images; **271:** Getty Images; **288:** ©Royalty-Free/Corbis; **290:** ©ThinkStock/SuperStock; **291:** ©Chase Swift/Corbis; **293:** ©Tom Brakefield/Corbis; **294:** ©Alan Schein Photography/Corbis; **295:** Brand X Pictures; **310:** ©Natalie Fobes/Corbis; **311:** (CR) ©Flip Nicklin/Minden Pictures, (BL) ©Gunter Marx Photography/Corbis, (BC) Alaska Stock; **312:** (TR) ©Royalty-Free/Corbis, (CR) ©Natalie Fobes/Corbis; **313:** (TR) ©Joel W. Rogers/Corbis, (BL) ©Jeffrey L. Rotman/Corbis; **315:** Getty Images; **316:** Getty Images; **317:** (T) ©Carlos Dominguez/Corbis, (B) ©Carl & Ann Purcell/Corbis; **339:** Corbis; **340:** (BC) Getty Images, (BR) ©Space Frontiers/Getty Images; **341:** ©Walter Rawlings/Robert Harding World Imagery; **342:** ©Warren Faidley/Weatherstock; **343:** (TR, BR, BL) Getty Images; **344:** (TR, BL, BC, BR) ©Warren Faidley/Weatherstock, (B) Getty Images; **345:** (B, BR) ©Warren Faidley/Weatherstock, (BR) Getty Images; **346-348:** ©Warren Faidley/Weatherstock; **349:** (T) Warren Faidley/Weatherstock, (TL) Getty Images; **350:** (TC, TL, TCL, CL) ©Warren Faidley/Weatherstock; **351:** (B) ©Warren Faidley/Weatherstock, (CR) Getty Images; **352:** (TR) Getty Images, (T) ©Warren Faidley/Weatherstock; **353:** ©Warren Faidley/Weatherstock; **354:** ©Warren Faidley/Weatherstock; **356:** Corbis; **357:** (T) Getty Images, (CR) ©Ralph Wetmore/Getty Images; **358:** (T, BR, BC) Getty Images, (CR) ©David R. Frazier/The Image Works, Inc.; **359:** Getty Images; **362:** ©Schafer & Hill/Getty Images; **363:** (T) ©Peter Lilja/Getty Images, (BR) ©Chase Swift/Corbis; **380:** (TR) Brand X Pictures, (BC) Digital Vision; **381:** (TC) Corel, (BR) Frank Greenaway/ Courtesy of the Natural History Museum, London/©DK Images; **382:** ©Tom Brakefield/Corbis; **383:** Corel; **386:** ©Todd Gipstein/NGS Image Collection; **388:** ©Stewart Cohen/Getty Images; **389:** (CR) ©Comstock Inc., (CC) Getty Images; **390:** ©ChiselVision/Corbis; **393:** ©Bettmann/Corbis; **394:** Comstock Production Department/©Comstock Inc.; **395:** (TL) Dave King/©DK Images, (TR) ©Royalty-Free/Corbis, (BR) ©Myrleen Ferguson/PhotoEdit; **417:** (TR) Brand X Pictures, (CL) ©Royalty-Free/Corbis; **418:** ©Bob Krist/Corbis; **419:** (TR) ©Royalty-Free/Corbis, (BR) Getty Images; **420:** ©Todd Pusser/Nature Picture Library; **422:** ©Wolfgang Kaehler/Corbis; **423:** Getty Images; **424:** Getty Images; **428:** Brand X Pictures; **429:** ©Andre Baertschi; **430:** ©Royalty-Free/Corbis; **433:** Getty Images; **434:** (TL) ©Buddy Mays/Corbis, (B) ©Hong Kong Dolphinwatch, Ltd.; **436:** (BR) ©Darek Karp/Animals Animals/Earth Scenes, (TR) ©Dr. Morley Read/Photo Researchers, Inc.; **437:** (TR, BR) Getty Images, (CR) Andy Crawford/©DK Images; **438:** ©William Grenfell/Visuals Unlimited; **466:** ©Gianni Dagli Orti/Corbis; **468:** ©Royalty-Free/Corbis; **469:** ©Archivo Iconografico, S.A./Corbis; **472-482:** Getty Images; **484:** ©Royalty-Free/Corbis; **486:** (BL) ©Ralph A. Clevenger/Corbis, (BC, CC, BC, BL) Getty Images, (BL) ©Lisa Henderling/Images, Inc.; **487:** (TL, BL) ©Comstock, Inc., (TC, TCL, TCR, CR) Getty Images, (TR) ©Images/Corbis, (CL) ©Rubberball Productions, (BC) ©Royalty-Free/Corbis; **490:** Getty Images; **491:** Getty Images; **505:** ©Royalty-Free/Corbis; **506:** (TL) ©Becky Shink/Lansing State Journal, (BC) Getty Images; **507:** Getty Images; **512:** ©ChiselVision/Corbis; **513:** (BR) Brand X Pictures, (CR) Getty Images, (TR) ©ChiselVision/Corbis; **514:** (C, Bkgd) ©Royalty-Free/Corbis; **515:** ©Jennifer Owings Dewey; **519:** (TC) Getty Images, (BR) ©Royalty-Free/Corbis; **532:** (BC) San Francisco Maritime National Historical Park, (BR) Jefferson County Historical Society; **533:** (BL) Jefferson County Historical Society, (BC, BR) Ena Marie Sroat; **536:** ©Harry Benson; **537** ©Kevin Horan/Time Life Pictures/Getty Images; **539:** (TL) Corbis, (TR) ©Lowell Georgia/Corbis; **541:** (T) Getty Images, (B) ©Roger Ressmeyer/Corbis; **556:** ©Jim Erickson/Corbis; **558:** (CR) ©Roman Soumar/Corbis, (B) ©Dave Wilhelm/Corbis; **559:** (CL) ©Kevin Schafer/Corbis, (TR) ©Francesco Venturi/Corbis; **561:** Corbis; **562:** Corbis; **563:** (TC) ©National Aviation Museum/Corbis, (CC) Corbis; **575:** National Air and Space Museum/Smithsonian Institution; **578:** (B) Corbis, (TR) Library of Congress; **580:** (CL) Bridgeman Art Library, (TL) Library of Congress; **581:** (TL) Courtesy, Marin History Museum, (T) Digital Vision; **583:** ©Ralph A. Clevenger/Corbis; **584:** Getty Images; **585:** ©Joel W. Rogers/Corbis; **586:** Digital Vision; **590:** ©Jennifer Owings Dewey; **592:** (TR, CL, BC) National Science Foundation, (BR) ©Jennifer Owings Dewey; **594:** (BL, BC) ©Jennifer Owings Dewey; **595-602:** National Science Foundation; **604:** Corbis; **605:** ©Gabriella Miotto; **606:** (TL) ©Gabriella Minotto, (BR) AP/Wide World Photos; **607:** Corbis; **610:** ©1996/Original image courtesy of NASA/Corbis; **611:** (T) ©1996/Original image courtesy of NASA/Corbis, (TL) ©NASA/Roger Ressmeyer/Corbis, (TR, BR) Corbis; **626:** Getty Images; **627:** Getty Images; **628:** (B) ©1996/Original image courtesy of NASA/Corbis, (CL) Getty Images; **629:** (TL) Getty Images, (CR) NASA/Corbis; **634:** ©Jerry Lofaro/Courtesy of Konica Minolta Business Solutions/American Artists Represents; **635:** (BR) Corbis, (TR) ©Jerry Lofaro/Courtesy of Konica Minolta Business Solutions/American Artists Represents; **636:** ©Jerry Lofaro/Courtesy of Konica Minolta Business Solutions/American Artists Represents; **639:** ©Bettmann/Corbis; **640:** ©Comstock, Inc.; **641:** (BR, TR) ©Comstock Inc.; **661:** (T) Corbis, (TC) Getty Images; **678:** (CL, CR, BR) Cumberland County Historical Society/Carlisle, PA, (TL) Getty Images; **679:** (TL, BR, CC) Cumberland County Historical Society/Carlisle, PA, (BC) Getty Images; **682:** (T) ©Joseph Sohm/ChromoSohm, Inc/Corbis, (BC) ©Reuters/Corbis; **683:** ©Stephane Cardinale/Corbis; **684:** (TL) ©Robert W. Ginn/PhotoEdit, (TR) ©Kathleen Kliskey-Geraghty/Index Stock Imagery, (B, BL) ©Jonathan Nourok/PhotoEdit; **685:** (TR) ©The Times/AP/Wide World Photos, (TC) ©The Daily Oakland Press/AP/Wide World Photos; **687:** (TL) Getty Images, (TR) ©Royalty-Free/Corbis; **688:** ©W. Cody/Corbis; **689:** (TL) Getty Images, (TR) ©Bass Museum of Art/Corbis; **715:** (T, B) ©Royalty-Free/Corbis; **734:** (BR) Corbis, (TR) ©Underwood & Underwood/ Corbis; **735:** Getty Images; **736:** (BR, TCL) Corbis, (TL, TCR) ©Bettmann/Corbis, (TC) ©Underwood & Underwood/Corbis; **737:** The Granger Collection, NY; **739:** Getty Images; **741** (T, B, BR) Getty Images; **743-751:** NASA; **752:** NASA; **753:** NASA; **754:** ©Time Life Pictures/Getty Images; **755:** ©Time Life Pictures/Getty Images; **758:** Getty Images; **759:** Getty Images; **760:** Getty Images; **761:** Getty Images; **766:** (CL) ©Hulton-Deutsch Collection/Corbis, (BCL, CR, BCR) Corbis, (BL) ©Jerry Lofaro/Courtesy of Konica Minolta Business Solutions/American Artists Represents; **767:** Getty Images; **773:** ©Ted Lewin; **774:** ©Laurie Myers; **775:** ©Wendy Barry/ Houghton Mifflin Company; **785:** JSC/NASA; **786:** ©E. R. Degginger/Animals Animals/Earth Scenes; **787:** ©Oliver Benn/Getty Images; **788:** ©Stouffer Productions/Animals Animals/Earth Scenes; **791:** ©Robert Amft; **793:** ©Bernard Desestres/Vandystadt/Photo Researchers, Inc.; **794:** SuperStock; **797** (CL) ©Amy and Chuck Wiley/Wales/Index Stock Imagery, (CR) ©Rob Crandall/Stock Connection; **798:** Corbis; **799:** ©H. Taylor/OSF/Animals Animals/Earth Scenes; **801:** ©Robert Frerck/Odyssey/Chicago; **802:** SuperStock; **805:** ©Tim Brown/Index Stock Imagery; **806:** ©Steve Vidler/SuperStock; **807:** ©Michael Fogden/OSF/Animals Animals/Earth Scenes; **808:** (BR) Getty Images, (BL) ©Don Mason/Corbis; **813:** (TL, TC) Getty Images.

Glossary

The contents of this glossary have been adapted from *Thorndike Barnhart Intermediate Dictionary.* Copyright © 1997, Pearson Education, Inc.

Student Tips for Making Top Scores in Writing Tests

1 **Use transitions such as those below to relate ideas, sentences, or paragraphs.**

in addition	nevertheless	finally	however
then	instead	therefore	as a result
for example	in particular	first	such as

2 **Write a good beginning. Make readers want to continue.**
- I shouldn't have opened that green box.
- Imagine being locked in a crate at the bottom of the sea.
- When I was four, I saw a purple dog.
- Have you ever heard of a talking tree?

3 **Focus on the topic.**
If a word or detail is off-topic, get rid of it. If a sentence is unrelated or loosely related to the topic, drop it or connect it more closely.

4 **Organize your ideas.**
Have a plan in mind before you start writing. Your plan can be a list, bulleted items, or a graphic organizer. Five minutes spent planning your work will make the actual writing go much faster and smoother.

5 **Support your ideas.**
- Develop your ideas with fully elaborated examples and details.
- Make ideas clear to readers by choosing vivid words that create pictures. Avoid dull *(get, go, say)*, vague *(thing, stuff, lots of)*, or overused *(really, very)* words.
- Use a voice that is appropriate to your audience.

6 **Make writing conventions as error-free as possible.**
Proofread your work line by line, sentence by sentence. Read for correct punctuation, then again for correct capitalization, and finally for correct spelling.

7 **Write a conclusion that wraps things up but is more than a repeating of ideas or "The end."**
- After all, he was my brother, weird or not.
- The Internet has changed our lives for better and for worse.
- It's not the largest planet but the one I'd choose to live on.
- Now tell me you don't believe in a sixth sense.

Rubric
4 3 2 1

Focus/Ideas

Organization/
Paragraphs

Voice

Word Choice

Sentences

Conventions

Writing Traits

- **Focus/Ideas** refers to the main purpose for writing and the details that make the subject clear and interesting. It includes development of ideas through support and elaboration.

- **Organization/Paragraphs** refers to the overall structure of a piece of writing that guides readers. Within that structure, transitions show how ideas, sentences, and paragraphs are connected.

- **Voice** shows the writer's unique personality and establishes a connection between writer and reader. Voice, which contributes to style, should be suited to the audience and the purpose for writing.

- **Word Choice** is the use of precise, vivid words to communicate effectively and naturally. It helps create style through the use of specific nouns, lively verbs and adjectives, and accurate, well-placed modifiers.

- **Sentences** covers strong, well-built sentences that vary in length and type. Skillfully written sentences have pleasing rhythms and flow fluently.

- **Conventions** refers to mechanical correctness and includes grammar, usage, spelling, punctuation, capitalization, and paragraphing.

Writing Workshop

- Develop an understanding of a personal narrative.
- Use a strong voice and vivid language to express feelings.
- Use time-order words to show clearly a sequence of events.
- Establish criteria for evaluating a personal narrative.

Key Features
Personal Narrative

In a personal narrative, a writer gives a firsthand account of an event in his or her life.

- Is about an interesting experience in the storyteller's life
- Tells the story using *I* or *me*
- Flows from beginning to middle to end
- Provides vivid details

Connect to Weekly Writing

Week 1	Memoir 39g–39h
Week 2	Journal Entry 65g–65h
Week 3	Post Card 87g–87h
Week 4	E-mail Invitation 111g–111h
Week 5	Narrative Writing 133g–133h

Strategic Intervention
See Differentiated Instruction p. WA8.

Advanced
See Differentiated Instruction p. WA9.

ELL
See Differentiated Instruction p. WA9.

Additional Resource for Writing
Writing Rubrics and Anchor Papers, pp. 40–47

Personal Narrative

Writing Prompt: This Land Is Your Land

Write a personal narrative about a time that you were a newcomer to a place or situation (a school, club, team, or neighborhood.) Explain how you felt and what you found challenging or exciting.

Purpose: Explain how you coped in a difficult situation

Audience: Classmates

READ LIKE A WRITER

Look back at *Because of Winn-Dixie*. Have students recall that the narrator told a story about making friends in a new neighborhood. Point out that a story in which a writer tells about an experience he or she had is a **personal narrative.**

EXAMINE THE MODEL AND RUBRIC

GUIDED WRITING Read the model aloud. Have students point out sentences in which the writer uses vivid words to show how he feels and acts. Discuss how the model reflects traits of good writing.

How to Make Friends

This was terrible! I looked out the window on my first morning in Springfield. It was a Saturday, but no one was in sight. Just rows and rows of houses full of strangers. I had to start school on Monday, I didn't know anyone, and my stomach was fluttering. What was I going to do?

My mom said she was tired of hearing me whine. She told me to take the dog for a walk and give her some space to unpack. I snapped the leash on Toby's collar and started along the street, trying to look like I knew where I was going.

I should tell you that Toby is a big strong Labrador, and he was pretty excited to be in a new neighborhood. He pranced along the sidewalk like a puppy. Suddenly he saw a cat. Zoom! Toby launched himself like a rocket across someone's lawn. I took off after him at the other end of the leash. The cat squeezed through a fence. Toby followed, but his head got stuck. Still holding the leash, I tried to yank him back.

That's how I met Pete. He was on the other side of the fence, playing catch with his dad. When Pete and his dad saw Toby's head wedged in their fence, they started to laugh. And after a while, so did I.

It turned out that Pete wanted a dog more than anything. What's more, he went to my school. Suddenly, the world wasn't so scary anymore. When I got home, my mom said I should take the dog out more often!

Unit 1 Personal Narrative • PREWRITE   Writing Process **1**

▲ **Writing Transparency** WP1

Traits of a Good Personal Narrative

Focus/Ideas — Narrative focuses on a specific experience and is full of lively supporting details.

Organization/ Paragraphs — Writer starts off by setting the scene and then tells a story with a beginning, middle, and end.

Voice — Writer expresses his feelings. (*Suddenly, the world wasn't so scary anymore.*) He speaks directly to readers in a friendly voice. (*I should tell you. . . .*)

Word Choice — Writer uses strong verbs (*snapped, pranced, launched, squeezed, yank*) and appeals to the senses (*my stomach was fluttering*).

Sentences — Sentences are of different lengths and types (declarative, interrogative, and exclamatory). They include simple, compound, and complex sentences. The writer has used an interjection. (*Zoom!*)

Conventions — Writer has good control of grammar, capitalization, punctuation, and usage. There are no run-on sentences.

Unit 1 Personal Narrative • PREWRITE   Writing Process **2**

▲ **Writing Transparency** WP2

FINDING A TOPIC

- Brainstorm with students occasions when they have done something for the first time. List their memories on the board.
- Suggest that students sort through their memories by talking to their families and reviewing journals and photograph albums.
- Encourage students to collaborate with others by having them get together in small groups and share stories of the first time they did something.

NARROW A TOPIC

First day in kindergarten   I don't remember it very well.

Moving to our new house   I don't think I could write about this briefly.

First time at Theater Workshop   That was really scary. I remember everything, and it's a good story.

PREWRITING STRATEGY

GUIDED WRITING Display Writing Transparency WP3. Model how to complete notes for a personal narrative.

Think Aloud **MODEL** This student's experience sounds really interesting. All the important parts of the story are mapped out. When the student writes a draft, he or she should add some vivid details to make the narrative fun to read.

PREWRITING ACTIVITIES

- Have students use Grammar and Writing Practice Book p. 160 to help them organize information about their chosen topic.
- Students can make lists of additional details for each part of their story.

Notes for a Personal Narrative
Directions Fill in the graphic organizer with information about the event or experience that you plan to write about.

Possible Title _"Help! Help!"_

Summary

What happened? _I went to Theater Workshop for the first time._
When? _Last year_
Where? _In my town_
Who was there? _Mr. Adler, the teacher, and lots of kids I didn't know_

Details

Beginning _I was really scared and didn't want to go._

Middle _Mr. Adler picked me to stand on a table and pretend I was on the roof of a burning building._

End _I shouted "Help! Help!" really loud and felt a lot better._

Unit 1 Personal Narrative • PREWRITE   Writing Process **3**

▲ **Writing Transparency** WP3

Taking Notes

Beginning

I was really scared | felt sick
told Mom I had homework
she didn't believe me

---

1 WRITING WORKSHOP   Personal Narrative

Name ___

Notes for a Personal Narrative
Directions Fill in the graphic organizer with information about the event or experience that you plan to write about.

Summary

What happened? _Answers should include_
When? _details about each part of_
Where? _student's personal narrative._
Who was there? ___

Details

Beginning

Middle

End

160 Unit 1   Grammar and Writing Practice Book

▲ **Grammar and Writing Practice Book** p. 160

Writing Workshop

WRITING THE FIRST DRAFT

GUIDED WRITING Use Writing Transparency WP4 to practice using words that tell about you.

- Point out that a vivid description helps readers see, hear, touch, taste, or feel something in their imagination.

- Encourage students to be true to their own feelings. Point out that there is no single "correct" way to write about yourself. Explain that the way one person feels when afraid, angry, or happy may not be the way another person feels.

MODEL Everyone's been nervous, but the word *nervous* doesn't really describe what happens to you when you have to sing on stage or read a report to the class. When I get nervous, my legs shake and my stomach starts to flutter as if it were full of butterflies! Describing it like that helps a reader share the writer's experience.

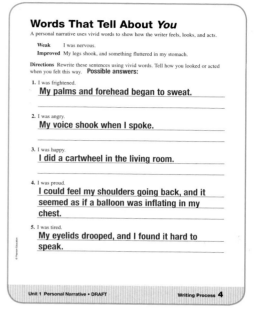

Words That Tell About *You*

A personal narrative uses vivid words to show how the writer feels, looks, and acts.

Weak   I was nervous.
Improved My legs shook, and something fluttered in my stomach.

Directions Rewrite these sentences using vivid words. Tell how you looked or acted when you felt this way. **Possible answers:**

1. I was frightened.
   My palms and forehead began to sweat.

2. I was angry.
   My voice shook when I spoke.

3. I was happy.
   I did a cartwheel in the living room.

4. I was proud.
   I could feel my shoulders going back, and it seemed as if a balloon was inflating in my chest.

5. I was tired.
   My eyelids drooped, and I found it hard to speak.

Unit 1 Personal Narrative • DRAFT   Writing Process **4**

▲ **Writing Transparency** WP4

Think Like a Writer

Select the Best Details Some students may have difficulty choosing details to include in their story. Encourage them to select only those details that contribute to the mood they are trying to describe. Good details should be memorable, brief, and easy for the reader to visualize or imagine.

Support Writing If students include home-language words in their drafts, help them find replacement words in English. Resources can include:

- conversations with you
- other home-language speakers
- bilingual dictionaries, if available
- online translation sources

Personal Narrative   WRITING WORKSHOP UNIT 1

Name _____

Words That Tell About *You*

Directions Your feelings probably changed during the course of the experience described in your personal narrative. Choose two or three words from the word bank to describe how you felt at different times. For each word, explain why you felt that way. Then use vivid details that *show* how you felt.

angry	excited	proud	sad
disappointed	embarrassed	satisfied	curious
nervous	anxious	delighted	upset

I felt **Answers should include adjectives from**
Reason: **the word bank, explain the choice,**
And here's how I looked and acted: **and give details that show the feelings the adjectives suggest.**

I felt _____
Reason: _____
And here's how I looked and acted: _____

I felt _____
Reason: _____
And here's how I looked and acted: _____

Grammar and Writing Practice Book   Unit 1 **161**

▲ **Grammar and Writing Practice Book** p. 161

WRITER'S CRAFT Sequence

Here are some ways to make sure your writing describes events in the order that they really occurred:

- Picture in your mind the order in which events happened.
- Use clue words such as *before, after, then, later,* and *next.*
- Refer to the dates or times of day that events occurred.

DRAFTING STRATEGIES

- Have students review their notes before they write.
- Students should use vivid language to describe their feelings.
- Remind students to keep their audience and purpose in mind.
- Students should follow the directions above in order to organize events in the correct order.
- Have students use Grammar and Writing Practice Book p. 161 to choose words that tell about themselves.

WRITER'S CRAFT Elaboration

COMPLEX SENTENCES Explain that one way to elaborate is to combine two short, simple sentences to make complex sentences. One of the simple sentences will become a dependent clause—a group of words that cannot stand alone as a sentence—by the addition of words such as *if, when, because, although, since,* or *as.*

Choppy	I'm nervous about going to the new school. I don't know anybody there. We've just moved here. I haven't had time to make friends.
Improved	I'm nervous about going to a new school because I don't know anybody there. Since we've just moved here, I haven't had time to make friends.

Use Grammar and Writing Practice Book p. 162 to practice elaboration by making complex sentences.

REVISING STRATEGIES

GUIDED WRITING Use Writing Transparency WP5 to model revising. Point out the Revising Marks, which students should use when they revise their work.

MODEL This is part of the narrative about going to Theater Workshop for the first time. Look how the writer has made sentence 1 stronger by explaining that he felt sick with nervousness. And do you notice that the original version has six short sentences? They make the writing sound choppy and dull. By combining sentences 2 and 3 with *when* and sentences 5 and 6 with *although*, the writer has created two complex sentences. This paragraph now sounds much smoother.

Think Aloud

PEER REVISION Write the Revising Checklist on the board, or make copies to distribute. Students can use this checklist to revise their personal narratives. Have partners read each other's first drafts. Remind them to be courteous and specific with suggestions.

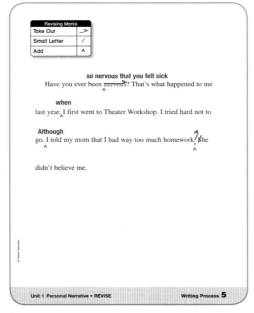

▲ **Writing Transparency** WP5

Trait Checklist

REVISING

Focus/Ideas
✔ Is the personal narrative focused?
✔ Are there enough details?

Organization/Paragraphs
✔ Do time-order words help make the sequence of events clear?

Voice
✔ Is the narrative interesting and lively?

Word Choice
✔ Does vivid language help describe the writer's feelings?

Sentences
✔ Should any simple sentences be combined into complex sentences?

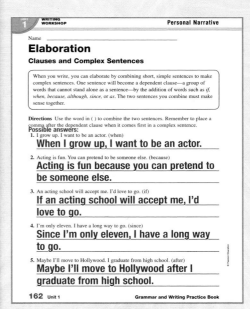

▲ **Grammar and Writing Practice Book** p. 162

Writing Workshop

1 PREWRITE 2 DRAFT 3 REVISE **4 EDIT** 5 PUBLISH

Monitor Progress

Differentiated Instruction

If... students are using only simple sentences,	then... review the grammar lesson on pp. 133e–133f.

Editing Checklist

✔ Did I spell words with the long *e* and *o* vowel sounds correctly?

✔ Did I use the correct end punctuation for each sentence?

✔ Did I indent for new paragraphs?

✔ Did I correct any run-on sentences?

Support Writing When reviewing a student's draft, emphasize ideas rather than errors. Observe whether there are consistent grammatical errors. If so, they may reflect the writing conventions of the home language. Choose one or two skills, and use the appropriate Grammar Transition Lessons in the ELL and Transition Handbook to explicitly teach the English conventions.

EDITING STRATEGY

SENTENCE BY SENTENCE Suggest that students use an editing strategy. They can check their work by examining each sentence individually. Encourage students to ask questions. Is this a complete sentence? (If not, is it an appropriate fragment?) Is it properly punctuated? Are all words spelled correctly? Have I run two or more sentences into one?

GUIDED WRITING Use Writing Transparency WP6 to model the process of checking a passage sentence by sentence. Indicate the Proofreading Marks, which students should use when they edit their work. Write the Editing Checklist on the board, or make copies to distribute. Students can use this checklist to edit their work.

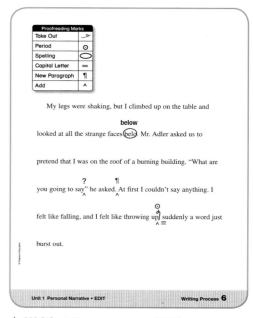

▲ **Writing Transparency** WP6

 MODEL I'll start with sentence 1. This looks fine, except for the spelling of *below,* which the writer has corrected. Sentence 2 is also complete and correctly punctuated. There's a problem in sentence 3, however. The writer has corrected it by adding a question mark before the quotation. And the next sentence makes more sense if it starts a new paragraph. You can see that the writer has added a paragraph symbol. Finally, this last long sentence contains a run-on sentence. The writer has corrected this by adding a period after the word *up* and capitalizing the *s* in *suddenly.*

USING TECHNOLOGY Students who have written or revised their personal narratives on computers should keep these points in mind as they edit:

- Computer grammar checkers are useful, but sometimes they make mistakes. Check your work with another reader and a good grammar book.

- Using a print preview or page layout feature can show you how your work will appear before it is printed.

- Save your work often and back it up. You've worked too hard to lose everything accidentally.

SELF-EVALUATION

Prepare students to fill out a Self-Evaluation Guide. Display Writing Transparency WP7 to model the self-evaluation process.

Think Aloud **MODEL** I would give the personal narrative a *4*.

Focus/Ideas This narrative is focused on the writer's first day at Theater Workshop.

Organization/Paragraphs The events are described in order.

Voice The narrator writes as if he is talking to the reader.

Word Choice The writer uses time-order words and phrases such as *then, last year, at first,* and *next week.*

Sentences Sentences are compound and complex as well as simple.

Conventions Grammar, capitalization, and spelling are excellent.

EVALUATION Assign Grammar and Writing Practice Book p. 163. Tell students that when they evaluate their own narratives, assigning a score of 3, 2, or even 1 does not necessarily indicate a bad paper. The ability to identify areas for improvement in future writing is a valuable skill.

"Help! Help!"

Have you ever been so nervous that you felt sick? That's what happened to me last year when I first went to Theater Workshop. I tried hard not to go. Although I told my mom that I had way too much homework, she didn't believe me.

There were lots of kids at the church hall, but I didn't know any of them. Then Mr. Adler, the teacher, walked into the room. Before he even introduced himself, he stared hard at all of us. His eyes fell on me, and he pointed to a big table. "Get up there," he said.

My legs were shaking, but I climbed up on the table and looked at all the strange faces below. Mr. Adler asked us to pretend that I was on the roof of a burning building. "What are you going to say?" he asked.

At first I couldn't say anything. I felt like falling, and I felt like throwing up. Suddenly a word just burst out.

"Help!" I said softly. Then I repeated it louder and louder. "Help! Help! Help!" The more I shouted, the better I felt. It was hard to stop.

The next week I couldn't wait to go back to Theater Workshop.

Unit 1 Personal Narrative • PUBLISH   Writing Process **7**

▲ **Writing Transparency** WP7

Ideas for Publishing

Picture Books Students can draw pictures or bring in photographs to illustrate their stories. They can create a cover and make their own book.

Writer's Circle Students can take turns reading their narratives aloud in a small group. Classmates may ask questions about the narratives.

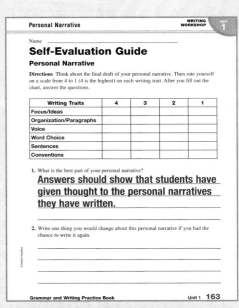

▲ **Grammar and Writing Practice Book** p. 163

Scoring Rubric — Personal Narrative

Rubric 4 3 2 1	4	3	2	1
Focus/Ideas	Personal narrative well focused and developed with many supporting details	Personal narrative generally focused and developed with supporting details	Personal narrative often off topic; lacks enough supporting details	Personal narrative without focus or sufficient information
Organization/ Paragraphs	Clear sequence of events with time-order words	Reasonably clear sequence with one or two lapses	Confused sequence of events	No attempt to put events into sequence, or sequence is incoherent
Voice	Natural-sounding, conversational voice	Pleasant voice but not very natural-sounding	Weak voice	Dull writing with no clear voice
Word Choice	Vivid language that describes feelings; sequence made clear by time-order words	Some language that describes feelings; fair use of time-order words	Little language describing feelings; little or no use of time-order words	No attempt to describe feelings; no use of time-order words
Sentences	Clear sentences, varied in type and style, including compound and complex	Mostly clear sentences with some variety	Some sentences unclear; little or no variety, no compound or complex sentences	Incoherent sentences; dull, choppy style
Conventions	Few, if any, errors	Several minor errors	Errors that detract from writing and/or interfere with understanding	Errors that prevent understanding

For 6-, 5-, and 3-point Scoring Rubrics, see pp. WA11–WA14.

Writing Workshop

Personal Narrative
Differentiated Instruction

WRITING PROMPT: This Land Is Your Land

Write a personal narrative about a time that you were a newcomer to a place or situation (a school, club, team, or neighborhood). Explain how you felt and what you found challenging or exciting.

Purpose: Explain how you coped in a difficult situation

Audience: Classmates

MODIFY INSTRUCTION

Pick One

ALTERNATIVE PROMPTS

ALTERNATIVE PROMPTS: Narrative Writing

Strategic Intervention Think about the first time you went to school or your first day in a new school. Was it frightening, exciting, or fun? Write a paragraph about what you did and how you felt.

On-Level Think of something you've recently done for the first time. It might be ice skating, making cookies, or going to a new store. Write an e-mail to a friend describing the experience. Make sure you explain to him or her how the experience made you feel.

Advanced You know how you felt when you were a newcomer to a situation. But how did other people feel about the same experience? Think of another person who was there on that occasion (a teacher, a coach, another student, etc.). Write about the experience in the words and voice of that other person. Choose a form (letter, essay, story, etc.) that best suits your purpose.

Strategic Intervention

MODIFY THE PROMPT

Help emerging writers think about suitable topics by brainstorming possible situations with the class. List these on the board, and then ask students how they felt on these occasions. Encourage students to explain why they felt nervous, sad, excited, or another emotion, and how their feelings changed over time.

① **PREWRITE** ② DRAFT ③ REVISE ④ EDIT ⑤ PUBLISH

PREWRITING SUPPORT

- Describe an experience of your own in which you were a newcomer to a place or situation.

- Encourage students to form pairs and tell each other about a situation in which they were a newcomer. Have the listening student ask questions.

- Have students dictate to you the event they want to describe in their personal narrative. Record their ideas, isolating key words or concepts. Elicit details about these key words.

OPTIONS

- Give students the option of writing a group narrative under your supervision.

CHECK PROGRESS Segment the assignment into manageable pieces. Check work at intervals, such as graphic organizers and first drafts, to make sure writing is on track.

MODIFY THE PROMPT

Expect advanced writers to produce work with strong elaboration and some analytic thought about the meaning of the personal experience. Students should vary sentences in style and length, combining short sentences with appositives, participial phrases, adjectives, adverbs, and prepositional phrases.

APPLY SKILLS

- As students revise their work, have them consider some ways to improve it.

  Read their narratives to a partner in order to listen to the flow and rhythm of the sentences.

  Look for opportunities to add sensory descriptions that show instead of tell about their experience.

  Add direct quotes or dialogue that helps show instead of tell.

OPTIONS

- Students can follow these steps to create their own class rubrics.

  1. Read examples of class personal narratives and rank them 1–4, with 4 the highest.

  2. Discuss how they arrived at each rank.

  3. Isolate the six traits and make a rubric based on them.

CHECK PROGRESS Discuss the students' Self-Evaluation Guides. Work with students to monitor their growth and identify their strengths and weaknesses as writers.

MODIFY THE PROMPT

Have students describe the main ideas they want to include in their narratives. Help them restate the ideas as complete sentences. Record the sentences and have students copy them.

BUILD BACKGROUND

- Write the word *personal* on the board. Explain that it describes anything relating to an individual. Write the word *narrative* and explain that it is another word for *story*. Discuss the fact that a personal narrative is simply a story about the writer. Discuss the list of Key Features of a personal narrative that appears in the left column of p. WA2.

OPTIONS

- As students write their personal narratives, guide them toward books, magazines, or Web sites that provide comprehension support through features such as the following.

  personal narratives illustrated with photographs and other pictures

  text in the home-language

- For more suggestions on scaffolding the Writing Workshop, see the ELL and Transition Handbook.

CHECK PROGRESS You may need to explain certain traits and help students fill out their Self-Evaluation Guides. Downplay conventions and focus more on ideas. Recognize examples of vocabulary growth and efforts to use language in more complex ways.

Scoring Rubric | Look Back and Write

2 points The response indicates that the student has a complete understanding of the reading concept embodied in the task. The response is accurate, complete, and fulfills all the requirements of the task. Necessary support and/or examples are included, and the information given is clearly text-based.

1 point The response indicates that the student has a partial understanding of the reading concept embodied in the task. The response includes information that is essentially correct and text-based, but the information is too general or too simplistic. Some of the support and/or examples may be incomplete or omitted.

0 points The response indicates that the student does not demonstrate an understanding of the reading concept embodied in the task. The student has either failed to respond or has provided a response that is inaccurate or has insufficient information.

Scoring Rubric | Look Back and Write

4 points The response indicates that the student has a thorough understanding of the reading concept embodied in the task. The response is accurate, complete, and fulfills all the requirements of the task. Necessary support and/or examples are included, and the information is clearly text-based.

3 points The response indicates that the student has an understanding of the reading concept embodied in the task. The response is accurate and fulfills all the requirements of the task, but the required support and/or details are not complete or clearly text-based.

2 points The response indicates that the student has a partial understanding of the reading concept embodied in the task. The response that includes information is essentially correct and text-based, but the information is too general or too simplistic. Some of the support and/or examples and requirements of the task may be incomplete or omitted.

1 point The response indicates that the student has a very limited understanding of the reading concept embodied in the task. The response is incomplete, may exhibit many flaws, and may not address all requirements of the task.

0 points The response indicates that the student does not demonstrate an understanding of the reading concept embodied in the task. The student has either failed to respond or has provided a response that is inaccurate or has insufficient information.

Scoring Rubric | Narrative Writing

Rubric 4 3 2 1

	6	5	4	3	2	1
Focus/Ideas	Excellent, focused narrative; well elaborated with quality details	Good, focused narrative; elaborated with telling details	Narrative focused; adequate elaboration	Generally focused narrative; some supporting details	Sometimes unfocused narrative; needs more supporting details	Rambling narrative; lacks development and detail
Organization/ Paragraphs	Strong beginning, middle, and end; appropriate order words	Coherent beginning, middle, and end; some order words	Beginning, middle, and end easily identifiable	Recognizable beginning, middle, and end; some order words	Little direction from beginning to end; few order words	Lacks beginning, middle, end; incorrect or no order words
Voice	Writer closely involved; engaging personality	Reveals personality	Pleasant but not compelling voice	Sincere voice but not fully engaged	Little writer involvement, personality	Careless writing with no feeling
Word Choice	Vivid, precise words that bring story to life	Clear words to bring story to life	Some specific word pictures	Language adequate but lacks color	Generally limited or redundant language	Vague, dull, or misused words
Sentences	Excellent variety of sentences; natural rhythm	Varied lengths, styles; generally smooth	Correct sentences with some variations in style	Correctly constructed sentences; some variety	May have simple, awkward, or wordy sentences; little variety	Choppy; many incomplete or run-on sentences
Conventions	Excellent control; few or no errors	No serious errors to affect understanding	General mastery of conventions but some errors	Reasonable control; few distracting errors	Weak control; enough errors to affect understanding	Many errors that prevent understanding

Scoring Rubric | Narrative Writing

Rubric 4 3 2 1

	5	4	3	2	1
Focus/Ideas	Excellent, focused narrative; well elaborated with quality details	Good, focused narrative; elaborated with telling details	Generally focused narrative; some supporting details	Sometimes unfocused narrative; needs more supporting details	Rambling narrative; lacks development and detail
Organization/ Paragraphs	Strong beginning, middle, and end; appropriate order words	Coherent beginning, middle, and end; some order words	Recognizable beginning, middle, and end; some order words	Little direction from beginning to end; few order words	Lacks beginning, middle, end; incorrect or no order words
Voice	Writer closely involved; engaging personality	Reveals personality	Sincere voice but not fully engaged	Little writer involvement, personality	Careless writing with no feeling
Word Choice	Vivid, precise words that bring story to life	Clear words to bring story to life	Language adequate but lacks color	Generally limited or redundant language	Vague, dull, or misused words
Sentences	Excellent variety of sentences; natural rhythm	Varied lengths, styles; generally smooth	Correctly constructed sentences; some variety	May have simple, awkward, or wordy sentences; little variety	Choppy; many incomplete or run-on sentences
Conventions	Excellent control; few or no errors	No serious errors to affect understanding	Reasonable control; few distracting errors	Weak control; enough errors to affect understanding	Many errors that prevent understanding

Scoring Rubric | Narrative Writing

Rubric 4 3 2 1

	3	2	1
Focus/Ideas	Excellent, focused narrative; well elaborated with quality details	Generally focused narrative; some supporting details	Rambling narrative; lacks development and detail
Organization/ Paragraphs	Strong beginning, middle, and end; appropriate order words	Recognizable beginning, middle, and end; some order words	Lacks beginning, middle, end; incorrect or no order words
Voice	Writer closely involved; engaging personality	Sincere voice but not fully engaged	Careless writing with no feeling
Word Choice	Vivid, precise words that bring story to life	Language adequate but lacks color	Vague, dull, or misused words
Sentences	Excellent variety of sentences; natural rhythm	Correctly constructed sentences; some variety	Choppy; many incomplete or run-on sentences
Conventions	Excellent control; few or no errors	Reasonable control; few distracting errors	Many errors that prevent understanding

Scoring Rubric — Descriptive Writing

Rubric 4 3 2 1	6	5	4	3	2	1
Focus/Ideas	Excellent, focused description; well elaborated with quality details	Good, focused description; elaborated with telling details	Description focused; good elaboration	Generally focused description; some supporting details	Sometimes unfocused description; needs more supporting details	Rambling description; lacks development and detail
Organization/ Paragraphs	Compelling ideas enhanced by order, structure, and transitions	Appealing order, structure, and transitions	Structure identifiable and suitable; transitions used	Adequate order, structure, and some transitions to guide reader	Little direction from beginning to end; few transitions	Lacks direction and identifiable structure; no transitions
Voice	Writer closely involved; engaging personality	Reveals personality	Pleasant but not compelling voice	Sincere voice but not fully engaged	Little writer involvement, personality	Careless writing with no feeling
Word Choice	Vivid, precise words that create memorable pictures	Clear, interesting words to bring description to life	Some specific word pictures	Language adequate; appeals to senses	Generally limited or redundant language	Vague, dull, or misused words
Sentences	Excellent variety of sentences; natural rhythm	Varied lengths, styles; generally smooth	Correct sentences with variations in style	Correctly constructed sentences; some variety	May have simple, awkward, or wordy sentences; little variety	Choppy; many incomplete or run-on sentences
Conventions	Excellent control; few or no errors	No serious errors to affect understanding	General mastery of conventions but some errors	Reasonable control; few distracting errors	Weak control; enough errors to affect understanding	Many errors that prevent understanding

Scoring Rubric — Descriptive Writing

Rubric 4 3 2 1	5	4	3	2	1
Focus/Ideas	Excellent, focused description; well elaborated with quality details	Good, focused description; elaborated with telling details	Generally focused description; some supporting details	Sometimes unfocused description; needs more supporting details	Rambling description; lacks development and detail
Organization/ Paragraphs	Compelling ideas enhanced by order, structure, and transitions	Appealing order, structure, and transitions	Adequate order, structure, and some transitions to guide reader	Little direction from beginning to end; few transitions	Lacks direction and identifiable structure; no transitions
Voice	Writer closely involved; engaging personality	Reveals personality	Sincere voice but not fully engaged	Little writer involvement, personality	Careless writing with no feeling
Word Choice	Vivid, precise words that create memorable pictures	Clear, interesting words to bring description to life	Language adequate; appeals to senses	Generally limited or redundant language	Vague, dull, or misused words
Sentences	Excellent variety of sentences; natural rhythm	Varied lengths, styles; generally smooth	Correctly constructed sentences; some variety	May have simple, awkward, or wordy sentences; little variety	Choppy; many incomplete or run-on sentences
Conventions	Excellent control; few or no errors	No serious errors to affect understanding	Reasonable control; few distracting errors	Weak control; enough errors to affect understanding	Many errors that prevent understanding

Scoring Rubric — Descriptive Writing

Rubric 4 3 2 1	3	2	1
Focus/Ideas	Excellent, focused description; well elaborated with quality details	Generally focused description; some supporting details	Rambling description; lacks development and detail
Organization/ Paragraphs	Compelling ideas enhanced by order, structure, and transitions	Adequate order, structure, and some transitions to guide reader	Lacks direction and identifiable structure; no transitions
Voice	Writer closely involved; engaging personality	Sincere voice but not fully engaged	Careless writing with no feeling
Word Choice	Vivid, precise words that create memorable pictures	Language adequate; appeals to senses	Vague, dull, or misused words
Sentences	Excellent variety of sentences; natural rhythm	Correctly constructed sentences; some variety	Choppy; many incomplete or run-on sentences
Conventions	Excellent control; few or no errors	Reasonable control; few distracting errors	Many errors that prevent understanding

Scoring Rubric | Persuasive Writing

Rubric 4 3 2 1	6	5	4	3	2	1
Focus/Ideas	Persuasive argument carefully built with quality details	Persuasive argument well supported with details	Persuasive argument focused; good elaboration	Persuasive argument with one or two convincing details	Persuasive piece sometimes unfocused; needs more support	Rambling persuasive argument; lacks development and detail
Organization/ Paragraphs	Information chosen and arranged for maximum effect	Evident progression of persuasive ideas	Progression and structure evident	Information arranged in a logical way with some lapses	Little structure or direction	No identifiable structure
Voice	Writer closely involved; persuasive but not overbearing	Maintains persuasive tone	Persuasive but not compelling voice	Sometimes uses persuasive voice	Little writer involvement, personality	Shows little conviction
Word Choice	Persuasive words carefully chosen for impact	Argument supported by persuasive language	Uses some persuasive words	Occasional persuasive language	Generally limited or redundant language	Vague, dull, or misused words; no persuasive words
Sentences	Excellent variety of sentences; natural rhythm	Varied lengths, styles; generally smooth	Correct sentences with variations in style	Carefully constructed sentences; some variety	Simple, awkward, or wordy sentences; little variety	Choppy; many incomplete or run-on sentences
Conventions	Excellent control; few or no errors	No serious errors to affect understanding	General mastery of conventions but some errors	Reasonable control; few distracting errors	Weak control; enough errors to affect understanding	Many errors that prevent understanding

Scoring Rubric | Persuasive Writing

Rubric 4 3 2 1	5	4	3	2	1
Focus/Ideas	Persuasive argument carefully built with quality details	Persuasive argument well supported with details	Persuasive argument with one or two convincing details	Persuasive piece sometimes unfocused; needs more support	Rambling persuasive argument; lacks development and detail
Organization/ Paragraphs	Information chosen and arranged for maximum effect	Evident progression of persuasive ideas	Information arranged in a logical way with some lapses	Little structure or direction	No identifiable structure
Voice	Writer closely involved; persuasive but not overbearing	Maintains persuasive tone	Sometimes uses persuasive voice	Little writer involvement, personality	Shows little conviction
Word Choice	Persuasive words carefully chosen for impact	Argument supported by persuasive language	Occasional persuasive language	Generally limited or redundant language	Vague, dull, or misused words; no persuasive words
Sentences	Excellent variety of sentences; natural rhythm	Varied lengths, styles; generally smooth	Carefully constructed sentences; some variety	Simple, awkward, or wordy sentences; little variety	Choppy; many incomplete or run-on sentences
Conventions	Excellent control; few or no errors	No serious errors to affect understanding	Reasonable control; few distracting errors	Weak control; enough errors to affect understanding	Many errors that prevent understanding

Scoring Rubric | Persuasive Writing

Rubric 4 3 2 1	3	2	1
Focus/Ideas	Persuasive argument carefully built with quality details	Persuasive argument with one or two convincing details	Rambling persuasive argument; lacks development and detail
Organization/ Paragraphs	Information chosen and arranged for maximum effect	Information arranged in a logical way with some lapses	No identifiable structure
Voice	Writer closely involved; persuasive but not overbearing	Sometimes uses persuasive voice	Shows little conviction
Word Choice	Persuasive words carefully chosen for impact	Occasional persuasive language	Vague, dull, or misused words; no persuasive words
Sentences	Excellent variety of sentences; natural rhythm	Carefully constructed sentences; some variety	Choppy; many incomplete or run-on sentences
Conventions	Excellent control; few or no errors	Reasonable control; few distracting errors	Many errors that prevent understanding

Scoring Rubric — Expository Writing

Rubric 4 3 2 1

	6	5	4	3	2	1
Focus/Ideas	Insightful, focused exposition; well elaborated with quality details	Informed, focused exposition; elaborated with telling details	Exposition focused, good elaboration	Generally focused exposition; some supporting details	Sometimes unfocused exposition needs more supporting details	Rambling exposition; lacks development and detail
Organization/ Paragraphs	Logical, consistent flow of ideas; good transitions	Logical sequencing of ideas; uses transitions	Ideas sequenced with some transitions	Sequenced ideas with some transitions	Little direction from beginning to end; few order words	Lacks structure and transitions
Voice	Writer closely involved; informative voice well suited to topic	Reveals personality; voice suited to topic	Pleasant but not compelling voice	Sincere voice suited to topic	Little writer involvement, personality	Careless writing with no feeling
Word Choice	Vivid, precise words to express ideas	Clear words to express ideas	Words correct and adequate	Language adequate but may lack precision	Generally limited or redundant language	Vague, dull, or misused words
Sentences	Strong topic sentence; fluent, varied structures	Good topic sentence; smooth sentence structure	Correct sentences that are sometimes fluent	Topic sentence correctly constructed; some sentence variety	Topic sentence unclear or missing; wordy, awkward sentences	No topic sentence; many incomplete or run-on sentences
Conventions	Excellent control; few or no errors	No serious errors to affect understanding	General mastery of conventions but some errors	Reasonable control; few distracting errors	Weak control; enough errors to affect understanding	Many errors that prevent understanding

Scoring Rubric — Expository Writing

Rubric 4 3 2 1

	5	4	3	2	1
Focus/Ideas	Insightful, focused exposition; well elaborated with quality details	Informed, focused exposition; elaborated with telling details	Generally focused exposition; some supporting details	Sometimes unfocused exposition needs more supporting details	Rambling exposition; lacks development and detail
Organization/ Paragraphs	Logical, consistent flow of ideas; good transitions	Logical sequencing of ideas; uses transitions	Sequenced ideas with some transitions	Little direction from beginning to end; few order words	Lacks structure and transitions
Voice	Writer closely involved; informative voice well suited to topic	Reveals personality; voice suited to topic	Language adequate but may lack precision	Little writer involvement, personality	Careless writing with no feeling
Word Choice	Vivid, precise words to express ideas	Clear words to express ideas	Topic sentence correctly constructed; some sentence variety	Generally limited or redundant language	Vague, dull, or misused words
Sentences	Strong topic sentence; fluent, varied structures	Good topic sentence; smooth sentence structure	Sincere voice suited to topic	Topic sentence unclear or missing; wordy, awkward sentences	No topic sentence; many incomplete or run-on sentences
Conventions	Excellent control; few or no errors	No serious errors to affect understanding	Reasonable control; few distracting errors	Weak control; enough errors to affect understanding	Many errors that prevent understanding

Scoring Rubric — Expository Writing

Rubric 4 3 2 1

	3	2	1
Focus/Ideas	Insightful, focused exposition; well elaborated with quality details	Generally focused exposition; some supporting details	Rambling exposition; lacks development and detail
Organization/ Paragraphs	Logical, consistent flow of ideas; good transitions	Sequenced ideas with some transitions	Lacks structure and transitions
Voice	Writer closely involved; informative voice well suited to topic	Sincere voice suited to topic	Careless writing with no feeling
Word Choice	Vivid, precise words to express ideas	Language adequate but may lack precision	Vague, dull, or misused words
Sentences	Strong topic sentence; fluent, varied structures	Topic sentence correctly constructed; some sentence variety	No topic sentence; many incomplete or run-on sentences
Conventions	Excellent control; few or no errors	Reasonable control; few distracting errors	Many errors that prevent understanding

Monitoring Fluency

Ongoing assessment of student reading fluency is one of the most valuable measures we have of students' reading skills. One of the most effective ways to assess fluency is taking timed samples of students' oral reading and measuring the number of words correct per minute (WCPM).

How to Measure Words Correct Per Minute—WCPM

Choose a Text
Start by choosing a text for the student to read. The text should be:
• narrative
• unfamiliar
• on grade level
Make a copy of the text for yourself and have one for the student.

Timed Reading of the Text
Tell the student: As you read this aloud, I want you to do your best reading and to read as quickly as you can. That doesn't mean it's a race. Just do your best, fast reading. When I say begin, start reading.

As the student reads, follow along in your copy. Mark words that are read incorrectly.

Incorrect	Correct
• omissions	• self-corrections within 3 seconds
• substitutions	• repeated words
• mispronunciations	
• reversals	

After One Minute
At the end of one minute, draw a line after the last word that was read. Have the student finish reading but don't count any words beyond one minute. Arrive at the words correct per minute—WCPM—by counting the total number of words that the student read correctly in one minute.

Fluency Goals
Grade 4 End-of-Year Goal = 130 WCPM

Target goals by unit

Unit 1 95 to 105 WCPM	**Unit 4** 110 to 120 WCPM
Unit 2 100 to 110 WCPM	**Unit 5** 115 to 125 WCPM
Unit 3 105 to 115 WCPM	**Unit 6** 120 to 130 WCPM

More Frequent Monitoring
You may want to monitor some students more frequently because they are falling far below grade-level benchmarks or they have a result that doesn't seem to align with their previous performance.
Follow the same steps above, but choose 2 or 3 additional texts.

Fluency Progress Chart Copy the chart on the next page. Use it to record each student's progress across the year.

See also Assessment Handbook, p. 166

Name _____

Fluency Progress Chart, Grade 4

	1	2	3	4	5	6	7	8	9	10	11	12	13	14	15	16	17	18	19	20	21	22	23	24	25	26	27	28	29	30
165																														
160																														
155																														
150																														
145																														
140																														
135																														
130																														
125																														
120																														
115																														
110																														
105																														
100																														
95																														
90																														
85																														
80																														
75																														
70																														

Timed Reading

Assessment and Regrouping Chart

		Day 3 Retelling Assessment		Day 5 Fluency Assessment				
		The assessed group is highlighted for each week.		The assessed group is highlighted for each week.				
		Benchmark Score	Actual Score	Benchmark WCPM	Actual Score	Reteach	Teacher's Comments	Grouping
WEEK 1 — *Because of Winn-Dixie* — Sequence	Strategic	1–2		Strategic — Less than 95		✓		
	On-Level	3		On-Level — 95–105				
	Advanced	4		Advanced* — 95–105				
WEEK 2 — *Lewis and Clark and Me* — Author's Purpose	Strategic	1–2		Strategic — Less than 95				
	On-Level	3		On-Level — 95–105				
	Advanced	4		Advanced* — 95–105				
WEEK 3 — *Grandfather's Journey* — Sequence	Strategic	1–2		Strategic — Less than 95				
	On-Level	3		On-Level — 95–105				
	Advanced	4		Advanced* — 95–105				
WEEK 4 — *The Horned Toad Prince* — Author's Purpose	Strategic	1–2		Strategic — Less than 95				
	On-Level	3		On-Level — 95–105				
	Advanced	4		Advanced* — 95–105				
WEEK 5 — *Letters Home* — Main Idea	Strategic	1–2		Strategic — Less than 95				
	On-Level	3		On-Level — 95–105				
	Advanced	4		Advanced* — 95–105				
Unit 1 Benchmark Test Score								

*Students in the advanced group should read above-grade-level materials.

- **RECORD SCORES** Use this chart to record scores for the Day 3 Retelling, Day 5 Fluency, and Unit Benchmark Test Assessments.

- **REGROUPING** Compare the student's actual score to the benchmark score for each group level and review the *Questions to Consider*. Students may move to a higher or lower group level, or they may remain in the same group.

- **RETEACH** If a student is unable to complete any part of the assessment process, use the weekly Reteach lessons for additional support. Record the lesson information in the space provided on the chart. After reteaching, you may want to reassess using the Unit Benchmark Test.

See also Assessment Handbook, p. 167

Unit 1
Assess and Regroup

FYI In Grade 4 there are opportunities for regrouping every six weeks—at the end of Units 2, 3, 4, and 5. These options offer sensitivity to each student's progress although some teachers may prefer to regroup less frequently.

Assess Unit 1

To assess student progress at the end of Unit 1, consider students' end-of-unit scores for

- Unit 1 Retelling
- Fluency (WCPM)
- Unit 1 Benchmark Test

Group Time

On-Level	Strategic Intervention	Advanced
For On-Level Unit 1 assessment, students should	**Students would benefit from Strategic Intervention if they**	**For Advanced group Unit 1 assessment, students should**
• score 3 or better on their cumulative unit rubric scores for Retelling	• score 2 or lower on their cumulative unit rubric scores for Retelling	• score 4 on their cumulative unit rubric scores for Retelling and demonstrate expansive vocabulary and ease of language in their retellings
• meet the current benchmark for fluency (95–105 WCPM), reading On-Level text such as Student Edition selections	• do not meet the current benchmark for fluency (95–105 WCPM)	• score 95% on the Unit 1 Benchmark Test
• score 80% or better on the Unit 1 Benchmark Tests	• score below 60% on the Unit 1 Benchmark Tests	• read above-grade-level material fluently (95–105 WCPM)
• be capable of working in the On-Level group based on teacher judgment	• are struggling to keep up with the On-Level group based on teacher judgment	• be capable of handling the problem solving and investigative work of the Advanced group based on teacher judgment

QUESTIONS TO CONSIDER

- What types of test questions did the student miss? Are they specific to a particular skill or strategy?
- Does the student have adequate background knowledge to understand the test passages or selections for retelling?

- Has the student's performance met expectations for daily lessons and assessments with little or no reteaching?
- Is the student performing more like students in another group?
- Does the student read for enjoyment, different purposes, and varied interests?

Benchmark Fluency Scores

Current Goal: **95–105 WCPM**

End-of-Year Goal: **130 WCPM**

Florida Everglades

◉ **SEQUENCE**

◉ **SUMMARIZE**

LESSON VOCABULARY grand, memorial, peculiar, positive, prideful, recall, select

---

SUMMARY This nonfiction book describes the special characteristics of many species native to the Everglades, including the black bear, alligator, mockingbird, egret, and mangrove and cypress trees.

INTRODUCE THE BOOK

BUILD BACKGROUND Locate the Everglades National Park on a map. Ask if any students have been to the Everglades, and have them describe the types of plants and animals they saw there. If no one has been to the Everglades, ask students to guess what types of species might live in the park.

PREVIEW/USE TEXT FEATURES Have students read the title and skim the book looking at pictures, captions, and headings. Have students tell what types of plants and animals they will read about in the selection.

ⒺⓁⓁ Have students draw pictures of the Everglades. Have them label plants, animals or other items in their home languages and English.

TEACH/REVIEW VOCABULARY Divide students into seven groups. Assign one vocabulary word to each group. Have each group read aloud the glossary entry for its word and write a sentence for the word. Then have groups share their words and sentences with the class.

TARGET SKILL AND STRATEGY

◉ **SEQUENCE** Remind students that keeping track of the *sequence,* or order, of events in a book may help them understand the facts that are presented. Write a list of clue words on the board, such as *first, then, after, now,* to help students as they read.

◉ **SUMMARIZE** Tell students that *summarizing,* or remembering the important information in a book, can help them keep track of the main facts of a selection. Have students stop reading at the end of each section of the book. Tell them to think of a summary sentence for each section using the section heading as a guide.

READ THE BOOK

Use the following questions to support comprehension.

PAGE 9 How does an alligator chase prey on land? *(It runs on its toes with its tail off the ground and sprints up to thirty miles an hour.)*

PAGE 10 How did the mockingbird get its name? *(It can mock the sounds of other birds.)*

PAGE 11 What happened after many egrets were killed for their feathers? *(They became a protected species.)*

TALK ABOUT THE BOOK

READER RESPONSE
1. Possible response: A bear might get hit by a car when it crosses the highway to find food and water.
2. Possible response: The mangrove tree grows in salt water, and its roots keep mud from being washed away; the cypress tree grows along the rivers and has "knees" that might help give it oxygen.
3. Possible response: Suffix: *–ful;* Base word: *pride* Other words: *actually, dangerous, beautiful, luckily*
4. Responses will vary but should be supported by details from the book.

RESPONSE OPTIONS

WRITING Have students choose their favorite plant or animal described in the selection. Then ask them to write a paragraph detailing what they learned about it.

CONTENT CONNECTIONS

SCIENCE Provide students with a list of other plants and animals that live in Everglades National Park. Divide students into small groups. Assign one plant and one animal to each group. Have groups research their plants and animals and write short summaries of the facts they discover. Ask each group to read its summaries to the class.

TIME FOR Science

Sequence

- **Sequence** is the order of events.

Directions Use *Florida Everglades: Its Plants & Animals*. Answer the following questions.

1. What is the sequence of the information the author presents about black bears in the Florida Everglades?

_____

_____

2. Reread page 11. What sequence of events led to the protection of egrets?

First, _____

Next, _____

Now, _____

3. Reread page 14. What sequence of events led to the protection of the Florida Everglades?

First, _____

Next, _____

Now, _____

4. In what sequence does the selection tell about the plants and animals in the Florida Everglades?

First, _____

Next, _____

Next, _____

Next, _____

Finally, _____

© Pearson Education 4

14

Vocabulary

Directions Use the vocabulary words in the box to fill in the blanks in the sentences below.

Check the Words You Know

___grand   ___memorial   ___peculiar   ___positive
___prideful   ___recall   ___select

1. I was _____ the black bear had not seen me.

2. Many people support putting up a _____ sign for all the black bears killed crossing highways.

3. Black bears like to _____ the tastiest berries.

4. Besides the armadillo, another _____ animal is the porcupine, with its unusual quills.

5. One of the most amazing habitats in North America is the _____ Florida Everglades.

6. Nina could not _____ where she had put her homework the night before.

7. People who live in Florida are _____ of many beautiful plants that grow in their state.

Directions Use a thesaurus to find antonyms for each of the words below.

8. **grand** _____

_____

9. **peculiar** _____

_____

10. **prideful** _____

_____

15

Something to Do

◉ **SEQUENCE**

◉ **SUMMARIZE**

LESSON VOCABULARY grand, memorial, peculiar, positive, prideful, recalls, selecting

SUMMARY In this story, the narrator is a boy whose grandfather comes to live with him and his father. The grandfather spends most of his days watching TV or sleeping, so the boy and his father try to find something for the grandfather to do. One day they discover the perfect activity.

INTRODUCE THE BOOK

BUILD BACKGROUND Ask students to describe what they like to do with their grandparents and what their grandparents do when they are not spending time with their grandchildren.

ELL This is an excellent topic for students to describe something they learned to do from an older relative. Encourage them to bring photographs to their presentations.

PREVIEW/USE ILLUSTRATIONS Have students look through all the pictures in the story. Ask: Who is this story mostly about? Point out that the grandfather appears more often in the pictures than any other character.

TEACH/REVIEW VOCABULARY Write the vocabulary words on the board. Have students work in pairs to find definitions and parts of speech for the words. Ask pairs to share their definitions with the class.

TARGET SKILL AND STRATEGY

◉ **SEQUENCE** Remind students that keeping track of the *sequence,* or order, of events in a story can help them understand what happens. Tell them that sometimes a sequence describes steps in a process. Suggest that they look for clue words as they read, such as *while, then, now, next, after.*

◉ **SUMMARIZE** Remind students that remembering the important information in a book can help them keep track of the main idea in the story. Tell students that while they read, they might note the activities suggested to the grandfather.

READ THE BOOK

Use the following questions to support comprehension.

PAGE 4 Why do the boy and his father try so hard to make Grandpa feel at home? *(They want him to be comfortable because he is moving from the city to the country, and he will probably miss Grandma and his old neighborhood.)*

PAGES 5–7 How do the boy and his father go about finding something for Grandpa to do? *(They buy him equipment for different activities, such as walking shoes and a pyrography set.)*

PAGE 15 What did Grandpa add to the mix after the flour and lard? *(an egg)*

TALK ABOUT THE BOOK

READER RESPONSE

1. Possible response: Mix together flour, salt, lard, and an egg; roll out dough; cut the dough into circles; spoon in filling; fold and seal the edges of the circles with a fork; fry the pies.
2. Possible response: walking, pyrography, and making fried pies
3. Possible response: filling, going, helping, selecting, enjoying; Sentences will vary.
4. Possible response: hobbies such as walking, golf, painting, knitting, and cooking

RESPONSE OPTIONS

WRITING Ask students to think of something they like to make. Have them create a chart similar to the one in question 1 of Reader Response. Tell students to write out the steps in making their special item.

CONTENT CONNECTIONS

SOCIAL STUDIES Have students interview a grandparent. Tell them to find out what life was like when he or she was a child. Invite students to share brief reports of their interviews.

Time for **SOCIAL STUDIES**

Sequence

- **Sequence** is the order of events.

Directions Use *Something to Do* to answer the following questions.

1. Skim through the book. Write down some of the clue words the author uses to indicate the sequence of events in the story.

_____

_____

2. Reread page 5. What was the usual sequence of events every day after Grandpa moved in?

_____

_____

_____

_____

3. Reread pages 7 and 8. What was the order of Grandpa's reactions to the pyrography set?

_____

_____

_____

4. What was the sequence of events that led to Grandpa making his first fried pie?

_____

_____

_____

_____

14

© Pearson Education 4

Vocabulary

Directions Rewrite each sentence using the form of the underlined word found in the box.

> ## Check the Words You Know
>
> ___grand   ___memorial   ___peculiar   ___positive
> ___prideful   ___recalls   ___selecting

1. Dad loves <u>recalling</u> the time when our family took a trip across the country.

_____

2. Grandpa <u>positively</u> couldn't get along all by himself.

_____

3. Grandma took <u>pride</u> in her fried pies.

_____

4. It's hard to <u>select</u> which flavor I want.

_____

Directions For each word below, write the meaning of the word. Then write a sentence using the word.

5. peculiar _____

_____

_____

6. grand _____

_____

_____

7. memorial _____

_____

_____

15

The Story of Libraries

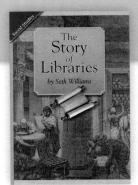

The Story of Libraries by Seth Williams

◉ **SEQUENCE**

◉ **SUMMARIZE**

LESSON VOCABULARY codex, grand, memorial, peculiar, positive, prideful, selecting, volume

SUMMARY This nonfiction book presents the history of libraries, from early collections of clay tablets to modern libraries. Featured are Benjamin Franklin and Andrew Carnegie, two important people in the creation of modern libraries.

INTRODUCE THE BOOK

BUILD BACKGROUND Draw a word web on the board with the word *library* at the center. Ask students to brainstorm all the words that come to mind when they think of libraries.

PREVIEW/USE TEXT FEATURES Have students skim the text, looking at the title, pictures, captions, and headings. Ask the students to brainstorm a list of facts they expect to learn about libraries from the selection, and write their predictions on the board.

TEACH/REVIEW VOCABULARY Divide students into two groups. Have one group find synonyms for each word, and direct the other group to find antonyms. Invite students to share what they found.

TARGET SKILL AND STRATEGY

◉ **SEQUENCE** Remind students that keeping track of the *sequence,* or order, of events in a book can help them understand the facts that are presented. Suggest that they look for clue words such as *first, next, then, last.*

◉ **SUMMARIZE** Remind students that *summarizing,* or remembering the important facts in a book, can help them keep track of information. Recommend that students make a mental summary of information in each section while reading.

ⒺⓁⓁ Pair students to do some extra research on Benjamin Franklin and Andrew Carnegie—especially if students are not familiar with these figures in U.S. history.

READ THE BOOK

Use the following questions to support comprehension.

PAGE 8 What happened to libraries after the fall of the Roman Empire? *(Muslims preserved libraries, which continued to thrive in the East.)*

PAGES 8–9 How was the codex important in making books look like they do today? *(The codex gave books the shape we know today.)*

PAGES 10–12 What prompted the Junto to form a lending library? *(The members needed books to write their essays, but not all members could afford to buy books.)*

TALK ABOUT THE BOOK

READER RESPONSE

1. Clay tablets created near Nippur; Royal Library at Alexandria founded; Trajan's library founded; movable type invented by Gutenberg
2. Possible response: Andrew Carnegie was born in 1835 in Scotland; he started school in 1843; he became a messenger and private investor; he used his money to create free libraries and other buildings.
3. Possible response: odd, strange, special
4. Possible response: The tall columns and the scrolls are different from the library at my school.

RESPONSE OPTIONS

WRITING Many libraries have procedures for borrowing books, using computers, or behaving in a respectful manner. Have students write paragraphs in which they describe the steps for one of these activities.

CONTENT CONNECTIONS

SOCIAL STUDIES Divide students into groups. Have each group research one of the famous libraries mentioned in the book that is not described in detail. Ask each group to write a description of its library.

Time for **SOCIAL STUDIES**

Sequence

- **Sequence** is the order of events.

Directions Use *The Story of Libraries* to answer the following questions.

1. Reread pages 3–7. The king of Assyria added tablets from conquered Babylon to his library. Where does this event fit in the following sequence of events?

    a) The first books were written on papyrus.
    b) The knowledge of how to write was lost in ancient Greece.
    c) King Ptolemy I founded the Royal Library at Alexandria.

    _____

2. Reread pages 8–9. In chronological order, list three important events in the history of libraries that happened between A.D. 400 and A.D. 1500.

    _____

    _____

    _____

3. Put the following events in the correct sequence in which they happened: the Library Company became the first lending library in America; the New York Library Society was founded; Ben Franklin formed the Junto.

1st _____

2nd _____

3rd _____

4. What was the sequence of events that led Andrew Carnegie's family to leave Scotland for America?

    _____

    _____

    _____

    _____

14

Vocabulary

Directions Each of the scrambled clue words in the puzzle below is a vocabulary word. Unscramble each of the clue words. Take the letters that appear in the circled boxes and unscramble them for the answer to this question: What word from the vocabulary list sounds as strange as its meaning?

Check the Words You Know

___codex   ___grand   ___memorial   ___peculiar
___positive   ___prideful   ___selecting   ___volume

S E P T I O V I

R N D A G

D O E C X

R A L M O I M E

S E I N T L E C G

M U V E O L

R D F E P L U I

Directions Use the words *grand, positive, prideful, selecting,* and *volume* in a paragraph titled "Something funny happened on my way to the library."

_____

_____

_____

_____

_____

15

The Long
Trip West

The Long Trip West — by Joseph Blaire — illustrated by Tom McNeely

Unit 1 Week 2

◉ **AUTHOR'S PURPOSE**

◉ **ANSWER QUESTIONS**

LESSON VOCABULARY docks, migrating, scanned, scent, translated, wharf, yearned

SUMMARY

The Long Trip West tells the story of the expedition led by Meriwether Lewis and William Clark to map and explore the territory acquired during the Louisiana Purchase.

INTRODUCE THE BOOK

BUILD BACKGROUND Use a map to point out the western part of the United States, from the Mississippi River to the Pacific Ocean. Discuss with students what they know about the landscape and the history of the West.

PREVIEW/USE TEXT FEATURES Point out the maps in the text. Explain that the book is about a journey into the American West when the region had just become part of the United States. Have students skim the illustrations in the book and predict what may have happened on this trip.

TEACH/REVIEW VOCABULARY Divide the class into six groups. Assign one vocabulary word to each group by having groups draw words from a box. Ask the groups to illustrate their words. Have groups present their illustrations while the rest of the class guesses the words.

TARGET SKILL AND STRATEGY

◉ **AUTHOR'S PURPOSE** Review with students that authors have purposes, or reasons, for writing that are not usually stated in the text. Point out that the reader can infer why the author wrote the book. Based on the genre and topic, have students discuss why they think the author might have written this book.

◉ **ANSWER QUESTIONS** Point out that knowing where to look in a text to find answers to questions can help them identify the author's purpose and understand what they read.

READ THE BOOK

Use the following questions to support comprehension.

PAGE 6 After reading this page, what do you think is the author's purpose for writing? *(to explain why Lewis and Clark made their trip through the American West)*

PAGES 10–11 Why was it important for the Corps to get horses? *(They needed the horses to cross the mountains.)*

PAGE 14 What question could you ask that is answered on this page? *(Possible response: When did Lewis and Clark and the Corps return to St. Louis?)*

TALK ABOUT THE BOOK

READER RESPONSE
1. Possible response: to inform us about the Louisiana Purchase and Lewis and Clark's voyage with the Corps of Discovery
2. Possible response: Sacagawea was able to translate the Native American languages into English. page 9
3. Possible response: Scents in My Life: popcorn, bubble gum, shampoo, chocolate cake; Scents on Lewis and Clark's Trip: smoke, fish, salt water
4. Possible response: The map shows the starting point and ending point of the trip.

RESPONSE OPTIONS

WRITING Have students imagine that they are members of the Lewis and Clark expedition. Tell them to choose one event from the selection and write a diary entry about it.

ELL Have pairs of students who speak the same home language dictate their diary entries to each other.

CONTENT CONNECTIONS

SCIENCE Have each student use the Internet, an encyclopedia, or other resources to write a brief report about one of the plants or animals documented by Lewis and Clark.

TIME FOR Science

Author's Purpose

- The **author's purpose** is the reason or reasons an author has for writing. For example, the author may want *to inform, persuade, entertain,* or *express* a mood or feeling.
- An author may have one or more reason for writing.

Directions Read the following passage from *The Long Trip West*. Think about the author's purposes as you read. Then, for each question below, circle the letter of the best answer.

On May 26, 1805, Lewis scanned the horizon. He saw the Rocky Mountains for the first time. They were rugged and tall. The Corps of Discovery traded with Sacagawea's Shoshone and with another Native American nation, the Salish. They got horses to ride through the mountains.

The trip over the steep mountains was tough. The weather was very cold. It was hard to find food. Many of the men were starving.

But the Corps of Discovery kept going. They made it over the mountains. Now they had to cross rivers. They left the horses behind and made canoes. The Corps of Discovery yearned to see the Pacific Ocean. In November of 1805 the Corps of Discovery finally reached the ocean.

1. The genre of this passage is
   a. science fiction.   b. poetry.   c. fiction.   d. nonfiction.

2. What do you think is the author's main purpose for writing this passage?
   a. to inform   b. to persuade   c. to express   d. to entertain

3. What do you think was the author's purpose for describing the trip over the mountains in the second paragraph?
   a. to persuade the reader that people should not ride horses
   b. to inform the reader about what the Rocky Mountains are like in the summer
   c. to entertain by making the reader feel fearful and worried about the Corps
   d. to express the feeling of joy that the men felt as they climbed the mountains

4. How do you think the author probably wants the reader to feel at the end of this passage?
   a. distrustful   b. sad   c. nervous   d. happy

© Pearson Education 4

18

Name _____

Vocabulary

Directions Choose the word from the box that best matches each definition. Write the word on the line. Use each word only once.

> ## Check the Words You Know
>
> ___docks   ___migrating   ___scanned   ___scent
> ___translated   ___wharf   ___yearned

1. _____ wharfs

2. _____ moving from one region to another

3. _____ to glance at; look over hastily

4. _____ felt a longing or desire; desired earnestly

5. _____ a platform built on the shore or out from the shore beside which ships can load and unload

6. _____ a smell

Directions Sort the words according to the description in each box.

Nouns
7. _____
8. _____
9. _____

Words with Endings
10. _____
11. _____
12. _____
13. _____
14. _____

© Pearson Education 4

19

Lewis and Clark

Biography
Lewis and Clark
by Cindy Swan

◉ **AUTHOR'S PURPOSE**

◉ **ANSWER QUESTIONS**

LESSON VOCABULARY docks, migrating, scan, scent, translated, wharf, yearned

---

SUMMARY This nonfiction book describes some of the interactions between Native Americans and the Lewis and Clark expedition as they explored the American West in the early 1800s.

INTRODUCE THE BOOK

BUILD BACKGROUND Explain to students that many Native American nations lived in North America long before European settlers arrived. Discuss with students what they know about how Native Americans and Europeans got along when they first met.

PREVIEW/USE TEXT FEATURES Have students skim the book, focusing on the map, headings, pictures, and captions. Discuss with students what they might learn about Lewis and Clark and the Native Americans.

ELL Explain to students that Lewis and Clark were not able to speak the languages of all the Native American nations that they encountered. Ask students to brainstorm ideas of how Lewis and Clark might have been able to communicate with Native Americans.

TEACH/REVIEW VOCABULARY Explain that endings can make a noun plural or change the tense of a verb. As an example, demonstrate that the noun *dock* is made plural by adding s at the end. Have students find the other vocabulary words with endings, tell the base word, the ending, and how the ending changes the word.

TARGET SKILL AND STRATEGY

◉ **AUTHOR'S PURPOSE** Review with students the different purposes an author pursues in writing—to persuade, to inform, to entertain, to express. Have students predict the author's main purpose for writing this book.

◉ **ANSWER QUESTIONS** Remind students that when questions arise while reading, it is important to be able to find answers. Explain that answers may be found in one or more places in the text and might not be stated directly. Have students think of questions that could be answered by carefully reading each section of the book.

READ THE BOOK

Use the following questions to support comprehension.

PAGES 6–7 What is the author's purpose for describing how Lewis and Clark met with the Missouri and Oto chiefs? *(to explain that their meetings with these chiefs set the pattern for their future meetings with all other Native American nations)*

PAGE 12 What question could be answered by the information on this page? *(How did Sacagawea help the Lewis and Clark expedition?)*

PAGES 14–15 What did the Shoshone and Nez Percé have in common? *(They did not possess firearms, and they were friendly to the Corps.)*

TALK ABOUT THE BOOK

READER RESPONSE
1. Possible response: to inform readers about the Native Americans Lewis and Clark met on their journey
2. Possible responses: How did the Teton Sioux make their rattles? search Native American instruments online
3. Possible response: She *yearned* for a ride on the roller coaster as she waited in line.
4. North: British Territory; South: Spanish Territory

RESPONSE OPTIONS

WRITING Have groups of students come up with questions and answers about the book. Use the questions for a quiz show in which teams are given a limited time to find the answers.

CONTENT CONNECTIONS

SOCIAL STUDIES Have pairs of students conduct research on one of the specific Native American nations that Lewis and Clark encountered during their expedition.

Time for **SOCIAL STUDIES**

Author's Purpose

- The **author's purpose** is the reason or reasons an author has for writing. For example, the author may want *to inform, persuade, entertain,* or *express* a mood or feeling.
- An author may have one or more reason for writing.

Directions Read the following passage from *Lewis and Clark*. Then answer the questions below.

The Tetons controlled a stretch of the Missouri River. The Tetons did not like the Corps because they saw these men as competitors. Also, no one in the Corps spoke the Sioux language. The two groups often misunderstood each other.

The Tetons did not want to make peace with their neighbors. They had a good relationship with one of their neighbors, the Arikaras, only because it was best for both groups. The Tetons traded clothes, guns, and other supplies with the Arikaras for horses and corn. The Arikaras, unlike the Tetons, were friendly to the Corps.

1. What is the topic of this passage? _____

2. What do you think is the author's main purpose for writing this passage?

_____

_____

3. What do you think might be another reason the author wrote this passage?

_____

_____

4. How did figuring out the author's purpose cause you to adjust the way you read the passage?

_____

_____

5. Think again about why the author probably wrote the passage. Do you think the author met his or her purpose for writing? Why or why not?

_____

_____

18

© Pearson Education 4

Name _____

Vocabulary

Directions Read each sentence. Write the word from the box that best completes each sentence. Use each word only once.

> ## Check the Words You Know
>
> ___docks ___migrating ___scan ___scent
> ___translated ___wharf ___yearned

1. The captain of the ship told the sailor to _____ the horizon for land.

2. The skies overhead are filled with the sounds of honking birds when the geese are _____ south for the winter.

3. The _____ was crowded with boxes of food.

4. Fishermen were lined up along the _____ trying to catch the evening's meal from the waters below.

5. The young girl _____ to travel to faraway places.

Directions For each word below, write a sentence that uses the word correctly.

6. migrating _____

_____

7. scan _____

_____

8. yearned _____

_____

9. translated _____

_____

Directions Imagine that you have taken a trip by boat. On a separate sheet of paper, write a brief story in which you describe where you have been and what it feels like to be home. Use as many vocabulary words as possible in your story.

19

Two
Great
Rivers

by Stephanie Sigue

🔊 **AUTHOR'S PURPOSE**

🔊 **ANSWER QUESTIONS**

LESSON VOCABULARY barges, conservationists, diminishing, expedition, reservoirs, route, silt, tributaries

Two Great Rivers

SUMMARY This book compares and contrasts the largest rivers in the United States, the Mississippi and Missouri Rivers.

INTRODUCE THE BOOK

BUILD BACKGROUND Discuss with students why rivers are important to people. Ask: What rivers are near your school? What rivers have you visited?

PREVIEW/USE TEXT FEATURES Read the title aloud, and turn to the map on page 3. Have students skim the book, focusing on headings. Discuss with students what they expect to learn about the two rivers.

TEACH/REVIEW VOCABULARY Have students use dictionaries to find as many different endings as they can for each of the vocabulary words. On the board, create word webs with the root words at the center surrounded by the different forms of the words and their parts of speech.

ELL Assist students who need help with the word webs. If necessary, put students in pairs and have them act out difficult words or use gestures to explain word meanings.

TARGET SKILL AND STRATEGY

🔊 **AUTHOR'S PURPOSE** Review with students that authors often have more than one purpose for writing: to persuade, to inform, to entertain, or to express a mood or feeling. Have students predict the author's purposes for writing this piece, and have them look for evidence to support their predictions.

🔊 **ANSWER QUESTIONS** Remind students that knowing where to look in a text to find answers to questions can help them understand what they read. Explain that answers may be found in one or more places in the text, might not be stated directly by the author, or may require the students' own knowledge.

READ THE BOOK

Use the following questions to support comprehension.

PAGE 7 What heading would you choose to describe the information found on this page? *(Possible response: Uses of the Mississippi Today)*

PAGE 11 One of the author's purposes in this section is to inform. What other purpose does the author pursue? *(to persuade the reader that farming and industry are serious threats to the river)*

PAGE 16 This section of the book answers the question, "What are some uses of the Missouri River?" What other question does this section answer? *(Why is the river so muddy?)*

TALK ABOUT THE BOOK

READER RESPONSE
1. Answers will vary.
2. Possible response: What happens when rivers flood? Reread the book or search online.
3. Possible responses: natural areas, wildlife, species, pollution, endangered
4. Possible response: Missouri River Wildlife, Plant and Animal Life, The Two Rivers, History of the River, Missouri River History

RESPONSE OPTIONS

WRITING Have students write letters to persuade the federal government to remove dams from the Missouri River and restore its natural flow. Students should use facts from the book to support their arguments.

CONTENT CONNECTIONS

SCIENCE Have groups of students prepare reports on topics related to the two great rivers, such as river ecosystems, levees, hydroelectric power, or the effects of pollutants.

TIME FOR
Science

Author's Purpose

- The **author's purpose** is the reason or reasons an author has for writing. For example, the author may want to *inform, persuade, entertain,* or *express* a mood or feeling.
- An author may have one or more reason for writing.

Directions Read the following passage from *Two Great Rivers.* Then answer the questions below.

Floods and Flood Control

Flooding along the Mississippi can be a problem. When melting snow or heavy rains add lots of water to the river, the river overflows its banks. If the surrounding land is unable to absorb the water, flooding occurs. Since many acres of wetlands along the river have been drained and turned into farmland, more water has been forced into the river. Paved roads, parking lots, and even the roofs on buildings prevent rainwater from soaking into the ground. This increases run-off into the river and the chance of flooding. Severe flooding often results in damage to nearby homes and communities.

Several methods are used to control floods. One way is to plant trees, grass, and other plants to absorb the water. Another way to control flooding is to build levees. Levees raise the banks of the river so that they can hold more water. Floodways are areas of land that provide outlets for draining water when the river reaches flood level. They help to decrease flooding elsewhere.

1–2. Give two reasons for the author's purpose in writing this passage.

_____

_____

3. Support why you think this.

_____

_____

4. Why does the author explain the human causes of flooding?

_____

_____

18

Vocabulary

Directions Read each sentence. Write the word from the box that has the same meaning as the underlined word or phrase.

Check the Words You Know

___barges	___conservationists	___diminishing	___expedition
___reservoirs	___route	___silt	___tributaries

1. We went on <u>large, flat-bottomed boats</u> to see how they operate. _____

2. A tree fell down in the storm and blocked the <u>road</u> to the store. _____

3. Waterways get cloudy from <u>deposited dirt or sediment</u>. _____

4. My hopes of getting a bicycle are <u>becoming smaller</u>. _____

5. The scientists planned a <u>trip with a specific purpose</u> to study. _____

Directions For each word, write a sentence that uses that word.

6. conservationists

_____

_____

7. reservoirs

_____

_____

8. tributaries

_____

_____

19

Grandpa's Scrapbook

by Peggy Bresnick Kendler
illustrated by Pamela M. Anzalotti

Unit 1 Week 3

◎ **SEQUENCE**

◎ **GRAPHIC ORGANIZERS**

LESSON VOCABULARY amazed, bewildered, homeland, longed, sculptures, still, towering

SUMMARY In this book, two of Mark Twain's grandchildren sit down with him and go through his scrapbook. They learn about Hannibal, Missouri, Twain's hometown. They learn about his friends and his adventures. They also learn about his days as a riverboat pilot.

INTRODUCE THE BOOK

BUILD BACKGROUND Ask students if they have ever talked with their grandparents about their grandparents' youth. What did they find out? What was surprising?

PREVIEW/USE ILLUSTRATIONS Have students look at the illustrations in the book. What can they learn from the illustrations about what will happen in the story?

ELL Talk with students about their grandparents. Do they live in this country? Have students talk about things they love to do with their grandparents.

TEACH/REVIEW VOCABULARY Have students write each vocabulary word and its definition on a note card. Have them find the words in the story. Have them write a sentence for each word.

TARGET SKILL AND STRATEGY

◎ **SEQUENCE** Remind students that the *sequence* is the order in which the story's events occur. To better understand what this means, ask students to write a short paragraph about what they do each morning to get ready for school. They should keep the actions in sequence. Have students read their paragraphs out loud to the class.

◎ **GRAPHIC ORGANIZERS** Remind students that *graphic organizers* can be used to organize information. Have students create a time line of how they spent last summer. The time line should start on the day school let out and end the day that school started again.

READ THE BOOK

Use the following questions to support comprehension.

PAGE 7 How wide is the Mississippi River? *(about one mile wide)*

PAGE 8 What did Grandpa like to do on the Mississippi River in the winter? *(go skating)*

PAGE 9 Where did Grandpa love to explore? *(the caves along the river)*

TALK ABOUT THE BOOK

READER RESPONSE
1. young explorer first, steamboat pilot second
2. Responses will vary: One picture shows New Orleans, where people are playing music in a group. The second shows St. Louis, Missouri, according to the label.
3. *amazed:* verb, adjective; *bewildered:* verb, adjective; *yearned:* verb; Sentences will vary.
4. Responses will vary: *homeland:* motherland, native soil; After months exploring distant islands in the Pacific, the explorer returned to his homeland. *sculptures:* statues, figures, monuments; My father loves to collect sculptures of ancient gods and goddesses.

RESPONSE OPTIONS

WRITING Have students imagine that they are one of Mark Twain's childhood friends. Have students write a paragraph or two about an adventure they had together.

CONTENT CONNECTIONS

SOCIAL STUDIES Have students research the life of Mark Twain. What was his childhood like? How many books did he write in his lifetime? Find an interesting Mark Twain quotation. Have students share their results with the class.

Time for SOCIAL STUDIES

Sequence

- The **sequence** of events means the order in which the events happen.

Directions Fill in the table below. The events of *Grandpa's Scrapbook* are divided into two stages: Grandpa's childhood years and his early adult years. Fill in as many examples as you can for each category.

Childhood Years	Early Adult Years

22

Vocabulary

Directions Fill in the blank with the word from the box that fits best.

Check the Words You Know
___amazed   ___bewildered   ___homeland   ___longed
___sculptures   ___still   ___towering

1. In Hannibal, Missouri, look for the _____ of Tom Sawyer and Becky Thatcher.

2. The pine trees were _____ over the raft as it moved downstream.

3. Sam Clemens's _____ was the area around Hannibal, Missouri.

4. Grandpa seemed _____ that we wanted to hear his stories again.

5. The water in this part of the river was deep and _____.

6. Grandpa _____ for the days of his youth.

7. Laura Hawkins looked _____ when I asked her to enter the cave.

Directions Write a brief paragraph discussing Mark Twain's childhood on the Mississippi, using as many vocabulary words as possible.

_____

_____

_____

_____

_____

_____

_____

_____

© Pearson Education 4

23

Childhood in Pre-War Japan

Childhood in Pre-War Japan
by Jana Martin

Unit 1 Week 3

◉ **SEQUENCE**

◉ **GRAPHIC ORGANIZERS**

LESSON VOCABULARY amazed, bewildered, homeland, longed, sculptures, still, towering

SUMMARY This book tells of life in Japan before World War II. It describes life not only in the big cities, but also in the country. This book looks at everyday life, as well as the history of this period.

INTRODUCE THE BOOK

BUILD BACKGROUND Ask students to tell what they know about Japan. What image do they have of Tokyo? What do they know about sports in Japan? automobiles? arts and crafts? Do they know what a Japanese home looks like? What do they know about the Japanese language?

PREVIEW/USE TEXT FEATURES Have students look at the chapter headings illustrations, and photos. Discuss how these text features help to organize the book.

ELL Ask students to skim the story and write down any unfamiliar words. Suggest they look up the words in the dictionary and write the meaning in their notebooks.

TEACH/REVIEW VOCABULARY Review the vocabulary words. Then play Vocabulary Master with students. Give students three different definitions for each vocabulary word, including one that is fantastical or silly. Have them select the correct definition and use the word in a sentence.

TARGET SKILL AND STRATEGY

◉ **SEQUENCE** Remind students that the *sequence* in a story is the order in which the events occur. Ask students to write a short paragraph about what they do each morning to get ready for school. They should keep the actions in sequence. Have students read their paragraphs out loud to the class.

◉ **GRAPHIC ORGANIZERS** Remind students that *graphic organizers* can be used to organize information. Have students create a time line of how they spent last summer. The time line should start on the day school let out and end the day that school started again.

READ THE BOOK

Use the following questions to support comprehension.

PAGE 8 According to the ancient tale, how did Japan come to be? *(Water dripped from a spear creating islands.)*

PAGE 11 How did Japanese writing develop? *(The Japanese adapted Chinese character writing.)*

PAGE 14 What significant thing happened in 1853? *(Admiral Perry sailed into a Japanese harbor wanting to trade with them.)*

TALK ABOUT THE BOOK

READER RESPONSE
1. Portugal
2. Girls learned to be polite, took care of little sisters and brothers, learned traditional dances. Boys learned martial arts, learned how to be strong, helped fathers with work.
3. b; *still* (verb): make quiet.
4. She longed to return to her homeland.

RESPONSE OPTIONS

WRITING Have students reread pages 15–18. Encourage students to imagine that they are a Japanese child living in traditional Japan. Have them write about a typical day, including work, school, and family life.

CONTENT CONNECTIONS

SOCIAL STUDIES Have the students research Matthew C. Perry's trip to Japan in 1853. How did the Japanese government receive him? What effect did Perry's trip have on Japan?

Time for SOCIAL STUDIES

Name _____

Sequence

- **Sequence** is the order of events.

Directions Put the following events in the boxes below in the proper sequence. Reread *Childhood in Pre-War Japan* to find the dates and sequence of events. If you can find a date, add that next to the event.

Matthew C. Perry arrives in Japan. Japan opens up to the West and becomes a powerful country.

Rice comes to Japan.

For 200 years, Japanese are forced to stay in the country.

Portuguese ship is wrecked on one of Japan's islands. Japanese people meet Europeans for the first time.

Japan becomes isolated again. People can't speak foreign languages.

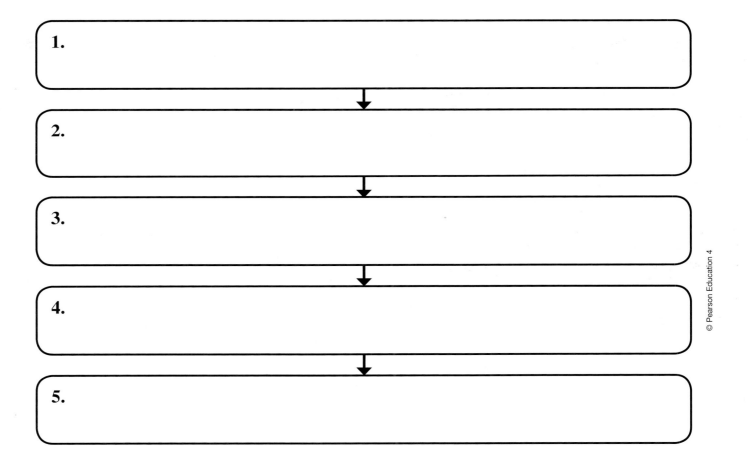

1.

2.

3.

4.

5.

22

Vocabulary

Directions Fill in the blank with the word from the box that fits the definition.

Check the Words You Know

___amazed   ___bewildered   ___homeland   ___longed
___sculptures   ___still   ___towering

1. _____ wanted very much

2. _____ to make quiet

3. _____ greatly surprised

4. _____ country that is one's home

5. _____ very high

6. _____ completely confused

7. _____ models made of stone or metal

Directions Write a brief paragraph discussing life in pre-war Japan, using as many vocabulary words as possible.

_____

_____

_____

_____

_____

_____

_____

_____

_____

23

Innocent Prisoners!

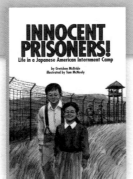

◉ SEQUENCE

◉ GRAPHIC ORGANIZERS

LESSON VOCABULARY barracks, elections, horizon, internment, naval

---

SUMMARY This story is about Yukiko, a young Japanese American girl imprisoned in a Japanese American internment camp in World War II. While in the camp, the adults often discuss why they have been imprisoned and what they will do when the war is over. Yukiko decides when she is released from the camp, she wants to stay in the United States.

INTRODUCE THE BOOK

BUILD BACKGROUND Discuss what students know about World War II, Pearl Harbor, and Japanese American internment camps. Did anyone in their family ever fight in a war? Have any students seen a film about World War II?

PREVIEW/USE ILLUSTRATIONS Have students look at the illustrations in the book. Discuss how the illustrations help the story.

ELL Ask students to skim the story and write down any unfamiliar words. Suggest they look up the words in a dictionary and write the meanings in their notebooks.

TEACH/REVIEW VOCABULARY Review the vocabulary words. Then play Vocabulary Master with students. Give students three different definitions for each vocabulary word, including one that is fantastical or silly, and have them select the correct definition and use the word in a sentence.

TARGET SKILL AND STRATEGY

◉ SEQUENCE Remind students that the *sequence* is the order in which the story's events occur. Have volunteers tell a sequence they do each day, such as prepare for school, help with dinner, prepare for an activity outside of school.

◉ GRAPHIC ORGANIZERS Remind students that *graphic organizers* can be used to organize information. Remind them that they can chart information on a time line, create a web, or create a chart or table as they read.

READ THE BOOK

Use the following questions to support comprehension.

PAGE 4 Where did Yukiko's family live before coming to the internment camp? *(on a farm)*

PAGE 4 Where did the families eat? *(in the mess hall)*

PAGE 5 What did Yukiko's mother not like about Americans' voices? *(that they were too loud)*

TALK ABOUT THE BOOK

READER RESPONSE
1. Possible responses should reflect the chronological order of events, noting that most of the story takes place over the course of one day.
2. Responses will vary.
3. Barracks are buildings in which people live on military bases or camps. Other words might be *relocation centers, mess hall, barbed wire, guard towers, soldiers,* and *govenment.*
4. Responses will vary.

RESPONSE OPTIONS

WRITING Have students put themselves in the place of Yukiko or Aki. How do they think it would feel to be unable to be with friends they grew up with? What would they do to occupy their time?

CONTENT CONNECTIONS

SOCIAL STUDIES Have students research Japanese American internment camps. Where were the camps located? Students should try to find interviews with people who had spent time in the camps. After finishing their research, students should share their findings with the class.

Time for SOCIAL STUDIES

Sequence

- **Sequence** is the order of events.

Directions Put the following events in the proper sequence. Write the sentences in order in the boxes below. Reread *Innocent Prisoners! Life in a Japanese American Internment Camp* to find the sequence of events.

After dinner Mama speaks English, and there is a dust storm.

Yukiko and Aki look at Mt. Whitney.

Yukiko goes to school, and the teacher talks about the new blackboard.

At dinner a group of men argue about whether to return to Japan after the war.

Yukiko meets an old man who has a drawing of Mt. Fuji.

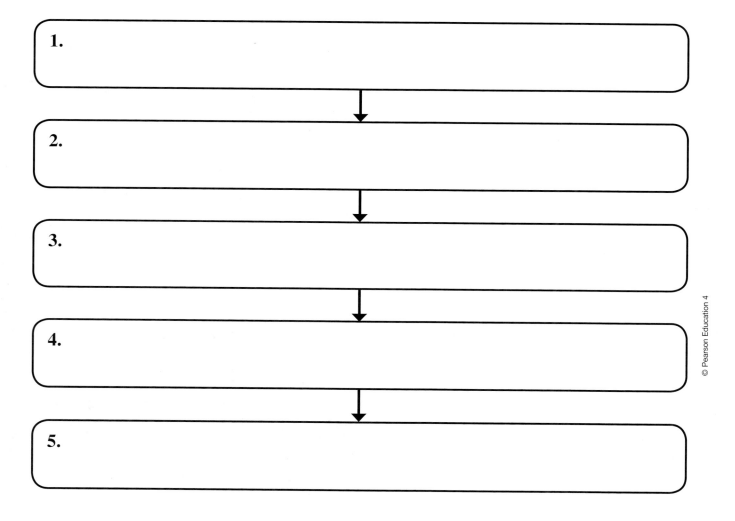

1.

2.

3.

4.

5.

© Pearson Education 4

22

Vocabulary

Directions Fill in the blank with the word from the box that fits the definition.

Check the Words You Know

___barracks	___elections	___horizon
___internment	___naval	

1. _____ an act of choosing by vote

2. _____ having to do with ships

3. _____ housing for soldiers or prisoners

4. _____ placing people in camps

5. _____ the line where earth meets sky

Directions Write a paragraph discussing life in an internment camp, using all the vocabulary words.

_____

_____

_____

_____

_____

_____

_____

_____

_____

_____

© Pearson Education 4

23

Flash Flood

SUMMARY Jimmy and his parents set out on a camping trip. They must keep safe from a flash flood.

INTRODUCE THE BOOK

BUILD BACKGROUND Ask students what they know about floods. How would they keep safe from a flood? Tell students that sometimes heavy rains can cause rivers to overflow very quickly, a flash flood.

PREVIEW/USE ILLUSTRATIONS Read the book title and the author's name aloud. Ask students to skim the book, looking at the pictures. Ask students: What do you think this story is about? Why? What do you think this story will be like—happy, sad, scary? What gives you that idea?

TEACH/REVIEW VOCABULARY Write the lesson vocabulary on the board. Divide the class into seven groups. Assign one word to each group. Have each group find its word in the book and define the word using context clues. Have groups share definitions with the class.

TARGET SKILL AND STRATEGY

AUTHOR'S PURPOSE Remind students that authors have reasons for writing stories. Tell them that an author often has more than one purpose—to persuade, to inform, to entertain, or to express a mood or feeling. As they read have them tell whether the predictions they made during the Preview part of the lesson were correct.

STORY STRUCTURE On the board, draw a *story-structure* diagram (an inverted V). Label the diagram as follows: *Conflict* (bottom of left-hand line); *Rising Action* (left side of the angle); *Climax* (peak of the angle); *Falling Action* (right side of the angle), and *Resolution* (bottom of right-hand line). Review with students these parts of story structure. Tell them to look for these parts of the story as they read.

ELL Point out the key words and phrases on the story-structure diagram for students. Have them work in pairs to complete this diagram.

READ THE BOOK

Use the following questions to support comprehension.

PAGES 6–7 What are Jimmy and his parents worried about? *(that a flood will wash out the road)*

PAGES 9–11 How do you know how the author wants you to feel at this point in the story? *(She wants us to feel scared and anxious, because she uses words like worried, gripping, gulped, and quickly.)*

PAGES 14–15 Summarize the resolution, or the end, of the story. *(Jimmy and his parents remain safe by leaving their camper behind and moving to higher ground. The camper stays safe too.)*

TALK ABOUT THE BOOK

READER RESPONSE
1. Possible response: to entertain and give information
2. Possible response: beginning: Jimmy's family leaves for vacation; middle: A storm causes dangerous flooding; end: The family moves to higher ground until the storm ends.
3. deal
4. Possible response: move quickly to higher ground; scared or worried

RESPONSE OPTIONS

WRITING Have students create a two-column, story-structure chart using the diagram on the board. The chart should have the parts of story structure in the left-hand column. In the right-hand column, have students write brief summaries of the action in the story that fits each part of the structure.

CONTENT CONNECTIONS

SCIENCE On a map, locate the prairie states. Divide students into groups and assign one state to each group. Have each group research the state's climate and landscape and present the information to class.

TIME FOR Science

Author's Purpose

- The **author's purpose** is the reason or reasons an author has for writing.
- An author may have one or more reasons for writing. He or she may want *to inform, persuade, entertain,* or *express* a mood or feeling.

Directions Read the following passage. Then answer the questions below.

Jimmy kept watching the river. The whipping wind shrieked outside the camper. Jimmy felt more and more nervous.

"The dry ground of these riverbeds can become almost as hard as rocks. When it rains, the hardened riverbed cannot absorb all the water," the radio announcer said.

"Riverbeds can overflow during rain storms, flooding roads and houses. It happens really fast. That's why they are called flash floods. Drivers beware: In a flood, it takes only two feet of water to wash away a car."

Jimmy pictured rushing water overflowing a dry riverbed as he stared out the window.

1. This text is
   a. fiction.
   b. nonfiction.
   c. poetry.
   d. drama.

2. The author's main purpose for writing this passage was probably to
   a. show the importance of radio announcers.
   b. explain how campers can float.
   c. entertain the reader by making the reader feel scared and nervous.
   d. express a feeling of calm by describing the wind and rain.

3. Another purpose the author may have had for writing this passage was to
   a. tell the reader that people should not worry about flash floods.
   b. express Jimmy's feeling of anger that he and his family were riding in a camper.

   c. entertain the reader by describing the fun and excitement Jimmy was having as he watched the river rise.
   d. inform the reader about what causes flash floods and how dangerous they are.

4. The author writes the passage from the point of view of the boy, Jimmy, so that the reader knows what Jimmy is thinking and feeling. Why do you think the author does this?
   a. to inform the reader about what boys think of adults
   b. to express the mood of nervousness that Jimmy was feeling
   c. to persuade the reader that Jimmy knows a lot about campers
   d. to entertain the reader by making fun of Jimmy

26

Vocabulary

Directions Match the words in column A with their synonyms in column B.

Check the Words You Know

___bargain   ___favors   ___lassoed   ___offended
___prairie   ___riverbed   ___shrieked

Column A

1. lassoed

2. shrieked

3. offended

4. bargain

5. favors

6. prairie

Column B

a. good deal

b. good deeds

c. roped

d. upset

e. cried out

f. flat grassland

Directions Write a brief story or poem about a cowboy or cowgirl using the words *prairie*, *riverbed*, and *lassoed*.

_____

_____

_____

_____

_____

_____

_____

_____

_____

© Pearson Education 4

27

From Spain to America

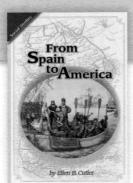

From Spain to America

by Ellen B. Cutler

◉ **AUTHOR'S PURPOSE**

◉ **STORY STRUCTURE**

LESSON VOCABULARY bargain, favors, lassoed, offended, prairie, riverbed, shrieked

---

SUMMARY This book details the influences of Spanish language and culture on the English language and American ways of life.

INTRODUCE THE BOOK

BUILD BACKGROUND Write these words on the board: *tortilla, patio, hammock, piñata.* Ask volunteers to tell what each word means. Then tell students that these words come from the Spanish language. Explain that some words, objects, and ideas that are part of American language and culture originally came from Spain.

ELL Take advantage of any Spanish-speaking students to assist the other students in understanding what the Spanish words mean.

PREVIEW/USE TEXT FEATURES Read the book title and the author's name aloud. Then ask students to skim the pictures, captions, and headings. Ask students: What information do you think the author presents in this book? Why do you think this?

TEACH/REVIEW VOCABULARY Divide the class into seven groups. Assign one word to each, and have groups use a thesaurus to find synonyms for their words. Have groups share synonyms with the class.

TARGET SKILL AND STRATEGY

◉ **AUTHOR'S PURPOSE** Remind students that authors often have more than one purpose for writing—to persuade, to inform, to entertain, or to express a mood. As they read, ask students to think about why the author wrote this book.

◉ **TEXT STRUCTURE** Explain that authors use many different ways of presenting information. One way is to provide group topics under headings and provide pictures with labels and captions. Ask students to look for these clues to understand the facts the author presents.

READ THE BOOK

Use these questions to support comprehension.

PAGE 5 How does the author use descriptions to inform the reader on this page? *(She describes what the people of the Bahamas ate. These descriptions help the reader understand what their lives were like.)*

PAGES 8 AND 9 What were some of the ways Spanish culture affected the native culture in America? *(The Spanish brought their architecture, language, and horses.)*

PAGE 14 To which three countries did the land of Texas belong? *(Spain, Mexico, United States)*

TALK ABOUT THE BOOK

READER RESPONSE
1. Possible response: to inform; how the Spanish first came to America; how Spanish culture influenced U.S. culture; how Spanish language influenced American English; history of San Antonio, Texas
2. Possible response: The labels help us see the influence of Spanish on the English language.
3. Sentences will vary.
4. Possible response: The time line helps us see when important events in Texas happened.

RESPONSE OPTIONS

WRITING Have students reread pages 15–16. Ask them to imagine they are part of the ten Spanish families who arrived in San Antonio in 1731. Have each student write a letter home describing life in San Antonio.

CONTENT CONNECTIONS

SOCIAL STUDIES Divide students into groups to research other cities in the Southwest that were settled by the Spanish. Reports should include information about architecture, local customs, and Spanish features.

Time for **SOCIAL STUDIES**

Author's Purpose

- The **author's purpose** is the reason or reasons an author has for writing.
- An author may have one or more reason for writing. He or she may want *to inform, persuade, entertain,* or *express* a mood or feeling.

Directions Read the following passage. Then answer the questions below.

Columbus and his crew set sail in search of *oro,* the Spanish word for gold. They hoped to land in Asia, where they could fill their pockets with gold and other riches. Columbus believed he could reach the Asian countries of the Far East by sailing due west from Spain. His crew did not believe him. His men were angry and scared. They may have shrieked in fear, not knowing what lay ahead. His crew's distrust offended Columbus, but he still felt confident.

1. Why do you think the author describes the riches that Columbus hoped to find in Asia?

_____

_____

_____

2. What do you think is the author's main purpose for writing this passage?

_____

_____

_____

3. What might be another reason the author wrote this passage?

_____

_____

_____

26

Vocabulary

Directions Read each sentence. Write the word from the box that has the same meaning as the underlined word or phrase. Some words may be used more than once.

Check the Words You Know

___bargain	___favors	___lassoed	___offended
___prairie	___riverbed	___shrieked	

---

1. _____ Yosh was <u>hurt</u> when Sarah left without saying good-bye to him.

2. _____ During the drought, you could see the floor of the <u>channel in which the river used to flow.</u>

3. _____ "Don't do me any <u>acts of kindness</u> by giving me a ride," huffed Mark.

4. _____ "You ruined my beautiful cake!" Milly <u>said in a loud, sharp, shrill voice.</u>

5. _____ It's hard to play hide-and-seek in a <u>large area of land with grass but few trees.</u>

6. _____ The smell of the burning tire <u>displeased</u> Ms. Pauly.

7. _____ Buying the used car for that amount of money was <u>a great deal.</u>

8. _____ The horse was <u>caught with a long rope with a loop on one end.</u>

9. _____ The crowd always <u>prefers</u> our team over any other.

10. _____ At a flea market, we usually <u>negotiate</u> for the best price.

© Pearson Education 4

27

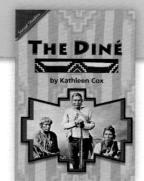

THE DINÉ
by Kathleen Cox

◉ **AUTHOR'S PURPOSE**

◉ **TEXT STRUCTURE**

LESSON VOCABULARY ancestors, cardinal points, edible, environmentalists, hogans, inhabited, nomads

The Diné

SUMMARY This book tells the history of a Native American people with a rich tradition.

INTRODUCE THE BOOK

BUILD BACKGROUND Ask students what they know about Native American culture in the United States. Have volunteers describe items or cultural practices they may have seen from various tribes.

PREVIEW/USE TEXT FEATURES Read the book title, emphasizing correct pronunciation of *Diné* (di-NAY). Have students look at the map and caption on page 3. Then have them skim through other photographs and captions in the book. Ask students what they can tell about the Diné from the map and pictures.

ELL Invite students to show others on a map where they have come from and pronounce the names of the places in the region.

TEACH/REVIEW VOCABULARY Talk with students about their understanding of the vocabulary words. Work out definitions. Then have students write cloze sentences, leaving out the vocabulary words. They may then exchange sentences and complete them.

TARGET SKILL AND STRATEGY

◉ **AUTHOR'S PURPOSE** Remind students that authors write with one or more purposes—to persuade, to inform, to entertain, or to express a mood or feeling. Ask students what the author's main purpose seems to be. Have them suggest what other purpose(s) the author might have.

◉ **TEXT STRUCTURE** Explain to students that the structure, or organization, of a book can help the reader understand information in the text. In nonfiction, authors often organize facts according to when they occurred. Write the following clue words on board: *on, at, now, after.* Ask students to suggest other clue words that can help them understand the book's information.

READ THE BOOK

Use these questions to support comprehension.

PAGES 4–7 How would you describe the Diné's attitude toward the land? *(The Diné respected all living things and celebrated nature as sacred.)*

PAGES 8 AND 13 The Diné borrowed practices and ideas from the Spanish and the Pueblo people. What does this tell you about the Diné? *(The Diné learned from others in order to adapt to their surroundings and become stronger.)*

PAGES 16–17 Why does the author describe the suffering of the Diné during the Long Walk and at Fort Sumner? *(Possible response: She wants reader to feel sympathy for the Diné.)*

TALK ABOUT THE BOOK

READER RESPONSE
1. Responses will vary.
2. Sentences will vary but should include factual references about the Diné before Columbus, the Diné and the Spanish, the Diné and the U.S. Army, and the Diné today.
3. Possible response: inhabited and lived
4. Arctic Ocean, Gulf of Alaska

RESPONSE OPTIONS

WRITING Ask students to imagine that they are Diné elders who must teach their children about the history of the Diné. Have students write brief histories of the Diné in any form they choose.

CONTENT CONNECTIONS

SOCIAL STUDIES Divide students into groups and have them research other Native American nations. Reports should include information about ancestors, history, homelands, and daily lives.

Time for SOCIAL STUDIES

Author's Purpose

An author may have one or more **purpose**, or reason, for writing. He or she may want to *inform, persuade, entertain,* or *express* a mood or feeling.

Directions Read the following passage. Then answer the questions below.

The U.S. government finally let the Diné sign a second peace treaty in 1868. In return the Diné were given land in the Southwest. Their new reservation included their sacred Dinétah. The Diné were also given some livestock to replace what had been taken. They were given the right to make their own laws on this new reservation. Their days of raiding were over. The Diné had to promise to keep the peace, and they could no longer fight against the U.S. government.

The cavalry had destroyed Dinétah. Weeds grew throughout the once-plowed fields, dirt filled the ditches where water once flowed, and the lovely peach trees were reduced to tree stumps. But the Diné still had their four sacred mountains.

The Diné wanted to repair the damage. They performed ceremonies in honor of their Mother Earth. They prayed that Mother Earth would bless them again. Over time the Diné made a comeback. By 1890 their population had doubled to eighteen thousand people. The Diné also increased the size of their reservation until they owned more than fifteen million acres of land.

1. What do you think is the author's main purpose for writing this passage? Explain.

_____

_____

2. What might be another reason the author wrote this passage? Explain.

_____

_____

3. Why do you think the author describes the way the cavalry had destroyed Dinétah?

_____

4. Why do you think the author describes how the Diné "performed ceremonies" and "prayed"?

_____

_____

26

Vocabulary

Directions Choose the word from the box that best matches each definition. Write the word on the line.

Check the Words You Know
___ancestors   ___cardinal points   ___edible   ___environmentalists ___hogans   ___inhabited   ___nomads

1. _____ safe to eat

2. _____ the four principal directions on the compass: north, south, east, and west

3. _____ people who want to protect the land

4. _____ lived in a place

Directions Write the word from the box that belongs in each group.

5. buildings, houses, _____

6. family, relatives, _____

7. wanderers, travelers, _____

Directions Write a brief history of some of your ancestors. Use as many vocabulary words as you can. Use a separate sheet of paper if necessary.

_____

_____

_____

_____

_____

_____

© Pearson Education 4

27

This Land Is Our Land

Unit 1 Week 5

This Land Is Our Land by Johanna Biviano

- **MAIN IDEA AND DETAILS**
- **GRAPHIC ORGANIZERS**

LESSON VOCABULARY glaciers, impressive, naturalists, preserve, slopes, species, wilderness

SUMMARY This nonfiction book introduces students to some of the important natural and historical parks in the United States.

INTRODUCE THE BOOK

BUILD BACKGROUND Locate on a map some of the important parks in the book, such as Yellowstone and Denali National Parks, the Grand Canyon, and Colonial National Historical Park. Discuss what students know about these places.

PREVIEW/USE TEXT FEATURES Read the title of the book aloud, and have students look at the pictures, captions, headings, and time line. Discuss what students think they might learn from this book.

TEACH/REVIEW VOCABULARY Read through the glossary with the class. Have groups of students locate the words in the book and write their own sentences for the words. Share sentences as a class.

TARGET SKILL AND STRATEGY

MAIN IDEA AND DETAILS Remind students that a topic is what a selection is about, while the *main idea* is the most important idea about the topic. Supporting *details* are the small pieces of information that tell more about the main idea. Tell students to look for the topic, main idea, and supporting details as they read.

GRAPHIC ORGANIZERS On the board, draw a flow chart with a box for the main idea at the top and boxes for three supporting details underneath. Point out that *graphic organizers* like this one can help students organize the main idea and supporting details of a selection. Have students copy the graphic organizer for a follow-up writing activity.

ELL To ensure comprehension of the text by speakers of other languages, have students use the Main Idea and Details graphic organizer to chart the information in subsections of the text.

READ THE BOOK

Use the following questions to support comprehension.

PAGES 6–7 What is the main idea on these two pages? *(Some national parks were set up to protect important historical places.)*

PAGES 8–9 Why do plants and animals in Denali National Park have to be tough? *(Most of the ground stays frozen, and the winters are long and harsh.)*

PAGE 13 What is the job of the National Park Service? *(to manage our national parks)*

TALK ABOUT THE BOOK

READER RESPONSE

1. Possible responses: Main idea: Our national parks preserve nature and history. Supporting details: Mesa Verde National Park preserves the cliff dwellings of the ancestral Pueblo people; Denali National Park protects mountains, plants, and animals in Alaska.
2. Responses will vary, but dates should appear in chronological order.
3. impressive, naturalist; Sentences will vary.
4. Possible response: when some state and national parks were founded

RESPONSE OPTIONS

WRITING Have students complete their Main Idea graphic organizers. Complete the class flow chart on the board with student responses. Then have students use their organizers to write paragraphs summarizing the selection.

CONTENT CONNECTIONS

SOCIAL STUDIES Have groups choose parks featured in the selection. Tell each group to learn more about its park and write a paragraph describing one special feature there. Have groups present their special places to the class.

Time for **SOCIAL STUDIES**

Main Idea and Details

- The **main idea** is the most important idea about the topic of a paragraph, passage, or article.
- Supporting **details** are the small pieces of information that tell more about the main idea.

Directions Read the following passage. Then tell the main idea of the passage and list the supporting details that tell more about the main idea.

Grand Canyon National Park is one of the most famous parks in the world. Scientists come from many countries to study the Canyon. They are interested in the Canyon's landscape. The Canyon was made millions of years ago. Its steep cliffs still hold fossils and rocks from times long gone. The Canyon is also home to many types of plants and animals. Many scientists visit the Canyon to study its wildlife. Of course, many tourists also travel to the Canyon just to admire its beauty.

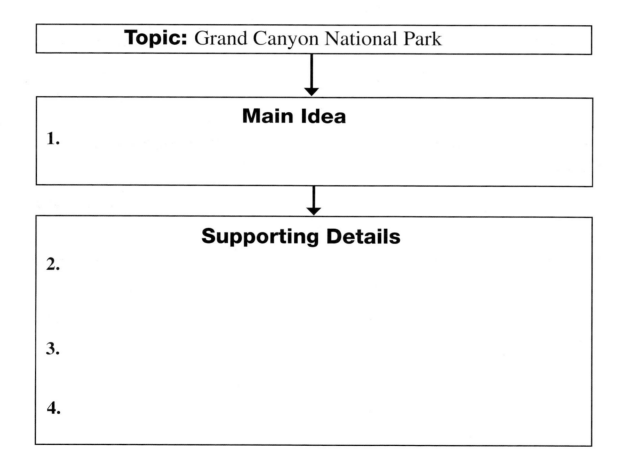

Topic: Grand Canyon National Park

↓

Main Idea

1.

↓

Supporting Details

2.

3.

4.

© Pearson Education 4

30

Vocabulary

Directions Match the word from Column A with its definition in Column B. Write the letter of the correct definition next to each word in Column A.

Check the Words You Know

___glaciers	___impressive	___naturalists	___preserve
___slopes	___species	___wilderness	

Column A

_____ **1.** naturalists

_____ **2.** slopes

_____ **3.** wilderness

_____ **4.** glaciers

_____ **5.** preserve

Column B

a. great masses of ice moving very slowly down mountains, along valleys, or over land areas

b. people who study living things

c. a wild, uncultivated region with few or no people living in it

d. to keep from harm or change; keep safe; protect

e. lines, surfaces, land, or other objects that go up or down at an angle

Directions Choose the word from the box that best completes each sentence. Write the word on the line.

6. Mt. McKinley in Alaska is the most _____ mountain in America.

7. There are many different _____ of plants and animals living in Yosemite National Park.

8. It is important to have national parks to _____ our most beautiful places.

9. The skier did not expect to find such steep _____ .

10. People who hike in the _____ need to take along a map and plenty of water.

31

The Amazing Geography . . .

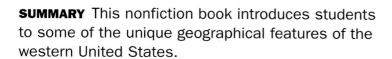

➤ **MAIN IDEA AND DETAILS**

➤ **GRAPHIC ORGANIZERS**

LESSON VOCABULARY glacier, impressive, naturalist, preserve, slopes, species, wilderness

SUMMARY This nonfiction book introduces students to some of the unique geographical features of the western United States.

INTRODUCE THE BOOK

BUILD BACKGROUND On a map of the United States, point out the states that make up the West. Ask students who have traveled to the West to discuss the unusual sites they visited. Have other students talk about natural features of the West they have learned about through books or school.

ELL Provide students with pictures of areas mentioned in the book. Have students label geographical features such as canyon or geyser.

PREVIEW/USE TEXT FEATURES Read the title of the book aloud, and have students look at the pictures. Discuss what students might learn from this book about the geography of the West.

TEACH/REVIEW VOCABULARY Assign vocabulary words to groups. Have each group read the word's definition in the Glossary, identify its base word and suffix if there is one, and write a sentence for the word. Share answers as a class.

TARGET SKILL AND STRATEGY

➤ **MAIN IDEA AND DETAILS** Remind students that a *main idea* is the most important idea about the topic of a selection. Supporting *details* are the small pieces of information that tell more about the main idea. Discuss with students the topic of this book: the geography of the West. Tell students to look for the main idea and supporting details about this topic.

➤ **GRAPHIC ORGANIZERS** Direct students' attention to question 1 in the Reader Response section of the book. Point out that *graphic organizers* like this one can help them organize and record the main idea and supporting details in a selection. Have students keep this graphic organizer in mind as they read the book.

READ THE BOOK

Use the following questions to support comprehension.

PAGE 5 What are two unusual features in Yellowstone National Park? *(yellow rock formations, geysers)*

PAGE 10 Where does the Pacific Ring of Fire get its name? *(These volcanoes lie close to the Pacific Ocean; many are still active, and they form the rough outline of a ring.)*

PAGE 15 Name two features that make Death Valley a special place. *(It is one of the hottest places on Earth and the lowest point in the Western Hemisphere.)*

TALK ABOUT THE BOOK

READER RESPONSE

1. Possible responses: Main idea: The western United States has some unusual and interesting geography. Supporting details: Yellowstone National Park has geysers; Mount Rainier is a volcano; Yosemite is home to giant sequoias.

2. San Andreas Fault, Yosemite National Park, Mojave National Preserve, Death Valley National Park

3. Possible response: The naturalist wrote a book about her studies of plant and animal life in Denali National Park.

4. *impressive,* adj., able to have a strong effect on the mind or feelings; able to influence deeply

RESPONSE OPTIONS

WRITING Have students write paragraphs about which natural wonders of the West are their favorites and why.

CONTENT CONNECTIONS

SCIENCE Have groups of students prepare reports about the following geographical features: volcanoes, glaciers, geysers, deserts, and faults.

TIME FOR Science

Main Idea and Details

- The **main idea** is the most important idea about the topic of a paragraph, passage, or article.
- **Supporting details** are the small pieces of information that tell more about the main idea.

Directions Read the following passage. Then write the topic of the passage. Tell the main idea of the passage and list the supporting details that tell more about the main idea. Then write a summary of the passage in one sentence.

Hawaii is a state with an amazing story. The state of Hawaii is made up of many islands. The Hawaiian islands were formed by erupting volcanoes. The largest island is called Hawaii. Two enormous volcanoes on the big island of Hawaii are still active. Kilauea and Mauna Loa add land to the island of Hawaii when lava oozes out, slides down their slopes, and cools.

Mauna Loa is actually the biggest mountain in the world! If you measure Mauna Loa's height from its base at the bottom of the sea to its very top, it is about thirty thousand feet tall! That's about a thousand feet taller than Mount Everest.

Topic

1. _____

Main Idea

2. _____

Supporting Ideas

3. _____

4. _____

5. _____

Summary

6. _____

© Pearson Education 4

30

Vocabulary

Directions Choose the word from the box that best matches each clue.
Write the word on the line.

> ## Check the Words You Know
>
> ___glacier   ___impressive   ___naturalist   ___preserve
> ___slopes   ___species   ___wilderness

1. _____ a person who studies plants or animals

2. _____ a mass of ice that moves slowly

3. _____ an outdoor place with more animals than humans

4. _____ able to have a strong effect on the mind or emotions

5. _____ living things in a group that are very much alike

Directions Write a sentence using the new form of the vocabulary word.

6. preserving _____

_____

7. sloped _____

_____

8. impressed _____

_____

9. glaciers _____

_____

31

John Muir: A Man of the Wilderness

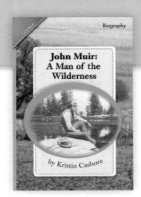

Biography

John Muir: A Man of the Wilderness

by Kristin Cashore

◉ **MAIN IDEA AND DETAILS**

◉ **GRAPHIC ORGANIZERS**

LESSON VOCABULARY botany, conservation, glaciers, naturalist, preserve, species

---

SUMMARY This biography of John Muir tells the history of the father of conservation in America, from his early life on a farm to his founding of the Sierra Club in 1892.

INTRODUCE THE BOOK

BUILD BACKGROUND Write the names of some locations from the book on the board, such as Yosemite National Park, the Sierra Nevada mountains, and the Grand Canyon. Discuss what students know about these places. Tell students that we enjoy these places today largely because of John Muir.

PREVIEW/USE TEXT FEATURES Read the title of the book aloud, and have students look at the pictures, captions, headings, and time line. Discuss what students might learn about John Muir from this book.

TEACH/REVIEW VOCABULARY Have students write sentences using the definitions of the vocabulary words from the Glossary but not the actual words. Have them exchange their sentences with partners and try to identify the vocabulary words in others' sentences.

TARGET SKILL AND STRATEGY

◉ **MAIN IDEA AND DETAILS** Remind students that a *main idea* is the most important idea about the topic of a selection. Supporting *details* are the small pieces of information that tell more about the main idea. Discuss with students the topic of this book: the life of John Muir. Tell students to look for the main idea and supporting details about this topic as they read.

◉ **GRAPHIC ORGANIZERS** Have students read question 1 in the Reader Response section of the book. Point out that *graphic organizers* like this one can help them organize and record the main idea and supporting details. Have students keep this graphic organizer in mind as they read.

ELL Draw a web on the board with *conservation* in the center circle. Have students contribute ideas on how to conserve nature to write in the outer circles.

READ THE BOOK

Use the following questions to support comprehension.

PAGE 7 Why did John Muir leave factory work? (*Losing his eyesight in an accident made him realize he wanted to spend his life outdoors.*)

PAGES 10–11 What is the main idea of these two pages? (*Muir started writing about the environment and begged people to protect nature.*)

PAGES 16–17 Summarize the fight over the Hetch-Hetchy Valley. (*The city of San Francisco wanted to flood the valley to create a reservoir, but Muir and the Sierra Club fought to protect the valley. Muir lost this fight.*)

TALK ABOUT THE BOOK

READER RESPONSE

1. Possible responses: Main idea: John Muir fought to protect the environment. Supporting details: Muir wrote articles asking people to protect nature; he asked President Roosevelt to save America's wilderness; he started the Sierra Club.

2. North America, South America, Australia, Asia, Africa

3. Possible responses: botany, conservation, glaciers, naturalist, preserve, species, wilderness, dam, fields, forests, mountains, wildlife, refuge, earthquake

4. Responses will vary.

RESPONSE OPTIONS

WRITING Ask students write letters to President Roosevelt in which they argue for the conservation of one of the places mentioned in the selection.

CONTENT CONNECTIONS

SOCIAL STUDIES AND SCIENCE Have groups prepare reports on national parks that include maps and descriptions of special features and wildlife. Compile the reports into a National Parks Guide.

TIME FOR Science

Main Idea and Details

- The **main idea** is the most important idea about the topic of a paragraph, passage, or article.
- **Supporting details** are the small pieces of information that tell more about the main idea.

Directions Read the following passage. Answer the following questions about the passage.

John Muir was one of our country's most important naturalists. Millions of people have read his books, and many have been influenced by his ideas. It is thanks to John Muir and others like him that many Americans today care about nature and the environment. People who work toward conservation today are acting in the spirit of this highly respected immigrant from Scotland.

John Muir is so admired that many parks, trails, and organizations are named after him. The John Muir Trust is a Scottish organization that works to protect the environment. The Muir Woods National Monument is a forest of protected redwood trees in California. The John Muir Trail runs for 211 miles through some of the most beautiful mountains in California. The John Muir Wilderness is a large area in California full of mountains, lakes, and streams. The Sierra Club that Muir established has also grown over the years, and today it does important conservation work all over the world.

1–2. What is the main idea of the first paragraph? Give one supporting detail.

_____

_____

3–4. What is the main idea of the second paragraph? Give one supporting detail.

_____

_____

5–7. What is the main idea of the entire passage? Give two supporting details.

_____

_____

_____

© Pearson Education 4

30

Vocabulary

Directions Choose the word from the box that best matches each definition.
Write the word on the line.

Check the Words You Know

___botany	___conservation	___glaciers
___naturalist	___preserve	___species

1. _____ to keep from harm or change

2. _____ a set of related living things that all have certain characteristics

3. _____ great masses of ice moving very slowly down a mountain, along a valley, or over a land area

4. _____ the science of plants; the study of plants and plant life

5. _____ a person who studies living things

6. _____ protection of natural resources

Directions Choose the word from the box that best fits each group. Write the word on the line.

7. protection, preservation, _____

8. biology, chemistry, _____

9. protect, defend, _____

10. cyclist, zoologist, _____

11. animals, plants, _____

12. mountains, ice, _____

31

Florida Everglades: Its Plants & Animals — LR1

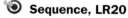 **Sequence, LR2**

1. bear facts, bear trouble, bear food **2.** many egrets were killed for their feathers. the feathers were used to decorate hats. the egret is protected. **3.** many animals and plants lived in the Florida Everglades. many animals and plants almost became extinct. the Florida Everglades is a protected habitat. **4.** black bears; other animals; birds; plants; plants and animals together

Vocabulary, LR3

1. positive **2.** memorial **3.** select **4.** peculiar **5.** grand **6.** recall **7.** prideful

Possible responses given. **8.** ordinary, poor, small, minor **9.** normal, ordinary, usual, common **10.** ashamed, humble

The Long Trip West — LR10

Author's Purpose, LR11

1. d **2.** a **3.** c **4.** d

Vocabulary, LR12

1. docks **2.** migrating **3.** scanned **4.** yearned **5.** wharf **6.** scent **7.** docks **8.** scent. **9.** wharf **10.** docks **11.** migrating **12.** scanned **13.** translated **14.** yearned

Grandpa's Scrapbook — LR19

Sequence, LR20

Childhood Years: adventures with Tim; swam in river; skating in winter; explored caves; Laura Hawkins went along.

Early Adult Years: cub pilot at age 22; pilot's license in 1859; saw New Orleans and St. Louis; worked on a steamboat; traveled on Mississippi River

Vocabulary, LR21

1. sculptures **2.** towering **3.** homeland **4.** amazed **5.** still **6.** longed **7.** bewildered

Responses will vary.

Flash Flood — LR28

Author's Purpose, LR29

1. a **2.** c **3.** d **4.** b

Vocabulary, LR30

1. c **2.** e **3.** d **4.** a **5.** b **6.** f

Responses will vary. Students' stories or poems should use all three words correctly.

This Land Is Our Land — LR37

Main Idea and Details, LR38

Possible responses provided. **1.** Grand Canyon National Park is one of the most famous parks in the world. **2.** Scientists come from all over the world to study the fossils in the canyon. **3.** Other scientists come to study the wildlife. **4.** Many tourists visit the park to admire it.

Vocabulary, LR39

1. b **2.** e **3.** c **4.** a **5.** d **6.** impressive **7.** species **8.** preserve **9.** slopes **10.** wilderness

Answer Key for On-Level Reader Practice

Something to Do — LR4

◉ Sequence, LR5

1. after, every morning, so, then, the next step, now **2.** Dad left to open the café; the boy left for school; Grandpa settled into his chair to watch TV and sleep; the boy and his dad returned home at the end of the day to find Grandpa still in his chair. **3.** He asked what it was; he said he couldn't draw; he said he couldn't even read his own writing with a pen; he made one sign that said "Do not disturb! Sleeping!" **4.** Dad gave Grandpa and the boy some pies to eat one night; Grandpa and Dad remembered the fried pies Grandma used to make; the boy suggested that they make some fried pies; the boy dragged Grandpa into the kitchen to try.

Vocabulary, LR6

Possible responses given. **1.** Dad often recalls the fried pies Grandma used to make. **2.** Grandpa was positive he couldn't get along all by himself. **3.** Grandma was prideful about her fried pies. **4.** Selecting a flavor is hard.

Sentences will vary. **5.** odd **6.** wonderful **7.** something done in honor of someone

Lewis and Clark — LR13

◉ Author's Purpose, LR14

Possible responses given. **1.** the Tetons **2.** to inform the reader about how the Tetons related to nearby groups **3.** to explain why the groups maintained a good relationship **4.** I figured the author was trying to explain something to me, so I read more slowly to make sure I understood the information. **5.** Yes, the author met her purpose by writing in a clear, factual way.

Vocabulary, LR15

1. scan **2.** migrating **3.** wharf **4.** docks **5.** yearned

Possible responses given. **6.** The migrating birds flew in V-formation. **7.** If you scan the sky at night, you might see Venus. **8.** The student yearned to travel to faraway places. **9.** My friend translated the Spanish signs for me.

Responses will vary.

Childhood in Pre-War Japan — LR22

◉ Sequence, LR23

1. around 300 B.C. Rice comes to Japan. **2.** 1543 Portuguese ship is wrecked on one of Japan's islands. Japanese people meet Europeans for the first time. **3.** For 200 years, Japanese are forced to stay in the country. **4.** 1853 Matthew C. Perry arrives in Japan. Japan opens up to West and becomes a powerful country. **5.** 1930s Japan becomes isolated again. People can't speak foreign languages.

Vocabulary, LR24

1. longed **2.** still **3.** amazed **4.** homeland **5.** towering **6.** bewildered **7.** sculptures

Responses will vary.

From Spain to America — LR31

◉ Author's Purpose, LR32

Possible responses given. **1.** to help the reader understand why Columbus and his crew took the trip, even though they didn't know what lay ahead **2.** to inform the reader of the reasons Columbus and his crew set sail for Asia **3.** to express the feelings that Columbus and his crew felt on their trip

Vocabulary, LR33

1. offended **2.** riverbed **3.** favors **4.** shrieked **5.** prairie **6.** offended **7.** bargain **8.** lassoed **9.** favors **10.** bargain

The Amazing Geography of the West — LR40

◉ Main Idea and Details, LR41

1. Hawaii's geography **2.** Hawaii has amazing geography. **3.** The islands were formed by erupting volcanoes. **4.** Two volcanoes on the island of Hawaii are active. **5.** Mauna Loa is taller than Mount Everest. **6.** Hawaii was formed by volcanoes that are still active.

Vocabulary, LR42

1. naturalist **2.** glacier **3.** wilderness **4.** impressive **5.** species

Possible responses given. **6.** Preserving special places in the United States is an important job. **7.** The hill sloped so much it was hard to climb. **8.** I impressed my teacher with my report. **9.** Many mountains are covered with glaciers.

The Story of Libraries LR7

 Sequence, LR8

1. between events b and c **2.** The fall of the Roman Empire marked the end of its libraries; followers of the Islamic religion translated books they found into Arabic; Johannes Gutenberg invented the printing press. **3.** 1st: Ben Franklin formed the Junto. 2nd: The Library Company became the first lending library in America. 3rd: The New York Library Society was founded. **4.** Steam-powered machines began to replace hand looms used for weaving; work became harder for Will Carnegie to find; Margaret Carnegie suggested they move to America; the family left Scotland for the United States in 1848.

Vocabulary, LR9

POSITIVE, GRAND, CODEX, MEMORIAL, SELECTING, VOLUME, PRIDEFUL, PECULIAR
Responses will vary.

Two Great Rivers LR16

 Author's Purpose, LR17

Possible response given. **1–2.** to inform the reader about Mississippi floods; to persuade that flooding is a serious problem along the Mississippi **3.** The author says flooding causes damage to homes and communities. **4.** The author wants to convince the reader that humans are a big part of the problem of flooding.

Vocabulary, LR18

1. barges **2.** route **3.** silt **4.** diminishing **5.** expedition
Possible responses given. **6.** Conservationists believe that more needs to be done to protect wildlife in Alaska. **7.** There are many good reasons to build reservoirs. **8.** The fish that live in the river swim into tributaries to breed.

Innocent Prisoners! LR25

Sequence, LR26

1. Yukiko goes to school, and the teacher talks about the new blackboard. **2.** Yukiko and Aki look at Mt. Whitney. **3.** Yukiko meets an old man who has a drawing of Mt. Fuji. **4.** At dinner a group of men argue about whether to return to Japan after the war. **5.** After dinner Mama speaks English, and there is a dust storm.

Vocabulary, LR27

1. elections **2.** naval **3.** barracks **4.** internment **5.** horizon
Responses will vary.

The Diné LR34

 Author's Purpose, LR35

Possible responses given. **1.** to inform the reader about what happened after the Diné signed the peace treaty in 1868 and returned to the Dinétah **2.** to persuade the reader that the Diné were hard-working by telling how they made a comeback **3.** show how much work the Diné had to do to repair the damage **4.** The author wants to inform the reader of how important religion and sacred ceremonies were to the Diné.

Vocabulary, LR36

1. edible **2.** cardinal points **3.** environmentalists **4.** inhabited **5.** hogan **6.** ancestors **7.** nomads
Responses will vary.

John Muir: A Man of the Wilderness LR43

 Main Ideas and Details, LR44

Possible responses provided. **1–2.** John Muir was one of our country's most important naturalists. Many people have been influenced by his ideas. **3–4.** John Muir is admired; many parks, trails, and organizations are named after him. **5–7.** Muir was so important to conservation in America that he is still remembered today. Millions of people have read his books. Muir's Sierra Club has grown. It still does important conservation work.

Vocabulary, LR45

1. preserve **2.** species **3.** glaciers **4.** botany **5.** naturalist **6.** conservation **7.** conservation **8.** botany **9.** preserve **10.** naturalist **11.** species **12.** glaciers

Routine Cards

Multisyllabic Word Routine

Teach students this Routine to read long words with meaningful parts.

1 Teach Tell students to look for meaningful parts and to think about the meaning of each part. They should use the parts to read the word and determine meaning.

2 Model Think aloud to analyze a long word for the base word, ending, prefix, and/or suffix and to identify the word and determine its meaning.

3 Guide Practice Provide examples of long words with endings (*-ing, -ed, -s*), prefixes (*un-, re-, dis-, mis-, non-*), and/or suffixes (*-ly, -ness, -less, -ful,* and so on). Help students analyze base words and parts.

4 Provide Feedback Encourage students to circle parts of the words to help identify parts and determine meaning.

Picture Walk Routine

To build concepts and vocabulary, conduct a structured picture walk before reading.

1 Prepare Preview the selection and list key concepts and vocabulary you wish to develop.

2 Discuss As students look at the pages, discuss illustrations, have students point to pictured items, and/or ask questions that target key concepts and vocabulary.

3 Elaborate Elaborate on students' responses to reinforce correct use of the vocabulary and to provide additional exposure to key concepts.

4 Practice For more practice with key concepts, have each student turn to a partner and do the picture walk using the key concept vocabulary.

Multisyllabic Word Routine

Teach students this Routine to chunk words with no recognizable parts.

1 Teach Tell students to look for chunks in words with no meaningful parts. They should say each chunk slowly and then say the chunks fast to make a whole word.

2 Model Think aloud to demonstrate breaking a word into chunks, saying each chunk slowly, and then saying the chunks fast to make a word.

3 Guide Practice Provide examples of long words with no meaningful parts. Help students chunk the words.

4 Provide Feedback If necessary, reteach by modeling how to break words into chunks.

Concept Vocabulary

Use this Routine to teach concept vocabulary.

1 Introduce the Word Relate the word to the week's concept. Supply a student-friendly definition.

2 Demonstrate Provide several familiar examples to demonstrate meaning.

3 Apply Have students demonstrate understanding with a simple activity.

4 Display the Word Relate the word to the concept by displaying it on a concept web. Have students identify word parts and practice reading the word.

5 Use the Word Often Encourage students to use the word often in their writing and speaking. Ask questions that require students to use the word.

Group Time

DAY 1

Leveled Reader Database ONLINE

PearsonSuccessNet.com

① Build Background

REINFORCE CONCEPTS Display the Diversity Concept Web. This week's concept is *diversity*. The United States is home to many different people—people from different countries, people of different ages, people with different incomes. Because the United States is a free country that belongs to all of its people, this land, the United States, is your land. Discuss the definitions of each word on the web on p. 18l and the Concept Vocabulary Routine on p. DI·1.

CONNECT TO READING This week you will read about the friendship that develops between a young person and an older person. Which young person and older person become friends in "Child of the Silent Night"? Why? *(Laura Bridgman and Asa Tenney become friends. Laura is deaf and blind and Asa wants to help her learn.)*

② Read Leveled Reader *Florida Everglades: Its Plants & Animals*

BEFORE READING Using the Picture Walk Routine on p. DI·1, guide students through the text, focusing on key concepts and vocabulary. Ask questions such as:

p. 3 Many different kinds of animals live in Florida. Which animal is pictured here? *(a black bear)* Scientists call the Florida black bear *Ursus americanus floridanus*. In which of these settings would you expect to find the Florida black bear? *(the swamp setting)* Why? *(Florida has a warm climate.)*

pp. 4–5 Sometimes black bears come in contact with people, such as campers. How might black bears be dangerous to people? *(Black bears have sharp claws and might attack people.)* Are there ways in which people might be dangerous to black bears? *(People might take over the black bear's land.)*

DURING READING Read pp. 3–5 aloud while students track the print. Do a choral reading of pp. 6–9. If students are capable, have them read and discuss the remainder of the book with a partner. Ask: What are some of the different plants and animals you can find in the Florida Everglades?

AFTER READING Encourage pairs of students to discuss the variety of plants and animals they might see on a trip to the Florida Everglades. We read *Florida Everglades: Its Plants & Animals* to learn about the Florida black bear and some of its plant and animal neighbors. Knowing something about Florida's animals and plants will help us as we read *Because of Winn-Dixie*.

Monitor Progress

Selection Reading and Comprehension

If... students have difficulty reading the selection with a partner,	**then...** have them follow along as they listen to the Online Leveled Reader Audio.
If... students have difficulty understanding the difference between mangrove and cypress trees,	**then...** reread p. 12 and discuss the photographs together.

For alternate Leveled Reader lesson plans that teach ⦿**Sequence,** ⦿**Summarize,** and **Lesson Vocabulary,** see pp. LR1–LR9.

On-Level

DAY 1

1 Build Background

DEVELOP VOCABULARY Write the word *understanding* and ask students to define it in their own words. *(the ability to understand something, the ability to explain what something means)* Imagine that you have just finished a science unit on electricity. How might your teacher check your *understanding* of electricity? *(She might give a test or assign a project.)* Repeat this activity with the word *comfortable* and other words from the Leveled Reader *Something to Do.* Use the Concept Vocabulary Routine on p. DI·1 as needed.

2 Read Leveled Reader *Something to Do*

BEFORE READING Have students create a Venn diagram with the labels Boy and Grandpa. This book tells the story of how a boy helps his grandfather find something enjoyable to do in his spare time. As you read, notice ways in which the boy and his grandfather are alike and different. Record this information in your Venn diagram.

DURING READING Have students follow along as you read pp. 3–8. Then let them complete the book on their own. Remind students to add information to their Venn diagrams as they read.

AFTER READING Have students compare the information in their Venn diagrams. Explain that understanding how a young person and an older person are alike and different will help them as they read tomorrow's story, *Because of Winn-Dixie.*

Advanced

DAY 1

1 Read Leveled Reader *The Story of Libraries*

BEFORE READING Recall the Read Aloud "Child of the Silent Night." Ask: Why does Asa Tenney take a personal interest in Laura Bridgman? *(Asa wants to help Laura learn. Laura is deaf and blind and her parents do not have the resources to help her.)* Today you will read about some of the people who helped make libraries a place of learning for all people.

CRITICAL THINKING Have students read the Leveled Reader independently. Encourage them to think critically. For example, ask:

- How have libraries changed over time?
- Are all books valuable? Why or why not?

AFTER READING Remind students that *library* comes from the Latin word *liber,* which means "book." Explain that the Latin word *liber* can also mean "free." Have students brainstorm a list of words, such as *liberate,* that come from this second meaning of *liber.* Meet with students to discuss the selection and to share their word lists.

2 Independent Extension Activity

NOW TRY THIS Assign "Now Try This" on pp. 22–23 of *The Story of Libraries* for students to work on throughout the week.

Because of Winn-Dixie
Group Time

Audio CD · AudioText

Strategic Intervention

ROUTINE

1 Word Study/Phonics

LESSON VOCABULARY Use p. 20b to review the meanings of *grand, memorial, peculiar, positive, prideful, recalls,* and *selecting.* Have individuals practice reading the words from word cards.

DECODING MULTISYLLABIC WORDS Write *experience,* saying the word as you write it. Then model how to use chunking to read longer words. I see a chunk at the beginning of the word: *ex.* I see a part in the middle: *per,* and another part: *i.* I see a chunk at the end of the word: *ence.* I say the chunks fast to make a whole word: *experience.* Is it a real word? Yes, I know the word *experience.*

Use the Multisyllabic Word Routine on p. DI·1 to help students read these other words from *Because of Winn-Dixie: arrival, trembling, embarrassed, snuffled, palmetto,* and *mosquitoes.* Make sure students understand the meanings of words such as *trembling, snuffled,* and *embarrassed.*

Use *Strategies for Word Analysis,* Lesson 1, with students who have difficulty mastering word analysis and need practice with decodable text.

2 Read *Because of Winn-Dixie,* pp. 22–27

BEFORE READING *Florida Everglades: Its Plants & Animals* described some of the many different plants and animals that can be found in the Florida Everglades. Think about these plants and animals as you read *Because of Winn-Dixie.*

Using the Picture Walk Routine on p. DI·1, guide students through the text, asking questions such as those below. Then read the question on p. 23. Together, set a purpose for reading.

pp. 22–23 What do you see in this scene? Where do you think this scene takes place? Why do you think so?

p. 24 This illustration shows a girl petting a dog. How does the girl seem to feel about the dog? How does the dog seem to feel about the girl? Does anything in this scene remind you of Florida?

DURING READING Follow the Guiding Comprehension routine on pp. 24–27. Have students read along with you while tracking the print, or do a choral reading. Stop every two pages to ask what has happened so far. Prompt as necessary.

- Who is India Opal Buloni? Where does she like to spend her time?

- What animal does Miss Franny mistake Winn-Dixie for? Why?

AFTER READING What has happened in the story so far? What do you think will happen next? Reread passages as needed.

Monitor Progress

Word and Story Reading

If... students have difficulty reading multisyllabic words in the selection,	**then...** have them look for and read meaningful parts in the words or have them chunk words with no recognizable parts.
If... students need practice reading words fluently,	**then...** use the Fluent Word Reading Routine on the DI tab.
If... students have difficulty reading along with the group,	**then...** have them follow along as they listen to the AudioText.

Advanced

1 Extend Vocabulary

WORD STRUCTURE Write this sentence from p. 3 of *The Story of Libraries:*

> **The information in a book could be as powerful as an army.**

Ask: What does *powerful* mean? *(full of power)* How did you figure out the word's meaning? *(I recognized the suffix -ful, which means "full of." I tried the meaning "full of power" in the sentence and it made sense.)* Discuss how using word structure is helpful, and remind students to use the strategy as they read *Because of Winn-Dixie.*

2 Read *Because of Winn-Dixie,* pp. 22–27

BEFORE READING Today you will begin reading a story about the friendship that develops between a girl and an older woman librarian. As you read, think about other stories you know, such as "Child of the Silent Night," in which a young person becomes friends with an older person.

Have students write their questions in their Strategy Response Logs (p. 22).

PROBLEM SOLVING Have students read pp. 24–27 independently. Encourage them to problem solve. For example, ask:

- How could Miss Franny Block make her library safe from unwanted visitors, such as wild animals?

AFTER READING Have partners discuss the story and share their Strategy Response Log questions and answers. Then invite them to recall a time when they had an unexpected encounter with a wild animal. What did they do to stay safe? Have individuals make a list of safety do's and don'ts for encounters with wild animals.

DAY 2

Audio CD   AudioText

Because of Winn-Dixie
Group Time

Audio CD AudioText

DAY **3**

ROUTINE

1 Reinforce Comprehension

SKILL SEQUENCE Have students explain what sequence is *(the order in which events happen)* and name clue words that often signal a sequence of events *(first, next, last; before, after)*. If necessary, review the meaning and provide a model. Sequence is the order in which events happen. Write the next day's morning schedule on the board (e.g., 9:00 Reading, 10:30 Math, 11:15 Recess). Say: Here is tomorrow morning's schedule. It is a list of activities in the order in which they will happen. It is a sequence of events. Review with students what they will do first, next, last, and so on.

Write the next day's afternoon schedule on the board, out of sequence. Ask students to help you rewrite the schedule so that the activities are in the correct order. Then review with students what they will do first, next, last, and so on.

2 Read *Because of Winn-Dixie, pp. 28–33*

BEFORE READING Have students retell what has happened in the story so far. Ask: How would you summarize what happens at the library that day? Reread the last two paragraphs on p. 25 and all of p. 26. Model how to identify the main events and retell them in order. This is what happens at the library that day: Opal teaches Winn-Dixie how to look in the library window so that he can see her choosing books. When Miss Franny Block sees Winn-Dixie in the window, she thinks he is a bear and screams and falls out of her chair. Opal comes to Miss Franny's aid and explains that Winn-Dixie is her dog. Remind students to pause to summarize as they finish reading *Because of Winn-Dixie*.

STRATEGY Summarize

DURING READING Follow the Guiding Comprehension routine on pp. 28–33. Have students read along with you while tracking print, or do a choral reading. Stop every two pages to ask students what has happened so far. Prompt as necessary.

- How does Miss Franny Block become librarian of the Herman W. Block Memorial Library?
- What happens when a bear gets into the Herman W. Block Memorial Library?

AFTER READING Why might people of different ages, such as a young person and an older person, become friends? Reread the story with students for comprehension as needed. Tell them that tomorrow they will read "Fast Facts: Black Bears," an article that gives more information about the black bear population in North America.

Monitor Progress

Word and Story Reading

If... students have difficulty reading multisyllabic words in the story,	**then...** have them look for and read meaningful parts in the words or have them chunk words with no recognizable parts.
If... students have difficulty reading along with the group,	**then...** have them follow along as they listen to the AudioText.

1 Extend Comprehension

◉ SKILL SEQUENCE Have students retell what happened at the library that day from the point of view of Miss Franny Block. Encourage them to consider how Miss Franny's account of what happened might be different from Opal's.

◉ STRATEGY SUMMARIZE Remind students that a chapter title often summarizes what a chapter is about. Have students suggest a chapter title for the first half of *Because of Winn-Dixie* that summarizes what it is about *(e.g., A Case of Mistaken Identity).*

2 Read *Because of Winn-Dixie*, pp. 28–33

BEFORE READING Have students recall what has happened in the story so far. Remind them to keep track of the sequence of events and to pause to summarize the main events as they read the rest of the story.

CREATIVE THINKING Have students read pp. 28–33 independently. Encourage them to think creatively. For example, ask:

- What might happen next in the story? What might Opal's next adventure be?

AFTER READING Have students complete the Strategy Response Log activity (p. 32). Give students the opportunity to meet with you and discuss the story. Then have them create a story map for the next chapter in the story.

DAY 3

AudioText

Because of Winn-Dixie
Group Time

ROUTINE

1 Practice Retelling

REVIEW STORY ELEMENTS Help students identify the main characters and the setting of *Because of Winn-Dixie*. Then guide them in using the Retelling Cards to list story events in sequence. Prompt students to include important details.

RETELL Using the Retelling Cards, have students work in pairs to retell *Because of Winn-Dixie*. Monitor retelling and prompt students as needed. For example, ask:

- Where and when does this story take place?
- Who are the main characters?
- Tell me what this story is about in a few sentences.

If students struggle, monitor a fluent retelling.

PEARSON Scott Foresman · Grade 4 · **Retelling Cards**

2 Read "Fast Facts: Black Bears"

BEFORE READING Read the genre information on p. 36. Hold up a copy of the Leveled Reader *Florida Everglades: Its Plants & Animals* and remind students that they have already read an example of expository nonfiction. Briefly review the Leveled Reader with students. Ask: What information does this book provide? Does it give a few facts about many things or many facts about one thing? Then have students preview the article "Fast Facts: Black Bears." Ask: What information does this article provide? In what ways is this article similar to the Leveled Reader *Florida Everglades: Its Plants & Animals*?

Read the rest of the panel on p. 36. Help students see that the article is divided into three sections. Have students scan the article to locate the three section headings in green, the individual paragraph headings in orange, and the map and map key.

DURING READING Have students read along with you while tracking the print, or do a choral reading of the selection. As you read, pause to discuss photographs that relate to the text.

AFTER READING Have students share their reactions to the selection. Then guide them through the Reading Across Texts and Writing Across Texts activities, prompting if necessary.

- Which facts about where black bears live could Miss Franny Block say are true?
- Which facts about black bear bodies could Miss Franny Block say are true?
- Which facts about what black bears eat could Miss Franny Block say are true?

DAY 4

Audio CD AudioText

Monitor Progress

Word and Story Reading

If... students have difficulty reading multisyllabic words in the story,	then... have them look for and read meaningful parts in the words or have them chunk words with no recognizable parts.
If... students have difficulty reading along with the group,	then... have them follow along as they listen to the AudioText.

Advanced

① Read "Fast Facts: Black Bears"

CRITICAL THINKING Have students read pp. 36–39 independently. Encourage them to think critically. For example, ask:

• Where, in the United States, might you have the best chance of seeing a black bear in the wild?

• Are zoos a good place for black bears? Why or why not?

AFTER READING Discuss the selection and Reading Across Texts with students. Have students complete Writing Across Texts independently.

② Extend Genre Study

RESEARCH Have students use print or online resources to find other expository nonfiction about black bears. Have them take notes on new information they find about where black bears live, what their bodies are like, and what they eat.

WRITE Have students use their notes to write one or more "fast facts" to add to the article. Tell them to provide a heading for each fact and an illustration, if possible. They should also decide where to place each fact in the article.

AudioText

Because of Winn-Dixie
Group Time

ONLINE

PearsonSuccessNet.com

ROUTINE

1 Reread for Fluency

MODEL Read aloud pp. 3–5 of the Leveled Reader *Florida Everglades: Its Plants & Animals*, using intonation to signal questions and full stops, show surprise at unexpected information, and emphasize negative words such as *not*. Have students note the rise and fall of your voice. Then read pp. 6–7 in a monotone. Have students tell you which model sounded better. Discuss how tone of voice can make factual information more appealing to listeners.

PRACTICE Have students reread passages from *Florida Everglades: Its Plants & Animals* individually or with a partner. For optimal fluency, they should reread three or four times. As students read, monitor fluency and provide corrective feedback. Students in this group are assessed in Weeks 2 and 4.

2 Retell Leveled Reader *Florida Everglades: Its Plants & Animals*

Model how to use the headings, photographs, and captions to retell what the book was about. Then have students retell what they learned from the book, using the headings, photographs, and captions. Prompt them as needed.

- What does the heading say? How does it relate to the Florida Everglades?
- How does the photograph relate to the heading? What information does the caption add?

Monitor Progress
Fluency

If... students have difficulty reading fluently,	then... provide additional fluency practice by pairing nonfluent readers with fluent ones.

For alternate Leveled Reader lesson plans that teach ↻**Sequence,** ↻**Summarize,** and **Lesson Vocabulary,** see pp. LR1–LR9.

On-Level

1 Reread for Fluency ROUTINE

MODEL Read aloud p. 3 of the Leveled Reader *Something to Do,* using tone of voice to emphasize negative words such as *never* and *couldn't* and repeated words such as *old.* Have students note the rise and fall of your voice and the words you emphasize. Discuss how tone of voice makes storytelling more exciting.

PRACTICE Have individuals or pairs reread passages from *Something to Do.* For optimal fluency, they should reread three or four times. As students read, monitor fluency and provide corrective feedback. Students in this group are assessed in Week 3.

2 Retell Leveled Reader *Something to Do*

Have students use the illustrations as a guide to retell the story. Prompt students as needed.

- What is the problem in this story? Who needs something to do? Why?
- How is the problem solved?

Advanced

1 Reread for Fluency ROUTINE

PRACTICE Have students reread passages from the Leveled Reader *The Story of Libraries* with a partner or individually. As students read, monitor fluency and provide corrective feedback. If students read fluently on the first reading, they do not need to reread three or four times. Assess the fluency of students in this group using p. 39a.

2 Revisit Leveled Reader *The Story of Libraries*

RETELL Have students retell the Leveled Reader *The Story of Libraries.*

NOW TRY THIS Have students complete and present the projects they have been working on all week. You may wish to display the projects in the classroom for the whole class to see and enjoy.

Group Time

ROUTINE

DAY 1

Leveled Reader Database
ONLINE
PearsonSuccessNet.com

1 Build Background

REINFORCE CONCEPTS Display the Exploration Concept Web. This week's concept is *exploration*. To explore is to travel over little-known lands or seas for the purpose of discovery. This land is our land, and it's natural for people to want to know about the land where they live. That's especially true when the land has not been explored, and nobody knows what's there. Discuss the meaning of each word on the web, using the definitions on p. 40l and the Concept Vocabulary Routine on p. DI·1.

CONNECT TO READING This week you will read about how some people explored the new land that the United States had just bought in 1803. How did Johnny Appleseed travel in the late 1700s? What other means of transportation were available to people in the early 1800s? *(horseback, wagon, boat, walking)*

2 Read Leveled Reader *The Long Trip West*

BEFORE READING Using the Picture Walk Routine on p. DI·1, guide students through the text focusing on key concepts and vocabulary. Ask questions such as:

p. 7 What are the people in this illustration preparing to do? *(They are loading supplies in a boat preparing to travel on the river.)* Yes, they had to carry their supplies out onto a wharf, which is a platform built out from the shore to help boats load and unload.

p. 9 Did the explorers meet any Native Americans on their journey? *(Yes, they visited a Native American village and met the people.)* They also had the help of a Shoshone woman named Sacagawea, who translated for them; that is, she told the Native Americans in their language what the explorers wanted to say and then told the explorers in English what they answered.

DURING READING Read pp. 3–5 aloud, while students track the print. Do a choral reading of pp. 6–8. If students are capable, have them read and discuss the remainder of the book with a partner. Ask: What did the Corps of Discovery do when they had to leave their horses behind? Was their journey successful? In what ways?

AFTER READING Encourage pairs of students to discuss the challenges of their journey. We read *The Long Trip West* to learn about the whole journey, beginning to end, made by the Corps of Discovery. Knowing this big picture will help us understand *Lewis and Clark and Me,* which covers only part of the journey but which focuses on one special member of the Corps of Discovery—the dog.

Monitor Progress

Selection Reading and Comprehension

If... students have difficulty reading the selection with a partner,	then... have them follow along as they listen to the Online Leveled Reader Audio.
If... students have trouble understanding why the trip was so difficult,	then... reread pp. 8–11 and discuss how the Corps of Discovery traveled and how the explorers lived on the way.

For alternate Leveled Reader lesson plans that teach
🔎 **Author's Purpose,** 🔎 **Answer Questions,**
and **Lesson Vocabulary,** see pp. LR10–LR18.

On-Level

ROUTINE

1 Build Background

DEVELOP VOCABULARY Write the word *territory* and ask students to list as many synonyms as they can. *(region, place, land, tract, district, section, locality)* These are all general synonyms for a piece of land. There is a more specific meaning for *territory:* "land belonging to a government," which is what the Louisiana Purchase was before it was divided into states. Repeat the synonym activity with the word *scent* and other words from the Leveled Reader *Lewis and Clark.* Use the Concept Vocabulary Routine on p. DI·1 as needed.

2 Read Leveled Reader *Lewis and Clark*

BEFORE READING Have students create time lines for the events of the Lewis and Clark expedition. As you read, record the most important events in your time line. In addition to the years, you can use divisions like *summer* and *fall* to help show the sequence of events.

DURING READING Have students follow along as you read pp. 3–7. Then let them complete the book on their own. Remind students to add events to their time lines as they read.

AFTER READING Have students compare the entries on their time lines. Point out that knowing the most important events of the Lewis and Clark expedition will help them as they read tomorrow's selection, *Lewis and Clark and Me.* In the main selection, some of the same events are covered, but they are covered from a different viewpoint—that of a dog!

Advanced

ROUTINE

1 Leveled Reader *Two Great Rivers*

BEFORE READING Recall the Read Aloud biography "Johnny Appleseed." In what ways was John Chapman an explorer? *(He went into new, unfamiliar places.)* Most of the early explorers in this country made use of rivers for part of their travel. Today you will read about two of the largest and most important rivers.

CRITICAL THINKING Have students read the Leveled Reader independently. Encourage them to think critically. For example, ask:

- Why was river travel so important, particularly in the early days of this country's history?
- What has been done to control flooding in the Missouri and Mississippi river systems? Why have these efforts been criticized?

AFTER READING Have students review the selection to find at least two unfamiliar words and determine their meanings. Then ask them to write questions or riddles about the words and exchange them with their classmates to answer or solve. Have students meet with you to discuss the selection and the questions or riddles they wrote.

2 Independent Extension Activity

NOW TRY THIS Assign "Now Try This" on pp. 22–23 of *Two Great Rivers* for students to work on throughout the week.

Lewis and Clark and Me
Group Time

Audio CD AudioText

Monitor Progress

Word and Story Reading

If... students have difficulty reading multisyllabic words in the selection,	**then...** have them look for and read meaningful parts in the words or have them chunk words with no recognizable parts.
If... students need practice reading words fluently,	**then...** use the Fluent Word Reading Routine on the DI tab.
If... students have difficulty reading along with the group,	**then...** have them follow along as they listen to the AudioText.

Strategic Intervention

ROUTINE

1 Word Study/Phonics

LESSON VOCABULARY Use p. 42b to review the meanings of *docks, migrating, scan, scent, wharf,* and *yearned.* Have individuals practice reading the words from word cards.

DECODING MULTISYLLABIC WORDS Write *unthinkable,* saying the word as you write it. Then model how to use meaningful parts to read longer words. First I ask myself if I see any parts I know. I see the base word *think.* I see the prefix *un-,* which I know means "not," and I see the suffix *-able.* Then I put them all together. I think the word *unthinkable* describes something you can't even think about.

Use the Multisyllabic Word Routine on p. DI·1 to help students read these other words from *Lewis and Clark and Me: exhausted, admiration, observations, patiently, impressed, politely, satisfaction.* Be sure students understand the meanings of words such as *admiration.*

Use *Strategies for Word Analysis,* Lesson 2, with students who have difficulty mastering word analysis and need practice with decodable text.

2 Read *Lewis and Clark and Me,* pp. 44–53

BEFORE READING *The Long Trip West* told of the events of the Lewis and Clark expedition from beginning to end. This selection also tells about Lewis and Clark, but there's another character added—*Me.* Read to find out to whom *Me* refers.

Using the Picture Walk Routine on p. DI·1, guide students through the text, asking questions such as those listed below. Read the question on p. 45. Together, set a purpose for reading.

p. 44 What character is featured in the selection opener on this page? *(a large dog)* Do you suppose that dog might be the *Me* referred to in the title?

p. 52 What is the dog doing in this picture? Why? *(It is jumping off the boat, maybe to hunt or fetch some animal the man is shooting.)*

DURING READING Follow the Guiding Comprehension routine on pp. 46–53. Have students read along with you while tracking the print or do a choral reading. Stop every two pages to ask what has happened so far. Prompt as necessary.

• When and where does this story take place?
• Why does Meriwether Lewis decide he wants a dog?
• Why does Lewis send Seaman to hunt squirrels?

AFTER READING What do you think will happen next? Reread for comprehension as needed.

Advanced

ROUTINE

1 Extend Vocabulary

WORD STRUCTURE Call attention to the word *exploration* in the Concept Web and in the question on p. 45. Once you recognize a suffix you can use your knowledge to read other words with that suffix. For example, the suffix in *exploration* is *-ation,* which means "act, condition, or result of," and the base word is *explore.* So *exploration* is "the act of exploring." Have students analyze these words that appear in *Lewis and Clark and Me: qualifications, admiration, observations.* Remind students to use the word structure vocabulary strategy as they read *Lewis and Clark and Me.*

2 Read *Lewis and Clark and Me,* pp. 44–53

BEFORE READING Today you will read about the journey of exploration led by Meriwether Lewis and William Clark in 1804. They led a group called the Corps of Discovery that was commissioned by President Thomas Jefferson to explore the lands west of the Mississippi that the United States had gained in the Louisiana Purchase. Because travel by water was so much easier—when it was available—than travel overland, the group made much use of the Missouri River, which you read about in *Two Great Rivers.*

Have students write out their predictions in their Strategy Response Log (p. 44). Encourage them to check their predictions as they read.

CRITICAL THINKING Have students read pp. 44–53 independently. Encourage them to think critically. For example, ask:

- Why do you suppose the author chose to write about these events from the point of view of a dog, rather than simply another crew member?

- In your opinion, does this point of view limit the story or make it more interesting? Explain.

AFTER READING Have partners discuss the story and share their Strategy Response Log entries. Encourage them to share other stories they know that are told from the points of view of animals instead of people. Challenge them each to come up with one important idea or insight that they have gotten from reading these stories in the animals' own words instead of those of a third-person narrator. Finally, ask volunteers to share their insights with the class.

DAY 2

Audio CD **AudioText**

Lewis and Clark and Me

Group Time

ROUTINE

DAY 3

Audio CD AudioText

Monitor Progress

Word and Story Reading

If... students have difficulty reading multisyllabic words in the selection,	**then...** have them look for and read meaningful parts in the words or have them chunk words with no recognizable parts.
If... students have difficulty reading along with the group,	**then...** have them follow along as they listen to the AudioText.

1 Reinforce Comprehension

SKILL AUTHOR'S PURPOSE The author's purpose is the reason or reasons the author has for writing a particular selection. Have students tell whether they think the author's purpose in writing this story was to persuade, to entertain, to inform, or to express ideas and feelings. Why? What is there about the story that makes you think that? Might the author have more than one purpose here? Why do you think so?

2 Read *Lewis and Clark and Me,* pp. 54–59

BEFORE READING Have students retell what happened in the story so far. Say: I'm going to ask a question, and then I want you to tell me where to look for the answer. Here is the question: *How does the dog Seaman demonstrate that he has been well trained before Meriwether Lewis meets him the first time?* Will you find that answer in one place in the text, in several places, or will you have to combine what you know with what you read? Allow some students to answer the question before you model: Yes, I remember that when Lewis first sees Seaman and throws a stick for him, Seaman won't fetch the stick until he is given permission by his owner. That shows he is well trained. That appears in one scene on p. 48. Remind students to think about how to answer questions as they read the rest of *Lewis and Clark and Me* **STRATEGY Answer Questions**

DURING READING Follow the Guiding Comprehension routine on pp. 54–59. Have students read along with you while tracking print or do a choral reading. Stop every two pages to ask students what has happened so far. Prompt as necessary.

• What does Seaman notice about the dog that accompanies the Indians?
• Why does the Indian offer Lewis three beaver skins? How does Lewis respond?
• Why are some of the lines on the map on pp. 58–59 in different colors?

AFTER READING How does this story carry out the theme of exploration? Reread with students for comprehension as needed. Tell them that tomorrow they will read "They Traveled with Lewis and Clark," about two other members of the Corps of Discovery.

Advanced

DAY 3

1 Extend Comprehension

⦿ **SKILL** **AUTHOR'S PURPOSE** Remember, an author's purpose is the reason or reasons the author has for writing. Do you think the author wrote *Lewis and Clark and Me* to persuade, to inform, to entertain, or to express ideas and feelings—or a combination of these? Why do you think so? Students may suggest a combination of purposes, such as to inform and to entertain. Then ask: Show me a section that you think is informative. Show me a section that you think is particularly entertaining.

⦿ **STRATEGY** **ANSWER QUESTIONS** You need to know where to look for the answers to questions. Answers might be found in one place in the text or in several places. Sometimes you must use what you've read plus what you know to answer a question. Here are two questions about what you've read so far. Where will you find the answers?

- What is special about Seaman's paws? *(They're webbed. The answer is in one place, on p. 47.)*
- What special talents does Seaman have that prove useful to the expedition? *(He loves to swim, and he loves to hunt. These talents prove useful when he catches a large number of squirrels for the men to eat. See pp. 49–53.)*

Audio CD **AudioText**

2 Read *Lewis and Clark and Me,* pp. 54–59

BEFORE READING Have students recall what has happened in the selection so far. Remind them to look for evidence of the author's purpose or purposes as they read the remainder of the story, and to think about what information might be used to answer certain kinds of questions.

CREATIVE THINKING Have students read pp. 54–59 independently. Encourage them to think creatively. For example: We learn that these Indians have no word in their language for *horse*, so they call a horse an *elk-dog*. Why would that be an appropriate term for these people to use? As you read, think about things the Europeans might bring with them on their expedition that the Indians would probably be unfamiliar with, and think of other new and imaginative terms the Indians might use to describe them.

AFTER READING Have students complete the Strategy Response Log activity on p. 58. Then have them retell the events on pp. 54–56 from the point of view of the Indians. Have them tell what characteristics they may have observed about Lewis, his men, and Seaman and what judgments they may have made, based on their interaction with them.

Lewis and Clark and Me

Group Time

ROUTINE

DAY
4

Audio CD   AudioText

① Practice Retelling

REVIEW STORY ELEMENTS Help students identify the main characters and the setting of *Lewis and Clark and Me.* Then guide them in using the Retelling Cards to list story events in sequence. Prompt students to include important details.

RETELL Using the Retelling Cards, have students work in pairs to retell *Lewis and Clark and Me.* Monitor retelling and prompt students as needed. For example, ask:

- How does Meriwether Lewis find the dog Seaman in the first place?
- What does Seaman do that proves his usefulness to the expedition?

If students struggle, model a fluent retelling.

② Read "They Traveled with Lewis and Clark," pp. 62–65

BEFORE READING Read the genre information on p. 62. Recall the Read Aloud "Johnny Appleseed," rereading portions of the text as needed. We have three examples of historical narrative this week. All of them have been about real people in real historical settings. Which are fiction? (*Lewis and Clark and Me*) Which are nonfiction? ("*Johnny Appleseed*" and "*They Traveled with Lewis and Clark*") What distinguishes the fiction from the nonfiction? (*Lewis and Clark and Me* is narrated by a dog, making it fantasy.)

Read the rest of the panel on p. 62. Then have students scan the pages, identifying the text features.

DURING READING Have students read along with you while tracking the print or do a choral reading of the selection. Stop to discuss the special qualities that both York and Sacagawea brought to the expedition and the special contributions they made.

AFTER READING Have students share their reactions to the selection. Then guide them through the Reading Across Texts and Writing Across Texts activities, prompting if necessary.

- How did the person help the expedition on a day-to-day basis? Was there one action the person did that was especially important?
- Of the three people or characters, which one do you think Lewis is most likely to write to?

Monitor Progress

Word and Story Reading

If... students have difficulty reading multisyllabic words in the selection,	**then...** have them look for and read meaningful parts in the words or have them chunk words with no recognizable parts.
If... students have difficulty reading along with the group,	**then...** have them follow along as they listen to the AudioText.

Advanced

1 Read "They Traveled with Lewis and Clark"

CRITICAL THINKING Have students read pp. 62–65 independently. Encourage them to think critically. For example, ask:

- How did York and Sacagawea help the expedition on a day-to-day basis?
- What did each do that was especially helpful?
- Describe the kinds of jobs that would be necessary to do every day in order to keep an expedition such as that of Lewis and Clark functioning smoothly.

AFTER READING Discuss the selection and Reading Across Texts. Have students do Writing Across Texts independently.

2 Extend Genre Study

RESEARCH Have students use online or print resources to find biographical information about other explorers of the North American continent during the 1700s or 1800s. Have them take careful notes from at least two sources, citing their sources.

WRITE Have students use their research on explorers to create American Explorer trading cards. Each student should choose one explorer and summarize that person's life and important deeds in just a few bulleted points. Then have students prepare trading cards, using 4-by-6-inch index cards. They should put the biographical information on one side and a portrait, if possible, on the other side. Finally, have students share their trading cards with classmates.

AudioText

Lewis and Clark and Me

Group Time

ONLINE

PearsonSuccessNet.com

1 Reread for Fluency

MODEL Read aloud pp. 3–5 of the Leveled Reader *The Long Trip West,* emphasizing pauses that separate meaningful phrases or word groups. Have students note how punctuation suggests where many of these pauses should come. Then read pp. 6–7 without pauses. Have students tell you which model was easier to understand. Discuss how paying attention to punctuation and pausing after meaningful phrases not only helps listeners understand what you are reading but sounds more natural, like common speech patterns.

PRACTICE Have students reread passages from *The Long Trip West* with a partner or individually. For optimal fluency, they should reread three or four times. As students read, monitor fluency and provide corrective feedback. Assess the fluency of students in this group using p. 65a.

2 Retell Leveled Reader *The Long Trip West*

Model how to skim the book, retelling as you skim. Then ask students to retell the book, one page at a time. They can use the illustrations as aids to retelling. Prompt them as needed.

- What was this selection mainly about?
- Tell me about the major events in order.

Monitor Progress

Fluency

If... students have difficulty reading fluently,	**then...** provide additional fluency practice by pairing nonfluent readers with fluent ones.

For alternate Leveled Reader lesson plans that teach
Author's Purpose, Answer Questions,
and **Lesson Vocabulary,** see pp. LR10–LR18.

On-Level

DAY 5

1 Reread for Fluency ROUTINE

MODEL Read aloud pp. 3–4 of the Leveled Reader *Lewis and Clark,* emphasizing pauses to set off meaningful phrases and word groups. Have students note how punctuation divides sentences into meaningful phrases and provides clues for where pauses should come. Discuss how reading with pauses not only sounds more like natural speech but actually helps a listener understand what you are reading.

PRACTICE Have students reread passages from *Lewis and Clark* with a partner or individually. For optimal fluency, they should reread three or four times. As students read, monitor fluency and provide corrective feedback. Students in this group are assessed in Week 3.

2 Retell Leveled Reader *Lewis and Clark*

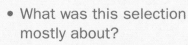

Have students use the map, heads, and illustrations as guides to summarize the important events they learned from the book. Prompt as needed:

- What was this selection mostly about?
- Tell me about the major events in order.
- What different Native American tribes did the Lewis and Clark expedition encounter?

Advanced

DAY 5

1 Reread for Fluency ROUTINE

PRACTICE Have students reread passages from the Leveled Reader *Two Great Rivers* with a partner or individually. As students read, monitor fluency and provide corrective feedback. If students read fluently on the first reading, they do not need to reread three to four times. Students in this group were assessed in Week 1.

2 Revisit Leveled Reader *Two Great Rivers*

RETELL Have students retell the Leveled Reader *Two Great Rivers.*

NOW TRY THIS Have students complete their projects. You may wish to review their sources and see whether they need any additional supplies or resources. Have them present their projects.

DAY

1

Leveled Reader Database ONLINE

PearsonSuccessNet.com

Strategic Intervention

ROUTINE

1 Build Background

REINFORCE CONCEPTS Display the Traveling America Concept Web. This week's concept is *traveling America*. What does "Going Places" tell us about traveling in America? Discuss the meaning of each word on the web, using the definitions on p. 66l and the Concept Vocabulary Routine on p. DI·1.

CONNECT TO READING This week you will read about a man who traveled America and told his grandchildren stories of his travels. What does "Going Places" tell us about traveling in America? *(how large it is; some of the places you might see)*

2 Read Leveled Reader *Grandpa's Scrapbook*

BEFORE READING Using the Picture Walk Routine on p. DI·1, guide students through the text focusing on key concepts and vocabulary. For example, say:

pp. 3–5 Look at these illustrations. What do you think the story is about? *(It's about a man showing his scrapbook to his grandchildren.)* That's right. Scrapbooks often contain souvenirs and mementos of people's travels.

pp. 12–13 How can you tell that the illustrations on these pages are supposed to be pages from the scrapbook? *(The background looks like pages, and the illustrations look like photos or postcards.)* Right. The illustration on p. 13 seems to be postcards from three locations.

DURING READING Read pp. 3–5 aloud, while students track the print. Do a choral reading of pp. 6–9. If students are capable, have them read and discuss the remainder of the book with a partner. Ask: What does this story tell you about Mark Twain and his travels around the United States?

AFTER READING Encourage pairs of students to discuss what made Mark Twain want to be a steamboat pilot. In *Grandpa's Scrapbook*, we learned about Mark Twain's desire for adventure and his love of the Mississippi River. Learning about one man's love of travel will help us as we read *Grandfather's Journey*.

Monitor Progress

Selection Reading and Comprehension

If... students have difficulty reading the selection with a partner,	**then...** have them follow along as they listen to the Online Leveled Reader Audio.
If... students have trouble understanding who Mark Twain is,	**then...** reread p. 16 and discuss the information together.

For alternate Leveled Reader lesson plans that teach
 **Sequence,** **Graphic Organizers,** and
Lesson Vocabulary, see pp. LR19–LR27.

On-Level

ROUTINE

① Build Background

DEVELOP VOCABULARY Write the word *route* and ask students to define it in their own words. *(a path or road for traveling)* Name a synonym for the word *route. (path, road, course, direction)* Repeat this activity with the word *rural* and other words from the Leveled Reader *Childhood in Pre-War Japan.* Use the Concept Vocabulary Routine on p. DI·1 as needed.

② **Read** Leveled Reader
Childhood in Pre-War Japan

BEFORE READING Have students create T-charts with the labels Japan and America. This book provides a great deal of information about the culture and customs of Japan. As you read, record this information under the column labeled Japan in your T-chart. Then record what you already know about the culture and history of America under the column labeled America.

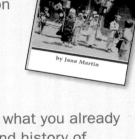

DURING READING Have students follow along as you read pp. 4–9. Then let them complete the book on their own. Remind students to add information to their T-charts as they read.

AFTER READING Have students compare the information on their T-charts. Point out that the information they have recorded will help them as they read *Grandfather's Journey.*

Advanced

ROUTINE

① **Read** Leveled Reader
Innocent Prisoners!

BEFORE READING Recall the Read Aloud "Going Places." How does "Going Places" help you better understand America? *(It describes the size and some of the things you'd find if you traveled America.)* Today you will read a fictional story that will tell you about one period in American history.

CRITICAL THINKING Have students read the Leveled Reader independently. Encourage them to think critically. For example, ask:

- Why do you think the government thought that Japanese Americans were a threat?
- Why is it unfair to imprison people based on their race or ancestry?

AFTER READING Review this week's vocabulary words with students. Then give students three different definitions for each vocabulary word, including one that is fantastical or silly. Have them select the correct definition and use the word in a sentence.

② Independent Extension Activity

RESEARCH INTERNMENT CAMPS Have students read "America Makes Amends" on p. 20 of *Innocent Prisoners!* Then have them begin research on Japanese internment camps, including the number of people who were sent to them and what life was like for the people who lived in them. Students will continue their research throughout the week.

Grandfather's Journey
Group Time

DAY 2

Monitor Progress

Word and Story Reading

If... students have difficulty reading multisyllabic words in the selection,	**then...** have them look for and read meaningful parts in the words or have them chunk words with no recognizable parts.
If... students need practice reading words fluently,	**then...** use the Fluent Word Reading Routine on the DI tab.
If... students have difficulty reading along with the group,	**then...** have them follow along as they listen to the AudioText.

Strategic Intervention

ROUTINE

① Build Background

LESSON VOCABULARY Use p. 68b to review the meanings of *amazed, bewildered, homeland, longed, sculptures, still,* and *towering.* Have individuals practice reading words from word cards.

DECODING MULTISYLLABIC WORDS Write *riverboat,* saying the word as you write it. Then model how to use meaningful parts to read longer words. *First I look to see if I know any of the parts of the word. I see river at the beginning of the word, and boat at the end. I know that a river is a flowing body of water and a boat is something that travels on water. So I think riverboat is "a boat that travels on rivers."*

Use the Multisyllabic Word Routine on p. DI•1 to help students read these other words from *Grandfather's Journey: steamship, reminded, factories, seacoast, songbird,* and *homesick.* Be sure students understand the meanings of words such as *reminded* and *homesick.*

Use *Strategies for Word Analysis,* Lesson 3, with students who have difficulty mastering word analysis and need practice with decodable text.

② Read *Grandfather's Journey,* pp. 70–77

BEFORE READING *Grandpa's Scrapbook* told a story about one man's experiences and travels around the United States. Think about that story as you read *Grandfather's Journey.*

Using the Picture Walk Routine on p. DI•1, guide students through the text asking questions such as those listed below. Read the question on p. 71. Together, set a purpose for reading.

pp. 72–73 What clues on these pages show you that the man in the illustration is on a journey? *(land on the water's horizon; the steamship)*

pp. 74–75 Do the illustrations on these pages appear to have the same setting? *(No, each one looks different.)* Right, the illustrations seem to be showing a movement from one place to another.

DURING READING Have students begin a time line of the important events in *Grandfather's Journey.* The first event will be "The grandfather leaves Japan as a young man." Follow the Guiding Comprehension routine on pp. 72–77. Have students read along with you while tracking the print or do a choral reading. Stop every two pages to add events to the time line. Prompt as necessary.

- What did the narrator's grandfather leave his homeland to do?
- Why did the narrator's grandfather return to his village in Japan?

AFTER READING What has happened so far? What do you think will happen next? Reread passages for comprehension as needed.

Advanced

ROUTINE

DAY 2

① Build Background

DICTIONARY/GLOSSARY Choose and read a sentence from the selection containing an unusual or difficult word, such as this passage from p. 3 of *Innocent Prisoners!:* "The U.S. government moved all Japanese and Japanese Americans to internment camps or relocation centers . . ." What does the word *internment* mean? Use a dictionary or glossary to help you if you don't know the meaning of the word. (Internment *is the confinement of someone regarded as a security threat.*) What did you do to figure out the meaning of the word? (*I looked for context clues, and looked the word up in a dictionary to see if my conclusion about its meaning was correct.*)

② Read *Grandfather's Journey*, pp. 70–77

BEFORE READING Today you will read a story about a Japanese man who leaves his home country to travel and live in America. As you read, think about what you already learned about traveling in America from "Going Places."

Have students create a T-Chart for their Strategy Response Log (p. 70). Encourage them to add to it as they read.

CREATIVE THINKING Have students read pp. 70–77 independently. Encourage them to think critically and creatively. For example, ask:

• How do you think the narrator's grandfather felt when he first arrived in America?

AFTER READING Encourage pairs of students to discuss *Grandfather's Journey* and discuss what they have noted in their Strategy Response Logs. Ask students to imagine that they are the narrator's grandfather, and have them write a letter to their family in Japan explaining what they have seen so far and what they have enjoyed most.

AudioText

Grandfather's Journey
Group Time

ROUTINE

DAY 3

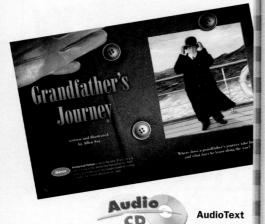

Audio CD AudioText

① Reinforce Comprehension

⊙ SKILL SEQUENCE Have students explain the meaning of *sequence (the order in which events happen)* and list some of the clue words that signal sequence *(first, last, next, then, finally, before, after, later, meanwhile).* If necessary, review the meaning of sequence and provide a model. Sequence refers to the order in which events happen. If someone says, "Before I went to school, I ate breakfast," I know that person first ate breakfast, and then went to school. Without the clue word *before,* I would have thought that the person went to school and ate breakfast afterward. The clue word *before* helps me to determine the sequence of events.

Review the clue words that signal sequence, and ask students to provide additional signal words. Have students take turns using each of the clue words in a sentence to demonstrate a sequence.

② Read *Grandfather's Journey,* pp. 78–81

BEFORE READING Have students retell what happened in the story so far. Ask: How can creating a graphic organizer such as a time line help you understand the sequence of events in the story? *(The time line shows each event in the order they happened.)* Right. Graphic organizers are meant to help you organize and better understand what you read. Remind students to add events to the time line begun yesterday as they read. **⊙ STRATEGY Graphic Organizers**

DURING READING Follow the Guiding Comprehension routine on pp. 78–81. Have students read along with you while tracking print or do a choral reading. Stop every two pages to ask students what has happened so far and add to the time line. Prompt as necessary.

- What happened to keep the narrator's grandfather from going on the trip to California that he planned?
- What did the narrator's grandparents do after the war ended?

AFTER READING Why did the narrator and his grandfather both love Japan and America so much? Reread with students for comprehension as needed. Tell them that tomorrow they will read "A Look at Two Lands," an informational article that explains how you might find out more about the two countries you've been reading about.

Monitor Progress

Word and Story Reading

If... students have difficulty reading multisyllabic words in the selection,	**then...** have them look for and read meaningful parts in the words or have them chunk words with no recognizable parts.
If... students have difficulty reading along with the group,	**then...** have them follow along as they listen to the AudioText.

Advanced

ROUTINE

1 Extend Comprehension

SKILL SEQUENCE Remind students that sequence is the order in which the story's events occur. Have volunteers explain a sequence that is part of their everyday routine, such as preparing for school, helping with dinner, or preparing for an activity done away from school.

STRATEGY GRAPHIC ORGANIZERS Remind students that graphic organizers can be used to organize information. Have students create a time line of how they spent last summer. The time line should start on the day school let out and end the day school started again.

2 Read *Grandfather's Journey*, pp. 78–81

BEFORE READING Have students recall what has happened in the selection so far. Remind them to pay attention to the sequence of events and to use a time line or sequence chart to help them keep track of the story's events.

THINK CREATIVELY Have students read pp. 78–81 independently. Encourage them to think critically and creatively. For example, ask:

• In what way do you think his grandfather's stories affected the author's decision to come to California?

AFTER READING Have students complete the Strategy Response Log activity (p. 80). Have students meet with you to discuss the selection and how the author makes both Japan and California sound desirable. Have students write a paragraph explaining how the story would have been different if the author had shown a strong preference for one or the other.

Audio CD   AudioText

Grandfather's Journey
Group Time

Audio CD AudioText

Strategic Intervention

ROUTINE

1 Practice Retelling

REVIEW STORY ELEMENTS Help students identify the main characters and the setting of *Grandfather's Journey*. Then guide them in using the Retelling Cards to list story events in sequence. Prompt students to include important details.

RETELL Using the Retelling Cards, have students work in pairs to retell *Grandfather's Journey*. Monitor retelling and prompt students to include important details. For example, say:

- Tell me what this story is about in a few sentences.
- Why do you think the author wrote this story?
- What is the author trying to tell us or teach us?

If students struggle, model a fluent retelling.

2 Read "A Look at Two Lands"

BEFORE READING Read the genre information on p. 84. Point out that students use online reference sources to find information and learn new things. As we read "A Look at Two Lands," look for interesting information about Japan and California.

Read the rest of the panel on p. 84. Have students read the title and identify the topic of this selection. *(Japan and California)* Call attention to the sequence question at the bottom of p. 85. Ask: Which type of online source might you use if you wanted to know where Japan can be found on a map of the world? *(an online atlas)*

DURING READING Have students read along with you while tracking the print or do a choral reading of the selection. Stop to discuss any text features that might be difficult to understand, such as the different web pages, the locator map, and the cursor arrow.

AFTER READING Have students share their reactions to the selection. Then guide them through the Reading Across Texts and Writing Across Texts activities, prompting if necessary.

- What do you think would be the best part of living in the place you chose?
- What do you think would be the best part of living in the place you didn't choose?

Monitor Progress

Word and Selection Reading

If... students have difficulty reading multisyllabic words in the selection,	**then...** have them look for and read meaningful parts in the words or have them chunk words with no recognizable parts.
If... students have difficulty reading along with the group,	**then...** have them follow along as they listen to the AudioText.

DI•28 This Land Is Your Land • Week 3

ROUTINE

Advanced

1 Read "A Look at Two Lands"

CRITICAL THINKING Have students read pp. 84–87 independently. Encourage them to think critically. For example, ask:

- What similarities do you see between the country of Japan and the state of California?
- Why do you think someone from one of these cultures might have a great appreciation for the other?

AFTER READING Have students meet with you to discuss the selection and Reading Across Texts. Have students do Writing Across Texts independently.

2 Extend Genre Study

RESEARCH Have students use online reference sources to find more information about Allen Say, the author of *Grandfather's Journey.* Have them find more information about the place where he was born and when he moved to the United States.

WRITE Ask students to use the information they've found about the author to write a short biography of his early life. Have them present their biographies to each other or to you.

DAY 4

Audio CD   AudioText

Grandfather's Journey
Group Time

ONLINE

PearsonSuccessNet.com

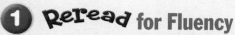

ROUTINE

1 Reread for Fluency

MODEL Read aloud pp. 3–5 of the Leveled Reader *Grandpa's Scrapbook,* pausing at commas and periods and using a rate appropriate to the story. Have students notice how your tempo matches the pace of the writing. Then read pp. 6–7 very quickly and without pauses. Have students identify which model sounded better. Discuss how reading at an appropriate tempo and rate creates a more enjoyable and engaging rhythm.

PRACTICE Have students reread passages from *Grandpa's Scrapbook* with a partner or individually. For optimal fluency, they should read three or four times. As students read, monitor fluency and provide corrective feedback. Students in this group are assessed in Weeks 2 and 4.

2 Retell Leveled Reader *Grandpa's Scrapbook*

Model how to skim the book, retelling as you skim. Then ask students to retell the book from beginning to end. Prompt them as needed.

- Where and when does this story take place?
- Tell me what this story is about in a few sentences.

Monitor Progress

Fluency
If... students have difficulty reading fluently,	**then...** provide additional fluency practice by pairing nonfluent readers with fluent ones.

For alternate Leveled Reader lesson plans that teach
⟳ **Sequence,** ⟳ **Graphic Organizers,** and
Lesson Vocabulary, see pp. LR19–LR27.

On-Level

1 Reread for Fluency ROUTINE

MODEL Read aloud pp. 4–5 of the Leveled Reader *Childhood in Pre-War Japan,* using a rate appropriate to the selection. Have students notice how your tempo matches the pace of the writing. Discuss how reading with the appropriate rate helps readers and listeners better understand what is being read.

PRACTICE Have students reread passages from *Childhood in Pre-War Japan* with a partner or individually. For optimal fluency, they should reread three or four times. As students read, monitor fluency and provide corrective feedback. Assess the fluency of students in this group using p. 87a.

2 Retell Leveled Reader *Childhood in Pre-War Japan*

Have students retell the book using chapter titles and subheads to summarize the most important information in the book. Prompt as needed.

- What was this selection mostly about?
- What did you learn from reading this selection?
- Why do you think the author wrote this selection?

Advanced

1 Reread for Fluency ROUTINE

PRACTICE Have students reread passages from the Leveled Reader *Innocent Prisoners!* with a partner or individually. As students read, monitor fluency and provide corrective feedback. If students read fluently on the first reading, they do not need to reread three to four times. Students in this group were assessed in Week 1.

2 Revisit Leveled Reader *Innocent Prisoners!*

RETELL Have students retell the Leveled Reader *Innocent Prisoners!*

RESEARCH INTERNMENT CAMPS Have students complete their research on internment camps. Students may then present their findings to you or to the class.

Group Time

DAY 1

Leveled Reader Database
ONLINE
PearsonSuccessNet.com

ROUTINE

1 Build Background

REINFORCE CONCEPTS Display The Southwest Concept Web. This week's concept is *the Southwest.* The Southwest is a region of the United States that includes the states of Oklahoma, Texas, New Mexico, and Arizona. It is rich in history and culture. Discuss the meaning of each word on the web, using the definitions on p. 88l and the Concept Vocabulary Routine on p. DI·1.

CONNECT TO READING This week you will read a modern fairy tale set in the Southwest. It shows the region's landscape and culture. "Growing Up in the Old West" talks about children's lives years ago in the Southwest frontier. How was life different for kids on the frontier than it is for you today? How is it the same? *(Responses will vary.)*

2 Read Leveled Reader *Flash Flood*

BEFORE READING Using the Picture Walk Routine on p. DI·1, guide students through the text focusing on key concepts and vocabulary. Ask questions such as:

p. 4 This story features people and places typical of the Southwest. What kind of job do you think the man on the horse does? *(He works as a cowboy.)* What is he doing? *(trying to put his rope over the bull's head)* Yes. Cowboys use lassoes—long ropes with a loop on the end—to herd cattle.

p. 8 This picture shows a landscape, including a riverbed, typically found in the Southwest. Do you know of any other things found in the southwestern landscape? *(Possible response: mountains)*

DURING READING Read pp. 3–5 aloud, while students track the print. Do a choral reading of pp. 6–9. If students are capable, have them read and discuss the remainder of the book with a partner. Ask: What features of the Southwest are written about in the story?

AFTER READING Encourage pairs of students to discuss the geographical and cultural features of the Southwest. We read *Flash Flood* to learn about the environment of the Southwest. This information will help us as we read *The Horned Toad Prince.*

Monitor Progress

Selection Reading and Comprehension

If… students have difficulty reading the selection with a partner,	**then…** have them follow along as they listen to the Online Leveled Reader Audio.
If… students have trouble understanding the dangers of flash floods,	**then…** reread p. 8 and discuss the illustration together.

For alternate Leveled Reader lesson plans that teach
🔵 **Author's Purpose,** 🔵 **Story Structure,** and
Lesson Vocabulary, see pp. LR28–LR36.

On-Level

ROUTINE

1 Build Background

DEVELOP VOCABULARY Write the word *rodeo* and ask students to define it in their own words. *(a show with horses and cowboys)* What activities occur at a rodeo? *(Cowboys rope cattle and ride horses.)* Repeat this activity with the word *traditions* and other words from the Leveled Reader *From Spain to America.* Use the Concept Vocabulary Routine on p. DI·1 as needed.

2 Read Leveled Reader
From Spain to America

BEFORE READING Have students create webs with the label Spanish Explorers. This book tells how Spanish explorers settled in the southwestern United States. As you read, look for information about their experiences and what they contributed to the culture of the Southwest.

DURING READING Have students follow along as you read pp. 3–9. Then let them complete the book on their own. Remind students to add information to their webs as they read.

AFTER READING Have students compare the information in their webs. Point out that information about Spanish explorers and their influence on the Southwest will help them as they read tomorrow's selection *The Horned Toad Prince.*

Advanced

ROUTINE

1 Read Leveled Reader
The Diné

BEFORE READING Recall the Read Aloud selection "Growing Up in the Old West." What do you think was the most difficult part of growing up in the Old West in the 1800s and early 1900s? *(not many children to play with)* Today you will read about a group of people who also settled in the Southwest, the Diné, long before people on the American frontier arrived.

CRITICAL THINKING Have students read the Leveled Reader independently. Encourage them to think critically. For example, ask:

- The author says on p. 4 that the Diné might be called early environmentalists. What are some of the ways they demonstrated this?
- In what ways were the Diné feared by others? Why did they eventually fear other people?

AFTER READING Have students review the selection to find five or more unfamiliar words and determine their meanings by looking at word structure, such as base words and prefixes, or by consulting a dictionary. Then ask them to write statements or questions that both include the words and convey their meanings. Encourage students to meet with you to discuss the selection and the statements or questions they wrote.

2 Independent Extension Activity

NOW TRY THIS Assign "Now Try This" on pp. 22–23 of *The Diné* for students to work on throughout the week.

The Horned Toad Prince
Group Time

Audio CD AudioText

Monitor Progress

Word and Story Reading

If... students have difficulty reading multisyllabic words in the selection,	**then...** have them look for and read meaningful parts in the words or have them chunk words with no recognizable parts.
If... students need practice reading words fluently,	**then...** use the Fluent Word Reading Routine on the DI tab.
If... students have difficulty reading along with the group,	**then...** have them follow along as they listen to the AudioText.

Strategic Intervention

ROUTINE

1 Word Study/Phonics

LESSON VOCABULARY Use p. 90b to review the meanings of *bargain, favor, lassoed, offended, prairie, riverbed,* and *shrieked.* Have individuals practice reading the words from word cards.

DECODING MULTISYLLABIC WORDS Write *tumbleweed,* saying the word as you write it. Then model how to use meaningful parts to read longer words. *First I ask myself if I see any parts that I know. I see tumble at the beginning of the word and weed at the end. I know that to tumble is "to roll end over end," and that a weed is a "wild plant." So I think a tumbleweed is "a wild plant that rolls around."*

Use the Multisyllabic Word Routine on p. DI·1 to help students read these other words from *The Horned Toad Prince: gully, vulture, whipping, splintered,* and *retrieved.* Be sure students understand the meaning of words such as *gully* and *splintered.*

Use *Strategies for Word Analysis,* Lesson 4, with students who have difficulty mastering word analysis and need practice with decodable text.

2 Read *The Horned Toad Prince,* pp. 92–99

BEFORE READING *Flash Flood* showed conditions typical of the Southwest. Think about this as you read *The Horned Toad Prince.*

Using the Picture Walk Routine on p. DI·1, guide students through the text asking questions such as those listed below. Read the question on p. 93. Together, set a purpose for reading.

p. 94 What characteristics of a cowboy does the girl in the picture have? *(She's wearing a cowboy hat, using a lasso, and riding a horse.)* Yes. She is wearing clothes and traveling the way cowboys do.

pp. 92–93 This animal is a small reptile called a horned toad or a horned lizard. What characteristics do you think it would need to survive in the Southwest? *(doesn't need much water, can live in high temperatures)* Yes. Parts of the Southwest are very dry and hot, so animals who live there must be able to survive in those conditions.

DURING READING Follow the Guiding Comprehension routine on pp. 94–99. Have students read along with you while tracking the print or do a choral reading. Stop every two pages to ask what has happened so far. Prompt as necessary.

• Why does Reba Jo's father warn her to stay away from dry riverbeds?
• What did Reba Jo do when the horned toad got her hat from the well?

AFTER READING What has happened in the selection so far? What do you think will happen next? Reread passages as needed.

DAY
2

Advanced

ROUTINE

1 Extend Vocabulary

CONTEXT CLUES Choose and read a sentence or passage containing a difficult word, such as this passage from p. 9 of *The Diné:* "The Diné raided the Spanish settlements. In time they became skilled raiders. They stole thousands of animals for their herds." What does the word *raider* mean? *(Raiders are people who steal from others.)* How did you determine the word's meaning? *(I used the context clue "stole thousands of animals.")* Discuss why context clues are helpful, and remind students to use the strategy as they read *The Horned Toad Prince*.

2 Read *The Horned Toad Prince,* pp. 92–99

BEFORE READING Today you will read a modern fairy tale set in the Southwest. It tells the story of a stubborn girl who learns a valuable lesson from an unusual toad. As you read, think about other stories set in the Southwest that you have read.

Have students develop a question about each of the characters pictured on pp. 92–93 and write them in their Strategy Response Log (p. 92). Encourage them to answer these questions as they read the selection.

CREATIVE THINKING Have students read pp. 92–99 independently. Encourage them to think critically and creatively. For example, ask:

• What parts and events in this story are similar to and different from other fairy tales you have heard, read, or even seen on TV and in movies?

AFTER READING Have partners discuss the selection and share their Strategy Response Log entries. Meet with students and ask them to imagine they are the horned toad telling his family what has happened and what he plans to do about it.

Audio CD   AudioText

The Horned Toad Prince
Group Time

DAY 3

Audio CD AudioText

ROUTINE

1 Reinforce Comprehension

⟳ SKILL AUTHOR'S PURPOSE Have students tell what author's purpose is *(the reason an author has for writing)* and cite various purposes an author may have *(to persuade, inform, express ideas or feelings, entertain).* Remind students that an author may have more than one purpose for writing. If necessary, review the meaning and provide a model. Author's purpose is the reason an author has for writing. If an author writes a recipe for making pancakes, the purpose is to inform.

Ask students to identify the purpose—to entertain, to inform, to persuade—of each writing topic.

> **The funniest story I ever heard**
> **What this school needs most**
> **How to write a research paper**

Then ask, based on what they have read of *The Horned Toad Prince* so far, what they think the author's purpose is. Challenge them to identify more than one purpose.

2 Read *The Horned Toad Prince*, pp. 100–105

BEFORE READING Have students retell what happened in the selection so far. Ask: How did Reba Jo and the horned toad meet? Reread p. 99 and model how to identify the problem in the story. Reba Jo promised the horned toad three things if he got her hat from the well. The horned toad returned Reba Jo's hat to her, but Reba Jo ran away without fulfilling her promise. The horned toad came to Reba Jo's house, and he wants her to keep her promise. This page shows the problem in the story. Remind students to identify elements of story structure as needed as they read the rest of *The Horned Toad Prince.* **⟳ STRATEGY Story Structure**

DURING READING Follow the Guiding Comprehension routine on pp. 100–105. Have students read along with you while tracking print or do a choral reading. Stop every two pages to ask students what has happened so far. Prompt as necessary.

- What was the last thing the horned toad asked of Reba Jo?
- Why had the prince been turned into a horned toad?

AFTER READING What elements of the Southwest does this story show? Did you enjoy the way it showed them? Reread with students for comprehension as needed. Tell them that tomorrow they will read "Horned Lizards & Harvesting Ants," a selection about several species that live in the southwestern United States.

ROUTINE

DAY 3

1 Extend Comprehension

◉ **SKILL** **AUTHOR'S PURPOSE** Review with students the author's purpose in *The Horned Toad Prince.* *(to entertain, to teach a lesson)* Encourage them to think of other purposes an author could have for writing a fairy tale.

◉ **STRATEGY** **STORY STRUCTURE** Have students reread pp. 98–99 independently. Ask them to identify key story elements such as the story's characters and setting. Then ask:

- What is the problem in this story?
- Can you describe the rising action?
- How does the story's organization help you identify the author's purpose?

2 Read *The Horned Toad Prince,* pp. 100–105

BEFORE READING Have students recall what has happened in the selection so far. Remind them to look for the author's purpose and to identify elements of the story's structure as they read the remainder of the selection.

CRITICAL THINKING Have students read pp. 100–105 independently. Encourage them to think critically. For example, ask:

- How has the author used characteristics of the geography and people of the Southwest and turned them into an enjoyable story?

AFTER READING Have students complete the Strategy Response Log Activity (p. 104). Then ask them to write their own fairy tale. Remind them to think about their purpose(s) for writing and to include elements of story structure such as characters, setting, main problem, and rising action.

Audio CD   **AudioText**

Group Time

Audio CD   AudioText

ROUTINE

1 Practice Retelling

REVIEW STORY ELEMENTS Help students identify the main characters and the setting of *The Horned Toad Prince*. List the ideas students mention. Then guide them in using the Retelling Cards to list story events in sequence. Prompt students to include important details.

RETELL Using the Retelling Cards, have students work in pairs to retell *The Horned Toad Prince*. Monitor retelling, and prompt students as needed. For example, ask:

- What is the problem in the story?
- Why do you think the author wrote this story?

If students struggle, model a fluent retelling.

2 Read "Horned Lizards & Harvesting Ants"

BEFORE READING Read the genre information on p. 108. Recall the Read Aloud "Growing Up in the Old West," rereading portions of the text as needed. We have read several selections about the Southwest this week. What is the focus of "Growing Up in the Old West"? *(what life was like for children growing up on the frontier)* As we read "Horned Lizards & Harvesting Ants," think about other aspects of the Southwest that the selection shows.

Read the rest of the panel on p. 108. Then have students scan the pages looking at the photo captions.

DURING READING Have students read along with you while tracking the print or do a choral reading of the selection. Stop to discuss difficult vocabulary, such as the words *saguaro, camouflaged, miniature,* and *armored.*

AFTER READING Have students meet with you to share their reactions to the selection. Then guide them through the Reading Across Texts and Writing Across Texts activities, prompting as necessary.

- Describe the way the horned toad acts in *The Horned Toad Prince*. How does the horned lizard act in "Horned Lizards & Harvesting Ants"?
- What does the horned toad look like? What does the horned lizard look like?

Monitor Progress

Word and Selection Reading

If... students have difficulty reading multisyllabic words in the selection,	**then...** have them look for and read meaningful parts in the words or have them chunk words with no recognizable parts.
If... students have difficulty reading along with the group,	**then...** have them follow along as they listen to the AudioText.

Advanced

1 Read "Horned Lizards & Harvesting Ants"

CRITICAL THINKING Have students read pp. 108–111 independently. Encourage them to think critically and to support their opinions. For example, ask:

- How does the use of photo captions enhance the author's purpose of informing readers about horned lizards and harvesting ants?
- What descriptive language does the author use to show what life is like in the Sonoran Desert?

AFTER READING Discuss the selection and Reading Across Texts. Have students do Writing Across Texts independently.

2 Extend Genre Study

RESEARCH Have students use online or print resources to find more expository nonfiction about unusual animal species or weather conditions in different areas of the United States. Have them make a list of titles, noting the unique features of the particular region that each selection includes.

WRITE Have students choose something unique to a region of the United States, such as a species of bird found in the West or a type of snowstorm typical of the Northeast, and write a report on it. Encourage them to use descriptive language.

DAY 4

Audio CD AudioText

The Horned Toad Prince

Group Time

Leveled Reader
Database
ONLINE

PearsonSuccessNet.com

ROUTINE

1 Reread for Fluency

MODEL Read aloud pp. 12–13 of the Leveled Reader *Flash Flood,* emphasizing the volume of your voice. Have students note the change in volume of your voice during different parts of the selection. Then read pp. 14–15, beginning at a high volume and ending at a low volume. Have students tell you which model sounded better. Discuss the importance of reading at a volume appropriate to the sizes of an audience and a room.

PRACTICE Have students reread passages from *Flash Flood* with a partner or individually. For optimal fluency, they should reread three or four times. As students read, monitor fluency and provide corrective feedback. Assess the fluency of students in this group using p. 111a.

2 Retell Leveled Reader *Flash Flood*

Model how to retell the selection using illustrations. Then ask students to retell the selection, one event at a time. Prompt them as needed.

- Tell me about the major events in order.
- Why do you think the author wrote this selection?

Monitor Progress

Fluency

If... students have difficulty reading fluently,	**then...** provide additional fluency practice by pairing nonfluent readers with fluent ones.

For alternate Leveled Reader lesson plans that teach
🔄 **Author's Purpose,** 🔄 **Story Structure,** and
Lesson Vocabulary, see pp. LR28–LR36.

For alternate Leveled Reader lesson plans that teach
🔄 **Author's Purpose,** 🔄 **Story Structure,** and
Lesson Vocabulary, see pp. LR28–LR36.

On-Level

DAY 5

1 Reread for Fluency
ROUTINE

MODEL Read aloud pp. 4–5 of the Leveled Reader *From Spain to America,* emphasizing the volume of your voice. Have students note the change in volume of your voice during different parts of the selection. Discuss the importance of reading at a volume appropriate to the sizes of an audience and a room.

PRACTICE Have students reread passages from *From Spain to America* with a partner or individually. For optimal fluency, they should reread three or four times. As students read, monitor fluency and provide corrective feedback. Students in this group were assessed in Week 3.

2 Retell Leveled Reader *From Spain to America*

Have students use heads as a guide to summarize the important facts they learned from the book. Prompt as needed.

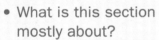

- What is this section mostly about?
- What did you learn from reading this selection?
- What was the author trying to teach us?

Advanced

DAY 5

1 Reread for Fluency
ROUTINE

PRACTICE Have students reread passages from the Leveled Reader *The Diné* with a partner or individually. As students read, monitor fluency and provide corrective feedback. If students read fluently on the first reading, they do not need to reread three to four times. Students in this group were assessed in Week 1.

2 Revisit Leveled Reader *The Diné*

RETELL Have students retell the Leveled Reader *The Diné.*

NOW TRY THIS Have students complete their projects. You may wish to review their work and see whether they need any additional supplies or resources. Have them present their projects.

Group Time

Leveled Reader Database ONLINE

PearsonSuccessNet.com

Strategic Intervention

ROUTINE

1 Build Background

REINFORCE CONCEPTS Display The West Concept Web. This week's concept is *The West.* The West is a region of the United States with a rich landscape, including mountains and volcanoes. Discuss the meaning of each word on the web, using the definitions on p. 112l and the Concept Vocabulary Routine on p. DI·1.

CONNECT TO READING This week you will read about some national parks in the United States, including Yosemite, one of this country's oldest national parks. Located in the West, Yosemite is known throughout the world for its beautiful scenery. What famous land formation was highlighted in "The Volcano Wakes"? *(Mount St. Helens)* How was this volcano formed? *(by many eruptions over thousands of years)*

2 Read Leveled Reader *This Land Is Our Land*

BEFORE READING Using the Picture Walk Routine on p. DI·1, guide students through the text focusing on key concepts and vocabulary. Prompt as needed.

p. 7 This selection tells about how the national park system began. What can you learn about the history and locations of national parks from the time line? *(They are located throughout the United States; some are much older than others.)* Yes. National parks are found in many states and offer a variety of natural features.

pp. 8–9, 14–15 These photographs show some animals found in national parks in the United States. What other animals do you know of that are found in national parks?

DURING READING Read pp. 3–5 aloud, while students track the print. Do a choral reading of pp. 6–9. If students are capable, have them read and discuss the remainder of the book with a partner. Ask: What can you learn about the landscape of the West by visiting Yellowstone, Yosemite, and the Grand Canyon?

AFTER READING Have pairs of students discuss national parks in the United States. We read *This Land Is Our Land* to learn about the national park system and how it began. Understanding how and why these parks were established will help us as we read *Letters Home from Yosemite.*

DAY 1

Monitor Progress

Selection Reading and Comprehension

If... students have difficulty reading the selection with a partner,	then... have them follow along as they listen to the Online Leveled Reader Audio.
If... students have trouble understanding the concept of the national park system,	then... reread pp. 4–7 and discuss the text together.

For alternate Leveled Reader lesson plans that teach **Main Idea, Graphic Organizers, and Lesson Vocabulary,** see pp. LR37–LR45.

On-Level

1 Build Background

DEVELOP VOCABULARY Write the word *volcano* and ask students to define it in their own words. *(a mountain that oozes lava)* What are some characteristics of volcanoes? *(They're large, and they erupt.)* Repeat this activity with the word *geyser* and other words from the Leveled Reader *The Amazing Geography of the West.* Use the Concept Vocabulary Routine on p. DI·1 as needed.

2 Read Leveled Reader
The Amazing Geography of the West

BEFORE READING Have students create webs with the center oval labeled Geography of the West. This book tells about the geographical features of the western United States, including the Rocky and Cascade mountain ranges, and about features found in national parks. As you read, look for facts about these places and features. Record them in your web.

DURING READING Have students follow along as you read pp. 3–9. Then let them complete the book on their own. Remind students to add information to their webs as they read.

AFTER READING Have students compare facts on their webs. Point out how these facts will help them as they read tomorrow's selection *Letters Home from Yosemite.*

Advanced

1 Read Leveled Reader
John Muir: A Man of the Wilderness

BEFORE READING Recall the Read Aloud "The Volcano Wakes." How did the summit of Mount St. Helens become hidden by clouds? *(Lava and ash formed new layers of the mountain, pushing the summit higher.)* Today you will read about naturalist John Muir and his efforts to preserve the natural resources in the West.

CRITICAL THINKING Have students read the Leveled Reader independently. Encourage them to think critically. For example, ask:

- How do national parks reflect the unique qualities of the West?
- How can we help preserve our national parks?

AFTER READING Have students review the selection to find five or more unfamiliar words and determine their meanings by looking at their structure, such as base words and suffixes, or by consulting a dictionary. Then ask them to write statements or questions that both include the words and convey their meanings. Have students meet with you and discuss the selection and the statements or questions they wrote.

2 Independent Extension Activity

GARDEN BUILDERS Assign "Now Try This" on pp. 22–23 of *John Muir: A Man of the Wilderness* for students to work on throughout the week.

Group Time

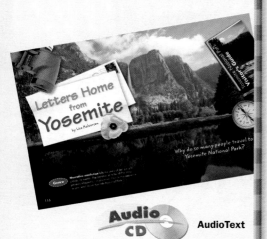

Audio CD AudioText

Strategic Intervention

ROUTINE

1 Word Study/Phonics

LESSON VOCABULARY Use p. 114b to review meanings of *glacier, impressive, naturalist, preserve, slopes, species,* and *wilderness.* Have individuals practice reading the words from word cards.

DECODING MULTISYLLABIC WORDS Write *waterfalls,* saying the word as you write it. Then model how to use meaningful parts to read longer words. I see *water* at the beginning of the word and *falls* at the end. I know *water* is "clear liquid found in nature," and that *fall* means "to drop." So *waterfalls* are "places where water drops."

Use the Multisyllabic Word Routine on p. DI·1 to help students read these other words from *Letters Home from Yosemite: horseback, formations, sometimes, designated, roadsides, endangered, actually, foothills,* and *reintroduced.*

Use *Strategies for Word Analysis,* Lesson 5, with students who have difficulty mastering word analysis and need practice with decodable text.

2 Read *Letters Home from Yosemite,* pp. 116–123

BEFORE READING *This Land Is Your Land* highlighted some natural and historical parks in the United States. Think about this as you read *Letters Home from Yosemite.*

Using the Picture Walk Routine on p. DI·1, guide students through the text asking questions such as those listed below. Read the question on p. 117. Together, set a purpose for reading.

pp. 116–119 What can you learn from the photos of Yosemite National Park? *(There are many mountains, meadows, trees, and rock formations.)* Yes. Yosemite has many natural features.

p. 122 Based on the photo, what can you infer about the tree? *(It is very tall and old.)* Yes. The Grizzly Giant is the name of this tree. It is a sequoia, a species of tree that is the largest in the world. The tree in the photo is about 2,700 years old.

DURING READING Begin a web with Yosemite National Park at the center. Each arm of the web should connect to a place visited, as indicated by the head for each section. Follow the Guiding Comprehension routine on pp. 118–123. Have students read along with you while tracking the print or do a choral reading. Stop every two pages to discuss the places. Prompt as necessary.

• Who were the first people to live in Yosemite?
• Why might people visit Yosemite in the winter?

AFTER READING What have you learned so far? What do you think you will learn about tomorrow? Reread passages as needed.

Monitor Progress

Word and Story Reading

If... students have difficulty reading multisyllabic words in the selection,	**then...** have them look for and read meaningful parts in the words or have them chunk words with no recognizable parts.
If... students need practice reading words fluently,	**then...** use the Fluent Word Reading Routine on the DI tab.
If... students have difficulty reading along with the group,	**then...** have them follow along as they listen to the AudioText.

Advanced

1 Extend Vocabulary

WORD STRUCTURE Choose and read a sentence or passage containing a difficult word, such as this sentence from p. 13 of *John Muir: A Man of the Wilderness*: "They sat under the trees in Yosemite and talked about conservation." What does the word *conservation* mean? *(protection from harm or from being used up)* How did you determine the word's meaning? *(I used the definition of the base word* conserve, *which means "to protect from harm or from being used up.")* Discuss how word structure can help you determine the meaning of unfamiliar words, and remind students to use the strategy for other words as they read *Letters Home from Yosemite*.

2 Read *Letters Home from Yosemite*, pp. 116–123

DAY 2

AudioText

BEFORE READING Today we will read about the geography and wildlife found in Yosemite National Park. As you read, think about the various physical features and wildlife of other national parks you have read about.

Have students write notes on what they already know about Yosemite and other national parks. Encourage them to add three new facts they have learned about Yosemite as they read, as well as questions they might have about their reading for the Strategy Response Logs (p. 116).

CRITICAL THINKING Have students read pp. 118–123 independently. Prompt them to think critically. For example, ask:

• What skills should a travel writer have?

AFTER READING Have partners discuss the selection and share their Strategy Response Log entries. Ask students to write a letter to their local newspaper urging the preservation of Yosemite and other national parks. Have them use facts and persuasive language to convince readers to preserve the area.

Letters Home from Yosemite

Group Time

ROUTINE

DAY 3

Audio CD AudioText

1 Reinforce Comprehension

SKILL MAIN IDEA Have students tell what the main idea of a paragraph is *(the most important thing an author has to say about the topic)* and how supporting details in a paragraph can help a reader identify the main idea. *(They provide other information that tells more about the main idea.)*

Ask students to identify the main idea and supporting details in the paragraph below. For example, ask: Which of the sentences shows the main idea of the paragraph, the sentence that the others tell more about? *(the first sentence)* What details support the main idea? *(Responses should include information from the other sentences.)*

> **Chicago is my favorite place in the world. I visit it twice a year. It has huge museums, great stores, and famous restaurants. Chicago is on Lake Michigan, so in the summer you can swim and play volleyball at the beach.**

2 Read *Letters Home from Yosemite*, pp. 124–127

BEFORE READING Have students summarize what they have read in the selection so far. Ask: Why did the Ahwahneechee call Bridalveil Fall "spirit of the puffing wind"? Remind students about the Yosemite National Park web they began yesterday. A web is a good way to see in a visual way a summary of what you have read or what you know. Have students add to the web as they read the rest of *Letters Home from Yosemite.* **STRATEGY Graphic Organizers**

DURING READING Follow the Guiding Comprehension routine on pp. 124–127. Have students read along with you while tracking print or do a choral reading. Stop after each page to ask students where in Yosemite the author has visited so far. Prompt as necessary.

- How long does it take to climb El Capitan?
- Why did people go to the rivers and streams of Yosemite years ago? Why do they go now?

AFTER READING Reread with students for comprehension as needed. Tell them that tomorrow they will read the song "This Land Is Your Land," a song that tells about the various landscapes of the United States.

Monitor Progress

Word and Selection Reading

If... students have difficulty reading multisyllabic words in the selection,	**then...** have them look for and read meaningful parts in the words or have them chunk words with no recognizable parts.
If... students have difficulty reading along with the group,	**then...** have them follow along as they listen to the AudioText.

Advanced

ROUTINE

DAY 3

1 Extend Comprehension

🎯 **SKILL MAIN IDEA** Have students reread the information about Badger Pass on p. 120. Discuss with them how to determine the main idea of each paragraph and brainstorm possible "titles" for the paragraph.

🎯 **STRATEGY GRAPHIC ORGANIZERS** Ask students to create a concept web with "Badger Pass" in the center. Each arm of the web should connect to a main idea in the text on p. 120, as indicated by a head for each. Then have students use additional arms to connect the main ideas to details that support them.

2 Read *Letters Home from Yosemite*, pp. 124–127

BEFORE READING Have students retell what they have learned in the selection so far. Remind them to think about the main idea of each section as they read. They can make a concept web or other graphic organizer to find the main idea of each section in the remainder of the selection.

CREATIVE THINKING Have students read pp. 124–127 independently. Encourage them to think creatively. For example, ask:

• What do the words *naturalist* and *geologist* have in common? Which other words have similar meanings?

AFTER READING Have students complete the Strategy Response Log activity (p. 126). Then have them create a 60-second radio announcement encouraging people to visit Yosemite National Park. Remind them to include details about the sights a visitor might see. Meet with students before they record their announcements.

Audio CD **AudioText**

Group Time

ROUTINE

DAY 4

Audio CD **AudioText**

1 Practice Retelling

REVIEW MAIN IDEAS Help students identify the main ideas in *Letters Home from Yosemite* by having them review the web they created. Then ask questions to help students differentiate between essential and nonessential information.

RETELL Using the Retelling Cards, have students work with partners to retell the important ideas. Show partners how to summarize in as few words as possible. Monitor retelling and prompt students as needed. For example, ask:

PEARSON Scott Foresman **Retelling Cards** Grade 4

- What was this selection mainly about?
- What did you learn from reading this selection?
- Why do you think the author wrote this selection?

If students struggle, model a fluent reading.

2 Read "This Land Is Your Land"

BEFORE READING Read the genre information on p. 130. Recall the Read Aloud "The Volcano Wakes," rereading portions of the text as needed. We have read selections this week about the geography and physical features found in the American West. What did "The Volcano Wakes" explain about how mountains in the West were created? *(Layers of lava and ash created summits over time.)* As we read "This Land Is Your Land," think about what the song tells about the physical features of the United States.

Read the rest of the panel on p. 130. Then have students scan the pages looking for the chorus and the rhymes and rhythms of the song.

DURING READING Have students read along with you while tracking the print, or do a choral reading or sing-along of the selection. Stop to discuss unfamiliar language, such as the proper noun *Gulf Stream waters.*

AFTER READING Have students share their reactions to the selection. Then guide them through the Reading Across Texts and Writing Across Texts activities, prompting if necessary.

- What natural wonder of Yosemite is your favorite? Why?
- Describe Yosemite using rhyming words that evoke images for the reader, such as those in "This Land Is Your Land."

Monitor Progress

Word and Selection Reading

If... students have difficulty reading multisyllabic words in the selection,	**then...** have them look for and read meaningful parts in the words or have them chunk words with no recognizable parts.
If... students have difficulty reading along with the group,	**then...** have them follow along as they listen to the AudioText.

DAY
4

Advanced

ROUTINE

1 Read "This Land Is Your Land"

CRITICAL THINKING Have students read pp. 130–133 independently. Encourage them to think critically. For example, ask:

- What was the author trying to say about the United States by writing this song?
- What effect does the repetition of the chorus have on the song?

AFTER READING Discuss the song and Reading Across Texts. Have students do Writing Across Texts independently.

2 Extend Genre Study

RESEARCH Have students use online or print resources to locate other traditional and patriotic poems or songs about the United States. Have them make a list of titles and note the images the author shares and the emotions they inspire.

WRITE Have students write song lyrics about their hometown using images that allow the reader to visualize the setting. Encourage them to use rhyming words.

Audio CD **AudioText**

Letters Home from Yosemite

Group Time

DAY **5**

ONLINE

PearsonSuccessNet.com

Strategic Intervention

1 Reread for Fluency

ROUTINE

MODEL Read aloud pp. 10–11 of the Leveled Reader *This Land Is Our Land,* emphasizing how punctuation marks are clues for grouping words together and for pausing. Have students note how you group words together and how pausing after punctuation marks makes your reading sound smooth. Then read pp. 12–13 without pausing. Ask students to compare the two styles and tell which sounded better. Discuss how phrasing makes sentences easier to understand.

PRACTICE Have students reread passages from *This Land Is Our Land* individually, with a partner or with you. For optimal fluency, they should reread three or four times. As students read, monitor fluency and provide corrective feedback. Assess any students you have not yet checked during this unit.

2 Retell Leveled Reader *This Land Is Our Land*

Model how to retell using photographs and headings. Ask students to retell what they have learned from the selection, one section at a time. Prompt them as needed.

• What was this selection mostly about?
• What did you learn from reading this selection?

Monitor Progress
Fluency

If... students have difficulty reading fluently,	**then**... provide additional fluency practice by pairing nonfluent readers with fluent ones.

For alternate Leveled Reader lesson plans that teach ◉**Main Idea,** ◉**Graphic Organizers,** and **Lesson Vocabulary,** see pp. LR37–LR45.

On-Level

1 Reread for Fluency ROUTINE

MODEL Read aloud p. 6 of the Leveled Reader *The Amazing Geography of the West,* emphasizing the punctuation clues for grouping words together and for pausing. Have students note the grouping of your words and your pausing. Discuss how reading *with* punctuation creates a more pleasing rhythm than without it.

PRACTICE Have students reread passages from *The Amazing Geography of the West* individually, with a partner, or with you. For optimal fluency, they should reread three to four times. As students read, monitor fluency and provide corrective feedback. Assess any students you have not checked during this unit.

2 Retell Leveled Reader *The Amazing Geography of the West*

Have students use photographs and captions as a guide to summarize the important facts they have learned from the selection. Prompt as needed.

- What is this selection mostly about?
- What did you learn from reading this selection?

Advanced

1 Reread for Fluency ROUTINE

PRACTICE Have students reread passages from the Leveled Reader *John Muir: A Man of the Wilderness,* with a partner or individually. As students read, monitor fluency and provide corrective feedback. If students read fluently on the first reading, they do not need to reread three to four times. Assess any students you have not checked during this unit.

2 Revisit Leveled Reader *John Muir: A Man of the Wilderness*

RETELL Have students retell the Leveled Reader *John Muir: A Man of the Wilderness.*

NOW TRY THIS Have students complete their projects. You may wish to review their work and see whether they need additional resources or ideas. Have them present their projects.

Sequence

Keeping track of the sequence of events helps students understand what they read. Use this routine to help students develop sequence skills.

1 DISCUSS SEQUENCE

Tell students it is important to keep track of the sequence, or order, of events to understand some stories and articles. Discuss a story recently read in which the sequence of events was crucial to a correct understanding of the story.

2 TEACH CLUE WORDS

Write clue words on the board that can signal sequence, such as *first, next, then,* and *finally.* Explain that these words show the order in which things happen. Also teach that dates and times of the day signal sequence.

3 SEQUENCE SENTENCE STRIPS

Write a clear sequence of events on sentence strips. Partners can work together to place the strips in the correct order. They can retell the events, inserting clue words to show the sequence.

4 RECORD A SEQUENCE ON A CHART

- After reading a story, students can work in pairs to create story sequence charts to show the order of events.

- For a nonfiction selection, partners can create time lines to show the chronological sequence of events.

Title
Because of Winn-Dixie

Characters
Opal, Miss Franny, and Winn-Dixie

Settings
Herman W. Block Memorial Library

Events
Winn-Dixie can't go into the library.
He watches Opal through the window.
Miss Franny screams. She thinks the dog's a bear.
Opal explains it's just her dog.
Miss Franny lets the dog in and tells a story: When she was a little girl, a bear came into the library. She was scared, but she threw a book at it, and it went away.
Opal decides they should be friends.

▲ Graphic Organizer 9

Research on Sequence

"Classes that read widely will encounter all sorts of ways authors play with time; recognizing flashbacks and attending to words and phrases denoting the passage of time or the sequential order of events are crucial to comprehension."

Sharon Kane,
"Teaching Skills Within Meaningful Contexts"

Kane, Sharon. "Teaching Skills Within Meaningful Contexts." *The Reading Teacher,* vol. 52, no. 2 (October 1998), pp. 182–184.

Author's Purpose

Evaluating the author's purpose for writing helps students decide how quickly or slowly and carefully to read. Use this routine to teach author's purpose.

1 DISCUSS AUTHOR'S PURPOSE

Explain that the author's purpose is the author's reason or reasons for writing. Four common reasons for writing are to persuade, to inform, to entertain, or to express ideas or feelings.

2 EXPLAIN ITS USE

Tell students that one reason they need to consider the author's purpose is to adjust their reading rate. If a story is meant to be fun, they may decide to read quickly. If the author wants to explain how something works, they may need to read slowly and carefully.

3 ASK QUESTIONS

Authors don't usually state their purposes for writing, and they often have more than one purpose. Before, during, and after reading a selection, ask questions to help students draw conclusions about the author's purposes: *Why do you think the author wrote this story? What reasons might the author have for writing the story this way? What is the author trying to tell you? Why is the author telling you that?*

4 USE A GRAPHIC ORGANIZER

Have students predict the author's purpose before reading by previewing the title, illustrations, and graphics. During and after reading, students should check and confirm their predictions. Have them record ideas and evidence in a three-column chart.

	Author's Purpose	Why Do You Think So?
Before you read: What do you think it will be?	To entertain	It says 'A Dog's Tale.' That seems like fun.
As you read: What do you think it is?	To entertain and inform	It's told by a dog, but it's about a real journey.
After you read: What was it?		

▲ **Graphic Organizer** 26

Research on Author's Purpose

"Younger and less proficient readers are unlikely to differentiate between 'study' reading and 'fun' reading."

Ruth Garner,
"Metacognition and Self-Monitoring Strategies"

Garner, Ruth. "Metacognition and Self-Monitoring Strategies." In *What Research Has to Say About Reading Instruction,* edited by S. J. Samuels and A. E. Farstrup. Second Edition. International Reading Association, 1992, p. 238.

Sequence

Keeping track of the sequence of events helps students understand what they read. Use this routine to help students develop sequence skills.

1 DISCUSS SEQUENCE

Tell students it is important to keep track of the sequence, or order, of events to understand some stories and articles. Discuss a story recently read in which the sequence of events was crucial to a correct understanding of the story.

2 TEACH CLUE WORDS

Write clue words on the board that can signal sequence, such as *first, next, then,* and *finally.* Explain that these words show the order in which things happen. Also teach that dates and times of the day signal sequence.

3 SEQUENCE SENTENCE STRIPS

Write a clear sequence of events on sentence strips. Partners can work together to place the strips in the correct order. They can retell the events, inserting clue words to show the sequence.

4 RECORD A SEQUENCE ON A CHART

- After reading a story, students can work in pairs to create story sequence charts to show the order of events.

- For a nonfiction selection, partners can create time lines to show the chronological sequence of events.

Title
Grandfather's Journey

Characters
The narrator and his grandfather

Setting
Japan and California

Problem
Grandfather can't visit America again.

Events
A grandfather travels all over America.
He likes California best. He settles his family there.
He lives there many years but misses home.
He moves back to Japan.
The grandfather plans a trip to California, but war breaks out. He never returns to California.
One day, the narrator/grandson moves to California. Then he understands his grandfather better.

▲ **Graphic Organizer** 9

Research on Sequence

"Classes that read widely will encounter all sorts of ways authors play with time; recognizing flashbacks and attending to words and phrases denoting the passage of time or the sequential order of events are crucial to comprehension."

Sharon Kane,
"Teaching Skills Within Meaningful Contexts"

Kane, Sharon. "Teaching Skills Within Meaningful Contexts." *The Reading Teacher,* vol. 52, no. 2 (October 1998), pp. 182–184.

Author's Purpose

Evaluating the author's purpose for writing helps students decide how quickly or slowly and carefully to read. Use this routine to teach author's purpose.

1 DISCUSS AUTHOR'S PURPOSE

Explain that the author's purpose is the author's reason or reasons for writing. Four common reasons for writing are to persuade, to inform, to entertain, or to express ideas or feelings.

2 EXPLAIN ITS USE

Tell students that one reason they need to consider the author's purpose is to adjust their reading rate. If a story is meant to be fun, they may decide to read quickly. If the author wants to explain how something works, they may need to read slowly and carefully.

3 ASK QUESTIONS

Authors don't usually state their purposes for writing, and they often have more than one purpose. Before, during, and after reading a selection, ask questions to help students draw conclusions about the author's purposes: *Why do you think the author wrote this story? What reasons might the author have for writing the story this way? What is the author trying to tell you? Why is the author telling you that?*

4 USE A GRAPHIC ORGANIZER

Have students predict the author's purpose before reading by previewing the title, illustrations, and graphics. During and after reading, students should check and confirm their predictions. Have them record ideas and evidence in a three-column chart.

	Author's Purpose	Why Do You Think So?
Before you read: What do you think it will be?	To entertain. But maybe I'll learn something about toads.	The pictures look funny.
As you read: What do you think it is?	To entertain	It's funny.
After you read: What was it?		

▲ **Graphic Organizer** 26

Research on Author's Purpose

"Younger and less proficient readers are unlikely to differentiate between 'study' reading and 'fun' reading."

Ruth Garner,
"Metacognition and Self-Monitoring Strategies"

Garner, Ruth. "Metacognition and Self-Monitoring Strategies." In *What Research Has to Say About Reading Instruction,* edited by S. J. Samuels and A. E. Farstrup. Second Edition. International Reading Association, 1992, p. 238.

Main Idea/Details

Determining the main idea in a text helps readers distinguish between important and less important information. When students can correctly identify the main idea, they understand the gist of what they read. Use this routine to teach main idea.

1 EXPLAIN ITS USE

Explain that finding the main idea is an important tool in helping students understand and remember what they read.

2 DEFINE THE TERMS

Explain that the topic is the subject, what the selection is all about. The main idea is the most important idea about the topic. The main idea can be stated in a sentence.

3 MODEL FINDING THE MAIN IDEA

Read a nonfiction paragraph with a stated main idea. Have students identify the topic by asking: *What is this paragraph about?* Then model how you determine the main idea.

4 FINDING SUPPORTING DETAILS

Explain that supporting details are small pieces of information that tell more about the main idea. Model how to identify supporting details.

5 USE A GRAPHIC ORGANIZER

Have students find the main idea and supporting details in a nonfiction selection. Use a main idea chart to help students organize their thoughts.

Choose passages carefully to practice this succession of skills:

- Paragraphs: stated main idea (Grades 2–6); implied main idea (Grades 3–6)

- Articles: stated main idea (Grades 4–6); implied main idea (Grades 4–6)

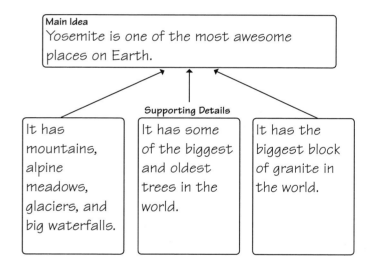

▲ **Graphic Organizer** 17

Research on Main Idea/Details

"When great readers are reading this stuff that has so many ideas in it, they have to listen to that mental voice tell them which words, which sentences or paragraphs, and which ideas are most important. Otherwise they won't get it."

Ellin Oliver Keene and Susan Zimmermann,
Mosaic of Thought

Keene, Ellin Oliver, and Susan Zimmermann. *Mosaic of Thought: Teaching Comprehension in a Reader's Workshop.* Heinemann, 1997, p. 86.

Providing students with reading materials they can and want to read is an important step toward developing fluent readers. A running record allows you to determine each student's instructional and independent reading level. Information on how to take a running record is provided on pp. DI•59–DI•60.

Instructional Reading Level

Only approximately 1 in 10 words will be difficult when reading a selection from the Student Edition for students who are at grade level. (A typical fourth-grader reads approximately 115–130 words correct per minute.)

- Students reading at grade level should read regularly from the Student Edition and On-Level Leveled Readers, with teacher support as suggested in the Teacher's Editions.
- Students reading below grade level can read the Strategic Intervention Leveled Readers. Instructional plans can be found in the Teacher's Edition and the Leveled Reader Teaching Guide.
- Students who are reading above grade level can read the Advanced Leveled Readers. Instructional plans can be found in the Teacher's Edition and the Leveled Reader Teaching Guide.

Independent Reading Level

Students should read regularly in independent-level texts in which no more than approximately 1 in 20 words is difficult for the reader. Other factors that make a book easy to read include the student's interest in the topic, the amount of text on a page, how well illustrations support meaning, and the complexity and familiarity of the concepts. Suggested books for self-selected reading are provided for each lesson on p. TR14 in this Teacher's Edition.

Guide students in learning how to self-select books at their independent reading level. As you talk about a book with students, discuss the challenging concepts in it, list new words students find in sampling the book, and ask students about their familiarity with the topic. A blackline master to help students evaluate books for independent reading is provided on p. DI•58.

Self-Selected/Independent Reading

While oral reading allows you to assess students' reading level and fluency, independent reading is of crucial importance to students' futures as readers and learners. Students need to develop their ability to read independently for increasing amounts of time.

- Schedule a regular time for sustained independent reading in your classroom. During the year, gradually increase the amount of time devoted to independent reading.
- Encourage students to track the amount of time they read independently and the number of pages they read in a given amount of time. Tracking will help motivate them to gradually increase their duration and speed. Blackline masters for tracking independent reading are provided on p. DI•58 and p. TR15.

Choosing a Book for Independent Reading

When choosing a book, story, or article for independent reading, consider these questions:

_____ 1. Do I know something about this topic?

_____ 2. Am I interested in this topic?

_____ 3. Do I like reading this kind of book (fiction, fantasy, biography, or whatever)?

_____ 4. Have I read other things by this author? Do I like this author?

If you say "yes" to at least one of the questions above, continue:

_____ 5. In reading the first page, was only about 1 of every 20 words hard?

If you say "yes," continue:

_____ 6. Does the number of words on a page look about right to me?

If you say "yes," the book or article is probably at the right level for you.

Silent Reading

Record the date, the title of the book or article you read, the amount of time you spent reading, and the number of pages you read during that time.

Date	Title	Minutes	Pages

Taking a Running Record

A running record is an assessment of a student's oral reading accuracy and oral reading fluency. Reading accuracy is based on the number of words read correctly. Reading fluency is based on the reading rate (the number of words correct per minute) and the degree to which a student reads with a "natural flow."

How to Measure Reading Accuracy

1. Choose a grade-level text of about 80 to 120 words that is unfamiliar to the student.
2. Make a copy of the text for yourself. Make a copy for the student or have the student read aloud from a book.
3. Give the student the text and have the student read aloud. (You may wish to record the student's reading for later evaluation.)
4. On your copy of the text, mark any miscues or errors the student makes while reading. See the running record sample on page DI·60, which shows how to identify and mark miscues.
5. Count the total number of words in the text and the total number of errors made by the student. Note: If a student makes the same error more than once, such as mispronouncing the same word multiple times, count it as one error. Self-corrections do not count as actual errors. Use the following formula to calculate the percentage score, or accuracy rate:

$$\frac{\text{Total Number of Words} - \text{Total Number of Errors}}{\text{Total Number of Words}} \times 100 = \text{percentage score}$$

Interpreting the Results

- A student who reads **95–100%** of the words correctly is reading at an **independent level** and may need more challenging text.
- A student who reads **90–94%** of the words correctly is reading at an **instructional level** and will likely benefit from guided instruction.
- A student who reads **89%** or fewer of the words correctly is reading at a **frustrational level** and may benefit most from targeted instruction with lower-level texts and intervention.

How to Measure Reading Rate (WCPM)

1. Follow Steps 1–3 above.
2. Note the exact times when the student begins and finishes reading.
3. Use the following formula to calculate the number of words correct per minute (WCPM):

$$\frac{\text{Total Number of Words Read Correctly}}{\text{Total Number of Seconds}} \times 60 = \text{words correct per minute}$$

Interpreting the Results

An appropriate reading rate for a fourth-grader is 115–130 (WCPM).

Running Record Sample

Running Record Sample

> All the maple trees that grow in the northeastern United States and parts of Canada have shaken off their slumber. During the next few months, they put all ^of^ their energy into growing. Maple trees can live for hundreds of years. During their first hundred years of existence, they grow about ~~a~~ ^one^ foot each year.
>
> The maple tree's roots anchor the tree to the ground. They burrow /bore/ deep in the soil and push out in every direction. The huge network of roots (has) spread like an <u>enormous</u> ^H^ open hand with dozens and dozens of outstretched fingers in the ground. The deep roots help keep the tree from toppling over during strong winds. The roots also gather (SC) nutrients the tree needs to make sap.
>
> —From *The Maple Tree*
> On-Level Reader 4.3.1

Symbols

Accurate Reading
The student reads a word correctly.

Insertion
The student inserts words or parts of words that are not in the text.

Substitution
The student substitutes words or parts of words for the words in the text.

Mispronunciation/Misreading
The student pronounces or reads a word incorrectly.

Omission
The student omits words or word parts.

Hesitation
The student hesitates over a word, and the teacher provides the word. Wait several seconds before telling the student what the word is.

Self-Correction
The student reads a word incorrectly but then corrects the error. Do not count self-corrections as actual errors. However, noting self-corrections will help you identify words the student finds difficult.

Running Record Results
Total Number of Words: **122**
Number of Errors: **5**

Reading Time: **61 seconds**

▶

Reading Accuracy
$\dfrac{122 - 5}{122} \times 100 = 95.9 = 96\%$

Accuracy Percentage Score: **96%**

▶

Reading Rate—WCPM
$\dfrac{117}{61} \times 60 = 115.08 = 115$ words correct per minute

Reading Rate: **115 WCPM**

Unit 1

Unit 1	Vocabulary Words	Spelling Words

Because of Winn-Dixie

Vocabulary Words: grand, memorial, peculiar, positive, prideful, recalls, selecting

Short vowels VCCV

admire	soccer	intend	happen
magnet	engine	fabric	cannon
contest	sudden	flatten	
method	finger	rascal	
custom	accident	gutter	
rally	mitten	mammal	

Lewis and Clark and Me

Vocabulary Words: docks, migrating, scan, scent, wharf, yearned

Long a and i

sigh	spray	tight	freight
right	braid	raisin	sleigh
weigh	bait	trait	
eight	grain	highway	
detail	slight	frighten	
height	thigh	dismay	

Grandfather's Journey

Vocabulary Words: amazed, bewildered, homeland, longed, sculptures, still, towering

Long e and o

sweet	throat	croak	seaweed
each	float	shallow	hollow
three	foam	eagle	
least	flown	indeed	
freedom	greet	rainbow	
below	season	grown	

The Horned Toad Prince

Vocabulary Words: bargain, favor, lassoed, offended, prairie, riverbed, shrieked

Long e

prairie	movie	collie	trolley
calorie	country	breezy	misty
honey	empty	jury	
valley	city	balcony	
money	rookie	steady	
finally	hockey	alley	

Letters Home from Yosemite

Vocabulary Words: glacier, impressive, naturalist, preserve, slopes, species, wilderness

Long u

usual	scooter	pupil
huge	juice	groove
flute	cruise	confuse
mood	truth	humor
smooth	bruise	duty
threw	cruel	curfew
afternoon	excuse	

Unit 2

Unit 2	Vocabulary Words	Spelling Words

What Jo Did — Vocabulary Words: fouled, hoop, jersey, marveled, rim, speechless, swatted, unbelievable

Adding -s and -es

monkeys	months	delays	batteries
friends	companies	scratches	donkeys
plays	costumes	counties	
supplies	sandwiches	teammates	
taxes	hobbies	memories	
holidays	daisies	bunches	

Coyote School News — Vocabulary Words: bawling, coyote, dudes, roundup, spurs

Irregular Plurals

videos	cliffs	cuffs	hoofs
teeth	roofs	beliefs	loaves
potatoes	halves	patios	
themselves	moose	banjos	
lives	radios	tornadoes	
leaves	sheep	tomatoes	

Grace and the Time Machine — Vocabulary Words: aboard, atlas, awkward, capable, chant, mechanical, miracle, reseats, vehicle

Words with ar, or

morning	story	Florida	garden
forest	argue	apartment	Arkansas
garbage	backyard	sport	
form	start	force	
alarm	partner	forward	
corner	storm	sharp	

Marven of the Great North Woods — Vocabulary Words: cord, dismay, grizzly, immense, payroll

Digraphs ng, nk, ph, wh

Thanksgiving	wheel	white	chunk
among	nephew	shrink	skunk
think	belong	wharf	
blank	whiskers	trunk	
graph	whisper	strong	
young	elephant	blink	

So You Want to Be President? — Vocabulary Words: Constitution, howling, humble, politics, responsibility, solemnly, vain

Words with ear, ir, our, ur

return	heard	nourish	hamburger
courage	early	purse	survey
surface	turtle	furniture	
purpose	birthday	search	
first	journal	curtain	
turkey	courtesy	burrow	

Unit 3   Vocabulary Words   Spelling Words

The Stranger

Vocabulary Words

draft	parlor
etched	terror
fascinated	timid
frost	

Adding -ed and -ing

watched	stopped	noticed	hurried
watching	stopping	noticing	hurrying
danced	dried	robbed	
dancing	drying	robbing	
studied	happened	slipped	
studying	happening	slipping	

Adelina's Whales

Vocabulary Words

biologist	massive
bluff	rumbling
lagoon	tropical

Homophones

piece	by	aloud	there
peace	bye	allowed	their
break	beat	past	
brake	beet	passed	
threw	thrown	weight	
through	throne	wait	

How Night Came from the Sea: A Story from Brazil

Vocabulary Words

brilliant
chorus
coward
gleamed
shimmering

Vowel sound in *shout*

however	towel	browse	eyebrow
mountain	ounce	announce	boundary
mound	coward	hound	
scout	outdoors	trout	
shout	flowerpot	drowsy	
couch	scowl	grouch	

Eye of the Storm

Vocabulary Words

destruction
expected
forecasts
inland
shatter
surge

Compound words

watermelon	upstairs	touchdown	loud-speaker
homemade	thunder-storm	campfire	laptop
understand	shortcut	skateboard	flashlight
sometimes	doorbell	anyway	
shoelace	jellyfish	fireworks	
highway		haircut	

The Great Kapok Tree

Vocabulary Words

canopy
dangle
dappled
fragrant
pollen
pollinate
slithered
wondrous

Possessives

its	men's	teacher's
ours	girl's	teachers'
mine	girls'	aunt's
yours	hers	aunts'
family's	theirs	boy's
families'	brother's	boys'
man's	brothers'	

Unit 4	Vocabulary Words	Spelling Words

The Houdini Box

Vocabulary Words:
appeared
bustling
crumbled
escape
magician
monument
vanished

Contractions

don't	doesn't	where's	when's
won't	I've	hadn't	haven't
wouldn't	here's	aren't	
there's	wasn't	they're	
we're	shouldn't	it's	
you're	couldn't	we've	

Encantado: Pink Dolphin of the Amazon

Vocabulary Words:
aquarium
dolphins
enchanted
flexible
glimpses
pulses
surface

Final -le, -al, -en

chicken	natural	paddle	tangle
eleven	needle	animal	frighten
given	single	spiral	
jungle	citizen	marble	
national	threaten	oval	
several	diagonal	mumble	

The King in the Kitchen

Vocabulary Words:
duke
dungeon
furiously
genius
majesty
noble
peasant
porridge

Words with final -er, -ar

brother	similar	filter	theater
together	regular	hangar	deliver
dinner	summer	never	
popular	clever	shelter	
center	supper	cellar	
calendar	pitcher	caterpillar	

Seeker of Knowledge

Vocabulary Words:
ancient
link
scholars
seeker
temple
translate
triumph
uncover

Consonants /j/, /ks/, and /k/

village	knowledge	Texas	quilt
except	question	fudge	expert
explain	equal	excellent	
quick	queen	exercise	
charge	excited	quart	
bridge	expect	liquid	

Encyclopedia Brown and the Case of the Slippery Salamander

Vocabulary Words:
amphibians
crime
exhibit
lizards
reference
reptiles
salamanders
stumped

Prefixes un-, dis-, in-

distrust	disorder	disrepair
uncertain	discount	inability
incomplete	indirect	disapprove
unlikely	unopened	unsolved
unfair	disrespect	disobey
discontinue	unimportant	unsuspecting
unaware	unlisted	

WORD LIST

Unit 5 | Vocabulary Words | Spelling Words

Sailing Home: A Story of a Childhood at Sea

Vocabulary Words: bow, cargo, celestial, conducted, dignified, navigation, quivered, stern

Multisyllabic words: reaction, prerecorded, incorrectly, incredibly, disobedient, disagreeable, refreshment, unbreakable, declaration, retirement, misdialed, undefined, unhappily, watchfully, gleefully, sportsmanship, repayment, questionable, displacement, midshipman

Lost City: The Discovery of Machu Picchu

Vocabulary Words: curiosity, glorious, granite, ruins, terraced, thickets, torrent

Syllable patterns V/CV and VC/V: basic, vacant, secret, honor, local, novel, olive, tiger, spinach, second, donate, locust, beware, emotion, cabin, tripod, dragon, habit, tribute, lizard

Amelia and Eleanor Go for a Ride

Vocabulary Words: aviator, brisk, cockpit, daring, elegant, outspoken, solo

Greek word parts: telephone, biography, telescope, photograph, microwave, diameter, barometer, microscope, headphones, microphone, autograph, microchip, telegraph, perimeter, paragraph, phonics, symphony, saxophone, periscope, megaphone

Antarctic Journal: Four Months at the Bottom of the World

Vocabulary Words: anticipation, continent, convergence, depart, forbidding, heaves, icebergs

Words with Latin roots: dictionary, abrupt, predict, import, locally, verdict, locate, portable, transport, bankrupt, dictate, location, erupt, passport, export, contradict, rupture, interrupt, disrupt, dislocate

Moonwalk

Vocabulary Words: loomed, rille, runt, staggered, summoning, taunted, trench, trudged

Related words: please, pleasant, breath, breathe, image, imagine, product, production, heal, health, triple, triplet, relate, relative, meter, metric, compose, composition, crumb, crumble

Unit 6	Vocabulary Words	Spelling Words

My Brother Martin

Vocabulary Words:
ancestors
avoided
generations
minister
numerous
pulpit
shielding

Schwa

stomach	remember	fortune	cement
memory	forget	giant	yesterday
Canada	suppose	architect	
element	iron	normal	
mystery	gravel	notify	
science	difficult	privilege	

Jim Thorpe's Bright Path

Vocabulary Words:
boarding school
dormitory
endurance
manual
reservation
society

Prefixes mis-, non-, re-

misplace	mishandle	nonfiction	nonstick
nonsense	nonstop	rebound	misquote
reread	recover	mistreat	
repack	reseal	readjust	
misfortune	misbehavior	misprint	
remove	reunion	nonprofit	

How Tía Lola Came to Visit Stay

Vocabulary Words:
affords
colonel
glint
lurking
palettes
quaint
resemblance

Suffixes -less, -ment, -ness

countless	statement	tireless	needless
payment	breathless	amazement	painless
goodness	restless	amusement	
fairness	enjoyment	greatness	
hopeless	pavement	punishment	
treatment	flawless	timeless	

To Fly: The Story of the Wright Brothers

Vocabulary Words:
cradle
drag
flex
glider
hangars
rudder
stalled

Suffixes -ful, -ly, -ion

careful	recently	yearly	correction
tasteful	extremely	successful	eagerly
lonely	certainly	playful	
powerful	wisely	thoughtful	
suggestion	harmful	actually	
peaceful	monthly	pollution	

The Man Who Went to the Far Side of the Moon: The Story of Apollo 11 Astronaut Michael Collins

Vocabulary Words:
astronauts
capsule
hatch
horizon
lunar
module
quarantine

Words with silent consonants

island	half	rhyme
column	calf	climber
knee	whistle	limb
often	autumn	plumbing
known	knuckles	ghost
castle	numb	clothes
thumb	Illinois	

Grade 3 Vocabulary

Use this list of third grade tested vocabulary words for review and leveled activities.

A
admire
airport
amount
antlers
anxiously
arranged
attention
attic
average

B
bakery
barrels
batch
bay
beauty
beneath
blade
blizzards
blooming
board
boils
boom
bottom
bows
braided
budding
bulbs
bundles
buried
burro
bursts
business

C
cardboard
carpenter
carpetmaker
celebrate
cellar
channel
cheated
check
chilly

chimney
chipped
chores
clearing
clever
clutched
coins
collection
college
complained
continued
cotton
crops
crown
crystal
cuddles
curious
current
custom
customer

D
dangerously
delicious
depth
described
deserts
dew
dimes
disappeared
discovery
dough
downtown
doze
drifting
drowned

E
earned
earthquakes
echoed
encourages
enormous
errands
excitedly
excitement

expensive
expressive

F
factory
famous
farewell
feast
festival
fetched
fierce
fined
fireflies
fireworks
flights
flippers
flutter
foolish
force
foreign
frozen

G
gardener
giggle
glaring
glassblower
goal
graceful
gully

H
handkerchief
hatch
homesick
humor

I
imagined
ingredients
interest

J
journey
joyful

K
knead
knowledge

L
labeled
languages
laundry
lazy
liberty
local
looping

M
marketplace
medals
melody
memories
mending
mention
merchant
million
mixture
models
motioned

N
narrator
narrow
native
nickels
notepad

O
outrun
overhead
overnight

P
paces
pale
partners
patch
peak

pecks
pegs
perches
pick
pitcher
plenty
poked
popular
preen
public
puffs

Q
quarters

R
raindrops
realize
recipe
recognizing
reeds
reply
rhythm
rich
ruined

S
sadness
scattered
scoop
scrambled
settled
shiny
shivered
shocked
showers
skillet
slammed
snug
snuggles
social
spare
spell
spoil
sprouting
stamps

steady
steep
stirred
stoops
strain
straying
strokes
struggled
supplies
support
surrounded
swooping
symbol
symphony

T
tablet
thousand
thread
tides
torch
treasure
trembles
tune
twist

U
unaware
unforgettable
unveiled
unwrapped

V
valley
value
volcanoes

W
waterfalls
wealth
wobbled
worth

Grade 5 Vocabulary

Use this list of fifth grade tested vocabulary words for leveled activities.

A
abdomen
accomplishments
achieved
acquainted
admiringly
adorn
advice
advised
agreement
algae
appreciate
architect
armor
artificial
assignment
astonished

B
background
barber
bass
behavior
benefactor
bleached
bluish
blunders
branded
bronze

C
cable
cannon
carcasses
cartwheels
caterpillar
cavities
choir
circumstances
civilization
clarinet
cleanse
cocoon
combination
complex

concealed
confidence
conservation
constructed
contribute
cramped
critical
criticizing
cruised

D
daintily
debris
decay
demonstrates
depressed
devastation
diplomat
disrespect
distribution
drenching
driftwood

E
economic
eerie
elbow
emerge
enables
encases
enthusiastic
environment
envy
episode
era
erected
essential
expanded
explosion
extinct

F
fashioned
fastball

fate
fearless
fidgety
fleeing
focus
forgetful
foundations

G
gait
glimmer
gnawed
gratitude
gravity
guaranteed
gymnastics

H
hammocks
handicapped
headland
hesitation
hideous
hustled
hydrogen

I
immigrants
independence
inspired
interior
intersection
investigation
issue

J
jammed

K
kelp

L
lair
lamented

landscape
lifeless
limelight
lingers
lullaby
luxury

M
magnified
midst
migrant
miniature
mocking
mold
monitors
mucus

N
newcomer
nighttime

O
occasion
ooze
outfield
overrun

P
parasites
peddler
permit
philosopher
pitch
plunged
pondered
precious
prehistoric
procedures
procession
profile
proportion

R
ravine
realm

reassembled
recommend
refugees
released
religious
representatives
reputation
resourceful
rival
robotic
role
rustling

S
sacred
scarce
scoundrel
scrawled
scrawny
sea urchins
secondhand
sediment
serpent
severe
shellfish
sinew
sketched
skidded
slavery
somber
somersault
sonar
specialize
specific
spectacles
spoonful
starvation
steed
sterile
sternly
strategy
strict
subject
superiors
suspicions

T
teenager
therapist
thieving
throbbing
tidied
traditions
tundra
tweezers

U
unique
unscrewed

V
vacant
veins
visa

W
weakness
wheelchair
wincing
windup
withered
workshop
worshipped
worthless

Legibility

When handwriting is legible, letters, words and numbers can be read easily. Handwriting that is not legible can cause problems for the reader and make communication difficult. Legibility can be improved if students are able to identify what is causing legibility problems in their handwriting. Focus instruction on the following five elements of legible handwriting.

Size

Letters need to be a consistent size. Students should focus on three things related to size: letters that reach to the top line, letters that reach halfway between the top and bottom line, and letters that extend below the bottom line. Writing letters the correct size can improve legibility. Often the letters that sit halfway between the top and bottom line cause the most problems. When students are writing on notebook paper, there is no middle line to help them size letters such as *m, a, i,* and *r* correctly. If students are having trouble, have them draw middle lines on their notebook paper.

Shape

Some of the most common handwriting problems are caused by forming letters incorrectly. These are the most common types of handwriting problems:

- round letters such as *a, o,* and *g* are not closed
- looped letters such as *i, e,* and *b* have no loops
- letters such as *i, t,* and *d* have loops that shouldn't be there

Have students examine one another's writing to indicate which words are hard to read, and then discuss which letters aren't formed correctly. They can then practice those particular letters.

Spacing

Letters within words should be evenly spaced. Too much or too little space can make writing difficult to read. A consistent amount of space should also be used between words in a sentence and between sentences. Suggest that students use the tip of their pencil to check the spacing between words and the width of their pencil to check the spacing between sentences.

Slant

Correct writing slant can be to the right or to the left, or there may be no slant at all. Slant becomes a legibility problem when letters are slanted in different directions. Suggest that students use a ruler to draw lines to determine if their slant is consistent.

Smoothness

Written letters should be produced with a line weight that is not too dark and not too light. The line should be smooth without any shaky or jagged edges. If students' writing is too dark, they are pressing too hard. If the writing is too light, they are not pressing hard enough. Usually shaky or jagged lines occur if students are unsure of how to form letters or if they are trying to draw letters rather than using a flowing motion.

D'Nealian™ Cursive Alphabet

a b c d e f g
h i j k l m n
o p q r s t u
v w x y z

A B C D E F G
H I J K L M N
O P Q R S T U
V W X Y Z . , ' ?

1 2 3 4 5 6
7 8 9 10

D'Nealian™ Alphabet

a b c d e f g h i

j k l m n o p q r s t

u v w x y z

A B C D E F G

H I J K L M N O

P Q R S T U V

W X Y Z . , ' ?

1 2 3 4 5 6

7 8 9 10

Manuscript Alphabet

Unit 1 *This Land Is Your Land*

	Below-Level	On-Level	Advanced

Because of Winn-Dixie

To Read Aloud!
Crocodiles, Camels, and Dugout Canoes: Eight Adventurous Episodes
by Bo Zaunders (Dutton, 1998) Eight real-life amateur explorers are profiled.

The Library
by Sarah Stewart (Farrar, 1995) This book recounts the story of a little girl with an intense love for books.

Watching Water Birds
by Jim Arnosky (National Geographic Society, 1997) Through text and illustrations, the author shares his feelings and knowledge about water birds.

Dick King-Smith's Animal Friends by Dick King-Smith (Candlewick, 1996) One man talks about the many animals he has known and how they have affected his life.

Lewis and Clark and Me: A Dog's Tale

To Read Aloud!
No Dogs Allowed!
by Bill Wallace (Holiday House, 2004) When a girl receives a puppy as a gift after losing her favorite horse, she is determined not to like it.

Puppy Love
by Dick King-Smith (Candlewick, 1997) The beloved author shares his experiences with dogs through-out his life.

Tornado
by Betsy Byars (HarperCollins, 1996) When a tornado lands a dog in their backyard, a family makes room for it in their lives.

My Dog, My Hero
by Betsy Byars, Betsy Duffey, and Laurie Myers (Henry Holt, 2000) Eight short stories relate the efforts of heroic dogs.

Grandfather's Journey

To Read Aloud!
My Name Is Maria Isabel
by Alma Flor Ada (Atheneum, 1993) Maria Isabel, newly emigrated from Puerto Rico, is upset when her teacher decides to call her Mary.

Tea with Milk
by Allen Say (Houghton Mifflin, 1999) The author relates the story of his American-born mother's return to Japan, where she falls in love with the Chinese man who eventually becomes Say's father.

Halmoni and the Picnic
by Sook Nyul Choi (Houghton Mifflin, 1993) Yummi worries about her Korean grandmother's adjustment to a new life in the United States.

The Happiest Ending
by Yoshiko Uchida (Atheneum, 1985) Rinko is startled to learn that a neighbor's daughter is coming to the United States from Japan to participate in an arranged marriage with a stranger.

The Horned Toad Prince

To Read Aloud!
Bubba, The Cowboy Prince
by Helen Ketteman (Scholastic, 1997) In this retelling of the Cinderella Story, Cinderella is a cowboy who has a very kind fairy godcow.

The Desert Is Theirs
by Byrd Baylor (Aladdin, 1987) This book describes the desert, its characteristics, and its inhabitants.

Desert Babies
by Kathy Darling (Walker, 1997) Colorful portraits of fourteen desert animals, including unusual facts about each.

Charro: The Mexican Cowboy
by George Ancona (Harcourt, 1999) A stunning photo-essay about a Mexican national sport, *la charrera,* and how it impacts the people of the West.

Letters Home from Yosemite

To Read Aloud!
Up North at the Cabin
by Marsha Wilson Chall (Lothrop Lee and Shepard, 1992) A girl loves the time she spends in the North Woods, swimming in the lake and canoeing on the river.

Postcards from Vietnam
by Denise Allard (Steck-Vaughn, 1998) Fictional postcards written by young people describe the culture and scenery of Vietnam.

Penguins at Home: Gentoos of Antarctica
by Bruce McMillan (Houghton Mifflin, 1993) Beautiful photo-graphs illuminate this profile of a specific species of penguins.

Market!
by Ted Lewin (Lee and Shepard, 1996) Six different markets across the world, from New York City to Morocco, are described in this beautifully illustrated book.

See also *Assessment Handbook*, p. 119

Unit 1 Reading Log

Name _____

Dates Read	Title and Author	What is it about?	How would you rate it?	Explain your rating.
From _____ to _____			Great Awful 5 4 3 2 1	
From _____ to _____			Great Awful 5 4 3 2 1	
From _____ to _____			Great Awful 5 4 3 2 1	
From _____ to _____			Great Awful 5 4 3 2 1	
From _____ to _____			Great Awful 5 4 3 2 1	

© Pearson Education

Unit 1 Narrative Retelling Chart

Selection Title ——————   Name ——————   Date ——————

Retelling Criteria/Teacher Prompt	Teacher-Aided Response	Student-Generated Response	Rubric Score (Circle one.)
Connections Has anything like this happened to you? How does this story remind you of other stories?			4 3 2 1
Author's Purpose Why do you think the author wrote this story? What was the author trying to tell us?			4 3 2 1
Characters Describe ———— (character's name) at the beginning and end of the story.			4 3 2 1
Setting Where and when did the story happen?			4 3 2 1
Plot Tell me what the story was about in a few sentences.			4 3 2 1

Summative Retelling Score   4   3   2   1

Comments ——————————————————
——————————————————
——————————————————

Unit 1 Expository Retelling Chart

Selection Title _____

Name _____

Date _____

Retelling Criteria/Teacher Prompt	Teacher-Aided Response	Student-Generated Response	Rubric Score (Circle one.)			
Connections Did this selection make you think about something else you have read? What did you learn about as you read this selection?			4	3	2	1
Author's Purpose Why do you think the author wrote this selection?			4	3	2	1
Topic What was the selection mostly about?			4	3	2	1
Important Ideas What is important for me to know about _____ (topic)?			4	3	2	1
Conclusions What did you learn from reading this selection?			4	3	2	1

Summative Retelling Score 4 3 2 1

Comments _____

Reading

Concepts of Print and Print Awareness	Pre-K	K	1	2	3	4	5	6
Develop awareness that print represents spoken language and conveys and preserves meaning	•	•	•					
Recognize familiar books by their covers; hold book right side up	•	•						
Identify parts of a book and their functions (front cover, title page/title, back cover, page numbers)	•	•	•					
Understand the concepts of letter, word, sentence, paragraph, and story	•	•	•					
Track print (front to back of book, top to bottom of page, left to right on line, sweep back left for next line)	•	•	•					
Match spoken to printed words	•	•	•					
Know capital and lowercase letter names and match them	•	• T	•					
Know the order of the alphabet	•	•	•					
Recognize first name in print	•	•	•					
Recognize the uses of capitalization and punctuation		•	•					
Value print as a means of gaining information	•	•	•					

Phonological and Phonemic Awareness	Pre-K	K	1	2	3	4	5	6
Phonological Awareness								
Recognize and produce rhyming words	•	•	•					
Track and count each word in a spoken sentence and each syllable in a spoken word	•	•	•					
Segment and blend syllables in spoken words			•					
Segment and blend onset and rime in one-syllable words		•	•					
Recognize and produce words beginning with the same sound	•	•	•					
Identify beginning, middle, and/or ending sounds that are the same or different	•	•	•					
Understand that spoken words are made of sequences of sounds	•	•	•					
Phonemic Awareness								
Identify the position of sounds in words		•	•					
Identify and isolate initial, final, and medial sounds in spoken words	•	•	•					
Blend sounds orally to make words or syllables		•	•					
Segment a word or syllable into sounds; count phonemes in spoken words or syllables		•	•					
Manipulate sounds in words (add, delete, and/or substitute phonemes)	•	•	•					

Phonics and Decoding	Pre-K	K	1	2	3	4	5	6
Phonics								
Understand and apply the **alphabetic principle** that spoken words are composed of sounds that are represented by letters	•	•	•					
Know letter-sound relationships	•	• T	• T	• T				
Blend sounds of letters to decode		•	• T	• T	• T			
Consonants, consonant blends, and consonant digraphs		•	• T	• T	• T			
Short, long, and r-controlled vowels; vowel digraphs; diphthongs; common vowel patterns			• T	• T	• T			
Phonograms/word families		•	•	•	•			
Word Structure								
Decode words with common word parts		•	• T	• T	• T	•	•	•
Base words and inflected endings			• T	• T	•	•	•	•
Contractions and compound words			• T	• T	• T	•	•	•
Suffixes and prefixes			• T	• T	• T	•	•	•
Greek and Latin roots						•	•	•
Blend syllables to decode words			• T	• T	• T	•	•	•
Decoding Strategies								
Blending strategy: Apply knowledge of letter-sound relationships to decode unfamiliar words		•	•	•	•			
Apply knowledge of word structure to decode unfamiliar words		•	•	•	•	•	•	•
Use context and syntax along with letter-sound relationships and word structure to decode	•	•	•	•	•	•	•	•
Self-correct		•	•	•	•	•	•	•

Fluency	Pre-K	K	1	2	3	4	5	6
Read aloud fluently with accuracy, comprehension, appropriate pace/rate; with expression/intonation (prosody); with attention to punctuation and appropriate phrasing			• T	• T	• T	• T	• T	• T
Practice fluency in a variety of ways, including choral reading, partner/paired reading, Readers' Theater, repeated oral reading, and tape-assisted reading		•	•	•	•	•	•	•

• instructional opportunity   T tested in standardized test forma

	Pre-K	K	1	2	3	4	5	6
Work toward appropriate fluency goals by the end of each grade			•T	•T	•T	•T	•T	•T
Read regularly in independent-level material			•	•	•	•	•	•
Read silently for increasing periods of time			•	•	•	•	•	•

Vocabulary (Oral and Written)

	Pre-K	K	1	2	3	4	5	6
Word Recognition								
Recognize regular and irregular high-frequency words	•	•	•T	•T				
Recognize and understand selection vocabulary		•	•	•T	•	•	•	•
Understand content-area vocabulary and specialized, technical, or topical words			•	•	•	•	•	•
Word Learning Strategies								
Develop vocabulary through direct instruction, concrete experiences, reading, listening to text read aloud	•	•	•	•	•	•	•	•
Use knowledge of word structure to figure out meanings of words			•	•T	•T	•T	•T	•T
Use context clues for meanings of unfamiliar words, multiple-meaning words, homonyms, homographs			•	•T	•T	•T	•T	•T
Use grade-appropriate reference sources to learn word meanings	•	•	•	•	•T	•T	•T	•T
Use picture clues to help determine word meanings	•	•	•	•	•			
Use new words in a variety of contexts	•	•	•	•	•	•	•	•
Examine word usage and effectiveness		•	•	•	•	•	•	•
Create and use graphic organizers to group, study, and retain vocabulary			•	•	•	•	•	•
Extend Concepts and Word Knowledge								
Academic language	•	•	•	•	•	•	•	•
Classify and categorize	•	•	•	•	•	•	•	•
Antonyms and synonyms			•	•T	•T	•T	•T	•T
Homographs, homonyms, and homophones				•	•T	•T	•T	•T
Multiple-meaning words			•	•	•T	•T	•T	•T
Related words and derivations					•	•	•	•
Analogies						•	•	
Connotation/denotation						•	•	•
Figurative language and idioms			•	•	•	•	•	•
Descriptive words (location, size, color, shape, number, ideas, feelings)	•	•	•	•	•	•	•	•
High-utility words (shapes, colors, question words, position/directional words, and so on)	•	•	•	•				
Time and order words	•	•	•	•	•	•	•	•
Transition words						?	•	•
Word origins: Etymologies/word histories; words from other languages, regions, or cultures					•	•	•	•
Shortened forms: abbreviations, acronyms, clipped words			•	•	•	•	•T	

Text Comprehension

	Pre-K	K	1	2	3	4	5	6
Comprehension Strategies								
Preview the text and formulate questions	•	•	•	•	•	•	•	•
Set and monitor purpose for reading and listening	•	•	•	•	•	•	•	•
Activate and use prior knowledge	•	•	•	•	•	•	•	•
Make predictions	•	•	•	•	•	•	•	•
Monitor comprehension and use fix-up strategies to resolve difficulties in meaning: adjust reading rate, reread and read on, seek help from reference sources and/or other people, skim and scan, summarize, use text features			•	•	•	•	•	•
Create and use graphic and semantic organizers		•	•	•	•	•	•	•
Answer questions (text explicit, text implicit, scriptal), including *who, what, when, where, why, what if, how*	•	•	•	•	•	•	•	•
Look back in text for answers			•	•	•	•	•	•
Answer test-like questions			•	•	•	•	•	•
Generate clarifying questions, including *who, what, where, when, how, why,* and *what if*	•	•	•	•	•	•	•	•
Recognize text structure: story and informational (cause/effect, chronological, compare/contrast, description, problem/solution, propostion/support)	•	•	•	•	•	•	•	•
Summarize text		•	•	•	•	•	•	•
Recall and retell stories	•	•	•	•	•	•	•	•
Identify and retell important/main ideas (nonfiction)	•	•	•	•	•	•	•	•
Identify and retell new information			•	•	•	•	•	•
Visualize; use mental imagery		•	•	•	•	•	•	•
Use strategies flexibly and in combination			•	•	•	•	•	•

Comprehension Skills

	Pre-K	K	1	2	3	4	5	6
Author's purpose			• T	• T	• T	• T	• T	• T
Author's viewpoint/bias/perspective					•	•	•	• T
Categorize and classify	•	•	•	•				
Cause and effect		•	• T	• T	• T	• T	• T	• T
Compare and contrast		•	• T	• T	• T	• T	• T	• T
Details and facts		•	•	•	•	•	•	•
Draw conclusions		•	• T	• T	• T	• T	• T	• T
Fact and opinion				• T	• T	• T	• T	• T
Follow directions/steps in a process	•	•	•	•	•	•	•	•
Generalize					• T	• T	• T	• T
Graphic sources		•	•	•	•	• T	• T	• T
Main idea and supporting details		• T	• T	• T	• T	• T	• T	• T
Paraphrase			•	•	•	•	•	•
Persuasive devices and propaganda			•	•	•	•	•	•
Realism/fantasy		•	• T	• T	• T	•	•	•
Sequence of events		• T	• T	• T	• T	• T	• T	• T

Higher Order Thinking Skills

	Pre-K	K	1	2	3	4	5	6
Analyze			•	•	•	•	•	•
Describe and connect the essential ideas, arguments, and perspectives of a text		•	•	•	•	•	•	•
Draw inferences, conclusions, or generalizations, support them with textual evidence and prior knowledge	•		•	•	•	•	•	•
Evaluate and critique ideas and text		•	•	•	•	•	•	•
Hypothesize						•	•	•
Make judgments about ideas and text		•	•	•	•	•	•	•
Organize and synthesize ideas and information		•				•	•	•

Literary Analysis, Response, & Appreciation	Pre-K	K	1	2	3	4	5	6
Genre and Its Characteristics								
Recognize characteristics of a variety of genre	•	•	•	•	•	•	•	•
Distinguish fiction from nonfiction		•	•	•	•	•	•	•
Identify characteristics of literary texts, including drama, fantasy, traditional tales		•	•	•	•	•	•	•
Identify characteristics of nonfiction texts, including biography, interviews, newspaper articles		•	•	•	•	•	•	•
Identify characteristics of poetry and song, including nursery rhymes, limericks, blank verse	•	•	•	•	•	•	•	•
Literary Elements and Story Structure								
Character	•	• T	• T	• T	• T	• T	• T	•
Recognize and describe traits, actions, feelings, and motives of characters		•	•	•	•	•	•	•
Analyze characters' relationships, changes, and points of view		•	•	•	•	•	•	•
Analyze characters' conflicts				•		•	•	•
Plot and plot structure	•	• T	• T	• T	• T	• T	• T	
Beginning, middle, end	•	•	•	•	•			
Goal and outcome or problem and solution/resolution		•	•	•	•	•	•	•
Rising action, climax, and falling action/denouement; setbacks						•	•	•
Setting	•	• T	• T	• T	• T	• T	•	•
Relate setting to problem/solution						•	•	•
Explain ways setting contributes to mood						•	•	•
Theme		•	• T	• T	•	•	•	•
Use Literary Elements and Story Structure	•	•	•	•	•	•	•	•
Analyze and evaluate author's use of setting, plot, character				•	•	•	•	•
Identify similarities and differences of characters, events, and settings within or across selections/cultures	•	•	•	•	•	•	•	•
Literary Devices								
Allusion								•
Dialect						•	•	•
Dialogue and narration	•	•	•	•	•	•	•	•
Exaggeration/hyperbole					•	•	•	•
Figurative language: idiom, jargon, metaphor, simile, slang			•	•	•	•	•	•

• instructional opportunity   **T** tested in standardized test forma[t]

	Pre-K	K	1	2	3	4	5	6
Flashback						•	•	•
Foreshadowing							•	•
Formal and informal language				•	•	•	•	•
Humor					•	•	•	•
Imagery and sensory words			•	•	•	•	•	•
Mood				•	•	•	•	•
Personification				•	•	•	•	•
Point of view (first person, third person, omniscient)					•	•	•	•
Puns and word play				•	•	•	•	•
Sound devices and poetic elements	•	•	•	•	•	•	•	•
Alliteration, assonance, onomatopoeia	•	•	•	•	•	•	•	•
Rhyme, rhythm, repetition, and cadence	•	•	•	•	•	•	•	•
Word choice				•	•	•	•	•
Symbolism				•	•	•	•	•
Tone							•	•

Author's and Illustrator's Craft

	Pre-K	K	1	2	3	4	5	6
Distinguish the roles of author and illustrator		•	•	•				
Recognize/analyze author's and illustrator's craft or style		•	•	•	•	•	•	•

Literary Response

	Pre-K	K	1	2	3	4	5	6
Recollect, talk, and write about books	•	•	•	•	•	•	•	•
Reflect on reading and respond (through talk, movement, art, and so on)	•	•	•	•	•	•	•	•
Ask and answer questions about text	•	•	•	•	•	•	•	•
Write about what is read	•	•	•	•	•	•	•	•
Use evidence from the text to support opinions, interpretations, or conclusions		•	•	•	•	•	•	•
Support ideas through reference to other texts and personal knowledge				•	•	•	•	•
Locate materials on related topic, theme, or idea				•	•	•	•	•
Generate alternative endings to plots and identify the reason for, and the impact of, the alternatives	•	•	•	•	•	•	•	•
Synthesize and extend the literary experience through creative responses	•	•	•	•	•	•	•	•
Make connections: text to self, text to text, text to world	•	•	•	•	•	•	•	•
Evaluate and critique the quality of the literary experience				•	•	•	•	•
Offer observations, react, speculate in response to text				•	•	•	•	•

Literary Appreciation/Motivation

	Pre-K	K	1	2	3	4	5	6
Show an interest in books and reading; engage voluntarily in social interaction about books	•	•	•	•	•	•	•	•
Choose text by drawing on personal interests, relying on knowledge of authors and genres, estimating text difficulty, and using recommendations of others	•	•	•	•	•	•	•	•
Read a variety of grade-level appropriate narrative and expository texts		•	•	•	•	•	•	•
Read from a wide variety of genres for a variety of purposes	•	•	•	•	•	•	•	•
Read independently		•	•	•	•	•	•	•
Establish familiarity with a topic		•	•	•	•	•	•	•

Cultural Awareness

	Pre-K	K	1	2	3	4	5	6
Develop attitudes and abilities to interact with diverse groups and cultures	•	•	•	•	•	•	•	•
Connect experiences and ideas with those from a variety of languages, cultures, customs, perspectives	•	•	•	•	•	•	•	•
Understand how attitudes and values in a culture or during a period in time affect the writing from that culture or time period						•	•	•
Compare language and oral traditions (family stories) that reflect customs, regions, and cultures		•	•	•	•	•	•	•
Recognize themes that cross cultures and bind them together in their common humanness						•	•	•

Language Arts

Writing	Pre-K	K	1	2	3	4	5	6
Concepts of Print for Writing								
Develop gross and fine motor skills and hand/eye coordination	•	•	•					
Print own name and other important words	•	•	•					
Write using pictures, some letters, and transitional spelling to convey meaning	•	•	•					
Dictate messages or stories for others to write	•	•	•					

	Pre-K	K	1	2	3	4	5	6
Create own written texts for others to read; write left to right on a line and top to bottom on a page	•	•	•					
Participate in shared and interactive writing	•	•	•					

Traits of Writing

Focus/Ideas

	Pre-K	K	1	2	3	4	5	6
Maintain focus and sharpen ideas		•	•	•	•	•	•	•
Use sensory details and concrete examples; elaborate		•	•	•	•	•	•	•
Delete extraneous information		•	•	•	•	•	•	•
Rearrange words and sentences to improve meaning and focus			•	•	•	•	•	•
Use strategies, such as tone, style, consistent point of view, to achieve a sense of completeness						•	•	•

Organization/Paragraphs

	Pre-K	K	1	2	3	4	5	6
Use graphic organizers to group ideas		•	•	•	•	•	•	•
Write coherent paragraphs that develop a central idea		•	•	•	•	•	•	•
Use transitions to connect sentences and paragraphs		•	•	•	•	•	•	•
Select an organizational structure based on purpose, audience, length						•	•	•
Organize ideas in a logical progression, such as chronological order or by order of importance	•	•	•	•	•	•	•	•
Write introductory, supporting, and concluding paragraphs				•	•	•	•	•
Write a multi-paragraph paper			•	•	•	•	•	•

Voice

	Pre-K	K	1	2	3	4	5	6
Develop personal, identifiable voice and an individual tone/style		•	•	•	•	•	•	•
Maintain consistent voice and point of view						•	•	•
Use voice appropriate to audience, message, and purpose						•	•	•

Word Choice

	Pre-K	K	1	2	3	4	5	6
Use clear, precise, appropriate language		•	•	•	•	•	•	•
Use figurative language and vivid words			•	•	•	•	•	•
Select effective vocabulary using word walls, dictionary, or thesaurus		•	•	•	•	•	•	•

Sentences

	Pre-K	K	1	2	3	4	5	6
Combine, elaborate, and vary sentences		•	•	•	•	•	•	•
Write topic sentence, supporting sentences with facts and details, and concluding sentence			•	•	•	•	•	•
Use correct word order			•	•	•	•	•	•
Use parallel structure in a sentence							•	•

Conventions

	Pre-K	K	1	2	3	4	5	6
Use correct spelling and grammar; capitalize and punctuate correctly		•	•	•	•	•	•	•
Correct sentence fragments and run-ons					•	•	•	•
Use correct paragraph indention			•	•	•	•	•	•

The Writing Process

	Pre-K	K	1	2	3	4	5	6
Prewrite using various strategies	•	•	•	•	•	•	•	•
Develop first drafts of single- and multiple-paragraph compositions		•	•	•	•	•	•	•
Revise drafts for varied purposes, including to clarify and to achieve purpose, sense of audience, precise word choice, vivid images, and elaboration		•	•	•	•	•	•	•
Edit and proofread for correct spelling, grammar, usage, and mechanics		•	•	•	•	•	•	•
Publish own work	•	•	•	•	•	•	•	•

Types of Writing

	Pre-K	K	1	2	3	4	5	6
Narrative writing (such as personal narratives, stories, biographies, autobiographies)	•	•	• T	• T	• T	• T	• T	• T
Expository writing (such as essays, directions, explanations, news stories, research reports, summaries)		•	• T	• T	• T	• T	• T	• T
Descriptive writing (such as labels, captions, lists, plays, poems, response logs, songs)	•	•	• T	• T	• T	• T	• T	• T
Persuasive writing (such as ads, editorials, essays, letters to the editor, opinions, posters)		•	• T	• T	• T	• T	• T	• T

Writing Habits and Practices

	Pre-K	K	1	2	3	4	5	6
Write on a daily basis	•	•	•	•	•	•	•	•
Use writing as a tool for learning and self-discovery			•	•	•	•	•	•
Write independently for extended periods of time			•	•	•	•	•	•

ENGLISH LANGUAGE CONVENTIONS in WRITING and SPEAKING	Pre-K	K	1	2	3	4	5	6

Grammar and Usage in Speaking and Writing

Sentences

	Pre-K	K	1	2	3	4	5	6
Types (declarative, interrogative, exclamatory, imperative)	•	•	• T	• T	• T	• T	• T	• T
Structure (simple, compound, complex, compound-complex)	•	•	•	•	•	• T	• T	• T

• instructional opportunity   **T** tested in standardized test forma

	Pre-K	K	1	2	3	4	5	6
Parts (subjects/predicates: complete, simple, compound; phrases; clauses)				•T	•	•T	•T	•T
Fragments and run-on sentences		•	•	•	•	•	•	•
Combine sentences, elaborate				•	•	•	•	•
Parts of speech: nouns, verbs and verb tenses, adjectives, adverbs, pronouns and antecedents, conjunctions, prepositions, interjections		•	•T	•T	•T	•T	•T	•T

Usage

	Pre-K	K	1	2	3	4	5	6
Subject-verb agreement		•	•T	•	•	•T	•T	•T
Pronoun agreement/referents			•T	•	•	•T	•T	•T
Misplaced modifiers						•	•T	•T
Misused words					•	•	•	•T
Negatives; avoid double negatives						•	•	•

Mechanics in Writing

	Pre-K	K	1	2	3	4	5	6
Capitalization (first word in sentence, proper nouns and adjectives, pronoun *I*, titles, and so on)	•	•	•T	•T	•T	•T	•T	•T
Punctuation (apostrophe, comma, period, question mark, exclamation mark, quotation marks, and so on)		•	•T	•T	•T	•T	•T	•T

Spelling

	Pre-K	K	1	2	3	4	5	6
Spell independently by using pre-phonetic knowledge, knowledge of letter names, sound-letter knowledge	•	•	•	•	•	•	•	•
Use sound-letter knowledge to spell	•	•	•	•	•	•	•	•
Consonants: single, double, blends, digraphs, silent letters, and unusual consonant spellings		•	•	•	•	•	•	•
Vowels: short, long, *r*-controlled, digraphs, diphthongs, less common vowel patterns, schwa		•	•	•	•	•	•	•
Use knowledge of word structure to spell			•	•	•	•	•	•
Base words and affixes (inflections, prefixes, suffixes), possessives, contractions and compound words			•	•	•	•	•	•
Greek and Latin roots, syllable patterns, multisyllabic words			•	•	•	•	•	•
Spell high-frequency, irregular words		•	•	•	•	•	•	•
Spell frequently misspelled words correctly, including homophones or homonyms			•	•	•	•	•	•
Use meaning relationships to spell					•	•	•	•

Handwriting

	Pre-K	K	1	2	3	4	5	6
Gain increasing control of penmanship, including pencil grip, paper position, posture, stroke	•	•	•	•				
Write legibly, with control over letter size and form; letter slant; and letter, word, and sentence spacing		•	•	•	•	•	•	•
Write lowercase and capital letters	•	•	•	•				
Manuscript	•	•	•	•	•	•	•	•
Cursive				•	•	•	•	•
Write numerals	•	•	•					

Listening and Speaking

Listening Skills and Strategies

	Pre-K	K	1	2	3	4	5	6
Listen to a variety of presentations attentively and politely	•	•	•	•	•	•	•	•
Self-monitor comprehension while listening, using a variety of skills and strategies	•	•	•	•	•	•	•	•
Listen for a purpose								
For enjoyment and appreciation	•	•	•	•	•	•	•	•
To expand vocabulary and concepts	•	•	•	•	•	•	•	•
To obtain information and ideas	•	•	•	•	•	•	•	•
To follow oral directions	•	•	•	•	•	•	•	•
To answer questions and solve problems	•	•	•	•	•	•	•	•
To participate in group discussions	•	•	•	•	•	•	•	•
To identify and analyze the musical elements of literary language	•	•	•	•	•	•	•	•
To gain knowledge of one's own culture, the culture of others, and the common elements of cultures	•	•	•	•	•	•	•	•
Recognize formal and informal language		•	•	•	•	•	•	•
Listen critically to distinguish fact from opinion and to analyze and evaluate ideas, information, experiences		•		•	•	•	•	•
Evaluate a speaker's delivery					•	•	•	•
Interpret a speaker's purpose, perspective, persuasive techniques, verbal and nonverbal messages, and use of rhetorical devices						•	•	•

Speaking Skills and Strategies

	Pre-K	K	1	2	3	4	5	6
Speak clearly, accurately, and fluently, using appropriate delivery for a variety of audiences, and purposes	•	•		•	•	•	•	•
Use proper intonation, volume, pitch, modulation, and phrasing		•	•	•	•	•	•	•
Speak with a command of standard English conventions	•	•	•	•	•	•	•	•
Use appropriate language for formal and informal settings	•	•	•	•T	•	•	•	•

Speak for a purpose	Pre-K	K	1	2	3	4	5	6
To ask and answer questions	•	•	•	•	•	•	•	•
To give directions and instructions	•	•	•	•	•	•	•	•
To retell, paraphrase, or explain information		•	•	•	•	•	•	•
To communicate needs and share ideas and experiences	•	•	•	•	•	•	•	•
To participate in conversations and discussions	•	•	•	•	•	•	•	•
To express an opinion	•	•	•	•	•	•	•	•
To deliver dramatic recitations, interpretations, or performances	•	•	•	•	•	•	•	•
To deliver presentations or oral reports (narrative, descriptive, persuasive, and informational)	•	•	•	•	•	•	•	•
Stay on topic	•	•	•	•	•	•		•
Use appropriate verbal and nonverbal elements (such as facial expression, gestures, eye contact, posture)	•	•	•	•	•	•	•	•
Identify and/or demonstrate methods to manage or overcome communication anxiety						•	•	•

Viewing/Media	Pre-K	K	1	2	3	4	5	6
Interact with and respond to a variety of print and non-print media for a range of purposes	•	•	•	•	•	•	•	•
Compare and contrast print, visual, and electronic media					•	•	•	•
Analyze and evaluate media			•	•	•	•	•	•
Recognize purpose, bias, propaganda, and persuasive techniques in media messages			•	•	•	•	•	•

Research and Study Skills

Understand and Use Graphic Sources	Pre-K	K	1	2	3	4	5	6
Advertisement			•	•	•	•	•	•
Chart/table	•	•	•	•	•	•	•	•
Diagram/scale drawing			•	•	•	•	•	•
Graph (bar, circle, line, picture)		•	•	•	•	•	•	•
Illustration, photograph, caption, label	•	•	•	•	•	•	•	•
Map/globe	•	•	•	•	•	•	•	•
Order form/application						•	•	•
Poster/announcement	•	•	•	•	•	•	•	
Schedule						•	•	•
Sign	•	•	•	•		•		
Time line				•	•	•	•	•

Understand and Use Reference Sources	Pre-K	K	1	2	3	4	5	6
Know and use parts of a book to locate information	•	•	•	•	•	•	•	•
Use alphabetical order			•	•	•	•		
Understand purpose, structure, and organization of reference sources (print, electronic, media, Internet)	•	•	•	•	•	•	•	•
Almanac						•	•	•
Atlas		•		•	•	•	•	•
Card catalog/library database				•	•	•	•	•
Dictionary/glossary		•	•	•	•T	•T	•T	•T
Encyclopedia			•	•	•	•	•	•
Magazine/periodical				•	•	•	•	•
Newspaper and Newsletter			•	•	•	•	•	•
Readers' Guide to Periodical Literature						•	•	•
Technology (computer and non-computer electronic media)		•	•	•	•	•	•	•
Thesaurus				•	•	•	•	•

Study Skills and Strategies	Pre-K	K	1	2	3	4	5	6
Adjust reading rate			•	•	•	•	•	•
Clarify directions	•	•	•	•	•	•	•	•
Outline				•	•	•	•	•
Skim and scan			•	•	•	•	•	•
SQP3R						•	•	•
Summarize		•	•	•	•	•	•	•
Take notes, paraphrase, and synthesize			•	•	•	•	•	•
Use graphic and semantic organizers to organize information		•	•	•	•	•	•	•

• instructional opportunity   **T** tested in standardized test format

Test-Taking Skills and Strategies

Test-Taking Skills and Strategies	Pre-K	K	1	2	3	4	5	6
Understand the question, the vocabulary of tests, and key words				•	•	•	•	•
Answer the question; use information from the text (stated or inferred)		•	•	•	•	•	•	•
Write across texts				•	•	•	•	•
Complete the sentence				•	•	•	•	•

Technology/New Literacies

Technology/New Literacies	Pre-K	K	1	2	3	4	5	6
Non-Computer Electronic Media								
Audio tapes/CDs, video tapes/DVDs	•	•	•	•	•	•	•	
Film, television, and radio		•	•	•	•	•	•	•
Computer Programs and Services: Basic Operations and Concepts								
Use accurate computer terminology	•	•	•	•	•	•	•	•
Create, name, locate, open, save, delete, and organize files		•	•	•	•	•	•	•
Use input and output devices (such as mouse, keyboard, monitor, printer, touch screen)	•	•	•	•	•	•	•	•
Use basic keyboarding skills		•	•	•	•	•	•	•
Responsible Use of Technology Systems and Software								
Work cooperatively and collaboratively with others; follow acceptable use policies	•	•	•	•	•	•	•	•
Recognize hazards of Internet searches		•	•	•	•	•	•	•
Respect intellectual property					•	•	•	•
Information and Communication Technologies: Information Acquisition								
Use electronic web (non-linear) navigation, online resources, databases, keyword searches			•	•	•	•	•	•
Use visual and non-textual features of online resources	•	•	•	•	•	•	•	•
Internet inquiry			•	•	•	•	•	•
Identify questions			•	•	•	•	•	•
Locate, select, and collect information			•	•	•	•	•	•
Analyze information			•	•	•	•	•	•
Evaluate electronic information sources for accuracy, relevance, bias					•	•	•	•
Understand bias/subjectivity of electronic content (about this site, author search, date created)						•	•	•
Synthesize information						•	•	•
Communicate findings				•	•	•	•	•
Use fix-up strategies (such as clicking *Back*, *Forward*, or *Undo*; redoing a search; trimming the URL)			•	•	•	•	•	•
Communication								
Collaborate, publish, present, and interact with others		•	•	•	•	•	•	•
Use online resources (e-mail, bulletin boards, newsgroups)			•	•	•	•	•	•
Use a variety of multimedia formats			•	•	•	•	•	•
Problem Solving								
Select the appropriate software for the task	•	•	•	•	•	•	•	•
Use technology resources for solving problems and making informed decisions				•	•	•	•	•
Determine when technology is useful					•	•	•	•

The Research Process

The Research Process	Pre-K	K	1	2	3	4	5	6
Choose and narrow the topic; frame and revise questions for inquiry		•	•	•	•	•	•	•
Choose and evaluate appropriate reference sources				•	•	•	•	•
Locate and collect information	•	•	•	•	•	•	•	•
Take notes/record findings					•	•	•	•
Combine and compare information				•	•	•	•	•
Evaluate, interpret, and draw conclusions about key information		•	•	•	•	•	•	•
Summarize information		•	•	•	•	•	•	•
Make an outline				•	•	•	•	•
Organize content systematically			•	•	•	•	•	•
Communicate information			•	•	•	•	•	•
Write and present a report				•	•	•	•	•
Include citations						•	•	•
Respect intellectual property/plagiarism						•	•	•
Select and organize visual aids		•	•	•	•	•	•	•

A

Abbreviations, 4.6 685e–685f.

Accountability. *See* **Adequate yearly progress.**

Achieving English proficiency. *See* **ELL (English Language Learners) suggestions.**

Activate prior knowledge. *See* **Prereading strategies.**

Adequate yearly progress (AYP), 4.1 16g–16h, 4.2 140g–140h, 4.3 266g–266h, 4.4 390g–390h, 4.5 514g–514h, 4.6 636g–636h

Adjectives, 4.4 537e–537f
  articles, 4.5 537e–537f
  comparative and superlative, 4.5 559e–559f
  proper, 4.4 537e

Advanced learners
  critical thinking, 4.6 654
  group time, 4.1 18f–18g, 40f–40g, 66f–66g, 88f–88g, 112f–112g, DI·3, DI·5, DI·7, DI·9, DI·11, DI·13, DI·15, DI·17, DI·19, DI·21, DI·23, DI·25, DI·27, DI·29, DI·31, DI·33, DI·35, DI·37, DI·39, DI·41, DI·43, DI·45, DI·47, DI·49, DI·51, 4.2 142f–142g, 162f–162g, 188f–188g, 212f–212g, 240f–240g, DI·3, DI·5, DI·7, DI·9, DI·11, DI·13, DI·15, DI·17, DI·19, DI·21, DI·23, DI·25, DI·27, DI·29, DI·31, DI·33, DI·35, DI·37, DI·39, DI·41, DI·43, DI·45, DI·47, DI·49, DI·51, 4.3 268f–268g, 292f–292g, 314f–314g, 338f–338g, 360f–360g, DI·3, DI·5, DI·7, DI·9, DI·11, DI·13, DI·15, DI·17, DI·19, DI·21, DI·23, DI·25, DI·27, DI·29, DI·31, DI·33, DI·35, DI·37, DI·39, DI·41, DI·43, DI·45, DI·47, DI·49, DI·51, 4.4 392f–392g, 416f–416g, 440f–440g, 466f–466g, 488f–488g, DI·3, DI·5, DI·7, DI·9, DI·11, DI·13, DI·15, DI·17, DI·19, DI·21, DI·23, DI·25, DI·27, DI·29, DI·31, DI·33, DI·35, DI·37, DI·39, DI·41, DI·43, DI·45, DI·47, DI·49, DI·51, 4.5 516f–516g, 538f–538g, 560f–560g, 582f–582g, 608f–608g, DI·3, DI·5, DI·7, DI·9, DI·11, DI·13, DI·15, DI·17, DI·19, DI·21, DI·23, DI·25, DI·27, DI·29, DI·31, DI·33, DI·35, DI·37, DI·39, DI·41, DI·43, DI·45, DI·47, DI·49, DI·51, 4.6 638f–638g, 660f–660g, 686f–686g, 712f–712g, 738f–738g, DI·3, DI·5, DI·7, DI·9, DI·11, DI·13, DI·15, DI·17, DI·19, DI·21, DI·23, DI·25, DI·27, DI·29, DI·31, DI·33, DI·35, DI·37, DI·39, DI·41, DI·43, DI·45, DI·47, DI·49, DI·51. *See also* **Grouping students for instruction.**
  leveled readers, 4.1 LR7–LR9, LR16–LR18, LR25–LR27, LR34–LR36, LR43–LR45, 4.2 LR7–LR9, LR16–LR18, LR25–LR27, LR34–LR36, LR43–LR45, 4.3 LR7–LR9, LR16–LR18, LR25–LR27, LR34–LR36, LR43–LR45, 4.4 LR7–LR9, LR16–LR18, LR25–LR27, LR34–LR36, LR43–LR45, 4.5 LR7–LR9, LR16–LR18, LR25–LR27, LR34–LR36, LR43–LR45, 4.6 LR7–LR9, LR16–LR18, LR25–LR27, LR34–LR36, LR43–LR45
  resources, 4.1 18i, 40i, 66i, 88i, 112i, 4.2 142i, 162i, 188i, 212i, 240i, 4.3 268i, 292i, 314i, 338i, 360i, 4.4 392i, 416i, 440i, 466i, 488i, 4.5 516i, 538i, 560i, 582i, 608i, 4.6 638i, 660i, 686i, 712i, 738i
  writing, 4.1 WA9, 4.2 WA9, 4.3 WA9, 4.4 WA9, 4.5 WA9, 4.6 WA9

Adverbs, 4.5 581e–581f
  comparative and superlative, 4.4 607e–607f

Advertisement. *See* **Graphic sources.**

Affective domain. *See* **Habits and attitudes, Literary response and appreciation.**

Affixes. *See* **Spelling,** word structure; **Word structure,** prefixes, suffixes.

Alliteration. *See* **Sound devices and poetic elements.**

Almanac. *See* **Reference sources.**

Alphabetical order, 4.2 253, 4.4 453, 4.6 662b. *See also* **Vocabulary strategies.**

Analogies. *See* **Vocabulary strategies.**

Analyzing. *See* **Reading across texts.** In addition, analytical thinking questions are raised throughout Guiding Comprehension and Reader Response.

Answering questions. *See* **Questions, answering.**

Antonyms, 4.2 242b, 4.4 394–395, 405, 415c, 490–491, 495, 507c. *See also* **Vocabulary strategies.**

Application. *See* **Graphic sources.**

Appropriate word meaning, 4.1 20b, 68–69, 79, 87c, 4.2 231, 4.3 270–271, 277, 291c, 316b, 4.4 418–419, 427, 439c, 457, 4.6 640b, 662–663, 669, 673, 685c, 714b

Art activities. *See* **Cross-curricular activities.**

Art, interpreting. *See* **Literary craft,** illustrator's craft/style.

Asking questions. *See* **Questions, asking.**

Assessment
  classroom-based. "If/then" assessment occurs throughout lessons and Guiding Comprehension.
  fluency, 4.1 39a, 65a, 87a, 111a, 133a, WA15–WA16, DI·57, DI·58, 4.2 161a, 187a, 211a, 239a, 259a, WA15–WA16, DI·57, DI·58, 4.3 291a, 313a, 337a, 359a, 383a, WA15–WA16, DI·57, DI·58, 4.4 415a, 439a, 465a, 487a, 507a, WA15–WA16, DI·57, DI·58, 4.5 537a, 559a, 581a, 607a, 629a, WA15–WA16, DI·57, DI·58, 4.6 659a, 685a, 711a, 737a, 761a, WA15–WA16, DI·57, DI·58
  formal, 4.1 35, 61, 83, 107, 129, 134a, WA7, WA10–WA14, 4.2 157, 185, 209, 235, 257, 260a, WA7, WA10–WA14, 4.3 287, 309, 333, 355, 379, 384a, WA7, WA10–WA14, 4.4 411, 435, 463, 483, 503, 508a, WA7, WA10–WA14, 4.5 535, 555, 577, 603, 625, 630a, WA7, WA10–WA14, 4.6 657, 681, 707, 733, 757, 762a, WA7, WA10–WA11
  scoring guide (rubric), 4.1 34, 35, 60, 61, 82, 83, 106, 107, 128, 129, 134a, WA7, WA10–WA14, 4.2 156, 157, 184, 185, 208, 209, 233, 234, 256, 257, 260a, WA7, WA10–WA14, 4.3 286, 287, 308, 309, 332, 333, 354, 355, 378, 379, 384a, WA7, WA10–WA14, 4.4 410, 411, 434, 435, 462, 463, 482, 483, 501, 502, 508a, WA7, WA10–WA14, 4.5 534, 535, 554, 555, 576, 577, 602, 603, 624, 625, 630a, WA7, WA10–WA14, 4.6 655, 656, 680, 681, 706, 707, 732, 733, 756, 757, 762a, WA7, WA10–WA14
  self-assessment, 4.1 WA7, 4.2 WA7, 4.3 WA7, 4.4 WA7, 4.5 WA7, 4.6 WA7
  spelling, 4.1 39j, 65j, 87j, 111j, 133j, 4.2 161j, 187j, 211j, 239j, 259j, 4.3 291j, 313j, 337j, 359j, 383j, 4.4 415j, 439j, 465j, 487j, 507j, 4.5 537j, 559j, 581j, 607j, 629j, 4.6 659j, 685j, 711j, 737j, 761j
  test-taking strategies, 4.1 34, 38, 60, 64, 82, 106, 110, 128, 133g–133h, 138, 4.2 156, 160, 184, 187, 208, 211, 233, 256, 259, 259g–259h, 4.3 286, 290, 308, 312, 332, 336, 354, 378, 382, 383g–383h, 4.4 410, 414, 434, 438, 462, 482, 501, 506, 507g–507h, 4.5 534, 551, 554, 558, 576, 602, 606, 624, 628, 4.6 655, 659, 680, 684, 706, 710, 732, 756, 760

writing, 4.1 WA7, WA10–WA14, 4.2 WA7, WA10–WA14, 4.3 WA7, WA10–WA14, 4.4 WA7, WA10–WA14, 4.5 WA7, WA10–WA14, 4.6 WA7, WA10–WA11

Atlas. *See* **Reference sources.**

Attitudes, personal. *See* **Habits and attitudes.**

Authors (of reading selections)
  Alvarez, Julia, 4.1 139d, 4.6 690–705
  Armour, Richard, 4.4 464
  Beecham, Cristina, 4.6 658
  Begay, Shonto, 4.3 386–387
  Beres, Samantha, 4.2 210–211
  Bova, Ben, 4.1 139l, 4.5 612–623
  Brown, John, 4.1 108–111
  Bruchac, Joseph, 4.1 139j, 4.6 664–679
  Cherry, Lynne, 4.1 139l, 4.3 364–377
  Chief Lelooska, 4.3 334–337
  Daniel, Claire, 4.5 604–607
  Dewey, Jennifer Owings, 4.1 139f, 4.5 586–601
  Díaz, Katacha, 4.5 556–559
  DiCamillo, Kate, 4.1 22–33
  Falkner, David, 4.6 708–711
  Farjeon, Eleanor, 4.4 509
  Farris, Christine King, 4.1 139j, 4.6 642–654
  Fisher, Aileen, 4.4 510
  Gavin, Susan, 4.2 258–259
  George, Kristine O'Connell, 4.5 630
  Gerson, Mary-Joan, 4.3 318–331
  Grimes, Nikki, 4.2 260
  Guthrie, Woody, 4.1 130–133
  Halvorsen, Lisa, 4.1 116–127
  Hoban, Russell, 4.2 261
  Hoffman, Mary, 4.1 139d, 4.2 192–207
  Holub, Miroslav, 4.5 632–633
  Hopkins, Jackie Mims, 4.1 92–105
  Hopkins, Lee Bennett, 4.1 136
  Hughes, Langston, 4.1 134, 4.6 762
  Kennedy, X. J., 4.5 631, 4.6 763
  Kepplinger, Bonnie, 4.4 504–507
  Khalsa, Ek Ongkar K., 4.6 659
  Klobuchar, Lisa, 4.2 186–187
  Kramer, Stephen, 4.1 139f, 4.3 342–353
  Kranking, Kathy, 4.1 36–39
  Lasky, Kathryn, 4.1 139j, 4.2 216–232
  Levy, Constance Kling, 4.4 511
  Lewin, Ted, 4.1 139f, 4.5 542–553
  Lewis, J. Patrick, 4.6 765
  Livingston, Myra Cohn, 4.4 465, 4.6 762
  Massie, Elizabeth, 4.1 62–65
  Montgomery, Sy, 4.4 420–433
  Myers, Laurie, 4.1 44–59
  Nayer, Judy, 4.5 626–629
  Oh, Sadaharu, 4.6 708–711
  Old, Wendie C., 4.6 716–731
  Perez, Marlene, 4.6 682–685
  Perry, Andrea, 4.2 262–263
  Peterson, Ruth De Long, 4.1 137
  Rand, Gloria, 4.5 520–533
  Rumford, James, 4.4 470–481
  Ryan, Pam Muñoz, 4.5 564–575
  Sandin, Joan, 4.1 139h, 4.2 166–183
  St. George, Judith, 4.2 244–255
  Say, Allen, 4.1 70–81, 139h
  Schyffert, Bea Uusma, 4.6 742–755
  Selznick, Brian, 4.4 396–409
  Singer, Marilyn, 4.3 385
  Slattery, Margaret E., 4.4 444–461
  Smith Jr, Charles R., 4.2 146–155, 158–159, 160–161
  Sobol, Donald J., 4.1 139d, 4.4 492–500
  Sobol, Richard, 4.3 296–307
  Soto, Gary, 4.6 764
  Sow, Fatou Ndiaye, 4.4 508
  Stone, Tanya Lee, 4.3 380–383

Strahinich, Helen, 4.3 288–291
Sutherland, Tui T., 4.4 412–415
Van Allsburg, Chris, 4.1 139l, 4.3 272–285
Wachter, Joanne, 4.3 310–313
Washington, Linda, 4.5 536–537
Weil, Ann, 4.4 436–439
Withrow, Dawn, 4.6 659
Wong, Janet S., 4.1 135
Zolotow, Charlotte, 4.3 384

Author's craft/style/language. See **Literary craft,** author's craft/style/language.

Author's perspective/viewpoint/bias, 4.1 88l–88m, 4.3 313b, 4.5 537a. See also **Literary craft.**

Authors, program, 4.1 xx, 4.2 iv, 4.3 iv, 4.4 iv, 4.5 iv, 4.6 iv
Afflerbach, Peter
Blachowicz, Camille
Boyd, Candy Dawson
Cheyney, Wendy
Juel, Connie
Kame'enui, Edward
Leu, Donald
Paratore, Jeanne
Pearson, P. David
Sebesta, Sam
Simmons, Deborah
Vaughn, Sharon
Watts-Taffe, Susan
Wixson, Karen Kring

Author's purpose, 4.1 31, 40l–40m, 40–41, 47, 57, 63, 65b, 88l–88m, 88–89, 95, 103, 109, 111b, DI·16, DI·17, DI·36, DI·37, DI·53, DI·55, 4.3 369, 4.5 516l–516m, 516–517, 523, 529, 537b, DI·6, DI·7, DI·52, 4.6 695

Author study, 4.1 139b–139l

Autobiography. See **Genres.**

B

Background, build. See **Concept development; Prereading strategies,** activate prior knowledge.

Base words with and without spelling changes. See **Spelling,** word structure; **Word structure.**

Bibliography
self-selected reading, 4.1 DI·59, DI·60, TR14–TR17, 4.2 DI·59, DI·60, TR14–TR17, 4.3 DI·59, DI·60, TR14–TR17, 4.4 DI·59, DI·60, TR14–TR17, 4.5 DI·59, DI·60, TR14–TR17, 4.6 DI·59, DI·60, TR14–TR17
trade book library, 4.1 18i, 40i, 66i, 88i, 112i, 4.2 142i, 162i, 188i, 212i, 240i, 4.3 268i, 292i, 314i, 338i, 360i, 4.4 392i, 416i, 440i, 466i, 488i, 4.5 516i, 538i, 560i, 582i, 608i, 4.6 638i, 660i, 686i, 712i, 738i

Bilingual students. See **ELL (English Language Learners) suggestions.**

Biography. See **Genres.**

Build background. See **Concept development; Prereading strategies,** activate prior knowledge.

C

Capitalization, 4.6 685e–685f
abbreviations, 4.6 685e–685f
adjectives, proper, 4.4 537e
letter conventions, 4.3 313g
nouns, proper, 4.2 161e–161f, 4.6 685e–685f
sentences, 4.6 685e–685f
titles, 4.6 685e–685f, 761e–761f
See also **Writing process,** edit.

Card catalog. See **Reference sources.**

Career awareness, 4.2 240j, 4.6 744

Categorizing. See **Classifying.**

Cause and effect, 4.1 49, 4.2 142l–142m, 142–143, 149, 161, 161b, DI·6, DI·7, DI·52, 4.3 268l–268m, 268–269, 275, 281, 291, 291b, 323, 338l–338m, 347, DI·52, 4.4 466l–466m, 4.6 638l–638m, 638–639, 645, 653, 659, 659b, 738l–738m, DI·6, DI·7, DI·52

Central message of text. See **Main idea, Theme (as a story element).**

Character, 4.4 401, 440l–440m, 440–441, 449, 455, 459, DI·26, DI·27, DI·54, 4.5 DI·54, 4.6 686l–686m, 686–687, 693, 699, 703, 711b, DI·26, DI·27

Character Counts! See **Character education.**

Character education (as demonstrated in literature selections)
attentiveness, 4.4 470–481, 492–500, 4.5 586–601, 4.6 716–731, 742–755
caring, 4.1 22–33, 4.2 192–207, 4.5 520–533, 612–623, 4.6 642–654, 664–679
citizenship, 4.1 130–133, 4.2 244–255
fairness, 4.1 92–105, 4.3 334–337, 4.6 642–654, 664–679
initiative, 4.1 70–81, 4.2 192–207, 210–211, 4.4 444–461, 470–481, 4.5 536–537, 542–553, 604–607, 4.6 642–654, 690–705, 716–731
patience, 4.3 296–307, 4.4 420–433, 470–481, 4.6 716–731
respect, 4.1 70–81, 4.3 364–377, 4.5 586–601, 4.6 664–679, 690–705, 708–711
responsibility, 4.2 166–183, 216–232, 244–255, 4.3 364–377, 4.5 612–623, 4.6 742–755
trustworthiness, 4.1 62–65, 92–105, 4.2 216–232, 4.5 612–623

Charts and tables. See **Graphic sources.**

Choral reading. See **Fluency, reading.**

Chronology. See **Sequence.**

Chunking. See **Word structure,** chunking.

Classifying
statements of evidence. See **Fact and opinion, statements of.**
words into groups, 4.1 20b, 90a, 4.2 144a, 144b, 190a, 242b, 4.3 294b, 4.4 394a, 4.5 518b, 562b, 4.6 662b

Classroom-based assessment. "If/then" assessment occurs throughout lessons and Guiding Comprehension.

Classroom management, 4.1 18d–18e, 18f–18g, 18g-1–18g-4, 40d–40e, 40f–40g, 40g-1–40g-4, 66d–66e, 66f–66g, 66g-1–66g-4, 88d–88e, 88f–88g, 88g-1–88g-4, 112d–112e, 112f–112g, 112g-1–112g-4, 4.2 142d–142e, 142f–142g, 142g-1–142g-4, 162d–162e, 162f–162g, 162g-1–162g-4, 188d–188e, 188f–188g, 188g-1–188g-4, 212d–212e, 212f–212g, 212g-1–212g-4, 240d–240e, 240f–240g, 240g-1–240g-4, 4.3 268d–268e, 268f–268g, 268g-1–268g-4, 292d–292e, 292f–292g, 292g-1–292g-4, 314d–314e, 314f–314g, 314g-1–314g-4, 338d–338e, 338f–338g, 338g-1–338g-4, 360d–360e, 360f–360g, 360g-1–360g-4, 4.4 392d–392e, 392f–392g, 392g-1–392g-4, 416d–416e, 416f–416g, 416g-1–416g-4, 416, 440d–440e, 440f–440g, 440g-1–440g-4, 466d–466e, 466f–466g, 466g-1–466g-4, 488d–488e, 488f–488g, 488g-1–488g-4, 4.5 516d–516e, 516f–516g, 516g-1–516g-4, 538d–538e, 538f–538g, 538g-1–538g-4, 560d–560e, 560f–560g, 560g-1–560g-4, 582d–582e, 582f–582g, 582g-1–582g-4, 608d–608e, 608f–608g, 608g-1–608g-4, 4.6 638d–638e, 638f–638g, 638g-1–638g-4, 660d–660e, 660f–660g, 660g-1–660g-4, 686d–686e, 686f–686g, 686g-1–686g-4, 712d–712e, 712f–712g, 712g-1–712g-4, 738d–738e, 738f–738g, 738g-1–738g-4

Colon, 4.2 236, 4.3 313h

Comma, 4.6 659e–659f, 711e–711f
appositives, 4.6 711e–711f
compound/complex sentences, 4.1 111e–111f, 133f, 4.6 659e–659f
items in a series, 4.6 711e–711f

Common word parts. See **Word structure.**

Communication, effective. See **Listening,** tips; **Speaking,** tips.

Community, involvement of. See **School-home connection.**

Comparing and contrasting, 4.2 197, 4.4 392l–392m, 392–393, 399, 407, 415, 415b, 416l–416m, 416–417, 423, 431, 439, 439b, 499, DI·6, DI·7, DI·16, DI·17, DI·52, DI·53, 4.5 538l–538m, 538–539, 545, 549, 557, 559b, DI·16, DI·17, DI·53

Composition. See **Six-trait writing, Writing forms/products, Writing Process, Writing purpose.**

Compound words, 4.1 68b, 4.2 214b, 4.6 662b. See also **Spelling,** word structure; **Vocabulary strategies.**

Comprehension skills, explicit/implicit instruction. See **Author's purpose; Cause and effect; Character; Classifying; Comparing and contrasting; Conclusions, drawing; Fact and opinion, statements of; Graphic sources; Main idea; Plot; Predicting; Sequence; Setting; Summarizing; Theme (as a story element).**

Comprehension strategies. See **Graphic and semantic organizers; Monitor and fix up; Questions, answering; Questions, asking; Self-check; Story structure; Text structure; Visualizing.**

Computers, using. See **New literacies (for student reading), Technology; Writing with technology.**

Concept development, 4.1 17a, 18a, 18l, 20a, 40a, 40l, 42a, 66a, 66l, 68a, 88a, 88l, 90a, 112a, 112l, 114a, 134a, 4.2 141a, 142a, 142l, 144a, 162a, 162l, 164a, 188a, 188l, 190a, 212a, 212l, 214a, 240a, 240l, 242a, 260a, 4.3 267a, 268a, 268l, 270a, 292a, 292l, 294a, 314a, 314l, 316a, 338l, 338l, 340a, 360a, 360l, 362a, 384a, 4.4 391a, 392a, 392l, 394a, 416a, 416l, 418a, 440a, 440l, 442a, 466a, 466l, 468a, 488a, 488l, 490a, 508a, 4.5 515a, 516a, 516l, 518a, 538a, 538l, 540a, 560a, 560l, 562a, 582a, 582l, 584a, 608a, 608l, 610a, 630a, 4.6 637a, 638a, 638l, 640a, 660a, 660l, 662a, 686a, 686l, 688a, 712a, 712l, 714a, 738a, 738l, 740a, 762a. See also **Prereading strategies,** activate prior knowledge.

Conclusions, drawing, 4.2 153, 162l–162m, 162–163, 169, 179, 181, 187b, 188l–188m, 188–189, 195, 203, 205, 211b, DI·16, DI·17, DI·26, DI·27, DI·54, 4.5 569, 591, 608l–608m, 608–609, 615, 619, 627, 629b, DI·46, DI·47, DI·56

Conjunctions, 4.6 659e–659f

Connections, making
text to self, 4.1 32, 46, 74, 98, 148, 4.2 192, 197, 218, 4.3 274, 302, 324, 4.4 400, 422, 460, 472, 4.5 548, 592, 618, 4.6 668, 696, 730, 746
text to text, 4.1 39, 58, 65, 87, 104, 111, 133, 4.2 161, 172, 182, 206, 230, 259, 4.3 291, 313, 330, 337, 368, 383, 4.4 415, 439, 450, 465, 487, 498, 507, 4.5 532, 537, 552, 559, 574, 581, 607, 622, 629, 4.6 646, 659, 678, 685, 737, 761

text to world, 4.1 30, 80, 126, 4.2 154, 254, 4.3 284, 306, 348, 352, 376, 4.4 408, 432, 480, 4.5 566, 600, 4.6 652, 704, 718, 754

Connotation and denotation, 4.4 442b

Content-area texts
  cultures, 4.1 16, 70–81, 84–87, 4.3 364–377, 4.5 542–553, 556–559, 4.6 690–705
  science, 4.1 36–39, 108–111, 130–133, 4.3 288–291, 310–313, 356–359, 380–383, 4.4 412–415, 436–439, 504–507, 4.5 626–629, 4.6 758–761
  social studies, 4.1 65, 4.2 186–187, 210–211, 258–259, 4.5 536–537, 556–559, 604–607, 4.6 682–685, 708–711

Content-area vocabulary, 4.1 36, 62, 108, 130, 4.2 186, 210, 258, 4.3 288, 310, 354, 380, 4.4 412, 436, 464, 504, 4.5 536, 540b, 556, 584b, 604, 626, 4.6 682, 708, 758

Context clues for meaning, 4.1 20b, 90, 101, 111c, 4.2 242b, 4.3 270, 277, 291c, 294, 305, 313c, 316b, 316–317, 325, 337c, 4.4 394–395, 405, 415c, 418–419, 427, 439c, 468b, 490, 495, 507c, 4.5 518–519, 525, 537c, 562–563, 573, 581c, 610b, 610–611, 617, 629c, 4.6 640b, 688–689, 701, 711c, 714b, 714–715, 721, 729, 737c, 740–741, 749, 761c
  antonyms, 4.2 242b, 4.4 394–395, 405, 415c, 490–491, 495, 507c
  appropriate word meaning, 4.1 20b, 4.3 270–271, 277, 291c, 316b, 4.4 418–419, 427, 439c, 4.6 640b, 714b
  definition and explanation, 4.6 714–715
  homographs, 4.5 518–519, 525, 537c, 761c
  homonyms, 4.3 294–295, 305, 315c, 4.5 518–519, 525, 537c, 4.6 740–741, 749, 761c, DI·45
  multiple-meaning words, 4.1 20b, 4.3 270–271, 277, 291c, 316b, 4.4 418–419, 427, 439c, 4.6 640b, 714b
  synonyms, 4.1 90–91, 101, 111c, 4.4 394–395, 405, 415c, 490–491, 495, 507c, 4.5 610b, 610–611, 617, 629c
  unfamiliar words, 4.1 DI·35, 4.3 316–317, 325, 337c, 4.4 486b, DI·5, DI·15, DI·45, 4.5 562–563, 573, 581c, DI·5, DI·25, DI·45, 4.6 688–689, 701, 711c, 714–715, 721, 729, 737c, DI·25, DI·35
  See also **Vocabulary strategies.**

Contractions, 4.4 507e–507f. See also **Spelling,** word structure.

Contrasting. See **Comparing and contrasting.**

Conventions of standard language. See **Capitalization, Grammar and usage, Punctuation.**

Creative/dramatic activities, 4.1 39d, 66j, 4.2 188j, 211d, 4.3 268j, 314j, 337d, 4.4 440j, 465d, 4.5 537d, 608j, 4.6 638j. See also **Speaking,** activities.

Creative thinking. Creative thinking questions appear throughout Differentiated Instruction Group Time lesson plans for each lesson.

Critical thinking
  analyzing, 4.1 34, 60, 82, 106, 128, 4.2 156, 184, 208, 233, 256, 4.3 286, 308, 332, 354, 378, 4.4 410, 434, 462, 482, 501, 4.5 534, 554, 576, 602, 624, 4.6 655, 680, 706, 732, 756. In addition, analytical thinking questions are raised throughout Guiding Comprehension and Reader Response.
  comparing and contrasting across selections (intertextuality), 4.1 39, 58, 65, 87, 104, 111, 133, 4.2 161, 172, 182, 206, 230, 259, 4.3 291, 313, 330, 337, 368, 383, 4.4 415, 450, 465,

498, 507, 4.5 532, 537, 552, 559, 574, 581, 607, 622, 629, 4.6 646, 659, 678, 685, 737, 761
  comparing and contrasting within a text, 4.2 196, 197, 4.4 392l–392m, 392–393, 398, 399, 407, 415, 415b, 416l–416m, 416–417, 422, 423, 431, 439, 439b, 498, 499, 4.5 538l–538m, 538–539, 545, 548, 549, 557, 559b
  evaluating and critiquing ideas and text, 4.1 34, 60, 82, 106, 128, 4.2 156, 184, 208, 233, 256, 4.3 286, 308, 332, 354, 378, 4.4 410, 434, 462, 482, 501, 4.5 534, 554, 576, 602, 624, 4.6 655, 680, 706, 732, 756
  inferring, 4.1 34, 60, 82, 106, 128, 4.2 156, 184, 208, 233, 256, 4.3 286, 308, 332, 354, 378, 4.4 410, 434, 462, 482, 501, 4.5 534, 554, 576, 602, 624, 4.6 655, 680, 706, 732, 756
  organizing ideas/information, 4.1 20a, 42a, 68a, 90a, 114a, 4.2 144a, 164a, 190a, 214a, 242a, 4.3 270a, 294a, 316a, 340a, 362a, 4.4 394a, 418a, 442a, 468a, 490a, 4.5 518a, 540a, 562a, 584a, 610a, 4.6 640a, 662a, 668a, 714a, 737g–737h, 740a
  synthesizing ideas from different texts and media, 4.1 39k, 58, 65k, 87k, 104, 111k, 133, 133k, 4.2 161k, 187k, 206, 211k, 239k, 259, 259k, 4.3 291, 291k, 313k, 330, 337, 337k, 359k, 383, 383k, 4.4 415k, 439k, 450, 465k, 487k, 498, 507k, 4.5 532, 537, 537k, 552, 559k, 574, 581k, 607, 607k, 622, 629k, 4.6 646, 659, 659k, 678, 685k, 711k, 737k, 761k
  synthesizing ideas within a text, 4.2 196, 197, 4.4 392l–392m, 392–393, 398, 399, 407, 415, 415b, 416l–416m, 416–417, 422, 423, 430, 431, 439, 439b, 498, 499, 4.5 538l–538m, 538–539, 545, 548, 549, 557, 559b
  See also **Conclusions, drawing; Generalizations, making; Problems, solving.** In addition, critical thinking questions appear throughout Guiding Comprehension in each lesson and Differentiated Instruction Group Time lesson plans for each lesson.

Cross-curricular activities
  art, 4.1 18j, 40j, 4.2 240j, 4.3 338j, 4.4 416j, 4.5 538j, 4.6 686j
  drama, 4.1 39d, 66j, 4.2 188j, 211d, 4.3 268j, 314j, 337d, 4.4 440j, 465d, 4.5 537d, 608j, 4.6 638j
  health, 4.1 88j, 4.2 212j, 4.4 392j, 4.5 516j, 4.6 738j
  listening, 4.1 18j, 40j, 66j, 88j, 112j, 4.2 142j, 162j, 188j, 212j, 240j, 4.3 268j, 292j, 314j, 338j, 360j, 4.4 392j, 416j, 440j, 466j, 488j, 4.5 516j, 538j, 560j, 582j, 608j, 4.6 638j, 660j, 686j, 712j, 738j
  math, 4.1 112j, 4.2 142j, 4.3 292j, 4.4 466j, 4.5 560j, 4.6 712j
  music, 4.2 162j, 4.3 360j, 4.4 488j, 4.5 582j, 4.6 660j
  science, 4.1 37, 109, 111, 119, 121, 125, 131, 4.2 199, 4.3 268k, 275, 281, 288, 289, 291, 292k, 299, 301, 305, 311, 314k, 321, 329, 335, 338k, 345, 347, 351, 360k, 369, 373, 375, 381, 4.4 392k, 399, 405, 413, 416k, 425, 431, 437, 439, 440k, 457, 459, 465, 466k, 488k, 495, 505, 4.5 516k, 523, 525, 529, 582k, 591, 595, 599, 608k, 615, 617, 621, 4.6 711, 712k, 719, 721, 727, 738k, 745, 747, 753
  social studies, 4.1 18k, 25, 29, 40k, 47, 51, 57, 63, 66k, 73, 75, 79, 88k, 95, 103, 4.2 142k, 149, 153, 159, 162k, 169, 173, 179, 187, 188k, 203, 205, 212k, 219, 225, 227, 229, 240k, 247, 249, 253, 259, 4.4 475, 479, 4.5 536, 538k, 545, 547, 551, 560k, 569, 573, 4.6 638k, 645, 651, 660k, 667, 669, 675, 686k, 693, 695, 701
  technology, 4.1 18k, 40k, 66k, 88k, 112k, 4.2 142k, 162k, 188k, 212k, 240k, 4.3 268k,

292k, 314k, 338k, 360k, 4.4 392k, 416k, 440k, 466k, 488k, 4.5 516k, 538k, 560k, 582k, 608k, 4.6 638k, 660k, 686k, 712k, 738k
  writing/vocabulary, 4.1 18k, 40k, 66k, 88k, 112k, 4.2 142k, 162k, 188k, 212k, 240k, 4.3 268k, 292k, 314k, 338k, 360k, 4.4 392k, 416k, 440k, 466k, 488k, 4.5 516k, 538k, 560k, 582k, 608k, 4.6 638k, 660k, 686k, 712k, 738k

Cross-Curricular Centers, 4.1 18j–18k, 40j–40k, 66j–66k, 88j–88k, 112j–112k, 4.2 142j–142k, 162j–162k, 188j–188k, 212j–212k, 240j–240k, 4.3 268j–268k, 292j–292k, 314j–314k, 338j–338k, 360j–360k, 4.4 392j–392k, 416j–416k, 440j–440k, 466j–466k, 488j–488k, 4.5 516j–516k, 538j–538k, 560j–560k, 582j–582k, 608j–608k, 4.6 638j–638k, 660j–660k, 686j–686k, 712j–712k, 738j–738k

Cross-textual comparisons. See **Connections, making; Reading across texts.**

Cultures, appreciating. See **Habits and attitudes,** toward other groups and people; **Multicultural connections.**

Cursive. See **Handwriting.**

Decoding. See **Phonics, Word structure.**

Denotation and connotation. See **Connotation and denotation.**

Details and facts, 4.1 75, 4.2 247, 4.5 589, 608

Diagram. See **Graphic sources.**

Dialogue. See **Fluency, reading; Literary devices.**

Dictionary/glossary
  definitions, 4.2 214–215, 221, 253, 4.5 537l, 4.6 711l
  guide words, 4.2 173, 177, 221, 231, 4.4 453, 465c, 4.6 711l
  multiple meaning words, 4.1 68–69, 79, 87c, 231, 4.4 457, DI·25, 4.6 662–663, 669, 673, 685c, DI·15
  pronunciation, 4.2 164–165, 214–215, 221, 239c, 242–243
  spelling, 4.4 WA6, 4.6 711l
  unfamiliar words, 4.2 164–165, 173, 177, 187c, 214–215, 221, 239c, 242–243, 253, 259c, DI·15, DI·35, DI·45, 4.4 442–443, 453, 465c, 468b
  See also **Reference sources,** dictionary/glossary; **Vocabulary strategies.**

Differentiated instruction, 4.1 DI·2–DI·51, 4.2 DI·2–DI·51, 4.3 DI·2–DI·51, 4.4 DI·2–DI·51, 4.5 DI·2–DI·51, 4.6 DI·2–DI·51. See also **Advanced learners, Intervention.**

Directions, following
  oral, 4.3 359
  written, 4.3 338k, 4.4 415l, 465l, 4.6 737l

Discussion. See **Speaking,** activities.

Drama. See **Cross-curricular activities, Genres.**

Dramatic activities, 4.1 39d, 66j, 4.2 188j, 211d, 4.3 268j, 314j, 337d, 4.4 440j, 465d, 4.5 537d, 608j, 4.6 638j. See also **Speaking,** activities.

Drawing conclusions. See **Conclusions, drawing.**

E

Echo reading. See **Fluency,** reading.

Electronic information. See **Technology,** skills for using technology.

ELL (English Language Learners) suggestions
  access content, 4.1 18m, 18, 20, 22, 36, 39b, 40m, 40, 42, 65b, 66m, 66, 68, 70, 74, 80, 85, 87b, 88m, 88, 90, 92, 94, 100, 109, 111b, 112m, 112, 114, 116, 118, 122, 133b, 4.2 142, 142m, 144, 146, 148, 161b, 162m, 162, 164, 166, 170, 174, 176, 187b, 188m, 188, 190, 196, 200, 211b, 212m, 212, 214, 218, 220, 228, 232, 239b, 240m, 240, 242, 248, 259a, 4.3 268m, 268, 270, 284, 288, 291b, 292m, 292, 294, 302, 313b, 314m, 314, 316, 322, 337b, 338m, 338, 340, 359b, 360m, 360, 362, 364, 374, 383a, 4.4 392m, 392, 394, 398, 412, 415b, 416, 418, 420, 439b, 440m, 440, 442, 444, 450, 465b, 466m, 466, 468, 470, 472, 480, 485, 487b, 488m, 488, 490, 492, 494, 498, 507b, 4.5 516m, 516, 518, 520, 524, 537b, 538m, 538, 540, 544, 550, 556, 559b, 560, 562, 572, 579, 581b, 582m, 582, 584, 590, 596, 604, 607b, 608m, 608, 610, 612, 618, 629b, 4.6 638b, 638, 640, 648, 659b, 660m, 660, 662, 664, 674, 678, 682, 685b, 686m, 686, 688, 711b, 712m, 712, 714, 728, 735, 737b, 738m, 738, 740, 742, 744, 759, 761b
  activate prior knowledge, 4.1 48, 104, 4.2 154, 180, 237, 244, 4.3 272, 296, 310, 318, 334, 342, 356, 4.4 396, 504, 4.5 522, 542, 564, 4.5 586, 616, 642, 676, 690, 754
  assessment, 4.2 156, 207, 4.3 354, 4.5 624, 4.6 732
  build background, 4.1 20a, 42a, 44, 63, 68a, 72, 90a, 114a, 130, 4.2 144a, 152, 159, 164a, 190a, 192, 214a, 216, 242a, 4.3 270a, 292m, 294a, 316a, 340a, 362a, 368, 381, 4.4 394a, 416m, 418a, 436, 442a, 468a, 474, 490a, 496, 4.5 518a, 526, 540a, 560m, 562a, 574, 584a, 598, 610a, 627, 4.6 640a, 650, 662a, 668, 688a, 692, 700, 709, 714a, 716, 740a, 748, 752
  check retelling, 4.1 34, 60, 82, 106, 128, 4.2 184, 233, 256, 4.3 286, 308, 332, 378, 4.4 410, 434, 462, 482, 501, 4.5 534, 554, 576, 602, 4.6 655, 680, 706, 756
  context clues, 4.1 28, 54, 78, 96, 124, 4.2 202, 226, 4.3 278, 300, 324, 348, 350, 366, 370, 4.4 422, 430, 446, 458, 4.5 524, 532, 592, 614, 622, 4.6 644, 652, 694
  extend language, 4.1 24, 26, 50, 56, 76, 120, 126, 4.2 172, 182, 194, 206, 230, 252, 4.3 276, 298, 304, 320, 330, 346, 4.4 402, 424, 426, 432, 454, 476, 500, 4.5 528, 530, 546, 552, 570, 588, 594, 600, 4.6 666, 672, 696, 702, 718, 720, 724, 726, 730, 746, 750
  fluency, 4.1 30, 39a, 65a, 87a, 111a, 133a, 4.3 326, 4.4 406, 452, 4.5 568, 620, 4.6 704
  grammar support, 4.1 39e, 65e, 87e, 111e, 133e, 4.2 161a, 161e, 168, 187, 187a, 211a, 211e, 239a, 239e, 259a, 259e, 4.3 282, 291a, 291e, 313a, 313e, 337, 337e, 359a, 359e, 383a, 383e, 4.4 415a, 415e, 439a, 439e, 465a, 465e, 487a, 487e, 507a, 507e, 4.5 537a, 537e, 559a, 559e, 581a, 581e, 607a, 607e, 629a, 629e, 4.6 659a, 659e, 685a, 685e, 711a, 711e, 737a, 737e, 761a, 761e
  guided practice, 4.1 38, 86, 132, 4.2 160, 238, 4.3 312, 358, 4.4 438, 486, 4.5 580, 606, 628, 4.6 736
  idioms, 4.1 32, 52, 98, 102, 4.2 150, 198, 204, 222, 246, 250, 254, 4.3 274, 280, 306, 328, 344, 352, 4.4 400, 404, 408, 428, 448, 456, 460, 478, 4.5 548, 566, 616, 4.6 646, 670, 698, 722

  independent practice, 4.1 64, 110, 4.4 414, 506, 4.6 684
  resources, 4.1 18g, 4.2 142g, 162g, 188g, 212g, 240g, 4.3 268g, 292g, 314g, 338g, 360g, 4.4 392g, 416g, 440g, 466g, 488g, 4.5 516g, 538g, 560g, 582g, 608g, 4.6 638g, 660g, 686g, 712g, 738g
  spelling/phonics support, 4.1 39i, 65i, 87i, 111i, 133i, 4.2 161i, 187i, 211i, 239i, 259i, 4.3 291i, 313i, 337i, 359i, 383i, 4.4 415i, 439i, 465i, 487i, 507i, 4.5 537i, 559i, 581i, 607i, 629i, 659i, 685i, 711i, 737i, 761i
  test practice, 4.3 290, 336, 382, 4.5 606
  use the strategy, 4.5 558, 4.6 710, 760
  vocabulary support, 4.1 39d, 65d, 87d, 111d, 133d, 4.2 161d, 187d, 211d, 239d, 259d, 4.3 291d, 313d, 337d, 359d, 383d, 4.4 415d, 439d, 465d, 487d, 507d, 4.5 537d, 559d, 581d, 607d, 629d, 4.6 659d, 685d, 711d, 737d, 761d
  writing support, 4.1 39g, 65g, 87g, 111g, 133g, WA4, WA6, WA9, 4.2 161g, 187g, 211g, 239g, 259g, WA4, WA6, WA9, 4.3 291g, 313g, 337g, 359g, 383g, 385h, WA4, WA6, WA9, 4.4 415g, 439g, 465g, 487g, 507g, WA4, WA6, WA9, 4.5 537g, 559g, 581g, 607g, 629g, WA4, WA6, WA9, 4.6 659g, 685g, 711g, 737g, 761g, WA4, WA6, WA9

E-mail. *See* **Genres; Technology,** new literacies.

Encyclopedia (as a reference source). *See* **Reference sources.**

Endings. *See* **Spelling,** word structure; **Vocabulary strategies; Word structure.**

End punctuation. *See* **Exclamation mark, Period, Question mark.**

English, conventions of. *See* **Capitalization; Grammar and usage; Punctuation; Writing process,** edit.

ESL (English as a Second Language). *See* **ELL (English Language Learners) suggestions.**

Essential message. *See* **Main idea; Theme (as a story element).**

Etymologies. *See* **Vocabulary development,** etymologies for meaning.

Evaluation. *See* **Assessment.**

Exaggeration. *See* **Literary devices.**

Exclamation mark, 4.1 65e–65f

Expository nonfiction. *See* **Genres.**

F

Fact and fiction. *See* **Fact and opinion, statements of.**

Fact and nonfact. *See* **Fact and opinion, statements of.**

Fact and opinion, statements of, 4.1 125, 4.2 212l–212m, 212–213, 219, 227, 229, 236, 239b, 4.2 DI·36, DI·37, DI·55, 4.3 292l–292m, 292–293, 299, 303, 311, 313b, DI·53, 660–661, 667, 675, 683, 685b, 747, DI·16, DI·17, DI·53

Family involvement. *See* **School-home connection.**

Fantasy. *See* **Genres.**

Figurative language
  idiom, 4.1 39b, 4.4 507b
  metaphor, 4.6 685b, 711b
  simile, 4.3 359b, 4.6 685b, 761b
  slang, 4.1 103

Fix-up strategies. *See* **Monitor and fix up.**

Flashback. *See* **Literary devices.**

Flexible grouping. *See* **Grouping students for instruction.**

Fluency, reading
  assessment, 4.1 39a, 65a, 87a, 111a, 133a, WA15–WA16, 4.2 161a, 187a, 211a, 239a, 259a, WA15–WA16, 4.3 291a, 313a, 337a, 359a, 383a, WA15–WA16, 4.4 415a, 439a, 465a, 487a, 507a, WA15–WA16, 4.5 537a, 559a, 581a, 607a, 629a, WA15–WA16, 4.6 659a, 685a, 711a, 737a, 761a, WA15–WA16
  characterization, 4.2 188l, 211a, 4.4 488l, 507a
  choral reading, 4.1 39a, 87a, 4.2 187a, 259a, 4.3 313a, 337a, 383a, 4.4 465a, 4.5 537a, 581a
  dialogue, 4.2 188l, 211a, 4.4 488l, 507a
  echo reading, 4.1 65a, 111a, 133a, 4.2 161a, 211a, 239a, 4.3 291a, 359a, 4.4 415a, 439a, 487a, 507a, 4.5 559a, 607a, 629a, 4.6 659a, 685a, 711a, 737a, 761a
  emotion, 4.2 162l, 187a, 4.4 392l, 415a, 4.5 582l, 607a, 4.6 686l, 711a
  emphasis, 4.2 240l, 259a, 4.4 440l, 465a, 4.6 660l, 685a
  modeling by teacher, 4.1 18l, 40l, 66l, 88l, 112l, 4.2 142l, 162l, 188l, 212l, 240l, 4.3 268l, 292l, 314l, 338l, 360l, 4.4 392l, 416l, 440l, 466l, 488l, 4.5 516l, 538l, 560l, 582l, 608l, 4.6 638l, 660l, 686l, 712l, 738l
  paired reading, 4.1 39a, 65a, 87a, 111a, 133a, 4.2 161a, 187a, 211a, 239a, 259a, 4.3 291a, 313a, 337a, 359a, 383a, 4.4 415a, 439a, 465a, 487a, 507a, 4.5 537a, 559a, 581a, 607a, 629a, 4.6 659a, 685a, 711a, 737a, 761a
  pauses, 4.1 40l, 65a, 4.3 338l, 359a, 4.5 516l, 537a
  phrasing, 4.1 112l, 133a, 4.4 439l, 466l, 487a, 4.5 538l, 559a, 4.6 638l, 659a
  pitch, 4.3 268l, 291a
  punctuation, attention to, 4.3 360l, 383a, 4.6 712l, 737a
  rate/pace, 4.1 66l, 87a, 4.5 608l, 629a, 4.6 738l, 761a
  rhythmic patterns of language, 4.2 142l, 161a, 4.3 314l, 337a
  stress, 4.2 240l, 259a, 4.4 440l, 465a, 4.6 660l, 685a
  tempo, 4.1 66l, 87a, 4.5 608l, 629a, 4.6 738l, 761a
  tone of voice, 4.1 18l, 39a, 4.3 292l, 313a, 4.5 560l, 581a
  volume, 4.1 88l, 111a, 4.2 212l, 239a

Folk tale. *See* **Genres.**

Following directions. *See* **Directions, following.**

Format (of text). *See* **Text structure.**

Free verse. *See* **Literary devices.**

Functional reading, 4.3 356–359, 4.6 708–711

G

Generalizations, making, 4.2 249, 4.3 301, 314l–314m, 314–315, 321, 329, 337, 337b, 360l–360m, 360–361, 367, 373, 383, 383b, DI·54, DI·55, 4.4 425, 4.6 712l–712m, 712–713, 719, 727, 735, 737b, DI·36, DI·37

Generate questions. *See* **Questions, asking.**

Genres
  autobiography, 4.1 139i, 4.6 708–711
  biography, 4.1 139a, 139i, 4.2 216–231, 4.4 470–481, 4.6 642–653, 664–679, 716–731
  drama, 4.2 192–207, 4.4 444–461
  e-mail, 4.2 236–239
  expository nonfiction, 4.1 108–111, 139a, 139e, 4.2 210–211, 244–255, 258–259, 4.3 288–291, 310–313, 342–353, 380–383, 4.4 412–415, 420–433, 436–439, 4.5 626–629, 4.6 682–685
  fable, 4.3 335, 383
  fairy tale, 4.1 139k, 4.4 392l–392m
  fairy tale, modern, 4.1 92–105
  fantasy, 4.1 139a, 139k, 4.3 272–285, 364–377, 383, 4.5 629b
  folk tale, 4.1 139k
  historical fantasy, 4.1 44–59
  historical fiction, 4.1 70–83, 139a, 139g, 4.2 166–183, 4.4 396–409, 4.5 520–533, 564–575
  how-to article, 4.2 186
  humorous fiction, 4.1 92–105
  Internet article, 4.1 84–87, 4.3 356–359, 4.4 484–487, 4.5 578–581, 4.6 734–737
  journal, 4.1 53, 57, 4.5 586–601
  legend, 4.1 139a
  letter, 4.5 592, 594–595
  lyric poetry, 4.1 139a
  mystery, 4.1 139a
  myth, 4.1 139a, 4.3 268m, 4.6 737
  narrative nonfiction, 4.1 62–65, 116–127, 4.5 536–537, 542–553, 604–607, 4.6 742–755
  narrative poetry 4.1 139a
  new literacies, 4.1 84–87, 4.2 236–241, 4.3 356–359, 4.4 484–487, 4.5 578–581, 4.6 734–737
  newspaper article, 4.4 504–507
  note, 4.4 403
  on-line reading, 4.1 84–87, 4.2 236–241, 4.3 356–359, 4.4 484–487, 4.5 578–581, 4.6 734–737
  personal essay, 4.1 119, 4.5 556–559
  photo essay, 4.3 296–307
  play, 4.2 192–207, 4.4 444–461
  poetry, 4.1 130–133, 134–137, 4.2 158–161, 260–263, 4.3 384–387, 4.4 464–465, 508–511, 4.5 630–633, 4.6 658–659, 762–765
  pourquoi tale, 4.3 318–330, 334–337
  realistic fiction, 4.1 22–33, 4.2 146–155, 4.4 492–500, 4.5 612–623
  science fiction, 4.1 139a, 139k, 4.5 612–623
  short story, 4.2 146–155
  song, 4.1 130–133
  textbook article, 4.6 758–761
  Web site, 4.1 84–87, 139c, 4.3 356–359, 4.4 484–487, 4.5 578–581, 4.6 734–737
Genre study, 4.1 139a–139k, DI·9, DI·19, DI·29, DI·39, DI·49, 4.2 DI·9, DI·19, DI·29, DI·39, DI·49, 4.3 DI·9, DI·19, DI·29, DI·39, DI·49, 4.4 DI·9, DI·19, DI·29, DI·39, DI·49, 4.5 DI·9, DI·19, DI·29, DI·39, DI·49, 4.6 DI·9, DI·19, DI·29, DI·39, DI·49
Gifted students. *See* **Advanced learners.**
Glossary. *See* **Dictionary/glossary.**
Goal and outcome. *See* **Plot, Story structure.**
Grammar and usage. *See* **Adjectives, Adverbs, Conjunctions, Contractions, Nouns, Prepositions and prepositional phrases, Pronouns, Sentences, Subject/verb agreement, Verbs.**
Graph. *See* **Graphic sources.**
Graphic and semantic organizers
  as comprehension tool, 4.1 18, 40, 66, 77, 81, 88, 112, DI·26, DI·46, DI·47, 4.2 142, 162, 188, 212, 240, 4.3 268, 292–293, 303, 307, 314, 338–339, 360, 4.4 392, 416, 440, 466, 488,

  4.5 516, 538, 560, 582, 608, 4.6 638, 660, 686, 712, 738
  as concept development tool, 4.1 18l, 39c, 40l, 65c, 68l, 87c, 88l, 111c, 112l, 133c, 4.2 142l, 161c, 162l, 187c, 188l, 211c, 212l, 239c, 240l, 259c, 4.3 268l, 291c, 292l, 313c, 314l, 337c, 338l, 359c, 360l, 383c, 4.4 392l, 415c, 416l, 439c, 440l, 465c, 466l, 487c, 488l, 507c, 4.5 516l, 537c, 538l, 559c, 560l, 581c, 582l, 607c, 608l, 629c, 4.6 638l, 659c, 660l, 685c, 686l, 711c, 712l, 737c, 738l, 761c
  as prereading tool, 4.1 20a, 42a, 68a, 90a, 114a, 4.2 144a, 164a, 190a, 214a, 242a, 265b, 4.3 270a, 294a, 316a, 340a, 362a, 4.4 394a, 418a, 442a, 468a, 490a, 4.5 518a, 540a, 562a, 584a, 610a, 4.6 640a, 662a, 688a, 714a, 740a
  as prewriting tool, 4.1 39h, 65h, 87h, 111h, 133h, WA3, 4.2 161h, 187h, 211h, 239h, 259h, WA3, 4.3 291h, 313h, 359h, 383h, WA3, 4.4 415h, 439h, 465h, 487h, 507h, WA3, 4.5 437h, 559h, 581h, 607h, 629h, 635b, WA3, 4.6 659h, 685h, 711h, 761h, WA3
  as vocabulary/word structure tool, 4.1 20b, 39c, 65c, 87c, 90b, 111c, 123, 126, 133c, 4.2 144b, 161c, 187c, 190b, 211c, 214b, 239c, 242b, 4.3 291c, 294b, 313c, 337c, 340b, 359c, 362b, 383c, 4.4 394b, 418b, 439c, 468b, 507c, 4.5 518b, 537c, 562b, 581c, 584b, 4.6 662b, 711c, 714b, 761c
  types
    cause and effect chart, 4.2 142, 268, DI·52, 4.3 DI·52, 4.6 638, DI·52
    column chart, 4.1 40, 65c, 87c, 90a, 111c, 111h, 133c, DI·53, DI·55, 4.2 144a, 144b, 161c, 187c, 187h, 211c, 214b, 242h, 4.3 291c, 294b, 313c, 337c, 359c, 383c, DI·55, 4.4 439c, 439h, 466, 487h, 507c, DI·55, 4.5 516, 518b, 537c, 537h, 559h, 581c, DI·52, DI·55, 4.6 662b, 686, 711c, 711h, 761c, DI·56
    comparison chart, 4.3 337h, 4.4 392, 4.5 538
    fact and opinion chart, 4.2 212, DI·55, 4.3 292–293, 303, 307, DI·53, 4.6 660, DI·53
    facts and details, 4.2 188, 4.5 608
    how-to chart, 4.2 WA3
    KWL chart, 4.1 42a, 114a, 4.2 242a, 4.3 294a, 340a, 4.4 418a, 468a, 4.5 584a, 607h, 610a, 662a, 4.6 714a, WA3, DI·47
    list, 4.1 65g, 4.2 162, 239h, 4.3 313h, 314, 338, 4.4 415h, 4.6 685h, 737h
    main idea chart, 4.1 112, 123, DI·56, 4.2 240, DI·56, 4.5 582, 4.6 712, DI·54
    map, 4.4 466, 4.6 738
    prediction chart, 4.4 442a
    sequence chart, 4.1 39h, 66, DI·52, DI·54, 4.3 359h
    story structure chart, 4.1 88, 4.3 360, 4.4 488, WA3
    T-chart, 4.1 68a, 77, 133h, 4.2 190a, 259h, 4.3 303, 383h, 4.4 394a, 416, 507h, 4.5 562b
    time line, 4.1 81, DI·26, DI·27, 4.5 560, 4.6 659h
    Venn diagram, 4.1 133h, 4.2 214a, 259h, 383h, 416, 4.3 WA3, 4.4 507h, DI·52, 4.5 562a, DI·53, 4.6 688a, 740a, DI·47
    vocabulary frame, 4.1 90b
    web, 4.1 18l, 39c, 40l, 65c, 66l, 87c, 87h, 88l, 111c, 112l, 133c, DI·46, DI·47, 4.2 142l, 161c, 161h, 162l, 164a, 187c, 188l, 211c, 211h, 212l, 239c, 240l, 259c, DI·54, 4.3 268l, 270a, 291c, 291h, 292l, 313c, 314l, 316a, 337c, 338l, 359c, 360l, 362a, 383c, DI·54, DI·56, 4.4 392l, 394b, 415c, 416l, 439c, 440l, 440, 465c, 465h, 466l, 487c, 488l, 490a, 507c,

  DI·54, 4.5 516l, 518a, 537c, 538l, 540a, 559c, 560l, 581c, 581h, 582l, 607c, 608l, 629c, 629h, DI·54, DI·56, 4.6 638l, 640a, 659c, 660l, 685c, 686l, 711c, 712l, 714b, 737c, 738l, 761c, 761h, DI·55
  word rating chart, 4.2 190b, 4.3 340b, 4.4 418b, 486b, 4.5 584b
  words in context chart, 4.3 362b
Graphic sources, 4.3 338–339, 345, 351, 359b, DI·55, 4.4 447, 466–467, 473, 477, DI·36, DI·55, 4.5 DI·55, 4.6 677, 723, 738–739, 745, 753, 758, DI·46, DI·56
  advertisement, 4.2 211l, 4.6 721
  application, 4.5 629l
  chart/table, 4.2 161l, 4.3 291l, 4.4 466–467, DI·36, 4.5 626, 4.6 753, 758, DI·26, DI·46, DI·47
  diagram/scale drawing, 4.4 412, 4.5 581l, 4.6 738–739, 4.6 DI·26, DI·46, DI·47
  graph, 4.2 239l
  illustration (photograph or art) and/or caption, 4.1 111l, 4.4 473, 477, DI·37, 4.6 745
  map/globe, 4.1 36, 39l, 4.5 556
  order form, 4.5 629l
  poster/announcement, 4.4 439l
  schedule, 4.3 383l
  time line, 4.2 259l
Greek and Latin roots. *See* **Vocabulary strategies.**
Grouping students for instruction
  advanced learners, 4.1 18f–18g, 40f–40g, 66f–66g, 88f–88g, 112f–112g, DI·3, DI·5, DI·7, DI·9, DI·11, DI·13, DI·15, DI·17, DI·19, DI·21, DI·23, DI·25, DI·27, DI·29, DI·31, DI·33, DI·35, DI·37, DI·39, DI·41, DI·43, DI·45, DI·47, DI·49, DI·51, 4.2 142f–142g, 162f–162g, 188f–188g, 212f–212g, 240f–240g, DI·3, DI·5, DI·7, DI·9, DI·11, DI·13, DI·15, DI·17, DI·19, DI·21, DI·23, DI·25, DI·27, DI·29, DI·31, DI·33, DI·35, DI·37, DI·39, DI·41, DI·43, DI·45, DI·47, DI·49, DI·51, 4.3 268f–268g, 292f–292g, 314f–314g, 338f–338g, 360f–360g, DI·3, DI·5, DI·7, DI·9, DI·11, DI·13, DI·15, DI·17, DI·19, DI·21, DI·23, DI·25, DI·27, DI·29, DI·31, DI·33, DI·35, DI·37, DI·39, DI·41, DI·43, DI·45, DI·47, DI·49, DI·51, 4.4 392f–392g, 416f–416g, 440f–440g, 466f–466g, 488f–488g, DI·3, DI·5, DI·7, DI·9, DI·11, DI·13, DI·15, DI·17, DI·19, DI·21, DI·23, DI·25, DI·27, DI·29, DI·31, DI·33, DI·35, DI·37, DI·39, DI·41, DI·43, DI·45, DI·47, DI·49, DI·51, 4.5 516f–516g, 538f–538g, 560f–560g, 582f–582g, 608f–608g, DI·3, DI·5, DI·7, DI·9, DI·11, DI·13, DI·15, DI·17, DI·19, DI·21, DI·23, DI·25, DI·27, DI·29, DI·31, DI·33, DI·35, DI·37, DI·39, DI·41, DI·43, DI·45, DI·47, DI·49, DI·51, 4.6 638f–638g, 660f–660g, 686f–686g, 712f–712g, 738f–738g, DI·3, DI·5, DI·7, DI·9, DI·11, DI·13, DI·15, DI·17, DI·19, DI·21, DI·23, DI·25, DI·27, DI·29, DI·31, DI·33, DI·35, DI·37, DI·39, DI·41, DI·43, DI·45, DI·47, DI·49, DI·51
  intervention, 4.1 18f–18g, 40f–40g, 66f–66g, 88f–88g, 112f–112g, DI·2, DI·4, DI·6, DI·8, DI·10, DI·12, DI·14, DI·16, DI·18, DI·20, DI·22, DI·24, DI·26, DI·28, DI·30, DI·32, DI·34, DI·36, DI·38, DI·40, DI·42, DI·44, DI·46, DI·48, DI·50, 4.2 142f–142g, 162f–162g, 188f–188g, 212f–212g, 240f–240g, DI·2, DI·4, DI·6, DI·8, DI·10, DI·12, DI·14, DI·16, DI·18, DI·20, DI·22, DI·24, DI·26, DI·28, DI·30, DI·32, DI·34, DI·36, DI·38, DI·40, DI·42, DI·44, DI·46, DI·48, DI·50, 4.3 268f–268g, 292f–292g, 314f–314g, 338f–338g, 360f–360g, DI·2, DI·4, DI·6, DI·8, DI·10, DI·12, DI·14, DI·16, DI·18, DI·20, DI·22, DI·24, DI·26, DI·28, DI·30, DI·32, DI·34, DI·36,

DI·38, DI·40, DI·42, DI·44, DI·46, DI·48, DI·50, 4.4 392f–392g, 416f–416g, 440f–440g, 466f–466g, 488f–488g, DI·2, DI·4, DI·6, DI·8, DI·10, DI·12, DI·14, DI·16, DI·18, DI·20, DI·22, DI·24, DI·26, DI·28, DI·30, DI·32, DI·34, DI·36, DI·38, DI·40, DI·42, DI·44, DI·46, DI·48, DI·50, 4.5 516f–516g, 538f–538g, 560f–560g, 582f–582g, 608f–608g, DI·2, DI·4, DI·6, DI·8, DI·10, DI·12, DI·14, DI·16, DI·18, DI·20, DI·22, DI·24, DI·26, DI·28, DI·30, DI·32, DI·34, DI·36, DI·38, DI·40, DI·42, DI·44, DI·46, DI·48, DI·50, 4.6 638f–638g, 660f–660g, 686f–686g, 712f–712g, 738f–738g, DI·2, DI·4, DI·6, DI·8, DI·10, DI·12, DI·14, DI·16, DI·18, DI·20, DI·22, DI·24, DI·26, DI·28, DI·30, DI·32, DI·34, DI·36, DI·38, DI·40, DI·42, DI·44, DI·46, DI·48, DI·50

Guiding Reading. *See* **Grouping students for instruction.** In addition, Guiding Reading and leveled readers are a part of every lesson plan.

H

Habits and attitudes
  consequences of actions/behaviors/choices (as demonstrated in literature selections). *See* **Character education.**
  humanity and compassion (as demonstrated in literature selections). *See* **Character education.**
  toward other groups and people (multicultural values), 4.1 16, 44–59, 70–81, 84–87, 4.2 140, 216–232, 4.3 266, 318–331, 334–337, 364–377, 4.4 390, 420–433, 470–481, 4.5 514, 542–553, 556–559, 4.6 636, 690–705. *See also* **Multicultural connections.**
  toward reading, writing, listening, speaking, viewing, 4.1 18l, 20a, 40l, 42a, 66l, 68a, 88l, 90a, 112l, 114a, 4.2 142l, 144a, 162l, 164a, 188l, 190a, 212l, 214a, 240l, 242a, 4.3 268l, 270a, 292l, 294a, 314l, 316a, 338l, 340a, 360l, 362a, 4.4 392l, 394a, 416l, 418a, 440l, 442a, 466l, 468a, 488l, 490a, 4.5 516l, 518a, 538l, 540a, 560l, 562a, 582l, 584a, 608l, 610a, 4.6 638l, 640a, 660l, 662a, 686l, 688a, 712l, 714a, 738l, 740a

Handwriting, 4.1 TR10–TR13, 4.2 TR10–TR13, 4.3 TR10–TR13, 4.4 TR10–TR13, 4.5 TR10–TR13, 4.6 TR10–TR13

Health activities. *See* **Cross-curricular activities.**

Higher-order thinking skills. *See* **Critical thinking.**

Historical fantasy. *See* **Genres.**

Historical fiction. *See* **Genres.**

Home-school connection. *See* **School-home connection.**

Homework. *See* **School-home connection.**

Homographs, 4.5 518–519, 525, 537c. *See also* **Vocabulary strategies.**

Homonyms, 4.3 294–295, 305, 313c, 4.5 518–519, 525, 537c, 4.6 740–741, 749, 761c. *See also* **Vocabulary strategies.**

Homophones, 4.1 42b, 4.6 688b. *See also* **Vocabulary strategies.**

How-to article. *See* **Genres.**

Humorous fiction. *See* **Genres.**

Hyperbole. *See* **Literary devices,** exaggeration/hyperbole.

I

Illustrations. *See* **Graphic sources,** illustration and/or caption; **Prereading strategies,** use illustrations.

Illustrator's craft/style. *See* **Literary craft.**

Illustrator study, 4.1 139m–139p

Implied message. *See* **Main idea, Theme (as a story element).**

Independent reading, 4.1 18f–18g, 18j, 40f–40g, 40j, 66f–66g, 66j, 88f–88g, 88j, 112f–112g, 112j, TR14, 4.2 142f–142g, 142j, 162f–162g, 162j, 188f–188g, 188j, 212f–212g, 212j, 240f–240g, 240j, TR14, 4.3 268f–268g, 268j, 292f–292g, 292j, 314f–314g, 314j, 338f–338g, 338j, 360f–360g, 360j, TR14, 4.4 392f–392g, 392j, 416f–416g, 416j, 440f–440g, 440j, 466f–466g, 466j, 488f–488g, 488j, TR14, 4.5 516f–516g, 516j, 538f–538g, 538j, 560f–560g, 560j, 582f–582g, 582j, 608f–608g, 608j, TR14, 4.6 638f–638g, 638j, 660f–660g, 660j, 686f–686g, 686j, 712f–712g, 712j, 738f–738g, 738j, TR14. *See also* **Bibliography,** self-selected reading.

Inferences. *See* **Author's purpose; Cause and effect; Comparing and contrasting; Conclusions, drawing; Fact and opinion, statements of; Generalizations, making; Predicting; Summarizing.** In addition, inferential thinking questions appear throughout Guiding Comprehension in each lesson.

Inflected endings. *See* **Spelling,** word structure; **Word structure.**

Informal assessment. *See* **Assessment.**

Integrated curriculum. *See* **Cross-curricular activities.**

Internet (as reference source). *See* **New literacies (for student reading), Reference sources, Technology.**

Internet article. *See* **Genres.**

Intervention
  answer questions, 4.6 654
  author's purpose, 4.1 40, 88, 4.5 516
  cause and effect, 4.2 142, 4.3 268, 4.6 638,
  character, 4.4 440 4.6 686,
  compare and contrast, 4.4 392, 416, 4.5 538
  conclusions, draw, 4.2 162, 188, 4.5 608,
  context clues, 4.1 90, 4.2 224, 4.3 270, 294, 316, 4.4 394, 418, 490, 4.5 518, 562, 610, 4.6 688, 714, 740
  dictionary/glossary, 4.1 68, 4.2 164, 214, 242, 4.4 442, 4.6 662
  English language learners. *See* **ELL (English Language Learners) suggestions.**
  fact and opinion, 4.2 212, 4.3 292, 4.6 660,
  generalize, 4.3 314, 360, 4.6 712,
  graphic sources, 4.3 338, 4.4 466, 4.6 738,
  group time, 4.1 18f–18g, 40f–40g, 66f–66g, 88f–88g, 112f–112g, DI·2, DI·4, DI·6, DI·8, DI·10, DI·12, DI·14, DI·16, DI·18, DI·20, DI·22, DI·24, DI·26, DI·28, DI·30, DI·32, DI·34, DI·36, DI·38, DI·40, DI·42, DI·44, DI·46, DI·48, DI·50, 4.2 142f–142g, 162f–162g, 188f–188g, 212f–212g, 240f–240g, DI·2, DI·4, DI·6, DI·8, DI·10, DI·12, DI·14, DI·16, DI·18, DI·20, DI·22, DI·24, DI·26, DI·28, DI·30, DI·32, DI·34, DI·36, DI·38, DI·40, DI·42, DI·44, DI·46, DI·48, DI·50,

4.3 268f–268g, 292f–292g, 314f–314g, 338f–338g, 360f–360g, DI·2, DI·4, DI·6, DI·8, DI·10, DI·12, DI·14, DI·16, DI·18, DI·20, DI·22, DI·24, DI·26, DI·28, DI·30, DI·32, DI·34, DI·36, DI·38, DI·40, DI·42, DI·44, DI·46, DI·48, DI·50, 4.4 392f–392g, 416f–416g, 440f–440g, 466f–466g, 488f–488g, DI·2, DI·4, DI·6, DI·8, DI·10, DI·12, DI·14, DI·16, DI·18, DI·20, DI·22, DI·24, DI·26, DI·28, DI·30, DI·32, DI·34, DI·36, DI·38, DI·40, DI·42, DI·44, DI·46, DI·48, DI·50, 4.5 516f–516g, 538f–538g, 560f–560g, 582f–582g, 608f–608g, DI·2, DI·4, DI·6, DI·8, DI·10, DI·12, DI·14, DI·16, DI·18, DI·20, DI·22, DI·24, DI·26, DI·28, DI·30, DI·32, DI·34, DI·36, DI·38, DI·40, DI·42, DI·44, DI·46, DI·48, DI·50, 4.6 638f–638g, 660f–660g, 686f–686g, 712f–712g, 738f–738g, DI·2, DI·4, DI·6, DI·8, DI·10, DI·12, DI·14, DI·16, DI·18, DI·20, DI·22, DI·24, DI·26, DI·28, DI·30, DI·32, DI·34, DI·36, DI·38, DI·40, DI·42, DI·44, DI·46, DI·48, DI·50. *See also* **Grouping students for instruction.**
  leveled reader, 4.1 LR1–LR3, LR10–LR12, LR19–LR21, LR28–LR30, LR37–LR39, 4.2 LR1–LR3, LR10–LR12, LR19–LR21, LR28–LR30, LR37–LR39, 4.3 LR1–LR3, LR10–LR12, LR19–LR21, LR28–LR30, LR37–LR39, 4.4 LR1–LR3, LR10–LR12, LR19–LR21, LR28–LR30, LR37–LR39, 4.5 LR1–LR3, LR10–LR12, LR19–LR21, LR28–LR30, LR37–LR39, 4.6 LR1–LR3, LR10–LR12, LR19–LR21, LR28–LR30, LR37–LR39
  main idea, 4.1 112, 4.2 240, 4.5 582
  main idea/details, 4.1 74, 118
  plot, 4.4 488
  resources, 4.1 18h, 40h, 66h, 88h, 112h, 4.2 142h, 162h, 188h, 212h, 240h, 4.3 268h, 292h, 314h, 338h, 360h, 4.4 392h, 440h, 466h, 488h, 616h, 4.5 516h, 538h, 560h, 582h, 608h, 4.6 638h, 660h, 686h, 712h, 738h
  sequence, 4.1 18, 66, 4.5 560
  setting, 4.4 440
  theme, 4.6 686
  word structure, 4.1 20, 42, 114, 4.2 144, 190, 4.3 340, 362, 4.4 468, 4.5 540, 584, 4.6 640
  writing support, 4.1 WA8, 4.2 WA8, 4.3 WA8, 4.4 WA8, 4.5 WA8, 4.6 WA8

Interview. *See* **Speaking,** activities.

Italics, 4.6 761e–761f

J

Journal. *See* **Genres; Logs, strategy response; Writing forms/products.**

Judgments, making. *See* **Author's purpose; Conclusions, drawing; Fact and opinion, statements of; Generalizations, making; Predicting.**

K

KWL reading strategy, 4.1 42a, 114a, 242a, 4.3 294a, 340a, 4.4 418a, 468a, 4.5 584a, 607h, 610a, 4.6 662a, 714a

L

Language arts. *See* **Capitalization, Creative/dramatic activities, Cross-Curricular Centers, Grammar and usage, Listening, Punctuation, Speaking, Spelling,** *all* **Writing categories.**

Language, oral. *See* **Fluency, reading; Listening; Speaking.**

Latin and Greek roots. See **Vocabulary development,** etymologies for meaning.

Learning Centers. See **Cross-Curricular Centers.**

Legend. See **Genres.**

Less-able readers. See **Intervention.**

Letter. See **Genres.**

Leveled readers, 4.1 18c, 40c, 66c, 88c, 112c, LR1–LR48, 4.2 142c, 162c, 188c, 212c, 240c, LR1–LR48, 4.3 268c, 292c, 314c, 338c, 360c, LR1–LR48, 4.4 392c, 416c, 440c, 466c, 488c, LR1–LR48, 4.5 516c, 538c, 560c, 582c, 608c, LR1–LR48, 4.6 638c, 660c, 686c, 712c, 738c, LR1–LR48

Levels of thinking. See **Critical thinking.**

Limited English proficient students. See **ELL (English Language Learners) suggestions.**

Listening
  activities
    advertisement/commercial, 4.1 87d, 4.4 439d
    announcement, 4.5 559d
    audio products, 4.1 20a, 42a, 68a, 90a, 114a, 4.2 144a, 164a, 190a, 214a, 242a, 4.3 270a, 294a, 316a, 337d, 340a, 362a, 4.4 394a, 418a, 442a, 468a, 490a, 4.5 518a, 540a, 562a, 584a, 610a, 4.6 640a, 662a, 688a, 714a, 740a
    debate, 4.1 133d, 4.6 711d
    demonstration, 4.6 685d
    description, 4.2 239d
    discussion, 4.1 34, 39d, 60, 82, 106, 128, 4.2 156, 184, 208, 233, 256, 4.3 286, 308, 332, 354, 378, 4.4 410, 434, 462, 482, 501, 4.5 534, 554, 576, 602, 624, 4.6 655, 680, 706, 732, 756
    dramatization, 4.1 39d, 4.3 337d
    interview, 4.3 313d, 4.4 415d, 4.5 607d, 4.6 737d
    introductions, 4.1 65d
    media, 4.3 313d, 4.5 537d, 629d
    music, 4.6 737d
    newscast, 4.2 187d, 4.3 359d, 4.4 507d
    opinions, 4.1 133d, 4.3 291d, 4.6 711d
    oral presentation/report, 4.1 111d
    persuasion, 4.1 133d, 4.3 291d, 4.6 711d
    poetry reading, 4.3 291d
    press conference, 4.2 259d
    radio advertisement, 4.1 87d
    read-alouds, 4.1 18m, 40m, 66m, 88m, 112m, 4.2 142m, 162m, 188m, 212m, 240m, 4.3 268m, 292m, 314m, 338m, 360m, 4.4 392m, 416m, 440m, 466m, 488m, 4.5 516m, 538m, 560m, 582m, 608m, 4.6 638m, 660m, 686m, 712m, 738m
    speech, 4.3 383d, 4.5 581d, 4.6 659d
    sportscast, 4.2 161d
    story, 4.1 39d, 4.4 487d
    TV and video, 4.5 629d
    weather broadcast, 4.3 337d
  purposes
    comparison and contrast, 4.3 337d, 4.5 537d
    comprehension, 4.1 18l–18m, 40l–40m, 66l–66m, 88l–88m, 112l–112m, 4.2 142l–142m, 162l–162m, 188l–188m, 212l–212m, 240l–240m, 4.3 268l–268m, 292l–292m, 314l–314m, 338l–338m, 360l–360m, 4.4 392l–392m, 416l–416m, 440l–440m, 466l–466m, 488l–488m, 4.5 516l–516m, 538l–538m,

560l–560m, 582l–582m, 608l–608m, 4.6 638l–638m, 660l–660m, 686l–686m, 712l–712m, 738l–738m
    enjoyment, 4.1 39d, 4.3 291d, 313d, 337d, 4.4 439d, 487d, 4.5 537d, 629d, 4.6 737d
    information, 4.1 87d, 4.2 187d, 239d, 4.3 383d, 4.4 439d, 4.5 581d, 4.6 659d
    persuasion, 4.1 87d, 4.3 383d, 4.4 439d, 4.6 659d
    tips, 4.1 111d, 4.2 161d, 211d, 4.6 685d, 711d, 761d

Literal comprehension. Literal comprehension questions appear in Guiding Comprehension in each lesson.

Literary craft
  author's perspective/viewpoint/bias, 4.1 88l–88m, 139b, 4.3 313b, 4.5 537a
  illustrator's craft/style, 4.1 139m–139p, 4.3 291b, 4.4 487b, 4.5 573, 4.6 669

Literary devices
  dialect, 4.1 111b, 4.2 179
  dialogue, 4.1 29, 4.4 449
  exaggeration/hyperbole, 4.4 405
  flashback, 4.2 211b
  free verse, 4.3 387
  imagery/sensory words, 4.1 65b, 4.3 337b
  mood, 4.2 262
  narration, 4.1 25
  point of view, 4.1 133b, 4.6 659b
  puns and word play, 4.4 497
  simile, 4.3 359b, 4.6 685b, 761b
  slang, 4.1 103
  symbolism, 4.6 753
  tone, 4.3 386, 387
  See also **Figurative language, Sound devices and poetic elements.**

Literary genres. See **Genres.**

Literary response and appreciation, 4.1 34, 60, 82, 106, 128, 139a–139p, 4.2 156, 184, 208, 233, 256, 4.3 286, 308, 332, 354, 378, 4.4 410, 434, 462, 482, 501, 4.5 534, 554, 576, 602, 624, 4.6 655, 680, 706, 732, 756

Literature selections
  "Adelina's Whales," Richard Sobol, 4.3 296–307
  "Amelia and Eleanor Go for a Ride," Pam Muñoz Ryan, 4.5 564–575
  "Ant and the Bear, The," Chief Lelooska, 4.3 334–337
  "Antarctic Journal," Jennifer Owings Dewey, 4.5 586–601
  "Because of Winn Dixie," Kate DiCamillo, 4.1 22–33
  "Coyote School News," Joan Sandin, 4.2 166–183
  "Difficult Art of Hitting, The," Sadaharu Oh and David Falkner, 4.6 708–711
  "Early Flying Machines," Internet article, 4.6 734–737
  "Earth and the Moon, The," from Scott Foresman Science, Grade 4, 4.6 758–761
  "Encantado: Pink Dolphin of the Amazon," Sy Montgomery, 4.4 420–433
  "Encyclopedia Brown and the Case of the Slippery Salamander," Donald J. Sobol, 4.4 492–500
  "Eye of the Storm," Stephen Kramer, 4.3 342–353
  "Fast Facts: Black Bears," Kathy Kranking, 4.1 36–39
  "Grace and the Time Machine," Mary Hoffman, 4.2 192–207
  "Grandfather's Journey," Allen Say, 4.1 70–81
  "Great Kapok Tree, The," Lynne Cherry, 4.3 364–377
  "Horned Lizards & Harvesting Ants," John Brown, 4.1 108–111

  "Horned Toad Prince, The," Jackie Mims Hopkins, 4.1 92–105
  "Houdini Box, The," Brian Selznick, 4.4 396–409
  "How Night Came from the Sea," Mary-Joan Gerson, 4.3 318–331
  "How Tía Lola Came to Stay," Julia Alvarez, 4.6 690–705
  "How to Start a School Newspaper," Lisa Klobuchar, 4.2 186–187
  "Jim Thorpe's Bright Path," Joseph Bruchac, 4.6 664–679
  "King in the Kitchen, The," Margaret E. Slattery, 4.4 444–461
  "Letters Home from Yosemite," Lisa Halvorsen, 4.1 116–127
  "Lewis and Clark and Me," Laurie Myers, 4.1 44–59
  "Living in a World of Green," Tanya Lee Stone, 4.3 380–383
  "Logging Camps," Internet article, 4.2 236–239
  "Look at Two Lands, A," Internet article, 4.1 84–87
  "Lost City: The Discovery of Machu Picchu," Ted Lewin, 4.5 542–553
  "Man Who Went to the Far Side of the Moon, The," Bea Uusma Schyffert, 4.6 742–755
  "Marven of the Great North Woods," Kathryn Lasky, 4.2 216–232
  "Moonwalk," Ben Bova, 4.5 612–623
  "My Brother Martin," Christine King Farris, 4.6 642–654
  "Mysterious Animals," Ann Weil, 4.4 436–439
  "Our National Parks," Susan Gavin, 4.2 258–259
  "Riding the Rails to Machu Picchu," Katacha Díaz, 4.5 556–559
  "Sailing Home: A Story of a Childhood at Sea," Gloria Rand, 4.5 520–533
  "Sea Animals on the Move," Joanne Wachter, 4.3 310–313
  "Seeker of Knowledge," James Rumford, 4.4 470–481
  "Severe Weather Safety," Internet article, 4.3 356–359
  "Sharing a Dream," Linda Washington, 4.5 536–537
  "So You Want to Be an Illusionist," Tui T. Sutherland, 4.4 412–415
  "So You Want to Be President?," Judith St. George, 4.2 244–255
  "Special Olympics, Spectacular Athletes," Marlene Perez, 4.6 682–685
  "Stranger, The," Chris Van Allsburg, 4.3 272–285
  "Swimming Towards Ice," Claire Daniel, 4.5 604–607
  "They Traveled with Lewis and Clark," Elizabeth Massie, 4.1 62–65
  "Time for a Change," Helen Strahinich, 4.3 288–291
  "To Fly: The Story of the Wright Brothers," Wendie C. Old, 4.6 716–731
  "Walk on the Moon, A," Judy Nayer, 4.5 626–629
  "What Jo Did," Charles R. Smith Jr., 4.2 146–155
  "What's There to Do?," Samantha Beres, 4.2 210–211
  "Women Explorers," Internet article, 4.5 578–581
  "Word Puzzles," Internet article, 4.4 484–487
  "Young Detectives of Potterville Middle School," Bonnie Kepplinger, 4.4 504–507
  See also **Poetry Selections.**

Logs, strategy response
  activate prior knowledge, 4.1 116, 4.2 146, 166, 4.3 296, 4.4 420, 4.5 520, 4.6 664
  answer questions, 4.1 27, 99, 4.2 201, 4.3 279, 371, 4.4 497, 4.5 549, 593, 4.6 649, 751

ask questions, 4.1 22, 92, 4.2 192, 4.3 272, 364, 4.4 492, 4.5 542, 586, 4.6 642, 742

check predictions, 4.1 53, 4.2 251, 4.3 349, 4.4 403, 451, 4.5 571, 619, 4.6 697, 725

graphic organizer, 4.1 70, 77, 4.2 216, 223, 4.3 318, 327, 4.4 470, 477

monitor comprehension, 4.1 123, 4.2 151, 175, 4.3 303, 4.4 429, 4.5 527, 4.6 671

predict, 4.1 44, 4.2 244, 4.3 342, 4.4 396, 444, 4.5 564, 612, 4.6 690, 716

summarize, 4.1 32, 58, 80, 104, 126, 4.2 154, 182, 206, 230, 254, 4.3 284, 306, 330, 352, 376, 4.4 408, 432, 460, 480, 502, 4.5 532, 552, 574, 600, 622, 4.6 652, 678, 704, 730, 754

M

Magazine (as reference source). See **Reference sources.**

Main idea 4.1 74, 75, 112l–112m, 112–113, 123, 133b, DI·46, DI·47, DI·56, 4.2 225, 240l–240m, 240–241, 247, 251, 259, 259b, DI·46, DI·47, DI·56, 4.4 475, 4.5 582l–582m, 582–583, 589, 595, 607, 607b, DI·36, DI·37

Making connections. See **Connections, making.**

Manual. See **Reference sources.**

Map/globe. See **Graphic sources.**

Mapping selections. See **Graphic and semantic organizers.**

Mass media. See **Viewing.**

Mathematics activities. See **Cross-curricular activities.**

Mechanics (of English grammar and writing). See **Capitalization, Punctuation.**

Media. See **Viewing.**

Metacognition. See **Monitor and fix up; Self-check.**

Modeling. Teacher modeling and think-alouds are presented throughout Skills in Context lessons and After Reading lessons.

Monitor and fix up, 4.2 212–213, 223, 227, 239, DI·37, 4.4 440–441, 451, 455, 461, 465, 4.5 608–609, 619, 623, 629, DI·47, 4.6 738–739, 751, 753, 755, 761
  adjust reading rate, 4.2 212-213, 223, 227, 4.5 608-609, 619
  ask questions, 4.2 DI·37, 4.5 619, DI·47
  read on, 4.5 609, 619
  reread, 4.2 223, 239, 4.4 DI·26, 4.5 608-609, DI·46
  retell, 4.2 DI·36, 4.6 DI·46
  skim/scan, 4.2 212–213, 223, 227
  summarize, 4.4 451, DI·27
  use a graphic organizer, 4.4 451
  use graphic sources, 4.5 629, 4.6 738–739, 751, 753, 755, DI·47
  use a reference source, 4.2 239
  use text features, 4.4 440–441, 451, 455

Monitor comprehension. See **Monitor and fix up, Self-check.**

Mood. See **Literary devices.**

Motivation, 4.1 18l, 20a, 40l, 42a, 66l, 68a, 88l, 90a, 112l, 114a, 4.2 142l, 144a, 162l, 164a, 188l, 190a, 212l, 214a, 240l, 242a, 4.3 268l, 270a, 292l, 294a, 314l, 316a, 338l, 340a, 360l, 362a, 4.4 392l, 394a, 416l, 418a, 440l, 442a, 466l, 468a, 488l, 490a, 4.5 516l, 518a, 538l, 540a, 560l, 562a, 582l,

584a, 608l, 610a, 4.6 638l, 640a, 660l, 662a, 686l, 688a, 712l, 714a, 738l, 740a

Multicultural connections, 4.1 16, 18l, 44–59, 70–81, 84–87, 4.2 140, 216–232, 4.3 266, 318–331, 334–337, 364–377, 4.4 390, 420–433, 470–481, 4.5 514, 542–553, 556–559, 4.6 636, 690–705. See also **Habits and attitudes.**

Multiple-meaning words, 4.1 20b, 68–69, 79, 87c, 4.2 231, 4.3 270–271, 277, 291c, 316b, 4.4 418–419, 427, 439c, 457, 4.6 640b, 662–663, 669, 673, 685c, 714b

Multisyllabic words. See **Spelling,** word structure; **Word structure.**

Music activities. See **Cross-curricular activities.**

N

Narrative nonfiction. See **Genres.**

Narrative poetry. See **Genres.**

New literacies (for student reading), 4.1 84–87, 4.2 236–241, 4.3 356–359, 4.4 484–487, 4.5 578–581, 4.6 734–737. See also **Technology.**

Newspaper (as reference sources). See **Reference sources.**

Newspaper article. See **Genres.**

Nonverbal communication. See **Listening,** tips; **Speaking,** tips.

Note. See **Genres.**

Note-taking, 4.4 403, 4.6 659l, 685g–685h

Nouns
  singular/plural, irregular, 4.2 211e–211f
  singular/plural, regular, 4.2 187e–187f
  possessive, 4.2 239a–239f, 259e–259f, 4.4 439e–439f
  proper, 4.2 161e–161f
  See also **Capitalization.**

O

On-line reading. See **Genres.**

Onomatopoeia. See **Sound devices and poetic elements.**

Opinion and fact. See **Fact and opinion, statements of.**

Oral reading ability
  appropriate phrasing, 4.1 112l, 133a, 4.4 439a, 466l, 487a, 4.5 538l, 559a, 4.6 638l, 659a
  attention to punctuation, 4.3 360l, 383a, 4.6 712l, 737a
  choral reading, 4.1 39a, 87a, 4.2 187a, 259a, 4.3 313a, 337a, 383a, 4.4 465a, 4.5 537a, 581a
  fluency, 4.1 39a, 65a, 87a, 111a, 133a, 4.2 161a, 187a, 211a, 239a, 259a, 4.3 291a, 313a, 337a, 359a, 383a, 4.4 415a, 438a, 465a, 487a, 507a, 4.5 537a, 559a, 581a, 607a, 629a, 4.6 659a, 685a, 711a, 737a, 761a
  paired reading, 4.1 39a, 65a, 87a, 111a, 133a, 4.2 161a, 187a, 211a, 239a, 259a, 4.3 291a, 313a, 337a, 359a, 383a, 4.4 415a, 439a, 465a, 487a, 507a, 4.5 537a, 559a, 581a, 607a, 629a, 4.6 659a, 685a, 711a, 737a, 761a

Order form. See **Graphic sources.**

Organizing information
  classifying, 4.1 20b, 90a, 4.2 144a, 144b, 190a, 242b, 4.3 294b, 4.4 394a, 4.5 518b, 562b, 4.6 662b

outlining, 4.5 559l, 4.6 659h, 737g–737h

summarizing, 4.1 18–19, 26, 27, 32, 33, 39, 65, 4.2 240–241, 251, 254, 255, 4.6 686–687, 697, 699, 705, 711

taking notes, 4.4 403, 4.6 659l, 685g–685h
  See also **Graphic and semantic organizers; Logs, strategy response.**

Outlining, 4.5 559l, 4.6 659h, 737g–737h. See also **Graphic and semantic organizers, Organizing information.**

Own life, text's relation to. See **Character education; Connections, making; Habits and attitudes.**

P

Paired reading. See **Fluency, reading.**

Paraphrasing, 4.1 87b. See also **Summarize.**

Parentheses, 4.2 211h

Parents. See **School-home connection.**

Parts of a book
  appendix, 4.5 537l
  bibliography, 4.5 537l
  glossary, 4.5 537l
  index, 4.3 291l, 4.4 415l, 4.5 537l
  table of contents, 4.3 291l, 4.4 415l, 4.5 537l
  title page, 4.5 537l

Penmanship. See **Handwriting.**

Period, 4.1 39e–39f

Personal essay. See **Genres.**

Personal reading programs. See **Bibliography,** self-selected reading.

Persuasion. See **Author's perspective/viewpoint/bias; Persuasive devices; Viewing,** uses of media.

Persuasive devices, 4.2 211l, 4.3 383b, 4.4 439b

Phonics
  chunking. See **Word structure,** chunking.
  consonant digraphs, final, 4.2 239i–239j
  consonants, hard and soft sounds of *c* and *g* 4.4 487i–487j
  consonants, silent, 4.6 761i–761j
  strategies. See **Spelling,** phonics, connection to.
  vowels
    common word (vowel) patterns
      VCCV, 4.1 39i–39j
      VCV, 4.5 559i–559j
    in final syllable, 4.4 439i–439j, 465i–465j
    long
      a, 4.1 65i–65j
      e, y, 4.1 87i–87j, 111i–111j
      i, igh, y, 4.1 65i–65j
      o, 4.1 87i–87j
      u, 4.1 133i–133j
    patterns, 4.3 337i–337j
    r-controlled, 4.2 211i–211j, 259i–259j, 4.4 465i–465j
    schwa sound, 4.4 439i–439j, 4.6 659i–659j
    short, 4.1 39i–39j

Photo essay. See **Genres.**

Phrasing. See **Fluency,** reading.

Pictures. See **Graphic sources,** illustration and or caption; **Prereading strategies,** use illustrations.

Pitch. See **Fluency,** reading.

Play. See **Genres.**

Plot, 4.1 88–89, 99, 103, 105, 4.4 401, 488l–488m, 488–489, 497, 507b, DI·46, DI·47, DI·56, 4.5 571, 575, 4.6 660l–660m

Poetic devices. *See* **Sound devices and poetic elements.**

Poetry selections

  "Allow Me to Introduce Myself," Charles R. Smith Jr., 4.2 160–161

  "Autumn," Charlotte Zolotow, 4.3 384

  "Best Paths, The," Kristine O'Connell George, 4.5 630

  "Carolyn's Cat," Constance Kling Levy, 4.4 511

  "City I Love," Lee Bennett Hopkins, 4.1 136

  "Confectioner, A," Myra Cohn Livingston, 4.4 465

  "Door, The," Miroslav Holub, 4.5 632–633

  "Dream Dust," Langston Hughes, 4.6 762

  "Early Spring," Shonto Begay, 4.3 386–387

  "Expert," Unknown, 4.4 465

  "Fall Football," Gary Soto, 4.6 764

  "Fast Break," Charles R. Smith Jr., 4.2 158–159

  "First Men on the Moon," J. Patrick Lewis, 4.6 765

  "Haiku," Christina Beecham, 4.6 658

  "His Hands," Nikki Grimes, 4.2 260

  "Homework," Russell Hoban, 4.2 261

  "Lem Lonnigan's Leaf Machine," Andrea Perry, 4.2 262–263

  "Man for All Seasonings, A," Richard Armour 4.4 464

  "Martin Luther King," Myra Cohn Livingston, 4.6 762

  "Martin Luther King Day," X. J. Kennedy, 4.6 763

  "Midwest Town," Ruth De Long Peterson, 4.1 137

  "My Life Is A Buried Treasure," Dawn Withrow, 4.6 659

  "Poetry," Eleanor Farjeon, 4.4 509

  "Roller Coasters," X. J. Kennedy, 4.5 631

  "Seed, The," Aileen Fisher, 4.4 510

  "Speak Up," Janet S. Wong, 4.1 135

  "This Land Is Your Land," Woody Guthrie, 4.1 130–133

  "We're All in the Telephone Book," Langston Hughes, 4.1 134

  "When You Hope, Wish, and Trust," Ek Ongkar K. Khalsa, 4.6 659

  "Who Knows?," Fatou Ndiaye Sow, 4.4 508

  "Winter Solstice," Marilyn Singer, 4.3 385

  See also **Genres.**

Point of view. *See* **Literary devices.**

Poster. *See* **Graphic sources.**

Pourquoi tale. *See* **Genres.**

Predicting

  confirming predictions, 4.1 53, 4.3 353, 4.4 409, 4.5 533

  outcomes, 4.3 338, 4.4 392, 403, 407, 409, 413, DI·6, DI·7, 4.5 516, 527, 529, DI·6, DI·7

  previewing and predicting, 4.1 22, 36, 44, 62, 70, 84, 92, 108, 116, 130, 4.2 146, 158, 166, 186, 192, 210, 216, 236, 244, 258, 4.3 272, 288, 296, 310, 318, 334, 342, 356, 364, 380, 4.4 396, 412, 420, 436, 444, 464, 470, 484, 492, 504, 4.5 520, 536, 542, 556, 564, 578, 586, 604, 612, 626, 4.6 642, 658, 664, 682, 690, 708, 716, 734, 742, 758

Prefixes, 4.2 144–145, 151, 161c, 190–191, 199, 211c. *See also* **Spelling,** word structure; **Word structure.**

Prepositions and prepositional phrases, 4.5 629e–629f

Prereading strategies

  activate prior knowledge, 4.1 20a, 42a, 68a, 90a, 114a, 4.2 144a, 164a, 190a, 214a, 242a, 4.3 270a, 294a, 316a, 340a, 362a, 4.4 394a, 418a, 442a, 468a, 490a, 4.5 518a, 540a, 562a, 584a, 610a, 4.6 640a, 662a, 688a, 714a, 740a

  ask questions, 4.1 42a, 114a, 4.2 242a, 4.3 294a, 340a, 4.4 418a, 468a, 4.5 584a, 610a, 4.6 662a, 714a

  graphic organizers

    chart, 4.4 442a

    column chart, 4.1 90a, 4.2 144a

    KWL chart, 4.1 42a, 114a, 4.2 242a, 4.3 294a, 340a, 4.4 418a, 468a, 4.5 584a, 610a, 4.6 662a, 714a

    T-chart, 4.1 68a, 4.2 190a, 4.4 394a

    Venn diagram, 4.2 214a, 4.5 562a, 4.6 688a, 740a

    web, 4.1 20a, 4.2 164a, 4.3 270a, 316a, 362a, 4.4 490a, 4.5 518a, 540a, 4.6 640a

    See also **Graphic and semantic organizers.**

  preview and predict, 4.1 22, 36, 44, 62, 70, 84, 92, 108, 116, 130, 4.2 146, 158, 166, 186, 192, 210, 216, 236, 244, 258, 4.3 272, 288, 296, 310, 318, 334, 342, 356, 364, 380, 4.4 396, 412, 420, 436, 444, 464, 470, 484, 492, 504, 4.5 520, 536, 542, 556, 564, 578, 586, 604, 612, 626, 4.6 642, 658, 664, 682, 690, 708, 716, 734, 742, 758

  set purposes for reading, 4.1 23, 45, 71, 93, 117, 4.2 147, 167, 193, 217, 245, 4.3 273, 297, 319, 343, 365, 4.4 397, 421, 445, 471, 493, 4.5 521, 543, 565, 587, 613, 4.6 643, 665, 691, 717, 743

  use illustrations, 4.1 22, 44, 70, 92, 116, 4.2 146, 166, 192, 216, 244, 4.3 272, 296, 318, 342, 364, 4.4 396, 420, 444, 470, 492, 4.5 520, 542, 564, 586, 612, 4.6 642, 665, 690, 716, 742

  use reading strategy (KWL, etc.), 4.1 42a, 114a, 4.2 242a, 4.3 294a, 340a, 4.4 418a, 468a, 4.5 584a, 610a, 4.6 662a, 714a

  use text features, 4.1 36, 62, 84, 108, 130, 4.2 186, 210, 236, 258, 4.3 288, 310, 334, 356, 380, 4.4 412, 436, 464, 484, 504, 4.5 536, 556, 578, 604, 626, 4.6 682, 708, 734, 758

Previewing. *See* **Prereading strategies.**

Prior knowledge. 4.2 142–143, 155, 159, DI·6, DI·7, 4.4 488–489, 505, DI·46, DI·47. *See also* **Prereading strategies,** activate prior knowledge.

Problems, solving, 4.1 DI·5, 4.2 DI·27, DI·33, DI·37, DI·39, DI·43, 4.4 484–487, DI·5, DI·15, DI·35, 4.5 DI·9, DI·23, DI·27, DI·33, DI·37, 4.6 DI·27, DI·39

Projects, 4.1 16–17, 134a, 138–139, 4.2 140–141, 260a, 264–265, 4.3 266–267, 384a, 388–389, 4.4 390–391, 508a, 512–513, 4.5 514–515, 630a, 634–635, 762a, 4.6 636–637, 766–767

Pronouns

  case, 4.4 439e–439f, 487e–487f

  pronoun/antecedent agreement, 4.4 465e–465f

  singular/plural, 4.4 415e–415f

Proofreading. *See* **Writing process,** edit.

Propaganda, 4.3 383b

Pun. *See* **Literary devices.**

Punctuation. *See* **Apostrophe; Colon; Comma; Exclamation mark; Italics; Parentheses; Period; Question mark; Quotation marks; Semicolon; Writing process,** edit.

Punctuation, attention to. *See* **Fluency,** reading.

Purposes for reading. *See* **Monitor and fix up; Prereading strategies,** set purposes for reading.

Put Reading First text comprehension strategies. *See* **Graphic and semantic organizers; Questions, answering; Questions, asking; Summarizing.**

Q

Question-answer relationship (QAR). *See* **Questions, answering.**

Question mark, 4.1 39e–39f

Questions, answering (QAR), 4.1 40, 41, 52, 53, 56, 57, 58, 59, DI·16, DI·17, 4.2 188–189, 201, 205, 207, 211, DI·26, DI·27, 4.6 638–639, 649, 653, 654, DI·6, DI·7

Questions, asking, 4.1 DI·53, DI·55, 4.2 DI·53, 4.3 268–269, 279, 281, 285, 289, 4.4 466–467, 477, 481, 485, 507, DI·36, DI·37, 4.5 DI·52, DI·56, 4.6 712–713, 726, 725, 727, 731, 737, DI·36, DI·37. *See also* **Prereading strategies,** set purposes for reading, **Speaking,** activities.

Quotation marks, 4.6 737e–737f, 761e–761f

R

Rate. *See* **Fluency, reading; Monitor and fix up.**

Read-aloud, 4.1 18m, 40m, 66m, 88m, 112m, TR14, 4.2 142m, 162m, 188m, 212m, 240m, TR14, 4.3 268m, 292m, 314m, 338m, 360m, TR14, 4.4 392m, 416m, 440m, 466m, 488m, TR14, 4.5 516m, 538m, 560m, 582m, 608m, TR14, 4.6 638m, 660m, 686m, 712m, 738m, TR14

Reader response. *See* **Connections, making; Response to literature.**

Reader's Guide to Periodical Literature. *See* **Reference sources.**

Reading across texts, 4.1 39, 58, 65, 87, 104, 111, 133, 4.2 161, 187, 206, 211, 239, 259, 4.3 291, 313, 330, 337, 359, 383, 4.4 415, 439, 450, 465, 487, 498, 507, 4.5 532, 537, 552, 559, 574, 581, 607, 622, 629, 4.6 646, 659, 678, 685, 711, 737, 761

Reading fluency. *See* **Fluency, reading.**

Reading rate. *See* **Fluency, reading; Monitor and fix up.**

Reading strategies. *See* **Strategies.**

Reading to students. *See* **Read-aloud.**

Realistic fiction. *See* **Genres.**

Recreational reading. *See* **Bibliography,** self-selected reading.

Reference sources

  almanac, 4.3 291l

  atlas, 4.1 39l

  card catalog/library database, 4.4 507l

  dictionary/glossary, 4.1 68, 79, 87c, 231, 4.2 164, 173, 177, 187c, 214, 221, 231, 239c, 242, 253, 259c, 4.4 442, 453, 457, 465c, 4.5 537l, 4.6 662, 669, 673, 685c, 711l. *See also* **Dictionary/glossary.**

  encyclopedia, 4.1 133l, 4.6 761l

  Internet and World Wide Web, 4.1 39k, 65k, 87k, 87l, 111k, 133k, 4.2 161k, 187k, 211k, 239k, 259k, 4.3 291k, 313k, 337k, 359k, 359l, 383k, 4.4 415k, 439k, 465k, 487k, 507k, 4.5 537k, 559k, 581k, 607k, 629k, 4.6 659k, 685k, 711k, 737k, 761k

  magazine/periodical, 4.1 133l, 4.2 239l, 4.6 685l

  manual, 4.4 415l, 465l, 4.6 737l

media, electronic, 4.1 87l
newspaper/newsletter, 4.1 133l, 4.2 187l, 211l
online manual, 4.6 737l
online telephone directory, 4.3 359l
pamphlets, 4.1 133l
parts of a book, 4.5 537l
Reader's Guide to Periodical Literature, 4.3 313l
technology. See **Technology, new literacies.**
telephone directory, 4.3 359l
textbook, 4.1 133l, 4.3 337l
thesaurus, 4.4 487l
trade book, 4.1 133l, 4.3 337l

Repetition. See **Sound devices and poetic elements.**

Rereading. See **Monitor and fix up.**

Research
activities, 4.1 39l, 65l, 87l, 111l, 133l, 4.2 161l,
187l, 211l, 239l, 259l, 4.3 291l, 313l, 337l, 359l,
383l, 4.4 415l, 439l, 465l, 487l, 507l, 4.5 537l,
559l, 581l, 607l, 629l, 4.6 659l, 685l, 711l, 737l,
761l
process and strategies
citing sources, 4.1 87d, 111d, 4.6 659l, 767b
evaluating, interpreting, and drawing conclusions
about key information, 4.1 211l
locating and collecting information, 4.3 359l,
383d, 4.4 507l, 4.5 607l
organizing content, 4.2 187l, 4.5 537l, 559l
outlining, 4.5 559l
pictures and captions, 4.1 211l, 4.2 211l
procedures and instructions, 4.4 415l, 465l,
4.6 737l
skimming/scanning, 4.1 65l
study strategy to find or learn information,
4.1 42a, 114a, 4.2 242a, 4.3 294a, 4.4 418a,
468a, 4.5 584a, 607l, 610a, 4.6 662a, 714a
taking notes/recording findings, 4.6 659l, 676b
using graphic sources, 4.1 39l, 4.2 161l, 239l,
259l, 4.3 383l, DI·55, 4.4 439l, DI·55,
4.5 581l, DI·55, 4.6 DI·56. See also **Graphic
sources.**
using reference sources, 4.1 41l, 87l, 133l,
4.3 291l, 313l, 337l, 4.4 487l, 4.6 685l, 711l,
737l, 761l. See also **References sources.**

Research and study skills, 4.1 39l, 65l, 87l, 111l,
133l, 4.2 161l, 187l, 211l, 239l, 259l, 4.3 291l,
313l, 337l, 359l, 383l, 4.4 415l, 439l, 465l, 487l,
507l, 4.5 537l, 559l, 581l, 607l, 629l, 4.6 659l,
685l, 711l, 737l, 761l

Response to literature
oral, 4.1 34, 39, 60, 65, 82, 87, 106, 111, 128,
133, 4.2 156, 161, 184, 187, 208, 211, 233,
239, 256, 259, 4.3 286, 291, 308, 313, 332,
337, 354, 359, 378, 383, 4.4 410, 415, 434,
439, 462, 465, 482, 487, 501, 507, 4.5 534,
537, 554, 559, 576, 581, 602, 607, 624, 629,
4.6 655, 659, 680, 685, 706, 711, 732, 737,
756, 761
written, 4.1 34, 39, 60, 65, 82, 87, 106, 111, 128,
133, 4.2 156, 161, 184, 187, 208, 211, 233,
239, 256, 259, 4.3 286, 291, 308, 313, 332,
337, 354, 359, 378, 383, 4.4 410, 415, 434,
439, 462, 465, 482, 487, 501, 502–503, 507,
4.5 534, 535, 537, 537g–537h, 554, 559, 576,
581, 602, 607, 624, 629, 4.6 655, 659, 680,
685, 706, 707, 711, 711g–711h, 732, 737, 756,
761

Retelling. See **Speaking,** activities.

Rhyme. See **Sound devices and poetic elements.**

Root words. See **Spelling,** word structure; **Word
structure,** Greek and Latin roots.

Rubric. See **Assessment,** scoring guide (rubric).

Running record, taking a, 4.1 39a, 65a, 87a, 111a,
133a, DI·57, DI·58, 4.2 161a, 187a, 211a, 239a,
259a, DI·57, DI·58, 4.3 291a, 313a, 337a, 359a,
383a, DI·57, DI·58, 4.4 415a, 439a, 465a, 487a,
507a, DI·57, DI·58, 4.5 537a, 559a, 581a, 607a,
629a, DI·57, DI·58, 4.6 659a, 685a, 711a, 737a,
761a, DI·57, DI·58. See also **Fluency, reading.**

S

Safety information. See **Character education.**

Scaffolded instruction, 4.1 19, 25, 41, 67, 73, 89,
95, 101, 113, 119, DI·1, 4.2 143, 163, 169, 179,
189, 195, 213, 241, DI·1, 4.3 269, 275, 277, 293,
305, 315, 325, 339, 361, DI·1, 4.4 393, 399, 405,
417, 423, 427, 441, 449, 467, 473, 489, 495, 497,
DI·1, 4.5 517, 523, 525, 539, 545, 561, 567, 573,
583, 589, 609, 615, 617, DI·1, 4.6 639, 645, 661,
687, 701, 713, 721, 739, 745, 749, DI·1

Scale drawing. See **Graphic sources,** diagram/scale
drawing.

Schedule. See **Graphic sources.**

School-home connection, 4.1 18i, 18m, 40i, 40m,
66i, 66m, 88i, 88m, 112i, 112m, 4.2 142i, 142m,
162i, 162m, 188i, 188m, 212i, 212m, 240i, 240m,
4.3 268i, 268m, 292i, 292m, 314i, 314m, 338i,
338m, 360i, 360m, 4.4 392i, 392m, 416i, 416m,
440i, 440m, 466i, 466m, 488i, 488m, 4.5 516i,
516m, 538i, 538m, 560i, 560m, 582i, 582m, 608i,
608m, 4.6 638i, 638m, 660i, 660m, 686i, 686m,
712i, 712m, 738i, 738m

Science activities. See **Cross-curricular activities.**

Science fiction. See **Genres.**

Science in reading, 4.1 36–39, 108–111, 130–133,
4.3 288–291, 310–313, 356–359, 380–383,
4.4 412–415, 436–439, 504–507, 4.5 626–629,
4.6 758–761

Self-appraisal and self-correction. See **Monitor
and fix up.**

Self-check, 4.1 33, 53, 59, 81, 99, 105, 127,
4.2 155, 175, 183, 201, 207, 223, 255, 4.3 279,
285, 307, 327, 331, 355, 371, 377, 4.4 403, 409,
429, 433, 451, 461, 481, 500, 4.5 527, 533, 553,
575, 593, 601, 623, 4.6 649, 654, 671, 679, 697,
705, 725, 731, 751, 755

Self-monitor and use fix-up strategies. See **Monitor and fix up.**

Self-selected reading, 4.1 DI·59, DI·60, TR14–
TR17, 4.2 DI·59, DI·60, TR14–TR17, 4.3 DI·59,
DI·60, TR14–TR17, 4.4 DI·59, DI·60, TR14–TR17,
4.5 DI·59, DI·60, TR14–TR17, 4.6 DI·59, DI·60,
TR14–TR17

Semicolon, 4.1 111e

Sentences
fragment, 4.1 87e, 4.6 659e
parts of
predicate, 4.1 87e–87f
subject, 4.1 87e–87f
run-on, 4.1 111e, 4.6 659e

structure
complex, 4.1 39e, 133e–133f
compound, 4.1 39e, 111e–111f
types of
declarative, 4.1 39e–39f
exclamatory, 4.1 65e–65f
imperative, 4.1 65e–65f
interrogative, 4.1 39e–39f

Sequence
directions, following, 4.4 415l, 465l, 4.6 737l
sequence of events (time sequence/chronology),
4.1 18l–18m, 18–19, 25, 27, 37, 39, 39b,
66l–66m, 66–67, 73, 77, 85, 87b, 97, DI·6, DI·7,
DI·26, DI·27, DI·52, DI·54, 4.5 531, 551, 560l–
560m, 560–561, 567, 571, 581, 581b, DI·26,
DI·27
steps in a process, 4.4 415b, 4.5 607b

Setting, 4.2 171, 4.4 440l–440m, 440–441, 449,
DI·26, DI·27, 4.5 582l–582m

Setting purposes for reading. See **Monitor and fix
up, Prereading strategies.**

Simile, 4.3 359b, 4.6 685b, 761b. See also **Figurative language.**

Six-trait writing
conventions, 4.1 39g, 65g, 87g, 111g, 129, 133g–
133h, WA1, WA2, WA6, 4.2 161g, 187g, 211g,
239g, 259g, WA1, WA2, WA6, 4.3 291g, 313g,
337g, 359g, 379, 383g–383h, WA1, WA2, WA6,
4.4 415g, 439g, 465g, 483, 487g–487h, 507g,
WA1, WA2, WA6, 4.5 537g, 559g, 581g, 607g,
629g, WA1, WA2, WA6, 4.6 659g, 685g, 707,
711g–711h, 737g, 761g, WA1, WA2, WA6
focus/ideas, 4.1 39g, 65g, 87g, 107, 111g–111h,
133g, WA1, WA5, WA7, 4.2 161g, 185, 187g–
187h, 211g, 234, 239g–239h, 259g, WA1, WA5,
WA7, 4.3 291g, 313g, 337g, 359g, 383g, WA1,
WA5, WA7, 4.4 415g, 435, 439g–439h, 465g,
487g, 507g, WA1, WA5, WA7, 4.5 535, 537g–
537h, 559g, 577, 581g–581h, 607g, 629g, WA1,
WA5, WA7, 4.6 659g, 681, 685g–685h, 711g,
737g, 761g, WA1, WA5, WA7
organization/paragraph, 4.1 39g, 65g, 87g, 111g,
133g, WA1, WA3, WA4, WA5, WA7, 4.2 161g,
187g, 209, 211g–211h, 239g, 257, 259g–259h,
WA1, WA5, WA7, 4.3 291g, 313g, 337g, 355,
359g–359h, 383g, WA1, WA3, WA4, WA5, WA7,
4.4 415g, 439g, 465g, 487g, 502, 507g–507h,
WA1, WA3, WA5, WA7, 4.5 537g, 559g, 581g,
607g, 629g, WA1, WA3, WA5, WA7, 4.6 659g,
685g, 711g, 733, 737g–737h, 761g, WA1, WA3,
WA5, WA7
sentences, 4.1 39g, 61, 65g, 65h, 87g, 111g,
133g, WA1, WA5, WA7, 4.2 161g, 187g, 211g,
239g, 259g, WA1, WA5, WA7, 4.3 291g, 309,
313g–313h, 337g, 359g, 383g, WA1, WA5, WA7,
4.4 411, 415g–415h, 439g, 465g, 487g, 507g,
WA1, WA5, WA7, 4.5 537g, 559g, 581g, 607g,
629g, WA1, WA5, WA7, 4.6 656, 659g–659h,
685g, 711g, 737g, 757, 761g–761h, WA1, WA5,
WA7
voice, 4.1 39g, 65g, 83, 87g–87h, 111g, 133g, WA1,
WA5, WA7, 4.2 161g, 187g, 211g, 239g, 259g,
WA1, WA5, WA7, 4.3 287, 291g–291h, 313g,
337g, 359g, 383g, WA1, WA5, WA7, 4.4 415g,
439g, 463, 465g–465h, 487g, 507g, WA1, WA5,
WA7, 4.5 537g, 559g, 581g, 603, 607g–607h,
629g, WA1, WA5, WA7, 4.6 659g, 685g, 711g,
737g, 761g, WA1, WA5, WA7
word choice, 4.1 35, 39g–39h, 65g, 87g, 111g,
133g, WA1, WA5, WA7, 4.2 157, 161g–161h,
187g, 211g, 239g, 259g, WA1, WA5, WA7,
4.3 291g, 313g, 333, 337g–337h, 359g, 383g,
WA1, WA5, WA7, 4.4 415g, 439g, 465g, 487g,

507g, WA1, WA5, WA7, 4.5 537g, 555, 559g–559h, 581g, 607g, 625, 629g–629h, WA1, WA5, WA7, 4.6 659g, 685g, 711g, 737g, 761g, WA1, WA5, WA7

Skimming and scanning, 4.1 65l

Slang. *See* **Literary devices.**

Social studies activities. *See* **Cross-curricular activities.**

Social studies in reading, 4.1 65, 4.2 186–187, 210–211, 258–259, 4.5 536–537, 556–559, 604–607, 4.6 682–685, 708–711

Solving problems. *See* **Problems, solving.**

Song. *See* **Genres.**

Sound devices and poetic elements
  alliteration, 4.6 763
  free verse, 4.3 387
  onomatopoeia, 4.1 136, 4.2 177, 4.5 631
  repetition, 4.2 260, 4.4 508
  rhyme, 4.4 465, 465b, 4.6 658

Speaking
  activities
    advertisement/commercial, 4.1 87d, 4.4 439d
    announcement, 4.5 559d
    ask questions, 4.3 268–269, 279, 281, 285, 289, 4.4 466–467, 477, 481, 485, 507, 4.6 712, 713, 726, 725, 727, 731, 737
    debate, 4.1 133d, 4.6 711d
    demonstration, 4.6 685d
    description, 4.2 239d
    directions, 4.3 359
    discussion, 4.1 34, 60, 82, 106, 128, 4.2 156, 184, 208, 233, 256, 4.3 286, 308, 322, 354, 378, 4.4 410, 434, 462, 482, 501, 4.5 534, 554, 576, 602, 624, 4.6 655, 659d, 680, 706, 732, 756
    dramatization, 4.1 39d, 4.2 211d, 4.5 537d
    interview, 4.3 313d, 4.4 415d, 4.5 607d, 4.6 737d
    introductions, 4.1 65d
    newscast, 4.2 187d, 4.3 359d, 4.4 507d
    oral presentation/report, 4.1 111d
    oral reading, 4.1 39a, 65a, 87a, 111a, 133a, 4.2 161a, 187a, 211, 239a, 259a, 4.3 291a, 313a, 337a, 359a, 383a, 4.4 415a, 439a, 465a, 487a, 507a, 4.5 537a, 559a, 581a, 607a, 629a, 4.6 659a, 685a, 711a, 737a, 761a
    persuasive, 4.1 133d, 4.3 291d, 383d
    press conference, 4.2 259d
    read aloud poetry, 4.1 134–137, 4.2 260–263, 4.3 384–387, 4.4 508–511, 4.5 630–633, 4.6 672–675
    Readers' Theater, 4.3 337d, 4.4 465d
    recitation, 4.2 260
    retelling, 4.1 35, 39d, 61, 83, 107, 129, 4.2 157, 185, 209, 234, 257, 4.3 287, 309, 333, 355, 379, 4.4 411, 435, 463, 487d, 502, 4.5 535, 577, 603, 625, 4.6 656, 681, 707, 733, 757
    round-table discussion, 4.6 659d
    speech, 4.1 133d, 4.3 291d, 383d, 4.5 581d, 629d, 4.6 761d
    sportscast, 4.2 161d
    story, 4.4 487d
    weather broadcast, 4.3 359d
  purpose/reasons for speaking
    descriptive, 4.1 65d, 187d, 4.2 239d, 4.5 629d
    expository, 4.1 111d, 4.3 313d, 359d, 4.4 415d, 439d, 507d, 4.5 559d, 581d, 607d, 4.6 685d, 737d, 761d
    expressive, 4.1 39d, 4.3 313d, 4.4 465d, 4.5 537d
    narrative, 4.1 39d, 4.2 161d, 211d, 4.3 313d, 4.4 465d, 487d

persuasive, 4.1 87d, 133d, 4.2 259d, 4.3 291d, 383d, 4.6 711d
  problem solving, 4.6 659d
  tips, 4.1 39d, 65d, 87d, 133d, 4.2 239d, 259d, 4.3 291d, 313d, 337d, 359d, 383d, 4.4 439d, 465d, 487d, 507d, 4.5 537d, 581d, 629d, 4.6 659d, 737d

Spelling
  common word (vowel) patterns
    VCCV, 4.1 39i–39j
    VCV, 4.5 559i–559j
  five-step plan for learning words, 4.1 39i–39j, 65i–65j, 87i–87j, 111i–111j, 133i–133j, 4.2 161i–161j, 187i–187j, 211i–211j, 239i–239j, 259i–259j, 4.3 291i–291j, 313i–313j, 337i–337j, 383i–383j, 4.4 415i–415j, 439i–439j, 465i–465j, 487i–487j, 507i–507j, 4.5 537i–537j, 559i–559j, 581i–581j, 607i–607j, 629i–629j, 4.6 659i–659j, 685i–685j, 711i–711j, 737i–737j, 761i–761j
  meaning relationships
    homophones, 4.3 313i–313j
  phonics, connection to
    consonant digraphs, 4.2 239i–239j
    consonants /j/, /ks/, /kw/, 4.4 487i–487j
    silent consonants, 4.6 761i–761j
    vowels
      diphthongs, 4.3 337i–337j
      in final syllables, 4.4 439i–439j, 465i–465j
      long,
        a, 4.1 65i–65j
        e, y, 4.1 87i–87j, 111i–111j
        i, igh, y, 4.1 65i–65j
        o, 4.1 87i–87j
        u, 4.1 133i–133j
      patterns, 4.3 337i–337j
      r-controlled, 4.2 211i–211j, 259i–259j, 4.4 465i–465j
      schwa sound, 4.4 439i–439j, 4.6 659i–659j
      short, 4.1 39i–39j
  word structure
    affixes, 4.4 507i–507j, 4.6 685i–685j, 711i–711j, 737i–737j
    compound words, 4.3 359i–359j
    contractions, 4.4 415i–415j
    Greek and Latin word parts, 4.5 581i–581j, 607i–607j
    inflected endings, 4.2 161i–161j, 4.3 291i–291j
    plurals, irregular, 4.2 187i–187j
    plurals, regular, 4.2 161i–161j
    possessives, 4.3 383i–383j
    related words (derivatives), 4.5 629i–629j
    roots, 4.5 607i–607j
    syllable constructions, 4.5 537i–537j, 559i–559j

Standard book features. *See* **Parts of a book.**

Steps in a process, 4.4 415b, 4.5 607b

Stereotypes, analyzing, 4.2 154, 4.5 574

Story elements. *See* **Character, Plot, Setting, Theme (as a story element).**

Story structure, 4.1 88–89, 99, 103, 105, DI·36, DI·37, 4.3 360–361, 4.5 560–561, 571, 575, DI·26, DI·27

Strategic intervention. *See* **Intervention.**

Strategies
  comprehension, 4.1 18–19, 40–41, 66–67, 88–89, 112–113, 4.2 142–143, 162–163, 188–189, 212–213, 240–241, 4.3 268–269, 292–293, 314–315, 338–339, 360–361, 4.4 392–393, 416–417, 440–441, 466–467, 488–489, 4.5 516–517, 538–539, 560–561, 582–583, 608–609, 4.6 638–639, 660–661, 686–687, 712–713, 738–739

concept development, 4.1 17a, 18a, 18l, 40a, 40l, 66a, 66l, 88a, 88l, 112a, 112l, 4.2 141a, 142a, 142l, 162a, 162l, 188a, 188l, 212a, 212l, 240a, 240l, 4.3 267a, 268a, 268l, 292a, 292l, 314a, 314l, 338a, 338l, 360a, 360l, 4.4 391a, 392a, 392l, 416a, 416l, 440a, 440l, 466a, 466l, 488a, 488l, 4.5 515a, 516a, 516l, 538a, 538l, 560a, 560l, 582a, 582l, 608a, 608l, 4.6 637a, 638a, 638l, 660a, 660l, 686a, 686l, 712a, 712l, 738a, 738l

context, 4.1 101, 4.3 305, 325, 4.4 405, 427, 495, 4.5 525, 573, 617, 4.6 701, 721, 729, 749

decoding, 4.1 39i–39j, 65i–65j, 87i–87j, 111i–111j, 133i–133j, 4.2 161i–161j, 187i–187j, 211i–211j, 239i–239j, 259i–259j, 4.3 291i–291j, 313i–313j, 337i–337j, 359i–359j, 383i–383j, 4.4 415i–415j, 439i–439j, 465i–465j, 487i–487j, 507i–507j, 4.5 537i–537j, 559i–559j, 581i–581j, 607i–607j, 629i–629j, 4.6 659i–659j, 685i–685j, 711i–711j, 737i–737j, 761i–761j

fluent reading, 4.1 39a, 65a, 87a, 111a, 133a, 4.2 161a, 187a, 211a, 239a, 259a, 4.3 291a, 313a, 337a, 359a, 383a, 4.4 415a, 439a, 465a, 487a, 507a, 4.5 537a, 559a, 581a, 607a, 629a, 4.6 659a, 685a, 711a, 737a, 761a

monitor and fix up, 4.2 212–213, 223, 227, 239, 4.4 440–441, 451, 455, 461, 465, 4.5 608–609, 619, 623, 629, 4.6 738–739, 751, 755, 761

prereading, 4.1 22, 44, 70, 92, 116, 4.2 146, 166, 192, 216, 244, 4.3 272, 296, 318, 342, 364, 4.4 396, 420, 444, 470, 492, 4.5 520, 542, 564, 586, 612, 4.6 642, 664, 690, 716, 742

research, 4.1 39l, 65l, 87l, 111l, 133l, 4.2 161l, 187l, 211l, 239l, 259l, 4.3 291l, 313l, 337l, 359l, 383l, 4.4 415l, 439l, 465l, 487l, 507l, 4.5 537l, 559l, 581l, 607l, 629l, 4.6 659l, 685l, 711l, 737l, 761l

spelling, 4.1 39i–39j, 65i–65j, 87i–87j, 111i–111j, 133i–133j, 4.2 161i–161j, 187i–187j, 211i–211j, 239i–239j, 259i–259j, 4.3 291i–291j, 313i–313j, 337i–337j, 359i–359j, 383i–383j, 4.4 415i–415j, 439i–439j, 465i–465j, 487i–487j, 507i–507j, 4.5 537i–537j, 559i–559j, 581i–581j, 607i–607j, 629i–629j, 4.6 659i–659j, 685i–685j, 711i–711j, 737i–737j, 761i–761j

vocabulary. *See* **Vocabulary strategies.**

Structural analysis. *See* **Word structure.**

Study strategies, 4.1 39l, 65l, 87l, 111l, 133l, 4.2 161l, 187l, 211l, 239l, 259l, 4.3 291l, 313l, 337l, 359l, 383l, 4.4 415l, 439l, 465l, 487l, 507l, 4.5 537l, 559l, 581l, 607l, 629l, 4.6 659l, 685l, 711l, 737l, 761l. *See also* **Assessment,** test-taking practice; **Content-area texts; Graphic sources; Organizing information; Parts of a book; Reference sources; Textbook-reading techniques.**

Style, illustrator's. *See* **Literary craft.**

Subject-verb agreement, 4.3 337e–337f

Suffixes, 4.1 20–21, 29, 39c, 114–115, 121, 133c, 4.2 144–145, 151, 161c, 4.3 362–363, 375, 383c, 4.4 394b. *See* **Spelling,** word structure; **Word structure.**

Summarizing, 4.1 18–19, 27, 33, 39, 65, DI·6, DI·7, 4.2 240–241, 251, 255, DI·46, DI·47, 4.6 686–687, 697, 699, 705, 711, DI·26, DI·27

Sustained silent reading. *See* **Self-selected reading.**

Syllables. *See* **Spelling,** word structure, syllable constructions; **Word structure,** chunking.

Symbolism. *See* **Literary devices.**

Synonyms, 4.1 90–91, 101c, 111c, 4.4 394–395, 405, 415c, 490–491, 495, 507c, 4.5 610b, 610–611, 617, 629c. *See also* **Vocabulary strategies.**

Synthesizing. *See* **Connections, making; Reading across texts.**

T

Tables. *See* **Graphic sources,** chart/table.

Taking notes. *See* **Note-taking.**

Target comprehension skills. *See* **Comprehension skills, explicit/implicit instruction** for a total listing of these skills.

Target comprehension strategies. *See* **Comprehension strategies, explicit/implicit instruction** for a total listing of these strategies.

Teaching strategies
  informal assessment. *See* **Assessment.**
  modeling. This strategy is part of every lesson.
  think-aloud. This strategy is part of every lesson.
  See also **Graphic and semantic organizers, KWL.**

Technology
  e-mail, 4.1 111g–111h, 4.2 236–239
  information and communication technologies. *See* **Technology,** new literacies; **Reference sources,** Internet and World Wide Web.
  Internet article, 4.1 84–87, 4.3 356–359, 4.4 484–487, 4.5 578–581, 4.6 734–737
  Internet/World Wide Web. *See* **Technology,** new literacies; **Reference sources,** Internet and World Wide Web.
  new literacies
    activities, 4.1 39k, 65k, 87k, 111k, 133k, 4.2 161k, 187k, 211k, 239k, 259k, 4.3 291k, 313k, 337k, 359k, 383k, 4.4 415k, 439k, 465k, 487k, 507k, 4.5 537k, 559k, 581k, 607k, 629k, 4.6 659k, 685k, 711k, 737k, 761k
    bookmarks, 4.1 85, 161k, 4.2 211k, 4.3 337k, 4.4 415k, 439k, 4.5 537k
    documentation of Web site, 4.1 111k
    electronic media, 4.1 20a, 26, 39k, 42a, 48, 65k, 68a, 80, 84, 85, 86, 87k, 87l, 90a, 96, 106, 111a, 114a, 118, 133k, 4.2 144a, 148, 161k, 164a, 172, 174, 187k, 190a, 200, 211k, 214a, 220, 228, 236, 237, 238, 239, 239k, 242a, 246, 259k, 4.3 270a, 278, 291k, 294a, 298, 313k, 316a, 320, 337k, 340a, 344, 352, 356, 357, 358, 359, 359k, 359l, 362a, 366, 383k, 4.4 394a, 415k, 418a, 422, 439k, 442a, 463k, 468a, 476, 484, 485, 486, 487k, 490a, 494, 507k, 4.5 518a, 537k, 540a, 546, 559k, 562a, 574, 578, 579, 580, 581k, 584a, 596, 607k, 610a, 614, 629k, 4.6 640a, 648, 659k, 662a, 678, 685k, 688a, 692, 711k, 714a, 724, 734, 735, 736, 737k, 740a, 748, 761k
    e-mail, 4.2 236–238
    etiquette, 4.1 85, 4.2 237, 4.3 357, 4.4 485, 4.5 579, 4.6 735
    evaluating Internet information and sources, 4.1 65k, 111k, 133k, 4.2 161k, 239k, 4.3 359k, 4.4 507k, 4.5 578–581, 629k, 4.6 659k, 734–737
    folder, 4.2 238
    graphic sources 4.1 86
    homepage, 4.1 84, 4.3 356, 357, 4.6 734, 735, 736
    Internet article, 4.1 84–87, 4.3 356–359, 4.4 484–487, 4.5 578–581, 4.6 734–737
    Internet inquiry, 4.1 20a, 26, 39k, 42a, 48, 65k, 68a, 80, 84, 85, 86, 87k, 87l, 90a, 96, 106, 111k, 114a, 118, 133k, 4.2 144a, 148, 161k, 164a, 172, 174, 187k, 190a, 200, 211k, 214a,

220, 228, 236, 237, 238, 239, 239k, 242a, 246, 259k, 4.3 270a, 278, 291k, 294a, 298, 313k, 316a, 320, 337k, 340a, 344, 352, 356, 357, 358, 359, 359k, 359l, 362a, 366, 383k, 4.4 394a, 415k, 418a, 422, 439k, 442a, 463k, 468a, 476, 484, 485, 486, 487k, 490a, 494, 507k, 4.5 518a, 537k, 540a, 546, 559k, 562a, 574, 578, 579, 580, 581k, 584a, 596, 607k, 610a, 614, 629k, 4.6 640a, 648, 659k, 662a, 678, 685k, 688a, 692, 711k, 714a, 724, 734, 735, 736, 737k, 740a, 748, 761k
    keyword, 4.1 20a, 26, 42a, 48, 65k, 68a, 80, 84, 85, 87k, 90a, 96, 106, 111k, 114a, 118, 133k, 4.2 144a, 148, 161k, 164a, 190a, 200, 211k, 214a, 220, 228, 242a, 246, 259k, 4.3 270a, 278, 291k, 294a, 298, 316a, 320, 340a, 344, 352, 358, 359l, 362a, 366, 383k, 4.4 394a, 418a, 422, 439k, 442a, 465k, 468a, 476, 484, 485, 486, 487k, 490a, 494, 507k, 4.5 518a, 537k, 540a, 546, 559k, 562a, 574, 581k, 584a, 596, 607k, 610a, 614, 629k 4.6 640a, 648, 659k, 662a, 678, 685k, 688a, 692, 714a, 724, 737k, 740a, 748, 761k
    links, 4.2 228, 237, 4.3 291k, 356, 4.4 439k, 484, 486, 4.5 559k, 4.6 659k, 734, 735, 736
    museum, online, 4.1 65k
    navigation 4.2 238
    reference sources and directories, online, 4.1 84–87, 111k, 118, 4.2 172, 200, 220, 4.4 422, 465k, 476, 4.5 562a, 578–581, 4.6 640a, 648, 678, 688a, 714a, 734–737, 737k
    search engines, 4.1 20a, 26, 42a, 48, 65k, 68a, 80, 87k, 90a, 96, 106, 111k, 114a, 118, 4.2 144a, 148, 164a, 174, 187k, 190a, 200, 214a, 220, 228, 242a, 246, 4.3 270a, 278, 294a, 298, 313k, 316a, 320, 337k, 340a, 344, 352, 359k, 362a, 366, 383k, 4.4 394a, 411, 415k, 418a, 439k, 442a, 465k, 468a, 484, 485, 486, 487k, 490a, 494, 4.5 518a, 537k, 540a, 546, 559k, 562a, 574, 581k, 584a, 596, 607k, 610a, 614, 629k, 4.6 640a, 648, 659k, 678, 685k, 688a, 692, 711k, 714a, 724, 736, 737k, 740a, 748, 761k
    search window, 4.1 84, 4.4 484
    searching and navigating the Internet, 4.1 20a, 26, 39k, 42a, 48, 65k, 68a, 80, 84, 85, 86, 87k, 87l, 90a, 96, 106, 111k, 114a, 118, 133k, 4.2 144a, 148, 161k, 164a, 172, 174, 187k, 190a, 200, 211k, 214a, 220, 228, 239k, 242a, 246, 4.3 270a, 278, 291k, 294a, 298, 313k, 316a, 320, 337k, 340a, 344, 352, 355, 356, 357, 359k, 359l, 362a, 366, 383k, 4.4 394a, 415k, 418a, 422, 439k, 442a, 465k, 468a, 476, 484, 485, 486, 487k, 490a, 494, 507k, 4.5 518a, 537k, 540a, 546, 559k, 562a, 574, 578, 579, 580, 581k, 584a, 596, 607k, 610a, 614, 629k, 4.6 640a, 648, 659k, 662a, 678, 685k, 688a, 692, 711k, 714a, 724, 734, 736, 737k, 740a, 748, 761k
    technology tools, 4.1 84, 4.2 236, 4.3 356, 4.4 484, 4.5 578, 4.6 734
    URLs, 4.1 84, 85, 111k, 4.2 161k, 187k, 211k, 239k, 259k, 4.3 291k, 313k, 359k, 4.4 439k, 487k, 4.5 537k, 559k, 578, 629k, 4.6 659k, 711k, 740a
    use graphic sources, 4.1 65k, 84, 86, 87k, 4.3 313k, 4.4 465k, 487k, 4.6 734
    use website features, 4.1 84, 4.3 356, 4.4 415k, 439k, 465k, 484, 485, 486, 4.6 659k
    Web site, 4.1 61, 65k, 68a, 84, 85, 87k, 87l, 111k, 133k, 4.2 161k, 187k, 211k, 237, 239, 239k, 259k, 4.3 291k, 313k, 337k, 355, 356–357, 359k, 383k, 4.4 415k, 439k, 465k, 484–487, 487k, 507k, 4.5 537k, 559k, 578, 579, 580, 581k, 607k, 629k, 4.6 659k, 685k, 711k, 734, 737k, 761k

Scott Foresman Reading Street technology
  Background Building Audio CD, 4.1 20a, 42a, 68a, 90a, 114a, 4.2 144a, 164a, 190a, 214a, 242a, 4.3 270a, 294a, 316a, 340a, 362a, 4.4 394a, 418a, 442a, 468a, 490a, 4.5 518a, 540a, 562a, 584a, 610a, 4.6 640a, 662a, 688a, 714a, 740a
  Leveled Reader Database, 4.1 18h, 40h, 66h, 88h, 112h, 4.2 142h, 162h, 188h, 212h, 240h, 4.3 268h, 292h, 314h, 338h, 360h, 4.4 392h, 416h, 440h, 466h, 488h, 4.5 516h, 538h, 560h, 582h, 608h, 4.6 638h, 660h, 686h, 712h, 738h
  professional development (PearsonSuccessNet. com), 4.1 18i, 40i, 66i, 88i, 112i, 4.2 142i, 162i, 188i, 212i, 240i, 4.3 268i, 292i, 314i, 338i, 360i, 4.4 392i, 416i, 440i, 466i, 488i, 4.5 516i, 538i, 560i, 582i, 608i, 4.6 638i, 660i, 686i, 712i, 738i
  Selection AudioText CD (Student Edition), 4.1 23, 45, 71, 93, 117, 4.2 147, 167, 193, 217, 245, 4.3 273, 297, 319, 343, 365, 4.4 397, 421, 445, 471, 493, 4.5 521, 543, 565, 587, 613, 4.6 643, 665, 691, 717, 743
  skills for using technology
    basic knowledge and skills, 4.1 65k, 84–87, 111k, 4.2 161k, 187k, 236–239, 239k, 259k, 4.3 337k, 356–359, 4.4 439k, 484–487, 4.5 559k, 578–581, 629k, 4.6 734–737
    communication, 4.1 111g–111h, 4.2 236–239
    compare and contrast, 4.2 211k, 4.5 537k, 574, 4.6 688a
    information acquisition, 4.1 39k, 65k, 87k, 111k, 133k, 4.2 161k, 187k, 211k, 239k, 259k, 4.3 291k, 313k, 337k, 359k, 383k, 4.4 415k, 439k, 465k, 487k, 507k, 4.5 537k, 559k, 581k, 607k, 629k, 4.6 659k, 685k, 711k, 737k, 761k
  See also **Cross-curricular activities, Reference sources.**

Telephone directory. *See* **Reference sources.**

Tempo. *See* **Fluency, reading.**

Testing, formal and informal. *See* **Assessment.**

Test-taking practice
  look back and write, 4.1 34, 60, 82, 106, 128, 4.2 156, 184, 208, 233, 256, 4.3 286, 308, 332, 354, 378, 4.4 410, 434, 462, 482, 501, 4.5 534, 554, 576, 602, 624, 4.6 655, 680, 706, 736, 756
  strategies for fiction/poetry
    identify theme, 4.1 132
    use figurative language, 4.6 659
    use plot and characters, 4.3 336
    use rhyme, 4.2 160, 4.4 465
  nonfiction
    use bold-faced words, 4.2 187
    use captions, 4.1 110
    use charts, 4.5 628, 4.6 760
    use diagrams, 4.4 414
    use quotations, 4.4 506, 4.6 710
    use graphics, 4.2 259, 4.3 312
    use illustration, 4.1 64
    use maps, 4.1 38
    use photographs, 4.5 558, 4.6 684
    use sidebars, 4.4 438
    use subheads, 4.2 211, 4.3 290, 382
    use tables, 4.5 606
  writing for tests, 4.1 133g–133h, 4.2 259g–259h, 4.3 383g–383h, 4.4 507g–507h
  See also **Assessment.**

Textbook (as reference source). *See* **Reference sources.**

Textbook article. *See* **Genres.**

Textbook-reading techniques, 4.3 337l

Text features, 4.1 36, 62, 84, 108, 111l, 4.2 186, 210, 211l, 236, 258, 4.3 288, 310, 334, 356, 380, 4.4 412, 415l, 436, 464, 484, 504, 4.5 536, 537l, 556, 578, 604, 626, 4.6 682, 708, 734, 758

Text structure (method of presenting information), 4.1 66l–66m, 111, 4.5 582–583, 593, 595, 601, DI·36, DI·37, 4.6 660, 661, 671, 675, 679, 685, 709, DI·16, DI·17

Theme (as a story element), 4.5 582l–582m, 621, 4.6 686l–686m, 686–687, 699, 703, 711b, DI·54

Themes for teaching and learning, 4.1 16–17, 17a, 18a, 40a, 66a, 88a, 112a, 138–139, 4.2 140–141, 141a, 142a, 162a, 188a, 212a, 240a, 264–265, 4.3 266–267, 267a, 268a, 292a, 314a, 338a, 360a, 388–389, 4.4 390–391, 391a, 392a, 416a, 440a, 466a, 488a, 512–513, 4.5 514–515, 515a, 516a, 538a, 560a, 582a, 608a, 634–635, 4.6 636–637, 637a, 638a, 660a, 686a, 712a, 738a, 766–767, DI·26, DI·27

Thesaurus. See **Reference sources.**

Think-aloud statements. Think-alouds and teacher modeling are demonstrated throughout weekly lessons as a basic teaching strategy.

Thinking strategies. See **Critical thinking.**

Time line. See **Graphic sources.**

Time sequence. See **Sequence.**

Tone. See **Fluency, reading; Literacy devices.**

Topic, recognizing. See **Main idea.**

Trade books
  as reference source, 4.1 133l, 4.3 337l
  trade book library, 4.1 18i, 40i, 66i, 88i, 112i, 4.2 142i, 162i, 188i, 212i, 240i, 4.3 268i, 292i, 314i, 338i, 360i, 4.4 392i, 416i, 440i, 466i, 488i, 4.5 516i, 538i, 560i, 582i, 608i, 4.6 638i, 660i, 686i, 712i, 738i

Types of literature. See **Genres.**

U

Unfamiliar word meaning, 4.1 114b, 4.2 164–165, 173, 177, 187c, 214–215, 239c, 242–243, 253, 259c, 316–317, 325, 337c, 4.4 442–443, 453, 465c, 468b, 4.5 562–563, 573, 581c, 4.6 688–689, 701, 711c, 714–715, 721, 729, 737c

Unit inquiry projects. See **Projects.**

Usage. See **Adjectives, Adverbs, Conjunctions, Contractions, Nouns, Prepositions and prepositional phrases, Pronouns, Sentences, Subject/verb agreement, Verbs.**

V

Venn diagram. See **Graphic and semantic organizers,** types.

Verbs
  action, 4.3 291e–291f
  helping, 4.3 313e–313f
  irregular, 4.3 383e–383f
  linking, 4.3 291e–291f
  main, 4.3 313e–313f
  tense, 4.3 359e–359f
  voice, 4.3 299

Viewing
  kinds of media
    art, 4.1 65d, 4.6 685d, 711d
    illustration, 4.1 65d, 4.6 685d, 711d
    movies/video, 4.2 161d, 211d, 4.4 415d, 465d, 507d
    multimedia, 4.5 607d
    photography, 4.1 62, 111d, 133d, 4.3 359d, 380, 4.5 536, 556, 559d, 626, 4.6 711d, 761d
    print media
      illustration, 4.1 65d, 4.6 685d, 711d
      speech, 4.2 259d
  responding to media
    analyzing, 4.1 65d, 4.2 161d, 211d, 4.4 439d, 465d
    oral, 4.1 65d, 111d, 133d, 4.2 161d, 211d, 259d, 4.3 352d, 4.4 415d, 465d, 507d, 4.5 559d, 607d, 4.6 685d, 711d, 761d
    written, 4.1 111d, 4.2 259d, 4.3 359d, 4.4 465d, 4.5 559d, 607d, 4.6 685d, 761d
  uses of media
    analysis, 4.1 65d, 111d, 133d, 4.3 359d, 4.6 685d, 711d
    enjoyment, 4.2 161d, 4.3 415d, 4.4 465d, 507d
    persuasion, 4.2 259d
    research, 4.5 559d, 607d, 4.6 761d

Visualizing, 4.3 314–315, 327, 329, 331, 4.4 416–417, 429, 431, 433, 437, 4.5 516l–516m, 538–539, 549, 553, 559, DI·16, DI·17

Vocabulary development
  classifying words, 4.1 42b, 4.2 144b, 242b, 4.3 270b, 294b, 4.5 518b, 562b, 610b, 4.6 662b
  concept vocabulary, 4.1 39c, 65c, 87c, 111c, 133c, 4.2 161c, 187c, 211c, 239c, 259c, 4.3 291c, 313c, 337c, 359c, 383c, 4.4 415c, 439c, 465c, 487c, 507c, 4.5 537c, 559c, 581c, 607c, 629c, 4.6 659c, 685c, 711c, 737c, 761c
  connotation and denotation, 4.4 442b
  content-area vocabulary, 4.1 36, 62, 108, 130, 4.2 186, 210, 258, 4.3 288, 310, 340b, 354, 380, 4.4 412, 436, 464, 504, 4.5 536, 540b, 556, 584b, 604, 626, 4.6 682, 708, 758
  etymologies for meaning, 4.2 164b, 4.4 418b, 468, 479, 487c, 490b, 4.5 540–541, 547, 559, 559c, 562b, 584–585, 597, 599, 607c
  graphic organizers for grouping, studying, and retaining, 4.1 20b, 42b, 90b, 4.2 144b, 190b, 214b, 242b, 4.3 294b, 340b, 362b, 4.4 394b, 418b, 442b, 468b, 4.5 518b, 562b, 584b, 4.6 662b, 714b
  introducing selection vocabulary, 4.1 20b, 42b, 68b, 90b, 114b, 4.2 144b, 164b, 190b, 214b, 242b, 4.3 270b, 294b, 316b, 340b, 362b, 4.4 394b, 418b, 442b, 468b, 490b, 4.5 518b, 540b, 562b, 584b, 610b, 4.6 640b, 662b, 688b, 714b, 740b
  listening for vocabulary development, 4.1 18l–18m, 40l–40m, 66l–66m, 88l–88m, 112l–112m, 4.2 142l–142m, 162l–162m, 188l–188m, 212l–212m, 240l–240m, 4.3 268l–268m, 292l–292m, 314l–314m, 338l–338m, 360l–360m, 4.4 392l–392m, 416l–416m, 440l–440m, 466l–466m, 488l–488m, 4.5 516l–516m, 538l–538m, 560l–560m, 582l–582m, 608l–608m, 4.6 638l–638m, 660l–660m, 686l–686m, 712l–712m, 738l–738m
  practice lesson vocabulary, 4.1 27, 33, 53, 59, 77, 81, 99, 105, 123, 127, 4.2 151, 155, 175, 183, 201, 207, 223, 231, 251, 255, 4.3 279, 285, 303, 307, 327, 331, 349, 353, 371, 377, 4.4 403, 409, 429, 433, 451, 461, 477, 481, 497, 499, 4.5 527, 533, 549, 553, 571, 575, 593, 601, 619, 623, 4.6 649, 653, 671, 679, 697, 705, 725, 731, 751, 755

Reading for vocabulary development, 4.1 20b, 42b, 68b, 90b, 114b, 4.2 144b, 164b, 190b, 214b, 242b, 4.3 270b, 294b, 316b, 340b, 362b, 4.4 394b, 418b, 442b, 468b, 490b, 4.5 518b, 540b, 562b, 584b, 610b, 4.6 640b, 662b, 688b, 714b, 740b

related words in meaning (derivatives), 4.1 87c, 4.2 190b, 4.6 740b

speaking for vocabulary development, 4.1 18l, 40l, 66l, 88l, 112l, 4.2 142l, 162l, 188l, 212l, 240l, 4.3 268l, 292l, 314l, 338l, 360l, 4.4 392l, 416l, 440l, 466l, 488l, 4.5 516l, 538l, 560l, 582l, 608l, 4.6 638l, 660l, 686l, 712l, 738l

specialized/technical words, 4.2 144b

writing vocabulary, 4.1 39g–39h, 65g, 87g, 111g, 133g, WA7, 4.2 161g–161h, 187g, 211g, 239g, 259g, WA7, 4.3 291g, 313g, 337g–337h, 359g, 383g, WA7, 4.4 415g, 439g, 465g, 487g, 507g, WA7, 4.5 537g, 559g–559h, 581g, 607g, 629g–629h, WA7, 4.6 659g, 685g, 711g, 737g, 761g, WA7

  See also **Vocabulary strategies.**

Vocabulary strategies
  alphabetical order, 4.6 662b
  analogies, 4.3 270b
  antonyms, 4.2 242b, 4.4 394–395, 405, 415c, 490–491, 495, 507c
  base words, 4.5 518b
  compound words, 4.1 68b, 4.2 214b, 4.6 662b
  connotation, 4.4 442b
  context clues, 4.1 20b, 90–91, 101, 111c, 4.3 270–271, 277, 291c, 294–295, 305, 313c, 316–317, 325, 337c, 4.4 394–395, 405, 415c, 418–419, 427, 439c, 490–491, 495, 507c, 4.5 518–519, 525, 537c, 562–563, 573, 581c, 610–611, 617, 629c, 4.6 662b, 688–689, 701, 711c, 714–715, 721, 729, 737c, 740–741, 749, 761c
  dictionary/glossary, 4.1 68–69, 79, 87c, 4.2 164–165, 173, 177, 187c, 214–215, 221, 231, 239c, 242–243, 253, 259c, 4.4 442–443, 453, 457, 465c, 4.6 662–663, 669, 673, 685c
  endings, 4.1 42–43, 51, 55, 65c, 68b, 4.3 270b, 340–341, 349, 359c, 362b, 4.4 394–395, 4.6 640–641, 647, 659c
  Greek and Latin roots, 4.4 418b, 468, 479, 487c, 4.5 540–541, 547, 559, 559c, 562b, 584–585, 597, 599, 607c
  homographs, 4.5 518–519, 525, 537c
  homonyms, 4.3 294–295, 305, 313c, 4.5 518–519, 525, 537c, 4.6 740–741, 749, 761c
  homophones, 4.1 42b, 4.6 688b
  multiple-meaning words, 4.1 20b, 68–69, 79, 87c, 4.2 231, 4.3 270–271, 277, 291c, 316b, 4.4 418–419, 427, 439c, 457, 4.6 640b, 662–663, 669, 673, 685c, 714b
  noun phrases, 4.3 294b
  nouns and verbs, 4.3 362b
  picture clues, 4.1 90b
  prefixes, 4.2 144–145, 151, 161c, 190–191, 199, 211c
  related words, 4.2 190b, 4.6 740b
  specialized vocabulary, 4.2 144b
  suffixes, 4.1 20–21, 29, 39c, 114–115, 121, 133c, 4.2 144b, 144–145, 151, 161c, 4.3 362–363, 375, 383c, 4.4 394b, 4.6 640b
  synonyms, 4.1 90–91, 101c, 111c, 4.4 394–395, 405, 415c, 490–491, 495, 507c, 4.5 562b, 610b, 610–611, 617, 629c
  unfamiliar words, 4.1 114b, 4.2 164–165, 173, 177, 187c, 214–215, 239c, 242–243, 253, 259c, 316–317, 325, 337c, 4.4 442–443, 453, 465c, 468b, 4.5 562–563, 573, 581c, 4.6 688–689, 701, 711c, 714–715, 721, 729, 737c
  word origins, 4.2 164b, 4.4 490b

word structure, 4.1 29, 39c, 42–43, 51, 55, 65c, 114–115, 121, 133c, 4.2 144–145, 151, 161c, 190–191, 199, 211c, 4.3 340–341, 349, 359c, 362–363, 375, 383c, 4.4 468–469, 479, 487c, 4.5 540–541, 547, 559c, 584–585, 597, 599, 607c, 4.6 640–641, 647, 659c
   See also **Context clues for meaning, Vocabulary development.**

Volume. *See* **Fluency, reading.**

W

Web site. *See* **Genres, Technology.**

Webbing. *See* **Graphic and semantic organizers,** types.

Word attack skills. *See* **Context clues for meaning, Dictionary/glossary, Phonics, Vocabulary strategies, Word structure.**

Word histories. *See* **Vocabulary development,** etymologies for meaning.

Word identification. *See* **Context clues for meaning, Dictionary/glossary, Vocabulary strategies, Word structure.**

Word structure
   base words
      with spelling changes, 4.1 43, 55, DI·15, DI·45, 4.2 DI·4, 4.4 DI·4, 4.5 DI·14, 4.6 641, 647
      without spelling changes, 4.1 DI·14, 4.2 DI·14, DI·24, 4.4 DI·14, 4.5 DI·24 4.6 DI·4, DI·14
   chunking, 4.1 68b, DI·1, DI·4, 4.2 144b, DI·1, DI·4, DI·44, 4.3 270b, DI·1, 4.4 394b, 419, DI·1, DI·24, DI·34, DI·44, 4.5 518b, DI·1, DI·34, 4.6 640b, DI·1, DI·24, DI·44
   compound words, 4.1 68b, DI·24, DI·34, DI·44, 4.2 214b, DI·34, 4.5 DI·4, DI·44, 4.6 662b, DI·34
   endings, inflected and uninflected, 4.1 42–43, 51, 55, 65c, 4.3 340–341, 349, 359c, 4.6 640–641, 647, 659c, DI·5, DI·14
   Greek and Latin roots, 4.4 418b, 468–469, 479, 487c, DI·35, 4.5 518b, 540–541, 547, 559, 559c, 562b, 584–585, 597, 599, 607c, DI·35
   plurals, 4.6 647
   prefixes, 4.2 144–145, 151, 161c, 190–191, 199, 211c, DI·5, DI·24, 4.6 DI·14
   root words, 4.5 547, 597
   suffixes, 4.1 20–21, 29, 39c, 114–115, 121, 133c, DI·5, DI·14, DI·15, 4.2 144–145, 151, 161c, DI·5, DI·14, 4.3 362–363, 375, 383c, 4.4 394b, DI·4, 4.5 DI·24, 4.6 DI·4
   syllabication, 4.4 419, 4.5 563
   word-learning. *See* **Vocabulary strategies.**
   See also **Spelling, Vocabulary strategies.**

Word study. *See* **Context clues for meaning, Dictionary/glossary, Vocabulary strategies, Word structure.**

Working with words. *See* **Context clues for meaning, Dictionary/Glossary, Vocabulary development, Vocabulary strategies.**

Work stations. *See* **Cross-curricular Centers.**

Writer's craft. *See* **Literary craft,** author's craft/style/language.

Writing assessment. *See* **Assessment,** scoring guide.

Writing forms/products
   article, 4.6 757, 761g–761h
   biography, 4.6 656–657, 659g–659h
   character sketch, 4.6 707, 711g–711h
   comparison/contrast, 4.3 333, 337g–337h, WA2–WA9

description, 4.2 234–235, 239g–239h, 4.3 287, 291g–291h
   editorial, 4.5 555, 559g–559h
   e-mail message, 4.1 107, 111g–111h
   explanatory paragraph/essay, 4.2 257, 259g–259h
   fantasy, 4.3 379, 383g–383h
   how-to report, 4.2 WA2–WA9
   informational article, 4.6 757, 761g–761h
   interview, 4.5 577, 581g–581h
   invitation, 4.1 107, 111g–111h
   journal, 4.1 61, 65g–65h
   letter, business, 4.4 463, 465g–465h, 4.5 603, 607g–607h
   letter, friendly, 4.3 309, 313g–313h
   memoir, 4.1 35, 39g–39h
   narrative writing, 4.1 129, 133g–133h
   news article/report/story, 4.2 185, 187g–187h
   note/card, 4.1 83, 87g–87h
   notes, 4.6 681, 685g–685h
   opinion paragraph/essay, 4.5 625, 629g–629h
   outline, 4.6 733, 737g–737h
   personal narrative, 4.1 WA2–WA9
   persuasive argument/essay/paragraph, 4.5 WA2–WA9
   play scene, 4.2 209, 11g–211h
   plot summary, 4.4 502–503, 507g–507h
   poem, 4.1 135, 137, 4.2 157, 161g–161h, 261, 263, 4.3 385, 387, 4.4 508, 511, 4.5 631, 633, 4.6 763, 765
   problem/solution, 4.3 355, 359g–359h
   research report, 4.6 WA2–WA9
   response log. *See* **Logs, strategy response.**
   review, 4.5 535, 537g–537h
   skit, 4.2 209, 211g–211h
   story, 4.4 411, 415g–415h, 483, 487g–487h, WA2–WA9
   summary, 4.4 502–503, 507g–507h
   travel brochure, 4.4 435, 439g–439h

Writing modes
   descriptive, 4.1 83, 87g–87h, 4.2 234–235, 239g–239h, 4.3 287, 291g–291h, 309, 313g–313h, 4.4 435, 439g–439h, 4.5 535, 537g–537h, 4.6 707, 711g–711h
   expository, 4.1 107, 111g–111h, 4.2 257, 259g–259h, WA2–WA9, 4.3 333, 337g–337h, 355, 359g–359h, WA2–WA9, 4.4 463, 465g–465h, 4.5 577, 581g–581h, 603, 607g–607h, 4.6 681, 685g–685h, 733, 737g–737h, 757, 761g–761h, WA2–WA9
   expressive, 4.1 35, 39g–39h, 61, 65g–65h, WA2–WA9, 4.2 157, 161g–161h, 209, 211g–211h, 4.3 309, 313g–313h
   narrative, 4.1 35, 39g–39h, 61, 65g–65h, WA2–WA9, 4.2 185, 187g–187h, 209, 211g–211h, 4.3 379, 383g–383h, 4.4 411, 415g–415h, 483, 487g–487h, 502–503, 507g–507h, WA2–WA9, 4.6 656–657, 659g–659h
   persuasive, 4.5 535, 537g–537h, 555, 559g–559h, 625, 629g–629h, WA2–WA9

Writing process
   assessing/scoring guide (rubric), 4.1 39h, 65h, 87h, 111h, 133h, WA7, 4.2 161h, 187h, 211h, 239h, 259h, WA7, 4.3 291h, 313h, 337h, 359h, 383h, WA7, 4.4 415h, 439h, 465h, 487h, 507h, WA7, 4.5 537h, 559h, 581h, 607h, 629h, WA7, 4.6 659h, 685h, 711h, 737h, 761h, WA7
   draft, 4.1 39h, 65h, 87h, 111h, 133h, WA4, 4.2 161h, 187h, 211h, 239h, 259h, WA4, 4.3 291h, 313h, 337h, 359h, 383h, WA4, 4.4 415h, 439h, 465h, 487h, 507h, WA4, 4.5 537h, 559h, 581h, 607h, 629h, WA4, 4.6 659h, 685h, 711h, 737h, 761h, WA4
   edit, 4.1 39h, 65h, 87h, 111h, 133h, WA6, 4.2 161h, 187h, 211h, 239h, 259h, WA6, 4.3 291h, 313h, 337h, 359h, 383h, WA6,

4.4 415h, 439h, 465h, 487h, 507h, WA6, 4.5 537h, 559h, 581h, 607h, 629h, WA6, 4.6 659h, 685h, 711h, 737h, 761h, WA6
   prewrite, 4.1 39h, 65h, 87h, 111h, 133h, WA3, 4.2 161h, 187h, 211h, 239h, 259h, WA3, 4.3 291h, 313h, 337h, 359h, 383h, WA3, 4.4 415h, 439h, 465h, 487h, 507h, WA3, 4.5 537h, 559h, 581h, 607h, 629h, WA3, 4.6 659h, 685h, 711h, 737h, 761h, WA3
   publish, 4.1 39h, 65h, 87h, 111h, WA7, 4.2 161h, 187h, 211h, 239h, WA7, 4.3 291h, 313h, 337h, 359h, 4.4 415h, 439h, 465h, 487h, WA7, 4.5 537h, 559h, 581h, 607h, WA7, 4.6 659h, 685h, 711h, 737h, WA7
   revise, 4.1 39h, 65h, 87h, 111h, 133h, WA5, 4.2 161h, 187h, 211h, 239h, 259h, WA5, 4.3 291h, 313h, 337h, 359h, 383h, WA5, 4.4 415h, 439h, 465h, 487h, 507h, WA5, 4.5 537h, 559h, 581h, 607h, 629h, WA5, 4.6 659h, 685h, 711h, 737h, 761h, WA5

Writing purpose
   clarify information, 4.3 333, 337g–337h, WA2–WA9, 4.4 435, 439g–439h, 4.5 577, 581g–581h, 4.6 733, 737g–737h
   express ideas, 4.2 234–235, 239g–239h, 4.4 463, 465g–465h, 4.5 555, 559g–559h, WA2–WA9
   respond to literature, 4.1 34, 39, 60, 65, 82, 87, 106, 111, 128, 133, 4.2 156, 161, 184, 187, 208, 211, 233, 239, 256, 259, 4.3 286, 291, 308, 313, 332, 337, 354, 359, 378, 383, 4.4 410, 415, 434, 439, 462, 465, 482, 487, 501, 502–503, 507, 4.5 534, 535, 537, 537h, 554, 559, 576, 581, 602, 607, 624, 629, 4.6 655, 659, 680, 685, 706, 707, 711, 711h, 732, 737, 756, 761
   share experiences, 4.1 35, 39g–39h, 61, 65g–65h, 83, 87g–87h, 129, 133g–133h, WA2–WA9, 4.3 287, 291g–291h, 309, 313g–313h
   share ideas/information, 4.1 107, 111g–111h, 4.2 185, 187g–187h, 255, 259g–259h, 355, 359g–359h, WA2–WA9, 4.4 502–503, 507g–507h, 4.5 535, 537g–537h, 4.6 681, 685g–685h, 757, 761g–761h, WA2–WA9
   share stories/poems, 4.2 157, 161g–161h, 211, 211g–211h, 4.3 379, 383g–383h, 4.4 411, 415g–415h, 483, 487g–487h, WA2–WA9, 4.6 656–657, 659g–659h, 707, 711g–711h
   specific audience, 4.1 WA2, 4.2 WA2, 4.3 WA2, 4.4 WA2, 4.5 555, 559g–559h, 603, 607g–607h, WA2, 4.6 WA2

Writing, six-trait. *See* **Six-trait writing.**

Writing strategies. *See* **Writing process.**

Writing with technology, 4.1 39h, 65h, 87h, 111h, 133h, WA6, 4.2 161h, 187h, 211h, 239h, 259h, WA6, 4.3 291h, 313h, 337h, 359h, 383h, WA6, WA7, 4.4 415h, 439h, 465h, 487h, 507h, WA6, 4.5 537h, 559h, 581h, 607h, 629h, WA6, WA7, 4.6 659h, 685h, 711h, 737h, 761h, WA6, WA7

ACKNOWLEDGMENTS

Teacher's Edition

Text

KWL Strategy: The KWL Interactive Reading Strategy was developed and is used by permission of Donna Ogle, National-Louis University, Evanston, Illinois, co-author of *Reading Today and Tomorrow*, Holt, Rinehart & Winston Publishers, 1988. (See also *The Reading Teacher*, February 1986, pp. 564–570.)

Page 18m: From *Child of the Silent Night: The Story of Laura Bridgman* by Edith Fisher Hunter. Copyright © 1963 and renewed 1991 by Edith Fisher Hunter. Reprinted by permission of Houghton Mifflin Company. All rights reserved.

Page 66m: From "Getting a Grip on the U.S.A." in *Going Places* by Harriet Webster. Copyright © 1991 by Harriet Webster. Reprinted by permission of Atheneum Books for Young Readers, an imprint of Simon & Schuster Children's Publishing Division.

Page 88m: From *Growing Up in the Old West* by Judith Alter. Copyright © 1989 by Franklin Watts. Reprinted by permission of Franklin Watts, an imprint of Scholastic Library Publishing, Inc. All rights reserved.

Page 112m: From "The Volcano Wakes" from *Volcano* by Patricia Lauber. Copyright © 1986 by Patricia Lauber. Reprinted with the permission of Simon & Schuster Books for Young Readers, an imprint of Simon & Schuster Children's Publishing Division.

Artists

Tim Jessell: cover, page i

Photographs

Every effort has been made to secure permission and provide appropriate credit for photographic material. The publisher deeply regrets any omission and pledges to correct errors called to its attention in subsequent editions.

Unless otherwise acknowledged, all photographs are the property of Scott Foresman, a division of Pearson Education.

Photo locators denoted as follows: Top (T), Center (C), Bottom (B), Left (L), Right (R), Background (Bkgd)

Page 18j: MapQuest;

Page 66k: Digital Wisdom, Inc.;

Page 87l: ©Royalty-Free/Corbis;

Page 133l: ©Royalty-Free/Corbis;

Page 162m: Hemera Technologies;

Page 188k: Digital Wisdom, Inc.;

Page 268j: Digital Wisdom, Inc.;

Page 268m: Getty Images;

Page 338m: Getty Images;

Page 516m: Digital Vision;

Page 608m: Ultimate Symbol, Inc.;

Page 685l: Getty Images;

Page 712m Getty Images;